HENRY J. WOOD

Maker of the Proms

By the same author

Music Lover's Anthology (editor)
Gilbert and Sullivan
The Penguin Dictionary of Music
Choral Music (editor)
The Pan Book of Opera (with Stanley Sadie)
The British Music Yearbook (editor, 1971–9)
A Short History of Western Music
The Music Education Handbook (editor)
Arthur Sullivan: A Victorian Musician
The Pan Book of Orchestral Music
The Penguin Dictionary of Musical Performers

and translations of libretti of
Monteverdi's *L'incoronazione di Poppea*,
Berlioz's *Benvenuto Cellini*, Tchaikovsky's
The Queen of Spades, Berg's *Lulu*
and other operas

Arthur Jacobs

HENRY J. WOOD

Maker of the Proms

Methuen

to my sons
and fellow-authors
Julian *and* Michael

First published in Great Britain in 1994
by Methuen London
an imprint of Reed Consumer Books Ltd
Michelin House, 81 Fulham Road London SW3 6RB
and Auckland, Melbourne, Singapore and Toronto

This paperback edition published by Methuen in 1995
Copyright © 1994, 1995 by Arthur Jacobs
The author has asserted his moral rights

A CIP catalogue record for this book
is available at the British Library
ISBN 0 413 69340 6

Typeset by Deltatype Limited, Ellesmere Port, Cheshire
Printed and bound in Great Britain by Clays Ltd, St. Ives plc

Contents

Henry J. Wood

Part III *Battling*

Part IV *Celebrating*

Note to the Proms Centenary Edition

The arrival of the Henry Wood Promenade Concerts at their centenary – or, as the BBC happily put it, 'the beginning of their second century' – and the recent spurt of CD reissues of Henry J. Wood's recordings combine to give special point to the timing of this second edition.

It was in 1895 that Henry J. Wood embarked, at Queen's Hall in London, on the series of concerts which he continued to conduct up to their fiftieth season in 1944. His death in the course of that Proms season, in wartime, left continuity in the hands of the BBC, under whose management the Proms have achieved their vast post-war expansion of repertory and of audiences (especially by television). In 1994 the BBC not only celebrated the achievement of a hundred seasons but commemorated the fiftieth anniversary of Wood's death with various special features in the programmes.

By contrast, the schedule for the 1995 season faced forward: an unusually high quota of new works was announced, many commissioned expressly by the BBC. That was a proper renewal of Wood's own dedication to whatever was new and challenging in music – from his early days, when Dvořák was still composing, until those when he brought the young Benjamin Britten to encounter the Proms audience as both pianist and composer.

For the opening concert of the 1995 season, the choice of Mahler's Symphony no. 8 likewise evokes Wood. Under his baton that gigantic choral fresco had its first hearing in Britain – not at the Proms but at a BBC Symphony Concert in 1930. More than 700 other first performances, or first performances in Britain, given by Wood are documented in an appendix to this book. It was indeed part of the author's task to reveal the breadth of Wood's musical activity *outside* the Proms, in choral as well as orchestral music, in the United States and on the continent as well as throughout Britain.

This second edition updates the first, makes some additions and corrections (for which the author acknowledges a debt to reviewers and other readers), and incorporates a thorough rewriting of the section on *The Recorded Legacy*.

Arthur Jacobs
Oxford, 1995

Acknowledgements

For the provision of copious and invaluable first-hand material pertaining to Sir Henry J. Wood, without any restraint on its use, I am particularly indebted to Wood's elder daughter, Mrs Tania Cardew, and to Mrs Eileen Calthrop and Mr Henry T. Calthrop, daughter and grandson of Lady Jessie Wood.

The chief public source of manuscript material, on which I have freely and gratefully drawn, is the Henry J. Wood collection in the Department of Manuscripts at the British Library, London. Further valuable material has been made available by the BBC Written Archives (Caversham, Reading) and by the Royal Academy of Music, reproduced here by permission.

To the Leverhulme Trust I am grateful for the award of an Emeritus Research Fellowship, which provided the chief funding for research leading to this book. Wolfson College, Oxford, by its award of a Visiting Fellowship, enabled the work to be done within an agreeable academic and social framework.

Rosamund Bartlett and Edward Morgan alerted me to the references in Russian sources. At the Royal Academy of Music I have been greatly helped by the Development Office, the library staff, and Michael Lloyd, the former orchestral librarian. Robert Philip kindly placed at my disposal his research into orchestral style as revealed by Henry J. Wood's and other conductors' recordings. The BBC Proms office and Music Information office kindly gave access to their files of programmes and to the computerized database of Proms performances.

Jerry Laurie, Stephen McClarence and my wife Betty Upton Jacobs have provided many suggestions and much stimulus to my work on the text, and Peter Joslin was my resourceful adviser on photographic material. Genealogical research on Henry J. Wood's family by Keith Gould has been gratefully used: in its fullest form, it has been deposited in the archive of the Society of Genealogists. For help with discographical problems I am grateful to Timothy Day, Jonathan Dobson, Christopher Dyment, Ruth Edge and Malcolm Walker. Sharon Owen has been an ideal research assistant.

Henry J. Wood

Information through interviews or in the provision of written material, including material newly incorporated into this 1995 edition, has also been gratefully received from:

Joan Abse
Frank Andrews
Arthur Ash
Iris Bisby
Edward Bor
D. J. Borthwick
Margaret Boys
A. D. P. Briggs
Michael Broadway
David Cahn
Lionel Carley
Raymond Carpenter
Norman Carrell
John R. Catch
David Chesterman
Charles Cleall
Hugo Cole
Edmund Cook MBE
David Cox
Sheila M. Craik
Michael Darke
Percy Davenport
Oliver Davies
J. S. Dearden
Alan Denson
John Dethick
Georgina Dobrée
John Drummond CBE
Bridget Duckenfield
Sir Vivian Dunn
Jeremy Eckstein
David Eden
Cyril Ehrlich
the late Sir Keith Falkner
Charles Fearnley
Brother Felix (Eric Norman Wood)
Christopher Fifield
the late Aileen Findlay
Lewis Foreman
Kurt Gänzl
Malcolm Gillies
Christopher Goldsack
Livia Gollancz

Sidonie Goossens
Laura Gray
the late Sir Charles Groves
Ida Haendel CBE
Barrie Hall
George Hall
Mary Stuart Harding
Keith Hardwick
Charles F. Hatfield
George Hauger
David Heald
Patricia Heath
Roy Henderson
Merryn and Columb Howell
Derek Hudson
David Russell Hulme
John Huntley
David Jackson
the late Josephine James
the late Mary Jarred
Lyndon Jenkins
Katherine Jessel
Edward Johnson
Brian Jones
Michael Jones
Michael Kennedy OBE
Peter King
Ruth Kitching
Anne Klar
Irene Kohler
Richard L. Kaye
Frances Lavender
Margaret Liebert
Stephen Lloyd
Rachel Lowe-Dugmore
Sir Charles Mackerras
Jacqueline Marcus
J. C. Matthews
Norman McCann
Jonathan Minns
Jerrold Northrop Moore
the late Harry Mortimer CBE
John Norman

Geoffrey Norris
Tony Obrist
Andrew Penny
Clarice E. Perry
Pam Poppleton
Patrick Prenter
the late Eric J. Pritchard
Charles Proctor OBE
June Rees
Christopher Regan
Brian Robins
Margaret Rogers
Lionel Salter
Lawrence A. Schoenberg
Joan Smyth

Diana Sparkes
Harry Spilstead
Frank Stokes
Anthony Storr
Mary Stratford
Ronald W. T. Thorns
Robert Threlfall
John Tyrrell
Christine Vann
Malcolm Walker
Nicolas Walter
John Warrack
Barbara Watson
Ursula Vaughan Williams
Patricia Young

Acknowledgements are also due to the following institutions:

Royal College of Music
Royal College of Organists
Slade School of Art (University College London)
Bartók Archívum, Budapest
Britten-Pears Library, Aldeburgh
Delius Trust
Dorothy Howell Trust
John Ireland Trust
Percy Whitlock Trust
British Library: Reference Dept
British Library: National Sound Archive
BBC: Research Collection, Record Library, Sound Archive, Written Archives, News Information
Westminster Music Library
Bodleian Library, Oxford (main collection and John Johnson collection)
Cambridge University Library
Sheffield City Libraries
Dorset County Libraries

Liverpool Public Libraries
Henry Watson Music Library, Manchester
Library of Congress, Washington, DC
Pierpont Morgan Library, New York
Schoenberg Institute, University of Southern California
British Engineerium
Madame Tussaud's
Musicians' Benevolent Fund
National Portrait Gallery
Savage Club
Charing Cross Hospital
BBC Symphony Orchestra
Hallé Concerts Society
Royal Liverpool Philharmonic Society
Los Angeles Philharmonic Association
Hull Philharmonic Society
EMI Records (UK)
EMI Music Archives
Decca Record Co., Ltd

The extract from a letter from Benjamin Britten to Sir Henry J. Wood is quoted by permission of the Britten–Pears Foundation, owners of the copyright. Unpublished letters from Ethel Smyth to Lady Wood are quoted by permission of David Higham Associates. Extracts from Sir Henry J. Wood's *My Life of Music* (1938), Jessie Wood's *The Last Years of Henry J. Wood* (1962) and Victor Gollancz's *Journey towards Music* (1964) are reproduced by permission of Victor Gollancz Ltd. Extracts from R. Vaughan

Henry J. Wood

Williams's *National Music and Other Essays* (1961) and from G.Roscow (ed.), *Bliss on Music* (1991) are reproduced by permission of the publishers, Oxford University Press.

Material from Robert Elkin's *Queen's Hall: 1893–1941* (1944) is reproduced by permission of Rider & Co; lines from a sonnet by John Masefield are reproduced by permission from the Society of Authors as the literary representative of the poet's estate. Sir Henry J. Wood's own article on Orchestration in *A Dictionary of Modern Music and Musicians* (1924) is quoted by permission of the publishers, J. M. Dent & Sons Ltd.

Every effort has been made to trace the holders of copyrights. Any inadvertent omissions of acknowledgement or permission can be rectified in future editions.

A Note on Spelling and Punctuation

Foreign proper names are generally given in currently standard forms: thus 'Schoenberg' in narrative reference (but 'Schönberg' where a contemporary letter with that spelling is quoted). Russian names follow the generally accepted British modern spelling – 'Skryabin', not 'Scriabin'; but an exception is made for the forms 'Koussevitzky' and 'Rachmaninoff', preferred by those people themselves, the latter often occurring in Wood's own letters.

Compositions are likewise given in the usual modern form – Tchaikovsky's 'Nutcracker' rather than 'Casse-noisette'. Word abbreviations formed by initial capitals (BBC, RAM) are given without intervening full stops, even though for most of Wood's life this would have been considered irregular. Dates have been homogenized in the form 1 January 1900.

Letters quoted have been lightly repunctuated where obscure. Typing errors (Henry J. Wood was prone to them, and did not bother to make obvious corrections) have been eliminated. These two editorial changes by the author, though departing from the strictest fidelity in transcription, seem appropriate as a courtesy both to the original writers and the present readers. In certain important citations, however, a verbatim transcription is made and identified as such.

List of Photo Illustrations

following p. 200:

following p. 280

Henry J. Wood

List of Line Illustrations

Chronology

(Events in Wood's life refer to London unless otherwise indicated.)

1869   Born, London, 3 March
         Janáček born 1854, Elgar 1857, Puccini 1858, Mahler 1860, Debussy 1862, Delius 1862, Richard Strauss 1864, Sibelius 1865, Busoni 1866, Vaughan Williams 1872, Rachmaninoff 1873, Schoenberg 1874, Ravel 1875

1883   Gives organ recitals at Fisheries Exhibition

1886–8   Student at Royal Academy of Music

1890   *Composers still living include Brahms, Bruckner, Verdi, Dvořák, Gounod, Tchaikovsky, Rimsky-Korsakov, Saint-Saëns, Grieg, Sullivan*

1892   Conducts first British performance of Tchaikovsky's opera *Yevgeny Onegin*

1895   First promenade concert with Queen's Hall Orchestra

1896   Conducts first British performances of Tchaikovsky's *Nutcracker* Suite and Rimsky-Korsakov's *Scheherazade*

1897   First symphony concert with Queen's Hall Orchestra

1898   Marriage to Olga Hillman, formerly Mikhailov (d.1909)

1902   First time as conductor of Sheffield Festival (last, 1936)

1903–6   Conducts first British performances of major works by Sibelius, Debussy, Strauss

1904   Guest conductor, New York Philharmonic Orchestra

1905   Conducts first performance of his *Fantasia on British Sea Songs*, but leaves his name off it

1911   Knighted; marriage to Muriel Greatrex (d. 1967)

1912   Conducts world première of Schoenberg's *Five Orchestral Pieces*

1914–18   *World War One*

1915   First orchestral recordings

1921   Conducts at Zurich Festival with Arthur Nikisch and Bruno Walter

1925   First season at Hollywood Bowl, California (again 1926, 1934)

Henry J. Wood

1927	First promenade concert season (at Queen's Hall) under auspices of BBC
1927–8	Treatise, *The Gentle Art of Singing*, published
1928	First BBC studio broadcast
1929	First performance of his orchestration, under the name 'Paul Klenovsky', of Bach's Toccata and Fugue in D minor
1934	Guest conductor, Boston Symphony Orchestra
1934	*Deaths of Elgar, Delius, Holst; Bartók is 53, Stravinsky 52, Prokofiev 43, Hindemith 39, Gershwin 36, Copland 34, Walton 32, Tippett 29, Shostakovich 28, Messiaen 26, Britten 21*
1935	Leaves his wife, sets up home with Jessie Linton, formerly Goldsack (d. 1979)
1938	His autobiography, *My Life of Music*, published
1938	Jessie Linton changes her name, by deed poll, to 'Lady Jessie Wood'
1939	He writes and signs 'My Confession'
1939–45	*World War Two*
1941	Queen's Hall destroyed by bombs; promenade concerts move to Royal Albert Hall
1942	Conducts in BBC studio the first performance outside USSR of Shostakovich's *Leningrad* Symphony
1944	Appointed Companion of Honour; celebrates his seventy-fifth birthday; participates in fiftieth season of promenade concerts
1944	Dies at Hitchin, Hertfordshire, 19 August

Conducting a Life

June 1936. On the balcony of the Palace Hotel, Lucerne, the British conductor contemplates the mountain-ringed waters of the Swiss lake. Within view is the villa of Tribschen, for many years Richard Wagner's home. The conductor is also a painter: his easel, palette and oils are to hand, and indeed he would count no holiday complete without them.

This is not, however, just a holiday for Sir Henry J. Wood. On the journey from London by ship and rail, relays of porters have been needed to handle heavy basketfuls of paper – the concert programmes and other documents of a life of musical performance. Now sixty-seven years old, he is to draw on these papers and on his memory to compile an autobiography, a testament of work which began in a precocious boyhood. A recurring thread will be what everyone calls the Proms – but nobody used that term in his youth, and in his autobiography they will be *promenade concerts*, in full. Many other types of performance are also to be recollected – concerts in a bare broadcasting studio or before an audience of 12,000 in the Hollywood Bowl; choral festivals, opera.

Composers are to be recalled in personal association as well as in his conducting of their once-new musical scores – composers such as Debussy and Ravel, Richard Strauss and Schoenberg, Sibelius and Elgar. Among soloists, the line of great violinists will stretch back to Joachim (Brahms's chosen interpreter) and forward through Kreisler to Menuhin; there will be pianists from Pachmann and Paderewski to Arthur Rubinstein and Myra Hess. The conductor's memory, impatient of the chronological time-frame, darts from one personality to another, from incident to similar incident.

His instrument is the baton. No literary gift is his. Other writings which have appeared under his name have been put into shape by various editors, usually yielding a rather formal prose. What Sir Henry J. Wood is now to dictate to the woman at his side, however, will emerge quite differently – chatty in tone, humorous, discursive.

This woman, his adored companion for the past year, he refers to in letters and conversation as 'Lady Wood' and 'my wife'. She is neither. The social deception into which Henry and Jessie have been led – both of them otherwise rather conventional people – casts its shadows into the auto-biography itself, which she will continue to write from dictation once they have returned to London. Finally she will cut it drastically in order to fulfil the requirement of Victor Gollancz, the publisher and Wood's devoted admirer.

The real Lady Wood, the conductor's second wife, is in Japan. She will remain unmentioned in those autobiographical pages, and so will the two daughters of that marriage. Professional and holiday trips shared by husband and wife will be disguised by singular forms of the verb: 'I went' instead of 'we went'. The conductor's happy first marriage to a Russian singer will be disguised in a different sense – Olga being given a surname which was not hers and the rank of princess which was not hers. Presumably with Jessie's consent, Wood's present, non-marital relationship will also go unmentioned.

Were the book's omissions a matter only of social tact, they could be excused by the reader and easily rectified by a later biographer. But there are also many mistakes of fact, names and chronology, springing from too great a reliance on unchecked memory. Occasional absurdities (the conductor Max Fiedler appearing as 'Fielded') suggest that the author could not be bothered with proofs.

More disquieting still, and fundamental to the book, is an element of deliberate deception – of pretending things happened which did not. It is as though Henry J. Wood were *conducting a life*, presenting a core of facts 'creatively' embellished. A fictitious boyhood journey to hear an orchestra in the United States would imply a precocious urge to be a conductor, whereas in fact he did not form that ambition until much later.

What need of such fantasies – it may be asked – when the man on the Lucerne hotel balcony could take such pride in the reality alone? No musician was more beloved by his countrymen, none played a longer or more distinguished role in expounding music's masterpieces. The fantasies tend to reinforce self-esteem, as if to compensate for perceived social dis-advantages – a humble background, an inadequate general education, a lack of cultural breadth and fluency, the spoken accent of a London tradesman rather than of the English public schoolboy. Sometimes the fantasies suggest an attempt to repay his parents – as if the book were to serve as 'a dutiful offering at the grave of parents who trained my childhood to all the good it could attain'.

That declaration of filial duty is not Wood's. It is from John Ruskin's comment on his own autobiography, *Praeterita:* 'It is – as you say – the "natural" me, only peeled carefully.' With Wood the 'natural me' was sometimes peeled (by removing persons from the surrounding scene), at other times given borrowed clothing. It would be far-fetched to suggest any modelling of Wood's pages on Ruskin's, but Ruskin above all others seems to have been chosen by the painter-conductor as his guide in the morality and philosophy of art. 'With a volume of Ruskin in his pocket', Wood was described in 1904 by his first biographer, Rosa Newmarch; in a letter of thirty years later he himself would cite Ruskin as the model for discipline in art. His personal act of homage in visiting Ruskin himself is described (perhaps partly fantasised) in *My Life of Music*.

That autobiography forms a kind of *Doppelgänger*, a phantom double, for the present work. Wood's pages become no less fascinating now that they have to be 'decoded' – to be treated sceptically as narrative, and primarily regarded as testimony of how their author wished in 1938 to be thought of. The plain facts of his life were to be subjected to further distortion in an autobiographical chapter ('My Early Start') included in Wood's later book, *About Conducting*. There his age on entry to the Royal Academy of Music is given as fourteen, rather than nearly sixteen as in *My Life of Music*: it was actually seventeen. A re-presentation of his art and life has become needed, particularly because Reginald Pound's *Sir Henry Wood* (1969) made no artistic judgements and took no critical stance towards *My Life of Music*. Moreover, a vast store of newly available evidence now claims examination.

What was he like, the man of the bronze bust which ceremonially presides at each year's Proms, and the only conductor ever to get into Madame Tussaud's? The nickname of Timber, not merely a play on words but a token of solid reliability, conceals a personality of complex layering. As for the assessment of his musical achievement, it depends on *how* a conductor's art is measured. If Henry J. Wood does not readily figure on most music-lovers' lists of, say, the dozen greatest conductors, perhaps it is the word *greatness* in this sense which will require re-scrutiny.

PART I

Building

'Orchestral virtuosity is now [1938]
a commonplace in this country, and
we are apt to forget to whom we
owe it.'

– Ralph Vaughan Williams, *Henry Wood*

Chapter 1

A Home in Oxford Street

1869–86

It was nothing less than the transformation of the conductor's art. As a music critic since the mid-1870s, Bernard Shaw noted the power exerted on London orchestras by the new wave of Continental masters – Hans Richter, Felix Mottl, and now in 1895 Hermann Levi, controlling the sound 'as if every nerve in the orchestra were in direct communication with his brain'. That power of command apparently belonged only to foreigners: 'Mottl says of the art of conducting that it cannot be learnt – that you step to the desk, and if you can do it, you do it. But when the Englishman steps to the desk he does *not* do it – cannot do it.' Bernard Shaw was about to be proved wrong. In August 1895, four months after that review appeared, the promenade concerts at Queen's Hall began under the conductorship of twenty-six-year-old Henry J. Wood. Within a few years he would be hailed by a German critic as 'Great Britain's only virtuoso of the conductor's desk'. A hundred seasons later, the Proms would still bear his name.

The new, more deeply interpretative role assigned to the conductor and his baton was indicated in Wagner's influential treatise, *About Conducting*, published in 1869: it was only the second work in its field, preceded by Berlioz's. On 3 March of that year (the very mid-year of Victoria's reign), Henry Joseph Wood was born in Oxford Street, London.

Oxford Street was not yet a thoroughfare of famous department stores. Small businesses crowded both sides, many of the owners and their families living on the premises. On the south side, just east of what is now called Oxford Circus (then Regent Circus), could be found an importer of snuff, a 'curer of deafness' and, at number 414, a public-house called the 'Mischief'. It had previously been 'The Man Loaded With Mischief', with an inn-sign depicting a man carrying a woman on his back, but the name had been shortened by the time that Henry Joseph Wood senior, the conductor's father, set up business next door at number 413A, as a master jeweller.

Henry senior was one of ten children, the son of Thomas Wood and his wife Eleanor, née Armstrong. Their family trade was pawnbroking, carried on after the deaths of Thomas and Eleanor by their eldest son Robert in partnership with his brother Henry. The conductor's autobiography suppresses a mention of the 'low' trade of pawnbroking, but records that the partnership of his father and uncle was broken by his father's marriage. Although thirty-seven years of age, Henry senior was considered insufficiently well off to marry. His wife, one year younger (they were married in Dover in 1865), was Martha Morris, daughter of a farmer or perhaps farm-labourer from Montgomeryshire. She was originally Welsh-speaking and Welsh-singing, too: her famous son would remember being sung to sleep with such melodies as 'The Ash Grove' and 'All through the night'. She taught him to memorize the lines of the treble staff (E, G, B, D, F) not as 'Every good boy deserves favour' but as 'Every good Briton deals fairly'. Just such an uncomplicated patriotism would remain with the future arranger of the *Fantasia on British Sea Songs*, later to become a staple of the ritual known (and, after his death, debased) as the 'Last Night of the Proms'.

Henry senior soon changed his entry in Kelly's Post Office Directory from 'master jeweller' to 'optician and engineering modeller', to which was later added 'wholesale and export'. The extension of a Victorian optician's trade (with precision metal-work required) into model engineering was not uncommon, and Henry senior was in any case developing a boyhood enthusiasm of his own. His model engines, both locomotive and stationary, now made his shop famous. With the unconscious deference of a trades-man's son to youngsters of higher social class, the conductor in his autobiography noted that 'Etonians and Harrovians' were among his father's customers. Today the British Engineerium, a national collection located at Hove, Sussex, shows two of Wood's engines as superior and beautiful examples of their types.

Henry junior was an only child – a rarity in the 1860s, when the average of births in a family exceeded six. If his birth certificate is to be believed, he was born at his father's work-place, 413A Oxford Street, the address which is also cited as the family's 'abode' on the baby's certificate of baptism on 9 January 1870 at St Sepulchre's, Holborn, and as their residence on the returns of the 1871 census. But he himself maintained that he was actually born at number 318 – which can be identified as accommodation within, or over, the 'Dolphin' public-house. It may be surmised that, with congestion at the family's work-plus-dwelling place, the Woods had taken extra accommodation at number 318 for the confinement. But Martha, it seems, preferred that not even the remotest association with the 'demon drink' should besmirch the birth certificate.

Around 1872–3 Henry senior's working premises became unavailable to him: number 413A disappears from the annual street directories. He relocated his business to number 429, a few doors off, dividing the premises with a wine and spirit merchant. It afforded no living accommodation, so the family's home was moved from inner London to 7 Pond Street in clean, high-lying, middle-class-favoured Hampstead, from which Henry senior travelled daily to his business address by horse-drawn bus.

Henry senior could not have afforded to buy or even to rent the spacious Hampstead house. The family which owned 7 Pond Street were the Bradshaws, including four unmarried sisters, among whom Harriet was a teacher of music. There – probably as boarders – the Woods stayed until, in 1875, Henry senior was able to move both the business and his family back to Oxford Street, where he took larger premises at number 355. At the beginning of the 1880s Oxford Street underwent a general renumbering and the new premises became number 185. The conductor's autobiography would locate the new house as 'a few doors east of Buzzard's'. He evidently expected his readers to recognize the famous confectioners of that name (properly Buszard's), perhaps still luminous in his own memory as a source of schoolboy delights. This was the home of which Henry J. Wood was to carry such vivid memories from the age of six.

At the new location Henry senior was able to devote his leisure to music as amateur singer and cellist; his famous son emulated his father in practical, constructive manual work as well as music. His middle-aged parents doted on young Henry (whom they sometimes called 'Joe' or 'Joey', to his dislike). To nourish his aptitude for music, painting, and scientific experiment (all, significantly, solitary pursuits), they endowed him with a miniature kingdom over the shop, they themselves moving into a 'cottage' at the rear. The boy's music-room accommodated a Broadwood grand piano, an Alexander harmonium, and a 'pianette' (a low-built upright French piano). In an upper-floor room, where two large plate-glass windows had been installed for the light, two easels were always set up. Round another room ran a steam-powered model railway on trestles, later discarded in favour of electrical apparatus by which he eventually succeeded in installing electric lights in the candle-sconces of the pianette.

The description of young Henry J. Wood's boyhood home comes from *My*

Life of Music, the autobiography which he published in 1938. Despite its unreliability in general, its depiction of an exceptionally warm domestic relationship rings true. 'What note's that, Joe?', Henry senior would demand, tapping on a tumbler or a cup at table. C.J.Bannister, son of the Woods' family doctor, was to recall frequent visits to the house, when the fascination of watching Henry senior's two workmen occupied in making the steam-engines would be followed, after shop hours, by listening to the family's music-making: 'Mr Wood practised on the cello, Mrs Wood the piano and Joey the violin . . . He played the same portion over and over until he was perfect.'

Bannister's reminiscences, dating from over sixty years later, are almost our only intimation that Martha Wood played the piano. She was presumably the first to guide her son's hands to the keyboard, though it was not until he was much older that he had formal lessons. The piano became his principal study, but an early acquaintance with the violin and viola, with tuition perhaps from his father or a family friend, invaluably helped the future conductor in his career.

Henry senior was a member of one of the leading London choirs, the Sacred Harmonic Society (until it disbanded in 1882), and sang also in the choir of St Sepulchre's, Holborn. On Sunday after Sunday the boy took the two-mile-long walk there and back with his parents, later counting himself fortunate to have heard 'one of the best mixed choirs in London rendering some of the finest English cathedral music'. ('Mixed' as distinct from the all-male choirs of St Paul's and other cathedrals.) As with many musicians, youthful exposure to church music seems to have left him with no inclination to religion, but with a lasting love of the sounds heard.

He was deeply stirred by the playing of the St Sepulchre's organist, George Cooper, and was made welcome in the organ-loft of St Sepulchre's by Cooper and his wife, who herself played for the earlier part of the service in order to allow her husband to earn another fee at another church. The Coopers took him home for dinner 'in a four-wheeler hired for the whole day'. The boy's wonder at this superior style of living is evident in his adult recollection. But Wood's assertion in *My Life of Music* that 'at the age of ten' he was allowed to practise 'as long as Mr Cooper was not giving lessons' makes no sense. Cooper died in 1876 when Wood was seven. Cooper can hardly have gone beyond introducing the six- or seven-year-old to the organ. The autobiographer probably wished to avoid giving credit to Cooper's successor at St Sepulchre's, Edwin M. Lott, whose lessons on both piano and organ he described as 'farcical'.

The organ became the boy's first public instrument. His uncle Thomas James Wood (misnamed in the autobiography as William Thomas Wood), a clockmaker with a shop at 18 Barbican, introduced him to the church of St Mary Aldermanbury in the heart of the commercial City of London. There, he relates, a half-crown was slipped into his hand after he had deputized at a service – his first 'professional' engagement, at the age of ten.

As in the case of Elgar – twelve years Wood's senior, struggling in provincial Worcester to build a career – the closeness in Victorian times between the amateur and the professional music-making could yield advantages. An established professional soprano, Margaret Hoare, sang alongside Henry senior at St Sepulchre's. Chamber music was a home pursuit for the Woods 'until I was seventeen', as *My Life of Music* puts it. Every Monday night (or 'every Sunday and Monday', according to the autobiographical chapter in Wood's later book, *About Conducting*), his father and friends met to rehearse. The young Henry's role was generally at the piano, but occasionally he played the violin or viola.

Soon enough, in a period where every district of London generated its own musical activities, came concerts. Not yet twelve, 'Master H. J. Wood' was the pianist in an ensemble with 'Mr H.J. Wood' (his father) as cellist, and five violinists, at St Andrew's Hall, Newman Street (near his home) on 24 February 1881. The programme included 'Airs from *Norma*' and a selection of 'Favourite National Melodies'. The participation of Agnes Larkcom, a soprano who would later be engaged by the Philharmonic Society, again shows the fluid frontier between modest amateurs and well-regarded professionals.

Apart from music-making, and painting (to remain a passion all his life), and his scientific experimenting at home, what was his boyhood like? Of games or reading, of trips to the zoo or to a fairground, no mention creeps into the autobiography. His mother took charge of his general education until he was nearly nine. Then, according to Wood, until he was fifteen (1884) he attended a school in Argyle Street, 'run by a Mr and Mrs Vie'. This is puzzling, since in successive annual directories, a *Miss* Vie listed her establishment at 4 Argyle Street as a school for 'ladies'. Was Miss Vie persuaded to take, exceptionally, a boy pupil – and for what reason, except that he lived just round the corner?

The parents were perhaps over-protective towards a boy who looked a little odd and might even be feared to be (a favoured Victorian expression) 'delicate' – although in fact his constitution was to prove herculean. A facial paralysis attacked him which was ascribed by Dr Bannister to overwork:

three months' rest was advised. This condition, Bell's Palsy, left him with what he called an 'inequality' between the left and right sides of his face which not even his later thickness of beard and whiskers could entirely mask. He had already acquired a crooked nose by a fall from an infant's chair – according to family tradition, while he was straining at the age of three to hear and see an organ-grinder and monkey in the street below.

The Welsh connection of his mother was preserved by holidays in Wales. But he tells us that he 'wore the kilt for best' (see plate 3), surely an eccentricity for such an English/Welsh family.

'My father never missed a chance of taking me to anything of importance in London – comedy, farce, drama, Shakespeare, concerts or opera. We saw and heard everything. Always in the pit or gallery [i.e. the cheaper, less comfortable seats].' Curiously, however, the pages of *My Life of Music* fail to cite any orchestral work heard. Nor is any opera named except Verdi's *Otello*, which reached London not during Wood's boyhood but after he had turned twenty (1889). But he did recall hearing the famous Joachim Quartet and the great baritone Charles Santley at the Saturday and Monday 'Pops' – London's famous series of chamber concerts (to be named satirically in *The Mikado*), which invariably juxtaposed vocal with instrumental performers.

Like so many other not very rich music-lovers, father and son were drawn to the Saturday afternoon series of orchestral concerts at the Crystal Palace in suburban Sydenham. Supervised by George Grove (of *Dictionary* fame) and conducted by August Manns, these concerts cultivated just the sort of pioneering, omnivorous repertory which Wood himself later emulated. More exclusive and much more expensive was the Philharmonic Society season, but a series of its printed programmes for 1881 and later years, now surviving among the bound volumes stamped with the name of Henry J. Wood at the Royal Academy of Music, suggests that his father found the money to allow him to attend those concerts too.

Apart from those at the Crystal Palace, however (then considered as *outside* London), symphony concerts were but sparsely dotted through the season. At the St James's Hall, Piccadilly, the Philharmonic Society usually gave six, occasionally seven or eight, concerts each year, entirely within the period March–June. When the conductor (and singer) George Henschel originated the 'London Symphony Concerts' at St James's Hall in 1886, the very title was new. No such thing existed as a permanent orchestral body with its own management. From a general pool of skilled musicians the Philharmonic Society drew its regular 'band' and so did the Royal Italian Opera at Covent Garden. The pool was likewise available to the promoters of other, occasional concerts, at which an eminent or aspiring soloist was more usually the attraction than the music as such.

Exceptionally, one concert series grew into a regular fixture with immense effect on London's perception of orchestral music. Hans Richter (1843–1916) had been the conductor of *The Ring* at its first complete performance at Bayreuth in 1876. When Wagner came to London in the following year, billed to conduct his own music at the Albert Hall, Richter was Wagner's associate conductor, and in effect the principal conductor. Richter's own yearly appearances began in 1879 and were credited by Bernard Shaw with rescuing London orchestral playing after 'a period of stagnation that cannot be recalled without a shiver'. Later to be the encourager of Elgar and the dedicatee of his Symphony no. 1, Richter exuded a new vigour and interpretative breadth. He was inevitably contrasted with his British counterparts such as Arthur Sullivan, who always conducted seated, or the Philharmonic conductor of the early 1880s, William G.Cusins, who (said the visiting Viennese critic Hanslick) 'looks exactly like an English clergyman and also conducts very piously'.

The young Wood reacted coolly to Richter, though later expressing warm admiration for 'my greatest of colleagues' in letters to Richter's London hostess, Marie Joshua. His own idol of the baton was to be Arthur Nikisch (1855–1922), who was yet to make his first appearance in London.

Henry J. Wood stood at just the point of British music-making to receive the new spirit of conducting. That this new spirit should stem from Wagner's circle was no accident. While Berlioz's treatise on conducting provided a practical how-to-do-it manual, Wagner's sought to define what the orchestral conductor seeks to convey in bringing the written score to performance. Richter, along with Felix Mottl and Hermann Levi, was a member of Wagner's humorously-named Nibelung Chancellery, his lieutenants in preparing and conducting the first Bayreuth Festival and, in 1882, the second. Nikisch, though not in that inner group, had been a violinist under the baton of Wagner himself in Beethoven's Ninth Symphony at the foundation-stone ceremony of the Bayreuth festival theatre in 1872.

Wagner's music, along with Tchaikovsky's, was to be a favourite battle-horse for Wood's conducting at Queen's Hall. The taste of the British concert public had already embraced Wagner. The various overtures from *Rienzi* onward (1842) had rapidly become standard, much-liked fare; *The Flying Dutchman*, *Tannhäuser* and *Lohengrin* entered the repertory of choral societies; *The Ring* was quarried for orchestral excerpts, with *The Ride of the Valkyries* leading the charge. Even the conservative Philharmonic Society of London managed to devote *half* a concert to Wagner as a tribute following his death in February 1883.

So Wagner made his conquest as a contemporary composer, as did Gounod, Verdi and other favourites of the Victorian era. At a time when music was all-pervasive – in street entertainment, in the 'respectable' home, in theatres of all kinds, in public ceremony – *most* music heard was contemporary music. New music was not thought frightening. New works commissioned from Sullivan, Gounod and Ferdinand Hiller as representative of Britain, France and Germany accompanied the Queen's opening of the Royal Albert Hall in 1871.

Musical entertainment was required also at those periodic exhibitions in the South Kensington area which attempted to renew, on a more modest scale, the impact of the Great Exhibition of 1851. Visiting the Fisheries Exhibition of 1883, the Henry J. Woods, senior and junior, found themselves at an organ which had been placed to provide performances in one of the galleries. They encountered 'a little man with jet-black hair, small head, flat nose and protruding jaw'. Hermann Smith was not only an acoustician and organ tuner, but had a widely speculative mind which would lead him to write a book on the music of ancient nations. His friendship with young Wood was to last for decades, and he wrote verses for many of Wood's first published songs (and others unpublished). With Smith's encouragement, the fourteen-year-old seated himself at the organ. He 'rambled on for half an hour or so', collected a small crowd of hearers and landed an invitation to give recitals throughout the exhibition during July, August and September 1883.

For this account of a spontaneous début as concert organist we have only Wood's word of fifty-five years later, but the printed programmes for the ensuing formal recitals at the Fisheries Exhibition are preserved in an outsize, bulging scrapbook now in the Royal Academy of Music collection. The meticulous compilation of this early scrapbook (even the smallest printed announcement being included) may well be the admiring work of Henry senior. Thoughts of music as a profession may have already been taking shape.

Of a concert in Westminster Chapel the *Musical Standard* reported on 31 May 1884 that 'the organ accompaniments of Master H. J. Wood (a pupil of Mr E. M. Lott) were excellently rendered'. The juvenile 'Master' had become 'Mr' by July 1885 when he completed a second series of Kensington organ recitals, this time at the Inventions Exhibition. Organ recitalists then were expected to produce orchestral music arranged for their instrument, but Wood's programming included an Andante from one of Mozart's string quartets and the Larghetto from Mozart's Clarinet Quintet – emerging, no doubt, from his home-influenced love of chamber music. He was engaged for similar recitals at the Folkestone Art Treasures Exhibition in 1886.

After Lott's 'farcical' lessons (which at least equipped him to earn money by deputising at church services), his father sent him for a course of private lessons in music theory from one of the great Victorian musical pedagogues, Ebenezer Prout (1835-1909), professor at the Royal Academy of Music. Prout has been somewhat unfairly pilloried for pedantry, but the instruction given by him and his son Louis – 'these two great teachers' – at their suburban house in Dalston was acknowledged by Wood as the foundation of his knowledge of harmony, counterpoint, form and instrumentation.

Prout's approval must have persuaded Henry senior to let his son proceed to the Royal Academy of Music itself – a recognition that the youth of seventeen was of suitable calibre for a high-flying musical career. The Academy's location was then in Tenterden Street, off Hanover Square and a few minutes' walk from the Woods' home. Naturally, Wood joined Prout's own class in harmony and composition. Tuition at the Academy was offered not by the year but by the term: he stayed for six, participating prominently in the Academy's public concerts. He was placed under one of the leading organ professors, Charles Steggall (1826–1905), and in November 1887, as a young recitalist, he made an entry into the pages of the *Musical Times*, the leading monthly journal which (to the advantages of this book) would so fully chronicle his career as conductor:

> Mr Henry J. Wood gave his first organ recital at St Katherine Cree, Leadenhall Street, EC, on the 17th ult., in aid of the Church funds. His programme included works by Bach, Handel, Muffat, Widor, Freyer, Guilmant, Krebs, Cuthbert and Nunn. His second recital was given on the 24th ult., in aid of the Choir Fund.

His piano professor at the Royal Academy of Music was Walter Macfarren, younger brother of the Academy's principal, Sir George Macfarren. Now seventy-three, refusing to let his blindness disable him, George Macfarren was no negligible composer but his rule at the Academy was weak as well as conservative. Very different was his successor as principal, Alexander Mackenzie. On taking over in February 1888, he was informed that no room had been allotted to him as an office, as it was not expected he would need to be present very often. With his bluff Scottish manner the forty-year-old

Building

Mackenzie got his office, asserted his authority by conducting the student orchestra, and quashed the rule which had forbidden 'boys' and 'girls' even to talk together, unless engaged in a musical task.

Mackenzie's reforms would touch Henry J. Wood only towards the end of his period at the Academy. But Wood made his own strides forward. He won favourable notice as soloist in the first movement of Prout's Organ Concerto in E minor on 9 July 1887 at one of the Academy's public concerts at St James's Hall. In the same concert, also favourably noticed, was the first performance of a symphony in E minor by Edward German, seven years Wood's senior but a fellow-student in Prout's class. Wood himself came forth as a composer in the Academy's chamber concert on 16 March 1888 with what the *Era* called 'two really charming songs', with words translated from Heine as 'The sea hath its pearls' and 'When on my couch I'm lying'. The baritone soloist was Ben Grove, an American fellow-student whom Wood accompanied at the piano and who was to become a trusted friend.

At a further Academy concert on 13 June 1888 another song of Wood's, 'Love thee as only a mother can love' (words by Hermann Smith), was performed – a ballad 'much above the average of its class', according to the *Musical Times*. The young musician's ambitions went further: he tells us that he wrote a symphony in C at this time, 'modelled on Schubert's in the same key', presumably no. 9. Henry J. Wood was in fact shaping himself to be a composer. A 'Romance in C' for violin and piano was performed at a miscellaneous concert of the Grosvenor Choral Society (in the Belgravia area of London) on 19 November 1886 and was three times repeated at other such concerts in the following month – in all cases with the composer partnering his violinist friend Henry Charles Tonking.

His period at the Academy laid the ground for a lasting aspect of Wood's career, that of a teacher of singing. He became an accompanist for several voice-teachers on the Academy's staff, notably the long-lived Manuel Garcia (1805–1906), perhaps the most famous vocal teacher of his time. Garcia was the inventor of the laryngoscope, an apparatus using a system of mirrors enabling physicians and others to inspect the larynx and thus the vocal cords. Already in his eighties, having taught at the Academy since 1848, he was a man of immense vigour who would be remembered for flying upstairs three steps at a time. Wood recalled Garcia's instant reaction when, as a student accompanist to a mezzo-soprano, he allowed the tempo to slacken. Garcia 'cannoned me to the floor, taking the keys from under my fingers. The singer went on, and any onlooker might have thought it part of the game, so naturally was it done.'

That Wood actually took a formal course of singing lessons himself seems unlikely, despite an implication to the contrary in *My Life of Music*. Had that been the case, he would have been required to sing in the choir at the Academy concerts, and the choir lists (which survive) do not mention his name. Nevertheless he received medals for sight-singing as well as for piano and organ. (These medals were not competitive: a bronze was awarded for the completion of a first-year study, a silver for the second year.) His new fascination with the voice led him also to become accompanist for the Academy's opera class, jointly directed by Manuel's son Gustave Garcia (1837–1925) and Ettore Fiori. Under Macfarren's conservative rule, opera excerpts at that time were permitted to be performed only 'in private dress', but Gustave Garcia had ambitions which were to promote Wood's abilities in other ways.

Meanwhile, Wood as organist was naturally eager to hear the celebrities of his instrument – none of them more in demand than the Liverpool City organist, W. T. Best. At one of the 'monster' Handel Festivals at the Crystal Palace, which attracted audiences of 20,000 people and more, Best was heard in May 1888 in Handel's Organ Concerto no.7 in B flat (with his own elaborate cadenza). Wood, impressed, resolved to offer the work in his own performance at the Academy. In rehearsal there, Mackenzie handed over the conducting to one of Wood's fellow-students, whose inadequate technique failed to maintain the ensemble. Rising furiously from the organ bench, Wood left the Academy building and (according to his own account) never returned as a student, leaving his hat and coat behind him.

It seems a needless way to have lost a hat and coat when one's home was only round the corner. Indeed, Wood's statement that he 'ran away' from the Academy is nonsense: as already noted, a song of his was performed at the end-of-term concert that June, and his name was on the programme as accompanist. He simply did not return for a further year's or part-year's study – his career being already in bud as piano accompanist, organist and vocal teacher. In mid-1887 he had become organist and choirmaster at St John's Church, Fulham (south-west London) and continued to be engaged to give organ recitals at other churches.

But that career had not yet taken its definitive direction. He was showing no inclination to be a professional conductor. It is curious, indeed, that even in narrating the above incident involving an incompetent student conductor (unnamed!), Wood says nothing of any wish of his own to have taken up the baton there. This being the case, what is to be made of the statement in *My*

Life of Music that – as if in preparation for a conductor's life - he was sent by his father to hear orchestral music on various trips abroad, in 'Germany, Bavaria, France, Belgium and America'?

In Boston he was supposedly thrilled to hear the Boston Symphony Orchestra 'under George Henschel', playing Beethoven's *Eroica* 'with woodwind and brass such as I had never dreamed of'. This is not narration; it is fabrication. The Boston Symphony, founded in 1881 with musicians brought from Europe, was at that time by no means the great orchestra it later became and Henschel was a fledgeling conductor in his first job. No one would have journeyed *from* Europe to hear it; rather, the rich and cultured Bostonian during the virtually obligatory transatlantic tour would hope to hear a performance by one of Europe's great orchestras. Henschel, moreover, held his post only up to mid-1884, and last performed the *Eroica* on 1 December 1883. At that date Henry J. Wood, aged fourteen, was a pupil at Miss Vie's girls' school, years away from any decision to pursue a conducting career.

Such accounts of travel must now be seen as Wood's retrospective fantasy – serving a desire, in the autobiography of 1938, to trace a predestination to a conductor's career. Perhaps there was also a wish to recompense with thanks a father whom he was actually to shift aside once he married. These boyhood voyages had not been invented when Rosa Newmarch wrote the first book about Wood in 1904. Nor was Wood to repeat them when he actually conducted in Boston thirty years after that.

Similarly absent from Newmarch's *Henry J. Wood*, and surfacing only in 1938, is his dubious claim to have been engaged as pianist for the rehearsals in 1888 for the latest Gilbert and Sullivan operetta, *The Yeomen of the Guard*. Certainly impossible to believe is his supporting anecdote, in which he claimed to have played over several of Sullivan's trial versions of 'I have a song to sing, O!' before one was found to satisfy Gilbert. Following his normal practice, that song would have been completed by Sullivan before rehearsals began, and the celebrated composer would never have exposed a trial-and-error process to a young assistant. This is surely a fanciful addition to the *correct* record that Wood was engaged two years later, in December–January 1890–1, to assist in rehearsals of Sullivan's 'grand' opera, *Ivanhoe*.

Wood's autobiography also claims that he was engaged as accompanist for the famous Sunday afternoon At Homes of Mrs (Mary Frances) Ronalds. Fashionable society knew her as a talented American amateur singer admired by the Prince of Wales and pretended not to know that she was the unmarried Sullivan's mistress. Such informal At Homes and more formal evening parties were – and for many decades continued to be – helpful to aspiring and even to eminent musicians as sources of fees and tastes of the grand life. Wood mentions a few other Society hostesses by whom he was engaged as a youthful piano accompanist, but we do not hear of him later seeking their patronage for any grander enterprise.

The art of painting, always in oils, remained an enthusiasm. He tells of Sunday morning painting expeditions with his cousin Edgar Thomas Wood, son of Thomas James Wood: this cousin was to win repute as a water-colourist. Generally, however, Henry J. Wood was poorly educated – that is, educated quite well enough had he pursued his father's trade, but disadvantageously for the artistic career which lay before him.

By his own account he had left school at fifteen. His work at the Academy had edged his knowledge into an appreciation of song-verses and theatrical matters, but no further. He had not learnt a foreign language – and never did. Outside music and painting he had developed virtually no curiosity. Through the rest of his life he showed not the smallest interest in public and political affairs of the day. Social issues as raised by the novels and plays of the Nineties such as Thomas Hardy's *Tess of the D'Urbervilles* and Ibsen's *Ghosts* were never his concern. His profession was everything, and he was a workaholic before that term had been invented.

One incident remains to characterize those youthful years and at the same time to show the unreliability of *My Life of Music*. By his own account, Wood abruptly and permanently broke off his friendship with Tonking on learning that he (an organist as well as violinist) had played a successful prank on a fellow-organist, changing the pre-selected groups of stops drawn by the composition-pedals so that an intendedly quiet voluntary came forth with a blast that shook the congregation. The incident was held important enough to recount in *My Life of Music*: ' "What a filthy trick!" I said in disgust, and left him there and then. I never saw him again.'

But he *did* see him again. Tonking was to be engaged several times as organ soloist during Wood's early seasons as conductor of the Queen's Hall Orchestra. Can Wood really have forgotten that renewal of relationship? It would have been more truthful but less colourful to have written that they ceased to be intimates. Friendship, we are meant to infer, could not survive an offence to musical seriousness and dignity.

Independence of judgement and an absolute confidence in one's own authority – these qualities are certainly those of a conductor, and they had already been shown by Henry J. Wood. The Royal Academy had assisted in

Building

his musical development and in later years he repaid that debt generously. But when he closed the door on it (with or without his coat), he did so without having identified his future role: none of his teachers would have referred to 'young Wood, who wants to be a conductor'. Not even in his own mind can he have made such a choice. Even three years later in the 1891 census he listed himself – still living with his parents – as 'music composer', and only that.

Chapter 2

Opera

1887–94

No more than any other musician of his generation did Wood receive formal lessons in conducting. No lessons were offered by the Academy or by its foreign counterparts. Every professional knew – if only by being on the receiving end – the conventional ways of beating four in a bar, three in a bar, and so on. The rest, if one had the gift of leadership and the requisite type of musical mind, was to be learnt by observation, intuition and practice. In Wood's case the opportunity arose in the course of his search for a livelihood as a musician-of-all-work – organist, choirmaster, piano accompanist, teacher of singing, composer.

The first occasion that he was actually paid to conduct, he later maintained, was a choral concert in Clapton (east London), at which the recently deceased George Macfarren was commemorated by a performance of his cantata, *May Day*. In old age, looking back at his youthful scrapbook, Henry J. Wood decided that this event of 12 December 1887 (when he was nineteen, and still a student at the Academy) should serve as the basis from which he would calculate a period of fifty years in conducting. Against the notice of this concert printed in the *Musical Times* he wrote in heavy pencil: 'This creats [*sic*] my 50th as a paid conductor.' By retrospectively supposing that he was not paid until the following month, he was able to pick 1938 as his jubilee year.

But such casual, low-level engagements as conductor came to almost every qualified organist. An immense gap stretched between that and the conductorship of a major orchestral series or choral festival. At the top of the British musical tree was a select flock of composers *who conducted as well*: Sullivan, Cowen, Stanford, Mackenzie. All of these, except Cowen, at some stage in their careers also took leading educational posts. They were not 'career conductors' – a state seemingly achievable only with the credentials of foreign birth. The Neapolitan Sir Michael Costa had been for twenty-one years (1847–68) the musical director of the Royal Italian Opera at Covent Garden. The German-born Sir Charles Hallé (originally Carl Halle) headed in Manchester the orchestra which still bears his name. German-born likewise, and likewise to be knighted, August Manns conducted the Saturday symphony concerts at the Crystal Palace for forty-six years until 1901.

Like many an organist Henry J. Wood formed a local amateur orchestra. But 'conductor' came only in third place when he advertised his services, perhaps at Gustave Garcia's suggestion, in *The Stage* on 14 June 1889:

> Mr Henry J. Wood (conductor of the Bayswater Orchestral Society), pianist, composer and conductor. Disengaged for town or country. 185 Oxford Street, London W.

Whether or not in response to this, the Arthur Rousbey English Opera Company engaged him as conductor. It was a decisive step – his *real* start as a professional conductor, requiring six or more performances per week plus rehearsals for his singers and orchestral players. So, where his Continental counterpart might have proceeded to learn the conductor's trade on the musical staff of an opera house – in a gradual rise, feeling his way as coach, rehearsal pianist, chorus-master and off-stage conductor – Henry J. Wood was plunged at a stroke into the musical direction of a touring company.

Of operatic organizations serving the provinces (and always performing in English) the Carl Rosa Opera Company was the most celebrated and the longest lasting (1875–1960). But the late Victorian age knew several others. The nation-wide diffusion of opera (as of Shakespeare) by live performers at fairly inexpensive prices is a phenomenon too easily missed by musical historians concentrating on London. Like the Carl Rosa, each of these other companies was owned by its musical leader, on the pattern of actor-managers such as Henry Irving in the playhouse. Such companies criss-crossed the country, presenting their repertory of plays or operas in towns large and small and travelling between locations on Sundays, commonly by specially chartered trains. The harpist Marie Goossens, grand-daughter and daughter and sister of three conductors all called Eugene Goossens, recalled her mother 'travelling every Sunday with thirteen packages, including two large skips (theatrical trunks made to order in Dewsbury, Yorkshire), a pram, a bath, and a sewing-machine'.

The repertory of the travelling opera companies went as far back as Mozart and up to the most modern works: Carl Rosa played Puccini's *La Bohème* in Manchester in 1897, before London heard it. There was

Valentine Smith's English Opera Company; there was the J. W. Turner Company, whose repertory included a revival of Macfarren's opera *Robin Hood*. Rousbey's troupe – Rousbey himself taking leading baritone roles – promised something even rarer, a new opera. The weekly *Musical Standard* on 2 November 1889 noted its miserably inadequate performance at South Shields of *Belphegor* ('for the first time on any stage'), with music by Alfred Christesen. The conductor is not named in the notice, which may have spared Henry J. Wood's blushes.

Belphegor (misspelt *Belphigore)* is mentioned in *My Life of Music* as part of Wood's assignment on being engaged as conductor of Rousbey's company. During 1889–90 *The Stage* recorded further performances of that opera at Stockport and Sheffield, similarly without reporting the conductor's name, alongside such works as *The Bohemian Girl, Maritana* (the popular English operas by Balfe and by Wallace) and *The Marriage of Figaro*. Wood's own account tells of the company's chorus of forty and 'a travelling orchestra of six', to be supplemented by local musicians.

That could be a dire hazard, as Eugene Goossens II (1867–1958) found when he took over the Rousbey company's conducting a few years later. As his son narrated it:

> In one small town, after a spell of bad business, the company's finances were so slender that he was reduced to conducting a performance of *Cavalleria* with five players – harmonium, cornet, horn, and two violins. The next day even the cornet and horn players deserted, and he had to conduct *Tannhäuser* with two violins and a harmonium.

Wood later wrote amusingly of his Rousbey tour. In a production of *Don Giovanni* in 'a small Lancashire town', the Commendatore's marble horse was too easily recognized as a cut-out cow, evoking cries of 'Milk-ho!' and 'Fourpence a quart!' On top of it was a bicycle saddle for the singer who, when the whole thing presently collapsed, was compelled to sing from the floor 'on the wrong side of the cow-horse'. The conditions must have been more often infuriating than comic.

Wood had not learnt – nor ever would learn – to handle money. He allowed himself to accept a three-year contract starting at two guineas (£2.10) *a week*, though he claims to have charged half a guinea for an hour's singing lesson at this time. His parents had still to supplement his income. Well might his mother feel concern: she apparently travelled ahead of the company to secure him lodgings at Ramsgate (where the tour opened) and to give him 'a tremendous tea' before returning to London. In mid-tour, according to Wood, Rousbey was induced to improve his terms. But before his first season was over the twenty-year-old musician understandably sought a way out of his contract: 'Some difficult letters had to be written.' No other post was on offer, but almost anything else would be better than Rousbey's blind alley.

He was still nourishing his career as composer. The respected firm of Weekes had published his 'Romance in C' for violin and piano in 1887 and now began to publish his songs, three of which had words by his friend, Hermann Smith: 'Love thee as only a mother can love', 'The Poacher' and 'My perfect love'. Only an already established composer could have insisted on a royalty (a percentage of price paid on each copy sold): Wood probably had to sell his songs outright for a few pounds each. The occasional concert performance would bring the composer no fee, since what later became familiar as 'performing right' was unenforceable in those days. Nevertheless such performances counted in pushing sales to the domestic music circle which was the prime target.

Wood's role as piano accompanist at small suburban concerts permitted a gentle promotion of his compositions. His song, 'To one I love' (another Weekes publication), was given in one such concert by the Grosvenor Choral Society in Belgravia, London on 20 July 1888, and on 9 February in the following year this society brought out Wood's oratorio, *St Dorothea*. He won the approval of an American soprano of some repute, Alice Esty, whose performance of 'My perfect love' in the Scottish town of Melrose on 17 November 1889 was perhaps the first performance of any of Wood's works without his own participation. He had a more ambitious goal in view – light musical entertainment for the stage.

Many indeed were the would-be rivals of the apparently unstoppable Gilbert and Sullivan, whose latest success was *The Gondoliers* (1889). Some of the hopeful new shows opened in London's West End, some in provincial or Scottish cities. In the inner-suburban obscurity of Kilburn Town Hall on 1 May 1890 was heard *Daisy*, 'a comic opera', with words by F. Grove Palmer and music by the twenty-one-year-old Henry J. Wood. The same librettist served him for the production of a one-act operetta entitled *Returning the Compliment* at the Royal Park Hall, Camden Town, on 5 November of the same year. Subsequent performances named 'Otto Waldau' as an additional librettist – which might be supposed a pseudonym for the composer himself (*Wald-au* = Wood-Meadow), if the slightest spark of literary talent on his part were known.

These were trial shots, their failure to reach the West End not deterring

Wood: two years later he would reload his guns as a stage composer. Meanwhile Gustave Garcia engaged him to conduct the young singers of his private vocal school in a performance of Ambroise Thomas's opera *Mignon* at the Royalty Theatre, London, on 23 May 1891. Next in Wood's operatic repertory came *The Mock Doctor*, as Gounod's *Le médecin malgré lui* was known in English. With Richard Temple (Gilbert and Sullivan's original Mikado) as its star and stage director, the production had won initial success in London at the Grand Theatre, Islington; Wood was engaged to conduct only a single performance on 14 July 1891 at the Crystal Palace.

More substantial was an engagement to conduct the Carl Rosa Opera, still vigorous despite the death of its founder two years before. Its provincial tour in 1891 was to be centred on the personality of the soprano Marie Roze and on *Carmen*. (Bizet's opera was enormously popular and had just enjoyed the tribute of parody in a stage piece called *Carmen Up-to-data*.) Married to a son of the London operatic impresario, James Henry Mapleson, Roze was – very unusually for a French artist – an accomplished performer in English and was much admired in such parts as Marguerite (*Faust*) and Carmen, often treated in those days as a soprano role. Henry J. Wood opened the four-month tour in Blackpool on 24 August.

Roze had a beauty of appearance which Wood compared to that of Edward VII's mistress, Lillie Langtry, but it is rather hard to credit English provincial audiences with the degree of enthusiasm for the forty-five-year-old prima donna which Wood narrates. After the opera, her admirers supposedly gathered at her hotel, 'often refusing to go away until she had appeared on the balcony and had sung them a song. They took the horses from the shafts of her carriage outside the theatre, the stage door of which was unapproachable for an hour after the performance.'

'We travelled with a splendid orchestra of ten,' wrote Wood in *My Life of Music* – not quite sarcastically, since that force was augmented *en route* by local musicians. Wood's recollection was that the quality of available players was better than for Rousbey's company, since the Carl Rosa did not descend to such small towns. Nevertheless the Carl Rosa took in Huddersfield and Bolton, towns which a later age would disdainfully wipe from the map of touring opera. The press-cuttings pasted into the young conductor's scrapbook show mainly praise for an orchestra unusually augmented to thirty or so, but the *Manchester Examiner* was critical:

> The weak point of the productions has been the orchestra. With the exception of *The Bohemian Girl* none of its performances have been first-rate, and while admitting the difficulties attending the orchestral production

of five operas in one week, we think that if Mr Henry T. Wood [*sic*], the conductor, had satisfied himself with a smaller but more efficient orchestra, the result would have been more acceptable to singers and audience.

Once again, he tried his hand as a stage composer with *A Hundred Years Ago*, a 'pastoral operetta'. His librettist was 'Alec Nelson', the pseudonym of Edward Aveling, who taught English diction at the Royal Academy of Music and, in private life, defied convention by living in unmarried state with Karl Marx's daughter Eleanor. Produced in a matinée performance at the Royalty Theatre, London, on 16 June 1892, the piece won a few favourable notices and a few later showings, but can have earned Wood nothing in either cash or prospects.

As conductor, however, 'the best-paid operatic engagement I ever held' came when two of the Carl Rosa company's leading singers broke off to set up their own touring enterprise. For Georgina Burns and Leslie Crotty, Henry J. Wood prepared the musical edition for a newly devised English version of Rossini's *La Cenerentola*. As was then common practice, he freely interpolated extra numbers from the composer's other works. The Georgina Burns Light Opera Company was bold enough to tour the one work (she playing Cinderella and he Dandini) on a night-after-night basis, instead of carrying the usual repertory of half a-dozen operas. Unfortunately the box-office response was unfavourable.

But now, in mid-1892, Wood was enabled to leap the gap that separated provincial touring from metropolitan grand opera. The most prestigious of London presentations were concentrated within what London Society called 'the season', between May and July. Here the greatest singers of Europe performed, almost invariably in Italian – in which language Wagner's *The Flying Dutchman* and *Lohengrin* had both been introduced to London. Under the powerful management of Sir Augustus Harris, Covent Garden was only now (1891) in the process of puncturing the primacy of Italian, renaming itself the Royal Opera House instead of the Royal Italian Opera House.

The title of 'Royal Opera' was, however, not exclusive to Covent Garden. It could be appropriated by any manager who had succeeded in getting one of the royal family to join his list of advance subscribers. The challenger in autumn 1892 was a 'Signor Lago', late of St Petersburg. In a similar challenge two years before, he had leased the Shaftesbury Theatre and brought off the coup of introducing London to Mascagni's sensationally successful *Cavalleria Rusticana*. In 1892 Lago resorted to a lesser theatre, the Olympic, for his Royal Opera with the seventy-year-old Luigi Arditi as

ROYAL LYCEUM THEATRE

PROPRIETORS & MANAGERS   MESSRS HOWARD & WYNDHAM.
ACTING MANAGER, . . MR ARTHUR WESTON.

MONDAY, 22nd AUGUST 1892

For Six Nights only,

GEORGINA BURNS

LIGHT OPERA COMPANY.

Proprietor, ... Mr LESLIE CROTTY

Under the Direction of . Mr T. W. ROBERTSON

Musical Director, Mr HENRY J. WOOD

Private Boxes, £2 2s.   Dress Circle, 5s.
Orchestra Stalls 4s.   Upper Circle, 3s.   Pit Stalls, 2s.
Amphitheatre, 1s.   Gallery, 6d.

Box Plan at Messrs PATERSON & SONS, also at the
Royal Lyceum Theatre Box Office, (Telephone No. 660),
and at both places Seats can be booked from 10 till 4 daily,
Saturdays 10 till 2.

23

principal conductor. An assistant conductor was also needed, and Lago's choice – apparently through consultation with Gustave Garcia – fell on the twenty-three-year-old who had won his spurs on the Carl Rosa's *Carmen* tour.

A Russian opera was Lago's bold choice as the novelty of his new London season. Tchaikovsky's *Yevgeny Onegin* (or *Eugene Onegin*, as it became known) had been produced in Moscow in 1879, and in St Petersburg from 1883; but apart from a Hamburg production earlier in 1892, it was virtually unknown in the West. Orchestral performances under such conductors as Richter, however, had made Tchaikovsky an increasingly well-known composer, though his music had not penetrated the conservative programmes of the Philharmonic Society.

On 17 October 1892 Arditi opened Lago's season at the Olympic by conducting the National Anthem; he then stepped down, and Henry J. Wood delivered London's first-ever performance of any Tchaikovsky opera. It was sung in English – quite a daring stroke on Lago's part. Glinka's *A Life for the Tsar* had been sung in Italian at Covent Garden five years before. The translation of *Onegin* had been commissioned from the music critic H. Sutherland Edwards and his wife, who was a scholar in Russian.

Principal singers well known to London audiences had been engaged – among them the American baritone Eugene Oudin in the title-role and the British soprano Fanny Moody as the heroine, Tatiana. By happy coincidence Tatiana's sister Olga was played by Fanny Moody's real sister, Lily Moody; and Tatiana's eventual husband, Prince Gremin, was played by Fanny Moody's real husband, Charles Manners. (In the following year these two would add to the roster of touring companies by establishing the Moody-Manners Opera Company.) A supporting member of the cast actually had a link with Tchaikovsky in person – though this seems not to have been pointed out at the time. Alexandra Svyatlovskaya, who sang the important role of the nurse Filipyevna in the new *Onegin*, had sung the main contralto role of Solokha in *Cherevichki* ('The Slippers') in Moscow under the composer's baton in 1887. Perhaps Lago had encouraged her to come to London.

The performance was extensively and favourably reviewed. In Wood's press-cuttings book, more than twenty large pages each of three columns of tiny print display reviews from such sources as *The Sportsman* and *The Ladies' Pictorial* as well as the principal newspapers. The *Daily Graphic* reproduced the scenes and 'close-ups' of the characters in exceptionally sympathetic line illustrations. Wood was judged to have conducted 'with

The first British performance of Tchaikovsky's *Yevgeny Onegin*, conducted by Henry J. Wood: from the *Daily Graphic*, October 1892.

skill' (*The Times*); 'Mr John [*sic*] Wood conducted ably' (*The People*); Wood's work was 'excellent', according to the *St James's Gazette*. Bernard Shaw, at that time reviewing for *The World*, was cooler: Wood's conducting was approved, 'but he did not succeed in getting any really fine execution out of the band'. The conductor in opera was often reviewed principally in terms of the orchestra; the idea of ranking a conductor's 'interpretation' on the plane of importance given to a prima donna or leading tenor would have seemed ludicrous.

The production 'made' Wood. It un-made Lago. The new work failed with the public; the season, due to include performances of *Die Zauberflöte*, *Der Freischütz* and *Lohengrin* (all in Italian), ended prematurely and the impresario bolted, apparently leaving conductor and singers unpaid. But Wood had discovered an affinity for Russian music which was strongly to mould his career. On 1 June 1893 he attended the concert at which Tchaikovsky (his death only five months distant) faced a London audience and conducted his Fourth Symphony for the Philharmonic Society: Wood made notes on the composer's tempos and expression, and claimed fifty years later to be still adhering to them. Many leading figures in London musical life were introduced to Tchaikovsky on that visit, but the young conductor of *Yevgeny Onegin* was not, apparently, among them.

The collapse of Lago's season had removed Wood's toehold in 'grand' opera, but the lighter, non-operatic stage still offered work. He was the conductor of a revival of the French operetta, Hervé's *Mam'zelle Nitouche*, which opened at the Trafalgar Square Theatre on 6 March 1893. Its American star, May Yohe, with a big personality and a vocal range of about ten notes, told him that he 'couldn't conduct for nuts'. Wood's *My Life of Music* omits all mention of this show but recalls *The Lady Slavey*, of which he conducted the London run (Avenue Theatre, from 20 October 1894). Yohe, who played the supposed 'slavey' (housemaid), is dubbed by Wood 'the most extraordinary prima donna I ever met', with not a word more. She went on to marry into the aristocracy as Lady Francis Hope, heiress to the title of Duchess of Newcastle.

Around this time, it would seem, Wood's devotion to painting led him to seek contact with leading teachers. It is characteristic of his autobiography to leave the dates obscure. He had begun by attending evening classes at Heatherley's school of art in Newman Street (near his parents' home in Oxford Street). 'I then studied under the great Legros and, later, under Brown and Tonks at the Slade School of Art. Two years afterwards I went to

St John's Wood Art School and studied under [Alfred] Ward . . . Later still I was under [Frederick D.] Walenn.'

If this account is accurate, it would indicate a training of some distinction. Alphonse Legros, a friend of Manet, Courbet and Degas during the 1860s, was principal of the Slade School of Art in London from 1876 to 1892; his *Le repas des pauvres* or *The Paupers' Meal* (1877, Tate Gallery) and Fred Brown's *Hard Times* (1886) are recognized as distinguished 'realist' paintings of the time. Henry Tonks, who abandoned a surgeon's career for a painter's and began instructing at the Slade in 1893, is classed as 'one of the foremost teachers of his generation' and was a friend of the British impressionist, Wilson Steer. Study with Legros at the Slade cannot have been *later* than 1892; study with Tonks, not *earlier* than 1893. Surprisingly, the records of the School (then, as now, part of University College London) indicate that he *never* enrolled there, at any rate in normal full-time attendance – but the possibility of his having attended part-time or casually cannot be excluded.

Wood's destiny now steered him away from the theatre, where no conductor could at that time make his reputation, towards the orchestral concert-hall and the large choral festival. Only in one further engagement would he conduct opera on the stage, but the experience of *Onegin* was crucial to his musical life. Twenty years later his first child was born: he named her, after the heroine of that work, Tatiana.

Chapter 3

Queen's Hall

1893–5

Theatrical engagements were welcome when they came, but Henry J. Wood derived his modest income mainly as a teacher of singing at the family home in Oxford Street. A few minutes' walk from there – as near, in fact, as the Royal Academy of Music was in another direction – stood the new hall where his professional identity was about to take its definitive shape.

Destined to be the chief home of London orchestral music for half a century, Queen's Hall opened its doors on 25 November 1893 – with a children's party in the afternoon and an evening entertainment in which the band of the Coldstream Guards and the organist W. T. Best were among the performers. At the official opening concert on 2 December, Mendelssohn's *Hymn of Praise* was conducted by Frederic Hymen Cowen. The soloists were Emma Albani and Edward Lloyd, as eminent a soprano and tenor as Britain could boast, along with the mezzo-soprano Margaret Hoare, whom Wood had known as his father's fellow-chorister at St Sepulchre's, Holborn.

The hall stood north of Oxford Circus, on the eastern side of Langham Place. The area was already distinguished, not so much by the inferior Thomas Nash church of All Souls as by the palatial seven-story Langham Hotel on the opposite side. Not far off, at 48 Great Portland Street, was Pagani's, a restaurant which was for decades beloved by musicians, Wood included. An advertisement for Pagani's would regularly appear in the programmes of the Queen's Hall promenade concerts.

The new concert-hall presented an odd approach to its patrons: from the street, they walked downstairs to reach the main floor. But once inside, there was no denying its superiority to the older St James's Hall in Piccadilly – not only in capacity (2500 as against 2127) but in comfort. Concert-goers at the St James's were seated on 'uncomfortable, long, narrow, green-upholstered benches . . . with the numbers of the seats tied over the straight backs with bright pink tape, like office files'. Queen's Hall offered individual seats on the main floor, 'armchair accommodation' in the principal balcony or grand circle, and less luxurious seating in a second balcony. In general amenity Queen's Hall established a newer standard for concert-going as Richard D'Oyly Carte's electrically lit Savoy Theatre had for theatre-going a dozen years before.

Its acoustics were agreed to be near-perfect. Less approval was given to its much-ornamented interior decoration, with its basic paintwork 'the colour of the belly of a London mouse'. (The architect, T. E. Knightley, kept a string of dead mice in the painting studio while work was in progress.) 'Much did she censure', E. M. Forster was to write in *Howards End*, 'the attenuated Cupids who encircle the ceiling of Queen's Hall, inclining each to each with vapid gesture, and clad in sallow pantaloons, on which the October sunlight struck.'

Henry J. Wood's was the name which, more than any other, would be associated with the Queen's Hall by concert-goers over fifty years. But the managerial and musical direction of the hall lay firmly in the hands of Robert Newman (1858–1926). In posters, newspaper advertising and concert programmes he ensured a conspicuous display of his name. He had been appointed by the original leaseholder of the hall, F. W. M. Ravenscroft, as its salaried manager for the first year, receiving a percentage of the takings, then took the hall on a tenancy from him.

As soon as the hall opened in 1893, he persuaded leading concert-giving bodies to reap its advantages. The Philharmonic Society moved from St James's Hall for its very next season (1894); likewise the Richter orchestral concerts and those promoted and conducted by George Henschel. So did the Boosey Ballad Concerts, offering broader programmes (mixed vocal and instrumental) than the name indicated. Ballad concerts, lasting up to four hours on a Saturday afternoon, 'the musical orgie of suburbia' as a derisive commentator called them, were nevertheless a firm fixture of the musical calendar and an important source of income for leading singers.

Robert Newman, operating a commercial enterprise at Queen's Hall, was not inexperienced in risk-taking: he had been an unsuccessful stockbroker. With musical training, however, he had turned to a singer's career as a bass before embarking on musical management. On the example of Ambrose Austin, the manager of the St James's Hall, he set out not only to make Queen's Hall attractive to other managements but to establish his own concerts. A Queen's Hall Choral Society was formed under the conductorship of Frederic Hymen Cowen, then of the equally well-known Alberto Randegger, an Italian who had been settled in London for forty years. A

Queen's Hall String Quartet (performing in the smaller hall of the building, with seating for 500) was led by the Spanish violinist-conductor-composer Enrique Fernández Arbós, lately appointed to a professorship at the Royal College of Music. Symphony concerts were also given under Randegger's baton, though with no permanent, named orchestra.

The institution which a future generation would call the 'Henry Wood Promenade Concerts' did not spring at once into existence. Wood was not the first orchestral conductor at Queen's Hall; Newman's series was far from being London's first promenade concerts; and they were never then called Proms, much less the Henry Wood Proms. They were Mr Robert Newman's promenade concerts, in which Mr Robert Newman's Queen's Hall Orchestra performed and his employee, Mr Henry J. Wood, conducted. The promenade concerts had a special role in Newman's calendar – aiming through lower prices at a less affluent audience while fashionable Society was 'out of Town' for the summer.

Founded originally on a French example (whence their name), promenade concerts had been intermittently promoted in London since 1838. Under the French showman-conductor Jullien, who often added military bands to his orchestral force in order to reinforce the thrill of overwhelming sound, they consolidated their appeal in the 1840s and '50s. Jullien, a dandy in appearance and an incarnation of energy on the rostrum, appealed to the eye as well as to the ear. He *demonstrated* the music, as the *Illustrated London News* observed in 1849:

> When the promenade conductor turns round with vehement gesture to animate his adroit executants of the parchment and brass, his pantomime is most intense and insinuating. He typifies a crescendo or a crash with astounding vigour – his stick rolling spasmodically and his body writhing convulsively.

For his promenade programmes Jullien relied heavily on dance music and showy instrumental solos, with a substantial component of classical overtures by such composers as Weber, Beethoven and Mendelssohn. There was a more cautious helping of symphonies or, more often, detached movements from them. The popularity of opera was evidenced not merely by vocal excerpts but by orchestral 'selections' in which various solo instrumentalists from the orchestra 'impersonated' the solo voices. Opera also often provided the tunes from which a set of quadrilles was arranged – though Jullien's greatest success in this line was with his *British Army Quadrilles*, based on popular military airs.

Jullien died in a French insane asylum early in 1860, but other managements continued to promote promenade concerts in London – with less magnetic conductors – through the following decades, particularly at Covent Garden Theatre in summer and early autumn. It became the custom to place any symphonic element in the first half of the programme, the second half being given over entirely to a popular miscellany.

Within a season of several weeks the occasional 'classical night' would give that component an extra emphasis. A so-called 'Mendelssohn Festival' during the season conducted by Alfred Mellon in 1863 offered Mendelssohn's Violin Concerto, the *Italian* Symphony, and others of his works (including piano solos) before the interval, then moved to the usual miscellany – beginning with an orchestral selection from Gounod's *Faust* and ending with a 'new Spanish waltz'. With the all-important features of refreshments available throughout the concert and an admission price as low as a shilling, here was the ready-made, well-tested model for the Newman–Wood programmes.

Among the lighter items there was a ready welcome for ballads and cornet solos, both redolent of the concert-goers' own ,humble music-making. Equally apt in reproducing 'vocal' sentiment and in the dazzle of fast articulation, the cornet was a 'people's' instrument – familiar in the theatre, in the street, in the domestic circle. Such bridging between 'high' and 'low' usages was long to remain an essential element of the popularity of the 'Proms' themselves. A succession of virtuoso players of the instrument wove their spell, typified at Covent Garden in the 1870s by 'Mr [Jules] Levy the cornet, looking as if not a cornet but a coronet were within his grasp, and as if that theatre and all its contents belonged to him'.

In 1878 and 1879 the promenade seasons at Covent Garden were promoted by the catering firm of Gatti's, with Sullivan engaged to conduct on 'classical nights'. Cowen functioned as conductor in 1880 – prophetically (in view of Wood's coming championing of Russian music) performing Glinka's *Kamarinskaya*. When the promenade concerts temporarily migrated to Her Majesty's Theatre, one of the soloists of the 1889 season was Robert Newman, bass, and the conductor was the operatically expert Enrico Bevignani. Cowen was again conductor when the promenade concerts returned to Covent Garden in 1893 – now under the management of the impresario Farley Sinkins, who had Robert Newman as his assistant.

Since Tchaikovsky's Piano Concerto no.1 and symphonies by Haydn and Mozart had been given even on evenings not specially denoted as 'classical', it could be maintained that promenade audiences' taste was already rising in the early Nineties. Nevertheless, London was without a promenade season in summer 1894: no management, it seems, could sense a continuing yearly demand for such concerts. Nor, since Jullien's day, had a conductor been found with the personality to reinvigorate them. Not, that is, until Robert Newman found Henry J. Wood.

At the beginning of 1894 Wood was once more enjoying an association with Marie Roze, who had engaged him to conduct on her 'farewell' concert tour and sang two songs of his in her programmes. But his own ventures as a theatrical composer were dribbling to an end. He had met further disappointment in his association with 'Alec Nelson' (Edward Aveling), whose play *The Frog* with Wood's incidental music achieved a grand total of three performances from 30 October 1893 at the Royalty Theatre. He must have seen that the conductor's baton was the instrument pointing his best way forward, though he had just one or two further occasions to show himself as a composer.

Already he had been accepted into a musically influential London circle. Roze's farewell tour had been under the management of 'N. Vert' – the name which Narciso Vertigliano had adopted in setting up London's first artists' agency. Vert was a member of the informal 'You Be Quiet' club which was run by the piano dealer Archibald Ramsden and met above his Bond Street showrooms. No less a celebrity than Hans Richter had accepted an invitation to membership. Wood, having joined, could expect from time to time to meet there such leaders of their profession as the violinist Arbós, the tenor Edward Lloyd, the acoustician A. J. Ellis, and the music critic Alfred Kalisch. At this time too Wood first met the brilliant but unclubbable Bernard Shaw.

Wood first appeared within Newman's domain in the supporting roles of pianist and organist. He did not, as he later claimed, take part in the first public concert at Queen's Hall on 2 December 1893 but his engagements there in 1894 included a St George's Day concert (23 April) when Robert Newman resumed his former role as bass singer to deliver 'The Roast Beef of Old England' to Henry J. Wood's no doubt energetic piano accompaniment.

In the second half Newman's voice again rose patriotically in a song by Lady Arthur Hill denouncing the campaign for Irish Home Rule on which Gladstone's government had met defeat in the previous month:

> Brothers, shall we sever? Never! Never! Never!
> But we'll cling for ever to Union and to Queen.
> No Home Rule shall bind us, but traitors ever find us
> With thousands more behind us for Union and for Queen.

Topicality would remain a favourite card for Newman to play, but he would in future steer away from such political partisanship as this.

More significant for Wood in that month was the brilliant London début, at Queen's Hall, of the conductor Felix Mottl (1856–1911). He had been brought to London under the management of Alfred Schulz-Curtius, who held a general London agency for the Wagner festivals at Bayreuth. Presumably on Mottl's invitation, Wood attended the Bayreuth Festival (where Mottl was conducting) in that summer of 1894. When Mottl reappeared at Queen's Hall on 22 May 1895, the programme included an excerpt from *The Flying Dutchman* in English, with 'an efficient choir of ladies which had been trained by Mr H. J. Wood, and which Mr Schulz-Curtius had imaginatively entitled "The Wagner Choir"(!)', as the *Musical Times* pointedly reported.

Newman, for his part, had found a capable and congenial pianist, organist and chorus-master. But how had he been convinced that the twenty-six-year-old Henry J. Wood was the right man to conduct the first long-term orchestral series at Queen's Hall?

There seems no evidence that he had ever previously conducted a professional orchestra in London, except in Lago's opera season of 1892. More than sixty years later the Russian-born pianist Mark Hambourg claimed that as a boy prodigy he and his father had attended that opera season and were impressed enough to engage Wood immediately to conduct Hambourg's own concert with orchestra at the St James's Hall. In sober fact Hambourg was studying with Leschetizky in Vienna at this period and did not perform with an orchestra in London until after 1900. Equally without basis is the statement that Wood appeared as orchestral conductor for the distinguished pianist Emil Sauer at Queen's Hall on 28 March 1895. This was a concert of instrumental and vocal soloists, without orchestra, with Sauer as the star on his own and Wood as one of two 'conductors' in the obsolete sense of 'director at the piano' for ensemble numbers.

In Newman's eyes, Wood must have compensated for inexperience in orchestral experience by his general musicianship and youthful confidence – supported, perhaps, by a testimonial from Marie Roze. After all, what was required? For the proposed season of close-packed nightly events with minimum rehearsal, the prime demand was for incisive leadership: depth and finesse were not on the agenda for promenade concerts. Not yet.

To underwrite his new enterprise, however, Newman needed capital. In inviting Wood to conduct, he asked him for an investment as well. (Richter, Henschel and Hallé all had financial involvement in their London concerts.)

Building

The sum proposed by Newman is impossibly recalled in *My Life of Music* as 'two or three thousand pounds', equivalent to more than £100,000 today. Wood in any case could not oblige – but fortune brought a financial rescuer in Dr George Cathcart, a London throat specialist with a special interest in singing. His meeting with Wood was apparently due to one of Wood's vocal pupils, the bass W. A. Peterkin. Cathcart's own account, published in 1944, insisted that he had kept an eye on Wood since noticing at the Fisheries Exhibition of 1883 'the little boy in the velveteen suit with curly black hair, whose feet barely touched the organ pedals'.

In Wood's categorical assertion, Cathcart by his financial backing was 'directly responsible' for the establishment of the promenade concerts. He made his investment conditional on the adoption of 'low pitch', which required not only new woodwind and brass instruments for the players, but the retuning of the pipes of the recently built Queen's Hall organ. It was a crucial step in British musical life. The matter of pitch had for decades troubled the musical scene. In Britain, a standard of pitch was in general use by which any (written) note was sounded at about half a tone higher than would have been heard on the Continent. As Cathcart and many others had remarked, singers reaching for high notes as written by composers were put to a strain which would not have faced them in France (from which a lower tuning, called in French the *diapason normal*, spread to other countries). Newman's acceptance of Cathcart's view was the decisive step in British acceptance of the *diapason normal*, with the A above Middle C at 439 Hz. Our present-day standard concert pitch was fixed in 1939 as A = 440 – though the public has now become acquainted with considerably lower pitches adopted by 'early music' ensembles for music of previous centuries.

In 1895 it fell to Cathcart himself – henceforth the conductor's close friend – to finance the purchase of the new, low-pitched wind-instruments required, in the face of the players' suspicions. But 'most of them . . . bought them from Dr Cathcart at the end of the first season – an acknowledgement that he had won his battle for the low pitch in England'. (Other bodies followed suit, including the Philharmonic Society in 1896.) Henry J. Wood would eventually have a machine designed (still extant at the Royal Academy of Music), with turning handles and bellows, by which to check the tuning of his players' instruments – to a pitch just *below* A=440 for strings, and a little below that for wind instruments, allowing for the rise in pitch which would result in a normally heated, normally full hall.

As momentous as the fixing of the new pitch, and far more conspicuous in public view, was the establishment of 'Mr Robert Newman's Queen's Hall

Orchestra': that description had never been used before. Though many of the players must have performed at various orchestral concerts in the hall, this was the first time they came together for a regular nightly engagement which turned out to be eight weeks long. After the first promenade season the orchestra's work rapidly grew to embrace concert engagements throughout the year. It thus became London's first 'permanent' orchestra – or almost permanent, in so far as engagements were still offered on a short-term basis, not on a salary.

Newman's invitation was Wood's great chance, and recognized by him as such before the series began. Habituated since his college days to providing the Press with helpful musical snippets – helpful to himself, that is – he was now able to plant a splendid puff in a professional journal. The reference to having conducted forty-six operas is one of its exaggerations. The press-cutting, retained in Wood's scrapbook without identification of source, is approximately datable because the orchestral leader is named as J. T. Carrodus, who had indeed been engaged but died on 13 July 1895, four weeks before the promenade season was due to open. It probably marks the first time that the word 'conductorship' was used in English to denote the art, not merely the position, of the conductor.

> In these days conductorship has been given increased importance. Mr Henry J. Wood is a conductor 'to the manner born' whose capabilities managers have recognized; his skill in this office has brought him rapidly to the front, although he had been earlier known as a composer of originality and refined taste, shown in opera, oratorio, and in songs full of charm and melody. Chiefly, however, of late years he has become sought after as a teacher of singing, more than half the prominent singers of the present time having studied under him, and in America his repute has spread, and many new arrivals at our shores find their way direct to the studio. Forty-six different operas, grand and comic, he has already conducted in public, and it is hardly an exaggeration to say that the whole repertoire of the lyric stage is at his fingers' ends, so that he is in readiness to take the baton at an hour's notice for any known opera. Consequently, singers who have heard of him from their comrades, upon offer of and acceptance of engagements, fly to him for training in their respective parts.
>
> His popularity with the profession 'goes without saying' for he is a hard worker, devoted to his pupils, sparing no pains on their behalf; no less is he popular and held in esteem by bands under his control. . .

Wood's youth formed no bar to his eligibility in Newman's eyes. August Manns had been only thirty when appointed to the conductorship of the Crystal Palace Orchestra, George Henschel only thirty-one when appointed to the Boston Symphony, Arthur Nikisch not yet twenty-four when he became principal conductor at the Leipzig Opera. Later to achieve immense authority as conductor of the Leipzig Gewandhaus Orchestra and simultaneously of the Berlin Philharmonic, Nikisch was introduced to British audiences in 1895, giving at one of his four concerts the first performance in London of Tchaikovsky's Fifth Symphony. Tchaikovsky himself heard Nikisch conduct in 1887:

> Herr Nikisch is elegantly calm, sparing of superfluous movements, yet at the same time wonderfully strong and self-possessed. He does not seem to conduct, but rather to exercise some mysterious spell; he hardly makes a sign, and never tries to call attention to himself, yet we feel that the great orchestra, like an instrument in the hands of a wonderful master, is completely under the control of its chief.

Much later, the violinist and pedagogue Carl Flesch (1873–1944) was to recall Nikisch's style by a comparison with that of a leading Parisian conductor, Charles Lamoureux (1834–99):

> To me he was a revelation. From the time of my work under Lamoureux, I was still used to the type of unimaginative stick-wagger who, strictly according to the compass, beat 4/4 time in the four cardinal points. Now for the first time I saw a musician who, impressionistically, described in the air not simply the metrical structure, but above all the dynamic and agogical nuances as well as the indefinable mysterious feeling that lies between the notes; his beat was utterly personal and original. With Nikisch began a new era of the art of conducting.

Preceding Nikisch by only a few weeks, Hermann Levi made his first and only London appearance on 25 April 1895. The new style of conducting was collectively seized upon by the critic of *The World* in dismissing the older English manner exhibited in October 1895 by Sir Arthur Sullivan at the Leeds Festival:

> We are so spoilt with our Richters and Levis and Mottls and Nikisches that Sir Arthur Sullivan sitting at his desk no longer impresses. . . Bands are now used to more impressive guidance than his undernourished beat can give, and the conductor whose eye is so much on the score is at a disadvantage.

The new style was, however, not merely a matter of more vigorous wielding of the baton: a sense of complete intellectual and bodily leadership was

· QUEEN'S HALL, W. ·

Lessee and Manager - ROBERT NEWMAN.

PROMENADE CONCERTS

SEASON 1895

(UNDER THE DIRECTION OF MR. ROBERT NEWMAN).

Programme for this Evening, Saturday, August 10th, 1895, at Eight o'clock.

DOORS OPEN AT 7 O'CLOCK EVERY EVENING.

MADAME MARIE DUMA.	MRS. VAN DER VEER-GREEN.
MR. IVER McKAY.	
MR. FFRANGCON-DAVIES.	MR. W. A. PETERKIN.
Flute -	MR. A. FRANSELLA.
Bassoon -	MR. E. F. JAMES.
Cornet -	MR. HOWARD REYNOLDS.

FULL ORCHESTRA. Leader - - MR. W. FRYE PARKER.

ACCOMPANIST - MR. H. LANE WILSON.

Conductor - MR. HENRY J. WOOD.

PROMENADE OR BALCONY - ONE SHILLING.

SEASON TICKETS (Transferable) ONE GUINEA.   GRAND CIRCLE SEATS (Numbered and Reserved) 2/6.

No Charge for Booking Seats.   Seats Reserved the whole Evening.

FLORAL DECORATIONS BY MESSRS. WILLS & SEGAR, ONSLOW CRESCENT, SOUTH KENSINGTON.

For Advertisements on these Programmes application should be made to

CHARLES DEWYNTER, Limited:

Agents and Contractors for Advertisements,

23, HAYMARKET, LONDON, S.W.

Price Twopence.

The printed programme (price twopence) for the first of Henry J. Wood's Promenade concerts.

37

conveyed. Richter was famous for the trick of ceasing to beat (controlling his orchestra by eye only) in the 5/4 movement of Tchaikovsky's Sixth. The finale of Beethoven's Seventh, according to Bernard Shaw, had been previously urged on like a chariot race, but Levi 'got the movement into its stride in two bars, and then, putting down his stick, proceeded to blow his nose, rub his hands, and otherwise convey to the audience that he was only the fly on the wheel of the English band. Of course the English band, knowing its master all the better for his consummate knowledge of when he was wanted and when he was not, obeyed the baton when it came into play again. . .'

Such a mastery, if not to be described in such picturesque terms, was to be Wood's, and would enable him to be Britain's first native-born career conductor.

Under Newman's management he began his first promenade concert at 8 p.m. on Saturday 10 August 1895 with the overture to Wagner's early opera, *Rienzi.* Not one in twenty of those present, he estimated, had ever heard him conduct before. The conductor's father and mother were there – standing close to the rostrum in the promenade itself, according to the recollection of Agnes Nicholls (later to become a celebrated soprano and the wife of another conductor, Hamilton Harty).

One shilling, which had long been the standard cheap price for popular orchestral or chamber concerts, gained admission to the promenade area on the main floor. Balcony seats at the same price were offered to 'those who did not care for ambulation', as a commentator put it. Better seats were priced from two to five shillings. A strong selling-point, but not an original one (it had been in operation at previous promenade concerts), was Newman's offer of a transferable season ticket at one guinea (£1.05) for the promenade and up to five guineas for the other parts of the hall. 'Handsome palms and shrubs, with tasteful arrangements of electrical fairy lights' appeared as a special platform decoration. Newman followed his predecessors in having refreshments available on the promenade floor itself, and smoking was permitted (a sign of relaxed atmosphere in those days). It became necessary to ask gentlemen not to strike matches while music was being performed.

How had the players been recruited for 'Mr Robert Newman's Queen's Hall Orchestra'? Probably not more than 150 first-class players were normally available in London at the time. The large number of foreigners in leading orchestral positions (and also in restaurant bands at the time) indicates a scarcity of home-grown abilities. Like every regular or occasional promoter, Newman must have maintained a private listing of available players and their capabilities, and Wood himself must have had an influential say. His players, like those of all leading professional orchestras, were at first all-male, except for the harpist – at first a Mrs Ap Thomas. Then in 1897 came the younger Miriam Timothy, 'undoubtedly an attraction to the male promenaders', as Wood recalled in 1938 – long after he had later burst open the general orchestral ranks to women.

Wood can have met little difficulty in persuading the best players in London to an engagement at an otherwise 'dead' time of year. His early programmes did not list the orchestra, but from the naming of principals who played solos in special selections it is clear that most of these were musicians seasoned in Richter's, Henschel's and other leading series of concerts. Some had already played for Wood in *Yevgeny Onegin*. 'The members of the orchestra are mostly English,' observed a commentator as late as 1902, having evidently expected a higher proportion of foreigners in a first-class London orchestra.

None the less, foreign names *were* conspicuous, a sign of the short-comings in the training of British players to first-class standards. Albert Fransella, the first flute, was Dutch – and was still reckoned the best player in England in 1919 when Gerald Jackson, the future first flute of Beecham's London Philharmonic Orchestra, became his pupil. Among other leading players in Wood's early orchestra were Manuel Gomez, clarinet; Henri de Busscher, oboe; Adolf Borsdorf, horn – their names indicating Spanish, Belgian and German origin.

The tuba-player W. Guilmartin also became conspicuous, swapping his instrument for the euphonium to reproduce the baritone vocal solos in the nightly 'grand operatic selections'. Another favourite from 1897 was the cellist W. H. Squire, who also functioned modestly as a composer. As second horn to Borsdorf's first, Wood engaged A. E. Brain, the founder of a remarkable horn dynasty – he was the father of Alfred and Aubrey Brain, Aubrey being the father of Dennis.

They *had* to be excellent players. The promenade season demanded six concerts a week from Monday to Saturday, each concert lasting three hours (including interval), yet with only three three-hour rehearsals *per week*. How could it have been done?

Some ways of saving orchestral time were available. Items played a second or third time in the season would not be rehearsed again. Solo piano pieces were frequently programmed, and occasionally organ solos too: prophetically for a certain adapter called Klenovsky, Bach's Toccata and

Fugue in D minor was given in its true organ version during the 1896 season. The lighter songs in the second half of the programme dispensed with orchestral support and used instead the 'resident' piano accompanist. Those vocal numbers which were due to be orchestrally accompanied at the concert could be *rehearsed* privately, to Wood's own piano accompaniment. But many fully orchestral items must have been only partially rehearsed or not rehearsed at all.

This is not the unheard-of or monstrous event which the lay person might imagine. Eugene Goossens III (1893–1962) was to note 'as a matter of cold record' that out of the sixty or more different operas he conducted in Britain, at least forty had no orchestral rehearsal. That new works are even today sometimes performed 'at sight', without rehearsal, was acknowledged by the first clarinettist of the Philharmonia Orchestra in an article in 1992. An expert conductor and expert players are expected to arrive at an acceptable performance – and usually will. The Australian pianist-composer Percy Grainger played Liszt's *Hungarian Fantasy* at the promenade concerts in 1906 and noted: 'Wood conducted excellently. We had no rehearsal.'

Would such concerts take the public's fancy in Queen's Hall, as compared with Covent Garden in the livelier theatrical district? Would the new series recapture the informality, the general jollity of the traditional promenade concerts? Significantly, the report of the first night in the *Monthly Musical Record* began with a mention of the 'arrangements' (that is, the physical disposition within the hall), later noting that the orchestra was not of the inflated size favoured in earlier promenade series:

> The arrangements were good, so was the music and the performance generally. The adoption of the French pitch was a novelty, and will no doubt prove successful, although at first causing a little difficulty. Lowering the pitch resulted in somewhat diminishing the brilliancy of the violins. But this has been remedied by increasing the number. An innovation was the permission to smoke, which appeared to please, as it gave the idea of a music hall performance. The excellent acoustic properties of the Hall enabled a smaller orchestra than usual to produce ample effect.

Henry J. Wood was now able to move himself and his parents from their home at 185 Oxford Street, barely a quarter of a mile from the site of the new hall, to within a few doors of it at 1 Langham Place. Henry senior had been induced to give up his own business and manage his son's professional career. Successive issues of *Kelly's Post Office Directory* suggest that the move took place in 1895, after Wood's connection with Queen's Hall had been cemented. Wood's autobiography speaks of 'installing my dear mother with an efficient staff so that she could indulge her flair for entertaining'. But Martha Wood was not long to enjoy that state. She died suddenly, of bronchitis, on 28 February 1896.

The promenade concerts were only one part of the prodigious realm which Henry J. Wood was to acquire in the coming decades. They were not his life-work but they were his springboard, and they gave him 'his' orchestra. 'Some may be in doubt,' wrote the composer and critic Havergal Brian in 1935,

> as to whether the Promenades made Wood, or whether Wood made the Promenades. There had been Promenade concerts before, but none so lasting as those organised by Henry Wood at Queen's Hall, so there can be no doubt that Wood made the Promenades and incidentally found himself in the process. The Promenades are a one-man show, and at the same time an epitome of Wood's artistic outlook and character. A similar object organized by a committee would have gone down after its first or second season.
>
> . . .The remarkable thing is that at the 'Proms' the native composer has never been pampered, and consequently we have been saved the bathos of nationality in art. Wood's policy has evidently been to take an average of all schools, both of familiar works and of novelties, giving indigenous works a fair share.

Wood's cosmopolitan baton would guide succeeding generations of concert-goers along an unparalleled path – with first performances (or first performances in Britain) spanning from Tchaikovsky through Elgar to Schoenberg in less than twenty years, and to Shostakovich and Britten after that.

Chapter 4

The Omnibrow Concerts

1893–5

Henry J. Wood's first promenade concert on 10 August was anything but revolutionary in content. The programme had sent a reassuring signal – that Robert Newman's management would continue the tradition of promenade seasons of the past:

OVERTURE, *Rienzi*	Wagner
SONG, Prologue (*Pagliacci*)	Leoncavallo
HABANERA	Chabrier
POLONAISE IN A	Chopin, arr. Glazunov
SONG, 'Swiss Song'	Eckert
FLUTE SOLO, Idylle and Valse, from Suite	Godard
SONG, 'Since thou hast come'	Kenningham
CHROMATIC CONCERT VALSES (*Eulenspiegel*)	Cyrill Kistler
SONG, 'My heart, at thy sweet voice' (*Samson and Delilah*)	Saint-Saëns
GAVOTTE (*Mignon*)	Ambroise Thomas
SONG, 'Vulcan's Song' (*Philémon et Baucis*)	Gounod
HUNGARIAN RHAPSODY no.2	Liszt

INTERVAL

GRAND SELECTION (*Carmen*)	Bizet, arr. Cellier
SONG, 'Largo al factotum' (*Il barbiere di Siviglia*)	Rossini
OVERTURE, *Mignon*	Ambroise Thomas
CORNET SOLO, 'Serenade'	Schubert
SONG, 'My mother bids me bind my hair'	Haydn
BASSOON SOLO, 'Lucy Long'	
SONG, 'Dear Heart'	Tito Mattei
THE UHLAN'S CALL	Eilenberg
SONG, 'Loch Lomond'	Old Scottish
SONG, 'A Soldier's Song'	Mascheroni
VALSE, Amoretten-Tanze	Gung'l
GRAND MARCH, Les enfants de la Garde	Schloesser

Here was the familiar multiplicity of items – carefully labelled ('Overture, Song, Flute Solo') to guide the novice listener, though the identification of *The Uhlan's Call* as a march had been overlooked. A 'Grand Selection' from an opera was to be found in its traditional place just after the interval. Likewise resurrected from earlier promenade seasons was the beloved set of semi-comic variations for bassoon on 'Lucy Long', a song-melody of obscure origin. A veteran cornetist, Howard Reynolds, had been specially engaged for his scheduled solo – and was persuaded to give an encore. For the other instrumental solos the orchestra's own players obliged: Albert Fransella, flute, and E. F.('Fred') James, bassoon.

Among the five singers was the bass W. A. Peterkin, who had introduced Wood to his financial provider, Dr Cathcart. A baritone of leading rank, David Ffrangcon-Davies, was entrusted with the first vocal item of each half, and Iver McKay was the tenor. The soprano Marie Duma contributed the imitation-yodelling 'Swiss Song', which would pass into the repertory of the celebrated Tetrazzini. From *Samson and Delilah* came the contralto aria (sung by Mrs Van der Veer-Green) later translated as 'Softly awakes my heart' – already well known, though the opera's biblical subject still barred it from the British stage. The composers Tito Mattei, Angelo Mascheroni and Charles Kenningham were established purveyors of ballads to the British public.

The roguish figure of Till Eulenspiegel had not yet been appropriated by Richard Strauss, but an older German composer, Cyrill Kistler (1848–1907), had made him the hero of an opera – from which an orchestral excerpt, rather eccentrically labelled *Chromatic Concert Valses*, was ticketed in Newman's programme as a 'first performance in London'. The implication is that there had been an earlier performance elsewhere in Britain – but no such performance is known. It would be pleasant indeed to suppose that Henry J. Wood's promenade concerts, later famous for their 'first performances' or 'first performances in Britain' (see Appendix 4, p.441), carried such an item on their very opening night.

This was programming far removed from that of a symphony concert. In present-day terms it is much nearer that of a military or brass band concert, targeting the widest possible audience with the maximum variety of items. Moreover, as with a series of band concerts at the park or by the seaside, items found to be popular would reappear in later programmes. (Successful solo singers would also earn their reappearance.) To the patrons of his early seasons of promenade concerts Newman offered no prospectus: the purchaser of a season ticket simply assumed that the fare would be ample and tasty, each programme being advertised only a few days in advance.

Building

A 'first classical night' was announced for the Wednesday after the opening Saturday, though on the Wednesday itself that epithet was not used. It began with a Beethoven overture – curiously enough it was the inferior *King Stephen*, which even the Philharmonic Society (its dedicatee) had by that time given up. Then came Schubert's *Unfinished* Symphony, a soprano aria from Goring Thomas's opera *Nadeshda* and the tenor's Prize Song from Wagner's *Die Meistersinger,* Weber's overture to *Der Freischütz*, the aria 'Dich, teure Halle' from Wagner's *Tannhäuser,* some ballet music from *Esmeralda* (another opera by Goring Thomas), an aria from Gounod's *La Reine de Saba,* and Liszt's Hungarian Rhapsody no.4. All in the first 'half'!

The second half followed the same pattern as before, beginning with the usual 'grand operatic selection', this time from Alfred Cellier's operetta, *Dorothy.* The audience was then regaled with soprano, tenor and baritone songs and a cornet solo, another operatic overture (Auber's *Le cheval de bronze)*, an orchestral *Meditation* by H. Lane Wilson, and two marches – one by Schubert, newly orchestrated from piano duet, and one by Meyerbeer. It can hardly be maintained, as David Cox does in his book *The Henry Wood Proms*, that 'the tone had changed completely' from the first night. Only a slight stiffening had taken place, even the 'classical' first half being safely stuffed with lighter elements.

It is indeed too easy for a modern commentator to place a big 'but' between the two halves of such concerts, with the implication that Newman and Wood were able to present masterpieces to their audience only at the cost of 'descending' to trivialities in the latter half of the programme. On the contrary, the vitality of the concerts was sustained by what the two halves *shared*. These were 'omnibrow' concerts. With no parallel to the modern chasm between 'pop' and 'classical', Victorian music was seamless between its more lofty and its 'lower' tastes. Of course some of the promenade audience must have relished a Wagner overture much more than a brisk military march, and vice versa. But enough people must have found both acceptable for the programmes to make sense.

On this point the contemporary press reviews are revealing for what they do not say. Neither the *Monthly Musical Record* nor the *Musical Standard* nor the *Musical Times* lifted pained eyebrows at the cornet's embrace of Schubert or the presence of such a simple, traditional song as 'Loch Lomond'. Nor was there denunciation next season of the Park Sisters, a quartet of cornet-players who would play the Pilgrims' March from *Tannhäuser* as well as 'The Lost Chord'. The promenade concert was recognized as broad by definition. Since the programmes lasted about three hours (the first 'half' being the longer), those to whom the more 'popular' second half did not appeal would not feel short-changed if they left at the interval. Music critics frequently did so, and did not spend space denouncing the music they chose to miss.

The seamlessness of Victorian music goes far to explain why the culture of Henry J. Wood's early promenade concerts was, in the main, a culture of contemporary music – on whatever level. In 1895 Brahms, Bruch, Dvořák, Massenet, Saint-Saëns, Verdi, Grieg and Rimsky-Korsakov were living composers; Tchaikovsky had but recently died. All of them were represented in Wood's programmes, along with the best of the ballad-composers. The many 'Sullivan Nights' represented the 'omnibrow' composer *par excellence.*

Given this 'contemporary' orientation, Wood could pass easily from such established composers to those still in their thirties, like himself – notably, Richard Strauss (1864–1949), represented in the first season by the prelude to his first opera, *Guntram.* It was not modern but 'classical' works – that is, works removed by fifty years or more – which had to be introduced cautiously to the promenaders, unless they were brief. The programme-note for Beethoven's Piano Concerto no.4 in the 1896 season soothed its readers: 'This beautiful work was composed in 1805. Yet it is difficult, while hearing it, to realize that it is 90 years old, so bright, fresh and youthful is the spirit which animates it – especially as regards the first and last movements.' The division of the programme into a heavier first half and a lighter second half remained a sacred principle, and even the designation of a 'Beethoven night' or a 'Wagner night' (Monday and Friday fixtures from 1896) referred to the first half only, the second keeping its miscellaneous character. Nevertheless the inclusion in the very first season of symphonies by Schubert (no.9), Mendelssohn (the 'Italian') and Schumann (no.4), as also of Mendelssohn's Violin Concerto and Schumann's Piano Concerto, indicated the desire to gratify listeners of a 'classical' taste.

To secure artistic results under the prevailing limits of rehearsal, what became Wood's famous technique of unmistakable gestures with the baton was indispensable. Technique was therefore from the outset the foundation of his success. Equally important was the most careful marking of his players' parts in advance, followed up by his rigid, almost military organization of rehearsal time. Indeed the heavy, precautionary marking of scores and parts became almost obsessional with him. As Sir Adrian Boult was to put it more than half a century later: 'He did not claim that it was a good thing to mark scores in this way, in fact I can remember him speaking in rather a disparaging way of the practice, but I am quite sure that I should do the same if I ever had to face the ordeal of eight or ten weeks of nightly concerts. The risk of a momentary loss of concentration would be considerable, and a gentle reminder amply justified.' This capacity for planning and discipline, universally remembered by players from his earliest to his latest years, hit a snag in the very first season. Custom allowed a player to send a deputy to rehearsals, and even to a performance, if a more pressing (that is, better paid) engagement arose. The *Musical Times* reported that the 'excellence' of Wood's performances was maintained even though the Leeds Festival in October 1895 'called away' many of his contracted players, including his leader. That leader, Frye Parker, was dismissed. Arthur Payne replaced him from September (suggesting that Parker must have been a truant even before the festival) and became one of the stalwarts of Wood's first orchestral decade.

What kind of public attended in such numbers as to justify the eight-week season at Queen's Hall? (By the end of the season the crowd was such as virtually to prevent any 'promenading' in its original sense.) The free-and-easy atmosphere – with refreshments available on every floor throughout the concert, not just during the interval – made a special attraction to those who might be intimidated by the formality of other occasions. So, of course, did the shilling admission fee to the promenade area. The young and the impecunious came, and those of 'progressive' artistic taste (as soon as it became clear that new music was to be prominently featured). A music-lover who was present at the very first of Henry J. Wood's promenade concerts recalled almost fifty years later that

> the type of audience was different from what it is today. There were comparatively few women – in the Promenade, at all events; not so many adolescents; a fair sprinkling of foreigners, some with flowing locks, floppy ties, loose clothes, and scores under their arms. The enthusiasm was there, but more restrained and judicious – none of the mass hysteria of recent years, which applauds everything indiscriminately; some unfamiliar items in those days got only perfunctory applause.

None the less it must have been the most lively musical audience in London, with the nightly succession of concerts encouraging musical discrimination on the one hand, and sociability and assignations on the other. Wood commanded that audience, but he was not yet the only conductor identified with Robert Newman's orchestral enterprise at Queen's Hall. Its Sunday afternoon concerts during the winter of 1895–6 and 1896–7 were still under the baton of Alberto Randegger, as were the concerts of the Queen's Hall Choral Society. Wood took the supporting role of organist at some of these, including a performance of Sullivan's *The Golden Legend* on 26 February 1896, and actually deputized for Randegger on 12 April 1896.

By that date he had begun what proved to be his last fully operatic engagement, conducting *Shamus O'Brien*, Charles Villiers Stanford's comic opera on an Irish theme, at the London theatre off the Strand called the Opera Comique. With stage direction undertaken by the veteran Augustus Harris himself, it was a conspicuous success. Unusually, as in the case of Sullivan's *Ivanhoe*, it was given on successive nights, not in a mixed opera repertory. The composer had conducted on the first night, 2 March 1896, but Wood piloted the work through its long run of eighty-two London performances (not 'over a hundred', as *My Life of Music* states).

The *Monthly Musical Record* heaped praise on Wood for his training of soloists, chorus and orchestra, adding that he was expected to conduct the opera in New York. (He did not, though it was produced there.) But Wood's 'recollection' that the young Gustav Holst was his first trombonist appears to be yet another instalment of fantasy – and with it his account of sending Holst to Margate for a week's holiday when he became sick. Holst was still a college student at the time: his genuinely first operatic experience as a trombonist was with the Carl Rosa company two years later, according to his daughter and biographer, Imogen Holst.

The success of *Shamus O'Brien* justified Wood's plucking the overture for inclusion in his second summer of promenade concerts. In place of the previous eight-week season, that of 1896 ran for only six weeks (or rather, as became traditional, for one day more, every series both opening and closing on a Saturday). Newman had increased the orchestral force to ninety players and more – reaching 103 for the final programme on 10 October, featuring Beethoven's rowdy potboiler, *Wellington's Victory*. 'An appalling work', Wood called it in *My Life of Music* (characteristically displacing the performance to 1897), offering a free gift of his score and orchestral parts to anybody prepared to risk a further performance.

Rousing, military-style music continued to be seen by Newman as a proper component of promenade programmes. Even Jullien's *British Army Quadrilles*, the very title so often held up to ridicule by later musical pundits, had been revived during the opening season. Patriotic topicality evidently attracted an audience. Mackenzie's *Britannia* overture, in which 'Rule,

Britannia!' receives a highly crafted treatment, was included in a tribute to Queen Victoria's reign on 23 September 1896 – Newman with typical showmanship anticipating the Diamond Jubilee celebrations of 1897, and getting the audience to encore their own performance of the third verse of the National Anthem.

The impetus generated by the second summer of promenade concerts led Newman to present Saturday-only promenade concerts in the winter and early spring of 1896–7. Wood used them adventurously, giving the first performances in Britain of Tchaikovsky's *Nutcracker* Suite, Rimsky-Korsakov's *Scheherazade,* and two of Dvořák's symphonic poems, *The Water Goblin* and *The Noonday Witch.* Amy Elise Horrocks was twice called to the platform after the first performance of her 'orchestral legend' *Undine* (6 February 1897); a *Liebeslied* by Dora Bright followed four weeks later. Such works remind us that Ethel Smyth (whose Mass in D had made a great impression when conducted by Joseph Barnby in 1893) was not unique in refusing to be limited to the traditional women composers' sphere of songs and piano pieces.

Nothing in Henry J. Wood's repertory was to prove more popular than the *Nutcracker* Suite. In it, the new sound of the celesta gave a special role to a musician who was to remain close to Wood as collaborator and friend. Percy Pitt, slightly Wood's junior (1870–1932), had been appointed the official piano accompanist and organist and had already been represented at the promenade concerts as a composer. His combination of business acumen with musicianship was to make him a valued associate also for Hans Richter and Thomas Beecham, and he would become the BBC's first director of music.

Queen's Hall as a place of entertainment had become more attractive through Newman's exploitation of the smaller hall within it. Sixpence bought admission to the 'animated pictures', a forerunner of the cinema, available in the interval of the promenade concerts, and again from 10.30 p.m., while the last musical items would have been still in progress in the larger hall. During other parts of the season the small hall continued to be in use for chamber concerts. Within a few years a Wind Quintet would be drawn from the Queen's Hall Orchestra, with Henry J. Wood as collaborating pianist.

'Truly, of all music-lovers, the London concert-goer is most favoured,' wrote the *Musical Times* in November 1896. 'He now has not only an abundance of orchestral concerts ably conducted by his own countrymen [among whom the foreign-born Manns, Henschel and Randegger were accepted] but Richter and Mottl seek his favour at frequent intervals.' There

had also been an opportunity to hear the two leading orchestras of Paris –
those conducted by Charles Lamoureux (April 1896) and by Edouard
Colonne (October 1896). Both appeared at Queen's Hall, where Newman
had nothing to fear in comparisons that would be made with his own
orchestra.

In early 1897 Newman decisively raised his stake in Wood's role at
Queen's Hall. As if the extension of the promenade concerts on successive
Saturday evenings were not enough, there would be concerts in the
afternoon of three of the *same* Saturdays. They were announced as
'symphony concerts' – not then a common term, but one which excluded the
lighter elements of programming and aimed to draw the connoisseurs.
'The band' (reported the *Musical Times*) 'is that which has made the
Saturday evening Promenade Concerts so successful, and the conductor, it
need scarcely be said, is Mr Henry J. Wood.' The first, on 30 January, drew
such a public response that a fourth concert was added, and another after
that.

The cheapest admission to these Saturday afternoon concerts was one
shilling, as for the promenade concerts – but only in the balcony, with
higher-priced seats up to 7s.6d. (and no promenading) on the ground floor.
The first programme in that series of symphony concerts must be judged, in
Wood's career, as no less of a landmark than his first promenade concert had
been. It began by honouring the centenary of Schubert's birth, the baritone
soloist being Watkin Mills:

Unfinished Symphony	
Overture, *Rosamunde*	
Entr'acte no. 2 in B flat	
Songs [in English]	Schubert
'The Erl King'	
'The Wanderer'	
'My Hawk is Tired'	

INTERVAL

Symphony no.5 (first performance in Britain)	Glazunov
Siegfried Idyll	Wagner
Malagueña from *Boabdil*	Moszkowski

The placing of the new symphony in the second half absolutely differentiated
this from a promenade concert programme, but it was still felt appropriate
(though not mandatory) to conclude with a 'light' piece.

Building

The second concert a week later served a generous helping of Wagner ('the most popular composer of any', said the reviewer in the *Monthly Musical Record*) coupled with the *New World Symphony* of Dvořák – a recent work (1893) but already a favourite. First performances were placed before this 'connoisseur' audience as before the broader promenade public. The Dvořák symphony was in fact a substitution for a symphony by Arensky of which the orchestral parts had failed to arrive in time. The third concert included first British performances of works by Humperdinck (whose *Hänsel und Gretel* was already well-known) and Draeseke; the fourth on 20 March introduced Franck's *Le Chasseur maudit*, long to remain a staple of the orchestral repertory.

The Saturday series made an obvious challenge to the Saturday concerts still offered at the Crystal Palace. Under the unflagging August Manns, now seventy-two, those Crystal Palace programmes remained as progressive as ever – as instanced in 1897 by the first British performance of Richard Strauss's *Also sprach Zarathustra* and the first London performance of Elgar's *King Olaf*. But in Wood's programmes, no less venturesome, Newman offered an escape from the rail journey to Sydenham and an orchestra now recognized as superior.

The Queen's Hall Orchestra – and its conductor with it – was also available for events promoted at the hall by other managements, so long as they did not interfere with Robert Newman's own. The impresario Daniel Mayer brought the already celebrated Paderewski for a concert on 9 April 1897. Wood recalled the great pianist at rehearsal:

'Mr Wood, will you permit me to suggest that you move your first clarinet to a position where I can see him?'

I made the requested adjustment and Paderewski appeared to devote himself to accompanying the flute, oboe, and clarinet solos of the Schumann concerto. I do not think these sections of that beautiful work have ever been played in quite the same manner since.

When he came to the Liszt concerto (E flat) he was a different man. The brilliance and force of his octave-playing were electrifying; his almost overpowering tone in the left hand was something I shall never forget. He received a tremendous ovation and among his encores played an arrangement of *The Erl-King* when, again, his left hand was almost a miracle.

A soloist's willingness to play two, sometimes three concertos in an evening was nothing unusual in those days, and the gracious addition of several (solo) encores was also expected. Presumably it was Liszt's well-known transcription of Schubert's 'The Erl-King' that Paderewski played.

In addition to the promenade concerts and the Saturday symphony concerts, from September 1897 Henry J. Wood was allotted a further slice of Newman's domain. Displacing the sixty-five-year-old Randegger, he became the conductor of the already existent Sunday afternoon concerts. Using a slightly reduced orchestra of about sixty-five players, assisted by at least one vocal soloist, these concerts were of about ninety minutes' duration. The items chosen being mostly familiar to the players, they had *no* rehearsal.

Of the three types of concert-promotion, the Saturday symphony concerts were the flagship of Newman's regime at Queen's Hall. More sedate in character and patronage than either the promenade or the Sunday concerts, they lasted about two hours (preceded by one three-hour rehearsal). They brought the orchestral musicians their best remuneration – a guinea per concert (including the single rehearsal), as against half a guinea for the unrehearsed Sunday concert and a total of £2.5s (£2.25) for a *week* of six summer promenade concerts, which had only three rehearsals per week.

At the symphony concerts one expected to hear the best works with the best soloists – often performers whose fees were beyond the budget of the promenade concerts. Occasionally there might be no soloists, as at an all-Wagner concert; exceptionally, a choir and soloists participated on 6 November 1897, when a concert version of *Samson and Delilah* under Wood's baton sidestepped the theatrical censor's continuing ban.

Wood's transformation was complete – no longer just the conductor engaged for the promenade concerts, but the most conspicuous orchestral conductor in London, and therefore in Britain. And this barely two years after taking up the baton at Queen's Hall! The Hallé Orchestra in Manchester dispersed every summer. No one rivalled his year-round command of a full symphonic force. Dan Godfrey was developing Bournemouth's venturesome municipal music, but his orchestra was only about forty strong. At Queen's Hall the orchestra listed for the symphony concerts of 1897 numbered over a hundred, with sixty-four strings, *four* each of flutes, oboes, clarinets and bassoons, four each of horns and trumpets, five (!) trombones, one tuba, six percussionists (a different man being allocated to timpani, bass drum, side drum, cymbals, triangle, and glockenspiel), harp, and organ (Percy Pitt). The full complement of wind players presumably participated only in Wagner and other 'heavy' orchestrations.

Building

The Queen's Hall Orchestra now had a consistency and cohesion unrivalled in the capital. The only inherent defect in Wood's musical organization of it was the deputy system, as described above. Now that sore was to be tackled at the root.

In September 1897 it was announced in the *Monthly Musical Record* that the orchestra 'will be made more efficient than ever by abolishing the practice of permitting "deputies" to appear in place of the performers regularly engaged. This system has led to much abuse, and is unfair to the conductor and to the audience.' At the same time it was learnt that 'no less than *thirty* new players have been introduced, to the displacement, we presume, of thirty of the old *personnel*' (*Musical Times*). This was the first of two 'purges' – the second to be even more far-reaching, seven years later – which were the price to be paid for the achievement of the orchestral discipline he required.

Henry J. Wood as a composer had not been quite obliterated under the spotlight now thrown on his conductorship. Two songs of earlier vintage ('Darling, how I love thee' and 'The King and the Miller') were heard during the promenade season of 1896. Virtually his final offering as a composer was a Latin Mass in E flat performed at St Joseph's Retreat in Highgate, north London, in June 1896. Dedicated to Cardinal Vaughan, Archbishop of Westminster, it was stated on publication to have been performed at London's 'principal Catholic churches', and won cordial commendation from the *Musical Times*. In *My Life of Music*, Wood linked the Mass (which he mis-remembered as being in C) with an undated period when he was himself organist at St Joseph's.

In 1894 a work of his called *Jacob's Dream*, for bass voice and orchestra, had been performed by an amateur orchestra at Kendal, on the edge of the Lake District. That location suggests a link with the chapter of homage to John Ruskin in *My Life of Music*. Wood supposedly addressed the sage in his lakeside garden: 'Sir, I have read everything you have written about painting and drawing' (which, if literally true, would have involved millions of words). Evidently having had the forethought to bring his gear with him, Wood was permitted to execute 'a little oil landscape' there. He tells of meeting various members of Ruskin's circle including 'Mr and Miss Severn with whom he lived, or who lived with him – I never actually discovered which'.

Amid the expression of hero-worship one can only wonder at such a casual description on Wood's part. Brantwood near Coniston was nationally famous as Ruskin's home. There – as was well known, particularly to devotees – he passed his final years, with increasing periods of mental breakdown, under the care of *Mrs* Arthur Severn (née Joan Ruskin Agnew, a distant cousin of his) and her husband.

Wood was supposedly presented to Ruskin by Mary Wakefield (1853–1910), previously a professional singer in London. In Westmorland she had pioneered a competitive musical festival which became a nationwide model. Wood portrays Mary Wakefield as enjoying an easy informality with Ruskin, hardly supported by the absence of her name from the principal biographical accounts of him. It is an impossibility that she could have told Ruskin that Wood was 'going to direct my festival next month', as alleged in *My Life of Music*. He never 'directed' such a festival, and did not begin participating in the Westmorland festivals (with his orchestra) until 1904, four years after Ruskin's death.

If indeed the meeting of John Ruskin with Henry J. Wood does not belong to fantasy, it cannot be dated. It is otherwise unmentioned in the voluminous Ruskin literature. Perhaps the memory of the garden, the presence of Mary Wakefield, and the 'little oil landscape' belong to a visit to Brantwood after Ruskin's death. There remains Mary Wakefield's anthology *Ruskin on Music* (1891) to remind us that the sage could touch Wood not only as painter but as musician: 'Every child should be taught, from its youth, to govern its voice discreetly and dexterously, as it does its hands; and not to be able to sing should be more disgraceful than not being able to read or write.'

One further stage of Henry J. Wood's career was now over. He 'destroyed the whole of his compositions and devoted himself entirely to conducting', as a later announcement put it. (Not quite truthfully: though he attempted to buy up the published copies he did not destroy the manuscripts of his compositions, now surviving at the Royal Academy of Music.) A young musician who had taken part in a performance of Wood's Mass put a higher value on it than did the composer himself and refused to part with his copy.

> The orchestration is virile and picturesque and when singing the work for the first time I was struck by the ease and fluency of the vocal parts. As compared with Stanford's Oratory Mass I can only say that I prefer Wood's flamboyancy to Stanford's immaculate academicism. His music might be 'in lighter vein' but it certainly had a more human touch in it.

Thus, forty years later in the *Radio Times*, wrote the celebrated Roman

Building

Catholic church musician Sir Richard Terry. But it was not to be expected that Henry J. Wood would ever regret his decision to quit the composer's path. He never did.

Chapter 5

'Are you quite English, Mr Wood?'

1896–1900

Wood was always a striking figure and a great draw. He had an unruly mane of black hair, which frequently fell over his forehead and was pushed back with a characteristic gesture of the left hand. His conducting mannerisms were more pronounced – the baton raised high above his head for the brass; his emphatic double nod to the strings in unison passages; his sensitive withdrawal, as if he had been stabbed, when a pianissimo was not pianissimo enough; these were more in evidence than they are now. There is no doubt that his dramatization of the music in this way excited people and made them come again. . .

Thus a veteran of Queen's Hall, J. P. O'Callaghan, who had frequented Wood's concerts since they began there. Writing in the early 1940s, he recalled Robert Newman as 'a bulky, commanding figure, with a heavy black moustache and a stern expression, very like Kitchener' (the field-marshal who appeared in newspaper advertisements of World War One with the slogan 'Your country needs you').

Newman . . . sometimes appeared in the vestibule at the Promenade Concerts, especially in the early days, but he was more in evidence at the Sunday afternoon concerts. At these, in order to comply with the law [on Sunday observance], a certain number of persons had to be admitted free. This number was usually about seventy, and they queued up at the back entrance in Great Portland Street, usually waiting from about 1.30 to 2.45. Then Newman appeared, in frock-coat and top hat, opened the door only just sufficiently to admit one person at a time, and counted them as they went in, one by one. Then, when the prescribed number had passed through, his black arm fell across the opening like the stroke of Fate, and the unfortunate thus excluded (sometimes more than a hundred) had either to go round to the front and pay or else wait until the following Sunday to try their luck again.

Building

Sunday concerts were part of a general extension of recreational facilities. Only in 1896 were London's state museums and art galleries permitted to be opened to the public on Sundays (in the afternoon). The provision of *some* free places was supposed to exempt a concert promoter from the offence of conducting trade for profit on a Sunday. It had worked since 1891 at the Albert Hall, where Sunday afternoon concerts built around the use of the organ had been very successful, with audiences up to 5600.

At Queen's Hall, Newman's first Sunday orchestral concerts tried out a similar plan, advertising 'admission free' (for a few!) but with reserved seats at a shilling. But in 1898 the Sabbatarians persuaded the London County Council not to renew Newman's licence unless with a clause prohibiting Sunday opening for profit. So the financing of the Sunday afternoon concerts was turned over (with Newman simply acting as their manager) to the National Sunday League, an energetic charitable body which existed to promote on a non-profit basis not only concerts of all kinds including band concerts in parks, but also cheap Sunday excursions by rail, and other 'intellectual and elevating recreation on that day'.

In addition to the Sunday afternoon concerts, a series of Sunday evening oratorio concerts was also placed on Wood's shoulders. Not infrequently that landed him with two performances on the same Sunday (and, presumably, a morning rehearsal for the evening concert, the afternoon concert being unrehearsed). He never seems to have objected to such a doubling of engagements – such as would also happen on 27 February 1898, when he conducted the final concert of the Saturday afternoon symphony series and then remounted the rostrum to begin a new Saturday evening series of winter promenade concerts. Each engagement, of course, represented a fee, though nowhere in his autobiography does he disclose the amounts.

The attention and skill which Wood lavished on Russian composers was unprecedented. At a Saturday symphony concert in April 1897 he gave the first British performance of what became a perennial favourite, the Polovtsian Dances from Borodin's *Prince Igor*; in the following February came one of Britain's first encounters with Musorgsky in *Night on the Bare Mountain*. In his first three years at Queen's Hall he conducted at least forty-two pieces by eleven composers including Arensky, Cui, Dargomizhsky, Rimsky-Korsakov, Anton Rubinstein, Nápravnik (the Czech-born conductor of the Imperial Opera) and Alexander Serov (1820–71), a composer almost unknown outside Russia. On 16 September 1896 his solo singer in an excerpt from Serov's opera *Rogneda* was named as 'Madame Swetloffski' – that is, Svyatlovskaya, one of the principals in his performances of *Yevgeny Onegin*.

Above all other Russians stood Tchaikovsky, one of the two composers whose music earned Wood his greatest following. Wood conducted twenty works by Tchaikovsky during those three years – the Byron-inspired *Manfred* Symphony at a promenade concert of 1896, the symphonies numbered 4, 5 and 6, extracts from opera and ballet, and shorter pieces including the *1812* overture. Extra 'Tchaikovsky Concerts' were Newman's response to the public. Repetitions of the *Pathetic* Symphony (no.6) were so many that critics began to complain it was hackneyed, but on stylistic matters Wood's touch was felt to be irresistible: 'Mr Wood has for years past identified himself with Slavonic music, with which his temperament would seem to be in entire accord, and no conductor has succeeded in so forcibly expressing the fierce and wild passion which surges like a mighty undercurrent in its strains, or in so brilliantly producing the barbaric glitter of its orchestration.' So the *Musical Times* in 1898.

Balakirev would be added to Wood's Russian composers in 1899, a further link in the chain of first British performances extending to Shostakovich's seventh and eighth symphonies during World War Two.

After conducting Tchaikovsky's Fifth Symphony during the 1898 promenade concerts, he received a letter from Sir Arthur Sullivan, who had been considering whether to include a Tchaikovsky symphony in his own concerts at the Leeds Festival:

> I have a fairly long experience of orchestral playing and orchestral conducting, and I say quite sincerely that I have never heard a finer performance in England than that of the Tchaikovsky symphony under your direction last Wednesday.
>
> It was a perfect delight to listen to such accent, phrasing, delivery and force, and I congratulate both the gifted conductor and the splendid orchestra. And what a lovely work it is! I could see that you and the band too revelled in bringing out its beauties.
>
> Forgive me this little outburst of honest admiration.

The newness of Wood's style of conducting could not be more clearly indicated than by that tribute from a conductor of the previous generation. Sir Adrian Boult was to make the judgement, after a lifetime of hearing performances of Tchaikovsky's orchestral music, that the greatest were those conducted by the Russian Vasily Safonov and by Henry J. Wood.

Building

The other composer for whom his public idolized Wood was Wagner. He was the prime inheritor of the tradition of 'concert-hall Wagner' first established in Britain by Richter. From Felix Mottl (with the implied sanction of Bayreuth itself) Wood borrowed those extracts from *The Ring* and other works which could make satisfactory entities once fitted with new closing bars, and added other selections of his own. Extracts such as *Siegfried's Funeral March* were already self-sufficient; others required the substitution of appropriate instruments for the missing voices, as in the passage from *Götterdämmerung* which Wood called *The Song of the Rhine-Daughters* – a long-lasting favourite in his programmes. (Donald Tovey's puritanical dismissal of 'bleeding chunks' of Wagner was not yet heard, much less heeded.) A Monday series of Beethoven–Wagner concerts was Newman's extra allocation to Wood in the autumn of 1898.

Wood's cultivation of Russian composers began just before his association with the pioneer British musicologist in the field, Rosa Newmarch. Born Rosa Harriet Jeaffreson in 1857, she used her married name in all her writings. Having mastered Russian, she was to write in English the first book on Tchaikovsky in any Western language (1900), which she dedicated to Wood. Before her first visit to Russia in mid-1897, she had written to compliment Wood on his performances and received a gratified reply. She returned that autumn and called at Langham Place, where 'on the doorstep of his flat I collided with a vivacious, tremendously energetic young man – the conductor himself. Heaven knows how long we discussed music on the pavement.'

In St Petersburg her mentor in Russian music was Vladimir Stasov (1824–1906), who had been the guide and stimulus to the whole circle of composers which had formed round Balakirev (the 'Mighty Handful'). Through her long, authoritative articles on major Russian composers in the second edition of *Grove's Dictionary of Music* (1904–10) together with her programme notes for Wood's and other concerts, Rosa Newmarch became the great educator of the British public in Russian music – a function comparable to that of Constance Garnett (1862–1943) as translator of Tolstoy, Dostoyevsky and Chekhov. She also became Wood's valued friend. Awkwardly formal though he often was with others, she became 'Dear Rosa' in his correspondence. A typical confusion in *My Life of Music* places his initial meeting with her in 1908, eleven years too late.

Henry J. Wood's identification with Russian music was further strengthened by his marriage in 1898 to a woman of Russian birth. Cultured, musically gifted, acquainted with several languages, Olga had apparently become one of Wood's vocal students in the mid-1890s. Born on 23 July 1868, she was some months his senior. Theirs was to be a marriage of perfect professional and private harmony.

In early allusions to her in the British press, Wood ennobled her as 'Princess Olga Ouroussoff' (Urusov, in today's customary transliteration), repeating that form in *My Life of Music*. Olga had no claim to the title of princess, nor did she use it; nor was Ouroussoff her surname. In places where she is correctly identified as the daughter of Princess Sofiya Ouroussoff, we find no reference to her father. Why not? Why is she not named as the daughter of Prince Grigory Alexandrovich Urusov and his wife Princess Sofiya Nikolayevna Urusova, née Naryshkin?

The inference must be that she was the daughter of the princess but not of the prince. Olga's maiden name, as declared on the certificate of her marriage to Wood, was not Ouroussoff but Michailoff (Mikhailov). An explanation might be that her mother was married a second time, and to a commoner; but no such marriage is known to have taken place. (The Prince himself did not die till 1888.) The inescapable conclusion is that Olga was the *illegitimate* daughter of the princess, taking as her surname that of her father, Mikhailov. In any case Olga was never a princess nor an Urusov, and only by a misleading invocation of her mother's name and title could Henry J. Wood pretend so. Not she but he, compensating his own feeling of social inferiority, was the presumed gainer in glamour and status.

What originally brought Olga to Britain is unknown. At Eastbourne in 1888 she married a solicitor (and coroner of East Sussex), Edward Hillman, her maiden name appearing in the local paper as 'Meikoff'. In 1896–7, she left her husband and took a trip back to her mother's home in Podolia in southern Russia. Her widowed mother died there on 24 February 1897, aged sixty-two. A letter from Ermilovka, site of the family estate, informed 'Dear Mr Wood' of Olga's longing to return to London and singing lessons. In London once again, Olga was divorced by Hillman in 1898, a Dr Nelson being cited as co-respondent. On 10 July 1898, two days after that decree became absolute, Olga Hillman and Henry J. Wood were married at Marylebone Register Office.

Olga's professional accomplishment and personal charm won immediate recognition. Rosa's Russian mentor, V. V. Stasov, visited London in 1900, referring to her in correspondence as 'the beautiful Madame Olga'. Yet Wood's own account in *My Life of Music* hints at nothing of Olga's personal attractiveness but only at her domestic virtues.

> She had become [before their marriage] a very welcome visitor and a dear friend who had helped my father and myself in the management of my home. Since my mother's death various housekeepers had worked their evil ways – undetected and unmolested – until one day when I seemed to think my weekly bill for food for my father, myself, and one maid must surely be excessive, considering the cost of a meal at any of our well-known restaurants. I asked Olga whether she considered my housekeeper could manage on less than £14 a week and learned to my surprise that half this sum would, or should, suffice.

According to his biographer Reginald Pound, Wood told a friend he was a virgin until marriage. The honeymoon took the form of 'a glorious six weeks at Braemar [in the Highlands of Scotland] even though it rained the whole time' – which must have cheated Wood of his usual open-air pursuit, painting. Back in London (for the time being still at 1 Langham Place), Olga set up the protective domesticity of which Henry had been deprived since his mother's death. Only under such care could he cope with the unrelenting work.

> I think I should have gone under myself (giving, as I did, every ounce of my vitality at each concert) but for the fact that Olga ran my home so perfectly. I was always sure of being given good food and good wines – and of enjoying perfect peace and comfort.
>
> There could have been a perpetual round of social pleasures. The temptation to accept some of the invitations we received was indeed great, but we had to risk offending people – even to forgoing all the pleasures of parties and country house weekends – in fact, all those delightful attractions in which we dare only participate on rare occasions. Many of our friends faded away because we neglected them in order to devote all our time to music. If we went out after concerts were over it meant late hours, so we simply cut off everything of the kind and got to bed as early as possible. Literally a life of work and sleep – but work was life to us.

Olga developed her public career as a singer, usually but not always with her husband as conductor or pianist. Nearly always she was designated as 'Mrs Henry J. Wood', though at one concert at Nottingham [14 December 1899] it was 'Madame Olga Wood' who sang 'Ombra mai fù', the so-called 'Handel's *Largo*', embellished with her husband's *obbligato* parts for violin and harp.

The city of Nottingham, with a population over a quarter of a million, had become an important secondary base for Wood. Ideally he could have wished for an appointment to one of Britain's large choral festivals (usually triennial), such as Hans Richter held in Birmingham, but no such opening was available. Wood seized the opportunities which Nottingham provided. Late in 1897 he began conducting the Nottingham Sacred Harmonic Society, a choral body which shared a common taste of that time for concert performances of opera, with orchestra. To that enthusiasm Wood responded eagerly. He presented not only Gounod's ever-popular *Faust* but also *Irene*, a new version of Gounod's *La reine de Saba* in which the biblical libretto was replaced; also *Tannhäuser,* announced as 'without cuts' and incorporating the Paris version of the Venusberg music, a particular favourite of his.

The orchestra for such performances, about fifty strong, had been recruited *ad hoc*, with leaders of sections imported from Queen's Hall. Wood now went further, persuading the Society to inaugurate the Nottingham City Orchestra and to present two orchestral concerts per season. 'The band numbered over ninety performers, of whom two-third were local musicians, including several ladies,' as the *Musical Times* noted in its report of the orchestra's debut on 8 December 1898. This use of women performers comes well before Wood's general welcoming of women to the Queen's Hall Orchestra in 1913. Moreover, whereas the initial female recruitment to Queen's Hall was of violinists and violists only, Nottingham opened its ranks to local women percussionists, and the listing of 1902 shows a woman cellist. Out-of-town professionals from Birmingham and London reinforced the local players.

The title of City Orchestra was a meaningful one. As the *Nottingham Daily Express* put it: 'The orchestra has received the cachet of municipal recognition, and also a substantial pecuniary proof of sympathy from the Council.' This may well be the first example in Britain of municipal subsidy for an orchestra, apart from the quite dissimilar case of a seaside resort such as Bournemouth subsidizing a band or orchestra to enhance the amenities.

Robert Newman retained his showman's eye for the topical touch. At the promenade concert on 13 October 1898 he personally led three cheers for the 37th Field Battery, Royal Artillery – acclaimed as heroes of Kitchener's victorious campaign in the Sudan – whom he had invited to attend. Though the general programme-planning for the concerts remained much the same, with the operatic fantasia and sundry ballads to lighten the second 'half', the 'classical' element was enlarged. 'The [Beethoven] *Pastoral Symphony* at a promenade concert was something to inspire wonder and gratitude,' gasped the *Monthly Musical Record* in October 1898. Even Brahms's Second Symphony was given, eased in by a programme-note: 'This noble and beautiful work has probably done more than any of its composer's compositions to win him admirers among those at first repelled by the frequent austerity and complexity of his style.' By the time that Brahms's violin concerto followed in 1901, none of the other three Brahms symphonies had been given. If one now asks what general qualities made Brahms repellent and Wagner attractive, the answer must be that open, strong emotion and rich orchestral colour were passwords for Wagner as they were for Tchaikovsky and Dvořák. Brahms's works, almost monochromatic in comparison and perceived as more classical in design, were 'difficult'.

Queen Victoria's taste evidently coincided with that of her promenading subjects. The 'command' to Robert Newman's orchestra to perform at Windsor Castle was not in itself unusual. By such invitations the sovereign honoured the chosen performers and – at the age of nearly eighty – took pleasure in keeping musically abreast. Operatic performances which she had 'commanded' at Windsor Castle ranged from *Cavalleria Rusticana* to *The Gondoliers;* early in 1895 she even summoned the entire Scottish Orchestra from Glasgow to perform under its conductor, George Henschel.

The royal choice of programme from Wood and his orchestra on 24 November 1898 was mainly of Wagner, whom the Queen had once received in person. Not only the *Meistersinger* Overture but the Good Friday Music from *Parsifal* was given (the stage performances of which were still confined to Bayreuth) and, as an encore, the *Ride of the Valkyries*. The final two movements of the *Pathetic* Symphony recognized the conductor's other specialization. Cathcart, the orchestra's great financial provider, had set his heart on being present, so Newman 'hit on the admirable idea of making out an extra contract for another triangle-player at the enormous fee of one guinea'.

Wood's joy in the occasion was marred only by his being obliged by court etiquette to conduct in white gloves ('I felt like a bandmaster on a seaside pier') and was enhanced by his conversation with his sovereign afterwards. 'Tell me, Mr Wood, are you quite English? Your appearance is rather un-English!' Naturally, Wood received this as a compliment: after all, he had taken Nikisch as the model for his looks as well as his performances! With his beard and dark, wavy locks – and the slight outlandishness of dress which he preferred – he did not conform to the stereotype of a British musician.

But the cosmopolitanism of Wood's repertory did not go unrebuked. 'LOST! BRITISH MUSIC AT QUEEN'S HALL' was the headline of the *Musical Times* when 'the programme of German, French and Russian music which was performed before Her Majesty the Queen' was repeated a few days later at 'the home of foreign music in Langham Place. And here is the crux! – these pieces were performed by the finest orchestra in England, while our best native composers are still waiting, waiting, wearily waiting.' Robert Newman, who 'seems to be gradually assuming the role of a monopolist in London', was reminded of his patriotic duty.

In targeting Newman, not Wood, the journal's attack was not misplaced. Newman was probably in a position to determine the general composition of programmes. It is important to remember, however, that Wood himself was no special champion of British music and at this stage tended to quarry it mainly for shorter, lighter pieces. He had given Mackenzie's rollicking *Britannia* overture and Cowen's *Four English Dances* but not, for instance, Cowen's *Scandinavian Symphony*, a work which had won some admiration. Elgar had been represented at the promenade concerts not by the big-scaled *Froissart* but only by the *Three Bavarian Dances*. Ethel Smyth, just turned thirty, had been taken up at the Crystal Palace, not yet at the Queen's Hall.

The *Musical Times* was able to cite a particular case in a performance of Edward German's symphonic poem *Hamlet* at the Saturday concerts in October 1898. A disparaging comparison was drawn with Richter's treatment of the same work at the previous year's Birmingham Festival. 'Mr Wood. . .takes enormous pains over novelties of the Russian school . . .When will he do the same for British works?'

Wood might, indeed, have had the distinction of an early London orchestral performance of a work by 'Fritz Delius', as the Yorkshire-born composer still called himself. Living in France, Frederick Delius had written to Percy Pitt in the hope of engaging Wood as conductor of an orchestral programme at Queen's Hall, but he made the tactical error of also approaching an impresario other than Newman, namely R. Norman-Concorde.

On 12 March 1899 Pitt replied to Delius in a letter which makes clear the extent to which Wood was contractually bound to Newman:

> With regard to your concert, I had already sounded Wood re conducting when your letter and that of Concorde Agency suddenly arrived. I fear that the fact of you having placed the arrangements in C.'s hands will prevent Wood from doing your thing as Newman will step in and refuse permission.
>
> You see, Wood is retained solely by Newman and cannot accept outside engagements. Had you waited, I was going to write to you – in fact I had done so but happening to call on W. before posting same, found the two letters. I had advised you to write Wood personally, applying for him and the Queen's Hall Orchestra. This would have been placed before Newman and I believe that between W. and myself, a favorable [*sic*] result wld have

been arrived at. As it stands however, I don't believe you will be able to
do much, for it will not be possible for you to have our men and all the
other good players will be required for Covent Garden. I wld advise you
to put off the concert for present, take it out of Concorde's hands and
wait until the Autumn. . .

Newman appropriated the grandiose title of London Musical Festival for his
Queen's Hall events of 8–17 May 1899, featuring the Lamoureux Orchestra
of Paris. It was the kind of enterprise which invited the word 'Napoleonic' –
and from the veteran critic Joseph Bennett he got it. Over three pages of the
Musical Times, using a first-person style very unusual in criticism at this
period, Bennett made some categorical comparisons.

> When engaged upon French music, dainty and delicate, piquant and
> engaging, the Paris band is almost out of sight of the Queen's Hall men. In
> like manner, Mr Wood's orchestra runs ahead in compositions of a robust
> character, as, for example, the Tchaikovsky Symphony and Coleridge-
> Taylor's Ballad. The distinction is mainly a matter of national temperament,
> which, in music, makes for value. We would not alter it if we could.

For the public the excitement must have paralleled those contests of a
former day at which Beethoven himself was pitted against such now-
forgotten rivals as Wölfl and Steibelt. The battle this time, as Wood
justifiably observed, was that of 'a four-year-old orchestra against one of
many years' standing whose great conductor was thirty-six [actually thirty-
five] years my senior'. For this festival Newman had hoped to secure for
Wood the première of Elgar's *Enigma Variations*, but the honour went to
Elgar's special champion, Hans Richter, in the following month.

E. A. Baughan, as the critic of the *Monthly Musical Record*, saw a clear
contrast between the visiting French conductor, 'who has made himself into a
perfect musical machine, a musical example of Carlyle's drill-sergeant ideal', and
Wood as a conveyer of *feeling*. 'He attempts to make his orchestra reflect his
own emotional view of a composition.' Baughan was dismissive (as was
Bennett) of one of the French novelties, Dukas's *The Sorcerer's Apprentice* – 'as
diabolically clever as it was intrinsically vulgar and empty', a verdict wholly to be
overturned by posterity. In the final concerts the two orchestras (the 'combined
bands' in Newman's advertising) occupied the platform with Lamoureux and
Wood sharing the conducting. Within the moderately-sized Queen's Hall, the
sound must have produced such aural excitement as to parallel the 'monster
concerts' given by Jullien half a century before.

The consolidation of Newman's and Wood's hold on London concert-giving proceeded irresistibly. An attempt at a rival series of promenade concerts (at Covent Garden, beginning on 2 September 1899) failed, although both Elgar and Coleridge-Taylor came to conduct their works. More importantly, for financial reasons the Crystal Palace was compelled to cease its Saturday orchestral programmes, for so long a fount of musical vigour. Not only did the Queen's Hall Orchestra absorb some of the leading players of the disbanded orchestra; on 13 October 1900, for the first time, the Saturday afternoon concert at Crystal Palace was given by 'Mr Robert Newman's band, conducted by Mr Henry J. Wood'.

Great esteem was enjoyed at this time by the Belgian violinist (and also conductor and composer) Eugene Ysaÿe, who 'outdated all the schools and trends of violin-players of his time,' said his fellow-artist Pablo Casals, '. . . not because he made more notes than his contemporaries but because he made them better'. Having proved himself as Ysaÿe's piano accompanist at a Queen's Hall recital in 1896, Wood was engaged as conductor of the Queen's Hall Orchestra for Ysaÿe's two self-promoted concerts on 30 May and 17 June 1899. At the second that jewel of the violin repertory, Chausson's *Poème*, had its first hearing in Britain.

Ysaÿe's pupil and compatriot, Henri Verbrugghen, appeared under Wood's conductorship in the rarely-heard Dvořák violin concerto and invited Wood to Berlin to conduct the same concerto for him on 18 November 1899. Wood began his Berlin programme with the overture to *Die Meistersinger* and ended with Percy Pitt's overture, *The Taming of the Shrew* – the pair surely forming an admirable compliment to his hosts and his home.

This concert with the Berlin Philharmonic Orchestra seems rather curiously to have had no sequel. Wood never returned to Berlin, though invited after World War One to conduct at many other continental centres. Verbrugghen was to become the regular leader of the Queen's Hall Orchestra in 1902, occasionally relieving his chief by conducting the last item of a programme, and in September 1907 he was soloist (with Wood conducting) in the first British performance of Sibelius's violin concerto. His later career saw him as a conductor and conservatory director in Australia and the USA.

Henry J. Wood's own account of the end-of-the-century years gives no inkling – any more than do the letters of Elgar – that Britain was at war. Soldiers and nurses embarked for South Africa in the presence of cheering crowds and the high-minded few who resisted the imperialist urge were reviled as 'pro-Boers'. Kipling's immediately popular poem about the soldier far from home, 'The Absent-Minded Beggar', was set to music by Sullivan, all proceeds from sales going to war charities. Not even Wood's admiration for Sullivan and Newman's nose for topicality got this song into the promenade concerts. But Mrs Beerbohm Tree, wife of the famous actor-manager, recited Kipling's poem, 'Soldier, Soldier', on 12 October 1900 and his 'Recessional' ten days later. The participation of a reciter (with or without musical acccompaniment) was not uncommon at this period of the promenade concerts, and in the coming greater war Elgar would provide another vehicle for the reciter's art.

Chapter 6

Olga, Rosa, Jessie

1900–2

His private life gave a happy renewal to Henry J. Wood's Russian musical connection. On 26 April 1900 at the Steinway Hall, Lower Seymour Street, a lecture on *The Art Songs of Russia* was given by 'Mrs Newmarch . . . with vocal illustrations by Mrs Henry J. Wood . . . assisted by Mr H. Lane Wilson and [at the piano] Mr Henry J. Wood'. The versatile Wilson, who had been the resident Queen's Hall accompanist for the first promenade season, was a singer on this occasion. Songs by Glinka, Dargomizhsky, Anton Rubinstein, Cui, Musorgsky and Rimsky-Korsakov were heard. Seldom (perhaps only once before, in a recital by Svyatlovskaya) had such a musical offering from Russia been laid before the London public.

For Olga, Robert Newman at Queen's Hall permitted a rule to be reversed. Except for those who were already celebrities, singers were usually first introduced at the promenade concerts; then, if they had shown sufficient distinction, they might be exposed to the more select audience of the Saturday symphony concerts. But 'Mrs Henry J. Wood, soprano' first appeared in a Queen's Hall programme on 3 May 1901 during Newman's most prestigious annual event, the London Music Festival. No provincial festival presented, as this did, four major conductors – Colonne, Ysaÿe, Felix Weingartner and Henry J. Wood – with the addition of Saint-Saëns as composer, pianist and conductor within the same concert.

Olga's 'sympathetic and polished' singing of Tatiana's Letter Song from *Yevgeny Onegin*, in Russian (with a verse translation by Rosa Newmarch in the printed programme), drew approval. In the second half of the programme, to her husband's piano accompaniment, she sang two French songs by the Russian composer César Cui and, again in Russian, Rimsky-Korsakov's 'Thou and You'. Her illustrious co-soloists that evening, in Bach's Two-Violin Concerto, were Lady Hallé (the widow of the conductor) and Ysaÿe. Among the Festival's other soloists was the revered violinist

Building

Joseph Joachim, a month off his seventieth birthday.

Olga's introduction to the promenade audience followed on 7 October with a substantial 'classical' item in the first half (Elisabeth's Greeting from *Tannhäuser)* and two ballads, by the popular Frances Allitsen and the lesser-known Max Stange, in the second. Reappearing on 30 October, she sang, remarkably for a soprano, Pauline's (mezzo-soprano) 'Romance' from Tchaikovsky's *The Queen of Spades* and two new English songs – 'When?' by Percy Pitt and 'April' by the otherwise unknown Maud Miller. With Rosa Newmarch, ready to provide Wood with shrewd advice, Olga remained on the most friendly terms.

Coincidentally it was at just this time that Wood's career first intertwined also with that of the much younger woman who was destined to be the beloved companion of his old age. Jessie Goldsack, contralto, was two months short of her eighteenth birthday when she sang for the first time at a Queen's Hall promenade concert on 25 September 1900. Evidently not yet ready to face the public in operatic or similar material, she was heard only in two lighter songs, Gounod's 'When all was young' and Cowen's 'The Children's Home' (the latter with verses ultra-mawkish even by Victorian standards: the children reach 'home' only by dying).

Jessie Amy Louise de Levante, as her birth certificate names her, was born in Ealing, London, on 23 November 1882. 'Goldsack' was her mother's surname, which she adopted for professional purposes. An audiotaped 'autobiography' which she made approximately ninety years later, apparently without anyone else being present, gives access to a wealth of recollections connecting her early years with those of her widowhood when she re-met Henry J. Wood.

The daughter of a railway clerk, she was guided in her musical studies by her father's brother Harry. Precociously, she learnt the piano, the guitar, and the violin; on tape she speaks of playing the violin at the age of seven (!) on tour with a women's orchestra conducted by her aunt Marie, Harry's wife (who was also his cousin). From the month of her fifteenth birthday she studied singing with Hilda Wilson – the sister of H. Lane Wilson, and herself a performer of repute. Jessie Goldsack remembered being taken by her teacher to Wood's flat 'just two doors from Queen's Hall, his mother's and father's home'.

On the audiotape of her old age she recalled her first sight of him as 'a little man, with a beard and lots of curly hair, [who] spoke with rather a nasal twang. "Come along, Miss Wilson, we'll go and hear her in Queen's Hall." '

QUEEN'S HALL, W.

Lessee and Manager - - ROBERT NEWMAN.

MR. ROBERT NEWMAN'S

Promenade

SEVENTH SEASON, 1901.
UNDER THE DIRECTION OF MR. ROBERT NEWMAN.

nearly 19 years old

EVERY EVENING FROM 8 till 11.
DOORS OPEN AT 7.30.

Concerts

Programme for Tuesday, November 5th, 1901.

Miss JESSIE GOLDSACK.				Mr. SAMUEL MASTERS.
Mr. HANS WESSELY	-	-	-	-	Solo Violin.
Mr. WALTER MORROW	-	-	-	-	Solo Trumpet.
Mr. PERCY PITT	-	-	-	-	Solo Pianoforte.

ROBERT NEWMAN'S QUEEN'S HALL ORCHESTRA.

PRINCIPAL VIOLIN - - - MR. ARTHUR W. PAYNE.
ORGANIST AND ACCOMPANIST - - MR. PERCY PITT.

Conductor - Mr. HENRY J. WOOD.

THE POLYTECHNIC ANIMATED PICTURES in the Small Hall during the interval. Admission 6d. extra.

Erard's Piano.   Metzler's Celesta.   Librarians, Messrs. Goodwin & Tabb.   Florists, Messrs. Wills & Segar.   Refreshments, Mr. J. Heywood.

PROMENADE - ONE SHILLING.   BALCONY, 2/-   GRAND CIRCLE, Numbered and Reserved, 3/- and 5/-

Jessie Goldsack ('nearly 19 years old') – the future Jessie Wood – is among the soloists during Henry J Wood's seventh Promenade season.

They went into the hall, where Wood initially sat down and accompanied the girl, then let her teacher accompany her while he went to the gallery to hear the pupil's voice. It was, he told Wilson, a very large voice for one looking so fragile – and to Jessie herself he gave a tip very characteristic of his emphasis on communication. '*Say* your lyric – *say* your words before you put it on to your tongue to sing.'

Encouraged and not a little dazzled, Jessie went again for advice, more than once. The conductor spoke of potential developments: 'He wanted to go forward and talk of things miles away from what we were doing then – it was all so beautiful.' He gave her further technical advice: 'Never – what I call – "shout"; sing always on your breath.' In the tape-recording of her old age she refers to an audition in 1899 *with orchestra* – very improbable, in all likelihood a confusion of memory with a rehearsal for an actual concert later on. Significantly, she mentions singing also for Robert Newman's approval.

Newman had become an artists' agent as well as concert promoter. On his small, distinguished list were the violinist Ysaÿe, the popular pianist Mark Hambourg, the contralto Louise Kirkby Lunn, and Ferruccio Busoni, that titan among pianists who first played under Wood's baton in November 1900 and whom Wood was to champion as composer. With such strong runners in his stable, Newman must have been impressed indeed with the young Jessie Goldsack to join her name to theirs. Rather than arrange for engagements in return for a commission, as presumably with his established artists, he decided to place her on salary, initially £250 annually.

Financially inexperienced, Jessie had already signed an agreement binding her to her teacher, Hilda Wilson. The salary from Newman had therefore to be paid to Wilson, to be passed (minus a commission) by Wilson to her pupil. The arrangement became an embarrassment but was not felt by Jessie to represent sharp practice on her teacher's part. 'She was the greatest friend I ever had in my youth, apart from my uncles.' It seems that Jessie performed personal services – dress-making, house-cleaning – for her teacher, in part-payment (at least) for lessons. In 1898 'I was still making Hilda Wilson's frocks – she was massive'.

Jessie Goldsack sang again at the promenade concerts on 5 October 1900 ('Slowly, slowly' from Sullivan's *The Golden Legend* and the traditional English song 'Come, lasses and lads'); next day she was heard in Handel's 'Lascia ch'io pianga' (from *Rinaldo*) and a song by Edward German. Engagements rained on her, since it was now to Newman's interest to promote her not only at his own concerts but elsewhere. She would be identified by the *Sunday Times* as 'the youthful contralto who has been doing so well at Queen's Hall' when she replaced the indisposed Clara Butt at a Crystal Palace orchestral concert on 10 November.

The same Handel aria and the Edward German song served her at the Queen's Hall promenade concerts on 11 October, and next day she reappeared there with a single traditional ballad, 'The Bailiff's Daughter of Islington'. Likewise at Queen's Hall, on St Andrew's Day that year (30 November) she delivered 'Annie Laurie' at a 'Scotch Concert' under N. Vert's management. On 2 December she sang in the commemoration of Sullivan (who had died ten days before) at one of the 'Sunday Evenings for the People' given by Wood and his orchestra in Queen's Hall.

For an intensive period of rather less than two years, Jessie Goldsack became the most frequently engaged of Henry J. Wood's young singers – primarily because of her contractual arrangement with Newman, but surely also because Wood approved of her artistry. In the 1901 promenade concerts, between 28 August and 9 November, she appeared on eleven occasions including the final night. She had also become, according to *My Life of Music*, 'one of my best pupils'. No other feeling towards her can be assumed on the part of the recently married conductor. Suddenly, however, in June 1902, she drastically if not quite completely cut short her career on marriage to an engineer, John Linton. It was 'not a love-match', she said later. The reason for her decision is not clear, but it is not impossible that the delicious proximity to Wood may have turned to pain.

Jessie made brief returns to concert-giving in 1904 and in 1905, in the latter year touring to English and Scottish provincial towns as one of the supporting artists for concerts centred on either the ageing, bejewelled Patti or the newer prima donna, Melba. The notices which Jessie received indicate that she might have won a star's ranking within a few seasons. But there was to be no such development. She sang under Wood's baton at a few promenade concerts in 1907 and 1908 and, in the latter year, at a *St Matthew Passion* at the Sheffield Festival and a Sheffield performance (15 December) of Dvořák's *Stabat Mater*. With that, her association with Henry J. Wood had come to an end. So it would seem. . . . and so, for twenty-five years, it was.

In the year of Jessie's first Queen's Hall appearances, 1900, Robert Newman again promoted a London Music Festival (30 April to 5 May). This time the 200 performers of Wood's and Lamoureux's orchestras appeared at Queen's Hall only in their combined form. Two of the concerts were conducted by Camille Chevillard, who had succeeded his late father-in-law, Lamoureux; the other three by Wood, who found a place for *Thalaba the Destroyer*, an early tone-poem by Granville Bantock. Almost Wood's exact contemporary (1868–1946), Bantock was a composer whose luxuriant orchestral works would be consistently championed in the coming years by Thomas Beecham as well as Wood. Bantock himself, as a conductor principally in Birmingham and Liverpool, was an energetic champion of new music.

Audiences' enthusiasm for Wagner was not confined to London. Act I of *Lohengrin* – in English, as always when amateur choralists took part – was on Wood's programme with the Nottingham Sacred Harmonic Society on 8 February 1900, involving 'an augmented band and chorus of 350 per-formers'. Four weeks later Wood's orchestral concert gave Nottingham more Wagner, including the 'Good Friday Music' from *Parsifal*. On 29 March the chorus was back on the platform for *Samson and Delilah* with Kirkby Lunn, who would be picked by Covent Garden for Delilah's role when the opera at last emerged (1909) from the Lord Chamberlain's ban on stage performances.

Nottingham's musical public would surely have been ready on 19 February 1900 to attend 'Mr and Mrs Henry J.Wood's Vocal Recital' with the assistance of the tenor Gregory Hast and Wood's leading cellist, W. H. Squire. Wood had also been engaged to give two lectures a year at Nottingham University College (the University, as it now is). In February 1899 Olga's voice illustrated his lectures on the art of singing; two years later his lecture on Bach had musical illustrations on period instruments including harpsichord, clavichord and viols, provided by Arnold Dolmetsch and his associates. The evening ended with a performance of the D minor Clavier Concerto using only six instruments – a type of performance which was an extreme rarity then. When Wood later became famous or notorious for 'inflated', big-orchestra Bach, it was not in ignorance of historical authenticity.

Additionally in 1900–2 Wood took on the conductorship of the Wolverhampton Festival Choral Society, but Queen's Hall remained the focus of his musical attention and that of the reviewers. Looking back on a promenade season which had been extended to 10 November 1900, the *Musical Times* declared 'unhesitatingly' that it was 'the most important ever given in this country . . . Towards the close of the season Mr Robert Newman's magnificent orchestra, from constantly playing under Mr Henry J. Wood's direction, acquired a oneness in attack and expression and a perfect responsiveness to Mr Wood's gestures that caused many performances of master-works to become memorable.'

There had been, as expected, new Russian works: a suite from Glazunov's ballet *Les Ruses d'Amour* (not yet two years old) and Rimsky-Korsakov's *Antar*. Perhaps most surprisingly of all, Rachmaninoff's Piano Concerto no.1 received not merely its first British performance, but what appears to have been its first full performance anywhere (though it was not so claimed), with Evelyn Suart as soloist. The composer must have met Henry J. Wood on his visit to London the previous year, though no such meeting is documented – the beginning of a long, cordial relationship.

New British music in that 1900 promenade series included a set of variations on 'Three Blind Mice' by Josef Holbrooke (a composer who later gained performances under both Nikisch and Beecham), and a venture into composition by Landon Ronald, who had been conducting comic opera at the Lyric Theatre, Shaftesbury Avenue. He termed his work a *Suite de Ballet*:

I sent it to Henry J. Wood, a complete stranger, and begged him to produce it at one of his famous 'Proms'. Within a week I got a reply from him accepting the work. . .

But I was yet to learn that Henry Wood was not only a genius as a conductor but a very severe taskmaster. On the eve of the production of my first orchestral work, I was indolently conducting at the theatre when a telegram was handed to me. It was from Wood and read: 'YOUR SCORE AND PARTS ARE LACKING ALL MARKS OF EXPRESSION, ALL MARKS OF BOWING AND PHRASING. IMPOSSIBLE TO REHEARSE TOMORROW MORNING OR PRODUCE TOMORROW NIGHT UNLESS YOU CAN RECTIFY.'

I handed my baton to the principal violin, left my seat as if I had been stung, and within five minutes was in a hansom cab on my way to Queen's Hall. With a beating heart, I asked the librarian for the score and parts of my *Suite de Ballet*. He gave it to me, and I reached my desk at home about 10:30. I sat up all night, marking score and parts with every imaginable mark of expression, and at eight o'clock the next morning duly delivered them at Queen's Hall.

I attended the rehearsal and marvelled at the grasp Wood had of my work, and the infinite pains he took over every bar of it. He was very cordial afterwards but (as a parting shot) said: 'Let it be a warning to you never to be careless over your work.'

Characteristically, Wood let the above account stand in *My Life of Music*, though stating on another page that the two men were *not* strangers but had met in 1891 when Wood had attended, 'not once but many times', performances of the mime-play *L'Enfant prodigue*, with Landon Ronald as the piano soloist in the musical score by André Wormser.

Ronald's piece was 'tersely knit, bright, and effectively scored', said the *Musical Times*, enhancing 'our none too large repertory of artistic, light music'. Dexterity of musical treatment also attracted Wood to the overture *The Butterfly's Ball* by a senior composer, Frederic Hymen Cowen, which he introduced at a Saturday symphony concert on 2 March 1901 and often performed in ensuing seasons. The re-emergence of this lively work on CD tends to reinforce Wood's critical approval – though the very title, redolent of fairies at the bottom of the garden, was probably enough to defeat his attempt to reinstate it in the BBC years which were to come.

Indeed, had not Wood cherished a place specifically for light music, would London have had a proper context to welcome Elgar's first two *Pomp and Circumstance* marches on 22 October 1901? Elgar was not present, but his friend A. J. Jaeger (the original of Nimrod from the *Enigma Variations)* wrote to him that the marches 'were the greatest success I have ever witnessed over a novelty at any concert'. 'Novelty' indicated a work new to *that* audience, the mainly amateur Liverpool Orchestral Society under Elgar's friend Alfred E. Rodewald having given the première four days before.

'With a sense of showmanship', remarks Elgar's biographer, Michael Kennedy, Wood reversed the order of the marches, playing no.2 in A minor before the now famous no.1 in D (to which the words 'Land of hope and glory. . .', so inspiring at the time and such an embarrassment since, had yet to be added). Wood's own account from *My Life of Music* bears requoting:

> I shall never forget the scene at the close of the first of them – the one in D major. The people simply rose and yelled. I had to play it again – with the same result; in fact, they refused to let me go on with the programme. After considerable delay, while the audience roared in its applause, I went off and fetched Harry Dearth who was to sing *Hiawatha's Vision* (Coleridge-Taylor); but they would not listen. Merely to restore order, I played the march a third time. And that, I may say, was the one and only time in the history of the Promenade concerts that an orchestral item was accorded a double encore.

But did that actually happen? Press reports record one encore, and the second seems to have happened only in the mind of the conductor.

Equally notable in Wood's association with Elgar was the symphony concert of 20 February 1901 which had introduced the 'Prelude and Angel's Farewell' from *The Dream of Gerontius* with Kirkby Lunn singing the Angel. The complete work, as conducted by Richter at the Birmingham Festival of a few months before, had been deemed a failure, but Wood's interpretation of the excerpted passage (which Elgar himself had edited for separate performance) delighted A. J. Jaeger: 'Wood conducted it with loving care; spent one and a half hours on it [at rehearsal] and the result was a performance which completely put Richter's in the shade.'

Visiting the Bayreuth Festival just before his summer promenade season of 1901, he (and Olga) could have heard *The Ring* conducted either by Richter or by Siegfried Wagner (the composer's son), with *Der fliegende Holländer* entrusted to Felix Mottl and *Parsifal* to Carl Muck. He proceeded to introduce his London audiences to the new sonority of Wagner tubas in his concert extracts from *The Ring* – a set of four having been specially made by the Brussels firm of Mahillon. To Wood's special orders, similarly, a set of 'real' bells was made for his extracts from *Parsifal*, replacing the conventional tubular bells.

Fridays continued to be hallowed as the promenaders' 'Beethoven nights' (that is, as regards the first half of the programme). On 15 October 1901 Wood even programmed the Ninth Symphony – cutting it short just before the vocal part of the finale, since the engagement and rehearsal of a choir was no part of a promenade season (or its budget). That such a castration was found acceptable on this and other occasions seems shocking. But for members of the audience not wealthy enough to attend the more expensive type of concert, this was no doubt the only opportunity of hearing the Ninth at all.

Bach was winning new interest, Wood himself coming forth as one of the four pianists (with Percy Pitt and two sisters surnamed Cerasoli) in the quadruple concerto in A minor. As for the miscellanous second halves of the promenade programmes, a successful formula was changed little. The cornet-player was less frequently seen warbling a vocal number from centre-stage, but he was invariably one of the named soloists for the nightly 'grand orchestral selection' from an opera. Ballads, too, remained a requirement in public expectations of a singer. Olga Wood contributed three Tchaikovsky songs in Russian to the first half of the concert on 30 October 1901, but after the interval she obliged with 'Those azure eyes' by one Garnet Wolseley Cox.

Apart from his name (no doubt after General Sir Garnet Wolseley, celebrated in W. S. Gilbert's *Patience* for 'thrashing a cannibal'), this composer merits at least a mention, since Wood was to give two of his orchestral suites in the promenade seasons in 1903 and 1907. He may stand as representative of the many British composers – then full of hope, now totally forgotten – whom Wood thought worth a trial. His programmes are remembered for their *successful* launches, naturally enough, but such successes could not have come about except as a winnowing from a vastly greater number of scores which he had to judge, rehearse and perform (or get the composers to conduct, always under his own supervision).

As if his orchestral commitment to Queen's Hall were not enough, on 13 November Wood inaugurated a series of Wednesday afternoon organ recitals there, with vocal solos by his wife. Three days later began another of Newman's enterprises in 'Napoleonic' vein - three fortnightly concerts on Saturday afternoons at the Royal Albert Hall with an instrumental force raised to 200. Under Wood's baton (and with Olga Wood as a soloist) the programmes were almost wholly devoted to Wagner, with the addition of two Beethoven symphonies. The combination of 'the usual Queen's Hall orchestra and many players who at some time have been under Mr Wood's baton' gratified the *Monthly Musical Record* with a sound 'more homogeneous than at the London Festival, when half the band was French'.

Building

On the crest of a wave of promotion, Newman then greatly extended London's winter promenade concerts. No longer confined to Saturday nights as in previous years, they were now nightly over a period of five weeks from 26 December 1901. Once again Wood accepted the load of double- performance days, a new series of Saturday afternoon symphony concerts beginning before the promenade concerts ended on Saturday 1 February 1902.

Wood's devotion to Elgar earned him a dedication. At a Queen's Hall symphony concert on 18 January 1902, Wood brought out a work under Elgar's title of *Grania and Diarmid*. As incidental music for a play by W. B. Yeats and George Moore, *Diarmuid and Grania*, it had been used for the production in Dublin in the previous October. If one were to believe *My Life of Music*, Moore had first sought music to the play from Wood himself; Wood declined and gave him a letter of introduction to Elgar. But a quite different account of the approach to Elgar, giving no role to Wood, appears in the pages of Moore's own *Hail and Farewell*. Wood, we know, admired Moore's novels: *Evelyn Innes*, rare in having a musician as its heroine, is among the works of fiction mentioned by Wood in his autobiography.

Revering Arthur Nikisch above all other conductors, Wood did not miss hearing his idol conduct at Queen's Hall (with 'Newman's orchestra of 110') on a Friday afternoon, 20 June 1902. Absence from London would keep him from hearing a celebrated German orchestra the following November – the Meiningen Court Orchestra under Fritz Steinbach – but he collected their printed programmes and evidently read the programme notes, which had been written by the young Donald Tovey. Against Tovey's note on Tchaikovsky's *Francesca da Rimini*, Wood scribbled his own comment: 'One of Tchaikovsky's poorest efforts at serious music. . . Why is it always dragged out instead of *Romeo* or the very pretty *Tempest* stuff?' An early Beethoven *Rondino* for eight wind instruments, introduced by that orchestra, became a favourite in Wood's own programming.

The opening of a new avenue for his gifts – especially as a choral conductor – was now before him. He had worked well with his Nottingham and Wolverhampton choralists and rewarded both by bringing them to Queen's Hall during 1901. But the Nottingham and Wolverhampton appointments were both to be given up for something grander. The invitation to conduct the Sheffield Festival of 1902 must have gleamed with the promise of a 'permanency' in one of the most conspicuous of musical events, a festival as firmly on the critics' calendar as any event in the capital.

In half a century (1851–1901) Sheffield, jocularly known as Steelopolis and mightily prosperous, had increased its population from 135,000 to over 400,000. As compared with Leeds, Birmingham and such cathedral-based festivals as Norwich and the Three Choirs, Sheffield's festival was a late arrival. Its impact on London critics in 1896 and 1899 had been principally achieved by a virtuoso choral trainer, Henry Coward. August Manns of the Crystal Palace had been the conductor of those festivals, bringing members of his famous orchestra with him. The Sheffield orchestra as selected for 1902 by Henry J. Wood was naturally based on that of Queen's Hall, though not identical with it.

A souvenir brochure for this festival reproduces a photograph of Wood in his most 'foreign' appearance - thick moustache and beard, black homburg hat. A biography, presumably self-compiled, lauds his achievements while deducting a year from his age. His association with Sheffield was indeed to be long, though his London commitments made him unavailable to the festival in 1905, when Weingartner took his place. The 1908 festival would see him taking a radical knife to choral traditions; at the festival of 1902 he was content to build on Coward's foundation.

There was a concentration of six concerts within three days, 1–3 October, the morning concerts starting at 11.30 and continuing after an hour's lunch-break. A chorus of 333 singers had been subjected to sixty-one rehearsals and were joined by a distinguished team of solo singers – including Ella Russell, Ada Crossley, Ben Davies and David Frangcon-Davies in *Elijah*; John Coates, the young Muriel Foster and Frangcon-Davies in *The Dream of Gerontius*; and Kirkby Lunn in works by Dvořák and Coleridge-Taylor, the young composer of mixed English and West African descent whom Wood continued to encourage. The pitch of the organ at Sheffield's Albert Hall had been lowered to the specification which London had long accepted.

The expectation of new or unfamiliar music at such festivals was fulfilled, and the public had sight of Parry, Cowen, Elgar and Coleridge-Taylor (as well as Henry Coward) conducting their own works. Appetites were assumed to be gargantuan: *The Dream of Gerontius* was to be swallowed before lunch on 2 October, followed by Beethoven's Violin Concerto (with Ysaÿe as soloist and Wood conducting) and Elgar's *Coronation Ode*. That same evening the repast included Richard Strauss's choral setting of Goethe's 'Wanderers Sturmlied' (first British performance), two orchestrally accompanied Strauss songs sung by the accomplished American tenor, David Bispham, Cowen's *Ode to the Passions* and a 'selection' from

Handel's *Israel in Egypt*. Elgar's Ode was unexpectedly brand-new, its planned London première having lapsed when the illness of the new king, Edward VII, had deferred his coronation.

Perhaps Wood's most unusual selection was a work of Bach new to the Festival, *Jesu meine Freude*, a long, contrapuntally complex motet which Wood properly chose to perform with organ reinforcement rather than unaccompanied. On the more familiar ground of *Israel in Egypt* he balanced his large string section by increasing the numbers of Handel's oboes and bassoons to six each.

'The Press indicates the throbbing of the pulse of the public; and it is a sign of the times when 35 leading papers in various parts of the kingdom send special representatives to report on Sheffield music,' as the *Sheffield Daily Telegraph* commented with some pride. The anonymous Special Correspondent of the *Birmingham Post* was on guard against the despoiling of masterpieces by artful contrivances of the baton. In Mendelssohn's *Hymn of Praise*, 'the symphony [i.e., the opening orchestral movement] was hurried in time, and the concluding *pianissimo* of the strings was almost dumb show. Mr Wood cannot apparently forget the little tricks of virtuosity which have made his Queen's Hall performances famous, but which are not in place in serious compositions.'

The authoritative J. S. Shedlock in the *Monthly Musical Record* had no such reservations. In Mendelssohn's *Elijah* the young conductor 'freshened up the music and threw into it many a dramatic touch – seemed, in fact, to give it new life. The oratorio is so hackneyed, and to modern music the conductor shows himself so partial, that one was scarcely prepared for so interesting and exciting a rendering.' The allocation of solo-quartet passages to selected members of the chorus was an innovation which 'deserves special note. If generally adopted it would create a proper spirit of emulation among the members of festival choirs, and thus tend to render the choral singing more artistic.'

A critic who could not be suspected of local or national partisanship was Otto Lessmann of the *Allgemeine Musik-Zeitung* of Berlin. He had notably saluted British music as far back as 1889, reviewing the triennial Leeds Festival and giving an unpatronizing welcome to the new works of Stanford, Mackenzie and Parry. Now, after a visit to the Sheffield Festival, he had an assessment to deliver on Henry J. Wood:

> If he is sometimes more animated in his movements than seems necessary when he has a well-trained orchestra before him, still he communicates a

truly artistic spirit to the players, and by the help of his strong musical perception carries the band along with him, so that they follow whereso-ever he leads – drawn, as it were, by the spell of his will and desire. Here we have a born conductor, a man with sensitive and vibrating nerves, who has made an intimate study of each work he performs, and breathes into them all a new tone-life. Mr Wood accomplished a giant's task at Sheffield, for besides the chief orchestral compositions he conducted the greater part of the choral works and solo pieces, and, in spite of all this labour, the freshness he managed to impart, even to the very last note, was something to marvel at. Two personalities now represent a new epoch in English musical life – Edward Elgar as composer and Henry J. Wood as conductor.

Never previously in Britain had a composer and conductor been so bracketed in esteem. Wood had built a house of music where none had been built before.

PART II

Broadening

'You don't expect that any human being could command the complete range of all schools of music – but *he* did, very nearly!'

– Sir Adrian Boult in a BBC television broadcast, 1969

Chapter 7

The New Wave

1902–12

By the time that Edward VII was crowned at last on 26 October 1902, public opinion had already begun to place the Victorian era firmly in the past. The old queen had died on 22 January 1901, so the sense of a break and a new beginning was reinforced by the arrival of a new century. With mathematical correctness, 1901 and not 1900 was treated in newspapers and elsewhere as the year when the twentieth century began.

With the new century, Wood's role altered too. When launching his career, he had seized on the already existent enthusiasm for Wagner and Tchaikovsky and had made more of their music than any other conductor in London, save possibly Richter in Wagner's case; but he did not discover or introduce them. Now within barely a dozen years he was conspicuously to introduce the new music of composers from Sibelius to Stravinsky. Moreover, as the new music increasingly tended to be disruptive of older notions of harmony, form and tonality, Wood marched with it. The often-cited first performance of Schoenberg's *Five Orchestral Pieces* in 1912 belongs in the context of Wood's espousal of other modernists of the time.

Yet that period of musical exploration began with an event which might have been a disaster for Wood: in 1902 Robert Newman went bankrupt. He had appeared perfectly secure in his musical enterprises, and at the Queen's (Small) Hall he also found success with daily matinées by the singing entertainer, Albert Chevalier. He was persuaded into presenting at the Comedy Theatre a play called *Memory's Garden* written jointly by Chevalier and Tom Gallon, for which members of the Queen's Hall Orchestra were engaged to play. The failure of this venture was enough to unbalance his finances. Proceedings in the bankruptcy court, as reported in *The Times* on 15 August, revealed that Newman found orchestral concerts to be profitable, choral concerts loss-making, and theatrical management disastrous.

Broadening

To Wood, the cessation of the enterprise which buoyed nearly all his current work must have been an incalculable shock. We are left to speculate whether it helped to bring on the bout of illness which kept him from the rostrum during October and November 1902 – a very rare failure on his part to maintain a promised schedule. Dr Cathcart sent him on a recuperative trip to Morocco. Olga did not accompany him. Did Cathcart offer himself as companion, or Wood's new friend Schwabacher – of whom more below?

In his absence the final four weeks of promenade concerts were conducted by his leader, Arthur W. Payne. Evidently the impetus which Wood had imparted to these concerts was such that they could freewheel under a deputy of no particular pulling-power. For the Saturday afternoon symphony concerts which Wood had to miss, more distinguished replacements were provided – Edouard Colonne on 25 October; Emil Paur from New York on 8 November, with Elgar as guest conductor of the *Enigma Variations*; and Elgar again for a complete programme on 22 November.

During Wood's absence abroad, his father died – on 29 November 1902. The event is mentioned with astonishing brevity in the conductor's autobiography. 'So passed my father – my friend,' wrote Wood, with barely a note of regret at having been absent. The reader is simply informed that Ben Grove, in whose house Wood senior had taken up residence after Henry's marriage to Olga, undertook 'all my responsibilities'. Why Henry and Olga had not concerned themselves more personally with his father's care is not explained, though Olga was 'in attendance' at the death in Fulham, according to the death certificate.

Fortune, however, was on the side of London music-lovers and disaster did *not* strike with Newman's bankruptcy. With surprisingly little fuss, concerts at Queen's Hall continued on a new basis. Promotion was taken over by a company called the Queen's Hall Orchestra Limited. It was financed by a wealthy German-born music-lover, Sir Edgar Speyer (1862–1932). Wood himself became one of the four other directors – his first involvement in such a function. Speyer, who became a good friend of Wood's, was the second husband of the violinist Leonora von Stosch, who had already been several times a soloist at the promenade concerts. Robert Newman, no longer proprietor of the enterprise, was retained as its salaried manager.

How Wood's own remuneration was fixed is undisclosed. Some idea of prevailing fees may be gathered from the fact that when Richter in 1908 withdrew from a Philharmonic Society engagement for two concerts at £60 each, Henry J. Wood and Landon Ronald as his replacements would receive just half as much. This was a time when a workman earned about £78 a year, and a series of articles in the *Cornhill Magazine* advised that even with an annual income as high as £1800 it was possible to do with as few as three servants.

Edgar Speyer's munificence allowed Wood more rehearsal time than ever before, in particular permitting sectional as well as full-orchestral rehearsals. Sharing Wood's enthusiasm for new works, Speyer supported the Queen's Hall Orchestra with lavish and significant hospitality towards Continental composers – in person as well as in their music. The regular Saturday afternoon symphony concerts took on a heightened importance. Looking back in 1928, Rosa Newmarch would describe this period as the zenith of the orchestra's work.

Speyer's open-handedness not only towards the Queen's Hall concerts but in other directions (he was a founder of the Whitechapel Art Gallery) earned him a baronetcy in 1906 and membership of the Privy Council. According to his cousin Edward Speyer, Sir Edgar spent £4000 on the concerts each year. The benefits he brought, and his role in establishing Wood as a leading interpreter of the newest wave of music, rendered all the more tragic Edgar Speyer's eventual severance from the London scene – and the more incomprehensible Wood's complaisant acceptance of it.

Guided by her husband, Olga's career as a performer continued to be advanced by carefully chosen engagements. Occasionally her work could be combined with that of the newly formed Queen's Hall Wind Instrument Quintet, of which 'Mr Henry J. Wood has consented to direct all the rehearsals and to act as pianist at the public performances'. At Oxford Town Hall on 26 November 1903, its programme began with Mozart's Quintet for Piano and Wind and included songs sung by Olga to her husband's accompaniment – songs not only by Borodin and Tchaikovsky but by Schumann, Strauss, Percy Pitt and the young Norman O'Neill (1875–1934), whose overture *In Autumn* Wood had already performed at the promenade concerts.

Wood and his wife had made their home at 25A Norfolk Crescent, north of Hyde Park. They now moved into a new home, away from central London, at 4 Elsworthy Road in the Primrose Hill district, north of St John's Wood. (A plaque on the house commemorates his residence there.) The conductor had already adopted the somewhat quaint telegraphic address of 'Conducteth, London', and the notepaper for his new home was to bear a telephone number (Hampstead 2078), the telephone at this period becoming common in social intercourse.

St. Anne's-on-the-Sea Lectures, 1904–5.

PUBLIC HALL, ST. ANNE'S-ON-THE-SEA.

ON

FRIDAY, DECEMBER 16th, 1904, at 8-0 p.m.,

A

LECTURE

ON

"THE WOOD-WIND OF THE ORCHESTRA"

BY

MR. HENRY J. WOOD,

ILLUSTRATED BY THE

QUEEN'S HALL WIND QUINTET.

Flute - - -	Mr. ALBERT FRANSELLA.
Oboe - - -	Mr. J. L. FONTEYNE.
Clarinet - - -	Mr. MANUEL GOMEZ.
Bassoon - - - -	Mr. E. F. JAMES.
Horn - - - -	Mr. A. BORSDORF.

Pianoforte - -	Mr. HENRY J. WOOD.

Cor Anglais - - - - - -	Mr. J. L. FONTEYNE.
Corno di Bassetto and Bass Clarinet - -	Mr. F. GOMEZ.
Double Bassoon - - - - - -	Mr. E. F. JAMES.

THE GRAND PIANOFORTE BY BLÜTHNER & CO.

86

As visitors to the Speyers' far more luxurious home at 46 Grosvenor Street, in the wealthy heart of Mayfair, the Woods gained acquaintance with the eminent musicians whom the Speyers delighted to make their guests. The Richard Strausses, old friends of the Speyers, stayed with them at the end of 1902. The behaviour of Strauss's 'vivacious and somewhat overbearing' wife, the singer Pauline de Ahna, is reported by Wood with what seems a mixture of shock and amusement:

> I remember one occasion when Speyer at his own hospitable table raised his glass to drink the health of 'our distinguished guest Dr Richard Strauss'. Before another glass could be raised Madame Strauss excitedly lifted her own. 'No, no!' she said, pointing to herself with her left hand – 'No, no! *To Strauss de Ahna.*' Everyone laughed – we just had to, for the dear man himself laughed more than any of us and seemed to enjoy his wife claiming the precedence.

Unlike the generality of composers, Strauss was a conductor of the highest class and commanded Wood's admiration:

> I have always modelled my Strauss on Strauss himself as I was fortunate in hearing him rehearse and produce all his important works for a period of years. He was always most complimentary to me over my direction of his tone-poems which he heard me conduct on several occasions as a member of the audience. I was chatting with him one day about music in general, *tempi* in particular, when he ended our exchange of views with: 'My dear Mr Wood, do whatever you like in music, but never be *dull.*'

At a Saturday symphony concert on 6 December 1902 Strauss himself conducted the Queen's Hall Orchestra in the first performance in Britain of *Ein Heldenleben* (A Hero's Life), typical of his ebullient style and brilliant orchestration. It was followed by Wood's own performances on the following 1 January and 29 March. According to Wood, Speyer's munificence allowed a barely credible total of seventeen rehearsals for this work.

In mid-1903 the Concertgebouw Orchestra of Amsterdam gave London a three-day Strauss Festival, when the composer shared the rostrum with the orchestra's regular conductor Willem Mengelberg. Then it was again Wood's turn. At a Saturday symphony concert on 25 February 1905 he unleashed the first British performance of Strauss's *Symphonia Domestica*, with its huge array of wind instruments (including oboe d'amore, soprano clarinet in D, four saxophones and eight horns). At Wood's hands, too, Strauss's choral ballad *Taillefer* received its first performance in London

Broadening

(though not the first in England) when the Leeds Choral Union visited Queen's Hall on 3 March 1906.

The promenade audiences were soon granted their own share of Strauss and took an exceptional liking to *Till Eulenspiegel*. With flexibility of programming (no advance announcements of programmes were made beyond about a week ahead), *Till* was given three times in September 1905, made it into a Saturday 'popular' night on 7 October, and was again brought out on the following Friday. On the Wednesday between the two, *Ein Heldenleben* was heard in a newly designated 'Tchaikovsky-Brahms-Richard Strauss Night'. Such a designation, it should be remembered, served only to indicate a special feature, not to exclude other composers from the programme. On that evening Henry J. Wood's beloved Sullivan was represented by 'Woo thou thy snowflake' from *Ivanhoe*, and the early Victorian overture to Wallace's *Maritana* respected an even older taste.

A survey of other composers whom Wood helped to recognition is required in order to show the importance of the Speyer era both in Wood's own career and in British musical life. Debussy was one of its first beneficiaries. His music was new when Speyer began to finance the Queen's Hall concerts, and Wood was the first in Britain to launch Debussy's orchestral works. He conducted the *Prélude à l'après-midi d'un faune* at a promenade concert on 20 August 1904, ten years after the Paris première of the work. Despite a coolness in the reaction of reviewers, Wood claimed to have received 'more letters asking for a repetition' than had ever happened with a new work.

His pleasure was, however, to have composers conduct their own works in their first performances. (Wood himself would meticulously undertake the initial rehearsing.) Sharing his conductor's enthusiasm, Edgar Speyer sent Wood to Paris in 1907 to offer Debussy a concert appearance at a fee of a hundred guineas, with the addition of hospitality at the Speyers' home. According to Wood, the composer refused indignantly, citing a fee of four hundred guineas allegedly paid in London to Caruso, but (after Wood had telegraphed to Speyer) yielded to an offer of two hundred guineas.

Debussy did indeed become the Speyers' house-guest, and found the London public ready for him. His piano works were already being cultivated by such forward-looking performers as Percy Grainger, who had arrived in London with a determination to put Australia – in the person of himself – on the musical map. Grainger was invited to the Speyers' house to play to Debussy. On 1 February 1908 'not even Strauss', wrote Wood, received a warmer welcome than the composer of *L'après-midi* and *La mer* when he conducted those works at a Queen's Hall symphony concert.

In the following year he returned – but his inexperience as a conductor precipitated a remarkable incident as he was conducting the first performance in Britain of his three *Nocturnes*. At a difficult point in the middle movement, *Fêtes*, he lost control: 'Disaster seemed imminent, and M. Debussy was disposed to stop, but the band went on resolutely and happily recovered. The audience, whether for sympathy or satisfaction, encored the movement, and it was performed for the second time with great success.'

So ran the account in the *Musical Times* – to which Wood in *My Life of Music* adds a tribute to his orchestral players:

> Here was a famous composer directing a work of his own and, having got into difficulties, was asking the orchestra to stop and was being met with refusal. They obviously did not intend to stop: they knew that the audience would think the fault was theirs. Moreover, the work (which they liked immensely) was going beautifully and they meant to give a first-rate performance of it; which they proceeded to do and succeeded in doing. I never knew them more unanimous.

Another distinguished composer was in London and in Debussy's audience: Jean Sibelius. Wood had begun to perform the Finnish composer's music long before, giving his promenade audience on 26 October 1901 the first performance in Britain of the suite *King Christian II*. What had been planned as the first *London* performance of Sibelius's first symphony on 13 October 1903 turned out to be likewise the first in Britain, a previously planned performance at the Three Choirs Festival in Gloucester having been cancelled.

Sibelius first visited Britain in November 1905, when Granville Bantock was his host. 'Today', wrote Sibelius to his wife, 'he is going to introduce me to Wood (England's Nikisch).' Finland still ranked as a Grand Duchy of the Russian Empire, and Sibelius was impressed to find a conductor whose wife was a Russian aristocrat, 'related to the Naryshkin family'. Rosa Newmarch also met him in London and became, in the words of Sibelius's Finnish biographer, 'an effective and knowledgeable advocate of his music [and] a sensitive and faithful friend'.

As with Strauss, so with the much older Grieg it was Speyer's hospitality that gave Wood the opportunity of a sociable meeting. In 1906, at the age of sixty-three, Grieg was in Britain to receive an honorary doctorate from Oxford University and was a house-guest of the Speyers. After a dinner when Wood was present, Grieg was about to accompany his wife in some of his songs when he tripped over a rug and fell headlong. He was too shaken to play, so Wood stepped in as Nina Grieg's accompanist in 'A Swan', 'From Monte Pincio' and 'A Dream': 'The first of these had already been scored for orchestra but the other two had never been sung except with piano. Grieg told Speyer he wished he had scored them, and added: "I wonder whether I dare ask Wood to score them for me?" *Dare* ask me? I felt deeply honoured that he should even think of entrusting such work to my care! I told him I should be only too pleased to score them for him.'

Of Mahler, Wood was the pioneer in Britain. The claim in *My Life of Music* that his performance in 1903 of Mahler's First Symphony was 'the first note of his music to be heard in England' is probably correct. When Wood introduced the Fourth Symphony to Britain in 1905, with the unique feature of an orchestrally accompanied song as its last movement, Olga was the singer. (Wood's introduction of the Seventh Symphony would follow in 1913.) It is worth remembering that Mahler was not principally identified as a composer at all. The *Monthly Musical Record*, noting in its first issue of 1912 the significant deaths of the previous year, listed 'Gustav Mahler and Felix Mottl, the eminent conductors'. He never returned to Britain after conducting Covent Garden's first-ever cycle of Wagner's *Ring* in 1892.

In the recognition of Busoni as a composer Wood had likewise an important role, having long known and admired him as a pianist. At the promenade concerts of 1906 he launched two of Busoni's orchestral compositions – the *Comedy Overture* and a suite from his opera *Turandot*, written long before Puccini's. Busoni also showed himself to be a gifted conductor. On 5 June 1912, at a 'Busoni Orchestral Concert', Wood conducted the Queen's Hall Orchestra in Beethoven's Fifth Symphony and, with Busoni as soloist, in Liszt's *Totentanz*; Busoni himself took the baton for the overture to Mozart's *Die Entführung aus dem Serail*, with Busoni's own ending, and two works of his own.

Like Busoni, it was in the guise of pianist that Maurice Ravel would first arrive in Britain, in 1909. Wood was already performing his music. Just as he had appropriated Saint-Saëns's *Septet* for orchestral presentation, so in 1907 he took Ravel's *Introduction and Allegro* (originally for harp and seven other instruments) as a display-piece for his harpist, Alfred Kastner, with orchestra. The popular *Rapsodie espagnole* had its first British performance during the promenade season two years later.

With the promotion of British music Speyer did not need to concern himself overmuch. Wood brought his own momentum and did not lack prodding from the press. A distinct British modernist movement was emerging: by 1907 Wood had given first performances of works by Bantock, Frank Bridge and Cyril Scott, all representative figures. Scott, sometimes seriously called the English Debussy (mainly for such piano pieces as *Lotus Land*), was first represented at the promenade concerts by a symphony in 1903; Bridge, whom Britten would revere as his teacher, by the symphonic poem *Isabella* in 1907. In 1904 an *English Dance* introduced the promenaders to H. Balfour Gardiner; in 1911 Gardiner's *Shepherd Fennel's Dance* (after an episode in Thomas Hardy's short story, 'The Three Strangers') was launched into a lasting popularity.

Ralph Vaughan Williams found early recognition, Wood conducting the first performance of the *Norfolk Rhapsody* 'no.1' in 1906. (No composer ever repaid a conductor more beautifully than Vaughan Williams would in composing his *Serenade to Music* for Wood's jubilee in 1938.) The overture *For Valour* by Havergal Brian, produced by Wood at the Proms in 1907, preceded the long period in which Brian was virtually forgotten as a composer, to re-emerge only in the 1950s. Likewise in that season's Proms Delius's Piano Concerto, newly revised (in a single movement instead of three), had its first British performance, with Theodor Szántó as soloist and the composer present.

Percy Grainger, his reputation as pianist already secure, was about to conquer the promenade audience with such robustly entertaining pieces as *Shepherd's Hey* and *Mock Morris*. Wood had noted his distinctive gift. *Green Bushes*, a *passacaglia* or set of variations on an English folksong, received its première not in a promenade season but at a Saturday symphony concert on 19 October 1912, Grainger himself conducting. This placing was, as he pointed out in a letter to Nina Grieg, 'a very great honor [*sic*], as they very seldom do English works at these important concerts'. The remark neatly shows both the higher prestige of the symphony series and Grainger's acceptance (despite his strenuously Australian 'otherness') of an 'English' status as a composer.

Occasionally, and not always successfully, Wood's programmes would exhume 'new' works from the past as well. The score of Wagner's *Rule Britannia* Overture, written when the composer was twenty-four, had been rediscovered (after being thought lost) in London in 1904. On 2 February 1905 Wood placed it alongside two even earlier Wagner overtures, *Columbus* and *Polonia*. Newman's continuing role in planning the Queen's Hall concerts is shown in Wood's lightheartedly blaming him for the failure of these performances: 'Had Robert Newman listened to me he would never have had them produced at all.'

Private wealth still played its part not merely in such long-term finance as Speyer's but in the engagement of leading singers and instrumentalists for private gatherings. One might even book the Queen's Hall Orchestra itself, complete with its conductor. The Countess of Stafford used to engage about forty members of the orchestra for her private annual concert. By 1904 the leader's position had passed from Arthur W. Payne to Maurice Sons, a Dutchman of the fiery temperament that Wood persisted in associating with Dutch musicians: 'I remember how I laughed when Sons presented himself at the front door of the house and the butler took his violin-case and told him the band used the side entrance . . . His fury at what he considered a flagrant insult was most amusing . . . As it happened, I had just come in and was standing in the hall. This put matters right. Even though the others had accepted the side entrance without a murmur, I am certain Sons would have gone home rather than use it.'

One can sense Wood's incomprehension of the point of honour but his admiration for someone who would have forgone his fee for it.

Wood himself remained a shy man. Intimate friends, such as in the idiom of the time might have been called 'cronies', were almost completely lacking in Henry J. Wood's life. Around this time, however, such an intimacy began in London with Siegfried Schwabacher, who became 'one of the most cherished and loved friends of my life'. Probably of German birth, he had made a fortune in diamonds in South Africa. Having settled in London, with a house first in Hammersmith and then in the Swiss Cottage area, not far from the Woods' house in Elsworthy Road, he sought no honours or prominence. A rare photograph (see plate 21) shows that he was perhaps twenty years older than Wood. Schwabacher financed at about £300 annually the 'Select Choir' of some 100 dedicated amateurs, which Wood founded in 1903. Its work was to be devoted to Bach, to unaccompanied singing and to such music as 'old glees and madrigals and the sacred works of Palestrina'.

It was thus a deliberately 'historical' enterprise of Wood's. Perhaps it was simply the available generosity of Schwabacher that determined him to start it at that particular time, but why he should have given it up after a few seasons of rehearsals – before considering it ready for performance – is not clear. The labour was not thrown away, however, since its membership was apparently put at the disposal of Charles Kennedy Scott when he was founding the Oriana Madrigal Society in 1904. Wood thus stands as a quasi-parent of that body, which contributed with distinction to British musical life and which Scott continued to conduct until 1961.

The striking individuality of Wood's face, hair and beard – whether or not he was wielding the baton – would later invite the caricaturist as well as the photographer. What was probably the first full-length photograph of him within Queen's Hall appeared in the *Tatler*, an illustrated magazine, on 16 December 1903 – 'taken by flashlight', as was indicated (see plate 26). In the previous week's issue the magazine noted that August Manns, the veteran conductor of the Crystal Palace concerts, had waited seventy-eight years for his recently conferred knighthood. Wood was to be so honoured in his early forties.

The *Tatler* had published two years previously an article headed 'The Queen's Hall Orchestra' dealing at greater length with Robert Newman than with Henry J. Wood. But the more Wood's reputation grew, the odder it must have seemed that neither in London's general nor musical press had he been accorded a signed article surveying his career. A biographical sketch had been promised in the *Musical Times* but the magazine announced in November 1901 that it was 'unavoidably postponed till early in next year' – and even then it did not appear.

Why not? The most likely author of such an article would have been Rosa Newmarch, and one wonders whether what she may have submitted to the magazine's editor savoured too much of hero-worship. Instead she gave her admiration full play in 1904 in her book of 100 pages, *Henry J. Wood* – the first of a series planned under her editorship, with the general title of *Living Masters of Music*. Ernest Newman's book on Richard Strauss was the second. Her intimate acquaintance with the conductor is conspicuous throughout its pages, though he deceived her over particulars of his birth, given one year late as 3 March 1870.

Evidently copying almost word-for-word from the anonymous 'puff' of 1895 (see p.35), she repeats the over-estimate that he 'has conducted forty-six operas, grand and comic'. Nevertheless her appreciation of Wood's qualities is infectious and her personal description vivid. Correctly, she identifies Olga only as 'daughter of the late Princess Sofie Ouroussov, née Narishkin [*her spelling*]', and never refers to Olga as a princess herself. She paints the picture of Wood's mental and physical vigour even off the concert platform: 'Wherever he goes, a volume of Ruskin is sure to make its appearance out of his pocket or travelling-bag. He is a good billiard-player, manages a punt as skilfully as an orchestra, and is fond of cycling. Those who picture him as suffering perpetually from nervous tension and over-fatigue should see him coast from the top of Beachy Head with a stiff breeze in his wake!'

She was evidently upset by 'such curious freaks of correspondence as that which recently appeared in the *Pall Mall Gazette* under the heading, IS MR

Broadening

WOOD A GOOD CONDUCTOR?' She does not quote from that correspondence, but 'curious' is indeed the word for it. Henry J. Wood's concerts had been appreciatively reviewed by the paper's music critic when – out of the blue – a letter appeared over the pseudonym 'F.' on 8 October 1903, querying not the conductor's technical efficiency but the musical sensibility of his results:

> Wagner made two classes: conductors and time-beaters. Mr Wood is an admirable, energetic time-beater. Look at him as he works – muscles, elbows, head in movement, everything gesticulates. The more noise and exertion required, the more gymnastically he moves. He assumes that his men will not respond save to the crack of the whip; like a muleteer, who at the foot of a hill rushes along beside his cattle, prodding, shouting, and whipping them up till they reach the top. Mr Wood has a special up-and-down movement of his elbows. Of his baton he makes a scourge.

A sheaf of ripostes from other readers more than redressed the balance, but the attack seems to have been extraordinarily ill-directed. One of those replying to 'F.' drew attention to Wood's regard for detail, to 'the manner in which the smallest passages are brought out – dragged out, as it were – from the soloist or block of instruments, not with the "stick" but with the eye, and the surrounding players made to subordinate themselves for the moment'.

Wood's other defenders, however, admitted imperfections in ensemble at the promenade concerts, due to short rehearsal time and the toleration of deputies in the orchestra. (Evidently the abuse was not yet stamped out.) At the Saturday concerts, however, it was claimed that he 'gives readings of the great masters which might rank with those of any other conductor in beauty, ripeness and intellectual subtlety'.

Were Wood to be criticized, it might be for the exact opposite of rigid time-beating, namely over-flexibility and exaggeration. Such a criticism was indeed voiced when he submitted himself to the approval of a new audience – in New York.

Chapter 8

In New York

1904–8

The name of Henry Wood has come to us across the seas from time to time as that of an evangel [*sic*] honored in his own country because of his teaching of things both new and great. We were told that he belongs to the small minority of conductors which has stopped seeking the 'hidden meaning' of Beethoven and the 'spiritual essence' of Brahms. It was proclaimed that Wood was serving strange musical deities, men of Russia who made music with their souls rather than with their pens. . . .

And the man, this Henry J. Wood, who helped to change the musical taste of his countrymen, who fed them iron in place of pap and blood instead of water, is himself something a world apart from every accepted standard of an English musician. . . .

The English leader looks like Nikisch – which means that Henry Wood is a man of good and graceful figure, with dark wavy hair and full black beard, that his gestures are sweeping, incisive and picturesque, and that he is a master of dynamics, a lover of the unexpected and of that piquancy without which no performance of Russian music is properly seasoned.

So the *Musical Courier* of New York reviewed the concert of 8 January when 'Henry J. Wood of London', as he was billed, first conducted the orchestra of the New York Philharmonic Society at Carnegie Hall. The front cover of the magazine carried the full-page picture of Wood himself. Olga Wood (as well as Dr Cathcart) accompanied the conductor on the trip, telling another interviewer, apropos her husband's manifest sympathy for Russian music, that he was 'Russian on his wife's side'.

The New York public had been stirred barely two weeks before by the first production there of Wagner's *Parsifal* – produced at the Metropolitan Opera on 24 December 1903 in defiance of the ban proclaimed by Wagner's family against any stage production outside Bayreuth. (Performances in concert form, however, had been given in both London and New York.) According to an interview in the Boston journal, *The Musician*, Wood himself arrived in New York in time to attend this performance and also journeyed 'immediately after his arrival' to Boston to hear a concert by the Boston Symphony Orchestra, at this time under the direction of Wilhelm Gericke.

Rather strangely, in view of Wood's choice of programmes for other 'ambassadorial' appearances, there was no British music on his Carnegie Hall programme. The overture to Weber's *Der Freischütz* was followed by Tchaikovsky's Symphony no.5. After the interval, the Violin Concerto no.3 by Saint-Saëns was played by the American violinist Maud Powell, and the concert ended with Rimsky-Korsakov's *Capriccio Espagnol* – 'new to this public', as the critic of the *New York Times* put it. Scheduled at 2 p.m. on a Friday afternoon, this event was not officially called a concert but a 'public rehearsal' of the Philharmonic, leading to the concert properly so called on the next evening. Such 'public rehearsals', however, were regarded as concerts in all but name, attracted their regular paying audience, and were attended by reviewers.

The patrons of the Friday matinée concerts were 'nine-tenths women, many of whom came from the towns and villages around about', as the *New York Times* reminded its readers when reporting Wood's evident power of stirring his audience. 'If a presage is to be drawn from the conduct of the audience yesterday, tonight is likely to witness scenes of almost boisterous enthusiasm.' (The 'almost' is a nice touch.)

But perhaps the Rimsky-Korsakov work was itself rather blatant in its appeal for such a dignified occasion:

> Popular audiences like music which is vivid in color, incisive in contrasts, pleasantly irritating to the nerves, stimulating and exciting to the fancy. The staid patrons of the Philharmonic were treated to those sensations yesterday, and, as has been indicated, manifested enjoyment of them, though some may have pondered afterward, and indulged in questionings as to whether or not the Russian composer's revel in Spanish rhythms mixed with a sort of barbaric splendour was altogether worthy of so dignified a function as a Philharmonic concert.

There was no lack of interest in the visiting conductor's physical appearance. The *New York Times* critic came as near as possible to suggesting sex-appeal:

> Mr Wood by no means corresponds to the conventional figure of an Englishman. Short, sallow, with a shock of black hair and a black pointed

beard, he has grace and elegance of manner, and in his motions before his orchestra these are united in a certain sinuosity, in graceful sweeps of the right arm and in a caressing fall of the left hand from the wrist. Yet his presence is authoritative, and he had full sway over the men in front of him – and, it might also be said, over the women behind him in the audience. It would be unfair, however, to lay too much stress on the latter: for Mr Wood is clearly a musician of vigorous fibre, deep feeling, and independent, robust, intellectual powers.

This critic seemingly found Wood's interpretation to be exaggerated, even for Tchaikovsky:

On occasion he will hold a poignant note in an expressive phrase as an Italian tenor would hold a high note in an aria before the footlights. He is fond of rounding off a phrase, explosively begun, with a dying fall. He seeks the extremes of contrast, both in dynamics and in tempo, sometimes with deep impressiveness, sometimes with so obvious a sense of effort and exaggeration as to disturb the forward sweep of the music, as at the entrance of the singing syncopated theme in the first movement. He routs out hidden melodies in inner instrumental voices – sometimes, in truth, when they are not there; and by bringing forward groups of notes intended only as harmonic material he confuses the texture of the music.

The *New York Tribune*, on the contrary, found that through all the variety of dynamics and tempo, the essential thread *was* maintained. Whether or not he was aware of Wagner's term *melos* to represent this notion of an inner thread (Wagner considered that the job of seeking out the *melos* was the essential function of the modern conductor), this critic expressed the point exactly in drawing attention to Wood's feeling for 'the broad orchestral song' – here in relation to his conducting of the *Freischütz* overture.

The *New York Herald*, which also noted his physical resemblance to Nikisch, found Wood's style of interpretation 'at once vigorous, poetic and refined. It abounded in individuality, in delicacy and in power'; weighty climaxes were achieved 'without the forcing of particular instruments'. His 'delicacy in accompanying the concerto' was also noted.

From Wood's autobiographical pages one might suppose that his presence on the rostrum of Carnegie Hall was due to the persuasiveness of the millionaire philanthropist who had endowed the hall, Andrew Carnegie, and who extended warm hospitality to Wood in New York. But the invitation to Wood was chiefly a product of a crisis in the Philharmonic management. Walter Damrosch (1862–1950), conductor of the Philharmonic in 1902–3, had moved to its rival body, the reorganized New York Symphony Society.

Broadening

To re-stimulate its public, the Philharmonic had decided to spread the 1903–4 season between seven guest conductors. The audience and the orchestra's directors could compare Wood with Colonne from Paris, Gustav Kogel from Frankfurt, Weingartner from Munich, Richard Strauss from Vienna, Vasily Safonov from Moscow and Victor Herbert (better known to posterity as the composer of *Naughty Marietta* and other operettas) from Pittsburgh.

In the following season some of these guests would be reinvited. Wood was not – and Safonov, who anticipated Stokowski in preferring to conduct without a baton, was eventually named the orchestra's regular conductor. The invitation to Wood, though confined to the two performances of the same programme, had the potentiality of an audition for the permanent post. Would he have accepted, had the offer been made? New York at that time was still considered inferior to London as a concert centre. Yet an opportunity to spend at least part of the year there – with the pickings of the London promenade concerts no doubt still available in summer – might well have tempted him at a comparatively early stage of his career.

He had been released by Newman, he tells us, only for a month, with the obligation to return in time for a rehearsal and concert with the violinist Marie Hall. With the Queen's Hall Orchestra (but at the St James's Hall) she was to play a Herculean succession of the Mendelssohn, Beethoven and Tchaikovsky concertos on 22 January 1904. The *Celtic*, on which Wood was travelling from New York, was scheduled to dock in Liverpool in good time, but was trapped by fog in the Mersey. Leaving his wife and Cathcart aboard (he tells us), he persuaded the captain to let him descend the rope ladder to the pilot's boat, was taken ashore, and by taking a night train arrived at Queen's Hall for the morning rehearsal as planned.

A farewell salute was now to be paid to the greatest violinist of his era. Joseph Joachim had first appeared in London at a Philharmonic concert on 27 May 1844, playing Beethoven's concerto under the baton of Mendelssohn; sixty years later, on 16 May 1904, he played it under Henry J. Wood. The occasion at Queen's Hall was not called a concert but a reception. The music-loving Prime Minister, Arthur James Balfour, presided. Wood opened the programme with Mendelssohn's *Hebrides* overture; Joachim followed the Beethoven concerto by playing his own arrangement of Schumann's 'Abendlied', and finally conducted his own overture to Shakespeare's *Henry IV, part 2* and the *Academic Festival Overture* of his great friend, Brahms.

Edward Speyer, an intimate of Joachim's as he had been of Brahms's, had made the arrangements.

In Fritz Kreisler a conquering new violinist had already won recognition. In 1902, aged twenty-seven, he had made his London début, under Richter. With Wood, as with Elgar, he was to develop a close collaboration in the concert-hall before finding a way via the gramophone record to the hearts of the middlebrow public as well as the sophisticates. At a Queen's Hall concert in aid of the Life-Boat Fund on 8 June 1904, Kreisler played Sarasate and Vieuxtemps in the company of Wood, his orchestra, and an extraordinary array of stars. Melba, Caruso and Pol Plançon ('the loveliest bass I ever heard', Wood declared) sang operatic arias, and Saint-Saëns was heard as piano soloist in his *Africa Fantasy*.

By this time Wood and Newman must have decided between them – prompted, perhaps, by the critical observations made in the *Pall Mall Gazette* (see p.94) – that a further dose of discipline in the orchestra's ranks was required on the vexed question of deputies. From the symphony concerts deputies had been eliminated; but not from the promenade concerts, for which the orchestra was engaged on a separate contract. According to *My Life of Music* the whip was applied in a famously terse announcement made by Robert Newman to his orchestra: 'Gentlemen, in future there will be no deputies. Good morning.'

There is no other source for this anecdote, which carries no date and savours strongly of myth: contractual arrangements would require paper. Notice of the new rule was probably given in May 1904. Applied to the approaching promenade season, due to last until 21 October, it would debar the players from participation in the Leeds Triennial Festival in early October. That was apparently the immediate cause of a large secession of players and of the formation of a new, rival body, the London Symphony Orchestra.

The partings were not without regrets nor without civilities. The celebrated, long-lived trumpeter, John Solomon (1856–1953), kept and treasured through the following decades the letter which Henry J. Wood sent him. It was indeed an astonishing expression of courtesy from a conductor about to be deserted by one of his most eminent players:

> Before leaving for my holidays allow me to take this opportunity of
> thanking you most sincerely for your superb services as Principal
> Trumpet in the Queen's Hall Orchestra. I need not say how I shall miss

99

> your face and your playing and deeply regret that owing to the new
> regulations we shall not be working together in the future.
>   Believe me, most faithfully yours

No wonder that orchestral players' affection for 'Timber' – as they nicknamed him – went beyond the ordinary.

He had also lost to the London Symphony Orchestra his violinist-leader Arthur W.Payne and such other eminent, long-standing principals as Manuel Gomez (clarinet), E. F. James (bassoon) and Adolf Borsdorf (horn). Among others faced with the choice of joining the new orchestra or remaining with the old was Lionel Tertis – at the age of twenty-seven already the leader of Wood's violas. He took neither option, instead deciding to concentrate on the solo work which gave him unique distinction. (He did, however, take a brief orchestral sojourn under Beecham.) In his reminiscences Tertis declared his debt to Wood: 'I learnt from him what good phrasing was, the accurate value of notes and rests, and many another detail of help to musicianship, not to speak of discipline and punctuality. . . He was a martinet, as he had need to be to get through all the enterprises he undertook.'

As if to show the seriousness of the ban on deputies, Wood was prepared to make sacrifices of his own:

> We are informed [announced *The Times* on 9 May 1904] that Mr Henry J. Wood has resigned the conductorship of the Sheffield Musical Festival of 1905, and has also cancelled his engagements with the Moscow Philharmonic Society in December and for six concerts in America next January. Musicians of the Queen's Hall Orchestra are by their contracts not permitted to send deputies to any of their concerts or rehearsals, and Mr Wood has cancelled the above engagements in order that he may himself conform to the conditions which are demanded from the members of the orchestra.

No details of this invitation from Moscow are known, nor of any subsequent invitations from there. Despite his close affiliation with composers of that country, Wood was never to set foot in Russia.

The newly-created London Symphony Orchestra gave its first concert on 9 June 1904 at Queen's Hall, under the baton of Hans Richter – with Wood, large-hearted, in the audience. There were ninety-nine players, of whom 'forty-six have recently seceded from the Queen's Hall Orchestra, while thirty-two others formerly played under Mr Wood's baton' (*Musical Times*) – a clear indication that in the campaign against deputies the move of 1904 was not the first, as all current histories of British musical life suppose it to have been.

At the promenade concerts of 1904 the 'newly reconstituted' Queen's Hall Orchestra (as it was seen to be) took its place on the platform. Not even Wood's prodigious skills as an orchestral trainer could rebuild his force overnight. With its infusion of fresh blood, the orchestra was judged at first to be 'vastly inferior to the old, both as regards the skill of the instrumentalists and the volume of tone produced'. The words are taken from the precocious William Maitland Strutt, then aged eighteen: his *Reminiscences of a Musical Amateur*, published shortly after his premature death in 1912, have a refreshing freedom from partisanship and were based on listening to music in France and Germany as well as in England.

The concerts of the London Symphony Orchestra – at first hardly amounting to one a month – might challenge the Queen's Hall Orchestra's standing in point of quality, but not of quantity. Nor could they damage Wood's own career. He was, in any case, not one to let that career stand still: he even announced in that year the formation of an 'orchestral society', that is, a training orchestra for amateurs or students. (Like his 'Select Choir', it seems to have been aborted.) Maintaining contact with Sheffield, he took over the joint conductorship of the city's Amateur Musical Society, on 19 December conducting the Brahms *Requiem* with Olga as the soprano soloist and Frederic Austin the baritone.

Other provincial visits also became regular. In 1904, for his first appearance at Mary Wakefield's festival at Kendal (see p.53), he had taken with him the Queen's Hall Orchestra to accompany *Elijah* and the *Alto Rhapsody* of Brahms. He was to continue yearly visits to that festival until 1913, not only conducting but, at least on one occasion, lecturing on the orchestral instruments. His description of the woodwind as 'the flower garden of the orchestra' was heard there and remembered by the composer and critic Havergal Brian, a keen gardener himself.

A fourteen-year-old schoolboy, Adrian Cedric Boult, had begun regular attendance at Wood's Saturday symphony concerts at Queen's Hall and noted Wood's assiduous attendance also at others' performances – at Richter's *Das Rheingold* (Covent Garden) in May 1903, and at a Berlioz centenary concert conducted by Richard Strauss at Queen's Hall in the following December. Already determined on a career in music, the boy had been introduced to Leo F. ('Frankie') Schuster, Elgar's patron (1840–1928), who was an acquaintance of Wood also. In Schuster's company Boult went to the Queen's Hall symphony concert on 12 November 1904, when

Broadening

Wood repeated *L'après-midi d'un faune*. 'Very difficult, though not much in it,' Boult thought. Shortly afterwards the drastic cuts made by Wood in Tchaikovsky's *Francesca da Rimini*, evidently in an attempt to improve a work he thought inferior (see p.76), scandalized the young conductor-to-be.

Wood and his orchestra were by no means confined to London. In March 1905 a Midlands-based promoter, Percy Harrison, sent them to give ten concerts in eleven days, each in a different provincial or Scottish city. At Dundee Olga sang the *Liebestod* from Wagner's *Tristan und Isolde*, and Percy Pitt was as usual the celesta soloist in Tchaikovsky's *Nutcracker Suite*.

Edgar Speyer was determined to see that the public appreciated Wood not only for his visible command but for his skill in preparing those performances at which composers conducted their own works. The Queen's Hall programme for 11 May 1905 reproduced a letter to Wood from Elgar, who had conducted *The Dream of Gerontius* and *The Apostles* at Leeds with the Queen's Hall Orchestra:

> I send my heartiest thanks to you for contributing to the magnificent performances at Leeds by preparing your Orchestra in such a wonderful way. Will you kindly convey to every member of your Orchestra, in terms which I leave you to choose, but which cannot be too warm and enthusiastic, my grateful appreciation of the splendid manner in which they interpreted my scores, and for the goodwill and patience with which they rehearsed.

The programme also contained a letter from Richard Strauss to Speyer after he had conducted a repeat performance of the *Symphonia Domestica* at Queen's Hall on 1 April 1905:

> . . . I cannot leave London without an expression of admiration for the splendid Orchestra which Henry Wood's master hand has created in so incredibly short a time. He can be proud indeed of this little colony of artists, who represent both discipline and quality of the highest order.
>
> After the thirty performances of the *Symphonia Domestica* which I have conducted this winter, and of which only very few indeed can compare with the masterly rendering of the new and, in that sense, youthful Queen's Hall Orchestra, I can well appreciate what an amount of hard work, expert knowledge, and sympathetic comprehension of my intentions have been expended on this performance through the energy and self-effacing labours of Mr Wood. Performances such as these mark days of rejoicing in a composer's life.

In its second season, the London Symphony Orchestra, still no rival to the Queen's Hall Orchestra, achieved only thirteen concerts between November 1905 and the following June. Only five were conducted by Richter: his British base now lay in Manchester with the Hallé Orchestra. Wood's exposure was meanwhile undiminished, with the occasional week-day afternoon concert (all-Tchaikovsky or all-Wagner) added to Newman's flag-carrying Saturday afternoon symphony concerts. Sunday concerts continued as charitable events under the National Sunday League, taking the orchestra to such venues as the Alexandra Palace in North London, the People's Palace in the East End, and the Alhambra Theatre in Leicester Square.

Anyone who lingered at the Alhambra on Sunday 23 April 1905 could have heard John Philip Sousa and his magnificent American band in the afternoon and Wood and his orchestra in the evening. Did Wood and Sousa never meet? The American 'march king' was keenly interested in the latest musical trends and knew Dan Godfrey of Bournemouth well. Godfrey arranged *Till Eulenspiegel* for Sousa's band and received the acknowledgement: 'I will not play *Till Eulenspiegel* on this trip over here, but will launch it on an unsuspecting public later on, in God's Own Country. Whether it will be God's Own Country after they have heard a lot of Richard Strauss is a debatable point.'

By summer 1905 the 'tone' of the promenade concerts had substantially altered. Saturday remained a 'popular' night, but on Friday 6 October there were no ballads, no operatic fantasia, no marches. A Haydn symphony *not* from the popular 'Salomon Set' was a remarkable opening: no complete edition of Haydn symphonies had yet been published. The programme (see next page) stands as an example of how the 'classical' element could now pervade a whole evening, not merely the first half.

Ballads had not suddenly been 'banned' – but if a singer now preferred to allot his or her piano-accompanied 'spot' (after the interval) to more artistic material, the audience was invited to respect that choice. The tenor Gervase Elwes, noted for just such refinement, had first met Wood in an unusual type of audition. Ushered into Wood's bedroom, he found a blind masseur at work. 'I hummed through my piece, he [Wood] following the while with the orchestral score, being massaged all the time.'

The violin soloist in the programme, Frederick Stock, was a member of the orchestra, not the German-born musician so named who became the illustrious conductor of the Chicago Symphony Orchestra. Wood complimented his leader, Henri Verbrugghen, by giving him the final item to conduct.

Broadening

Symphony [no.60] in C, *'Il distratto'*	Haydn
Songs:	
'Absence'	Berlioz
'Non so più' [*Le nozze di Figaro*]	Mozart
EMMA HOLMSTRAND	
Two Equali [for four trombones]	Beethoven
Piano Concerto no.3	Beethoven
ARCHY ROSENTHAL	
Recitative and Air, 'Waft her, angels' (*Jephtha*)	Handel
GERVASE ELWES	
Symphony no.4 in A (*'Italian'*)	Mendelssohn

INTERVAL

Overture, *Carnaval romain*	Berlioz
Songs:	
'Der Doppelgänger'	Schubert
'Pastourelle' (*La Basoche*)	Messager
EMMA HOLMSTRAND	
Violin solo, Ballade et Polonaise	Vieuxtemps
FREDERICK STOCK	
Piano solos:	
Prelude no.17	Chopin
Etude (on the black keys)	Chopin
ARCHY ROSENTHAL	
Song, 'O mistress mine'	Quilter
GERVASE ELWES	
English Dances in the Olden Style	Cowen

How ironic that Wood should be remembered less for such innovative programmes as this than for an item which – a few days later – deliberately reverted to the older promenade tradition, an item to which he did not even bother to affix his name. Henry J. Wood's *Fantasia on British Sea Songs*, today the climax of celebration on the Last Night of the Proms, appeared anonymously in the printed programme of a promenade concert which was unprecedentedly held on a Saturday afternoon, 21 October 1905 – the centenary of the Battle of Trafalgar.

Trafalgar Day was always a nationally marked anniversary, but the centenary especially so: naval power and the image of the bold and free Jolly Jack Tar were important to Edwardian imperialism. At Queen's Hall, flags representing the famous Nelson signal ('England expects every man will do his duty') floated above the orchestra and Nelson's picture fronted the printed programme. The musical fare conformed to Newman's old style of topical hotch-potches. The patriotic-nautical note allowed the favourite Victorian ballad 'Rocked in the cradle of the deep' (by Joseph Knight) to sit alongside the overture to *The Flying Dutchman*.

Wood's *Fantasia* was equally a hotch-potch. Naval bugle-calls (on horns and trumpets, on and off the platform) preluded a sixteen-minute parade of short items performed by various instrumental soloists, in the style of the old-fashioned operatic 'Grand Selection'. 'The Anchor's Weigh'd', 'The Arethusa', and 'Tom Bowling' were evidently culled from a popular parlour album, J. L. Hatton's *Songs of England.* (Wood even borrowed Hatton's six-bar introduction for 'The Anchor's Weigh'd'.) Next came genuine shipboard material –'Jack's the lad', better known as the Sailor's Hornpipe, and 'Farewell and adieu to you, fair Spanish ladies'. The concluding items were Bishop's 'Home, sweet home' and Handel's 'See, the conquering hero comes', in which not even Nelson's telescope would have found maritime content, and 'Rule, Britannia!' – not (as today) as a separate item with vocal soloist and chorus, but allotted to the orchestra only, the organ joining in towards the end.

Just before the final refrain Wood wrote in an early manuscript score (now at the Royal Academy of Music): 'Conductor turn to public'. The opportunity of lending their voices to 'Rule, Britannia!' was evidently the only intended participation by the audience. Only when the item had shifted to the final night of much later seasons did Wood embrace the phenomenon he had unwittingly created, with the audience foot-tapping as the hornpipe was accelerated – and 'when it comes to the singing of "Rule, Britannia!", we reach a climax that only Britons *can* reach, and I realize I can be nowhere in the world but in my native England'.

Neither *The Times*, mentioning the original concert in its review of other events of Trafalgar Day, nor the *Musical Times* recorded the birth of the new Fantasia, which was also performed at the regular promenade concert on the evening of the same day. Musically, the only remarkable thing about the *Fantasia* (apart from keeping alive for a modern audience such fine tunes as 'The Saucy Arethusa' and 'Tom Bowling', respectively by Shield and Dibdin) is Wood's superb harmonization of 'Spanish Ladies' for four trombones – a combination he perhaps took from the Beethoven *Equali*, included in his programme listed opposite and in many others.

Four days before, on 17 October, the sensational Mischa Elman, aged fourteen but stated to be twelve, was heard in what was advertised as the 'first public performance' of Glazunov's violin concerto (actually given its

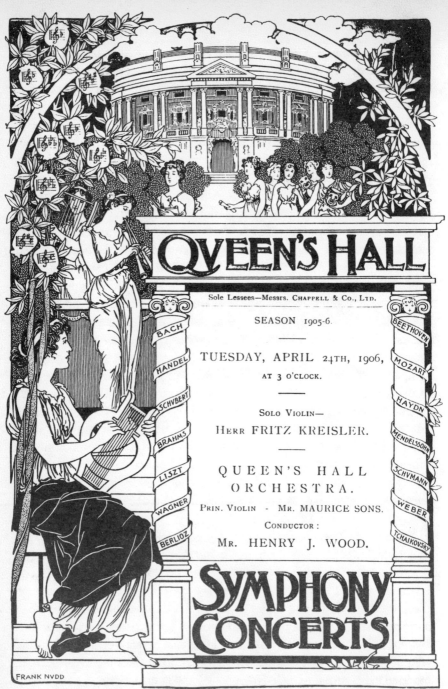

ANALYTICAL PROGRAMME, PRICE SIXPENCE.

Printed programme for a weekday afternoon symphony concert in 1906.

first performance by Leopold Auer in St Petersburg the previous year). Wood retained all his life a liking for the music of Glazunov, who at this date seemed to be directly in line to inherit Tchaikovsky's mantle.

Continuing what seemed to be a one-man crusade for Bach, Wood in the ensuing season of symphony concerts claimed a 'first performance in England' for Bach's Brandenburg Concerto no. 6 on 4 November 1905 – but the *Musical Times* identified a less conspicuous London performance of ten years previously. Wood's performances of 'the Brandenburgs' were famous and popular, and would continue so until a later taste reacted against the heavy, full-orchestral approach to such works. No.6, scored for lower strings only, was apparently his favourite: by his choice, its slow movement was played at his funeral.

Two deaths were to be solemnly marked during the 1907 promenade season. For such tributes, the funeral march from Chopin's piano sonata in B flat minor was still the regularly preferred piece, as *Nimrod* from the *Enigma Variations* would be for the next generation. Rejecting the orchestration published by Breitkopf & Haertel, Wood had rescored Chopin's movement – using a large orchestra with bells, organ and four trombones, and shifting the key by a semitone to B minor so that the cellos by retuning their lowest string from C to B could give extra sonority on the bass-line. On 17 August, the entire audience stood while Wood and the orchestra honoured Joachim, who had died two days before. To Wood's obvious pleasure, Breitkopf later published his version.

The death of Grieg on 4 September 1907 was likewise keenly felt. (Much more of his music was then current than it now is.) Not Chopin's funeral march was used at the Queen's Hall commemoration on 16 October, but Grieg's own funeral march in memory of his friend Richard Nordraak – originally written for military band, newly scored by Wood for the orchestra. These two, Chopin's and Grieg's, in Wood's imaginative arrangements might well be reclaimed for the modern repertory, as also his arrangement of Debussy's *La cathédrale engloutie*.

Wood continued to find time for the occasional appearance in chamber music at smaller halls than Queen's Hall. At the Bechstein Hall, a concert held on 27 January 1906 to mark the 150th anniversary of Mozart's birth found Wood playing on the piano the glass-harmonica part in the Adagio and Rondo, K.617. At the Aeolian Hall on 1 May 1906 both Henry (at the piano) and Olga were among the artists giving their services to help raise funds for the endowment of Bach's birthplace at Eisenach as a Bach museum.

But in approaching Bach's (and Handel's) music, what challenged and excited him was the problem of communicating major works to large, modern audiences in large, modern halls built to project the blended sound of a large, modern choir and orchestra. Wood could and did evoke Mozart's revision of Handel's *Messiah* to justify his own freedom in updating. The *St Matthew Passion* was the work in which he would put forward his principles and the Sheffield Festival of 1908 (5–9 October) would be his testing-ground. Newman evidently permitted his absence this time, as not in 1905. He had the incalculable advantage of bringing the Queen's Hall Orchestra with him while the London Symphony Orchestra acted as substitutes at the promenade concerts, with Edouard Colonne conducting.

Thirty years later, in a chapter of *My Life of Music*, he re-expounded his approach to the *St Matthew Passion*. It is the only chapter containing music-type illustrations, enabling the reader to glimpse the detailed markings of volume, phrasing and expression which Wood habitually presented to both singers and orchestral players. The performance was assumed to be in English. British choruses did not expect to sing in foreign languages, and for British singers to address biblical words to British audiences in German would have been thought ridiculous. A new translation was commissioned from Claude Aveling. In such words as: '(*pianissimo*) Leave Him, leave Him, (*forte*) bind Him (*piano*) not!' Wood insisted on his choir 'singing to the words', as the *Sheffield Daily Telegraph* was to put it. The critic precisely identified Wood's approach, with full application of colour and nuance as suggested by the changing sense and feeling of the text – even to sarcasm: 'and build it in (*fortissimo, exaggerated*) three days!' This was post-*Gerontius* Bach.

Wood enriched his woodwind with two *oboi d'amore* and two *oboi da caccia* corresponding to Bach's specifications (or rather to what these specifications were thought to mean around 1900). For its single *obbligato* number a seven-string bass viol (viola da gamba) was 'lent by Mr Wood'. But how to balance the choir of several hundred voices with an orchestra of sufficient strength? The German composer Robert Franz had brought out an edition augmenting the orchestra with modern, non-Bach instruments, much as Wood's own teacher Prout had done for *Messiah*. Wood preferred simply to multiply Bach's own instruments in proportion as his own choir (and his own string section) was bigger than Bach's. Bach's two flutes and two oboes were replaced by eight of each, with eight bassoons on the bass-line.

Rejecting the anachronistic piano and 'the jingle-jangle of tinny sound from a harpsichord', Wood judged that to accompany the recitatives 'the only instrument to use is the instrument of the church – the organ'. But the decision in principle was overridden by a concession to *variety*: at some points the Evangelist's words were accompanied not by organ but by four cellos and one double-bass. Similarly, some of the chorales were taken out of the hands of the chorus and allotted to a quartet of the soloists. Under the surface of Wood's own written instructions can be seen a struggle between a desire to penetrate a difficult, archaic score and a desire to 'bring it off' in terms of the current audience.

The point was illuminated, in a critical yet appreciative way, by the critic who was to be the most influential of the next half-century in Britain. Ernest Newman (1868–1959) was at that time still working for the *Birmingham Daily Post* before his move to London. Most newspaper criticism of the pre-1914 era was anonymous, but Newman's long report bore his initials. It is remarkable for its *rationale* of a conductor's liberty to 'be himself':

> Some of the chorales were over-elaborated to the point of being sentimentalized. It was beautiful singing, but one would have preferred the chorales in their native grand simplicity without all these refinements of emotional expression and verbal accentuation in the chorus and of the organ. There were one or two effects that came a little too near the theatrical for some tastes, and yet, in spite of there being so many things in the performance that ruffled one's sense of the fit and proper, as a whole it was one of the most impressive and affecting things I have ever heard. Part of this good effect came from the admirable work of the principals, who, rising to the height of their great task, gave us the best that was in them; part also from the ravishing beauty of the orchestral playing. . .
>
> But the main reason why, after all, the performance was a notable one is to be sought in Mr Wood himself. If it was not always the real Bach that he gave us, we had an extraordinarily vivid and unified picture of Bach as he appears to Mr Wood. We felt his personality there all through the performance, as we used to feel it all through the acting of Irving. We might dislike this gesture or that stride of the great actor, or smile at the obvious artificiality of some of his intonations, but, upon the whole part there was imposed a powerful and compelling personality that, in the end, made us give up thinking how far the acting was congruous with the ideas of the author, and left us simply admiring the strange vividness of the actor himself.
>
> So it was today. Even when we lost sight of Bach, as we did for a moment now and then, there was something absorbing, entrancing in the concentrated play of Mr Wood's personality upon the music. Once we granted his dramatic point of view with regard to the work, the performance was intensely interesting. Even in quite little things, such as the way he kept us in suspense at times waiting for the organ chord after a recitative, he

made us catch our breath as we do at some brilliant piece of virtuosity in acting.

Dramatic the performance might be: indeed, in *My Life of Music* Wood expressed interest in Gordon Craig's idea of staging the work, adding that in that case 'we might have established an Oberammergau Passion Play in England'. His Sheffield audience was requested not to applaud after either part of the work, divided between morning and afternoon. Jessie Goldsack and Olga Wood both sang in this performance. Neither they nor the other soloists of the *Passion* were required to perform in the concert which concluded the festival on the same evening. After Henry Coward as festival chorus-master had directed a miscellany of vocal items, Wood returned to the rostrum to deliver what Newman recorded as 'a highly individual reading of Beethoven's Ninth Symphony. . . charged with a peculiar electrical nervous energy that extended even to the slow movement, where Mr Wood drew a kind of *Tristan*-like passion from the strings'.

Not only the critics had been on duty that day. 'Our Lady Correspondent' in the *Sheffield Daily Telegraph* described in some detail the fashions on parade. In the balcony of the city's Albert Hall during the evening concert the Lady Mayoress sat in her blue taffeta gown, and so did 'Mrs H. J. Wood, gowned in white satin, rich with pearl embroideries, and carrying the bouquet of shaded pink carnations presented to her by the chorus'.

Nothing in the previous days of the festival drew quite so much attention as these two concerts. After Delius's *Sea Drift*, receiving its first British performance after its German première, 'many of the audience shook their heads' (said the *Musical Times)* 'and failed to catch its note, perhaps because it was performed somewhat perfunctorily'. The composer himself, in a letter to his wife, nevertheless called it 'a huge success – although I don't believe anyone really understood it. . . Wood's orchestra knew it perfectly, but he did not always take the right *tempi* - sometimes too slow and then too fast.' Frederic Austin proved an admirable baritone soloist but the choralists were largely out of sympathy with their task. *The Times* faulted the composer in contrast with the poet: 'We have not yet found a Walt Whitman in music.' Despite which, the poetic qualities of the score were to gain it an endurance in the British choral repertory above that of any of Delius's other works.

Wood put forth yet another addition to the Russian repertory in the unusual form of a suite from Rimsky-Korsakov's opera *Christmas Eve* for soloists, chorus and orchestra, Newmarch having translated the Russian text. Debussy's *L'enfant prodigue* had long provided sopranos (including

Olga Wood) with a favourite excerpt, the so-called 'Air de Lia', but had never previously been performed entire in Britain. Debussy reorchestrated it for Wood, having decided that his original youthful orchestration smelt of 'exams, the Conservatoire, and tedium'. As it required three solo singers (Agnes Nicholls, Felix Senius, Frederic Austin) but no chorus, Wood 'startled Yorkshire', as he put it, by performing the work in French. Admirers of the fifty-one-year-old Elgar were well served. Wood gave *The Dream of Gerontius*, the *Enigma Variations*, and *King Olaf*, the last of them in the composer's presence.

A festival public such as Sheffield's expected a distinguished component of instrumental as well as vocal soloists. They got Kreisler, playing Bach's Concerto in E major and *Chaconne*, and Teresa Carreño, whose powerful technique hammered nails into any lingering suspicion that it took a man to play Tchaikovsky's Piano Concerto no.1.

Wood, his orchestra, Olga, Jessie Goldsack, Kreisler and Carreño (and some other Sheffield soloists too) reassembled later that month at the Norwich Triennial Festival. Though it was a much older festival than Sheffield's, founded in 1824, Wood was only its fifth conductor. Beethoven's Ninth was given, apparently for the first time in the city. Bach was represented not by the *St Matthew Passion* but by the Magnificat in D. Norwich heard the first performance in Britain of *Christmas Night,* a choral work by Hugo Wolf, who had died five years before. It had stirred no very high recommendation even from Ernest Newman (whose book on Wolf had appeared in 1907) and sank with the verdict of 'dull vulgarity' from *The Times. Cleopatra*, a 'prize' work by Julius Harrison (both he and the librettist, Gerald Cumberland, having been selected by competition), likewise made small effect: the twenty-three-year-old composer later destroyed the work.

On 30 October Olga was the soprano soloist in the first performance in Britain of *The Blessed Damozel*, Debussy's cantata-setting of Dante Gabriel Rossetti's pre-Raphaelite vision. Olga's singing of the English text charmed the *Times* critic: she 'gave the right touch of spiritual beauty to the utterances of the Damozel, never allowing the expression of human love to swallow up that of a higher devotion'. Such appreciation for an *intellectually* guided performance was often evoked by listeners to Olga's voice. It was to be stilled too soon.

So much in sympathy with Elgar and Delius was Wood that he could hardly refuse to sign the letter fronted by their names which appeared in *The Times* on 23 March 1908, announcing the formation of the Musical League. Vague on finance, its objects were thus summarized:

Broadening

(a) To hold an annual festival of the utmost attainable perfection in a town where conditions are favourable.
(b) To devote the programmes of these festivals to new or unfamiliar compositions, English and foreign.
(c) To make use, as far as possible, of the existing musical organisations of each district, and of the services of local musicians.
(d) To establish a means by which composers, executive musicians, and amateurs may exchange ideas.

Among the other signatories were Mackenzie, Bantock, Adolph Brodsky (first performer of Tchaikovsky's Violin Concerto, and by this time principal of the Royal Manchester College of Music), and W. G. McNaught, who in 1910 would become editor of the *Musical Times*. Its announcement that 'Dr Hans Richter has kindly consented to direct the first festival of the league' may have caused Henry J. Wood to gulp down a certain amount of pride, and in the event its one and only festival (in Liverpool, September 1909) had neither Richter's nor Wood's participation.

Richter's name had lost no power. Only he could have persuaded the management of Covent Garden, against all conventional practice, to let him conduct *The Ring* in January 1908 *in English*. Conductor of the Hallé Orchestra since 1899, he gave his Manchester audience the first performance of Elgar's Symphony no.1 (dedicated to him) on 3 December 1908, four days before conducting the work in London with the London Symphony Orchestra. Following that, three performances with Elgar himself as guest conductor were given on 1, 7 and 16 January 1909 in the course of Henry J. Wood's concerts with his regular orchestra at Queen's Hall.

Wood was himself to give many performances of that long, emotionally laden symphony, the first of them at Queen's Hall on 3 February 1909 – a reading 'more virtuosic than those of Dr Richter and the composer', commented the *Musical Times*. 'Virtuosic': this was an early, perhaps the first, use of the adjective. It was summoned into existence in order to indicate the power of a conductor to 'play on' an orchestra with maximum flexibility of tempo, volume, and nuance, and still to maintain what the *New York Tribune* had called 'the broad orchestral song'. That was Wood as his public knew him.

On matters outside music he made hardly any display of his opinions. There is one striking exception. In June 1906 he enrolled as a member of the Rationalist Press Association, at that time the principal outlet for intellectual opposition to the claims of religion – a mode of thought now more generally known as humanism. In 1937 the RPA would elect Wood an Honorary Associate, previous elections to that rank having included Albert Einstein, Somerset Maugham and the royal physician Lord Horder, a figure prominent in later pages of this book.

Chapter 9

Recording – and a Choral Triumph

1907–13

'No home is complete without a Gramophone,' the readers of the *Graphic* were told by an advertisement in 1902. *Gramophone*, always spelt with a capital letter, was the trade name of a particular manufacturer ('There are many kinds of Talking Machines; there is only one *Gramophone')* and the company which invited readers to bring into their homes such British singers as Kirkby Lunn and Ben Davies, such foreign stars as Caruso and Plançon, was called the Gramophone and Typewriter, Limited. It was as an accompanist to his wife's soprano voice that Henry J. Wood first made records, seven years before he did so as an orchestral conductor.

In July 1908 Olga Wood recorded three songs in the company's studios, though her contract with the G. & T. company was not signed until the following year. On the labels, as in her concert appearances, she was 'Mrs Henry J. Wood'. She made eleven further song-recordings between February and June 1909, mostly in English but including Mendelssohn's 'On Wings of Song' in German and Debussy's 'Air de Lia' in French.

It was not to be expected that all the recordings would pass the critical ear of the performers and the record company, and be judged fit for issue. In fact only one of the 'takes' from 1908 and five from 1909 were issued, all on single-sided records. Two sides were devoted to a young composer's work: the *Four Old English Songs*, to Shakespearean lyrics, by Eric Coates (1886–1957).

The recordings sustain the impression of a finely schooled technique and a feeling for the musical phrase. Particularly remarkable is the quality of the tone, without perceptible 'breaks' between higher and lower registers. With a lightly trilled 'r' (in such words as 'more') which was then standard in English song, the diction is accurate, if not as forceful as with some other singers of the period. Her husband's accompaniments are – need it be said? – immaculate and the balance of voice and piano admirable.

What Mr. HENRY J. WOOD
says of the
GRAMOPHONE

Mr. HENRY J. WOOD, in the course of a speech at Sheffield last month, addressing 350 members of the Sheffield Festival Chorus, remarked:—

"Have you all got a Gramophone? If not, get one at once, as it is of the utmost educational value to all musicians. In listening to the records of such great artistes as Patti, Melba, Caruso, Plancon, Battistini, etc., you will hear what true, right vocal tone is. As a vocal teacher of twenty-five years' experience, and as a devotee of the great Garcia method, I can assure you of the tremendous value of this invention, and how grateful we vocal teachers are for the aid it gives us in showing our pupils what right and beautiful tone is; especially in the Provinces, where it is often impossible to hear the greatest voices.

I firmly believe that if all teachers of singing had a Gramophone in their studios as well as the finest vocal records as published by the City Road Gramophone Company, and could let their pupils hear the brightness and ring of good voice production, it would do more to dispel and eradicate our fluty, hooty, breathy, dull, weak English voices, than hundreds of pounds spent on useless lessons and in fruitless argument and controversy."

His Master's Voice

A pre-1912 advertisement.

114

Such judgements can be more confidently made since the discovery – at the Royal Academy of Music in 1991 – not only of the published records but of a complete set of the unpublished 'takes'. Hidden among the latter (see Appendix 2, pp.418–31) is a private joke. Though attributed on the company's label to 'Mrs Henry J. Wood', two items are sung unmistakably in a male voice and in a parody of bad style – Schumann's 'Die Lotosblume' (in English) with emotions heavily pasted on, and Hatton's 'To Anthea', a favourite Victorian song, splashed with *tempo rubato* and exaggerations of diction. The voice is that of Henry J. Wood himself, with his own piano accompaniment. It is a delicious example of what might be called negative pedagogy, and one would only like to find elsewhere some account of a serious singing-lesson with Wood. Vocal teaching never ceased to be part of his work.

Happy indeed was the partnership of the Woods, whether in the concert-hall and studio or at their home in Elsworthy Road. They had no children, and *My Life of Music* reveals no visits by relatives on either side, but they delighted in welcoming a visit by Saint-Saëns, displaying the buffoonery of which he was capable at the age of seventy or so. 'When Olga apologised because the drawing-room curtains had not come back from the cleaners he dashed to the piano and proceeded to improvise a free *fantasia* to express the horror of his feelings at being asked into a drawing-room without curtains.'

Olga's appearances were not confined to those at which her husband conducted or accompanied. In October 1907 she sang at the Leeds Festival, where Stanford had succeeded Sullivan as conductor. Her pianist in Grieg songs was Percy Grainger, who went on to play Grieg's piano concerto. But for his death in the previous month, Grieg himself would have been Olga's accompanist.

With Delius, too, Olga was on the most cordial terms as an interpreter. 'Henry thanks you very much for your letter', she wrote to the composer on 14 September 1907, 'and hopes you will excuse his not writing – I am singing on 25 March 1908 at the last of the new concerts organized at Birmingham and Bantock is very keen I should sing something of yours with orchestra.' The Birmingham Orchestral Concerts were under Bantock's supervision – though their conductor was Wood himself, employing a mixture of Queen's Hall and local players.

Evidently Delius was happy to orchestrate his piano accompaniments for Olga. She wrote again on 28 January 1908 to thank 'My dear Mr Delius' for scoring 'Das Veilchen'. (Delius's settings of Norwegian and Danish texts were often referred to by the German translations of their titles.)

> Now will you be very kind and score 'Abendstimmung' [better known as
> 'Twilight Fancies'] and 'Eine Vogelweise' and if you will kindly send me the
> scores I will get the parts done [copied] here as I don't want you to have any
> trouble over it. I shall sing these three songs at Liverpool on 21 March
> [when Bantock himself would share the conducting with Wood] and at
> Birmingham on 25 March and hope very much to do them justice – and also
> during the 'Proms' sing them in London. . . .

'Proms' was an abbreviation which Henry J. Wood himself never used at this
time, though it was to become common. 'My wife made a great success of
your songs in Liverpool and Birmingham,' wrote Wood to Delius on 30
March 1908. The performance at the promenade concerts seems not to have
taken place. On 2 July Henry J. Wood wrote congratulating Delius on the
successful Munich première of Part II of *A Mass of Life*, regretting that
insufficient rehearsal time prevented him from giving it in London. 'The only
chance would be at some future festival.'

Stanford likewise orchestrated two songs for Olga: 'I think that we were
children' and 'O flames of passion'. She sang them under Wood's baton at
the last night of the 1909 promenade season, 23 October. It was her last
public performance, after little more than eleven years of married happiness.
Olga Wood (her husband recalled) had been 'in great pain' at that last
concert. She was removed to a nursing home on 3 or 4 December ('I cannot
remember which') and was operated on, but died on 20 December. The
operation had been deemed 'not serious' according to the *Musical Times* in
the following month. In press notifications of her death, its medical cause
was not mentioned.

> Her passing [wrote Henry J. Wood] left a greater blank than that of even my
> dear mother in that I had now lost a comrade and the love of my life . . . It is
> not often given man and woman to find such a perfect union as ours had
> been, for Olga was so much all that I ever wanted musically and artistically,
> coupled with a worldly sophistication with which her upbringing had
> endowed her (and which was so lacking in me) that she was able to help me
> form plans for a future I could never have conjured up for myself at that
> time.

When entering this account into his autobiography Wood made no attempt to
clarify his remembrance of those days. He left unmentioned the date and
place of the funeral (it was at Highgate Cemetery, London, on 23 December)
– though he kept the service-book of that ceremony, later found among his
own papers. It names the deceased simply as Olga Wood. He recorded that

his friend Dr Cathcart had taken him away for a few days, 'but I am not sure when this actually was because I notice from programmes that I directed a concert on Boxing Day and another on New Year's Day [1910]'. The recollection was in fact mistaken: Mackenzie conducted the concert at Queen's Hall on Sunday 26 December and there was no such concert on 1 January.

With his wife's death, Henry J. Wood's gramophone recording as piano accompanist was halted and was not resumed. But the possibility of recording with an orchestra was already within view. In March 1904 Landon Ronald had squeezed a forty-five-piece orchestra into Melba's drawing-room to accompany her recorded voice; in January 1910, as musical adviser to the Gramophone company, Ronald would conduct the first-ever recording of a concerto, or rather part of it (Grieg's, with the twenty-five-year-old Wilhelm Backhaus as soloist). As early as January 1909 Wood's record company was apparently negotiating with him over the formation of an international orchestra, but not until 1915 did his orchestral recordings begin.

The memory of Olga remained green to Eric Coates when he came to write his own autobiography, *Suite in Four Movements,* half a century later. During an attack of influenza Olga had been his 'ministering angel':

> She herself was convalescing after an illness and, on hearing that I was ill, insisted on sending her nurse round to look after me for an hour or so each day. She had already sung my songs, and sung them beautifully, at the previous Promenade Concerts, and since then I had been to the house in Elsworthy Road several times to play her my latest efforts in the song line and sometimes to have tea with her and Henry Wood. One afternoon, I remember being taken for a motor-car run somewhere north of London, seated with her at the back while he sat in front with the chauffeur and played with what, at that time, was the latest novelty in motor-car hooters, a four-note bugle-call. I felt that Mrs Wood was faintly shocked at the maestro's show of boyish enthusiasm for his latest toy and the exuberance with which he 'sounded the alarm' at the least possible provocation.

Henry J. Wood at this time had enjoyed several years of virtually unchallenged command. A change of policy by the Philharmonic Society of London – whose seven concerts a year still commanded prestige – came happily for him. Previously the Society had used a single conductor for its whole season (latterly Cowen) but now decided to stir its sluggish box office by sharing its concerts between different conductors. Wood was engaged for two concerts in its 1908 season, increased to three when Richter precipitately withdrew his undertaking to appear. In the first of them, Wood gave the *Enigma Variations* for the first time at the Philharmonic, ten years after it had first appeared! That engagement may have prompted the German *Musikalisches Wochenblatt* for 30 January 1908 to devote its leading article, with a photograph, to him. It was noted that 'the secret of Henry J. Wood's great success lies in his tireless creativity and his gigantic enthusiasm', and that 'the whole of the orchestral library is his domain'. It was in this article that Fritz Erckmann hailed him as 'Great Britain's only virtuoso of the conductor's desk'.

A year later that qualification could not have been sustained. Thomas Beecham, born in 1879 (ten years Wood's junior), and a virtuoso conductor from the start, established himself on the London scene in an eclectic orchestral repertory. He appeared with the recently established New Symphony Orchestra, then launched his own Beecham Symphony Orchestra at Queen's Hall in January 1908. His commitment to Delius was signalled by the first complete performance of *A Mass of Life*, one of the composer's largest and most complicated scores, with his own orchestra and the North Staffordshire Choral Society at Queen's Hall on 7 June 1909.

The wealth of his father's pharmaceutical business sustained this orchestral enterprise ('Beecham's Pill-harmonic') as it did his epoch-making London operatic seasons at Covent Garden – beginning in 1910 with the first British performances of Strauss's *Elektra*, Delius's *A Village Romeo and Juliet*, and Smyth's *The Wreckers*. These were no pills: they were a tonic.

Wood and Beecham were antithetical in class, upbringing, temperament, and not least in their attitude to institutions and orchestras. Beecham had just that 'worldly sophistication' which Wood had noted as a deficiency in himself; Beecham possessed, and Wood did not, the confidence of a businessman as well as that of a musician. In the concert-hall, as later on record, the younger conductor was rapidly seen as Wood's challenger. Their rivalry mainly took the form of ignoring each other: Beecham's name has not one mention in *My Life of Music*, nor Wood's name in Beecham's *A Mingled Chime*, subtitled 'leaves from an autobiography', published in 1944.

Experiencing the finesse and attack of Beecham's orchestral per-formances, Ethel Smyth was 'transported with admiration'. She would write in 1940 of his 1908 concerts: 'Never in England, indeed only in Vienna under Mahler, had I heard music rehearsed to such a pitch of perfection.' As words such as 'brilliance' began to attach themselves more and more to Beecham's performances, so such soberer qualities as conscientiousness and reliability were increasingly attributed to Wood's. Beecham splashed out; Wood ploughed on. The difference, not always in Beecham's favour, may be glimpsed in Coates's autobiography. Not only a composer but a professional violist, Coates provides one of the liveliest accounts of London orchestral life.

Coates was at first a freelance player, glad to earn the occasional 'one-one' (a fee of one guinea, written as one pound, one shilling). He then became a founding member of the Beecham Symphony Orchestra but moved to Wood's Queen's Hall Orchestra in 1910, from 1912 as principal viola. Of Beecham's orchestra he was to say (in 1953) that 'never before or since' had he heard an orchestra play with greater brilliance. But he was shocked by Beecham's irresponsibility, especially in cutting Elgar's First Symphony from fifty to thirty-five minutes on tour – with the words 'I don't know how it sounds and I don't *care*!'.

> After having played with Beecham, who did not seem to understand the first meaning of time from the point of view of keeping an appointment or turning up for rehearsal at the appointed hour, it was a relief to have as conductor a man who, besides being a fine musician, was business-like and to all appearances orthodox in his ways. It was an object-lesson to hear Wood take a rehearsal and to watch him tackling some difficult passage until it was note-perfect. His score-reading was remarkable and when rehearsing a new work, no matter how intricate it might be, you could see that he was familiar with every bar before getting up on to the rostrum, and you could imagine the hours of thought which he must have given to it in the quiet of his study beforehand. Many were the invaluable tips I picked up from him while watching the way in which he got his various effects; tips which were to be useful to me in later years when conducting my own works. His beat was clear and easy to follow and you were never in doubt as to the meaning he wished to convey, and if he conducted a work in a certain manner at the rehearsal you could be sure that the rendering at the actual performance would be exactly the same.

Coates was frank enough, though, about the overwork entailed by the Queen's Hall Orchestra's schedules. It was not unknown for sleep to overtake players during concerts – especially at 'those Saturday three-o'clocks and the Sunday three-thirties'. (One begins to appreciate the story of the cellist who 'dreamt that he was playing in a performance of the *Messiah* and woke up to find he was'.) Wood himself, however, was indefatigable. He was 'a fiend for rehearsing', '. . . and the more difficult the work the more he seemed to thrive on it. At 9.55 a.m. sharp he would be on the platform, his tuning-fork in hand, almost tumbling over the music-stands in his eagerness to hear the A of every member of the orchestra and still be able to start rehearsing on the first stroke of ten.'

Ballads – those songs which had domestic music-making as their main target – continued to be in demand. The publishing firms of Chappell and Boosey were still presenting their rival Saturday afternoon series – now at the Queen's Hall and the Royal Albert Hall respectively – with such stars as John McCormack and Kirkby Lunn and instrumental 'supporting artists', sometimes of the highest class, such as Kreisler and the pianist Raoul Pugno. So it was no wonder that ballads lingered on in the second halves of the promenade concert. But progressively heavier weighting of the orchestral component continued. Where once nothing but an operatic fantasia would do to start a second half, one might now encounter such a 'classical' work as Beethoven's overture *Leonora* no.3 – or, even more surprisingly, such a long work as Elgar's *Enigma Variations* on 9 September 1907.

On 12 September Wood himself made an unusual appearance as pianist, joining with York Bowen and Frederick Kiddle to give the first British performance of Mozart's early Three-Piano Concerto. His orchestral players too were still allowed their occasional displays of virtuosity. On 14 October Handel's 'O ruddier than the cherry' as a euphonium solo evidently signalled no incongruity, even though another aria from the same work, *Acis and Galatea*, had been allotted to a singer a few weeks before.

While the promenade concerts offered – if only by their sheer length – a more accessible launching-pad for new works, the higher prices charged at Saturday symphony concerts made them the place where star performers were generally to be found. Here in the 1908–9 season came the French violinist Jacques Thibaud and the pianists Raoul Pugno and Teresa Carreño; here, too, as guest conductors of their own music, came Elgar (the Symphony no.1 on 16 January), Sibelius (the perennially popular *Finlandia* on 13 February), Bantock with his first London performance of his overture *The Pierrot of the Minute* (30 January 1909). Earlier in the series Wood claimed a 'first performance in England' for Bach's Brandenburg Concerto no.1 on 28 November, a claim which – this time! – does not seem to have been disputed.

Beyond his Sheffield Festival commitment, Wood retained his position as conductor-in-chief of that city's Amateur Musical Society (a choral body), begun in 1905–6. Drawing instrumentalists from Queen's Hall and from Manchester as well as locally, he programmed such unusual works as Dvořák's *Stabat Mater* and, in December 1910, Liszt's *St Elisabeth*. In

Manchester itself he challenged the hegemony of the Hallé Orchestra under Richter: the same Dvořák work and *Spring* from Haydn's *The Seasons* were among his performances for the old-established subscription series called the Gentlemen's Concerts. On 27 February 1911 in that same series he gave the first British performance (which was also the first performance anywhere) of Ravel's *Pavane pour une Infante défunte* in its orchestral version. He also continued to conduct Manchester concerts for the impresario G. W. Brand Lane, early in 1910 giving the city its first hearing of Dukas's *L'apprenti sorcier* – in the teeth of Richter's neglect of French music.

Elgar's new Violin Concerto was also the occasion of a challenge to the Hallé. As its dedicatee, Kreisler had given the first two performances under the composer himself at Queen's Hall on 10 and 30 November 1910. Then, eager to exploit the work further, he himself engaged Wood to conduct a further London performance on 28 December and to take it to Manchester on 6 March 1911. With fifty members of the Queen's Hall Orchestra, Kreisler played not only the new work but concertos by Tchaikovsky and Mozart as well. 'Manchester stayed at home that night,' as Wood put it, indicating the exclusivity of devotion to the Hallé. But a *Musical Times* correspondent was enthusiastic: 'This concert has fixed the standard of excellence in Manchester as regards concertos and their accompaniment.'

Manchester mustered a full house, however, in the following season when Kreisler played the Elgar concerto with the Hallé Orchestra itself on 2 November 1911, with Wood as guest conductor. Soloist and conductor repeated the concerto in Bradford on the following day. To Manchester audiences, however, Wood remained chiefly identified with the Gentlemen's Concerts and with the Brand Lane Concerts. Apart from orchestral rivalry with the Hallé, Brand Lane also promoted choral and miscellaneous concerts. Olga Wood was heard in the same programme on 16 January 1909 as the Manchester pianist Edward Isaacs, whom Wood had already brought to London to play his own piano concerto at the promenade concerts.

In the promenade season of the following year, the *Fantasia on British Sea Songs*, now credited to Wood, was moved to the last night – but only to the beginning of the second half, not as the final item. In the same season the inclusion of a Fantasia by Wood on Scottish traditional melodies – performed on two different evenings – served to introduce a Highland bagpiper among the season's soloists. So the appearance of such a piper in a work by Peter Maxwell Davies in the 1992 promenade concerts was not quite the novelty it seemed.

121

Broadening

The programme of 10 August 1910 introduced a composer with whose music Wood was to be intimately linked until his death. Though English by birth, Arnold Bax had already begun to embrace Celtic mythology for inspiration, and a symphonic poem called *In the Faery Hills* was the first of many works given by Wood at Queen's Hall. The twenty-six-year-old composer had been previously summoned to Wood's home at 4 Elsworthy Road and 'discovered to my relief that he was actually no more than life-size. Like Elgar, Sir Henry on the rostrum always appeared, by sheer force of personality, to be very much taller than he actually was. . . . At the concert he gave a beautifully balanced performance of a piece which was at that time considered dangerously modern and uncomfortably difficult to play.'

'Sir Henry': the knighthood was conferred in January 1911 by the new king, George V. 'The new knight', declared the *Musical Times* in the following month, 'has done more than any other man living to create, educate, and feed the taste for orchestral music that is now a great factor in the musical life of the nation.' In March the magazine redeemed at last its promise of ten years before, and devoted an unsigned article to him in highly complimentary terms, acknowledging its debt to Newmarch's book of 1904. Next month an article was justly devoted to the achievement of Newmarch herself. In her collected programme-notes she would describe herself merely as 'the fly on the wheel' for which Wood supplied the motive power. Her true importance as prompter to Wood and an enlightener of British taste was more than that.

Still misdating the year of his birth as 1870, the *Musical Times* article mentioned Wood's study at the Slade School of Art (see p.26–27) and was accompanied by a reproduction in black and white of Wood's picture of a seaside scene. Interviewed, Wood seems to have been rash enough to express disgust with what he had seen at the first London exhibition of Post-Impressionism the previous year: 'He went at once to the National Gallery to get the taste out of his mouth.' His own paintings remained strongly literal in image, with landscape predominating. Nevertheless, in a few years he would value Schoenberg as a painter sufficiently to beg a sample of his work.

In May 1911, Wood's own paintings went on show in London at the Piccadilly Arcade Gallery, under the direction of Philip Burne-Jones. Rosa Newmarch – a factotum indeed! – wrote the annotated catalogue. An amateur's exhibition, it did not rate a critical review in such journals as *The Times*, but photographs of Wood in painter's smock appeared on the front page of the *Daily Mirror* on 26 May 1911. An unofficial account surfacing in the archives of the Slade School speaks of Wood's dropping in to study shortly before he became a knight, in the hope of improving his painting of figures. (His landscapes are markedly bare of them.)

Not only because of his knighthood, the year 1911 marked a peak in the recognition of his status. The New York Philharmonic, having apparently rejected him after his 'trial' in 1904, now offered him its conductorship, but he declined. 'Universal satisfaction, or rather relief, will be felt throughout England at Sir Henry Wood's decision to reject the opportunity of becoming conductor of the New York Philharmonic Concerts,' commented the *Musical Times* in June. Left conductorless by the death of Mahler, the New York orchestra eventually appointed Josef Stransky in his place, to the fury of Richard Strauss, who thought it would give German conducting a bad name.

The 1911 Sheffield Festival was in itself a demonstration of Wood's gargantuan capacity. For the first time in the entire history of British festivals, every item was conducted by a single person who had also assumed the role of chorus-master and undertaken the weekly choral rehearsals. In order to free Wood for the summer promenade season in London, the festival had been brought forward from October to 26–8 April and he brought his own orchestra to participate in it.

Wood did *not*, as he wrote in *My Life of Music*, give at Sheffield 'probably. . .the first concert performance in England of *The Ring*': he merely included the closing scene from each of its four components in the course of a single concert. More significant was the care he took over the excerpts from *Parsifal* at the festival's closing concert. He had previously sent a forewarning to Herbert Thompson, the art and music critic of the *Yorkshire Post* (and an amateur painter, like Wood), who was to write the programme note. The evident object was to simulate conditions at the shrine of Bayreuth itself:

> Kindly note that we carry out Wagner's intentions in the concert room as regards the placing of the three choirs. The full chorus of tenors and basses sing the parts allotted to the Knights of the Grail. The youths' voices consisting of altos and tenors will sing from a mid-height above the organ and, of course, out of sight and the boys' voices, with a few contraltos, page 12, will be sung from the roof over the Orchestra to give it its proper distant effect. I am naturally very proud and happy that, with the assistance of the architect and the committee, the Albert Hall, Sheffield, is being specially arranged to get the right effect.

A Sheffield cartoonist sketches the Festival conductor, 1911.

Later, Wood's complete concerts devoted to *Parsifal* would become a Good Friday tradition at Queen's Hall, but here the excerpts were confined to the Grail Scene and Finale from Act I, and formed the incongruous second half of a programme which began with Bantock's *Omar Khayyam*. Gervase Elwes, singing the title-role in *Parsifal* and also the Narrator's part in the *St Matthew Passion*, participated in the festival roster alongside other singers of such high standing as Agnes Nicholls, Kirkby Lunn and Ben Davies.

What created a sensation, however, was neither the solo singing nor the orchestral work, nor a new oratorio (*Ruth*, by the German composer Georg Schumann) but Wood's choral delivery of *Messiah*, Bach's Mass in B minor and the *Passion*. Here Wood's patient drilling of the chorus enabled him to exhibit a controlled virtuosity as remarkable as that which he drew from his orchestra at Queen's Hall. The critic writing in the *Musical Times* objected to dynamic 'excrescences' in some of the choruses of *Messiah*, but reported that 'the diction of the choir was almost miraculous and has never in my experience been equalled by any other English festival choir, while the precision and sensitive modelling of the expression was a triumph of discipline'. The choral entries in the Mass were judged to be 'as sensitive and differentiated as are the thematic and counterpoint lines of a well-played fugue from the *Well-Tempered Clavier*'.

Wood had, moreover, deliberately modified the broad, 'open-throated' vowels cultivated by Northern choirs, insisting on 'a more closed cavity, greater palatal and nasal resonance, and, especially in the men's voices, a more concentrated, almost glittering tone'. Such a sharper-edged tone no doubt aided the detail of interpretation. The resultant press notices, together with those of the previous (1908) Sheffield Festival, left Britain in no doubt that Henry J. Wood now stood as one of the great choral, as well as orchestral, conductors. The impressiveness of his performances of Bach and Handel owed something to his habitual (but anonymous) rewriting of the string parts, achieving a more brilliant orchestral sound by taking advantage of the centuries' advance in the technical ability of string players. But it is of some interest, in view of today's revival of natural, unvalved brass, that 'Mr A.E.Brain junior', i.e., Aubrey Brain, played the *obbligato* to the 'Quoniam' on 'a specially made *corno da caccia*'.

Next month came yet another of the London Music Festivals at Queen's Hall which Robert Newman had instituted in 1899 and which were still described as 'under the MANAGEMENT of Mr ROBERT NEWMAN' on the printed programmes. Of six remarkable concerts between 22 and 27 May 1911 Wood conducted every item except those entrusted to their own composers. (Strauss was to have conducted one programme but was indisposed.) The choral component was especially strong, perhaps unprecedently so for London. The Sheffield Festival Chorus was heard in Bach's Mass in B minor, the Leeds Choral Union in the *St Matthew Passion*, and the Norwich Festival Chorus in the *Dream of Gerontius*. Elgar's failure to attend that performance of *Gerontius* was a disappointment for which Wood himself charitably found an excuse: 'Elgar was a curiously shy man; on the other hand, I think he only believed in performances he himself conducted.'

Elgar did, however, conduct the première of his own new symphony – no.2 in E flat, with its enigmatic motto from Shelley, 'Rarely, rarely comest thou, spirit of delight!' – on 24 May. His disappointment with the reaction of the audience is well attested. Even after being recalled several times, he said pathetically to his future biographer, W.H.Reed: 'What is the matter with them, Billy? They sit there like a lot of stuffed pigs.'

On the previous day Wood gave a programme which deserves to be recalled in full. Opening with the first performance of Percy Pitt's *English Rhapsody*, conducted by the composer, it proceeded to display Casals playing Haydn's Cello Concerto in D, Kreisler playing Elgar's Violin Concerto and, after the interval, Kreisler and Casals in Brahms's Double Concerto. Finally came the first performance in Britain of a major orchestral work of Debussy's, the *Rondes de Printemps*. In the first item Wood had no doubt been over-indulgent to his friend Pitt's talents as a composer, but the combination in this programme of the greatest performers and the exposure of new music (the Elgar concerto being only six months old) speaks eloquently of what Newman's festival had come to represent.

Wood had learnt, when Casals was playing, to keep the string accompaniment at a low level of volume, thus avoiding 'endless stoppages and many scowlings and hisses' from the soloist at rehearsal. With understandable pride Wood claimed to be the only conductor 'with whom Casals has risked playing the Boccherini concerto *without a rehearsal*'.

The concert of 25 May, originally allotted to Strauss's baton, included the *Dance of the Seven Veils* and Closing Scene from *Salome* with Aïno Ackté, the Finnish soprano. She had won a sensational success in Beecham's first British performances of the opera during the previous year. According to the *Musical Times*, Wood's reading of the orchestral part was 'the most lucid that had been heard in London, and the significance of the music was thereby heightened'. Even more up-to-date was the inclusion of a waltz from *Der Rosenkavalier* in Wood's ensuing 1911 promenade season: that latest opera of Strauss's had yet to reach the London stage.

Taking pride in his knighthood, Wood could scarcely have declined an invitation to participate in a Festival of Empire held at the Crystal Palace to honour the coronation of King George and Queen Mary. Its inspirer and chief conductor was Charles Harriss, with his Imperial Choir of some four thousand voices. The 'Grand Canadian Concert' which Wood conducted on 30 May exhibited Canadian performers led by the celebrated soprano Emma Albani – but there were no Canadian orchestral compositions. Australia did only a little better on 13 June: at a 'Grand Australian Concert', Wood revived a symphony by the English-born Australian composer Marshall Hall, which he had already given at the promenade concerts. Grainger (but only as pianist) and the young, already popular Australian baritone Peter Dawson were among the soloists.

The proceeds of an 'Endowment Fund Concert' on 17 June aided a pension fund to which members of the orchestra were themselves contributing: both Wood and the distinguished American violinist Efrem Zimbalist gave their services. The care for sick and retired orchestral players was to become Henry J. Wood's principal charitable activity, and the Endowment Fund had been the beneficiary of the exhibition of his paintings in the previous month.

The orchestra was again summoned away from London to perform under Wood's baton at the Norwich Festival on 25–8 October. Very exceptionally for such a festival, no new works were offered, either vocal or orchestral. Elgar's *The Kingdom*, only five years old, may have been considered a form of substitute. The composer conducted. The greatly admired Ysaÿe disappointed by promising to play Elgar's even newer violin concerto and then side-stepping it, substituting Saint-Saëns's well-known concerto in B minor. He had already played Elgar's concerto on the Continent but, according to Michael Kennedy's biography of the composer, jibbed at the high fee which he said was being demanded by the publishers, Novello, for performances in Britain.

Wood himself recalled that Ysaÿe's performance of the Beethoven concerto at Norwich was

easily the worst I ever directed. In the slow movement his memory went to pieces – indeed, I do not know what he would have done had not Maurice Sons [leading the orchestra] prompted him as he went along, playing the solo part on his own violin. Ysaÿe managed to get through but, fond as I was of him, I did think he walked away with two hundred and fifty guineas that night at the expense of much anxiety on my part. Fortunately the Norwich audience did not know its Beethoven well enough to appreciate what had happened.

127

Broadening

Wood's own retrospective reckoning (1938) of the work done in 1911 is worth quoting.

> There were twenty-nine Sunday afternoon concerts; thirty-eight of various artists in London and of certain provincial societies; sixty-one Promenade concerts; twelve [Saturday] Symphony concerts. That makes a total of one hundred and forty concerts. In addition there were the festivals at Sheffield and Norwich; also the Empire Festival in the Crystal Palace at which I directed four out of the six concerts as well as the London Musical Festival. Besides the necessary rehearsals for these London concerts, I directed some forty chorus rehearsals in the Provinces.

Ignoring rehearsals, but calculating also the number of festival concerts, this gives a total of about 160 performances – not counting his occasional appearances as pianist, for instance with the Queen's Hall Wind Quintet. Always of an omnivorous curiosity, Wood may also have attended the London International Musical Congress in late May and early June 1911 – the first such musicological event ever held in Britain. He was certainly among its financial supporters.

About 140 performances was a normal annual quota for him. In his autobiography he was to recall Nikisch amiably chiding him for taking on more performances in a month than he (Nikisch) gave in a year. Wood never seems to have faced the probability that by the sheer number of his appearances he was depressing his status (and, no doubt, his fee) in comparison with harder-to-get conductors. It is as if, with his humble origins in mind and no feeling for finance, he could not see beyond the security of piling up fees *now*.

Pressure of work had led him to begin using the services of a musical assistant – a copyist, but much more than that. Francis G. Sanders was a London organist and occasional concert pianist to whom Wood entrusted many jobs of orchestration. A postcard thanking Sanders for 'all your help and assistance' in the 1911 Sheffield Festival added: 'I don't know what I should do without you – you are always so kind, reliable and prompt.'

Sanders's own name appeared in the 1918 promenade schedule as orchestrator of one of Bach's masterpieces for organ, the *Passacaglia* in C minor. In general, however, his services were anonymous, in fulfilment of Wood's instructions, and Wood took the credit. Such was, and is, a recognized role for the assistant (as a kind of 'devil') to a perpetually busy conductor. It must be said, however, that the single mention of Sanders in *My Life of Music* gives no inkling of the closeness and length (at least from

1907 to 1939) of their collaboration. Only when a collection of letters from Wood to Sanders came to light (they were put up for sale at Sotheby's in December 1992, withdrawn, and sold privately) was this essential aspect of Wood's working life revealed.

A reticence more remarkable yet in Wood's autobiography is a total failure to mention his second marriage – to Muriel Ellen Greatrex, on 19 June 1911. Nor is there a mention of their two daughters, Pauline Tatiana, known as Tania (b.1912), and Hermione Avril (1915–83). The family home in London continued to be at Elsworthy Road, with the addition in 1915 of Appletree Farm House – a rural retreat in Chorley Wood, Hertfordshire, some twenty miles north-west of London.

The marriage was to end in bitter separation in 1935, with a divorce sought by Wood and refused. The decision to make his second wife a non-person in *My Life of Music* means that in references to travel and other matters the reader must interpret many an 'I' as 'we'.

Born on 5 December 1882, Muriel was the only daughter of a retired army major, Ferdinand William Greatrex, and his wife Adela Florence, née Manuelle (pronounced as Manuelli). The maternal family were quarry-owners and stone merchants. Aged twenty-eight at the time of her marriage, Muriel had been working as Wood's secretary – according to Reginald Pound's biography, since a few months before Olga's death. (Pound, however, mis-stated her age on marriage as twenty-one.) The circumstances of their original contact are not known. Muriel's first cousin, Doris Manuelle, was a contralto whom Wood engaged for the promenade concerts in the 1914 season and who 'has lately taken her place among singers of distinction', said the *Musical Times* in 1921; but there is not even anecdotal evidence to cast her as an intermediary.

Well educated, speaking French and German, competent in money matters, a good manager, a skilled letter-writer, Muriel was able to offer Wood the organising skills that he needed. If Wood had any further reason to marry Muriel beyond the obvious relief of having someone to cope with all the tiresome clutter of life apart from music-making, it is not clear. At the bitter end of their marriage, seeking justification for having left her, Wood ascribed all the pressure to *her* family's side: a young unmarried woman could not decently continue daily association with a youngish widower (aged forty-one) – and what a catch a famous, newly-knighted husband would be! No documents of the period survive from Muriel's side which might give a different and less calculating account.

Broadening

Among Henry J. Wood's accusations of 1935 (in a document called *My Confession* reproduced in Appendix 1, pp. 415–17) is the allegation that the marriage was unsatisfactory almost from the beginning – indeed that on the honeymoon itself Muriel insisted on bringing a friend, the author Helen Douglas Irvine. Muriel's good intentions were not in doubt, but the objective disqualification for her married role was that she had apparently no musical appreciation whatever. As the celebrated conductor's wife she would be seen regularly occupying the seat reserved for her at his Queen's Hall concerts, but under the fox fur on her lap (as their elder daughter Tania was to observe) would be a novel for surreptitious reading. Music was in a literal sense her husband's business: she would help him manage it but in no sense could participate in his musical thoughts as Olga had done. She would run his household too, but with no enthusiasm for domestic routine.

A curious photograph survives of Tania's first birthday party in June 1913 (see plate 12). The child is carried not by the mother but by one of Muriel's formidable-looking Manuelle aunts. The birthday cake is held by a uniformed nanny. Bearded Henry is being embraced by another relative or friend in the background. At the side, detached, pops out the tall, smiling figure of Muriel, as though to say, 'Look! my show!' It was a 'show' that could survive, and did survive, long enough to allow what Tania insisted (in interviews granted to the present author between 1990 and 1993) was a happy childhood for her and her sister. To particular friends of her own Muriel could reveal charm, sympathy and humour. But the incompatibilities of the marriage were to grow, not lessen, with the years.

Chapter 10

'My dear Mr Schönberg . . .'

1911–14

The pre-1914 Queen's Hall Orchestra presented a distinctive look. Wood massed all the orchestral violins on his left side – a layout unusual for the time, though generally adopted later. Hitherto the first violins had customarily been on the left, the seconds on the right, on the supposition that composers wanted to hear them in antiphony. (Always a dubious justification, it was certainly meaningless if applied to the musical texture of Tchaikovsky or Elgar.) An individual touch of Wood's was to position the harp, or harps, well forward and almost central in order not to lose the fragile sound.

If permitted to travel back in time to that period, a modern concert-goer would have various other peculiarities to note. The conductor would lead a female soloist by the hand on to the platform. The orchestra's principal violin (Wood did not use the term 'leader') was not granted the privilege of entering later than his colleagues to a special round of applause. That custom, even today peculiarly British, seems to have arisen only at some point of W. H. Reed's long occupancy (1912–35) of the first desk of the London Symphony Orchestra. No ritual of a public handshake between conductor and principal violin was expected before a programme could begin. But Wood was noted 'for having introduced the fashion of the entire band to stand up and share in the applause which follows an orchestral performance', as was remarked in 1918 in the *Monthly Musical Record*. This gesture had indeed been noted during his Nottingham concerts before 1900.

A fanatic for correct intonation, Wood had already established a routine of checking each instrumentalist's 'A' on the way to the platform. An oft-repeated story tells of violinists tricking him as they marched past – passing from one to another an instrument of which the tuning had already been approved but which their chief would now declare out of tune. This story never seems to have been told, however, by anyone who had actually carried out the trick and Wood was probably too wily for such a deception to have been carried out more than once – if that. He was known for leaving a secret mark on scores which he rejected, so that their composers could not hope to send them back, re-titled, for a fresh consideration.

Wood conspicuously pushed for the integration of performances by suppressing intermediate applause. In 1911 Samuel Langford, the celebrated music critic of the *Manchester Guardian*, had noted (during that Hallé concert when Kreisler played the new Elgar concerto) that Wood stopped the audience from clapping between the movements of Mozart's *Haffner* symphony. Similarly, his performances of the *St Matthew Passion* carried a request not to interrupt concentration by applauding before the final chorus, and in April 1914 the *Monthly Musical Record* noted that 'Sir Henry Wood managed to play Beethoven's Eighth Symphony without the usual interruption of applause between the movements'. It would be a long time, however, before his audiences fell automatically into line. As late as November 1923 a London programme of Wood's containing Beethoven's Symphony no.7 bore the printed announcement: 'The audience is requested to refrain from applause between the movements of the symphony.' With concertos, however, no such abstention was asked for or expected.

With a professional music librarian attending at his house, Wood kept his personal library of scores and complete orchestral parts, which he marked copiously (in heavy blue pencil) with directions of emphasis, expression and so on. Marks which he wrote on his own conducting scores served to 'cue' him to shout his directions to the players while rehearsing (he did not waste time by stopping). Players under his command might complain privately when directions known all too well from previous seasons were flung yet once more at their heads – but this was part of that complete certainty of a Wood performance, as described by Eric Coates (p.119).

Coates was not the only budding composer-conductor to sit in Wood's pre-1914 band. The name of 'B. Hindenberg' among the violins conceals the identity of Basil Cameron (as he later became). Eugene Goossens III, already referred to in these pages, joined the ranks of violinists in 1912. Though British-born, Goossens had begun his musical training at the Bruges Conservatory: the number of Queen's Hall musicians who were of foreign birth or training or both was still considerable, and Coates went so far as to ascribe the special blend of the orchestra to its cosmopolitanism.

The Dutch first flute, Albert Fransella, who had been in Wood's orchestra since its inception, was mentioned by the *Musical Times* (September 1911) as among the musicians whom the free-and-easy promenaders liked to 'spot' and personally welcome. The orchestral listing as printed in programmes of the London concerts had signally expanded. Eight bassoonists were named, Wood's quota for massed choral Handel and Bach.

An up-to-date addition was a player of the heckelphone – the baritone oboe which had been required during the London Music Festival of 1911 for the excerpts from *Salome*. A further performance of those excerpts, again with Aïno Ackté's powerful portrayal of the principal figure, would be one of the sensations of the Birmingham Festival of 1912 - yet another major provincial event which Henry J. Wood was called on to direct, in succession to Hans Richter. Ackté was one of the singers of this period particularly admired by Wood; another was the contralto Ernestine Schumann-Heink, whom he declared to be the only singer able to perform Mozart's 'Non più di fiori' (from *La clemenza di Tito)* to perfection.

The Birmingham Festival of 1912 was obviously bidding to match the significance of Sheffield's in the previous year. Elgar conducted his new work, *The Music Makers*, as well as *The Apostles;* Wood repeated Delius's *Sea Drift,* the composer travelling from his French home at Grez-sur-Loing to hear it, though declining Wood's invitation to conduct it himself. Sibelius, not a frequent visitor to these shores, conducted his Fourth Symphony (its first performance in Britain) and found time for a pleasure-trip to Stratford-on-Avon in the company of Rosa Newmarch. Chronicling the festival in *My Life of Music*, Wood also listed the first British performance of Skryabin's *Poem of Fire*. Not so: although announced, it was found impossible within the available rehearsal time. The standard of the 'band' at Birmingham – a mixed bag of players raised locally, with some Queen's Hall principals included – was judged inferior to that at Sheffield, to which Wood was able to bring his entire Queen's Hall Orchestra.

In tackling *Messiah*, Wood seems to have allowed himself at Birmingham a greater freedom than ever, particularly in sudden variations of pace within numbers. The *Musical Times* correspondent checked (by his metronome) the speeds in the Hallelujah Chorus and found the pulse varying from forty-eight to ninety-six crotchets per minute: 'When it was over not a few in the hall felt wounded.' But not a few did *not. The Times* found the Hallelujah Chorus

so moving that one could hardly stand still and listen to it. To hear the sopranos putting the trumpets to shame in the words 'King of Kings and Lord of Lords' was an unforgettable experience. When a conductor can inspire a choir to such heights as those to which Sir Henry Wood has brought the Birmingham Chorus, one has little heart left for quarrelling with his *tempi*.

The *Monthly Musical Record* likewise conceded to the doubters only that Wood's treatment 'was too modern to please those used to the ordinary style of singing the work'. It similarly defended Wood's freedom of treatment in the *St Matthew Passion*, with the chorus in the chorales sometimes unaccompanied, sometimes replaced by a solo quartet. 'A concert-room performance, however, differs from one in a Cathedral; in the latter, Bach's accompaniments should be given; in the former a conductor may surely give what he considers the most artistic rendering.' It is worth noting the absence of any fruitless argument about what the composer 'would have' wanted. The interpreter's autonomy was seen as limited only by his or her artistic taste. The attitude of Wood in choral Bach was similar to that of Busoni in Bach at the piano keyboard.

Manchester, unlike Birmingham, had no periodic festival: it needed none, since the general level of its orchestral life throughout the year was so much higher. Though Wood had allied himself with the impresario Brand Lane in orchestral rivalry with the Hallé, he was again summoned by the Hallé management itself in the interim between Richter's departure and the arrival of Michael Balling, his successor. On 12 February 1912, Wood typically brought Gardiner's new *Shepherd Fennel's Dance* from Queen's Hall and gave Saint-Saëns's Third Symphony – which in Manchester was just as new, never having previously been performed by the Hallé.

In London, not the Queen's Hall but the larger Albert Hall was needed for the concert of 24 May 1912 which mourned the sinking of the liner *Titanic* in the previous month. Players from the Queen's Hall, the London Symphony, and other London orchestras made up an instrumental force of nearly 500, variously conducted by Wood, Ronald, Elgar, Beecham, Pitt, Fritz Ernaldy and Willem Mengelberg, 'who had travelled expressly from Berlin to lend his assistance'. It was a typical gesture of Wood's to orchestrate for the occasion the hymn 'Nearer, my God, to Thee' (by J. B. Dykes), which – according to a legend rapidly born – the band on the *Titanic* itself had played as the ship went down.

The boy prodigy who delighted Londoners that season was himself a Londoner. Solomon (he used his forename only), born on 9 August 1902, played 'with all the glory of orchestral accompaniment under Sir Henry Wood' (*Musical Times*) at Queen's Hall on 24 June 1912 and was presented with a watch and a tricycle. He performed Beethoven's piano concerto no.3

Sir Henry Wood, and did. 11 Oct. 1912

A cartooning colleague
exaggerates an
injury, 1912.

and Liszt's *Hungarian Fantasia*, with a Chopin waltz as an encore. The audience, according to *The Times*, was 'delighted with everything about him from his little thin bare legs to his little thin piano tone'. No artist was to be dearer to Wood than Solomon in his mature years; none would show greater affection for Wood than Solomon did.

The promenade concerts 'probably never opened more brilliantly' (said the *Musical Times)* than on 17 August 1912, when 'enthusiasm was spontaneous, eager, and thoroughly impartial'. Frank Bridge's *The Sea* was among the more important of British works to receive a first performance (24 September), shortly before Wood was relieved by George Henschel as guest conductor to fulfil his Birmingham Festival engagement. Resuming the Proms, Wood for once failed his criterion of punctuality. A fog caused the taxi taking him from Elsworthy Road to the Queen's Hall to crash into a wall 'with the result that my head came into sharp contact with a window':

> I was rather badly cut and had to return home. Robert Newman was telephoned and told that I would come as soon as my wounds were dressed. I suggested that the concert should begin without me but Newman said he would wait. I arrived at twenty minutes past eight – the only time in my whole career I have been late for a concert – and walked on to the platform with my head bound up, to receive a tremendous welcome from the waiting audience.

'Sir Henry *Wood*, and did' was the title of a cartoon sent him by a fellow-musician, Herbert Godfrey, showing a figure bandaged into immobility (see p.135).

Of all the promenade concerts of that 1912 season, that which generated the most heat – both in anticipation and in reception – took place on 3 September. Henry J. Wood's performance of Schoenberg's *Five Orchestral Pieces* constituted not merely their London première but their first performance anywhere. This was not quite the first of Schoenberg's works to reach Britain. On 23 January 1912 the American pianist Richard Buhlig had introduced London to the *Three Piano Pieces*, op.11, in a recital at the Steinway Hall.

The programming of the *Five Orchestral Pieces* was an act of huge courage on Wood's part, not simply in the realization that it would provoke an extreme reaction but in the investment of time required in preparation. As Eugene Goossens, among Wood's orchestral violinists at that performance, was to recall:

> This baffling novelty . . . aroused the gravest misgivings among the members of the orchestra during rehearsals, and consequently necessitated three consecutive rehearsals of an hour each (an unprecedented amount of time to be expended on a new work) before it was considered fit for presentation. Wood, cutting, thrusting, parrying and dissecting with that long white baton, fighting down the thing that all conductors have to fight sooner or later in varying degrees – the hostility of an orchestra which has fatally prejudged a novelty – eventually secured order out of chaos.

Wood's own supposed exhortation at rehearsal, 'Stick to it, gentlemen! This is nothing to what you'll have to play in twenty-five years' time', has the savour of truth about it, though its first appearance in print came as late as 1969.

Beginning with the overture to Humperdinck's *Hänsel und Gretel*, the programme was not in any other way remarkable, but the reaction to the Schoenberg pieces showed an unfamiliar vehemence.

'It is not often that an English audience hisses the music it does not like, but a good third of the people at Queen's Hall last Tuesday permitted themselves that luxury after the performance of the five orchestral pieces of Schoenberg. Another third of the audience was only not hissing because it was laughing, and the remaining third seemed too puzzled to laugh or to hiss.' So Ernest Newman wrote in *The Nation*. His own verdict, nothing like as decisive in *pro* or *con* as when he had confronted successive works by Richard Strauss, showed an open mind, at least. The composer was 'a man of undoubted gifts who, in his later works, is aiming at the transcription of new shades of emotion into a musical language that he has not yet succeeded in making logical and lucid. . .whether he succeeds or not in doing what he is now trying to do, it will have to be done some day by some one. The next vital development of music will be along the lines of the best of Schönberg.'

According to H. H. Stuckenschmidt's biography of the composer, Wood was not among the half-dozen conductors to whom a score of the *Five Orchestral Pieces* had been sent by the publishers, but he had somehow got hold of it. On reading an announcement of the coming performance – which was not merely the first British performance, but the first anywhere – Schoenberg expressed alarm to his publishers, regarding it 'as almost inconceivable that the performance would be good without his personal presence and advice'. He evidently wrote to Wood *after* the performance, eliciting a typewritten reply from Wood dated 24 January 1913:

> Regarding your Five Orchestral Stücke, in the first instance I played them at one of my popular concerts, but it was almost impossible for me to let you know the date of the performance as I kept on rehearsing them continually beforehand and was only able to arrange the date of performance a very short time beforehand. I do, however, appreciate your great kindness in saying that you would have come over had you known.
>
> Personally I cannot tell you how deeply interested I am in your wonderful music and you will be happy to hear that the members of the Queen's Hall Orchestra carried through their difficult task with enormous enthusiasm. There were several musicians present at the performance at Queen's Hall who had heard the work in Vienna, and who were most complimentary to our performance. Please do not imagine that the pieces were not played to the end; they were played in their entirety and listened to in all seriousness, and at the end of the performance there was terrific applause, which completely drowned the slight hissing which proceeded from some half dozen people not in sympathy with your music. I was recalled several times and the orchestra had to rise in a body and acknowledge the applause. It was the

press in London who tried to work up this slight display of unfriendly
feeling; they always do this in England but we never take any notice of it.

Wood's performance was introduced in the printed programme only as a
'first performance in England', he and his advisers not being in a position to
know whether a previous performance elsewhere *might* by that date have
taken place. None the less, the categorical reference in the above letter to
'musicians. . .who had heard the work in Vienna' is extremely puzzling. It is
now known there had been *no* performance in Vienna, and none elsewhere
save a performance of three of the pieces in an arrangement for two pianos
(four players) in Berlin on 4 February 1912. That Wood should be so careless
with facts in writing *to the composer* seems incredible.

The composer's offer to conduct an entire programme of his own works
had to be tactfully declined, but Wood promised 'a very warm welcome both
from the public and the members of the Queen's Hall Orchestra' if he would
conduct a further performance of the *Five Orchestral Pieces*.

As regards rehearsals, you would find the work excellently prepared by
myself, and my orchestra is exceedingly well disciplined. They have
played under all the greatest conductors in the world, and Dr Richard
Strauss considers them a most flexible body of musicians; in fact, I think
you have no fear of not having a fine performance. Our usual rehearsal is
from 10am to 1pm (three hours) on the morning of the concert, and I
could in all probability arrange for a rehearsal in the afternoon of the day
before. Further during the rehearsals for my popular concerts in
August, September and the beginning of October I should make a point
of keeping your work in rehearsal.

As regards the financial arrangements, I am sorry that I cannot offer
you a proper fee; but if you would care to accept the sum of £25 towards
your expenses we shall be most happy if you can see your way to accept
our invitation. If you are pressed for time you need not arrive until
Friday morning and could leave after the concert on Saturday afternoon.
Also if you do not care to stay in hotels and prefer staying with friends, I
could easily arrange for some of my friends to put you up.

Unfortunately I do not speak or write German, but my wife does, and
therefore you can always correspond with me in German.

During the time it took to arrange that visit, the diversity of Wood's musical
activities expanded yet further. In June 1913 Sir Oswald Stoll of the London
Coliseum induced him to conduct a forty-minute selection from *Parsifal* to
accompany 'tableaux' from the opera (without singing) as part of the daily
variety bill. With a workmanlike rather than purist temperament, he set

about reducing the scoring of *Parsifal* for what he calls in his autobiography 'this forty minutes' pastiche', referring to its twice-daily showing for five weeks as 'one of the most pleasurable engagements of my long career'. Sullivan's *The Golden Legend* would, he thought, succeed if given a similar treatment in tableaux.

Skryabin's music was as liable as Schoenberg's to arouse fierce reactions. The *Poem of Fire (Prometheus)*, abandoned at Birmingham, was unveiled in London instead – though lacking the 'keyboard of light' (throwing a play of light on a screen) stipulated by the composer. It was given at a Saturday concert on 1 February 1913 and – apparently at the suggestion of the *Musical Times* – was performed twice over. 'I shall *never* forget the performance of *Prometheus* at Queen's Hall last February, under Wood,' wrote the composer Kaikhosru Shapurji Sorabji later that year. 'It was so sublime to me as to be almost painful: the ecstasy and gloriousness of it! And people hissed and laughed!!!!'

Wood's characteristic response to such a reception was to programme the work yet again, on 14 March 1914. The composer himself undertook the important piano part, and in the same concert was the soloist in his Piano Concerto in F sharp minor. Skryabin's Symphony no.3, otherwise *The Divine Poem*, had been heard in the opening concert (18 October 1913) of the Saturday series in the previous autumn. A cult of Skryabin seemed to be in gestation, but was aborted under the greater impact of Stravinsky – particularly *The Rite of Spring*, brought to London in June 1913 as part of the Russian ballet season.

The following which Wood established for Delius was nourished further. A revival at the promenade concerts of 1913 of Delius's Piano Concerto, again with Szántó as soloist, had a 'splendid success', Wood assured the composer. Beecham, however, had become an even more assiduous promoter of Delius's music. Moreover, through his mistress Lady (Maud) Cunard, he was able to ensure that Delius in person was lionized in high social circles – among which Wood never showed any desire to move. Delius now quite properly made use of the support of *both* leading British conductors. He was to stay with Beecham at his London and Watford homes in 1914–15 and, as will be noted, at the Woods' London home in 1918.

Delius's admirer Philip Heseltine (the composer 'Peter Warlock') thought that Wood performed Delius's first *Dance Rhapsody* 'disgracefully badly' at a Saturday symphony concert on 14 February 1914. Nevertheless Wood cherished the work and was to record it in 1923. Before the 1914 performance he had written to Delius regretting that he could not undertake a London performance of a new work which had been offered (probably *A Song of the High Hills*) 'as we are not bringing up any Northern choirs this season, and I never conduct a chorus composed of Londoners'. The distinct tonal vigour of a Northern choir, from Yorkshire especially, was well recognized.

The most-discussed event of the symphony concert series in early 1914 was, however, Schoenberg's promised visit as composer-conductor. He delivered a performance of the *Five Orchestral Pieces,* now renamed in an advance announcement as *Five Characteristic Pieces for Orchestra*, at Queen's Hall on 17 January 1914. Wood conducted Brahms's *Tragic Overture*, Haydn's Symphony no.7 ('*Le Midi*'), Tchaikovsky's Piano Concerto no.1 (with Adela Verne) and – as the final item, preceded by Schoenberg's work – Gustave Charpentier's *Napoli*. Evidently with the promenaders' earlier reaction to the work in mind, the printed programme at the symphony concert came with a warning note: 'Herr Arnold Schönberg has promised his co-operation at today's concert on condition that during the performance of his *Orchestral Pieces* perfect silence is maintained.' In the event the precautions seemed unnecessary, though *The Times* was dismissive about the appreciative reaction: 'There was applause at the end of each number save the first, but everyone knows how much a London audience's applause is worth. It is mostly compounded of nervousness, anxiety to be polite, and affectation.'

In 1987, assessing the impact of Schoenberg on British audiences, David Lambourn in the *Musical Times* ascribed the greater cordiality of the 1914 reception to the difference made by the composer's conducting. But the work's smoother passage must also have been aided by increased familiarity on both the audience's and the orchestra's part. The composer paid public tribute to the orchestra's capabilities. Shortly afterwards, Wood wrote again (from Brighton on 2 February 1914) with an allusion to Schoenberg's work as a painter:

My dear Mr Schönberg,
    I am sending you a typewritten letter, because I think it will be clearer to you than my handwriting.
    First, let me thank you for your splendid letter to the Queen's Hall Orchestra, which gave them such *very* great pleasure, and I am happy to say that the whole of the London press inserted it in their various papers, and your visit altogether has been a most memorable event.
    May I thank you too most sincerely for the splendid signed photograph which arrived quite safely, and please do not think me

greedy, but if at any time you could possibly spare even a *tiny* sketch, it would give me such great happiness to possess a souvenir of your other art, in which I am so deeply interested. I daresay you might some time have [made] a very trifling sketch, which you might not perhaps think anything of, but which by me would be highly valued as a lasting souvenir. Please do not think I am trespassing on your good nature. Of course I am only too pleased to send you my photograph.

In my spare moments I am studying your *Gurre Lieder*, and I have made all arrangements to attend the performance at the Albert Halle, Leipzig, on the evening of 6 March. Whether I will be able to have a word with you is doubtful, as I shall only arrive in time for the concert and shall have to catch a train immediately afterwards for London.

I have been so terribly busy this last week producing Gustav Mahler's *Das Lied von der Erde*, which I am happy to say was a great success last Saturday [31 January 1914], that I have not yet had time to look through your pupil's work, but I hope to do so this week.

With kindest regards and renewed thanks for the pleasure which your visit gave us,

> Believe me,
> Sincerely yours,
> Henry J. Wood

The 'pupil' was Anton Webern – an introduction which bore fruit. According to Stuckenschmidt's biography of Schoenberg, Wood did indeed attend the Leipzig performance *and* found it possible to meet Schoenberg there.

Later, having been approached by the Austrian singing actress Albertine Zehme with a view to her performing *Pierrot Lunaire*, Wood wrote to ask Schoenberg whether that would be a suitable item for the Queen's Hall symphony concerts and whether it required a conductor. Unfortunately, in this as in all other citations from Wood's letters to Schoenberg, there are no surviving letters in the other direction.

Schoenberg never allowed his admiration of Wood to diminish. In the symposium *Homage to Sir Henry Wood*, published to salute his seventy-fifth birthday in 1944, Schoenberg recalled the occasion of conducting for Wood in 1914:

Besides being very amiable he was also very helpful to me – which I needed badly. Struggling with the little English I had been taught in school, I had tremendous difficulties to present my ideas, demands or suggestions to the orchestra. I have today a fairly correct idea how funny my pronunciation must have sounded at that time. In recollection I still hear myself addressing the orchestra: 'Bliss tchentlmenn, nember fifffe', whereupon

141

Sir Henry Wood in the softest *dolcissimo con sordino*, with the most delicate pronunciation of the 'G' and the 'V', and a long extended 'I', would repeat: 'Please, gentlemen, number fi-eve.'

On that occasion Schoenberg also reaffirmed his tribute to the orchestra:

These men supported me by their ability, attentiveness and willingness to the greatest extent. Of course they were trained technically, mentally and morally to respect a composer even when his music was daring, and even if they would not like it. They were trained by this man Henry Wood, a perfect musician, a great educator, a great benefactor of music and a most charming gentleman.

'These men', wrote Schoenberg: but in 1913 Henry J. Wood had taken the step of admitting women to a major orchestra. His admirer Ethel Smyth, composer and autobiographer extraordinary, hailed it as 'mixed bathing in the sea of music'. He later recalled receiving 137 applications to fill six vacancies. In the symphony concert season which opened that October, Dora Garland, Jessie Grimson, E. M. Dudding and Jean Stewart took their places among the violins, S. Maturin and Rebecca Clarke (later known also as a composer) among the violas. Fears that their salaries would undercut those of men were squashed: Newman paid at a uniform rate. Although the Paris orchestras had already opened their ranks to women and although women players participated in the mixed amateur-and-professional provincial orchestras which Wood encountered, this was a breakthrough for London.

A breakthrough, indeed, which other conductors – notably Beecham and Ronald – did *not* follow. Beecham's reputed epigram about women players exists in several forms (all equally nasty) on the lines of 'If they are pretty, they distract the men; if they are ugly, they distract me'. In Manchester Hamilton Harty, appointed conductor of the Hallé Orchestra in 1920, actually purged the orchestra of the women players who had entered during the war, later admitting only a harpist. In 1921 Wood affirmed his position: 'I shall never conduct an orchestra without them in future, they do their work so well. They have great talent for the violin and wonderful delicacy of touch . . . They are sincere, they do not drink, and they smoke less than men. In the Queen's Hall they have given a certain tone to our rehearsals, and a different spirit to our performances.'

'Generous-minded Sir Henry Wood', as Smyth hailed him, had performed her own music since 1902. He treated her imperious eccentricities with good humour:

I remember her conducting one of her own works at Queen's Hall one night at a promenade concert. She went up to my rostrum, took up my baton and surveyed its length critically. Deciding that it was more than she could manage, she calmly snapped it in two, threw away one half and conducted with the other.

It sounds like an incident in rehearsal rather than performance, but Smyth's impetuousness is recognizable. When 'the famous Dr Ethel Smyth', as the *Musical Times* described her (she would not become a Dame until 1922), conducted the overture to her opera *The Wreckers* at a promenade concert on 21 August 1913, 'the rare spectacle of a lady, and a particularly energetic specimen of her sex, acting in this capacity evidently absorbed attention, and the ability displayed in the music drew enthusiastic approbation'.

Between Smyth and Wood, nevertheless, there was a certain edge in personal relationship, exacerbated by his later walk-out from his marriage. One of Smyth's later volumes of recollections hurt the conductor with a reference to 'the once faithful Henry Wood' (characteristically his pages misquote the remark as 'Henry J. Wood who was once my friend'). Elsewhere, contrasting it with Beecham's 'frontal attack on Philistinism' in promoting new music, she appeared to belittle Wood's achievement in conceding only that 'in spite of protests from whoever was backing his concerts, [he] had often succeeded in slipping novelties into his concerts'.

Other women composers besides Smyth won no more than a transitory interest from Wood's audiences – Ethel Barns appearing as violin soloist in her own *Concertstück* on 17 October 1907, Kathleen Bruckshaw performing the solo part in her own piano concerto on 10 September 1914. Better known on the London scene was 'Poldowski' (Lady Dean Paul, daughter of the great violinist-composer Wieniawski), whose *Nocturne* was remarkably orchestrated - with two piccolos, three flutes and alto flute; three oboes, oboe d'amore, cor anglais and bass oboe; three clarinets, basset horn and contrabass clarinet. Its first performance, at a promenade concert on 8 October 1912, moved the critic of the *Monthly Musical Record* to wonder unsympathetically 'how Debussy's Faun had found his way into a picture of night off an island on the west coast of Scotland'.

Wood's performance of *Das Lied von der Erde* at a Saturday symphony concert in January 1914 was a landmark in the British acceptance of the still controversial Mahler. Wood had filled Queen's Hall to overflowing in giving the first British performance of the Symphony no. 7 in the previous year. But the reaction to the vocal-orchestral work was 'so much more favourable than that accorded to any previous work of his that we shall probably have further opportunities of hearing this composer', noted the *Monthly Musical Record*. The soloists were Doris Woodall and Gervase Elwes. The third movement ('Von der Jugend' – 'Of Youth') was encored, but the finale, with its long-drawn-out fade into nothingness, was faulted by the same critic for a 'too insistent melancholy'. He suggested simply lopping off this finale in order to make the work 'a useful addition to the promenade programmes'.

In May and June Wood was in Italy. His new wife Muriel, whose love of travel much exceeded his, had evidently persuaded him to take a more substantial holiday than he was used to. Nevertheless he made it a working holiday. The inscription 'Roma, 27 May 1914' is found on a music manuscript book in which he was, apparently, composing a score for a short play which Edgar Speyer had written for presentation at home on his wife's birthday in the following November. From Genoa on 7 June Wood wrote again to Schoenberg:

> You will remember kindly sending me some months ago a composition by your pupil Anton Webern. I should very much like to try it over with the Queen's Hall Orchestra during the next month, and would you mind sending me (or asking him to send me by registered post) to 4 Elsworthy Road, London, NW, the complete band parts – strings 7–6–4–4–3, as I have every reason to think that I shall perform it in public shortly, so I should be glad if you would let me know the performing fee and the fee for the hiring of the material.
>
> Some months ago I bought a full score of your *Kammer Symphonie*, and I have put it down for performance at my Promenade Concerts, but a short time ago when I tried to hire or purchase the band parts through Breitkopf & Haertel, your publisher in Vienna said that you are rescoring the work and making many changes. Do you think that I can rely upon getting the new score and band parts by August 1st? Otherwise I fear I shall have to give up the idea of playing it this season, unless you allow me to play it from the existing band parts which agree with my score. I would then afterwards give your revised version.
>
> A reply to this (in German) at your earliest convenience will be deeply appreciated.
>
> Please do not think that I have forgotten about the photograph which I will send as soon as I return to England. I was obliged to order some, which is the reason of [*sic*] the delay.
>
> PS I have no cover to the von Webern score and no title: would you be so kind as to let me know what he calls his pieces.

The work by Webern was the *Five Pieces* (without further title!) for small orchestra, a score which at the beginning of July Webern was indeed ready to send to Wood. But the summer of 1914 was seized by historical events which brought such planning to a halt. Wood's projected music for Speyer's play remained unfinished, and anti-German hysteria engulfed Speyer despite his British baronetcy. The upheaval caused to British musical life by the outbreak of World War One on 4 August demands a separate chapter.

Chapter 11

War

1914–18

The First World War was not 'total war' in the sense that was often applied –
with reference to the involvement of the civilian population – to the Second.
Yet it would be quite wrong to see it as merely sending hundreds of
thousands to battle abroad while the rest got on with 'business as usual' as
best they could. On 16 December 1914 Germany's naval bombardment of
north-east coastal towns such as Scarborough gave a sense that the enemy
was not far off. In the following month the Zeppelin (airship) raids began:
there were to be fifty-seven such raids, and twenty-seven by German
aeroplanes, before the war ended. The total of deaths amounted to fewer
than 1500 but the threat was persistent.

From the first weeks of war, bellicose feeling turned on German elements
in British life at all levels. 'Harmless old men', as A. J. P. Taylor was to put it,
'who had forgotten to take out naturalization papers during their forty years'
residence in England, found their sons in the army and themselves interned
in the Isle of Man.' Announcing a series of lectures on non-European music
by Kathleen Schlesinger, the British Museum identified the scholar as 'a
British subject by birth and parentage'.

The surname of Henry J. Wood's cherished friend Siegfried Schwabacher
underwent a tactful change into Shaw-Baker. Likewise the veteran critic and
vocal teacher Hermann Klein, born in Norwich in 1856, changed the spelling
of his first name to Herman and publicly proclaimed a joint Russian and
French descent. Just as the royal family itself threw off its German names,
becoming the House of Windsor in 1917, so the Bechstein Hall in Wigmore
Street, London, became the Wigmore Hall.

The different destinies of the two musically prominent Speyers illustrated
the prevalent uncertainties. Both men had taken British citizenship and
played a part in public life. Edward (formerly Eduard) Speyer, the friend of
Brahms and Joachim, had settled in Britain as far back as 1860, becoming

146

naturalized in 1869. In 1885 he took as his second wife Antonia Kufferath (born 1857), of a distinguished Belgian, originally German, musical family.

> I had been a member of the Conservative Club since 1886, and one day, some six months after the outbreak of war, saw a notice in the hall requesting members of enemy origin to resign. I immediately sent in my resignation, but the committee asked me to withdraw it, which I naturally did.

Edward Speyer's autobiography *My Life and Friends* also records that 'in spite of my German birth, which was a matter of common knowledge, not one amongst the great number of our friends and neighbours showed any change in their friendly attitude towards us.'

The Edward Speyers' home, a large estate called Ridgehurst near Shenley in Hertfordshire, continued to give musical hospitality to many British and other visitors. Chamber music was the prevailing passion. Elgar was a frequent guest (and keen snooker-player); Casals arrived on a fine summer morning, racquet under his arm, exclaiming: 'Now, six sets of tennis first and then the two Brahms sextets!'

Very different was the case of Edward Speyer's considerably younger cousin Sir Edgar Speyer, banker and baronet, the munificent supporter of Henry J. Wood. His wife, the violinist Leonora von Stosch, could hardly conceal where her patriotism lay, to judge by Wood's own anecdote. In Hyde Park they watched young army recruits marching and drilling: 'I remember Lady Speyer turning to me and saying, "My dear Henry, how can these young, untrained boys hope to conquer our [*sic*] armies of trained soldiers? It is dreadful." '

Amid the general suspicion of all those of German origin, the links between the Speyer banking house in London and those of New York and Frankfurt cast additional odium on Edgar Speyer. He was attacked in the newspapers and obliged to resign from hospital boards lest subscribers should withdraw. He was told that unless his children ceased to attend certain classes, other children would be withdrawn from them. It was even said that from his house on the Norfolk coast he was flashing signals to German warships. After months of silent endurance, he wrote in May 1915 to his friend the Prime Minister, Herbert Asquith, offering to resign his baronetcy and Privy Councillorship. Asquith replied that his offer was declined by the King, and added: 'I have known you long and well enough to estimate at their true value those baseless and malignant imputations.'

It may surely be thought amazing that Wood neither made public testimony on Speyer's behalf at the time nor expressed, in his autobiography of two decades later, any regret at the turn of events.

In December 1915 a private initiative brought Speyer's membership of the Privy Council before a court; his status was upheld, and re-upheld on appeal. Nevertheless, before the month was out Speyer and his family had left England for the United States, there to spend the rest of the war. Smarting under what must have seemed ingratitude, he then *did* range himself on the German side. His brother James, in charge of the New York banking house, was already and openly pro-German (as were many Americans, two years before their country's entry into the War). In 1921 Edgar Speyer was stated to have been 'disaffected and disloyal' to the Crown: his British naturalization was revoked and his name removed from the roll of the Privy Council.

Until he left England, Edgar Speyer continued his financial support of the Queen's Hall concerts. According to the *Dictionary of National Biography* he had spent on them 'some £2000 a year for many years' (a sum which might compare to £100,000 today). In a final gesture of generosity on leaving, he handed the title-deeds of the Queen's Hall Orchestra to Wood. 'I still hold them,' the conductor wrote in 1938 in *My Life of Music*; and indeed it was by this means that he was able to revive the orchestra's title for his Decca recording series in 1935.

In wartime Britain it had become unpatriotic not merely to have a German name but to be associated with German goods. The veteran Liberal politician John Morley, reproved for drinking hock, had the wit to answer: 'I am interning it.' British piano-makers, who since about 1900 had been recovering ground against the best German makes, found buoyant opportunities with the removal of new German instruments from the market.

But what of German music? On the opening night of the promenade concerts on Saturday 15 August it could hardly have been surprising to find that Richard Strauss – as the pre-eminent living German composer – had been dropped from the advertised programme. The British work receiving its première that night was Elgar's *Sospiri* for strings, harp, and organ, a work of sweet melancholy, as remote from combat as could be.

The next concert, however, raised the political question in acute form. For many seasons past, Monday night had been Wagner night. Would it, should it, continue to be so? On 17 August the answer appeared to be 'No'. A French, Russian and British selection was given instead, including the *Nutcracker* Suite and *L'Après-midi d'un faune* (with the *Marseillaise* to end the concert). But the battle of the repertory had not been conceded. A printed slip was to be found inserted in the printed programme: 'Sir Henry Wood begs the kind indulgence of those members of his audience who may be disappointed at the non-performance of the customary Monday evening Wagner programme, the postponement of which has been rendered necessary by a variety of circumstances. He confidently hopes for a continuance of their valued support.'

On the following Friday the printed programme carried a further announcement from the directors of the Queen's Hall Orchestra Ltd, disclaiming 'any narrow, intolerant policy' and ascribing Monday's change to 'outside pressure brought to bear upon them at the eleventh hour' by the publishing firm of Chappell as the hall's leaseholders. Over Robert Newman's signature as manager of the concerts, it continued:

> With regard to the future, the Directors hope – with the broadminded co-operation of their audience – to carry through as nearly as possible the original scheme of the Concerts as set forth in their Prospectus. They take this opportunity of emphatically contradicting the statements that German music will be boycotted during the present season. The greatest examples of Music and Art are world possessions and unassailable even by the prejudices and passions of the hour.

'Normal' programmes, including Wagner as Monday's diet, were resumed. A weaker line was adopted by the Philharmonic Society, now prefixed 'Royal', with Beecham both as conductor and financial backer: it banned all German music after Mendelssohn. But at Brighton the municipal orchestra's conductor, Henry Lyell-Tayler, defiantly coupled Wagner and Handel for three concerts of its five-day festival in November 1914. Wood, with extracts from *The Ring* as well as an *Elijah* to open the festival, was one of the guest conductors.

Amazingly enough, the Queen's Hall promenade concert on 1 September 1914 had accommodated an orchestral suite by Bartók – the citizen of an enemy country, Austria-Hungary. But other music by Bartók fell from Wood's projected schedule, as did six new works by Mahler, including the *Kindertotenlieder*. The legacy left by deceased German and Austrian composers was welcomed; understandably, the work of their living successors was not. The 1915 season of promenade concerts would carefully introduce the composer Charles Martin Loeffler as one 'who was born in Alsace prior to the Franco-Prussian War of 1870'. Because they would have generated fees for 'enemy' publishers, Sibelius's symphonies also came under a wartime ban; his *Valse Triste* and *Finlandia*, under a different publishing arrangement, did not.

Not from every listener did the promenade concerts earn commendation simply for carrying on. Philip Heseltine, writing to Delius in October 1914, was scathing (and may well have influenced Delius's shift of favour away from Wood towards Beecham as interpreter):

> The programmes have been worse than usual, and the audiences – as a result – proportionately larger. It is difficult to escape Walford Davies's *Solemn Melody* or Gounod's *Hymne à Ste Cécile* or some such tosh, which invariably gets encored. Whenever the organ is used the Britisher applauds, presumably because it reminds him of church! Your two little pieces [*On hearing the first cuckoo in spring* and *Summer night on the River*] were mangled in the most execrable way; the strings played just anyhow, and the cuckoo came in at the wrong moment nearly every time. . .

Like other conductors, Wood faced the attrition of orchestral ranks as musicians entered the Forces – voluntarily, until conscription was introduced in January 1916. Those musicians who remained faced severe threats to their livelihood as the number of concerts fell. As early as November 1914 a Committee for Music in Wartime (soon to have Wood among its members along with Stanford, Elgar and Vaughan Williams) initiated a register of musicians, 'British subjects who have been adversely affected by the War, and unfit for military service'. It appealed for funds so that these musicians, organized into 'concert parties', could perform at army camps and elsewhere – and get paid for doing so. Vaughan Williams himself (aged nearly forty-two) was to volunteer for military service within a few weeks.

The cause of distressed musicians was one of many charitable drives which levied tribute on Wood and other leading musicians. 'H.M. the Queen's Work for Women Fund' was the beneficiary of an Albert Hall concert on 4 October 1914 organized by Clara Butt and her husband, the baritone Kennerley Rumford, at which Wood, Elgar, Ronald, Stanford, Cowen and Sir Frederick Bridge (the organist of Westminster Abbey and conductor of the Royal Choral Society) shared the conducting of the Queen's Hall Orchestra. Four weeks later, again on the initiative of Clara Butt (whose work for war charities would win her a post-war DBE), Wood and the orchestra participated in a concert for 'artists and musicians who were suffering by War'.

The plight of the Belgians after the German invasion of their country aroused much sympathy. Elgar was stirred to compose a piece for reciter and orchestra called *Carillon,* with its allusion to Belgium's famous keyed bell-chimes. The composer himself conducted the first performance in December 1914 and early in the following year took the London Symphony Orchestra on tour with it. Wood embraced the work, more than once rousing the promenaders' emotions as the celebrated French actress Réjane declaimed the poem by Emile Cammaerts: 'Chantons, Belges, chantons!'

The image of the conductor himself as warrior must have entered not a few heads, as in W. P. N. Barbellion's *The Journal of a Disappointed Man.* In December 1914 he sat *behind* the orchestra at a Queen's Hall concert and observed the conductor 'through a forest of violins':

However swift and elegant the movements of his arms, his splendid lower extremities remain as firm as stone columns. While the music is calm and serene his right hand and baton execute in concert with the left, perfect geometric curves around his head. Then as it gathers in force and volume, when the bows begin to dart swiftly across the fiddles and the trumpets and trombones blaze away in a conflagration, we are all expectant – and even a little fearful, to observe his sabre-like cuts. The tension grows. . . I hold my breath. . . Sir Henry snatches a second to throw back a lock of his hair that has fallen limply across his forehead, then goes on in unrelenting pursuit, cutting and slashing at hordes of invisible fiends that leap howling out towards him. There is a great turmoil of combat, but the Conductor struggles on till the great explosion happens. But in spite of that, you see him still standing thro' a cloud of great chords, quite undaunted. His sword zigzags up and down the scale – suddenly the closed fist of his left hand shoots up straight and points to the zenith – like the arm of a heathen priest appealing to Baal to bring down fire from Heaven. . . . But the appeal avails nought and it looks as tho' it were all up for Sir Henry. The music is just as infuriated – his body writhes with it – the melanic Messiah crucified by the inappeasable desire to express by visible gestures all that he feels in his heart. He surrenders – so you think – he opens out both arms wide and bearing his breast, dares them all to do their worst – like the picture of Moffat the missionary among the savages of the Dark Continent!

And yet he wins after all. At the very last moment he seems to summon all his remaining strength and in one final and devastating sweep mows down the orchestra rank by rank. . . . You wake from the nightmare to discover the victor acknowledging the applause in a series of his inimitable bows.

One ought to pack one's ears up with cotton wool at a concert where Sir Henry conducts. Otherwise, the music is apt to distract one's attention. R.L.S. wanted to be at the head of a cavalry charge – sword over head – but I'd rather fight an orchestra with a baton.

Broadening

Among those who had arrived as refugees from Belgium was the composer Joseph Jongen (1873–1953), whose *Fantasia on Two Popular Walloon Christmas Carols* Wood introduced to the promenaders on 18 August 1915. The Belgian Piano Quartet was formed in London, with Jongen as pianist, Désiré Defauw (later well-known as conductor) as violinist, Emile Doehaerd as cellist, plus Lionel Tertis on the viola. That most famous of Belgian musicians, Ysaÿe, was also in London, and joined in the all-night chamber-music sessions in the Chelsea basement of an American hostess, Muriel Draper.

Such celebrities as Tertis, Eugene Goossens and Arthur Rubinstein were to leave glowing reminiscences of Muriel Draper's hospitality. Her musical parties had begun some years earlier. In 1913 Pierre Monteux, conductor of the sensational programmes of the Diaghilev Ballet (including *The Rite of Spring*), had joined in – on the viola. Cortot, Casals and Sammons were among other frequenters, as were the visiting Polish composer Szymanowski, the Russian bass Shalyapin (the sensation of London's seasons of Russian opera in 1913 and 1914), the dancer Nijinsky, the painter John Singer Sargent and the novelists Henry James and Norman Douglas. But not Wood. It was not that he was too old, for Ysaÿe was even older; it was evidently that the quasi-Bohemian informality of such gatherings held no more attraction for him than the moneyed salons in which Beecham moved with ease.

As for the concerts at Queen's Hall, Chappell's as leaseholders were wise enough not to repeat the bullying which had marred the opening week of the War. Liberality in programme-making was seen to command public assent. Moreover, Chappell's stepped into the breach left by the hounding-out of Edgar Speyer, and under the direction of William Boosey took over the actual running of the orchestra and the Queen's Hall concerts. The Queen's Hall Orchestra ceased formally to exist, its pensioned members drawing their due sums from the Endowment Fund which Wood had established. The *New* Queen's Hall Orchestra took its place, and as such was first greeted by promenaders when the second wartime season opened on 14 August 1915.

With London streets darkened as a deterrent to air raids there was some decline in audiences, and a subsequent transfer of some concerts from evening to afternoon did not regain them. From 1916 a shift of the evening starting-time from 8 to 7.30 was more persuasive.

Patriotism, as distinct from empty anti-Germanism, found an echo in Wood's wartime concerts. 'A welcome note of colour was added to Queen's Hall' (says the historian of the hall, Robert Elkin) by the appearance of large flags of the Allies, draped in front of the organ, of which the console had not at this time been moved to a central position. 'As the number of Allies increased, so the display of bunting grew, until it became quite an imposing and not inartistic composition.' The Allied national anthems resounded, dressed in full orchestral guise by Wood. At this time, according to *My Life of Music*, he also 'decided to re-score our own notable tune' – though his own earlier arrangement of it had evidently satisfied Nikisch, who used it at the Philharmonic Society. Wood himself was persuaded to compose in 1914 a hymn of suitable wartime fervour, beginning 'O God our strength'. In his autobiography he called it 'a *dreadful* tune': 'My only consolation was that a footnote in the programme intimated that copies were purchasable, at 1s.9d. for twenty-five, from the owners of the copyright, Skeffington's of Southampton Row. I never heard anything more of it.'

Chappell's had no compunction – and as a business firm, why should they? – in pushing their wares at the promenade concerts. Chappell pianos were used and prominently advertised in the printed programmes. In singers' choices of piano-accompanied solos during the second halves of concerts, a remarkably high proportion turned out to be ballads published by Chappell, advertised with their prices in the printed programme. Nevertheless the concerts remained essentially what they were, with Robert Newman retained as manager under the new proprietors. The *Musical Times* in June 1915 recorded 112 concerts by Wood and the Queen's Hall Orchestra over the past nine months – sixty-one promenade, thirty Sunday afternoon, fourteen symphony concerts, and seven private concerts. Sunday concerts still being required to claim a charitable basis, those at Queen's Hall had been entrusted since 1912 to a body called the Sunday Musical Union.

From the provinces, however, came news of the cancellation of major festivals. Included were those of Norwich, Birmingham and Sheffield (where Wood was to have given the first British performance of Rachmaninoff's *The Bells*). Wood nevertheless continued to give occasional concerts in Sheffield and to fulfil guest engagements for the Liverpool Philharmonic Society. A typical Liverpool programme on 12 January 1915 included the Fauré *Pavane*, Grainger's *Irish Tune from County Derry* and *Shepherd's Hey*, and the overture to Rimsky-Korsakov's *Ivan the Terrible*, introduced to the Queen's Hall promenaders in the previous year.

In Manchester, his regular concerts for Brand Lane's management likewise continued with programmes of a more miscellaneous type than the Hallé Orchestra provided. Hallé players nevertheless took their seats in Wood's Manchester orchestra alongside a few principals brought from

Broadening

Queen's Hall, among them the oboist Léon Goossens, still only seventeen years old. Wood did not delay Manchester's introduction (9 January 1915) to Stravinsky's *Fireworks*, which he had already given at Queen's Hall; at the same concert a Japanese soprano, Tamaki Miura, was heard in a Verdi aria and in three traditional Japanese songs which Henry J. Wood had notated (presumably from her informal singing) and fitted with an orchestral accompaniment. Japan, it is worth remembering, had joined the Allied coalition against Germany from the very first month of the War.

The alliance with Russia was, of course, capable of stronger musical expression. Always alive to the possibilities of orchestral transcription, Wood made his own rather free version of Musorgsky's *Pictures at an Exhibition* (originally for piano solo), first performed at a Saturday concert in Queen's Hall on 17 April 1915. Rosa Newmarch again visited Russia, reporting enthusiastically for the *Musical Times* in September 1915. Increasingly, however, Russian music in Britain meant the Russian music of the past, or of Russia's two great living exiles. Rachmaninoff's symphonic poem, *The Isle of the Dead*, had its first London performance under Wood during the 1915 promenade season; Stravinsky, now resident in Paris, was represented by a not-quite-new *Scherzo Fantastique*.

A fresh name came up too, that of the young Prokofiev: his music was improbably introduced to the promenaders in 1916 in the shape of a *Humoresque-Scherzo* for four bassoons. (The composer had probably met Wood or Newmarch or both when visiting London just before the outbreak of war, aged twenty-three.) Early in 1916, when a Russian Music Committee was formed 'to promote the use of Russian music in this country', the names both of Wood and Newmarch were inevitably to be found alongside those of Rachmaninoff and Glazunov.

French music was equally welcome during the war years. Debussy had been persuaded to provide for Wood's 1915 promenade concert a set of 'symphonic fragments' from his stage music for D'Annunzio's play, *Le Martyre de St Sébastien*. Franck's symphony and other works enjoyed something of a boom – though Wood later took a dislike to Franck and thought the British would do much better if they developed a passion for Berlioz instead.

What had been the regular round of visits by eminent foreign instrumentalists now almost dried up. Even non-enemy foreigners faced difficulties in travel, though the ageing Vladimir de Pachmann, the young Arthur

Rubinstein, and Guilhermina Suggia, already hailed as 'princess of cellists', were among those who overcame them. Against Germans, Austrians and Hungarians the frontier was absolute. 'The barring of the alien enemy has laid bare the fact that we have amongst us English executants of the first rank who have not hitherto had their fair chance owing to the infatuation of so many concert-goers for foreign names,' as the *Musical Times* put it. Albert Sammons was now recognized as a first-class interpreter of Elgar's violin concerto, and when he was later conscripted for the armed services the same magazine commented: 'Whether such an asset should be exposed to risk is a matter for much difference of opinion, but the call is inexorable.'

Among the newly prominent British contingent, a group of much-loved pianists was of Jewish origin. The Russian-born Benno Moiseiwitsch (at that time spelt 'Moiseivitsch', a little less German-seeming) began his long-lasting popularity, playing not only the traditionally favourite concertos but also Delius's (8 February 1915 under Beecham, as well as on 12 February 1916 under Wood). The London-born child prodigy, Solomon, already referred to, played Tchaikovsky's First Piano Concerto on 17 October 1914 in the first symphony concert of the season. Myra Hess had given her first performance with Wood in 1908: she was to give ninety-two. Her cousin Irene Scharrer began in October 1915 her long association with the Scherzo from Litolff's Concerto Symphonique no.4.

Vocal solos continued to be heard at every promenade concert and most other orchestral occasions. Under Wood's guidance the choice of such items embraced an extraordinary range of periods and styles. At the promenade concert of 23 September 1914 a woman singer, Hayward Webb, performed an aria attributed to Francesco Sacrati (1605–50). That name would hardly cross the lips of musicians again until the 1980s, when research identified Sacrati as the part-composer (with Monteverdi) of *L'Incoronazione di Poppea*.

Curiously it was during the stressful times of war that Wood was invited to embark on a new development of his career, and one of historic importance – orchestral recording for the gramophone. He received from Clara Butt, already celebrated as a recording artist, a letter dated 29 July 1915:

> The Columbia Co. know they have no real good orchestral records and that is why they are anxious to secure you. They are sure you would get some fine results. I am empowered now to make you this offer, that you sign a contract for 3 years. They guarantee you 300 guineas a year. Will

> pay your men a guinea per man each session. When you accompany me
> (apart from the above) they will pay you 10 guineas per record. I have made
> six this aft [*sic*].

On 31 August 1915 Wood took the decisive step and signed with Louis
Sterling, the European general manager of Columbia, an exclusive recording
contract:

> . . . 3. The artist shall be paid for conducting one hundred guineas
> (£105.0.0) per session of three hours. Columbia guarantee to engage the
> artist for at least six sessions of three hours per year during each year of the
> period of engagement.
> 4. At the request of Columbia the artist will conduct for record-
> making purposes the accompanying Orchestra for such singers as may be
> mutually agreed upon between the artist and Columbia for a fee of twelve
> guineas (£12.12.0) per record.

He conducted a special series of recordings for Clara Butt, including the
earliest recorded selection from Elgar's *The Dream of Gerontius*. His entry
into this field rather surprisingly antedates that of Leopold Stokowski, who
began recording only in 1917 – but who was to take an intense and creative
attitude to the actual process of recording, which Wood (thirteen years his
senior) never did.

Before the end of 1916, sufficient records had been marketed to warrant
an advertisement in the programmes of Brand Lane's concerts in
Manchester:

SIR HENRY J. WOOD
Conducting his Famous Orchestra
has made a series of Columbia Records that attain a standard of perfection
never before achieved in Orchestral recording. . . . Ask to hear 'Till's
Merry Pranks' at your dealers.

Strauss's *Till Eulenspiegel*, abbreviated to one double-sided record, was
accompanied by descriptive notes 'specially written by Sir Henry J. Wood'.
Drastic abbreviation was also applied in a two-record issue of Elgar's Violin
Concerto with Albert Sammons as soloist.

Columbia advertised 'his' orchestra, rather than that of Queen's Hall by
name, because a contract had been signed with Wood and not with the
orchestral management. By the end of the war in November 1918 Columbia
had issued his recordings of music by (among other composers) Beethoven,

Wagner and Tchaikovsky as well as Elgar, Gardiner, Grainger and Holbrooke. An abbreviated version of the Prelude to Act 3 of *Lohengrin* was backed by Wood's own orchestration of Rachmaninoff's Prelude in C sharp minor. A letter of 18 April 1916, thanking Francis G. Sanders once again for his musical services, probably refers to the task of *reducing* full-orchestral strength down to what the studio could accommodate: 'Many, many thanks for all you did for me last week, in scoring all that stuff for my Gramaphone [*sic*] work. You did it splendidly and I had nothing to change at all. I am sending you a pot-boiler that I had to score – will you kindly correct score and parts; I hope my MS is all right. I never had time to read it through carefully, so make any changes you like.'

In July 1918 he signed a renewal of the contract – with the significant addition of an extra payment in advance of £500 – as an exclusive Columbia artist for a further three years.

The success of the promenade concerts at Queen's Hall prompted a rival series at the Albert Hall at which Beecham and Ronald were joint conductors of the New Symphony Orchestra for four weeks beginning 29 May 1916. It failed – mainly, Ronald afterwards said, because the organizers of that series had banned *all* German music, even Bach and Beethoven. It was a failure which can only have reinforced the Newman-Wood empire. As the musical adviser to the Columbia recording company, and since 1910 principal of the Guildhall School of Music, Ronald was always treated by Wood as a friendly colleague. Beecham – 'Sir Thomas' from 1916, first as a knight and later that year succeeding to his father's baronetcy – was, on the contrary, always the rival.

Ballad concerts were by now in danger of losing their appeal, but 'the Emperor' (as William Boosey of Chappell's was known) had the idea of enhancing his Saturday series at Queen's Hall by the addition of an orchestra. The New Queen's Hall Light Orchestra (about forty-five players selected from the larger group) appeared at these concerts from 1916 under the baton of the excitable but highly gifted Alick Maclean. With four or more singers at each concert and with such solo pianists as Moiseiwitsch, the attraction had certainly been heightened. An advertisement in June 1918 announced the augmenting of the orchestra to sixty for a programme conducted by Edward German, with Marguerite d'Alvarez and Robert Radford among the vocal soloists.

Wood was indefatigable if not quite invincible. Illness had compelled the engagement of Beecham as substitute for a promenade concert on 9 October

Broadening

1915; Landon Ronald deputized at a Saturday symphony concert on 21 April 1917, when Wood was suffering from influenza and depression. Earlier, Wood took over a London Symphony Orchestra concert (thus reuniting himself with the 'seceders' of 1904) on 8 May 1916 at Queen's Hall when Beecham became unavailable.

Mid-1916 was a dark time for British military fortunes. From the Somme came news of 19,000 killed, 57,000 casualties on 1 July – 'the greatest loss in a single day ever suffered by a British army and the greatest suffered by any army in the First World War'. At home, to keep pace with the demands of the military machine, women increasingly took over 'men's work' in factories and offices. Just before the opening of the 1916 promenade season it was announced that the orchestra would include 'lady players'. Though women had participated since 1913 in the Queen's Hall Orchestra's other concerts, the nightly grind of promenade concerts had been supposed to be too strenuous for them – but their services now stopped the hole in the dike.

Despite the earlier starting-time of 7.30, on one occasion the concert-goers did not escape the air-raids – as recalled by Mrs M. Currie, a member of the Oriana Choir, which was participating in a concert on 29 September 1917. After the choir performed Norman O'Neill's *Before Dawn* in the first part of the evening,

> some of us went into the balcony to hear the rest of the concert. Carmen Hill was singing, when we heard the ominous sounds outside, but we all sat tight. The next item was a bassoon solo. In the middle of it there was a crash, and then a cracking sound, and a shower of plaster began to fall from the roof of the Promenade, which was packed.
>
> There was a bit of a rush from the centre of the hall for a moment. One or two of the orchestra disappeared from their seats. Even Sir Henry Wood himself glanced rather anxiously up at the roof, though still wielding his baton. The bassoonist, however, kept merrily on; and we realized it could only be shrapnel which had dislodged the plaster. The soloist got a rousing encore and treated us to 'We Won't Go Home Till Morning', amidst cheers and laughter.
>
> After the concert no one was allowed to leave the Hall. We prowled round the passages and had some coffee, until one of the orchestra nobly returned to the platform and struck up a waltz. We were soon dancing over the floor and really enjoying the experience. We were not released [by the official 'All Clear' signal] until about 1 a.m.

As soon as war was declared, Percy Grainger had taken himself off to the neutral United States: convinced of his destiny as history's first major

Australian composer, he was not going to put it at risk in Europe's conflict. Promenade audiences, far from being outraged, continued to welcome his works. A new addition in 1916 was *Handel in the Strand*, with Grainger's slender original instrumentation metamorphosed to full-orchestral dimensions by Wood himself. Grainger, although such an individualist in orchestration, declared himself delighted – as well he might have been by Wood's chirpy-cheery use of the xylophone, or hammerwood as the anglicizing Grainger renamed it.

Despite its neutrality, the United States protested at the German sinking of the British liner *Lusitania* in May 1915 and of the *Sussex* in March 1916. Travelling aboard the *Sussex* was the Spanish composer Enrique Granados: he was picked up by lifeboat but dived into the sea to save his wife and was drowned. Wood commemorated him with the first British performance of his symphonic poem *Dante and Beatrice* at the opening of the symphony concert season on 28 October 1916. In the following year's Proms Wood unveiled his own orchestration of a set of Spanish Dances by Granados. These were to remain a favourite in Wood's programmes, and he would twice record them.

At a symphony concert on 11 November 1916 Wood won his audience's approval with another Spanish novelty, Joaquin Turina's *La procesión del Rocío* (programmed under a French version of the title). Such events showed an increasing welcome at this time for Spanish music. Arthur Rubinstein proved a powerful advocate in his performances of works by Albéniz, Granados and Falla (especially his transcription of the *Ritual Fire Dance* from Falla's *El Amor Brujo*). The coming theatrical success of Falla's *The Three-Cornered Hat* (see p.167) would seal the matter.

War was eventually declared on Germany by the United States in April 1917, producing one of the oddest juxtapositions ever made in one of Wood's programmes – a concert performance of extracts from *Parsifal* (using only one singer, the soprano Carrie Tubb) followed by 'The Star-Spangled Banner' (Good Friday, 6 April). America's new belligerent status threw the Boston Symphony Orchestra into a crisis of organization. Anti-German feeling forced its distinguished German conductor, Carl Muck, to resign. (He was then briefly interned before being allowed to return to Europe.) Emissaries came to London and offered Wood the vacant post, by this time as prestigious as any in the world.

It was an offer he might well have accepted. The Boston position would have allowed him to make music 3000 miles away from the battlefield, in conditions free from air raids, blackout, rationing, conscription of players and a hundred lesser inconveniences of war. A season lasting less than half the year in Boston might be combined – when peace returned – with several months' concert-giving in Britain. Wood was evidently tempted. His auto-biography mentions 'rather a stormy interview with Newman and William Boosey [of Chappell's]', when he told them he had not made up his mind.

The announcement of his eventual decision was curiously bungled. On 24 May *The Times* announced that he had accepted the offer; on 29 May its readers learned that, on the contrary, 'while greatly appreciating the compliment that America has paid to British music, he has decided to remain in London'. He was stated to have signed a new contract (presumably a more remunerative one!) with Chappell's. The monthly magazines being bound by their deadlines, readers of the *Musical Times* were told in the June issue that he was going, in the July issue that he was not. He found himself unexpectedly summoned to meet the music-loving Foreign Secretary, A. J. Balfour, with whom he had shared the Queen's Hall platform at the Joachim jubilee celebrations ten years before. If that meeting was as late as 27 June (as Wood's pages have it), then Wood's story that Balfour urged him to take the Boston appointment is unbelievable: it would have been impossible to announce a *second* change of mind after the pronouncement of 29 May.

The first months of 1918 brought no military comfort to Britain. 'With our backs to the wall and believing in the justice of our cause each one of us must fight to the end': the message of the British Commander-in-Chief, Lord Haig, hardly had Nelson's Trafalgar touch. Not until the latter half of the year would the land battles in France and Flanders turn to the Allied advantage. To Frederick Delius – still living in his French home at Grez under some hardship under war conditions – a return to Britain seemed nevertheless the best way to promote his compositions.

'My dear Delius' begins a typewritten letter of 16 January 1918 bearing Henry J. Wood's signature, but probably typed by his wife Muriel:

> Delighted to receive your note of the 8th and to hear there is some chance of seeing you over here again soon.
>
> *Brigg Fair* was a great success both at the Promenade and Symphony Concerts: I also played the *Dance Rhapsody* in Birmingham a short time ago, but I have no longer a good bass oboe player, as the original man Horton, has been called up.
>
> I do hope you and Mrs Delius will run down to Chorleywood and see us: it is only 35 minutes from Baker Street. Our little London house, 4 Elsworthy Road, N. W., has just been vacated by its last tenants: how would it suit you?
>
> With kindest regards, in which my wife joins . . .

The Deliuses' arrival was delayed. The composer's deteriorating health had made spa treatment at Biarritz advisable – after which, on returning to Grez, they found their house (which had been requisitioned by the French army) vandalised and filthy. Not until 3 September 1918 did the Deliuses get to London. They did in fact become tenants of 4 Elsworthy Road, the composer on his arrival extracting page after page of music-paper from inside his clothes before the eyes of his astonished host. He had feared that his current composition, if discovered by Customs, might have been seized on suspicion of being coded material.

From 4 Elsworthy Road the composer's wife Jelka wrote on 19 September to her American friend Marie Clews of hearing Wood perform Delius's *Dance Rhapsody* at a promenade concert: 'It was delightful!' The same letter gives a glimpse of Beecham's Society hostess:

> We were at Selfridge's yesterday with Lady Cunard. She at once introduced us to a head man there as most important persons and so we obtained a pot of jam without standing in line. It was killing, the way she cross-examined this *chef de rayon* as to *how* she could give luncheon parties on only four meat coupons at 5d. each per week. 'But what are my friends to *eat*? You *must* find something, etc. Oh, but I *must* give luncheon parties.'

No account survives, in either angry or comic vein, of Henry or Muriel Wood's way of coping with such wartime restrictions. (Sugar was rationed from January 1918, meat some months later.) It is impossible to imagine either of them publicly bullying their way to special treatment.

After a few weeks, however, the Deliuses were to move to another London address. 'At the Woods it was so chilly and trees right in front hiding the sun and whipping against the windows in the night,' Jelka complained to the same friend, Marie Clews. Henry J. Wood was probably glad to have the London home at his disposal again (in addition to Appletree Farm) but Muriel was more inclined to see the financial advantage of renting it out. Later he accused her of letting the London house inconveniently and without warning.

The young Adrian Boult, to whom Wood was always kind, had been found unfit for active military service and was working at the War Office. He obtained permission to further his conducting career by giving four concerts of British music (4 and 18 February, 4 and 18 March 1918), during the second of which there was an air raid, when orchestra and audience took temporary refuge in the basement of Queen's Hall. In the second programme was Vaughan Williams's *A London Symphony*, which had not been heard in the capital since 1914; in the fourth concert that symphony was repeated, with cuts newly made by the composer. The letter which Wood wrote to Boult while staying with a friend near Kendal on 29 July 1918 is reproduced here verbatim, the loose construction and casual, uncorrected punctuation being typical of Wood's informal, handwritten correspondence:

> Dear Mr. Boult
>
> I am so sorry never to have replied to your very kind letter about the Full Score of the Vaughan William's [sic] Symphony, but I have got very much behindhand in my correspondence, but I am hoping to cope with some of it, during my two weeks holiday up here.
>
> I only want the V. W. score for a few days, in order to see how much rehearsal it will require in London & the provinces & I can only judge this by looking it through.
>
> Unfortunately I missed both your splendid performances of it. Could you arrange for me to have a look at it, anytime after my return to town on August 10th or shall I communicate with Mrs. Vaughan Williams & save you all further trouble & bother – perhaps you can oblige me with her address on a postcard – but it is a precious score and must not be trusted to the post.
>
> May I be allowed to offer you my sincerest congratulations upon your recent splendid series of Orchestral Concerts; the programmes were most interesting, & I hear on all sides, that you made a great personal success
>
> > Believe me
> > Sincerely yours
> > [signed Henry J. Wood]
>
> P.S. Do let me have the cuts.
>
> P.S. How very kind of you to write me about the Boston appointment, it was hard to refuse, but I felt it was a patriotic duty to remain in my own country, at the present moment, & in my long interview with Mr. Balfour only a few weeks ago, he quite sympathised with me in my ideas.

To the end of his life Boult maintained an affection and respect for Henry J. Wood, founded on the encouragement received from him as a young man. On a Sunday morning, 29 September 1918, Wood was among the listeners at Queen's Hall for a historic event - the first performance of *The Planets* by Gustav von Holst (as he was then known), conducted by Boult in a private performance funded by the generosity of another composer, H. Balfour Gardiner. Exactly a week after the war ended on 11 November 1918, Wood wrote to Boult from the Prince's Hotel, Brighton (again reproduced verbatim here):

I don't know what you will think of me, for not replying to your kind note until now, but you know that since the last week of the Promenades, I have not been very well, & have spent most of the days that I have not had a Concert, in bed, resting. That, & my three weeks stay down here, has put me right, & I now feel as fresh & fit as ever.

As regards the Conducting lessons, how can you teach Conducting except with an Orchestra in front of you, to play on. I was *delighted with your direction* of the Van Holst [*sic*] work, all you want is opportunity, & that will come to you, now that war is over. If I can be of any assistance to you, over any knotty points, in the direction of Choral or Orchestral works, just send me a line, & we can always arrange a meeting – but a course of lessons – No! No! No! certainly not – ridiculous.

Sincerely yours

'Riotous joy and triumph and flags and motor-lorries of drunken Dominion soldiers and crowds and crowds. . .' So Jelka Delius wrote, describing the London street scene after the Armistice was declared on 11 November 1918. Neither the concert 'for the Fallen' (including the funeral march from Beethoven's *Eroica*) which he conducted for Newman at Queen's Hall nor his own personal reactions to the ending of the War are mentioned in Wood's autobiography. According to Pound, Wood later alleged (in setting down his grievances against his wife) that he had wanted to go out and join the crowds but that Muriel, thinking it 'a vulgar idea', had restricted his celebrations to 'a high tea of boiled eggs'.

Chapter 12

Under Chappell's Banner

1918–23

To the general scheme of promenade concerts the immediate post-war years seemed to bring no change. A typical week as advertised in the 1919 season announced: 'Monday, Wagner etc; Tuesday, Russian etc; Wednesday, Operatic etc; Thursday, Popular; Friday, Beethoven etc; Saturday, Popular' – with significance in the 'etc', since the latter part of the programme was always a miscellany. A broadening of public taste was nevertheless proceeding – in particular an incipient 'Bach cult', as Rosa Newmarch saw it. 'Concerts consisting almost entirely of Bach's music became – and still are [1928] – the most reliable "draws" of the season.'

Such was Wood's power of leading his audiences. He privately admitted, however, that he had 'little or no say' in the choice of piano-accompanied songs which fell in the second part of the programmes. That choice fell first of all to the singer, but the singer might be overruled by the Chappell management. 'That is why we all miss dear [Gervase] Elwes so much,' wrote Wood after the tenor had been killed in a train accident in 1921, 'because he put these splendid songs down and they were not cut out by the powers that be.' Other singers were content to milk the ballads for their sentiment. The distinguished tenor Ben Davies, past his sixtieth birthday, might declaim 'Deeper and deeper still' and 'Waft her, angels' from Handel's *Jephtha*, but later in the programme would stand by the piano and confidentially warble:

> Ah, if you only loved me, dear,
> How easy all would be,
> I'd take the music of the stars,
> The song of bird and sea. . .

to the strains of the popular ballad-composer Hermann Löhr. An advertisement in the programme drew attention to the publication of that song among

164

others in Chappell's catalogue. Audiences continued to draw amusement from the names of Kiddle (F. B.) and Liddle (S.), the alternating piano accompanists.

According to Edward Speyer's *My Life and Friends*, it had cost Chappell & Co. £35,000 to keep the New Queen's Hall Orchestra afloat during the war (just over four years), as compared with an annual average of £4000 which his cousin Sir Edgar Speyer had spent on the Queen's Hall concerts when he was financing them. That the three series – the promenade concerts, the Saturday symphony concerts and the Sunday concerts – should have survived the war with no season interrupted was, in retrospect, remarkable. Probably less of a loss to Chappell's, or even profitable, was the survival of the Saturday afternoon ballad concerts, which continued to have the participation of the New Queen's Hall Light Orchestra under the baton of Alick Maclean. Later Wood himself was to conduct some of these concerts.

But even before the war's end – while a ban was still in force on all modern German and Austrian music – there were those who criticized an excess of routine as Wood paraded his warhorses at the promenade concerts and in other series. 'The eternal Tchaikovsky, Grieg, Mendelssohn, Liszt, Saint-Saëns, Handel – the same old *Peer Gynt*, Hungarian Rhapsodies, *Pathetic* Symphony' complained an anonymous letter-writer to the *Daily Telegraph* (7 September 1918). 'Far too little' was being done, wrote Robin Legge, music critic of that newspaper, 'to encourage potential native musical ability'. Chappell's answer was couched in terms which show the relative share of Chappell's, Newman and Wood in decision-making:

> The moment we are convinced by receipts that the public prefer Mr Joseph Holbrooke's music to that of Beethoven, or Mr Granville Bantock's compositions to those of Tchaikovsky, we are perfectly prepared radically to alter the character of the Queen's Hall programmes.
>
> Mr Legge asks who is responsible for the drawing up of these programmes. They are drawn up by Mr Robert Newman, whose long experience thoroughly qualifies him for the task. Mr Newman has general instructions from us to draw up the programmes upon the most popular lines, and they are finally submitted to us for our approval.
>
> The musical public, which quite well knows what it wants, will not be dictated to by us, or even by eminent musical critics. Sir Henry Wood every season submits to us a large number of novelties, including English works. We have to point out to Sir Henry Wood that novelties, particularly British ones, do not attract, and that as, more particularly during such a war as this, it costs thousands of pounds to run orchestral

concerts, it is not possible, unless you are a millionaire, to exploit novelties
and at the same time find the money to pay your artists.

Wood himself, interviewed by the *Sunday Telegram*, was not at all apologetic
in regard to his quota of new British work, and from the point of view of box-
office common sense declared himself firmly opposed to 'all-British'
programmes as advocated by some. The 1918 promenade concerts had in
fact included a substantial helping of British music. As well as Delius's *Dance
Rhapsody* (no.1), Wood gave William Wallace's symphonic poem *Villon*,
Bantock's *Sappho* prelude, York Bowen's piano concerto no.3, and Edward
German's *Welsh Rhapsody*. All of these performances were revivals,
gestures of sustained confidence without invoking the special novelty of a
première.

Incidentally, 'gentlemen' (as in the very first season) were still requested
in the printed programme 'to refrain from striking matches during the
performance of the various items'. The free-and-easy atmosphere associated in those days with 'the mollifying influence of the weed' was credited
with attracting audiences which other concerts repelled. 'It is safe to assume
that a large number of men, particularly young men, go to the "Proms" chiefly
because smoking is allowed, and that they stay away from other concerts
because it isn't.' But the reason why packed houses were so often observed
at the Proms (an abbreviation now becoming general) in contrast with the
empty spaces often observed at other concerts must have been in some
degree a question of price. Promenaders paid two shillings to stand; at
regular concerts a seat in the same area might cost five times as much.

A Delius première was due – the work which the composer had unpacked
in manuscript from under his clothes on arrival at the Woods' house (see
p.161). Under the title of *Once Upon a Time*, it had been scheduled for
Wood's symphony concert on 23 November 1918, but the illegibility of the
manuscript score had compelled a postponement. It was produced instead
on 11 January 1919 and now bore the Norwegian title *Eventyr* (i.e., *Tales of
Adventure*) in recognition of the inspiration which the composer had drawn
from the Norwegian writer Asbjørnsen: the English nursery-tale phrase
became a subtitle. 'The Queen's Hall Orchestra have tried your work and I
think it will come out *very well indeed*,' wrote Wood to the composer on 2
January, inviting him to an extra rehearsal for strings alone. 'Before this I will
run in [i.e. drive by car to London from Chorleywood] and see you about one
or two doubtful passages as regards phrasing, etc.; the full final rehearsal will
be at 10 a.m. on 11 January.'

Eventyr was dedicated to Wood. A large audience was secured by the fact that the same programme marked the return to London (after fourteen years) of the celebrated French singer Emma Calvé. The surprise in Delius's score was a wordless 'wild shout', supposed to be delivered by about twenty male voices from *behind* the orchestra. That this shout was accepted as a matter of course by the audience, and not even mentioned in some press notices, was seen by the critic Harvey Grace as a change in public susceptibilities:

> What a hullabaloo there was over the Strauss wind-machine, the bleating of the sheep in *Don Quixote* and the battle music in *Ein Heldenleben*! Following the Delius work, we had Calvé singing the *habanera* from *Carmen*, and very audibly snapping her fingers as a substitute for the tambourine. Can you imagine these things being done at a symphony concert a few years ago without protest?

'At a symphony concert': once more the differentiation of atmosphere from the free-and-easy Proms was marked.

Another Delius première was to follow. The cellist Beatrice Harrison had been a child prodigy and had now returned as a mature and sensitive artist. (Her distinction has been somewhat obscured by the popular celebrity she won in radio broadcasts 'accompanied' by the nightingales in her Sussex garden.) For her and her violinist sister, May Harrison, Delius wrote his Double Concerto. 'The girls played superbly and Wood surpassed himself,' wrote the composer after the performance at a symphony concert on 21 February 1920.

Just as in pre-war days, a visit to London of the Paris-based Diaghilev Ballet could be relied on for musical stimulus. The Alhambra Theatre housed the première of *The Three-Cornered Hat*, with choreography by Massine and music by Falla, on 22 July 1919. The company later transferred to the Empire Theatre and engaged Adrian Boult as conductor. Knowing that Boult intended to present himself formally for a doctorate of music at Oxford, Wood wrote in his best jovial manner on 5 October:

> My dear Mr Boult,
>   Do accept my *very sincerest congratulations*, on your conducting of 'Russian Ballet' in London – this settles it, you can never be a Doctor of Music after this, can you? Please send me a postcard of the date of the

first Matineé of De Falla's Ballet, I can only attend Matineés, and I missed it at the Alhambra.
>With all good wishes
>>Sincerely yours
>>>Henry J. Wood
P.S. I am back home again for six months, 4 Elsworthy Road, N. W.

This handwritten letter was sent from the Langham Hotel – which, with the postcript, probably indicates that Wood's London home had been temporarily let to a tenant.

In 1920 Boult evidently sent him a draft of what was to be published as *A Handbook of Conducting*. Wood suggested adding 'a few remarks about the legs and the feet':

> . . .my experience is that very few British conductors, even after years of experience, are able to cure themselves of that abominable habit of 'giving' at the knees. Of course this causes the head and body to bob up and down with the first beat of the bar, and the scissors-like opening which generally accompanies this action is certainly not graceful to watch or helpful to the players.
>
> Another point which I think ought to be carefully watched is that of getting on the toes, because if this becomes a habit and you conduct several hours a day, it leads to cramp. Personally I am in favour of the heels being pressed on the platform, as it gives a central pose to the body, and with a little practice the body can be swung round as on a pivot without moving the feet position, and I found this personally to be of great benefit, as in the provinces I have often had to conduct even big choral performances standing on a champagne box! and it gives the audience a feeling of confidence if they see that the conductor does not step forward or backward on his platform.

What would have been Henry J. Wood's reaction to the prancing and leaping of conductors in the television age hardly bears thinking about. But they, of course, do not take on Wood's load of up to seven concerts a week.

Richard Strauss's works were restored to the Queen's Hall in 1920, and in the following year Sibelius renewed his warm relationship with Wood and the British public. 'Dear Sir Henry,' he wrote from an address in South Kensington on 8 March 1921,

> Before leaving England for my tour in Norway, I write to thank you and Lady Wood for your friendly hospitality. But above all I want to express to Mr Maurice Sons, and the other gentlemen and ladies of the New Queen's Hall Orchestra, my appreciation of their cordial reception, and

of the sympathy and insight they have shown in their performances of my
works – especially my Fourth and Fifth Symphonies. Thanks to you all, I
carry away very happy memories of this visit to London, and I hope to have
the honour of conducting the New Queen's Hall Orchestra again before we
have time to forget our good understanding,
>Yours sincerely
>Jean Sibelius

It was with memories of such a close understanding that Wood was to
resent, in later years, Sibelius's seeming to favour Thomas Beecham as his
London interpreter.

London's taste for Wagner, so far from being on its way to exhaustion,
found new stimulus after the War. Up to the end of 1913 Wagner's family in
Bayreuth had restricted concert performances to what were called 'normal'
extracts – 'but now there are no obstacles', as Alfred Kalisch noted in the
Musical Times. On 13 September 1920 parts of *Götterdämmerung* never
previously performed at a London concert were heard. 'Sir Henry Wood',
Kalisch added, 'always rises to an occasion like this'.

Singers remained an important element in Wood's programmes, and the
management did not stint their engagement. The Australian poet W. J.
Turner, who had become music critic of the weekly *New Statesman*, was
suspicious of Chappell's business morality but in 1921 conceded that there
had been 'no lowering of the standard of music performed. There has even
been an improvement in the quality of the vocalists engaged, which is a really
astonishing achievement.' Those vocalists included the New Zealand
soprano Rosina Buckman, who joined the much admired tenor John Coates in
the love-duet from Ethel Smyth's opera *The Wreckers* on 30 April 1921, the
final Saturday symphony concert of the season. Another composer,
Bantock, conducted his own *Hebridean Symphony,* leaving as Wood's share
of the concert Beethoven's *Egmont* Overture, Schumann's Piano Concerto
with Myra Hess, and Wagner's *Prelude and Death Song* from *Tristan and
Isolde* (as the programme put it). The war had de-Germanized many such
titles.

An internationally known operatic contralto who found Wood 'the most
enchanting of all conductors' was Marguerite d'Alvarez, Liverpool-born of
Peruvian and French parentage, a Carmen and Delilah of striking beauty. In
concert she cultivated an adventurous repertory almost without parallel. On
4 May 1918 her Queen's Hall programme, with Wood conducting, included
items by Cavalli and Monteverdi and ended with what may well have been
London's first hearing of Borodin's ballad for voice and orchestra, 'The Sea'.

Broadening

Her memoirs (*Forsaken Altars*, 1954), would accord to him a touching tribute which he would never read:

> He was a simple, intelligent man, modest and jovial, and the hardest worker one could possibly meet. He managed to be erudite in his work and constructive towards the artist he was conducting. Like a lover, he breathed one's phrases with one and looked anxiously to see if one was at ease with his tempo. To sing Bach under his guidance was a prayer, and made me feel so elevated that I thought God might one day pull me up through a hole in the roof to Heaven just as I was, without having to experience the agonies of death.

The prima donna saw her conductor as a lover; an effusive article which appeared in November 1919 in *Musical Opinion* portrayed him as a medicine-man, a 'skin-changer', transforming himself to inhabit one composer's personality after the next. The author was H. Orsmond Anderton, a friend and biographer of Bantock, who found it necessary to evoke Icelandic mythology, Milton, Ruskin, G. K. Chesterton and the Book of Samuel in order to make his point on Wood's many-sidedness. He had been granted an interview and a visit to 4 Elsworthy Road. The interview seems to have been the first time that Wood divulged his correct year of birth (1869 rather than 1870) but he still fantasized the rank of princess for his late wife Olga. The magazine misprinted her supposed surname as Ouranoff.

Other conductors besides Beecham now challenged Wood's position as the champion of the newest orchestral music. Returned from Russia, Albert Coates (1882–1953) conducted the first complete, *public* performance of Holst's *The Planets* in 1920 and in the same year introduced London to Prokofiev's *Scythian Suite*. Eugene Goossens conducted his own work at the promenade concerts and in 1921, with his own specially-enlisted orchestra, was to give Stravinsky's *The Rite of Spring* its first British concert performance. Curiously enough Wood seems never to have conducted *The Rite of Spring*, though late in life he performed its competing block-buster in barbarism, Prokofiev's *Scythian Suite*.

At the promenade concerts of 1920, Wood gave Prokofiev's Piano Concerto no.1 its first British performance with Ellen M. Jensen as soloist. Then the composer himself came to play his more characteristic Concerto no.3 at a Saturday symphony concert on 24 November 1923 (having already performed it under Albert Coates eighteen months before). The *Musical Times* was little impressed:

It is a queer thing to see and hear a Prokofiev concerto. None but the composer has yet been known to play one. [But see above!] In a way it is infantile. You think of a singularly ugly baby solemnly shaking a rattle. But no; it is not so human as that. . . Prokofiev's art takes all the natural warmth out of the pianoforte and orchestra, but inspires them with a jerky, elfin cleverness.

Before arriving in England, Prokofiev had pressed Wood to perform two works by his prolific compatriot Nikolay Myaskovsky – the symphonic poem *Alastor* (after Shelley) and the Symphony no.5. Wood duly introduced *Alastor* to British audiences during the 1923 promenade season and his symphonic poem *Silence* (under the title *Silentium)* in 1929. It was an unfruitful advocacy before the court of British musical taste, but Wood's persistence with Russian music was to be gratefully remembered in Moscow.

Elgar invariably treated Wood as a close brother-musician, as his letters to 'My dear Henry' show. ('Dear Wood', or the still more formal 'Dear Sir Henry', was the style adopted in correspondence by most of his colleagues.) The death of his wife Alice on 7 April 1920 was to have a deep effect on Elgar's professional as well as private life. On 15 January 1921 Elgar conducted a concert at Queen's Hall in which Beatrice Harrison played his Cello Concerto. Evidently Wood was at hand, since it was 'his' orchestra. A letter from the composer followed on 18 January:

> My dear Henry
>   One line to thank you for your kindness & help at the rehearsals & Concert: it was delightful to be with you again after the sad break in my life: such friendly acts as yours go far to soften the very trying conditions of life.
>   Best regards
>   Yours sincerely
>   Edward Elgar

On 9 May both Elgar and Wood were at the Aeolian Hall for the first performance of a string quartet composed by Fritz Kreisler. Conspicuously, Wood continued to attend other artists' performances: on an October day in 1922 he was spotted at Nellie Chaplin's exposition of old dances and music in the afternoon, and at an early evening organ recital at Westminster Cathedral, before going on to direct his promenade concert at Queen's Hall! If he did not make the journey to Glastonbury in Somerset, where the composer Rutland Boughton was trying to establish a national music-drama based as much on socialist ideals as on Bayreuth's example, he at least found it worth encouragement. Wood's name went forward with those of Elgar, Thomas Hardy and Bernard Shaw in support of an appeal in 1919 for £10,000 to build a permanent festival theatre at Glastonbury. The appeal failed miserably.

Having squeezed Bartók's Suite no.1 into his 1914 promenade concerts (see p.149), Wood repeated it in 1920. Next year he gave the Rhapsody no.1 in the version for piano and orchestra, Auriol Jones being the soloist. Two years later Bartók himself arrived in England to find his reputation much enhanced, thanks in part to the advocacy of the critic Cecil Gray – who, as a teenager, had been catapulted into music by the single, shattering experience of hearing Wood conduct Wagner. Bartók presented himself both as pianist and composer in a London recital with Jelly d'Arányi, a much-admired Hungarian violinist resident in Britain, and then called on Wood at Queen's Hall on Sunday 25 March to leave with him the score of his *Four Pieces*, op. 12. In a letter Wood expressed his 'deepest interest' in the work with a hope to perform it in the following season. For whatever reason, he failed to·do so, but won a considerable success for Bartók with the British première of the *Dance Suite* at the promenade concerts in 1925.

The music of Bartók's fellow-Hungarian Ernö Dohnányi became more quickly familiar to London audiences. He was the piano soloist in his own *Variations on a Nursery Song* when Wood introduced this work – long to remain a favourite – at a Queen's Hall symphony concert on 27 January 1923. In the previous promenade season another work was introduced which took a deep hold on British audiences: Ernest Bloch's *Schelomo* (*Solomon*) for cello (May Mukle) and orchestra. Wood remained a keen advocate of Bloch's music, including the *Israel* Symphony, and Bloch himself was among the musicians welcomed as a visitor to Henry and Muriel Wood's country home, Appletree Farm.

Not all the most significant new works were coming to birth within the domain of the symphony orchestra or, indeed, that of the conventional chamber concert. The British composition which best seized the spirit of the impertinent, iconoclastic early Twenties was *Façade* by the twenty-one-year-old William Walton, on near-nonsensical verses by Edith Sitwell. Arthur Bliss, eleven years older, had similarly experimented with a small instrumental ensemble and a nonsense text in *Rout*, but embraced the full orchestra in his *Mêlée Fantasque*, which he himself was to conduct at a promenade concert. The preparation aroused his admiration for Wood as 'a man free of conceit or megalomania, one wholly devoted to music, and generous to those younger and less secure than himself':

> The rehearsal schedule of the Promenades in 1921 was like some nightmare jigsaw puzzle. How Henry Wood managed to complete his long and exhausting programmes in the short hours of preparation allotted remains a miracle to me: yet skimping the better-known works he would allow the younger composer the fullest measure of time he could. There was one endearing feature he showed at performance; as I nervously waited to go on the platform he would hold me back: 'Just a moment till I get to my seat' he would say, and then bounding up to the dress circle he would sit overlooking the first violins and watch your performance. It gave me a warm feeling of support. It was Henry Wood who, two years later, sent me a telegram to Gloucester when I was rehearsing the performance of my *Colour Symphony* telling me he wanted to include the work in one of his forthcoming symphony concerts: and this *before* the performance [conducted by Bliss himself] had taken place, a performance that bitterly disappointed me. When I think of the arrogant attitude of some other 'famous' conductors in their dealings with me I gladly pay tribute to this warmhearted and dedicated man.

War's legacy of hostility between the nations took some time to heal. The founding of the International Society for Contemporary Music in 1922 – at Salzburg, following an international festival of modern chamber music there – would rightly be considered a landmark. Preceding it by a year, a notable orchestral festival at Zurich would give Wood the compliment of appearing alongside his idol, Nikisch. It was the first time such a festival had been held in Zurich, and the local orchestra was augmented for the occasion. Bruno Walter conducted opera (*Parsifal* and Mozart's *Die Entführung aus dem Serail*) and Nikisch the first two orchestral concerts. The French conductor-composer Gabriel Pierné was entrusted with the third concert and Wood with the fourth (5 July 1921), a final concert being conducted by Volkmar Andreae, the resident conductor at Zurich.

Wood's concert began with Weber's *Oberon* overture and ended with Tchaikovsky's *Francesca da Rimini*, enclosing a threesome of British works – Wood's own *Purcell* Suite (compiled from the earlier composer's stage works and string sonatas), Elgar's *Enigma Variations*, and George Butterworth's *A Shropshire Lad*. Among Britons, Butterworth's death in the recent war had lent to this work a halo comparable to that conferred on Rupert Brooke's 'If I should die, think only this of me. . .'. The reviewer in the *Neue Zürcher Zeitung* found in it a 'folk-like melancholy' which might

173

remind one of the shepherd's piping in *Tristan und Isolde*. Wood's choice of programme and his conducting alike roused the reviewer's enthusiasm. As to Weber's overture, 'never has the tenderness of the elfin march been more purely and daintily conveyed in musical tones', and in the sounding of Oberon's horn and the evoking of tempestuous passion Wood showed himself 'the most delicate of poets'.

Characteristically (and significantly enough for the Swiss critic to note it), Wood insisted on sharing plaudits with the orchestra:

> The tumultuous applause refused to die down until the renowned guest, unselfishly acknowledging our orchestra – which, indeed, fully deserved this tribute for its truly admirable work during these days – had taken one bow after another. The ovation was the reward for an artist who showed himself capable of combining truly fiery and rousing energy with that most subtle delicacy which gives the smallest detail its rightful significance and importance – an artist, moreover, who is capable of bringing the works he conducts to life in their full and vital concentration and yet far transcending any earthy realism, entirely in the spirit of art of the noblest sort. Zurich will remember him and his great gifts with a feeling of gratitude.

Wood and Nikisch were travelling-companions for part of their homeward journey. 'When we parted on the quay at Ostend' Wood received from Nikisch, as from a teacher, a saying that he quoted *twice* in *My Life of Music*: 'Make all your performances a grand improvisation!' Nikisch died five months later, remaining in Wood's pantheon as 'the most inspired of all conductors'.

The Zurich Festival gave Wood a taste for Swiss scenery, not least in its inspiration to an amateur painter. He would make many further visits to Switzerland on holiday. But his professional engagements in foreign parts were to remain comparatively rare, to be planned and treated as matters of special prestige. His provincial calendar was, on the contrary, a vessel for perpetual replenishment. He continued his commitment to Brand Lane's enterprise in Manchester, presenting orchestral programmes of a more mixed and occasionally more operatic type than those promoted by the Hallé Orchestra. Mascagni's *Cavalleria Rusticana*, as part of such a concert in January 1921, made the critic of the *Manchester Guardian* 'conscious of a regret that Sir Henry Wood had not devoted his gifts as a conductor entirely to opera. For such vividness and directness are what we mean when we speak of anything as essentially dramatic, and these are gifts which are so innate with Sir Henry Wood that we can never forgo them.'

Such powerful, long-remembered singers as the soprano Florence Austral, the tenor Frank Mullings and the bass Norman Allin were engaged for these concerts at Manchester's Free Trade Hall. The instrumental soloists who played concertos with Wood were of no lesser rank – the pianists including Busoni, Egon Petri, Frederick Lamond and Moiseiwitsch, the violinists Bronislaw Huberman and young, dazzling Jascha Heifetz, who had only lately (1920) made his London début. Wood received a cordial letter from the former Jessie Goldsack, now Mrs John Linton, residing in the Cheshire area just south of Manchester, inviting him to make their house his overnight base – an offer he declined, as it had become his habit to return to London by railway sleeping-car.

The locally recruited New Brand Lane Symphony Orchestra was advertised as 'the largest professional orchestra in the kingdom'. But for what Brand Lane considered his most important orchestral concerts the Hallé Orchestra itself with its more refined musicianship was hired and put at Wood's disposal. On 21 January 1921 Richard Strauss as guest conductor shared a concert with Wood; on 8 April Wood was ill and was replaced as conductor by Frank Bridge. New or newish works were not easily admitted by Brand Lane's commercial enterprise, but Delius's pre-war *Brigg Fair* was heard on 6 January 1923 – in an evening of no less than twenty orchestral pieces, constituting 'something like a record for a Manchester programme', as the *Manchester Guardian* mildly observed. At a time when its critic was the revered Samuel Langford, the appreciative reviews in that newspaper show what a distinctive counterpoint to the Hallé Orchestra's own concerts was woven by Wood. The Hallé's concerts, in turn, were broadened and polished after the appointment in 1920 of Hamilton Harty as conductor.

At Liverpool, where the Philharmonic Orchestra continued not to engage any titular chief, Wood's guest engagements continued. The first British performance of Rachmaninoff's *The Bells* (that massive choral setting of Edgar Allan Poe, the text translated into Russian and then back-translated) had been frustrated by the war but now took place in Liverpool on 15 March 1921. According to Stainton de B. Taylor, the historian of Liverpool's music:

> Misprints and almost unreadable passages in the Russian choral and orchestral parts caused many difficulties, and there was a near-disastrous breakdown at one point. But Sir Henry was never a man to be outdone, and six years later he retrieved everyone's honour by a repeat performance at which all went well – in the mean time more civilized parts, with the English words properly printed instead of being badly written in, had materialized.

Broadening

The Liverpool Philharmonic Choir spent almost two seasons preparing Bach's Mass in B minor for a performance scheduled to be conducted by Wood in March 1923, but after several visits to rehearsals Wood insisted on postponement until the following December. It was typical of Wood that he should also give Liverpool its first-ever Mahler symphony (no.4) in November 1922 and its first hearing of Skryabin's Symphony no.2 the previous January.

Occasionally, a local promoter would invite Wood to take the Queen's Hall Orchestra to a provincial centre. At the De Montfort Hall in Leicester on 3 February 1921 the programme included a new work by a Leicestershire composer, who (Wood suggested) should conduct it himself. And so he did. The work was an *Allegro impetuoso* subtitled *An Impression of a Windy Day* and the composer was Malcolm Sargent, aged twenty-five. Wood subsequently brought the piece to Queen's Hall (11 October 1921), Sargent again conducting. So Wood's future successor as the emperor of the promenade concerts made his bow there in the primary role of composer.

London, Manchester, Liverpool – all these were major centres where Wood could expect full fees, major professional orchestras and appropriate publicity. All the more remarkable, amid the plethora of such engagements, that he should have accepted in 1923 the conductorship of an amateur orchestra in the East Yorkshire city of Hull. A letter arrived asking him to propose terms for taking over a single concert when the local conductor had fallen ill. He took the concert; the local man died and Wood was asked to stay on for the remaining two concerts of the season. Then, season by season, he was re-engaged until giving it up in 1938/9. It was a commitment of great generosity, particularly because he appears never to have pushed up the fee agreed for his earliest season – 55 guineas, *including* hire of music and all other expenses. (In the mid-1930s the BBC in London paid him 100 guineas per studio concert, involving him in almost no expenses.)

Three times a year, after the regular course of weekly rehearsals under a local assistant conductor, Wood arrived at Hull's railway station, took the final rehearsal on a Thursday afternoon, and then conducted the evening concert. He also made it a practice to attend one of the intermediate rehearsals, again with no addition to his fee. Alongside the local amateurs were local professionals, some of them regularly engaged in the city's theatres and cinemas; and there were three or four London or Manchester players in crucial positions, Laurance Turner of the Hallé being engaged as leader. In his autobiography Wood thanked such fellow-musicians as Clifford

Curzon, Moiseiwitsch and Solomon for coming to play concertos in Hull on the basis of expenses only.

If the pressure of provincial engagements prevented his attending another conductor's London performance – from which he might derive useful preparation for his own – then Sanders might be asked to help. A double postcard from Elsworthy Road on 11 March 1923 not only makes it clear that Sanders would precisely understand Wood's needs, but shows the kind of self-preparation Wood undertook.

> Would you kindly buy a ticket and go to the Albert Hall next Wednesday afternoon 14th at 3 p.m.: buy also a new vocal score of Mass in D Beethoven (Novello's edition). Try to get a seat in the back row of raised stalls under first tier of boxes, I should say near the chorus and orchestra where you can see Sir Hugh Allen's beat. I want you to mark any rocky points – to see if you think the 3/2 *Et vitam* too fast, etc; and the six crotchet beats in the *Grave* too slow. Carrie Tubb is fairly safe. I have given a lot of lessons to Margaret Balfour and I think she will be the best in the quartet – the bass I don't know *but I believe he is a very bad musician*. I want all the critical information about this performance from a conductor's point of view as I think we are going to have the same cast at the Norwich Festival, except of course that [Robert] Radford will be the bass. Be sure and charge me for all your time and expenses, ticket, etc., and if your engagements cannot allow you to attend *never mind* in the least. I am conducting in the Provinces every night next week.

The confidentiality of Wood's tone, from an eminent musician to a lowly one, is also surely remarkable. Sir Hugh Allen, conductor of the (London) Bach Choir, had become director of the Royal College of Music and professor of music at Oxford; he was exactly of Wood's age and would contribute an admiring preface to *My Life of Music*.

Scarcely less self-sacrificing in nature than the commitment to Hull, and far more demanding of his time, was Wood's acceptance of the direction of the student orchestra at the Royal Academy of Music. Beginning in 1923 by directing only one of the twice-weekly rehearsals, he eventually took on both, regarding his Wednesday and Friday afternoons as dedicated to that task throughout the academic terms. The work extended also to the training of student conductors. That one of his eminence should shoulder such responsibility – not giving it up until his last years – was, and is, unparalleled. Thoroughness was his motto. It was reported that he kept the students for a whole term on the overture to *Oberon*, interchanging every individual part among the strings and among the wind.

THE

Royal Philharmonic Society.

OCTOBER 30th, 1921.

MEDAL PRESENTATION.

ORDER OF PROCEEDINGS.

Address by SIR ALEXANDER C. MACKENZIE.

Presentation of Medal by

H.R.H. PRINCESS BEATRICE

to

SIR HENRY J. WOOD.

Vote of Thanks to H.R.H. PRINCESS BEATRICE
Moved by THE LADY SWAYTHLING
Seconded by LADY COOPER.

Vote of Thanks to SIR ALEXANDER C. MACKENZIE
Moved by PROF. SIR HUGH P. ALLEN
Seconded by MR. NORMAN O'NEILL.

Vote of Thanks to the ARTISTES
Moved by SIR ALEXANDER C. MACKENZIE
Seconded by MR. LANDON RONALD.

The Academy conferred a fellowship on Wood in 1920, the Royal College of Music an honorary fellowship in 1923. In that year too came an honorary doctorate in music from Manchester University, Oxford following suit in 1926, Birmingham in 1927 and Cambridge in 1935. But of all honours none can have pleased him more than the gold medal of the Royal Philharmonic Society – then, as now, the highest salute of musicians to a fellow-musician. Queen Victoria's youngest daughter, Princess Beatrice, presented it to him, at a small ceremony in the Grafton Gallery (on 30 October 1921) which he sealed by conducting Wagner's *Siegfried Idyll* in its original miniature orchestration. In 1920 he had been awarded the Order of the Crown of Belgium and in 1926, perhaps at the prompting of the French violinist Jacques Thibaud, France too made him an officer of the Légion d'honneur.

When he found a British composer to believe in, Wood was ready to back that composer with considerable force. The most notable case is that of Dorothy Howell – today a virtually unknown name, deleted from *Grove's Dictionary* in its newest (1980) edition. Twenty-one years old (born 25 February 1898), she had studied at the Royal Academy of Music and was pursuing a joint career as pianist and composer. As performer she received in mid-June 1919 the standard typewritten letter addressed by Robert Newman (on behalf of the Queen's Hall Orchestra, proprietors Messrs Chappell & Co. Ltd) inviting her to audition at Queen's Hall as a pianist.

But a few days later a letter from Wood to 'Dear Miss Howell' made it clear that her gift as composer had taken precedence: 'I have put down *Lamia* for the promenade concerts.' A further letter was dated 14 August 1919: 'I should be glad if you would run over the score with me.' With the première fixed for 10 September, she was invited to come to 4 Elsworthy Road on the preceding day for a 'piano rehearsal' (which must have been a further consultative session on how the score should go). An orchestral rehearsal, perhaps not the first, presumably took place on the day of the concert. Wood could have taken no greater care in preparation had it been the most celebrated composer in Europe instead of a novice.

'All musical London is talking about Miss Dorothy Howell, the girl composer, whose symphonic poem *Lamia* created such an instantaneous effect at Queen's Hall,' wrote the *Daily Express* two days afterwards. Such was the flexibility of arrangements at the promenade concerts that Wood repeated the work three days later in the traditionally popular programme of a Saturday night (13 September). Moreover he put it down also for his Sunday series (where new works were practically unknown) on 5 October, playing it at both the afternoon and evening concerts.

Broadening

Between the repetitions came a social engagement which placed the young woman on the highest pedestal of acceptance: 'So glad you can come to lunch with us tomorrow [25 September] – besides my wife, my oldest friend Mr Shaw-Baker [Schwabacher] and Miss [Myra] Hess have promised to come. Café Royal. . .1.30 p.m.'

Later Wood reported to Dorothy Howell that *Lamia* had been 'a very great success' in his performance at a Liverpool Philharmonic Society concert (30 October) and on 3 February 1920 he wrote to her again: 'I am *so* glad you can be present at Birmingham on Wednesday evening for the performance of *Lamia*. Don't expect much – the orchestra is not good.'

This projected Birmingham performance had to be 'postponed', but Wood gave *Lamia* instead at a concert of the Birmingham Festival Choral Society in the following December. Acknowledging the composer's dedication of the work to him, he wrote: 'It is my little baby, in a way, and I want to always give it a chance whenever I can.'

He was likewise to give first performances, at the promenade concerts, of her *Koong Shee* (1921), described as a ballet though never produced as such; a piano concerto (1923), in which she herself was soloist; and another orchestral work, *The Rock* (1928). In 1924, having begun his commitment to orchestral training at the Royal Academy of Music, Wood wrote to Howell (though she was well past her student period):

> Dear Miss Howell,
>   As you know, I have wanted you for some years past to direct one of your compositions with the Queen's Hall Orchestra. Could I not persuade you just to join the conductors' class at the RAM for it would take up very little of your time, and you would get the necessary experience, and then in 1925 you could conduct at the Promenade Concerts for me. So far, we have no ladies in the conductors' class at the RAM which I think is a great pity.
>   With kind regards,
>   Sincerely yours,
>   Henry J. Wood

She never did conduct at Queen's Hall, however. That she achieved only a small output as a composer cannot be ascribed to lack of encouragement. Henry J. Wood continued to perform her music, and the score of *Lamia*, at least, invites scrutiny today. In a signed and framed testimonial, now at the Royal Academy of Music, from 'the younger school of British composers' congratulating Wood in 1919 on twenty-five years of promenade concerts,

Dorothy Howell's name is among the signatories with others including Delius, Vaughan Williams, Bridge, Holst and Bantock.

The 1922 promenade concerts opened with 'a prolonged and affectionate roar' for Wood on his entrance, the *Monthly Musical Record* also observing that 'the so-called "promenade" more nearly resembled a packing-case'. The same commentator noted 'the rare sound of hissing' when Darius Milhaud's Second Symphonic Suite was found over-discordant. Wood extended the repertory backwards as well as forwards. Few at Queen's Hall on 17 August 1922 could have heard previously *any* Monteverdi when he delivered the *Sonata sopra 'Sancta Maria'* for organ and orchestra, taken from the *Vespers* of 1610. (The *Monthly Musical Record*, evidently anxious not to get out of its depth, noted it as 'interesting mainly on antiquarian grounds'.) The 1918 Proms season had included an *Ave Maria* doubtfully ascribed to the Flemish composer Arcadelt (d. 1568) – a vocal work which Liszt had transcribed for piano and for organ, and which now appeared in Wood's own orchestral version.

Among those who attended the promenade season of 1922 was the novelist Arnold Bennett, a keen music-lover and the librettist for two operas by Eugene Goossens. His frequent companion was the musician he called 'the other A.B.' – not Adrian Boult, but Arnold Bax. Bennett's lively published diaries make several references to the pianist Harriet Cohen, nicknamed 'Tania'. She 'gave an astonishing performance of his [Bax's] new concerto at the Queen's Hall on Tuesday [18 October 1922] and was recalled seven times. Such an ovation I have never before seen at a Prom.' The Bax 'concerto' was actually the Symphonic Variations, of which she had given the first performance two seasons before under Wood's baton. Arnold Bax and Harriet Cohen, for whom Bax left his wife, were frequent Sunday visitors of Henry and Muriel at Appletree Farm.

On 27 October 1922 a non-playing, non-singing, non-speaking soloist joined Henry J. Wood on the platform of Queen's Hall. The Aeolian Company had engaged Wood and his orchestra to demonstrate their player-piano in its most advanced model, the Duo-Art. The technique of perforated piano 'rolls' had been refined to reproduce not merely the composer's notes but a particular performer's expression. Harold Bauer was the pianist who had 'cut' the piano-roll of Saint-Saëns's Piano Concerto no.2, to which Wood smoothly fitted the accompaniment: 'the timing was impeccable', reported Kalisch. That type of technical innovation never seriously challenged live performance. But the concert world was to be threatened by a monster – or so radio broadcasting was perceived by some of the most powerful minds in the business of music-making. The BBC began its broadcasts in 1922, but not until five years later would Henry J. Wood participate in them.

The Birmingham Festival had never restarted since the war, but Wood continued to hold the conductorship of the Choral Society, which survived as a rump. On resigning early in 1923, he gave a strong hint that the Society should choose Adrian Boult as his successor. From a holiday address in Lausanne he wrote to 'Dear Dr Boult' on 20 June:

> Birmingham has just sent me a cutting in which I read that you have been appointed conductor of the Birmingham Festival Choral Society. I congratulate them upon securing your very valuable services, and I am glad my desires and feelings in the matter have been carried out.
>
> We leave at 9 a.m. tomorrow for our motor tour in North Italy, so shall be lost to the world for a short time.

Since neither Henry nor Muriel learnt to drive, the tour must have had the service of a chauffeur. Assuredly Henry's painting equipment was among the baggage. They were back, of course, in time for the promenade season of 1923, which began with Elgar's *Cockaigne* overture. 'All we Londoners have a feeling of pride in the "Promenades",' wrote Richard Capell in the *Monthly Musical Record*:

> We all resent the sight of a 'thin house' and rejoice on the nights when there appears to be no room for one more pair of feet on the floor, when there is not one chair-seat visible, when the tobacco clouds of the devotees show us H. J. W. and his men [and women?] vague as figures in a hashish-smoker's dream and let us quite forget the ghastly blue of the *post-bellum* Queen's Hall decoration. . .Generally of course there have been great crowds: invariably on Mondays for Wagner, on Fridays for Bach, Mozart and Beethoven, and on Saturdays for general fun.

On one Saturday of that season, 11 August 1923, Wood introduced to Britain what was to become a perennial favourite, Saint-Saëns' *Carnival of the Animals*. (The composer had restricted it to private performances, except for *The Swan*, during his lifetime: he died in 1921.) Wood kept a special corner of affection for such 'humorous' music: Gounod's *Funeral March of a Marionette* he often gave in concert and twice recorded. But woe betide the would-be 'humorist' in the orchestra. A reprimand went in May 1923 to Léon Goossens:

> . . . No one enjoys a joke more than I do, but I fear you do not realize that if

all the leaders of our woodwind department, whenever they are not playing, indulged in these humorous and dramatic asides and these little 'back-handed' conversations with their neighbours, we should have to give up concerts altogether, or I should have to ask Messrs Chappell to find another conductor for ours.

No one appreciates more than I do the buoyancy of your spirits, which I hope you may long keep, but there is a time and a place for everything, and it is certainly not either the band rehearsal or when you are under the eyes of several thousand members of an audience.

Contrite, the twenty-five-year-old offender drove to the Woods' house in Chorley Wood, found Sir Henry not in, and left a note promising to mend his ways 'if given the chance'. Which, needless to say, he was.

PART III

Battling

'Labour is the contest of the life of man with an opposite; – the term "life" including his intellect, soul and physical power, contending with question, difficulty, trial, or material force . . . and labour of good quality, in any kind, includes always as much intellect and feeling as will fully and harmoniously regulate the physical force.'

– John Ruskin, *Unto this Last*

Chapter 13

A Family Man

1924–7

Wood had since 1919 changed his appearance in photographs: he looked neater, the old floppy tie replaced by a spruce bow. But the dark beard, the felt-collared or fur-collared overcoats, the broad hat unlike the stand-up British trilby, all combined to suggest – still! – an exotic, perhaps Russian origin. (In contrast, musicians such as Stanford, Elgar, Edward German and Wood's fellow-conductor Sir Dan Godfrey had the image of the British country solicitor or retired army officer.) Away from concerts and festivals, Wood might be photographed in cheerful informality, hatless and jacket-less in the garden of Appletree Farm; if his wife Muriel appears, she will be hatted, erect, taller than he. (She was five foot nine inches to his five foot eight according to their 1920 passports; his 1924 passport unbelievably gives him only five foot four.)

The three-storied London house at 4 Elsworthy Road was commodious, a place where Henry could not only work on his scores but receive his singing pupils in a first-floor studio. On the same floor were the matrimonial bedroom, a spare bedroom, and Muriel's 'boudoir' (as her daughter Tania called it in conversation with the present writer). Downstairs were the dining-room and the large drawing-room (the latter containing a full-size concert grand piano), with double doors leading to the garden. On the top floor, as well as Wood's library, were the children's day nursery, night nursery, servants' and governess's rooms. As Tania was to recall, there were 'a living-in cook, a living-in house-parlourmaid, a daily housemaid and a daily kitchenmaid'. The function of a governess seems to have been mainly to talk French to the girls.

Almost adjacent to the house stood the church of St Mary the Virgin – though, as an observer put it, the family 'rarely if ever darkened its doors'. (Not surprisingly, perhaps, in view of Henry J. Wood's adherence to Rationalist principles.) The Woods' younger daughter Avril later set down her memories of schoolgirl life:

Escorted by a series of French and Swiss governesses, I used to cross Primrose Hill and Regent's Park every morning to attend, in company with numerous doctors' children from Harley Street, the Open Air Kindergarten School which was held on the verandah of the large conservatory which stood in the middle of what was then the Royal Botanical Gardens, and is now Queen Mary's Garden.

There was quite a country village atmosphere in Elsworthy Road in those days – the butcher's boy in striped apron and straw boater going up the road at a fast trot in a high dogcart, singing at the top of his voice as he delivered the meat from house to house: the white-aproned muffin man with his bell and his wares piled high on a linen-covered tray balanced on his head walking down the road on winter afternoons: the postman delivering letters 4 times a day (!): frequent telegrams to my father (who conducted a great deal of his business by telegram) delivered at the door at all hours by a small telegraph boy on a bicycle wearing a blue pillbox hat. If needed, he would wait at the door to take the telegraphed reply back to the Post Office. Most of our household shopping was done in England's Lane, and most of the shops must have delivered to the house for I never remember carrying loaded shopping baskets (or sitting in pram or pushchair surrounded by bags and parcels) down the hill, as we would certainly have to do now. My parents banked at Barclays on the corner of England's Lane, and my impression is that the manager of the day called on them when they had any business to transact, rather than them calling on *him*. . . .

We were burgled one night, the thieves forcing an entry through the skylight on the top landing, and climbing down the fire-escape ladder on the nursery floor. They must have been remarkably skilled for no-one in the house was roused – children, governess, maids, or my parents sleeping on the floor below, and they got away with two fur coats of my mother's and, strangely, an assortment of gramophone records (*very* heavy things to carry in those pre-electric, pre-long-playing days!) and they managed to force the door of my father's music library on the top floor where they created havoc by pulling hundreds of orchestral parts out of the shelves and scattering them all over the floor, presumably in search of money or jewels. My father's music librarian was reported to have burst into tears when confronted with the scene next day and swore that it would take him six months to get the parts back into order and on the shelves again. . . .

Parked outside No.4 stood our enormous Renault 'landaulette' (we always had to have a car with a roof which let down at the back since my mother insisted on being able 'to see the tops of the trees' while she was being driven along) usually waiting to take my father down to the Queen's Hall for a rehearsal or a concert. Our chauffeur was in fact a 'chauffeuse' (but always dressed in the conventional dark blue uniform, with skirt not trousers, but with a stiff peaked cap). My father (who was an early supporter of Women's Lib – he was the first conductor in this country to introduce women players into the professional orchestra) always maintained that women were more punctual and more reliable as drivers than men, and punctuality was an obsession with him. He was never a minute late for anything. . . .

As children we never knew, of course, what the neighbours thought of the distinguished but noisy resident at No.4. When he was at home my father spent hours of the day pounding on the piano in his first-floor music room, either going through his scores for the next day's rehearsal or accompanying his many singing pupils. These pupils' often excruciating vocal exercises must have penetrated clearly to the outside world but, so far as I know, we never had any complaints from any of the other residents. They must have been a kind and tolerant lot, as I have no doubt they still are today. . . .

Appletree Farm House (it had been a genuine old farmhouse) was used mainly as the Woods' extended summer residence, from about Easter each year. With less extensive accommodation than the London house, it still allowed Henry a study of his own, but Muriel's business-desk was placed in the drawing-room – a cause for Henry's subsequent irritation. (In later years, to escape a certain amount of domestic friction, he tended during the eight-week promenade concert season to spend weekday nights in London at the Langham Hotel, returning to Appletree only after the Saturday concert.) Muriel absorbed herself in cultivating her garden, gaining advice and help from her friend the celebrated garden-designer Gertrude Jekyll, a woman much older than she (1848–1932).

To Henry, Appletree gave the opportunity of indulging in his hobbies of painting and heavy carpentry. Tania recalled her school-age pleasure in helping him. 'He liked things solid . . . I used to hold the end of the bit of things he was sawing, and things like that.' In the great barn where the family entertained large parties on summer Sundays, the cross-beams for a large window had been carpentered by Wood himself from disused railway sleepers. His younger daughter Avril, recording for the BBC in 1975, enlarged on the scene:

> He had turned one of the small barns into a very well-equipped carpenter's shop and he would spend hours there, standing in shirt sleeves and often singing loudly to himself in a rather raucous voice – sawing away at huge railway sleepers for a staircase he was making to reach to an upper gallery in the big barn which he had turned into a very fine music room. He had had a parquet floor put in and had himself made a vast window to the barn and this was the scene of the large parties which my parents gave throughout the summer, and to which came, I suppose, in the course of the years, almost every famous musician of the day. I certainly remember such

illustrious people as Janáček, Kodály, Bloch and Hindemith, and there were certainly many others. My father was a most enthusiastic and lively host, trotting about the place with bottles of hock – his favourite wine – for the guests and climbing into a pair of frightful old once-white flannels to play appalling games of tennis with anyone foolish enough to join him.

I once, at the age of about eleven, took a photograph, which I treasure to this day, of Sir Adrian Boult and my father and Dame Ethel Smyth (in a large straw hat with a velvet bow, a manly-looking shirt and a long skirt) standing on our tennis court holding their rackets and having obviously finished one of those dreadful sets. My father was a rabbit on the court and missed the ball more often than he hit it but each time he made an even worse shot than usual he would relapse into helpless fits of laughter, tears would pour down his face and we would all have to stop while he got out a large handkerchief, mopped his eyes and regained some kind of composure. This performance greatly irritated poor Dame Ethel, his partner, who rather fancied herself as a player, and she would reprove him sternly – 'Oh, Henry, there's *nothing* to laugh at – stop it at once and let's try to concentrate on winning the game!' Because of him, they very rarely did!

Tania was to maintain in 1991 that the failure to mention their harmonious childhood was a grave blemish in Pound's biography. A Swiss family holiday, in which her father essayed the gentle art of tobogganing, remained a happy memory. But Tania's mother told her that it was she, not he, who wanted children. Seeking no contact with his numerous relatives on his father's side, Wood did not speak of them to his daughters: Tania was astonished, when the present writer revealed it to her in 1993, to learn how large that family was. The girls were allowed to grow up supposing that Tania owed her Russian name to being born on a night when her father had been deputising as conductor for Tchaikovsky himself – though Tchaikovsky had in fact died nine years earlier. Avril repeated the error in a broadcast talk; Tania learnt only from the present writer the true derivation of her name, from that of Tchaikovsky's operatic heroine (see p.27).

Musically gifted, Avril was sent in the autumn of 1925 to join the Saturday morning Junior class at the Royal Academy of Music, her piano teacher being none other than Dorothy Howell – to whom Wood wrote on 28 September:

> My wife and I are *so* delighted to learn that our little daughter, Avril, is joining your class at the R.A.M. . I think you will find her a good little worker and keen, but of course she is only 10.
>
> I am very keen upon her becoming a good *all-round musician*, and I am so happy you are able to take charge of her.
>
> My wife joins me in kindest regards.

Tania, though she started going to Saturday promenade concerts at the age of six and grew to love the privilege and bustle of the artists' room, was marked down not for music but for painting or sculpture. From about the time when she was fifteen, Henry pushed this supposed destiny with increasing obsessiveness, as she was to recall: 'I used to have *Film Weekly* delivered to the house and I had to make sure I was downstairs to get it first; otherwise my father tore it to shreds the minute he saw it. . . . He said the only thing I should read was the lives of the great artists. His bedside reading was. . . purely music stuff; I don't believe he ever read a novel in his life.'

She went, for one afternoon a week while she was still at school, to the Slade School of Art, then full-time to the Royal College of Art – failing to accumulate sufficient work to pass the examination, and later ascribing that failure to the demands made on her as her father's driver. Her own inclination was to craftwork, not fine art, but this would not have satisfied her ambitious father.

For himself, as hardly needs emphasising, work was the object of a total dedication; he would have regarded anything less as weakness. Muriel Wood accepted that concentration and served it but she could not share it. It is not surprising if she felt driven into herself. She deserves more sympathy than she is given in Reginald Pound's biography. A less forbidding portrait is drawn in a typed memoir by the singer Dora Foss (née Stevens), wife of Hubert J. Foss of Oxford University Press's music department. That firm was shortly to publish Henry J. Wood's remarkable treatise, *The Gentle Art of Singing* (1927). The sociable contact was ripened when the Fosses moved to become neighbours of Henry and Muriel at Chorley Wood in 1929.

My dear Mrs Foss
   A note seems a silly sort of way to welcome you to the neighbourhood, but I can't think of any other as your garden is sure to be full of flowers, so just let me say that we hope you will be as happy at Nightingale Corner as we have been at Appletree Farm and that we shall see you more often than one sees one's neighbours. (*What* a sentence to send to someone connected with the OUP!)
   With *very* best wishes
    Yours v. sincerely
    Muriel Wood

Muriel Wood was 'not an easy person to know', wrote Dora Foss:

. . . She appeared austere and aloof at first sight, but Hubert and I were allowed, for some reason, behind the barriers of her reserve and we loved

her for her thoughtfulness for us and for her loyal friendship and we revelled
in her slightly salty wit and her sprightly and discerning comments on the
many and varied people who crossed her path. We admired her too for her
unswerving devotion to her husband and all his activities.

Dora Foss's observations as quoted in Pound's biography add up to
something of an adverse portrayal. But she left an annotated copy of the
relevant pages of that book, claiming some of her phrases to have been
misquoted.

The garden, tended by Muriel, was remembered for 'the largest, most
brilliant and quite perfect flowers' – sheets of daffodils, bluebells, roses 'and
madly tall and exotic lilies'. No less vividly remembered were Sir Henry's
'merry, twinkling blue eyes' and his 'small, rather plump' figure when Dora
Foss was first welcomed by the Woods to Appletree Farm. At the Sunday
parties ('every Sunday in summer, if Sir Henry was at home'), Dora Foss
noted 'the invasion of the well-known in the musical world'. Just inside the
wide door of the great barn stood a huge round table with a delicious tea-time
spread, where Muriel presided, with Tania and Avril as 'attendant under-
hostesses'. The girls, in Dora Foss's recollection, had little opportunity as
they moved into their teens to invite friends of their own age. It was Sir
Henry's circle, with Muriel 'keeping a guardian angel's eye on her husband.
He was never allowed even to have the chance of sitting in a draught, and
scarves and coats were always at hand in case a breeze arose or the
temperature fell.'

It sounds like a protective, even over-protective regime for the
conductor. Muriel cocooned his private life. 'He took no interest in his home,
really,' Tania was to recall. 'He expected everybody to run round after him
the whole time, and that's what we were for! . . . Our entire home life was
geared to his music; never was anything else to be even considered to be of
importance.' At the age of seventeen, whatever might have been a young
woman's desire for independence, Tania willy-nilly became her father's
car-driver, allowing him to save the expense of a professional chauffeuse. As
for business, that was entirely Muriel's domain: he wanted nothing to do
with money.

He signed, in advance, whole books of blank cheques for Muriel to dispose
of. A similar method was likewise applied to correspondence. 'She would
open the letters and read them to him, write notes in shorthand and then she
would write the [answering] letters – he would never see them again,' since
he had placed his signature in advance on blank sheets of notepaper. Right up
to the 1990s Tania kept some of these signed (and otherwise blank) sheets,

some with the signature well up the page so as to suit a short letter. The consequence is (let the biographer beware!) that a typed letter 'signed' by Henry cannot be assumed to be such – unless the typing is also the work of Henry, distinguished by its irregular spelling and punctuation.

A highly capable businesswoman ('Today she would be a top executive,' Tania claimed in 1990), Muriel was minimally interested in housekeeping. She hated shopping, did no needlework (except darning); 'she was never interested in running a home; she didn't cook – couldn't make a cup of tea.' In volunteering that information Tania added loyally that a woman of her mother's class in the 1920s would expect servants to do that kind of work for her. But with her imperious ways she was inefficient in managing and retaining servants, and domestic amenities suffered. The memory of being occasionally forced to go out for a meal to a teashop in nearby Rickmansworth rankled heavily in her husband's later catalogue of grievances.

By bicycle from the post office at Rickmansworth, some three miles away, a succession of telegrams was delivered at Appletree Farm by messenger-boys, one of whom in 1990 still remembered Wood 'always in a grey suit with a big floppy bow tie', painting in the garden or, hammer in hand, repairing fences. 'He often gave me a sixpenny tip and sometimes apples.' Lady Wood 'never gave a tip'.

In the public gaze, Wood was already an institution – too much so, perhaps; too liable to be considered part of the very fabric of Queen's Hall, especially during promenade seasons. The thirtieth such season was reached in 1924. How often, in the diaries of the music-addicted poet Siegfried Sassoon, comes a record of hearing Bach, Handel, or other composers at Queen's Hall, with no mention of Wood's presence at all!

His players, of course, were ever conscious of his methods of command. At rehearsal he would often hand the baton to Charles Woodhouse, his leader since 1920, while he himself listened from the back of the hall, interrupting with a peremptory bell. The violist Bernard Shore joined the Queen's Hall Orchestra in 1922 and left vivid recollections of Wood in his deservedly popular book of 1937, *The Orchestra Speaks*:

> With much to be rehearsed there is not time for a moment's relaxation between the pieces. As one comes to an end he announces the next, and he is away again before the horns can empty their instruments. Working at this terrific pressure, he yet loses his temper extraordinarily rarely, even when tried to the limits of human endurance.
>   . . .When really pressed for time and his singers are due to rehearse

their aria at 12.41, Sir Henry will at 12.39 exclaim with penetrating voice, whilst still playing: 'M—s, get the singers ready!' And precisely at 12.41 they will be pushed on the platform, with the last chord still echoing round the hall, and the stick upheld for the aria.

. . . Few conductors, if any, help their players so much; whenever possible he looks at the player at the very moment when he needs a lead, his left hand ever ready to emphasize it. He never forgets a bad mistake. If once a department fails at an entry, through a miscount of bar or any other reason, that department may be sure that when next the work is performed the conductor's eye will be upon it like a hawk's. And these particular players will probably have eyes, stick, left hand and the whole of Sir Henry's body focussed upon them, if the original catastrophe was a bad one.

Shore recalled a rehearsal of Beethoven's Symphony no.8 when Wood's handbell rang out at bar 23 as the players were negotiating a 'black patch' – a cluster of rapid notes which looks very dense in the music-copy: 'I don't hear that black patch – it must be played with the utmost ferocity. I want a tearing *fortissimo*. Don't be afraid of it. You're always so nervous at a black patch because it looks black on paper. Don't be nervous – I'm never nervous! Rip it out and make the old ladies jump!'

Instructions like 'Make the old ladies jump!' were fondly remembered by Wood's former orchestral players when they were interviewed by the author of this book more than fifty years later. Gerald Jackson's auto-biography, *First Flute*, recalls the orchestral players anticipating the remark by calling it out, to which Wood retorted (rehearsing the end of Liszt's second piano concerto), 'It's a pity, since you know it so well, that you can't play it a bit better.'

His principal harpist from 1922, Marie Goossens, recalled other Woodisms at rehearsal, 'General crescendo!' and 'Logical retard!' – the latter, she commented, 'has remained in my memory and has helped so much in playing and teaching'. Bernard Shore was to quote Wood's phrase 'It shows – it shows!' as an explanation why a Haydn symphony with its apparent simplicity of texture had to be rehearsed in the most thorough detail, while the Tchaikovsky *Pathétique* could if necessary be performed entirely without rehearsal.

Henry J. Wood was the least literary or intellectual of conductors, so it is surprising – and a tribute to his authority – that a distinctive one-volume *Dictionary of Modern Music and Musicians* (1924) should bear his name as one of the editorial committee. The others were Sir Hugh P. Allen and Edward J. Dent, professors respectively at Oxford and Cambridge; the composer Granville Bantock; and the practical working editor, Arthur Eaglefield-Hull. Though soon to be outdated, the *Dictionary* vividly illumines the musical world of its period.

There is no entry for *Conducting,* on which Wood's views would have commanded great interest. Nor is there an entry on *Orchestration* as such. But Wood's six-column article headed 'Orchestral Colour and Values' is one of the longest in the book. Eaglefield-Hull may have guided Wood's hand, amplifying here and modifying there, but Wood's is certainly the initial distinction between a painter's and a composer's mixture of colours (the former is a blend, the latter is not). He continues with an attack on 'the so-called black-and-white test', by which an orchestral work was supposed to be judged good if it sounded well on the piano.

> The orchestral works of the older masters do indeed sound well on the pianoforte, which is a colourless instrument, because their significance is mainly a matter of form and design. . . . [But] some of the most beautiful modern orchestral compositions convey nothing, or worse than nothing, when they are arranged as four-handed pieces for the pianoforte. The fact is that the colour, obtained from the orchestra but not from the piano, can entirely change harmonic ideas. Thus on the modern orchestra the most violent harmonic clashes, the juxtaposition of several keys at once, can give perfect aesthetic pleasure. Therefore the black-and-white test is discredited. As well judge a modern painting by a sketch of it! How poor and trivial, even ugly, might the drawing be of a painting that was luminous, scintillating, ethereal by the wonder of its colour! Its whole emotional, and therefore artistic, effect may have depended upon colour. Modern orchestral composition, like modern painting, does not have form and design for its only essential elements, but it is, on the contrary, mainly a matter of colour.

As modern masters of orchestral colour Wood names Strauss, Elgar, Ravel, Malipiero, Stravinsky and, more surprisingly, Delius:

> whose *Sea-Drift*, a work for soli, chorus and orchestra, is unique in the colour of its various musical combinations which truly reflect the elusiveness of Walt Whitman's poem.
>   . . .The composer of the future must not only use the orchestra in its present state of development but must expect that it will be further changed; for there is much room for improvement. The most perfectly disposed concert orchestra still has some very nasty holes in it. There is no strong tenor voice in the strings; the brass-bass needs reinforcement, the quality of the bass tuba is clumsy and hooty and does not blend with the trombone timbre. It is to be hoped that someone shortly will invent a

bright, clear-toned brass-bass instrument of good intonation which will carry down the bass-trombone scale chromatically, and which will blend perfectly with the trombone quality in chordal work. There is at present a great difficulty in carrying one streak or seam of colour up and down a long range.

'The proofs of the whole *Dictionary* have been read by all the members of this committee,' stated the preface. In Wood's case the assertion is doubtful, since the article 'Queen's Hall Orchestra' contains a conspicuous error relating to its early years and to Lamoureux. The article about Wood himself (written by Eaglefield-Hull) gives a solid documentation with the correct year of birth, and a just tribute to his pioneering of new works of the various Continental schools.

The passage quoted above which seeks to mend 'some nasty holes' in orchestral texture enshrines an important aspect of Wood's aesthetic. The constant drive to improve orchestral tone-quality involves the progressive modernization of instruments. That a commercial promoter in the 1990s should have attached the name of 'the New Queen's Hall Orchestra' to a body seeking to freeze the tone-quality to what it was before 1914 represents a comical misunderstanding of how Wood treated his orchestral palette.

Wood continued to enlarge the orchestral repertory by transcriptions from other media. A suite of three movements orchestrated from Bach's organ works (1909) he had rather presumptuously called 'Bach's Suite no.5' – the composer himself having written four. It was followed in 1916 by 'Bach's Suite no.6', six movements from a greater variety of sources including two preludes from the *Well-Tempered Clavier*, and five years later by another Bach compilation, a 'Suite in G' with a solo oboe part specially written for Léon Goossens. Few at the time denied the legitimacy of such compilations, or of Wood's *Purcell Suite*: similar suites culled from Purcell's theatre works and other pieces were produced by Arthur Bliss (1921), John Barbirolli, and others.

In a rather different category was Wood's orchestral version of Musorgsky's *Pictures at an Exhibition* – a highly coloured orchestral score, incorporating that most un-Russian of instruments, the organ. Since its wartime première, already noted, it had continued to find favour with promenade audiences. (Wood also tried out an earlier arrangement by an otherwise unknown Russian, Tushmalov.) In 1920 it also entered Wood's catalogue of recordings. It was typical of Wood's boldness that he should go beyond mere orchestration and make occasional changes in the actual bar-structure of the piece. His arrangement remained unpublished, and was understandably overtaken in public favour by Ravel's published version, more faithful to Musorgsky's actual notes, which was commissioned and first performed by Serge Koussevitzky in 1922.

A letter sent by Wood in July 1924 to Walter Damrosch, conductor of the New York Symphony Orchestra (not yet amalgamated with the New York Philharmonic), refers to another of his Musorgsky transcriptions – *Rayok* (*The Peepshow*), originally for voice and piano:

> I shall be delighted to lend you the parts of *The Musician's Peepshow*, but please do not mention anywhere who has scored it, because I have so often refused to lend these and other parts, which I keep exclusively for my own concerts at Queen's Hall, but I should very much like *you* to have them.
>
> We have both been greatly interested in your autobiography; it, and that of Dame Ethel Smyth, are far and away the most interesting records I have ever read in the musical line.

Wood continued to be invited to lend distinction to special provincial events. Emulating Bournemouth, the Sussex resort of Eastbourne supported a municipal orchestra with an annual festival as its showpiece. Henry G. Amers was its conductor, but at the final concert of the 1924 festival (29 November) he shared the conducting with Henry J. Wood, who typically offered his own Bach suite ('no.6'), Strauss's *Death and Transfiguration*, and an ever-popular *Hungarian Rhapsody* (no.2) of Liszt to finish. A different kind of guest appearance, sharing the baton with Elgar, found him at Covent Garden on 25 May 1925 in a benefit concert for one of the great prima donnas of a past generation – Emma Albani, now seventy-seven and impoverished.

Gramophone recordings of orchestral music were on a flood tide, and Wood's recording of Delius's *Dance Rhapsody* (no.1) even prompted the use of a new verb. 'As the work has been gramophoned by Sir Henry Wood and the Queen's Hall Orchestra it is probably well known,' wrote Havergal Brian in an article of 1924. Wood's contract with Columbia was renewed for a further three years from the beginning of 1925, with the fee unchanged (£105 per three-hour session, on top of a retainer) but the number of sessions per year increased from six to seven. During the next few years his records would include many short, popular works such as Rossini's *William Tell* overture and Sibelius's *Finlandia*, but also a Haydn symphony (no.94), Elgar's *Enigma Variations,* and – with Harriet Cohen, a pianist noted for Bach as well as for Bax – Bach's concerto in D minor. A full-length *Eroica* on fourteen sides atoned for an earlier, ill-advisedly abbreviated recording on six sides.

All these new recordings gained immeasurably from the process of electrical (as distinct from acoustic) recording which was just becoming standard, giving an improved orchestral fidelity. But even before this Wood had ranged himself with those who recognized the gramophone record as a precise educational tool. In a prescient address to a conference of the music industry held at Folkestone in 1924 he spoke with the serious student in mind:

> [In listening to a recorded string quartet] open your miniature score and follow the first and second violins with concentrated attention, then close your miniature score and hear these two parts only. Then repeat the record and follow from miniature score the second violin part and the viola; close the score and listen, fixing attention on these two parts only. Repeat the record, open miniature score again, and follow, with great attention, the viola and cello parts only; close the score and concentrate upon hearing these two parts by ear alone. Repeat the record: now following three parts in your score: second violin, viola and cello, covering perhaps the first violin line over with a slip of paper. Then close the score and repeat the record again, listening to the second violin, viola and cello parts, training your ear to blot out the first violin part.
>
> Finally, take your score again and repeat the whole record, now following the *four* parts. Then listen to the record again, and you will find your ear has probably become alert enough to hear the *real four parts*, no matter what melodic or contrapuntal line they may take. If you are able to do this daily for a few months you will be quite surprised at the result. I specially recommend this practice to all vocalists whose ears and hearing are too often in such a comatose condition – alas! as we vocal teachers and conductors know to our sorrow.

In the typescript from which he read this speech, Wood took the unusual step of marking the spoken prose with quasi-musical directions. The inflexion of the spoken word, and indeed phonetics generally, were of lasting interest to him.

A symphony concert conducted by Wood on 10 October 1925 unveiled Vaughan Williams's newest work, *Flos Campi*, rather obliquely based on the biblical Song of Solomon. It had the distinction of Lionel Tertis's solo viola-playing, still regarded as one of the wonders of instrumental performance. Tertis also contributed to a Wigmore Hall concert marking the recent death of the composer Gabriel Fauré, with Wood as his piano accompanist – a role he had rarely assumed since Olga's death. The prime mover of that memorial (9 June 1925) was that indefatigable octogenarian, 'Frankie' Schuster, the benefactor of Elgar. Siegfried Sassoon observed him, on that hot afternoon 'in his frock-coat, bowing over the hands of the French, Italian and Austrian ambassadors. Schuster in a flower-garden of richly- attired elderly dames of wealth and distinction – to whom he'd sold 160 seats at a guinea each. Schuster shouting "Bravi" at the end of each item. Schuster enraptured by the familiar cadences of "Soir", "Clair de Lune" etc. An exquisite concert of almost too refined music.'

Wood had long been acquainted with Schuster but the latter's cultivation of Society held no appeal for him. It is tantalizing to realize that a single step closer towards such a patron would have brought Wood within a circle which embraced such artists as Walter Sickert, John Singer Sargent and Jacob Epstein, along with the ageing Thomas Hardy and the Bloomsbury hostess (and lover of Bertrand Russell) Lady Ottoline Morrell.

The musical content of the promenade concerts was changing. It had to. The ballad, the march and similar 'light' pieces of the older type now had a decreasing appeal. The new, Americanized dance music – 'syncopated' was its label – had become the prevalent popular idiom. Eric Coates' *Moon Magic* and *Samarkand*, conducted by the composer himself, were described on the programme of 5 September 1925 as 'Two Light Syncopated Pieces', a tribute to the vogue-word. But the exponents of the new dance music broke away from the genteel tradition which could allow even so 'serious' a composer as Elgar to create a sentimental ballad like *Pleading*. By no possibility could the new popular music ('American atrocities' to Wood) take its place alongside the more weighty elements of a promenade programme, as the old kind had done. Musical taste was becoming increasingly polarised between the 'serious' (sometimes called 'classical') and 'popular' – or between 'highbrow' and 'lowbrow'.

So the programmes became yet more solid, the cultivation of a 'classical' taste more marked, with hardly more than a vestigial role for the occasional 'light' piece by such composers as Coates, Haydn Wood and Montague Phillips. Saturday programmes were still designated 'popular', and the Chappell ballad still had its place, but the Saturday opening of the 1923 season moved the *Musical Times* to observe:

> The programme was remarkable for a 'popular' night: fifteen, even ten, years ago, it would have been called 'classical'. The fact is strong proof of the educational effect the Promenade Concerts have had on their audiences. The principal numbers were Elgar's *Cockaigne* Overture, the second Pianoforte Concerto of Rachmaninoff (with Miss Myra Hess as

soloist), and Massenet's ballet music from *Le Cid*. There was also – and this too was a departure from precedent – a novelty in the programme [Saint-Saëns' *Carnival of the Animals*, as noted in the last chapter]. . .

This 'upward' trend was evident well before the BBC's take-over.

The 1924 Proms offered not only improved lighting at Queen's Hall and a renovated organ, but a change on Tuesday evenings from a popular miscellany to a 'classical' programme. Haydn, thanks to the gradual progress of the Austrian complete edition, was favoured with ten symphonies including such rarities as the *Philosopher* (no.22) and the *Horn Signal* (no.31). Bach flourished. A few years previously, in a book called *The Promenade Ticket*, it was noted that Wood made the orchestra *stand up* to play the *Brandenburg* Concerto no.3 (anticipating some post-1945 chamber orchestras). In the Brandenburg Concerto no.5 a piano rather than harpsichord was still preferred. The combination of Myra Hess with Charles Woodhouse and Robert Murchie (the orchestra's principal flute) was one of 'perfect felicity and mutual understanding', according to the critic W. R. Anderson.

The notion of the Proms as a 'repertory', a virtually self-contained, self-renewing parade of all that was most interesting in both older and newer music *of the classical kind*, seems to have established itself at this time – though without self-congratulating claims of 'first time at a Promenade concert', such as became common under BBC auspices after World War Two. The cycle of Beethoven's nine symphonies was annually delivered complete or near-complete, the Ninth (when not excluded) still coming to a stop before its choral section, no choir being on hand. In 1924 it was announced that the 'long-standing custom' of presenting the 'Nine' in chronological order would be dropped, out of regard for country-dwelling music-lovers who, if they took their holidays in London in August, would annually hear the same selection of symphonies, 'and the early ones at that'.

Never till now had a Sovereign visited the Proms. But in this thirtieth season (not, as *My Life of Music* has it, the 25th!) a packed audience was joined by King George V and Queen Mary on 15 October 1924. It was a signal honour for Wood, whose twelve-year-old daughter Tania presented a bouquet. Elgar took the baton for his *Cockaigne* and Frank Bridge for two movements from *The Sea*. Wood's own *Fantasia on British Sea Songs* was also included. After the concert, according to *My Life of Music*, the King asked him jocularly whether 'Rule, Britannia!' (which climaxed the fantasia) was not 'a better tune than "The Red Flag", eh?' A topical remark, since this

1 The conductor's father, Henry J. Wood senior: a photograph taken three years after the first of his son's Promenade concerts

2 His mother, Martha Wood

3 'I wore the kilt for best': Henry J. Wood at about three years of age

4 One of the model steam-engines made by Henry J. Wood senior – with Dr Peter Skeggs, son of the physician who attended the conductor in his last years

5 Hans Richter, the establisher of Wagner's popularity in Britain

6 Arthur Nikisch, on whose style and appearance Henry J. Wood modelled his own

Fellow-conductors

7 August Manns, conductor of the Crystal Palace concerts for over fifty years until 1901

8 Sir Dan Godfrey, pioneer in Bournemouth of municipal music and a champion of new compositions

9 A group at the Westmorland Music Festival, 1905, with Henry J. Wood (centre) and Mary Wakefield, founder and president (second from left)

10 Jessie Goldsack as a young singer: about 1900, more than thirty years before she changed her name to Lady Jessie Wood

11 Wood's first wife, born Olga Mikhailov, a gifted soprano under the name Mrs Henry J. Wood

12 The first birthday, 1913, of Pauline Tatiana Wood ('Tania'), elder daughter of Henry and Muriel Wood. The conductor is in the doorway, the baby is held by one of her mother's aunts, the birthday cake is displayed by a nurse. Muriel Wood occupies an almost detached position at extreme right

13 Outside the barn at Appletree Farm: the conductor's younger daughter Avril is seated at extreme left, her mother Lady Wood (Muriel) third from left, his elder daughter Tania third from right, Rosa Newmarch second from right. Wood stands in front of the window which he himself carpentered

14 Henry and Muriel on the lawn

15 Muriel Wood's basket of gardening tools exemplifies her passion for gardening

Appletree Farm was the Woods' country home at Chorley Wood, Hertfordshire

16 Avril, the Woods' younger daughter, with her parents

17 The carpenter's hut where Henry J. Wood worked at his hobby

18/19 Among welcome visitors to Appletree Farm were the composers Leoš Janáček in 1928 (left) and Arnold Bax at about the same time.

20 The composer Ethel Smyth with Pan

21 The rarely photographed Siegfried Schwabacher (left), Henry J. Wood's financial patron and close friend, with Wood's orchestral leader Charles Woodhouse (centre) and Wood himself

22 On Charlie Chaplin's set in Hollywood during Wood's season at the Hollywood Bowl, 1925: Muriel is seated centre, her relaxed husband at extreme right

23 With an informality rarely caught (Jessie was the photographer) Wood is seen when the couple were staying at a hotel at Ostend for his concerts of 1936

24 The platform of Queen's Hall with Wood and Robert Newman's Queen's Hall Orchestra in the early 1900s

25 The exterior of Queen's Hall. The church of All Souls, Langham Place, is glimpsed on the left

was the year of Britain's first, short-lived Labour Government – but it is not to be presumed that the monarch would actually have recognized the socialist rallying-song, since his musical knowledge was on the level of supposing that Stanford was the composer of the *Hallelujah Chorus*.

The *Sea Songs* Fantasia reappeared two days later on the final night of the season. It is a little curious that Henry J. Wood did not seize the opportunity to restore the correct melody of 'Rule, Britannia!', since in 1922 Sir Frederick Bridge as Gresham Professor at the University of London had drawn attention to the distortion which the passing of generations had imposed on Arne's original tune. (Wood wrote the descending melody of 'Britannia, rule the waves' as a succession of even crotchets instead of dotted crotchets and quavers.) The restoration was left for Malcolm Sargent to make, some thirty years later.

The King's visit occasioned a jolly article by an observant journalist from the London *Evening News*, W. Crawford Snowden, in the form of 'a letter from an old Promenader most improperly addressed to a certain august personage visiting Queen's Hall tonight for the first time'. He draws the King's attention to the 'fierce-eyed young men and women with long hair and unconventional attire' and (once again!) points out the informality signalled by the permission to smoke:

> I should get your pipe going, sir, if I were you, because Sir Henry Wood will be here in half a shake, and he wastes no time. . . Didn't I tell you? Before the clock's done striking eight his baton is in the air and everybody stops talking. See, all heads turned in his direction. . . .
>
> Hot? I should think he must be. Many's the time Sir Henry puts on a fresh collar at the interval. And that isn't his only dress suit, either. In fact, I believe he has three – and yet Lady Wood, they say, has a job to have a dry one ready for him every evening. . . .
>
> If you were to slip round to the back door after the concert you might meet Sir Henry staggering out to his car carrying a couple of suitcases, followed by someone carrying two more. The scene suggests departure for a longish weekend, but the suitcases are really full of orchestra parts Sir Henry is taking home with him to correct from his score. He does it all himself. Every bit of music on those stands has been cleaned of printers' errors by Sir Henry's own hand. . . .

On the first Monday of the 1925 promenade season (10 Aug 1925) another article of Snowden's would add further details, beginning with the previous Saturday's rehearsal:

Battling

. . .On every stand, as usual, there was a blue pencil, sharpened (for the correction of parts); every string player was provided with one of Sir Henry's special mutes (a metal one which clips when not in use on to the music stand – he doesn't rely on musicians bringing their own, though they have them, of course). . . .

He attends [other] orchestral concerts as a member of the audience (invariably buying his ticket) with a stop-watch and a pair of binoculars. With the former he times each item; the latter he uses to aid him in identifying any member of the orchestra whose playing of a passage arrests his attention.

This article was headed SIR HENRY, THE EVERGREEN. There were twenty more evergreen years to come.

Chapter 14

Hollywood and the BBC

1925–30

'We are having a lovely passage to New York on our way to Los Angeles, where I direct four concerts with their symphony orchestra of one hundred – back 4 August!' So Wood wrote to the composer Thomas Dunhill from the SS *Homeric* on 20 June 1925. From aboard ship he also wrote to thank his musical assistant Francis G. Sanders, who had not only helped with preparation of scores and parts but had unexpectedly appeared, along with his wife, at Waterloo Station to see the Woods to the boat train. It was proving a 'most delightful' voyage over calm waters: 'my wife has not missed a single meal. It is *the most perfect ship* in the world. . .The food and service is as good as the Savoy Hotel.'

As far from New York as New York is from London, Los Angeles was to be the most distant location in which Henry J. Wood conducted, and he was to go three times – in each case to conduct at the 'Symphonies under the Stars' series in the Hollywood Bowl. (*My Life of Music* actually gives the wrong year, 1926, for his first Hollywood season.) The musicians of the Los Angeles Philharmonic Orchestra were engaged to play for the Bowl season, giving Wood the pleasure of a reunion with some of his best players who had been lured years before from Queen's Hall – including the horn-player Alfred Brain, the oboist Henri de Busscher and the harpist Alfred Kastner.

When symphony concerts had begun at the Bowl in 1922 the original conductor was Alfred Hertz, who came from no further than San Francisco, but in 1925 the engagement of guest conductors began. The distinguished Hungarian-born Fritz Reiner (who had become conductor of the Cincinnati Symphony Orchestra) opened the season; Wood, the first to be invited direct from Europe, immediately followed. His four concerts began on Tuesday 14 July and continued on the Thursday, Friday and Saturday of the same week. At that time the vast natural amphitheatre had been adapted to seat 15,000.

Battling

The *Los Angeles Times* of 16 July reported a speech made by Wood to a Los Angeles club. The flowery language perhaps does credit to the journalist's capacity to deliver what his readers expected:

> Los Angeles people have music in their souls. In fact, one could almost hear the singing in the heart of that vast throng as, with lips closed and ears open, the devotees of music drank in the precious wine of harmony dispensed by your wonderful orchestra. I wish to say also that Mother Nature has provided you with the most excellent temple of music, scenically and acoustically speaking, in all the world. No architectural wisdom, short of that of the Maker of the Universe, could have created so large and so perfect a home for music.

The 'attentive' qualities of the listeners were to be tested. It was in fact an unsophisticated, 'holiday' kind of audience. As noted by Grace Koopal, the historian of the Bowl, when Reiner had included Stravinsky's *Petrushka* in his opening concert, 'the Bowl patrons actually laughed', thinking that it was 'some sort of *put-on*'. Wood's programmes were not to offer anything quite so challenging, but they included a high proportion of modern British music – all new to the area. As well as Elgar's *Enigma Variations*, Delius's *Dance Rhapsody* and Vaughan Williams's *A London Symphony*, Wood put forward three numbers from Holst's *The Planets*, Eugene Goossens' *Tam O'Shanter*, Ethel Smyth's *On the Cliffs of Cornwall* (the prelude to Act 2 of her opera *The Wreckers*), and what was called the 'Luring Scene' from Rutland Boughton's *The Immortal Hour,* an opera which had enjoyed 216 consecutive performances in London in 1923.

Other pieces, including three of Granados's Spanish Dances and an Andante from a Mozart cassation (suite), were also marked in the programme as 'new here'. Tchaikovsky's *Francesca da Rimini* stirred the newspaper's critic, Bruno David Ussher:

> Wood irresistibly drags orchestra and audiences miles into the bowels of the earth within the second circle of Dante's *Inferno*, where violent winds toss about hapless souls of sinners in a sombre, dark atmosphere of fearfulness.
>
> Svengali-like Wood transports us from darkest into daylight realm. I will long see before me those mighty, meaningful, conjuring gestures, tremendous impelling upward sweeps of both arms, as if lifting literally, hoisting us from this dark, Hades-bound scene.

Readers of *My Life of Music* were told that 'Naturally everyone in the cinema world attends these concerts. Charlie Chaplin was in my audience one night and I was delighted to find him so full of enthusiasm for British works.' Strangely he failed to mention his own visit to Chaplin 'on the set' at his film studio, a meeting preserved in a photograph (plate 22).

To the pleasure of those who ran the Bowl (Mrs Artie Mason Carter was the organization's president), Wood's concerts attracted notably good audiences and a high level of enthusiasm for his style of conducting. The result was an invitation to return in the following year for double the number of concerts. By that time Artie Mason Carter, the 'Mother of the Hollywood Bowl', had been ousted after a tussle with her board of directors, and it was under her successor Florence Behm Irish that the Bowl opened its season in 1926. As 'the sensation of last year's season' (*Los Angeles Times*), Sir Henry arrived in Los Angeles on Sunday 18 July, he and Lady Wood having previously taken a sightseeing trip through the Yellowstone and Yosemite National Parks.

He rehearsed next day with the orchestra, and again on the morning of his opening concert, 20 July. It was the start of an astonishing display of British music. Evidently given *carte blanche* on the strength of the previous season's success, he had programmed – out of fifty-one items in the eight concerts – thirteen works by living British composers, not counting as British two short pieces by Grainger. Surely never outside the shores of Britain itself, and rarely within them, has British music been so paraded within twelve days. Stanford, Delius, German, McEwen, Holst, Vaughan Williams, Gardiner, Bridge, Coleridge-Taylor and the more recently emergent Herbert Howells (*Puck's Minuet*) were each represented by a single work, Elgar by three. In addition, Purcell was represented by the suite which Wood himself had fashioned out of movements from the stage works.

Bach's Brandenburg Concerto no.4 and a Concerto Grosso of Handel's (opus 6, no.12 in B minor) were announced as 'new here'; so was the overture to Glinka's *Ruslan and Lyudmila*. More remarkably, Wood's opening concert included the first performance in the United States of Haydn's Symphony no.26, the *Lamentatione*, such earlier Haydn symphonies being still in the process of discovery. From Gluck to Sibelius, the remainder of the programmes was chosen with equal flair.

The auditorium had been remodelled, the capacity extended from 15,000 to 20,000, and the stage equipped with a 'totally ugly and overly decorated' concert shell which *worsened* the acoustics. 'DEAR OL' LUNNON WINS BOWL CROWD' ran the headline when Wood repeated Vaughan Williams's *A London*

Symphony, which he had introduced in the previous season. It was prefaced by 'well-chosen remarks in the British accents of Robert Nichols, the poet'. Nichols had been present at the previous season too, writing with enthusiasm to his friends the Deliuses about the success Wood had won with the *Dance Rhapsody*.

In the 1926 series, Hollywood farce invaded Hollywood music-making and Elgar's Symphony no.1 was the occasion of it. Lasting some fifty minutes, it was the longest single work in Wood's programmes and must have strained the patience of unsophisticated listeners, of whom there was an extra component in the audience on 29 July. It was the annual 'Lions Night', a rallying-point for members of the male community-charity organization so named. On previous such nights at the Bowl a real, caged lion had been displayed on stage. This time there were ferocious-looking lions in cages, stationed around the entire footlit perimeter of the stage.

> Sir Henry apparently had not been told that they were stuffed and when the lights were turned on them and the assembled Lions' Club members roared in their traditional ceremony, he was quite obviously apprehensive.
>
> He had already been visibly annoyed by a last-minute change in the programme to permit the addition of an ill-advised *Romeo and Juliet* aria by an amateurish though beauteous blonde Lions' Club 'Mascot' and, to cap the climax, an electrician inadvertently (or perhaps deliberately, since Sir Henry's 'grand manner' did not exactly endear him to the stage crew) turned the stage lights *off* and the lion spotlights *on* just as the famous conductor turned with great dignity to take his bow at the conclusion of his beloved Elgar symphony!
>
> Sir Henry looked out into utter darkness, blinded by the lights blazing on the lions, while the audience reaction was raucously geared to the lions rather than reverently to him. He was outraged, to say the least, and refused to go on with the concert.

The account in Grace Koopal's book describes Mrs Irish pleading in vain with him, and being 'near tears when her husband rushed to her aid and had to be physically restrained from "planting one" on the august chin of the eminent conductor. . . Taking his equally haughty Lady with him, Sir Henry stalked out of the Bowl into his waiting Rolls-Royce.' It was announced to the audience that he had become indisposed, and the concertmaster (leader) conducted the remaining items of the programme.

Wood did not, however, decline to conduct the remaining two concerts, and the fact that he was to return in 1934 – with Florence Irish also returning in that year as chairman of the organization – shows that (with blows to the chin not delivered) no bones were broken.

In June, before crossing the Atlantic, Wood had undertaken an old-style Handel Festival at the Crystal Palace. Loathing the accepted custom there of a 'public rehearsal', he insisted – public presence or no – on stopping 'half-a-dozen times in the opening chorus of *Israel in Egypt* – they were all over the place and the contraltos decidedly flat'. The enlarged orchestration was presented as Wood's own, though he had placed his customary reliance on the ability of Francis G. Sanders: 'I have spent the day on your score of *Israel in Egypt* and am perfectly delighted with it,' he wrote from Appletree Farm.

On his return he introduced his promenaders to Paul Hindemith (the recently composed Concerto for Orchestra) on 14 September. At the first Saturday symphony concert of the 1923 season Wood had already given the first British performance of Hindemith's *Nuschi-Nuschi Dances,* a suite drawn from music for a Burmese puppet-play. The perceived 'dryness' of Hindemith's style did not appeal to British taste. In the promenade concerts of 1927 a concerto for piano and twelve instruments (one of his *Kammermusik* series) inspired the *Musical Times* critic to the jocular plea: 'Will nobody revive for us the gay days of *Heldenleben* and *The Rite of Spring*?'

Wood's name was invoked for various causes. Along with Sir Hugh Allen, Sir Landon Ronald (knighted in 1922) and Percy Pitt, he accepted nomination to a committee endorsing the Community Singing movement, promoted by Lord Beaverbrook's *Daily Express.* Beyond its aim of raising that newspaper's circulation, it was no doubt intended to resurrect the myth of 'one nation' which had been realistically shattered by the General Strike in May 1926. 'The levelling-up of all sorts and conditions, rubbing shoulder to shoulder – with no class distinction – must exert great influence on society in general,' as Sir Herbert Brewer put it with the political correctness expected of a cathedral organist. Ronald conducted the movement's opening concert at the Royal Albert Hall on 20 November 1926; the publication of the *Daily Express Community Song Book* (of national songs) followed. Whether the committee ever met – its membership additionally blessed by the participation of a bishop and a Society hostess – is unknown, and Wood's adherence seems to have been nominal.

In March of that year when Ronald was ill, Wood had obliged him by taking over some of his Sunday concerts at the Palladium. To another colleague, Sir Dan Godfrey (knighted in 1922), he lent support by an appearance at the

Battling

Bournemouth Municipal Orchestra's festival on 9 April. Next day the *Daily Telegraph* noted the inclusion in his Bournemouth programme of another Haydn rarity, the overture to the opera *L'isola disabitata*. More significant in the critic's notice, however, was its reference to broadcasting. The topic was now inescapable in musical discussion, the performance in another case being of Vaughan Williams's *A London Symphony*:

> Incidentally I should be glad to hear that this performance, which was broadcast, reached the ears of listeners-in as, so to speak, it left the Winter Gardens. But, while I am prepared to bow to the opinion of wireless experts, I doubt very much whether the beautiful *pianissimo* – hardly more than a dying whisper – Sir Dan Godfrey obtained at the close of the symphony was properly heard by anybody actually outside the concert hall.

The BBC had begun to take its microphones out of the studio and into the concert-hall in 1924, in that year using its own musicians (as 'the Augmented Wireless Orchestra') for a series of concerts at the Central Hall, Westminster, with Elgar and Harty among the conductors. In the winter of 1926–7 it promoted 'National Symphony Concerts' with an orchestra of 150 in the Albert Hall. So far, however, Henry J. Wood had never broadcast. His distancing from the new medium reflected the attitude of his boss, William Boosey of Chappell's; his eventual embrace of it was smoothed by one of his oldest friends and musical associates, Percy Pitt. Serving with distinction as opera administrator at Covent Garden, Pitt first assumed musical duties in the BBC on a part-time basis, and from 1924 was the BBC's first full-time musical director.

The opposition to broadcasting, manifested not only by Chappell but by a swathe of other parties in theatrical and concert management, was based partly on claims that the BBC was infringing copyrights, partly by fears that potential audiences would absent themselves from the concert-hall, beguiled by the lure of the domestic loudspeaker. If broadcasting were allowed to continue its 'devilish work', then 'in ten years' time the concert halls will be deserted', declared Beecham.

Management turned the screws. A speech by the Prince of Wales, the future Edward VIII, was to have been broadcast from a concert held under the auspices of the British Legion at Queen's Hall: according to Percy Pitt's biographer J. D. Chamier, Chappell's refused to permit the laying of a broadcasting cable to the hall. Chamier also reproduces a letter sent to the press by William Boosey which paraded the army of those who had closed ranks against broadcasting 'under present conditions'.

Every concert-giver of importance is opposed to it. I include the names
of Messrs Boosey & Co., Enoch & Sons, Cramer & Co., Lionel Powell,
with his enormous series of celebrity concerts both in London and the
provinces, and Mr Henry Mills, the organizer of the popular Sunday
League Concerts, also all the important concert agents, such as Messrs
Ibbs & Tillett, Daniel Mayer & Co., L. G. Sharpe, E. L. Robinson and
the directors of the Albert Hall, the Aeolian Hall, the Wigmore Hall, the
Central Hall, Westminster. Sir Henry Wood and Sir Landon Ronald are
on our side, as also Sir Dan Godfrey and Mr Walter Hedgcock of the
Crystal Palace.

Ronald had broadcast as early as 1924, so the citation of his name was
dubious. As for Wood, still under contract to Chappell's, he could not have
protested. But it would not be long before he was given his freedom to
perform on 2LO, as the BBC's London station was identified. By a
dramatic announcement on 7 March 1927 Chappell's declared that it would
henceforth maintain neither the symphony concerts nor the promenade
concerts. The symphony season about to end would be the orchestra's
last.

That statement threatened the whole future of music at Queen's Hall. If a
famous cartoon by Sir Bernard Partridge in *Punch* is to be taken as
representative, the chief concern of the general public was for the Proms.
Against the background of the Queen's Hall, with a poster proclaiming 'No
More Proms', the cartoonist imagined the ghost of Beethoven saying to Sir
Henry J. Wood: 'This is indeed tragic, but I cannot believe that this rich city,
once so generous to me, will fail to find us a permanent home.'

The date arrived for the last of the season's Saturday symphony concerts
(which Wood had conducted since 1896), the last time that the New Queen's
Hall Orchestra was publicly heard under that name in its own hall. On 17
March 1927 no valedictory programme was given. Wood made no speech.
The inference in Reginald Pound's biography that he was too emotionally
affected to do so is surely wide of the mark. Henry J. Wood was, up to the
end of that concert, Chappell's man.

Nor was he inclined to blame Chappell's for its withdrawal after spending
what he estimated as £60,000 on maintaining orchestral music at Queen's
Hall. (Had it not pulled out then, it must certainly have done two years later,
when severe economic depression hit Britain and even the BBC suffered
cuts in its musical establishment.) Wood must have been well forewarned.
More than a year before, he had been in contact with the BBC as an obvious
alternative employer, as its written archives make clear. These

archives, preserved at Caversham near Reading, become an invaluable source for Wood's biography from this point: they were made available to the present writer, though apparently not consulted by Pound.

The BBC's negotiations with Wood were conducted at the highest level by John Reith, its general manager – styled Director-General from 1927, in which year he was knighted. On 19 February 1926 Reith noted in a memorandum: 'Sir Henry Wood came to see me two days ago.' Seeking a three-year contract, he had seemed to be more concerned with the size of the annual fee than with the number of concerts. 'I imagine he would be quite ready to conduct once a fortnight for £2000 [per annum].'

It was two months before Reith actually offered such a contract (three years at £2000 p.a.; twenty concerts yearly, nine of them in London). By then Wood, remarking that a long time had elapsed since 'our chat', decided to decline, saying he had made other arrangements for the coming season. Negotiations continued into 1927, Wood finally accepting on 12 May of that year a contract for three years at £2500 p.a., with a maximum of twenty-five concerts each year. He would become, in effect, a BBC artist: 'In all concerts. . .under auspices other than the BBC it is agreed that your name shall appear on bills and programmes as "by courtesy of the BBC".'

By this time the BBC's potential role in London's concert life had been thrown wider by Chappell's abandonment of orchestral music at Queen's Hall. Would there indeed be 'No More Proms' – or would the BBC step in? The Proms did not have to be at Queen's Hall, if Chappell's (who remained the leaseholder) were to impose too high a rental. The Central Hall, Westminster, was considered as an alternative. But in May 1927 a BBC announcement under the heading 'Saving the Promenades' made it clear that an accommodation with Chappell's had been reached. The BBC would present a six-week promenade season at Queen's Hall that summer (nothing was said about future summers) under Sir Henry J.Wood. A series of symphony concerts would be given in the ensuing months. 'Moreover, the microphone is no longer banned from Queen's Hall on other occasions.'

Amazingly, at the time of the announcement the BBC had not yet formally contracted Wood for the Proms. On 2 June the terms were fixed – £150 per week for six concerts; 'the sixth concert in each week will count as an engagement under his contract with us'. (That is, it would be deducted from the maximum number of concerts covered by Wood's yearly fee.) Moreover, the BBC was to pay Wood additionally for the hire of scores and parts from the vast library he had personally built up.

The programmes would continue to bear Wood's distinctive mark, as in the revival of Dorothy Howell's piano concerto during the opening week, with the composer as soloist. But he now had to consult the BBC's own music administrators. On 18 June he had written to the twenty-one-year-old composer William Alwyn that he had scheduled his *Five Preludes* for performance at the Proms 'and as soon as the Advisory Board of the BBC accept and confirm my programmes I will write and let you know the date of performance'. A letter of 13 July made it definite, inviting Alwyn himself to conduct and asking him to 'get out the parts at once . . . parts note-perfect, please'.

Chappell's, obstinate to the last, refused to allow the BBC the use of the name, New Queen's Hall Orchestra. (But it would reappear at the Norwich Festival and on Wood's gramophone records.) When the six-week season of promenade concerts opened (traditionally, on a Saturday) on 13 August 1927, the odd, dance-band-like formula of 'Sir Henry J. Wood and his Symphony Orchestra' was used. This performance apparently marked Wood's first BBC broadcast. His own autobiographical dating of his first broadcast as 20 January 1927 springs from an evident confusion with his first broadcast *from a BBC studio* a year later (20 January 1928).

The whole programme of the BBC's first promenade concert was broadcast, with an introductory talk by Dame Ethel Smyth. The Belgian pianist Arthur de Greef, the soprano Rosina Buckman and the baritone Dale Smith were the soloists:

National Anthem	
Overture, *Cockaigne*	Elgar
Minuet in A for strings	Boccherini
'Elisabeth's Greeting' from *Tannhäuser* (soprano)	Wagner
Piano Concerto	Grieg
Three Sea Songs (baritone)	Stanford
Valse Triste	Sibelius
Largo	Handel
Overture, *William Tell*	Rossini

INTERVAL

Hungarian Rhapsody no.2	Liszt
Songs (soprano)	Schubert, Quilter, Parry
Three Old Scottish Airs (baritone)	
Prelude and Mazurka (*Coppélia*)	Delibes

The first 'half' was, as of old, enormously long, one hour and forty minutes; during the interval the BBC broadcast the news and weather forecast; and the second 'half' lasted only thirty-five minutes.

Battling

FIRST BBC PROM: QUEEN'S HALL NOT BIG ENOUGH was the headline in the *Weekly Dispatch* (London had many more daily, Sunday and weekly newspapers then). Reports spoke of 'hundreds' being turned away. In the ranks of the orchestra, along with the familiar women players among the strings, a 'feminine oboist' (Helen Gaskell) was noticed for the first time. Wood triumphed, and relished the occasion: 'I do not think I ever conducted Elgar's joyous *Cockaigne* overture with greater spirit than on this occasion.' The *Monthly Musical Record*, however, found his reading of Elgar to have 'hard competence and no joy'. Subtitled 'In London Town', that overture surely signalled that the plea of the ghost of Beethoven to 'this rich city' had been answered.

'The trash in the Prom programmes [was] eliminated,' wrote David Cox, referring to 'the sentimental ballads about Mother of Mine, the cottage by the waterfall, June and so on'. But that simply marked the end of the blatant commercial link between Chappell's as (former) concert-promoter and Chappell's as ballad-publisher. In other respects this programme with its twelve separate items shows the BBC – at this stage – stressing continuity and not reform. The Scottish traditional songs and the *Hungarian Rhapsody* were like echoes of Wood's very first promenade programme (1895). The so-called *Largo* of Handel, not in its original vocal version but in Wood's own arrangement with solo parts for violin, harp and organ, met a broad popular taste, as did the *Valse triste* and the *William Tell* overture.

The BBC timing of the first half had allowed for De Greef taking an encore, Chopin's Grand Valse in E flat. Encores in the second half do not appear on the BBC's internal schedule, but Watson Lyle in the *Musical Standard* reported that the soprano and baritone soloists took their three encores apiece – 'or was it four? they seemed to be unending'. A few evenings later Lyle deserted his domestic wireless set for the auditorium, noting that 'above the heads of the promenaders' hung that new visitant to Queen's Hall, a pair of microphones – 'a rectangular metal frame enshrining two objects of sinister appearance, two (apparently) small bleached skulls, gleaming white, with big black eye-sockets'.

Admission to the promenade area now cost two shillings, as compared with a lowest admission price of seven shillings and sixpence to a 'normal' symphony concert. Instead of twopence for the old single sheet, sixpence was demanded for a booklet-type programmme in which the audience read an advertisement for Wood's recent recordings of Tchaikovsky's *1812* Overture, Schubert's *Unfinished* and Beethoven's *Leonora* no.3.

As manager for the concerts, the BBC had taken over the services of

W. W. ('Tommy') Thompson, who had been Robert Newman's assistant – and who was to remain in the BBC's service until 1953. The BBC's chief music planner was Edward Clark (later the husband of the composer Elisabeth Lutyens), whose acquaintance with modern composers and their music was international. Also on the BBC's staff was Julian Herbage, taking what he described as 'a very minor role in the Prom deliberations', to be followed by much closer collaboration with Wood from 1935.

To call Wood's promenade performances 'invariably workmanlike', as *The Times* did on 20 August 1927, was something of a qualified compliment. The critic continued: 'To demand of a single conductor an absolute standard of perfection in all styles of music would be to ask the impossible' – with the implication that, somewhere out there if it could only be grasped, there *was* an absolute standard. In the eyes of the more sophisticated, opinion-forming section of the public, such remarks tended to lower the esteem for Wood, *especially at the Proms*. To the generality of audiences his magnetism was undiminished, as measured by the numbers and enthusiasm of his audiences. He and the BBC must have experienced a little bump, however, from what became known as the Daisy Kennedy incident.

The Australian violinist Daisy Kennedy, previously married to the pianist Moiseiwitsch and now the wife of the poet John Drinkwater, was engaged to play the Brahms Violin Concerto on 24 August. She came to a temporary standstill during the course of the first movement and publicly put the blame on not having had a rehearsal. Wood denied it but the BBC spokesperson's defence was more circumspect: 'All new and difficult works are rehearsed . . . The Brahms concerto has been performed by the Queen's Hall Orchestra about a hundred and fifty times, so I really do not see that a rehearsal is necessary.'

It transpired that Wood had given the soloist a rehearsal with piano before the day of the concert, and that on the day she and the orchestra had rehearsed some passages only. The circumstance allowed the critic Ernest Newman to offer gleeful advice to soloists: 'Do not be afraid to come to England to play your concertos . . . Take it from us that you and the orchestra will rehearse – *though perhaps not together.*'

If the BBC's director-general was more than momentarily displeased, he did not show it. On 9 September 1927 Reith came 'to hear Wagner at the Proms, seeing Sir Henry Wood in the interval. He was delighted with everything, and said it was the most successful season he had had.' With more than two and a quarter million licence-holders at the time, the public audience had been vastly multiplied by radio, the programmes being announced with suitable prominence in the Corporation's journal, the *Radio Times*.

Yet as an outlet for new music the first BBC season had the air of a dampened enterprise. There were few new compositions, of which the *Monthly Musical Record* dismissed as 'preposterously empty and pretentious' a work for organ and orchestra by Marcel Dupré in which the soloist was not the distinguished French organist himself but the long-serving accompanist of the Proms, F. B. Kiddle. Walton's breezy overture *Portsmouth Point*, conducted by the composer, was the only British work which would anchor firmly in the concert repertory. It had first been heard in the previous year at the festival held in Zurich by the International Society for Contemporary Music.

Henry J. Wood's final night mirrored the first in having a popular pianist in a favourite concerto – Solomon, in Tchaikovsky's no.1. A Bach-Elgar arrangement (*Fugue in C minor*) showed the continued acceptance of brilliant modernizations of Bach. At the end of the evening the *Sea Songs* Fantasia and *Pomp and Circumstance* no.1 did not run in sequence, as in the patriotic inebriation of later years, but were soberly separated by solo songs with piano – Wolf and Strauss sung by Miriam Licette, Glinka and Musorgsky by Norman Allin. During the series only four Beethoven symphonies were given, and the Ninth was not among them: the compromised version which stopped short of the choral part (still tolerated as late as the 1924 and 1925 Proms) was shelved. Hardly had the Proms ended, however, when Wood conducted the Ninth at Queen's Hall on 7 October in the first concert of the BBC's winter series, with a chorus mainly drawn from the Royal Academy of Music.

Some of these 'National Symphony Concerts', as the BBC commandingly called them, were broadcast not from Queen's Hall but from the People's Palace in the East End of London. Wood had a prominent presence in both locations, as well as in the studio. The instrumentalists were those of the old Wireless Orchestra, augmented as necessary. In some announcements the title 'BBC Symphony Orchestra' was prematurely used: the formal establishment of such an orchestra, with full-time contracts for the players, was yet to come.

Among European music catching British interest at the time was that of the Swiss composer Ernest Bloch, some but not all of it with an overt Jewish content. At Queen's Hall on 13 April 1928 Wood gave for the BBC the first performance in Britain of Bloch's *Israel* Symphony with its five solo voices. It must have evoked sufficient interest to have justified Wood in repeating it at a concert of the Royal Philharmonic Society on 18 April 1929, also at Queen's Hall – but it seems never to have been heard in Britain since.

The self-governing Royal Philharmonic Society, though confining itself to eight concerts a season, still carried on. With no permanent conductor, it engaged such distinguished guests as Bruno Walter, Ernest Ansermet, Pierre Monteux, Václav Talich – and Wood. Its orchestra 'has been brought to a high pitch of efficiency by Sir Henry Wood's training', reported the *Musical Times*. 'Some of the best playing heard in London for a long time' was encountered on 3 November 1927, when Maria Olszewska, a major operatic star, sang Mahler's *Lieder eines fahrenden Gesellen* under Wood's baton. On 8 December 1927 the Society gave him the honour of the first British performance of Sibelius's Symphony no.7, in C – that tersely eloquent single-movement work which turned out to be the last of its composer's symphonies.

The Society's financial position was perilous, however. To raise money, it decided to sell its reputation. Although it had no formal list of contracted orchestral musicians, its concerts traditionally attracted the best London players – and the 'Royal' prefix could be called on to exert its usual hypnotizing effect on the British public. The label of the 'Royal Philharmonic Orchestra' (no connection with the present orchestra of that name) was authorized to appear on recordings made for Columbia by various conductors, among whom Beecham was prominent. Now Beecham put himself at the centre of a plan to involve the Royal Philharmonic Society and Columbia Records with the foundation of a new, salaried, first-class symphony orchestra which the BBC wished to create.

The need for such an orchestra was indicated by adverse criticism of the standard of playing in the BBC's 1927–8 season (when its orchestra was enlisted *ad hoc*, in collaboration with the management of Covent Garden Opera). Comparisons with the Berlin Philharmonic, which won golden notices for its London performances in December 1928 under Wilhelm Furtwängler, reinforced the point. The moment for such a new enterprise seemed propitious, since the BBC for its part had for some time been hopeful of persuading Beecham to reverse his hostility to the 'wireless'. In March 1928 Sir Landon Ronald, by then a member of the BBC's musical advisory committee, was able to write to Roger Eckersley, director of programmes: 'I have really at last entirely broken down Beecham's opposition to broadcasting.'

A scheme was mooted for an orchestra which would assume the title of Royal Philharmonic Orchestra but would be financed mainly by the BBC. It would not only broadcast and give a hundred public concerts a year, including those of the Royal Philharmonic Society; it would also participate in opera at Covent Garden and it would record extensively for Columbia. No need to ask who would be its chief conductor. Negotiations advanced far enough for Beecham to agree with Percy Pitt, still the BBC's musical director, a list of twenty-seven key players to be recruited for the orchestra. But after two years, not least because of Beecham's evasiveness and his disposition to prime the Press to his own advantage, the BBC felt that negotiations could go no further – Eckersley writing to Reith on 24 January 1930: 'Beecham has not replied and his time is up.' The Royal Philharmonic Society and the BBC went their own ways – and, as Asa Briggs put it in his authoritative history of British broadcasting, 'Beecham remained an angry judge of everything the BBC tried to do.' Plans for a new concert-hall were likewise abandoned, and the BBC proceeded with plans to create a national, salaried orchestra which would be exclusively at its own disposal.

Wood himself had good reason to be thankful to the BBC. Financial uncertainty had been removed from the Proms and, consequently, more generous rehearsal time allotted to them. As Wood exclaimed: 'The joy of a *daily rehearsal* and, a little later on, *preliminary* rehearsals on four days before the opening concert!' The Proms had indeed been saved, and an era had begun in which the BBC's resources would allow it to assume the leadership in setting musical taste.

But Henry J. Wood's life was at a watershed. For the first time in thirty-five years, he no longer had 'his' orchestra. The BBC would probably, he might suppose, allow him to retain the Proms; but even of that he could not be sure. For the rest of the year he could hope only for a modest share in the BBC's schedules and would similarly be competing for engagements offered by other concert organizations and festivals. Younger conductors who had already passed the age when *he* had begun – Malcolm Sargent was thirty-five in 1930, John Barbirolli thirty-one – would stake out their claims. The gramophone record market was being increasingly saturated as rival conductors' versions of the same works were compared, and foreign orchestras' performances became available. Coincidentally, Manchester's impresario G. W. Brand Lane had died in November 1927, aged seventy-three; the orchestral enterprise associated with his name did not long survive him, and Wood's regular Manchester schedule was over.

He had already stamped musical history so distinctively that his prestige was unassailable. But his income was not, and that is where the prospect must have seemed uncertain. To be seen as a grand old man was not a livelihood. Nevertheless the ensuing decade, the decade of his sixties, was to embrace some of the peaks in his life's achievement. It was also to bring about a violent domestic crisis.

Chapter 15

The Gentle Art

1926–31

> When I got to my chair for the rehearsal of the concert I noticed that Sir
> Henry was already there, marking his parts. He looked up and gave me a
> cheery Cockney welcome: 'Mornin', Mr Jackson. Welcome to the Proms.'

Cockney, was it? A northerner like Gerald Jackson, who first played his flute
under Wood's direction at the Norwich Festival of 1930, would easily attach
the label to any London accent. But if 'cockney' means what Alfred Doolittle
spoke in Shaw's *Pygmalion* (and its latter-day musicalization, *My Fair Lady*),
Wood's utterance was different. 'Lower-middle-class London' probably
identifies his accent: he was, after all, nurtured well out of range of Bow
Bells. 'Vahlins' for 'violins' is a rare distortion of vowels on one of his
surviving recordings of a rehearsal.

The invention of exaggeratedly cockney 'Woodisms', sometimes
flavoured with an authentic nasal delivery, proceeded naturally from the
length of his players' service – and the affection that went with it. 'Stop
sawrin' away regardless!' he is supposed to have said to his string-players,
and 'Horns, what are you a-doing of?' – amended, when he learnt it was
incorrect, to 'Horns, what are you a-doing?', which elicited a unison
response of 'OF!'. The 'sawrin' ' was given a posthumous lease of life by
James Agate's obituary of Wood in the *Daily Express* – but, not surprisingly,
nobody has testified to actually being present on such legendary occasions.
The viola-player Norman Carrell, however, remembered with amusement
Wood's pronunciation of 'pikkulo' for the instrument which Beecham used to
call a 'pikkilo'. Such an odd phrase of Wood's as 'Both sides of the orchestra
aren't together' was recalled by the trumpeter-turned-timpanist, Eric
Pritchard.

The *Musical Times* in 1927 eavesdropped on a rehearsal not at Queen's
Hall but at the Royal Academy of Music – where Henry J. Wood is observed,

jacket off and in full voice: 'Up-bow! *Up*-bow, firsts!. . . Point of the bow! Heel! Press the bow! Hit the string! That cello *spiccato* bowing is no good against the brass. . . Feel it in your fingers!'

And above all: 'Listen!' – meaning, 'Listen to what your colleagues are playing.' His schooling is directed mainly to the strings, less to the woodwind and brass, in which several places are filled by teachers – presumably because not enough sufficiently advanced students are available. When a student conductor is bidden to take over the baton, Wood seats himself at a piano, with a full score, in the middle of the string section, 'prompting' from the keyboard.

Such twice-weekly afternoon rehearsals at the Academy, of three hours each, were entered as a priority in Henry J. Wood's calendar. The correspondent from the *Musical Times* (probably the editor, Harvey Grace) observed that Wood never lapsed into sarcasm or witticisms at the expense of the young players. Instead, there was 'stable good-humour'.

For Mary Stratford (at that time Mary Fouracre), a cello student of the Academy from 1926, those two orchestral rehearsals were the highlights of the week, along with chamber music under the tuition of Lionel Tertis. As for Wood, 'We all loved him – he could do no wrong for us.' He would stride into the Duke's Hall – wearing, if it was winter, an almost ankle-length coat lined with expensive musquash fur. Throwing the coat over the back of a chair, he would immediately begin to hear each individual player's tuning, using not the tuning-machine kept at Queen's Hall but an ordinary tuning-fork. The pieces to be rehearsed had not been individually studied with the students' teachers; the students confronted them for the first time at the orchestral rehearsal. Within the string sections, the players' positions were rotated, so that everyone got a chance to be at the front desk. Mary Stratford also recalled that Muriel Wood was a constant attender at rehearsals – 'grim-faced, always abominably dressed'.

Proud of his students' achievement, at various times he brought to the rehearsals Elgar, who conducted the *Enigma Variations*, Edward German, Ethel Smyth in her buttoned boots, and Nellie Melba – 'and didn't she roast Sir Henry! Something went wrong and she turned round and gave him what for. I think he didn't take [the aria] at the tempo she liked it. "Of course, if you're going to do that sort of thing, it's quite impossible for me to sing at all!" '

Public concerts were given by the Academy orchestra at Queen's Hall – where on one occasion, full of nerves, Mary Stratford could hardly get herself to mount the platform as one of two cello soloists in a Handel concerto. But as soon as she and her partner were seated, and looked up at Sir Henry to indicate they were ready to begin, 'he gave a prodigious wink, and that was it! Suddenly the nerves fell off like a discarded mantle – you wanted to play as well as you could because he was looking after you.'

Mary Stratford remembered, as many of Wood's professional players did, his phrase 'One hair of the bow!' to indicate the softest possible string sound; and also, 'Ladies and gentlemen, *pianissimo, pianissi-nissi-nissimo*!' As with his professional orchestras, he would call out directions and warnings while continuing to conduct, wherever possible avoiding halts and short-range repetitions. After a bout of illness had put the students under various less inspiring deputies, Mary Stratford recalls that on his return his young players welcomed him with a huge box of chocolates.

In 1926 Wood brought the Academy's orchestra, choir and solo singers to give Bach's *St Matthew Passion* at Queen's Hall – apparently the first time that it had ever been given in London without cuts. (Two items, numbers 50 and 51 in the score, were reversed.) The performance began at 2 p.m. and ended at 6.45, with a break of forty-five minutes. 'We hope that it will not remain unique,' commented the *Musical Times*, 'but that every year London will have the opportunity of learning the full stature of the *St Matthew Passion*.' This was indeed the model for later uncut performances by such bodies as the Bach Choir. On 4 June 1930 he took the student orchestra as far as Liverpool to perform.

Another pedagogical enterprise was a four-volume work – sized like twelve-stave music-paper, not like the usual printed book – entitled *The Gentle Art of Singing* and painstakingly supervised by Hubert J. Foss for publication in 1927–8 by the Oxford University Press. Recognized as an authority on the voice, Henry J. Wood found a lively welcome for his precepts. At this time, when even the most eminent concert soloists were expected to deliver most of their repertory in English and audiences were alert to strengths and deficiencies in delivery, vocal technique was a matter of fairly general musical discussion. An article by Dawson Freer in the *Musical Times* on 'The Composer and the Larynx' (May 1927) and a subsequent letter headed 'More about the larynx' were typical.

The majority of Wood's pages were devoted to a series of about 1500 progressively graded, written-out technical exercises. A preface acknowledged the help of Francis G. Sanders and of Helen Douglas Irvine, 'in reading the proofs and exercises'. Doubtless Sanders was given the task of actually writing out the vocal exercises on patterns the author laid down. The aim of Wood's pages was immediately clear to the student: to make the singer an artist. The singer needed to develop those qualities which were taken for granted in instrumental study – technical accuracy, the availability of a range of tone-quality, and a dedication to the composer's demands. Part of Wood's message was to warn the student against *bad* teaching:

> Walk through the passages of fashionable teaching studios and listen to the exercises and the quality of tone you hear through the green baize doors. A walk in the Zoo is more pleasing to the ear and mind. . .
>
> Foundational tone should always be bright, ringing and clear as a silver trumpet; it should even have a metallic ring, but it should never be hard, dry or throaty. Forward, bright ring, full of joy; this is the foundation to build. Never put one dull, veiled tone into these exercises. The colouring of vowels must be left until later, when real words are introduced. To my ear, dramatic colour, real emotional singing, is a development from the fundamental bright quality. You can darken and veil any bright ringing tone by admixture of breath, by a halo of breath round the tone, but to try to make a dull, breathy-toned voice bright is to try to sink your foundations after you have decorated your walls. . . .
>
> Only by a long, slowly graded course of musical exercises can a voice be tuned, made even throughout its compass, and a fine equal quality of tone upon all vowels at all pitches be obtained. . . For the first three years, singing students should be trained to make their voices like a beautiful, even instrument. There are registers in every musical instrument, but they must not show. There are muscles, there are reeds, but they must never be perceptible in an artist. There is breath, but never, except at the will of the singer and for a dramatic purpose or a colour effect, must the hearers be aware of it. . . .
>
> We have no use in the singing world for dull, hooty, phlegmy, breathy tone. In fact, it is ring in the tone which distinguishes the highly trained, cultivated voice from the merely pretty amateur voice. All qualities of tone are used and required by an artist, especially in opera, but they must all be under the mental and ear control of the singer. Dull, sombre quality has its uses, but prolonged dullness is death to all art. . . .

Wood's suggested DAILY TIME-TABLE FOR STUDENTS OF SINGING struck some reviewers as rigorous beyond the likelihood of fulfilment. But it was, after all, an attempt to give vocal students some counterpart to the routine of a dedicated instrumental student – who could, as a singer cannot, plunge into continuous hours of practice. On each morning of a six-day week the routine would run (in part):

Battling

A.M.

8.30 to 9.00 Walk in all weathers.

9.00 Paper work. At first this will consist of the elements of music, elements of harmony, etc. Later, harmony and counterpoint. Transposing your songs, arias and exercises.

Writing out the words of all your songs and arias as written by the various authors, not as set by the composer with repetitions, etc. Making your own literal translations of all foreign songs and arias, etc.

10.00 10 minutes' breathing exercises for singing, without voice.

10.10 Vocal exercises (after one year this can be increased to 15 minutes).

10.20 Rest voice.

10.30 Work mentally at your vocal exercises; do not hum or sing, but you can play them through many, many times on the piano, always slowly and in perfect rhythm.

10.50 Vocal exercises (this after the first year can be increased to 15 minutes).

11.00 Rest. . . .

Never let a week pass without attending a string quartet chamber concert. Your ear will thus be attuned to just intonation; you will hear music of the first order; and you will become accustomed to hearing and following four parts. . . .

In bed every night at 10 p.m. when not out at a musical performance.

Sunday was a day of rest – of a kind:

Entirely rest your voice. Don't talk all day. If you live in a cathedral city or London, ring the changes by attending different services every Sunday morning. By this means you will hear a pure, dignified church style, become acquainted with all schools of church music, and learn to love and know the great church services, the anthems by Palestrina, Tallis, Purcell, Gibbons, de Lassus, Wesley. You will learn a host of very fine things which will much help to form your musical taste. . . .

Sunday afternoon: If in London, attend a classical orchestral concert, so as to get accustomed to the sound of an orchestra. . . .

Sunday evening: You may be permitted to call and see your friends, or they may call and see you, provided you have faithfully carried out your six days' work, and are not in arrears with your studies.

I find dozens of singing students fritter away their time (and their poor parents' money) by paying calls, surrounding themselves with useless acquaintances. It is impossible ever to make up for the time lost during student days. The present dancing craze, with its many late nights, is especially upsetting to a serious student's work. Your musical studies will fatigue you quite enough without the fatigue of frivolous amusements. . . .

In 1927, when three of the four parts of *The Gentle Art of Singing* appeared (the fourth would appear in 1928), a magazine-publisher capitalized on Henry J. Wood's popularity by naming him as editor of a fortnightly part-work, *Music of all Nations*, with his photograph prominent on the cover. (No doubt the actual editorial work was allotted to other hands.) Songs and piano pieces as well as interviews and articles on musical history made up its contents. His name was thus associated with self-guided musical education, as well as with his work at the Academy and, above all, the work of educational popularisation via the promenade concerts.

One particular campaign which he had begun before World War One had ended in victory: reviewing one of his performances of Elgar's Symphony no.1, the *Musical Times* noted that 'audiences have learnt, chiefly at the suggestion of Sir Henry's upraised baton, to put their applause in its place. We do not interrupt symphonies nowadays, even if it means sitting like poor relations for nearly an hour.'

The triennial Norwich Festival called on him once again in 1927. This time there was a shift of emphasis – no new choral works, but a first performance on 27 October for Frank Bridge's latest orchestral work, *Enter Spring*. The New Queen's Hall Orchestra, though it was no longer heard under that name at Queen's Hall itself, still figured on the Norwich announcements, and the Bayreuth-like fanfares summoning the audiences were heard (as before the war). Walter Gieseking, a German pianist strongly favoured by Wood, was among the soloists.

Rosa Newmarch, whose knowledge of Russian and contact with Russian musicians had so well supported him before 1914, had now learnt Czech and became his enthusiastic adviser in his championing of Janáček and other composers of Czechoslovakia. (That state had been created in 1918 from part of the dismembered Austrian Empire.) Wood and his wife, as their passports reveal, had themselves spent a few days in Prague at the end of June and the beginning of July 1920, but there is no record of what musical contacts he may have had. A visit by the seventy-one-year-old Leoš Janáček to London in 1926 was followed two years later by Wood's pioneering performances of the *Sinfonietta* (10 February) and the orchestral rhapsody, *Taras Bulba* (16 October), both in BBC-promoted concerts at Queen's Hall. The seed did not germinate, and a subsequent performance of the *Wallachian Dances*, later known as the *Lachian Dances* (19 August 1930), made almost no impression: Janáček would achieve no firm British popularity until the discovery of his operas in the 1950s.

Battling

Wood tried out another Czech composer on his Liverpool Philharmonic audience, on 20 March 1928 introducing a work by Ladislav Vycpálek (1882–1969), the *Cantata of the Last Things of Man*. The four soloists were among the most distinguished of the inter-war period, the soprano Bella (later Isobel) Baillie, the contralto Elsie Suddaby, the tenor Walter Widdop and the baritone Roy Henderson. Wood's edition of *Five Operatic Choruses* by Handel, with English words by Helen Douglas Irvine, was also given at Liverpool that season. What other conductor of the time would have quarried such obscure Italian operas as *Lotario*, *Atalanta*, *Admeto*, *Rinaldo* and *Deidamia* for the delight of choralists and their audiences?

At this time, too, Wood conferred a vast popularity on what was known as *Purcell's Trumpet Voluntary*. Following another editor, Wood mistakenly attributed this keyboard piece to Purcell (it is really by Jeremiah Clarke) when he arranged it with enormous panache for brass, organ and timpani. In the printed programme for the BBC's concert of 27 November 1928 is an advertisement for a recording of the 'Purcell-Wood' *Trumpet Voluntary* performed not by Wood but by Sir Hamilton Harty and the Hallé Orchestra. Since Wood's version had not yet been printed, he had presumably given exceptional permission for his score and parts to be used.

By now the formation of the BBC's long-planned new orchestra had become a matter of pressing necessity. The interim BBC Wireless Orchestra had encountered some devasting criticism for performances at public concerts: 'the worst orchestral performances ever heard in London', 'an orchestra which sounds as if it were composed in great part of substitutes'. In the hope of attracting the very best instrumentalists to the new body, it was announced that a nucleus of most-desired players would be excused an audition. The remaining players would be recruited partly by fresh selection and audition, partly by honouring the contracts of certain members of the Wireless Orchestra.

Back from a holiday trip with Muriel to Norway, Wood wrote in mid-1928 to the BBC's director-general complaining that the BBC's advertising for its public concerts was inadequate, with too much reliance on broadcast announcements. 'Many regular concert-goers do not "listen-in" at all, and you want these in your audience as much as your wireless listeners.' He had the coming promenade concerts in mind, but also the poor attendances at Glasgow and other centres where he had conducted BBC concerts. 'I realize that the BBC organization is young,' he continued, but now was the time to grasp the opportunities which were theirs for the taking.

Pending the recruitment of its new orchestra, the BBC again fielded 'Sir Henry J. Wood and his symphony orchestra' – that is, his own seasoned players from Queen's Hall – for the 1928 and 1929 seasons of Proms. The BBC's budget allowed Wood to hold *two* rehearsals daily from the Tuesday to the Friday preceding the Saturday opening, and thereafter a morning rehearsal every day (Sundays alone excepted) throughout the eight weeks of the concerts – requiring prodigious stamina on the players' as well as the conductor's part. No event in the 1929 season was more remarkable than the première of William Walton's viola concerto, which Lionel Tertis had over-hastily rejected. The solo role was 'gallantly acccepted' by Paul Hindemith (an accomplished player of the instrument), not only to help a fellow-composer but to show his high regard for Wood. In the audience sat the 19-year-old Benjamin Britten, recording in his diary 'slack and incompetent performances' that night. His general response to Wood as conductor and arranger was highly critical – 'meaningless vandalism' being his view of Wood's Wagner extracts earlier in the year. Wood's reputation for vigour and sheer quantity was increasingly vulnerable to such charges of rough-and-readiness.

As the BBC's director of music, Wood's friend Percy Pitt found his position suddenly terminated by Sir John Reith on reaching the age of sixty in January 1930. In his place came Adrian Boult, whom Reith saw as an efficient administrator and orchestral trainer but never intended as chief conductor. (Reith was not initially prepared to tolerate 'sending for his director of music in the afternoon only to be told that he had gone home to rest as he was conducting in the evening'.) At the time when Boult was first approached, it was still envisaged that Beecham would become chief conductor.

The regime of creative energy which Pitt had already instituted at the BBC was typified by the decision to give the first British performance of Mahler's Symphony no.8, the so-called 'Symphony of a Thousand'. Recognizing (as it would later fail to do) the need to help its radio audience in following such a work, the BBC had commissioned a translation of the Goethe text. To have been entrusted with that vast fresco of nearly eighty minutes must have gratified Wood immensely. And who better? He had, after all, pioneered Mahler's work since 1903.

Wood proceeded to make known to the BBC's chorus-master his wishes for the most thorough vocal preparation. His letter (11 September 1928) is characteristically careless in mis-spelling the surnames of the conductors Carl Schuricht and Leopold Stokowski.

Dear Mr Stanford Robinson,

I shall require for the production of Gustav Mahler's 8th Symphony 250 mixed voices divided into two perfectly equal choirs – 125 singers on the right hand of the conductor and 125 singers on the left hand of the conductor; also 100 choir boys. I believe it is intended to invite these to take part from the various City churches. They will sit at the extreme end of the grand circle – 50 boys on each side.

Of course you know how intensely difficult this work is and that there is nearly one hour's choral singing in it, and when Schurich at Wiesbaden gave it recently (and German choirs are good musicians and readers as a rule) he found that fifty rehearsals were only just enough and Mr Stowkowski told me two Sundays ago that he gave it six months continuous preparation. It is therefore very imperative that from October to April you hold one rehearsal a week with the female voices and one rehearsal a week with the male voices, as it would be a useless waste of time to combine the two bodies until they are nearly note perfect.

Such a demand, however, had to go much higher in the BBC than the chorus-master. Wood was told that this extended schedule of rehearsals was more than the BBC could afford. He wrote to Sir John Reith on 28 November 1928 that 'in the circumstances' it would be 'impossible' for him to conduct the concert. A BBC annotation to his letter, for internal reference, retorted: 'This is nonsense! and the chorus *can* do it [with fewer rehearsals]. Wood's demands are childish and I don't see why our chorus should help him to learn the work!'

The last sentence, whoever wrote it, travestied the position. Everyone familiar with Wood's methods knew of his rigorous self-preparation when tackling new music. Never was a rehearsal used to help him 'learn the work'. It is clear that despite the 'impossible' of Wood's letter, negotiations continued and Wood was persuaded to accept a smaller number of rehearsals. The projected performance was postponed from the 1928–9 season to 1929–30, and on 10 September 1929 the BBC was still considering Wood's 'full and final demands' for extra rehearsals and other expenses – including the engagement of understudies for the eight solo singers required by the score.

The BBC's own amateur choral society was reckoned capable enough, but what of the composer's stipulation of exceptionally low bass voices able to descend to a sustained low B flat? Wood suggested to the BBC that amateur singers of this range 'might be found in the East End of London among the Jewish synagogues'. But they were not unearthed there and it

proved necessary to add to the bill by engaging four specialized professionals. For the boys' chorus Wood was induced to lower his demand from a
hundred voices to fifty or perhaps sixty on the technical grounds put forward
by the BBC's Balance and Control department – that more than fifty 'would
be muzzier instead of clear-cut in tone and would cause peaks in the
modulation that would upset the whole of the remainder of the transmission'.

By December 1929 the BBC was communicating with Wood on the Nile
steamship *Delta* (care of Thomas Cook, Luxor, Egypt) and next month at the
Hotel Majestic, Tunis – an extended holiday for the conductor and his wife,
with a return journey overland from Italy. New difficulties with the boys'
chorus led to the suggestion from the BBC that the Mahler performance be
deferred for yet another season, but that idea was dropped. So on 15 April
1930, at Queen's Hall, the colossal symphony was given. Beethoven's
Leonora no.3 overture opened the concert, followed by Part 1 of the Mahler;
Part 2 was performed after the interval, when the BBC 9 o'clock news was
broadcast. The participating soloists were Elsie Suddaby, May Blyth, Irene
Mordin, Muriel Brunskill, Clara Serena, Walter Widdop, Harold Williams
and Robert Easton.

As regards the choral complement, the sequel was ironic. Leslie
Woodgate, who had been put in charge of the boys' chorus, wrote an internal
BBC memorandum on the very day of the concert:

> In spite of the fact that Sir Henry Wood asked for 100 boys to sing in the
> Mahler Symphony, he was advised that 50 would be ample. At the
> rehearsals, the boys have been completely swamped by the orchestra and
> chorus, and Sir Henry has continually asked for more sound from them
> when they have been singing their utmost. I think it would have been
> possible for Balance & Control to have arranged to eliminate any blasting
> that might have taken place had there been 100 boys. It is obviously
> impossible for such a small number of boys to make any definite impression
> against such a large number of older voices and instruments.

Writing a few days after the concert, Stanford Robinson as principal chorus-
master concurred:

> I must say I support this view and feel also that Sir Henry well knew what he
> was talking about when he said that it was necessary for the chorus to have
> 50 rehearsals. The music meeting was rather inclined to pooh-pooh him and
> I myself thought he was being rather on the extravagant side, but to get a
> really first-class performance, he was quite right – 50 rehearsals would not
> have been one too many.

Battling

Press reaction still showed that suspicion of Mahler which was to be prevalent in Britain for many years. The influential Eric Blom, later to be the editor of the fifth edition of *Grove's Dictionary*, wrote in reaction to the Eighth Symphony:

> Quite disinterestedly considered, Gustav Mahler has no chance whatever to be ranked with the great composers by posterity. He is a composer of extraordinary artistic imagination, but without a vestige of specifically musical invention that can be called out of the ordinary. . . . [The symphony is] exactly the sort of music we all dreamed of writing at the age of fifteen, when nothing less than Goethe's *Faust* (part 2) would do.

The Mahler performance ended a series of thirteen spring concerts (January-April 1930), in the middle of which the inauguration of both a 'National' and a 'Regional' programme marked a major expansion of BBC transmissions. Of these concerts six were allotted to Beecham (one being shared with Elgar) and three to Wood, including Mahler's purely orchestral Seventh Symphony, a work as long as the Eighth. The concert of 14 March included an important première: Bax's Symphony no.3, which was dedicated to Wood and which he would continue to champion in Britain and abroad. On 14 February his performance of Bartók's first Piano Concerto had the composer as soloist – but the broader public never responded to Bartók with the warmth they bestowed on his friend and compatriot Kodály for the *Háry János* suite. This, with its strikingly novel part for *cimbalom* or Hungarian dulcimer, had received its first British performance from Wood's baton at the 1928 Proms and would never lose its place in the Proms repertory.

In an 'extra' concert on Good Friday (18 April 1930) Wood conducted what was to become a regular feature, a *'Parsifal* concert', almost entirely orchestral but with soprano and baritone soloists, respectively in Kundry's 'Herzeleide' aria and Amfortas' prayer. Then, at last, the prospectus for the 1930 season of BBC Promenade Concerts proclaimed the presence of 'Sir Henry J. Wood and the BBC Symphony Orchestra'. This was its first appearance under that name, with a playing strength of ninety. An additional component of players (making the total 114) was to appear at the following series of BBC symphony concerts.

Many members of what had been the New Queen's Hall Orchestra found a place in the new BBC orchestra, though Wood in *My Life of Music* was hardly accurate in saying that the one simply 'merged' into the other. His leader, Charles Woodhouse, retained that place at the 1930 Proms but, from the beginning of the ensuing symphony concerts, took second place to Arthur Catterall. The first horn was Aubrey Brain, as in Wood's old orchestra. But the first oboe, Alec Whittaker, had been lured from the Hallé Orchestra; Frederick Thurston, first clarinet, and Ernest Hall, first trumpet, were among other new names, soon to be famous. Lauri Kennedy, an Australian, was the new first cello. The *Manchester Guardian* of 11 August 1930 was in no doubt about the improved quality at the Proms: 'The tone in every section is improved beyond comparison. One had the impression of walking in a garden that had been thoroughly weeded . . . There is not the smallest doubt about it, the new orchestra is something in the nature of a glorious adventure for musical London.'

The new orchestra's first (1930) season of Proms had a strong representation of British music – partly through the designation of certain concerts as 'British Composers' Concerts', a kind of special pleading which took its initiative from the BBC, not from Wood. Bax's recent Third Symphony was given, and Léon Goossens (another adornment of the new orchestra) played the new Oboe Concerto composed for him by his brother Eugene. There was also a new, though minor, work by Elgar – the *Pomp and Circumstance* March no.5 on 20 September. Though kept away from that première by sciatica, Elgar mounted Wood's rostrum as the conductor of his Symphony no.2 on 2 October. On that same evening came the première of John Ireland's piano concerto, a work long to remain popular. The solo part was undertaken by the composer's young protégée Helen Perkin – and not by Arthur Rubinstein, whose memoir *My Many Years* has the fictitious 'reminiscence': 'Sir Henry Wood . . . had given me a score of a concerto by the English composer John Ireland. "My dear Rubinstein, why don't we give the first performance of it?" Sir Henry gave two full rehearsals to the work, which helped me to become quite familiar with it, and the performance was a success.'

Rubinstein's performance of the concerto was in fact a later one, on 1 September 1936 on the occasion of his first appearance at the Proms.

The players of the BBC Symphony Orchestra became habituated to a tight schedule in preparing for the annual Proms. Assembling on a Tuesday, the day after the August Bank Holiday, they underwent a preliminary period of intense rehearsals – six hours a day for four days. After that, all preparation had to be fitted into the morning rehearsals on each day of the concerts themselves. The only work to win an exception was Bach's Brandenburg Concerto no.6, for which Wood called an afternoon rehearsal at his own expense, with tea and cake provided – as a young member newly recruited would later recall. Norman Carrell was one of the violinists reallotted (since that score excludes violins) to function as an extra viola-player. Carrell retained great admiration for Wood as 'the absolute tops' among technicians of conducting, while sensing that the BBC hierarchy viewed him as a 'workman', a lesser artist than such visiting conductors as Mengelberg and Walter.

The Proms, at least, were 'his'. So the public ovation told him as he mounted the rostrum to conduct the first concert of the 1930 promenade season on 9 August, flower in his buttonhole as usual. So too his BBC contract assured him – thus far, though such contracts would have to be periodically renegotiated. In June 1930 he had accepted a figure of £3900 p.a. as remuneration for conducting the promenade concerts for three more years, plus up to sixteen more BBC concerts each year (in concert-hall or studio). In the BBC's schedule of such concerts in winter and spring he would have to compete with the perceived specialities of other British and foreign conductors.

He also faced a battle to maintain orchestral standards at provincial festivals. Norwich beckoned once again in October 1930 for what turned out to be Wood's last appearance in the city's long-lived triennial series. Interest was evidently falling (were those predictions of the greater lure of the domestic loudspeaker coming true?) but the festival still served an area largely out of range of major orchestral performances for the rest of the year. The twenty-one-year-old Benjamin Britten was among those who attended, as well as his principal teacher in composition, Frank Bridge. The level of playing was criticized both in the *Monthly Musical Record* (Richard Capell) and *Musical Opinion* (A. J. Sheldon). It was noted that this was not the orchestra Wood had lately spruced up for the Proms but a motley assembly 'euphemistically called the Queen's Hall Orchestra'.

On 22 October Arthur Bliss – now confirmed as a representative British composer – conducted at Norwich his hour-long symphony called *Morning Heroes* (the reference was to World War One) for orator, chorus and orchestra. Though with a precedent in Elgar's *Carillon*, the speech-and-music combination failed to strike root. Next day Wood's continuing enthusiasm for new Czech music yielded the first performance in Britain of Janáček's *Glagolitic Mass*. The Janáček failed of effect: Wood's advocacy was simply twenty-five years in advance of British readiness to accept the spiky unconventionalities of the composer's style. Richard Capell had heard a Czech choir give the Mass in Geneva where it sounded 'rather jolly, like a Balkan insurrection without the danger'; whereas at Norwich, 'sung to

230

selected phrases from the English Communion service, it sounded ridiculous, but no one dare[d] even smile'.

The Norwich Festival of 1930 also served to introduce Wood's new, freely-orchestrated version of Handel's *Solomon* – tit-for-tat to Beecham, who had brought an equally individualistic treatment to the work in the Royal Philharmonic Society season of 1927–8. Wood's firm belief in amplifying the orchestral palette in such works was gathering opposition from some critics while continuing to convince others. Frank Howes, later to be chief music critic of *The Times*, made an attack on grounds of taste in 1929:

> Sir Henry's orchestral arrangements and transcriptions (mostly of the earlier composers like Bach and Purcell) are out of character, and . . . we wish he would not do it. He appears to think that all composers' scoring ought to sound alike, viz., like Wagner, and Wagner played turgidly at that. He ruthlessly adds clarinets, doubles string parts with wind, adds trombones to Bach, and destroys all sense of lines in the contrapuntal type of scoring by sheer weight of redundant notes. Not only is it bad, it is wrong; not only is it wrong, it is unnecessary. Why, then, do it?

On the other hand Havergal Brian in *Musical Opinion* wrote of a Bach *sinfonia* 'modernized by Sir Henry Wood' as 'one of the most completely satisfying things yet experienced . . . The apparent concern of Sir Henry Wood was to give the music a free hand and to let the music tell its own story.' A distinction should nevertheless be made (as Howes failed to do) between Wood the modernizer, adding to the baroque orchestra what was not already in it, and Wood the transcriber for orchestra of works originally written for a keyboard instrument. The most celebrated of such transcriptions came to birth at a promenade concert on 5 October 1929: Bach's celebrated organ work, the Toccata and Fugue in D minor, in an orchestration ascribed to one Paul Klenovsky and dated 'Moscow, 1923'.

Supposedly a pupil of Glazunov who had died young, 'Klenovsky' had orchestrated the work in a 'monster' version, with quadruple woodwind, six horns, four trumpets, four trombones, multiple percussion and, at the climax, organ! Much less of an array had been demanded by Leopold Stokowski in his already well-known orchestration. Wood's successful first performance was followed by many others in London and elsewhere. The Klenovsky scoring provided 'the most magnificent piece of music [in the programme]', wrote Richard Capell of a later Proms performance. A Liverpool performance of what was frequently referred to as Bach's 'great D minor' led the *Liverpool Echo* of 26 February 1930, in an inspired misreading of its reviewer's handwriting, to refer to Wood's conducting of Bach's 'great Dimmer organ toccata and fugue'.

Not until 1934 did Hubert Foss of the Oxford University Press, wishing to publish the orchestration, ask Wood for further identification of the arranger or his surviving relatives. Wood divulged the secret, which his own family already shared. *He* was Klenovsky. Across the manuscript full score he had scrawled in a hasty hand:

> This is my *original copy* of the scoring of Bach's Toccata and Fugue in D minor. I only announced it scored by Paul Klenovsky, *as a blind to the Press*, as I got *very fed up with them*, always finding fault with any arrangement or orchestrations that I made – 'heavy Wagner handling', 'spoiling the original' etc: etc: *but directly this piece appearing, with my untrue concocted story* which of course I had put in all the programmes, the Press, the musicians of the Orchestra, and the officials of the BBC fell into the trap, and said the scoring was wonderful, Klenovsky had the real flare [*sic*] for true colour etc. – and performance after performance was given and *asked* for. Had I put it out under my own name the result would have been one performance (after spending £33 on score and parts) – slated and shelved. So for the future all my scoring will be announced as by Paul Klenovsky – although such a person never existed.
>
> Henry J. Wood

It was surely curious that the music critics and others involved were so indolent as not to have investigated the identity of 'Paul Klenovsky' in the first place. They would have found that there was no such person, though a Russian composer called Nikolay Klenovsky had died in 1915. Henry J. Wood did not proceed to re-use the pseudonym Klenovsky for future orchestral arrangements: the cover once having been blown, he could not. The fact that not all the reviewers had actually praised the transcription in the first place was irrelevant. The hoax had worked, just as had Kreisler's cheeky attribution to Pugnani and other composers (genuine eighteenth-century figures in his case) of pieces he had composed himself. The 'Bach-Klenovsky' arrangement, duly published, was widely performed and remained a favourite of Wood's audiences at the BBC's promenade concerts. It was to involve him tangentially with two other great conductors.

In confronting the higher management of the BBC, Wood had a staunch champion within the organization – Adrian Boult, who remained in the administrative position of director of music while accepting from 1931 the additional (and, initially, unexpected) role of chief conductor. Boult's admiration for Wood as an orchestral trainer and the sustainer of the night-by-night promenade season had been forthrightly stated in 1925:

> . . .I have often said (and I have never been contradicted) that in my opinion the average standard of performance throughout the Promenade season is higher under Sir Henry Wood's direction than could be possible under any other living conductor. The worst performance one could ever hear at the Promenade concerts would do credit to many well-known concert-giving institutions, and the best will bear comparison with anything to be heard throughout the world.

In the years that now followed, Boult was not required to negotiate with Wood on fees and similar matters. But he could mediate between musical and administrative claims. The question of whether Wood claimed perquisites beyond his due, or presumed too heavily on being indispensable, would periodically irritate BBC executives. Boult had a way of cushioning such prickles, as when he was asked why the BBC was paying Wood for the use of his own (Wood's) parts:

> I believe that wherever he goes he makes a practice of using his own material and charging current [hire] rates for it. It is not usually done by conductors, but I think it can be considered reasonable in view of the fact that Sir Henry has built up his library at considerable capital expenditure, has increased its value musically by the most careful marking, and the society for whom he conducts gets the benefit of this in the reduction of rehearsal time owing to this marking.

Wood's dedication to the *mission* of music was too acute for him not to appreciate the social benefits brought by the BBC. In *The Golden Age of Wireless*, Asa Briggs aptly quotes a remark of Wood's of a few years later: 'With the whole-hearted support of the wonderful medium of broadcasting I feel that I am at last on the threshold of realizing my life-long ambition of truly democratizing the message of music and making its beneficent effect universal. . . .'

There was another good reason for Wood to show himself thankful to the BBC. Already in the position of Britain's largest musical paymaster, the BBC seemed uniquely immune from the effects of the prevailing economic recession (1929–32). Its fortunes stayed buoyant as the total number of licence-payers climbed unstoppably, from just over two million in 1927 to more than nine million just twelve years later. Moreover 'the biggest percentage increase in a single year was in the gloomy months from March

Battling

1930 to March 1931'. No other organization was available to give Wood the financial shelter of which, particularly since stripped of his 'own' orchestra in 1927, he stood in need.

Chapter 16

Squeezed Out?

1930–34

To accept the shelter of the BBC's umbrella was one thing; to secure his own territory within the BBC's operations was another. Vigilance and exertion would be needed to ensure not only that the Proms kept their musical importance, but that his was a conspicuous place in the BBC's year-round schedule of studio concerts and 'symphony' (public) concerts with the new orchestra at Queen's Hall. And just because the BBC had now become his main source of income, his power of negotiation against it was frail. Within a few years, a feeling of being both artistically and financially squeezed by its demands would come to a head.

At first he was given generous treatment. Three successive symphony concerts in November 1930 displayed him as a Bach conductor (all six Brandenburg Concertos, plus other items, in a single evening); as an exponent of Strauss and Mahler; and in a programme which once again united him with Bartók, this time as soloist in his Rhapsody for Piano and Orchestra. Further symphony concerts came his way in the new year. But the summer of 1931 saw the BBC dampening down the characteristic enterprise of Wood's promenade concerts. Only two new works by composers of foreign nationality were given – Webern's *Passacaglia* (the first-ever Webern at the Proms) on 22 August, an *Aubade* by Poulenc two weeks later.

The promotion of new British works was equally sluggish, with seniority weighing heavily in the selection. The ailing Delius heard, by radio at his French home, the first performance of *A Song of Summer* on 17 September. On 20 August Elgar himself conducted his *Nursery* Suite, written in honour of the two little princesses, Elizabeth (later Queen Elizabeth II) and Margaret, and first performed privately two months before. Wood was angered (relieving his feelings in a letter to the composer John Ireland) by an article in the *Radio Times* seeming to imply that in matters of orchestral standards the Proms were 'of no use at all, that not one performance was of any account, and that only in the BBC Symphony Concerts could you hear perfection'. Sir John Reith received 'a strong letter' from him in protest.

By the following May (1932), when a more potent omen had arrived on Wood's desk, Adrian Boult had been appointed the chief conductor of the BBC Symphony Orchestra, while still retaining his administrative post as the BBC's director of music. A letter from Reith advised Wood of the BBC's intention to increase the number of concerts 'given to our permanent conductor, Dr Boult' and to reduce the number of appearances by guest conductors. The same letter offered Wood two more seasons of Proms, but was silent on any commitment beyond that.

The Proms that summer showed the BBC even more strongly determined to deprive the Proms of their pioneering character. There were *no* first performances of British works: never since the very beginning in 1895 had such a thing been known at the Proms. There was only one work of new Continental vintage. It was, admittedly, a considerable novelty: Ravel's Piano Concerto for the Left Hand, introduced on 16 August by the one-armed Austrian pianist for whom it was written, Paul Wittgenstein. It can then hardly have been guessed how many normally equipped pianists would take on the challenge of this extraordinary work – and would surpass, by all accounts, its original exponent's performance.

In the judgement of the *Musical Times*, by ceasing to identify the Proms with new music the BBC had reduced them to featureless 'mass concert-giving'. *The Times*, under the heading NO NEWCOMERS NEED APPLY, castigated not only the failure to bring forward absolutely new pieces but a more general, debilitating conservatism: 'The question is whether, in becoming higher-class, [the programmes] have not become something less than they formerly were. . . . This year's season has made no venture at all in the matter of composers, and practically none in the matter of solo performers.'

The newspaper presented this change firmly in the context of a battle between Wood and the BBC planners: 'His hands are tied while the programmes are being made up, and untied only just in time to allow him to wave them before the performers when the rehearsals begin. He, like everyone else, is caught in the machine which caters [only] for existing public taste.'

If in 1932 BBC policy was tying Wood's hands, a drastic change at the Royal Philharmonic Society would also place him at a marked disdvantage. Hitherto his place on the Society's roster of conductors had been maintained, alongside Beecham and such younger British figures as Basil Cameron and Malcolm Sargent. On 10 March 1932 his was the honour of conducting the concert at which the Society's gold medal was presented to Rachmaninoff, after Rachmaninoff himself had been heard as soloist in his Piano Concerto no.3.

Once again, however, the Society was in financial trouble – and once again it grasped the lifeline offered, not without benefit to himself, by Sir Thomas Beecham. Its concerts would be given by the new and brilliant assembly of players which Beecham created as his personal fief under the name of the London Philharmonic Orchestra. To this orchestra (giving the public a confusion of names and identities from which it has still not recovered) the Royal Philharmonic Society handed its programmes, and Beecham rapidly secured contractual arrangements also from Covent Garden Opera House and from both the Columbia and HMV recording companies. Beecham's personal prestige and entrepreneurial flair had now established a firm base. He again had 'his' orchestra: Wood had not.

The effect of Beecham's *coup* on the Society's roster of conductors was palpable. Of ten concerts in the 1932–3 season Beecham conducted nine and the Russian Nicolai Malko the other. Wood was not again engaged until 1934 (once) and 1939 (twice). He must have felt the slight deeply.

Before the advent of the London Philharmonic Orchestra, its predecessor, the so-called 'Royal Philharmonic Orchestra', had been engaged to reinforce the BBC Symphony Orchestra at an Albert Hall concert in aid of the Musicians' Benevolent Fund, a charity which could always count on Wood's sympathetic ear. But Wood had greeted sceptically the initial proposal by Frank Thistleton, organizer of the Fund, to invite the participation of seven major world stars – McCormack, Shalyapin, Elisabeth Schumann, Lotte Lehmann, Lauritz Melchior, Kreisler and Rachmaninoff. The daily *News Chronicle*, of which Landon Ronald had become 'music editor' and a regular columnist, was to sponsor the event. 'Dear Sir Landon,' wrote Wood (who stuck rather oddly to formal modes of address, even to colleagues):

> I told him [Thistleton] that it would be impossible to get any of these artistes to appear, as they are all artistes too big to appear in concerts with other artistes. They are 'lone hunters'. I have had experiences in soliciting benefit appearances from them, and have always met with refusals.
>
> In this connection, I attended two concerts in which the massed LSO [London Symphony Orchestra] and the New Symphony gave benefit concerts – one at the Palladium, and the other at the Albert Hall, and

neither of these concerts were properly featured by the Press, and the houses were practically empty. The musicians gave their services.

But Ronald and Thistleton persisted. They were able to secure the presence of King George V and Queen Mary for the event on 26 May 1932. Of the originally invited soloists only Kreisler and McCormack accepted (thus far Wood was right!) but estimable substitutes were secured – the singers Elena Gerhardt and Friedrich Schorr, the pianist Backhaus and the cellist Suggia. Wood shared the conducting with Elgar, Ronald and Boult. Students of the Royal Military School of Music joined the orchestral brass and percussion in fanfares by Bliss and Bax. Nearly at the end of a very long evening, the audience was invited to join in the singing of Parry's 'Jerusalem' – almost in anticipation of the modern 'Last Night of the Proms', but in this case with words and music provided in the printed programme.

The *Musical Times,* having so severely censured the BBC over the programming of the 1932 Proms, cast an equally disapproving look at the announcement of what was to follow:

> The eighteen Symphony concerts of the BBC also seem to imply that contemporary music is at a standstill. There are only four novelties, and three of them (as might be expected) come from Central Europe, the composers being those BBC favourites Schönberg, Hindemith, and Berg; the English novelty is Vaughan Williams's Pianoforte Concerto. Those of us who defended the lack of enterprise in the Promenade programmes on the supposition that the BBC was reserving its enterprise for the Symphony concerts are thus shown to have been wrong.

Exceptionally the BBC interrupted that winter–spring season by giving Wood a two-week season of winter promenade concerts (from 31 December 1932), but did not seize the opportunity to rebut the charge of narrowness. The only new work was Hindemith's *Philharmonic Concerto.* Wood's revival on the same evening (10 January) of Vaughan Williams's *A London Symphony* was 'one of the best performances of the fortnight', according to Richard Capell in the *Monthly Musical Record.* Capell was dismissive, however, of a sequence of sixteen choruses from *Messiah,* sung by the Sheffield Musical Union, with Wood's characteristic reinforcement of the orchestral palette. Wood was said to be 'strangely out of sympathy with Handel, whose style he endeavoured to recast in some sort of nineteenth-century mould, Tchaikovskian perhaps'.

Yet another work by Hindemith was allotted to Wood by the BBC

planners, this time no doubt in the hope of grafting a distinctive Continental
modernity on to the stem of the British choral tradition. But if ever the text of
a choral work was designed *not* to appeal to British audiences it was that of
Hindemith's *Das Unaufhörliche* (*The Perpetual*), a kind of secular oratorio:

> The one Perpetual, greatest of laws, on days and nights
>   sustained, it sports itself from sea to sea. . .
> . . . Transition always,
> Marble fanes, then beasts and mortals converted soon
>   to ashes and flowery scent. . .

So ran the English version which had been commissioned from Rose and
Cyril Scott. The *Monthly Musical Record* printed a six-page preliminary
analysis of the work by Edmund Rubbra: thus *two* British composers were
involved, the ageing Scott and the young Rubbra, soon to win respect as a
substantial symphonist. But the same journal eventually reviewed 'the first
performance, which no doubt was also the last' (22 March 1933) with
maximum distaste. The solo vocal parts were 'about as charming as a
barbed-wire entanglement', though the choruses were 'well built'. With
stubborn independence Wood was to maintain, in *My Life of Music,* that this
was Hindemith's best work. He was to repeat an aria from it at the coming
summer's Proms.

With Schoenberg and Webern already in his bag, Wood came last of all to
the remaining member of the 'second Viennese school', Alban Berg. The
authorized three *Fragments* from *Wozzeck* formed part of his BBC concert at
Queen's Hall on 8 March 1933, after they had been less conspicuously
broadcast from the studio with Webern conducting. With May Blyth as the
soprano soloist, this 'first public performance' by Wood anticipated Boult's
much-reported complete concert performance of the opera in the following
year. In respect of both the Hindemith and the Berg performances Wood's
place is insufficiently recognized in Nicholas Kenyon's book of 1981 on the
BBC Symphony Orchestra: they are mentioned there with no conductor's
name in a chapter headed 'Boult's Great Orchestra, 1930–5'.

The BBC's orchestra was not, however, the only one with which Wood
appeared in London at this time. The New Symphony Orchestra was the
name under which Landon Ronald regularly assembled his choice of players,
and Wood took a share in its Sunday concerts at the London Palladium. On 19
March 1933 his programme was of Beethoven's *Pastoral* Symphony,
Brahms's Violin Concerto with Jelly d'Arányi, and Elgar's *Dream Children*
and *Cockaigne*. Such a programme was far more 'classical' than would have

been thought appropriate for such a middlebrow public before World War One. Reserved seats were available for as little as 1s 3d, as compared with 2s for unreserved admission to the promenade concerts in that year.

Other events in Wood's calendar formed a miscellany. Regularly bringing the Royal Academy of Music orchestra to Queen's Hall, he programmed in November 1931 the Symphony no.2 by Edward German, his own fellow-student of Academy days: it had never previously been given in London. Maintaining his commitment to the amateurs of the Hull Philharmonic Orchestra, he enlisted the twenty-seven-year-old Clifford Curzon to play Dohnányi's *Variations on a Nursery Song* in March 1932. In the following month he conducted another amateur body, the Herbert Ware Symphony Orchestra of Cardiff. He conducted *The Dream of Gerontius* in Leicester. None of such engagements can have been money-making; they simply showed his continuous, omnivorous desire to make music. Looked at in a different way, however, they depreciated his value at a time of life when selectivity and specialisation would have enhanced it.

Life with Muriel continued to involve holidays in distant places. In *My Life of Music*, where her name is never mentioned, Wood records only that 'I left England again for a holiday in South Africa' (December 1930), 'I was on holiday in Costa Rica and Trinidad' (Christmas 1932), and so on. But there is little doubt that Muriel not only accompanied him but largely initiated the trips, adding some extensions for herself alone – from Trinidad to Bermuda, for instance. The autobiography makes mention of visits to Montreux in 1928, Biskra (in the interior of Algeria) in 1929, Bermuda in December 1933, all without a word to convey a sightseer's agreeable or disagreeable impression. 'Three weeks in Morocco' in January–February 1933, mentioned in an anticipatory letter to Sanders, slipped the autobiographer's memory.

These were Muriel's 'annual scamps abroad', as Henry was to describe them, with considerable irritation, in *My Confession*. He seems to have been pleased only when the nominal holiday in South Africa turned out to involve him in concerts with the City Orchestra of Capetown. 'I had one or two batons with me – merely because I always take them wherever I go in order to keep in practice' [!]. He – or rather they – visited South Africa again in the summer of 1934, returning via Canada, 'reaching London on 6 August in time to take the first rehearsal for the Promenades the following morning'.

The years had provided other occasions of travel specifically to fulfil concert engagements – in Nice in April 1927, in Monte Carlo in January 1928, in Paris the following November; in Zurich in June 1932 and at Scheveningen in Holland the following month.At Zurich, his offering of Bax's Symphony no.3, Delius's *First Cuckoo* and two of Holst's *Planets* earned him no less praise than had his appearance in the city a decade before. The report of the concert by 'Sir Wood' on 26 April 1932 was literally front-page news in the city's principal daily newspaper, the *Neue Zürcher Zeitung*. In the Zurich *Tages-Anzeiger*, the critic Fritz Gysi made a familiar comparison: Wood was 'to some extent an English Nikisch, but with a more masculine attack'. He classified Wood as 'one of those fortunate creatures who can wholly express themselves in the work of art, who instinctively hit the mark without recourse to technical tricks or intellectual over-subtleties. Wood makes his point not with dictatorial gestures but in a natural, honest artistic impulse.'

Gysi welcomed not only the British works but the rarity of a Haydn symphony, Wood's choice being *The Clock* (no.101). 'Only an interpreter of ripe years, with most of his journey through life and art already past' could bring to life a work of such purity, refreshing to heart and mind.

A tour in November 1933 took him to conduct in Hamburg, Copenhagen, Gothenburg and Oslo. In a letter to Sanders from the Hôtel d'Angleterre, Copenhagen, on 7 November he wrote that he and Muriel were having 'a wonderful time, lunches, dinners, and a special banquet after my concert here tonight'.

His arrival at the railway station in Copenhagen was watched by a reporter from the *Berlingske Tidende*: 'When [Louis] Armstrong arrived, the entire platform was filled with people giving him a rapturous welcome. When Sir Henry Wood arrived last night, there were only the pianist from the orchestra, Miss Stockmeir, and the composer Hakon Børresen to do him honours.' (Johanne Stockmeir, who had performed with Wood in London, was to play the Schumann concerto at his Copenhagen concert on 8 November.) Plainly with the famous jazz trumpeter still in mind, the reporter teasingly asked the visitor: 'How do you regard jazz?' and received the answer 'Whatever you may say, jazz is for dancing and has nothing to do with music' (a sentiment which he sometimes put more crudely, and from which he never diverged).

In his notice of that concert, the paper's music critic would have liked a British work less familiar than the *Enigma Variations* and diplomatically referred to Wood's own *Purcell* Suite as 'a little too organized' (i.e., over-scored). Richard Strauss's *Don Juan* was said to have been the work 'where Sir Henry most clearly revealed his personality as a conductor'. It was a review slightly less enthusiastic than might have been hoped for – but the whole tour satisfied Wood. From the Grand Hotel, Oslo, on 16 November he wrote to Hubert Foss with congratulations on Foss's new book, *Music in My Time*, adding: 'My concerts in Copenhagen, Oslo and Gothenborg [*sic*] have all been sold out – not bad, think you?'

To perform at such events abroad did not materially help in enhancing a conductor's image at home. The making of gramophone recordings would do so. In this respect Wood was falling behind the competition offered not only by Beecham but by Mengelberg, Weingartner, Koussevitzky and others. A seriously musical public stood ready to accept works as much as an hour long, no matter how many 78 r.p.m. sides had to be allotted to them. Twelve sides were devoted by Pierre Monteux to Berlioz's *Symphonie Fantastique*. Schoenberg's and Stravinsky's music became available on record. Wood's Columbia recordings of the early 1930s, however, gave no more than a hint of his range in either older or newer music. His Bach was properly represented by the *Brandenburg* Concertos nos.3 and 6, but the record-buyer too easily identified him with the cheaper section of the record catalogue and with short works by Grainger, or with Järnefelt's *Praeludium*, or his own transcription of the 'Volga Boat Song'.

The gramophone record played a crucial role in establishing one of the most sensational performers to enter the British scene in those years. Yehudi Menuhin was only thirteen years old (some accounts wrongly say twelve) when he made his London début under the baton of Fritz Busch in November 1929. In 1932 came his famous recording of Elgar's Violin Concerto, with the composer conducting. Menuhin's own recollections of meeting Henry J. Wood, set down in a BBC interview of 1969, are among the most interesting of any:

> The strongest impression I have of Sir Henry is of an ebullient, vigorous, and if I might say, Continental quality in relation at least to music. At that time I didn't realize his close association with the Russian musical literature, but being of Russian origin myself, although born in New York, I must have instinctively found in this typical Englishman an approach to music which rhymed with my own childish instinctive feeling about Tchaikovsky and the rather heavier, more garishly coloured music which at that time I particularly favoured.
>
> Although I loved Mozart, my tastes in childhood were hardly subtle, shall I say? Not that Sir Henry didn't have great subtlety, but our association at that time was soldered, as it were, by this tremendous vigour that I found in him and this unashamed quality of being himself, being absolutely himself. Later I learned how very characteristic he was of the people to whom he

belonged, especially his musical career, which like the career of many great English musicians was based solidly on the organ, the choir and the English opera, Gilbert and Sullivan and later on Wagner and Tchaikovsky. It just proves how important it is for a very great conductor to have a broad base. And I can't imagine anyone who had a broader base, and that came through not only in talking to him but simply by his presence, he was a broad man, he was a man who spread space and strength about him.

All four Woods (Henry, Muriel and their daughters) had accepted an invitation to meet Menuhin at a lunch party in London and to proceed to a performance of his on that same afternoon. But how, with due politeness, was their acceptance to be reconciled with the claims of a christening in Chorley Wood? Muriel was to be godmother to Diana, the newly-born child of her friend and neighbour Dora Foss.

Her letter of 29 November 1933 – beginning with the same formality in address as Henry used – bears the heading 'In train', evidently Brighton-bound.

> My dear Mrs Foss,
> I *am* glad you have been able to arrange everything so nicely. I will be at the church on time as I will go straight from a lunch party in town arranged *ages* ago round Menuhin and his father and I will explain to my host that I cannot go to the Albert Hall concert afterwards. Tania says she too will 'cut' the concert in favour of Diana – leaving Henry and Avril to carry out the full lunch-concert programme. (If there is a more wobbly-knobbly train than the 10 a.m. London to Brighton I hope I shan't meet it!)
> Now *please* be kind and tell one whether you think Diana will prefer a porringer mug or small piece of jewellery. It would be such a help if I may put the blame on you afterwards!
> I *do* hope you feel every day a good deal better.
> Love from
> – Yours ever,
> Muriel Wood.

Such a letter indicates yet again the warmth and liveliness which her friends found in Lady Wood, and which doubtless permeated the Sunday hospitality which continued to be extended at Appletree Farm to musical celebrities and others. She struck up a personal, informal relationship with Sanders. After Wood had sent Sanders £2 to help a musician in distress, Muriel followed up with her own note: 'But how sad it all is, and one fears there must be many such cases . . . (P.S.) By the way, did *you* pay anything towards the redemption [from the pawnbroker's] of Mr Coenen's violin and clothes? A feeling comes over me that perhaps you did! and of course Henry would like to pay it all. I know you would have been kind enough to do it.'

She was writing in April 1931 from Torquay, where Wood was conducting a concert. Such solicitude makes a mockery of Wood's later complaint that his wife 'hated and despised musicians'. The phrase smacks of petulance. Muriel was soon adopting a warm personal tone in letters to Mrs Sanders also:

> I really must write and tell you how *very* sorry I am to hear that Mr Sanders has been ill; somehow one feels that neither you nor he deserve *ever* to be ill, but as he says I suppose we must all come to it if we live long enough, but I *do* hope that he will soon be quite himself again. I had 'flu – the first time for ages – as soon as I got back from Bermuda, but did not spend one whole day in bed as there was plenty of correspondence to attend to and also I did not yet want to break my record of never a whole day in bed since we came here sixteen years ago!

Henry J. Wood likewise shed his reserve in a way most unusual for him. 'My dear Sanders,' he wrote in June 1932, 'Please let us drop for the future all Sirs and Misters, and do call me Wood . . .' His delegation of work to Sanders continued: '(24 June 1933) I do hope you can score for me Handel's first organ concerto in G minor [opus 4 no.1]. The BBC have put it down for Cunningham [to play at the Proms] and over a year ago I sketched out the scoring in my Best [W.T.Best's] edition, and this you can have if you care to have it – it conveys *how* I was going to do it, but do it entirely off your own bat if you care to do so.'

In the summer of 1933 he was severely ill and confined to his bed at Appletree Farm – 'a sharp attack of pneumonia', he called it in reply to a solicitous letter from Edward German. 'What a sudden and wretched thing it is, but I am told that I have been exceptionally lucky in making such a quick and good recovery, for they called it an "acute" attack, but it kept to one lung fortunately and there is no trace of anything now, they tell me.'

A few years later, after the break from his wife, he would complain of a lack of domestic care during that illness. Not only is that denied by his daughter Tania, who remembers a succession of nurses, but Muriel's own letter of 15 May 1933 to Francis G. Sanders shows her solicitude – and tact as well. 'You are such an old friend that I should like you to know that my husband is ill, I am afraid I must add "very ill" because pneumonia is serious whatever the condition of the patient. It has all come so suddenly. Please will you not spread it about . . . As you know, he dislikes publicity and we are so grateful for the quiet for him. . .'

Muriel had called in a consultant to pronounce a second opinion – 'for my own satisfaction':

> I find it difficult to believe that eight days ago he was carpentering hard and standing (alas) in cold draughts when very hot . . . The BBC do not know, unless Mr Godfrey Brown (to whom I was obliged to write about a concert at the end of the month) has told them. He stayed in bed as he did not feel well enough to get up and go to Sheffield, just a week ago, [and] was of course obliged to abandon a lecture in Leicester on the following day, but could not be considered really ill until last Wednesday. The consultant tells me that he has 'everything in his favour' and that he is 'years younger than his age' and has an excellent heart and pulse. As an old friend I felt I should like to write to you and I know you will treat my letter as confidential. Please tear it up.
>
> P.S. I have not written to Mr Woodhouse [Charles Woodhouse, the orchestral leader] because as he is in daily touch with musicians it might be a little difficult for him.

The danger from publicity was, of course, that such an illness might be taken as an indication of a general weakening. If Muriel was herself alarmed, she kept her counsel. To the promenaders who assembled for the new season on 12 August 1933 he was the same old 'Henry J.'. On 3 October, four nights before the season ended, he conducted the first performance of Delius's *Idyll*, the composer's last orchestral work (with two voices, those of Dora Labbette and Roy Henderson). Once again the composer, at his home in Grez-sur-Loing, heard the broadcast. There was also the first British performance (16 September) of Honegger's *Symphonic Movement* no.3 – which, unhelped by its title, failed to match the impact of the composer's preceding *Pacific 231* (the reference was to a railway locomotive).

Brahms was becoming a promenaders' favourite: as the *Monthly Musical Record* noted, 'The hall is as crowded on Brahms nights as it is for Bach, Beethoven and Wagner.' A 'Bach night' or 'Brahms night' or the like was still understood as one which allowed for other composers' music towards the end of the programme. It was quite exceptional, and no doubt a deliberate test of the audience, to present on 30 August 1933 a programme which consisted of nothing but Bach from first note to last.

To Sheffield again! The revival in 1933 of Sheffield's once triennial festival, lapsed since 1911, was a bold civic effort. Its concentration into two days hardly lessened Wood's burden, for there were two densely laden concerts on both Thursday 26 and Friday 27 October and he conducted every item but one. The afternoon concerts were of three hours, with the words 'Motors at 5 p.m.' in the printed programme; the evening concerts lasted two-and-a-half hours. Mahler's Symphony no.8 (the second performance in Britain), as the opening item of the opening concert, was followed by Strauss's *Don Juan*, Handel's organ concerto 'no.10' (op.7 no.4 in D minor) with G. D. Cunningham as soloist, and Kodály's *Psalmus Hungaricus* (entrusted to the festival chorus-master, J.Frederic Staton).

It was typical of Wood, and of the festival's expectation of him, that he should offer on Thursday evening a full-scale Wagner programme (vocal and orchestral excerpts from *Die Meistersinger, Parsifal, Das Rheingold,* and *Götterdämmerung,* with Florence Austral as Brünnhilde) and on Friday afternoon Bach's Mass in B minor. But it was on the final evening that the fare was piled highest. Brahms's *Song of Destiny* was followed by Beethoven's Piano Concerto no.4 (with Myra Hess, the only instrumental soloist of the festival) and by Delius's *A Song of the High Hills*. And *then* came Handel's *Israel in Egypt*, to most choral societies a full evening's work, but here abridged, and reorchestrated by Wood with Sanders' (unacknowledged) help.

'Having frequently disagreed with Sir Henry's practice in rearranging old scores,' Ferruccio Bonavia was to write in the *Monthly Musical Record,* 'I take pleasure in paying him tribute for the very able and entirely fitting orchestral setting which he provided for Handel's *Israel in Egypt* . . . There was absolutely nothing to which one could take exception.' Here is a further indication of contemporary critical stance. Wood was not usually taken to task simply for adding to Bach, but only when the additions exceeded what was 'fitting', as the critic saw it.

Bonavia also voiced the regret that 'so admirable a conductor of Wagner as Sir Henry Wood should never have had the opportunity to display his talents at Covent Garden'. To support the Festival's choral force of 400 adult voices and 100 boys' voices Wood could no longer summon his New Queen's Hall Orchestra, now defunct; Beecham's London Philharmonic, available for engagement without their chief, had been contracted instead – with Paul Beard as leader, and with Léon Goossens and Reginald Kell as principal oboe and clarinet. 'I have never heard from an *oboe d'amore* such lovely tones as Leon Goossens drew from it,' Bonavia wrote after hearing the Bach Mass.

In returning to conduct for the Hallé Orchestra in Manchester Wood likewise resumed a thread broken by World War One. A quarrel between the orchestra's management and its conductor since 1920, Sir Hamilton Harty, led to the latter's resignation in 1933 after his return from a trip to the United States. Individual guest conductors were summoned in his place, including Pierre Monteux, Albert Coates and the thirty-three-year-old John Barbirolli. Wood's return in the Verdi *Requiem*, preceded by Brahms's *Song of Destiny*, was so unexpected that Neville Cardus, music critic of the *Manchester Guardian*, wrongly wrote that Wood had 'never before' conducted at a Hallé concert. Cardus proceeded with praise for Wood's Verdi: 'Sir Henry gave us a magnificent performance of the masterpiece. He reaped the good sowing done by him at rehearsals which the Hallé Choir will discuss enthusiastically for many a day to come. Sir Henry is a worker and has the faith that moves mountains – and the average choir is nothing less than a mountain. Seldom has the Hallé Chorus sung with more life and point than last night.'

According to Michael Kennedy's *The Hallé Tradition*, it had been 'an agitation by the choir's supporters' which had led to Wood's engagement for the occasion, but the Free Trade Hall was barely half full – a sign of a general decline in the public following for choral music, 'no longer the staple entertainment in the home and village hall'.

Crowning all the invitations Wood had recently received from abroad was one from the Boston Symphony Orchestra. Nearly a decade of training and inspiration from Koussevitzky had raised the orchestra to rare excellence. The invitation reinforced Wood's bargaining counters when, at the beginning of 1933, he had to face negotiations with the BBC about a new contract for his work from late 1933. He spoke of an offer of a 'nine months' tour abroad in the United States and other countries' which would be 'far more remunerative to him than the engagements which he seems likely to get by staying at home'.

Whether such an extensive tour was ever really on offer is not known: in the event he would make two separate visits to the United States in 1934. But the hint was clear. If the BBC wanted him (and it did!) to continue shouldering the immense load of the promenade concerts, then in compensation he was entitled to no smaller share than before, and perhaps a greater share, in the symphony concerts of the winter and spring seasons which were now the BBC's flagship. The BBC's planning was moving in exactly the opposite direction.

Having decided to allot a greater proportion of its concerts to Boult, the BBC proposed to give Wood only three public symphony concerts at £100 each, three studio concerts at £75 each, a lump sum of £2300 for the summer promenade season and a further lump sum of £600 for a projected two-week series of winter promenade concerts (afterwards dropped). The BBC's Assistant Director of Programmes, Gerald Beadle, had evidently been entrusted with the delicate personal negotiations. Wood invited him to lunch on 21 December 1932, after which Beadle reported back to Sir John Reith on 3 January 1933:

> His [Wood's] vanity has been wounded in three ways:
>
> 1. The reduction in the number of Symphony dates.
> 2. The reduction in the number of guaranteed studio dates.
> 3. The reduction of his fees for the latter.
>
> It is very important that we get our own way over (1), but (2) and (3) are of relatively small importance. We shall very likely use him for 10 studio dates anyway, so I think we might safely guarantee them. With regard to his fee, he wants £100, which is more than we should pay to anyone else for such work. However, Sir Henry has done such unique and wonderful work for British music that I think we should be justified in treating him rather differently from the others. In any case, Wood's value to us in the matter of the Proms is so immense that I feel it would be wise to keep him as happy as possible by meeting him on either (2) or (3), or both.
>
> He has reached a very sensitive age – still young enough to carry on, but feeling himself on the threshold of old age. He is very ready to interpret any diminution in his work or fees as an indication that his age is against him. I have noticed on other occasions that he refers much too often to the subject of his age and gets quite heated about press reporters who refer to him as a 'wonderful old man'.
>
> So long as we do nothing to suggest that we think he is getting old, our relations with him ought to be perfectly smooth.

Wood persistently claimed that the BBC *owed* him recognition. As he put it in a letter of 26 February to Reith himself:

> The policy of the BBC in allotting practically all their symphony concerts to their permanent conductor is one that can be understood, even though it seems very strange to many people that a body such as the BBC should offer me at my time of life all the very hard work with limited rehearsal in the Promenade Concert season *and take from me* the opportunity of conducting the concerts for which plenty of rehearsal is provided; – an opportunity which, if it has been earned by *any* man through his work and services to music during past years, has certainly been earned by me during long years of work under difficult rehearsal conditions. . . .

> It also seems strange to my friends that at a time when you have set up this wonderful 'Empire' broadcasting (upon which many congratulations; I thought Christmas afternoon was very marvellous and touching) there is not *more* scope than ever for my services . . . Mine is one of the names which is most familiar, after that of Elgar and Clara Butt. I have constant proofs of this wherever I go – some of which have touched me deeply. However, this may be a question of policy with the BBC – to build up for the future and to dwell little upon what has been accomplished in the past; but I am going to be candid and say frankly what my friends are saying to me, which is that the whole thing seems a somewhat poor return for what I have accomplished for music in England and for the musicians and people of England. . . .

Wood added a complaint (though it had nothing to do with the contractual matters under discussion) that his former policy of encouraging young British composers had fallen into abeyance. 'During the next two seasons I should like to resume my former policy and select at least six *new* works by British composers (not necessarily of the *front* rank) and also six foreign novelties *of various schools and nationalities*, as I consider that of late years these novelties have been confined too much to one school.'

To Beadle's suggestion of a further lunch he reacted on 25 March with apprehension, especially on learning that Roger Eckersley, BBC Director of Programmes, would also be present:

> I should be delighted to accept for some other day (I am sorry to say that the 31st is not possible) if it is just a friendly meeting with you, but as you mention 'discussing' several points and that Mr Eckersley will be there, I am going to be perfectly frank with you and tell you that I could not come *alone* if any points about which I have lately written to Sir John Reith are to be discussed. After all, I am only a musician, and although I can paint a fairly decent landscape and do a moderately good job of *rough* carpentering I cannot meet expert businessmen and 'negotiators' on equal ground, and I feel I must have someone with me to jog my memory and to help me to remember what is said.
>
> It is only since I became connected with the BBC that I have had the experience of 'negotiating' in a way so foreign to most artists, for I always had that great manager Robert Newman to take all this kind of thing off my shoulders, *to act in my interest* and to leave me the musical side only, and it is not easy for me to remember that what is to all appearance just a friendly luncheon is at the same time a meeting for discussing points at issue, so I know you will understand that I feel that I too need support and to have my 'second' with me *if* the luncheon has anything of this kind in view. Please forgive the mixed metaphors; I am

> not suggesting that it is anything in the nature of a duel, but I know you will understand what I mean!!

Wood's severe illness had interrupted the negotiations. From May onwards, however, further suggestions from Wood evidently shortened Beadle's patience, as his memorandum of 19 June to Reith made clear:

> After our conversation the other day I wrote to Sir Henry Wood in the terms you approved. This produced a telegram from him with a new request, namely that he should be offered five studio dates during the second year, i.e. 1934/35. I replied that I could not answer that question at short notice. This morning I have received a further letter in which he questions the fee for the Promenade Concerts, in addition to repeating his demand for studio dates in 1934/35.
>
> It seems to me that either Sir Henry is becoming quite impossible or else he is deliberately procrastinating in order to extort still further concessions. If the former is the case I take it that a break with him is inevitable, if the latter I think we have got to the point where we ought to call his bluff. If you agree would you approve of my sending the attached letter.
>
> This course would mean that if Wood does not accept the offer by return Boult would have to conduct the Promenade Concerts. I was hoping to be able to stave this off until after Wood's fortieth season, but I see no alternative now.

Accordingly, the BBC sent Wood an ultimatum to accept or reject its terms within three days. On 22 June he capitulated:

> Dear Mr Beadle
>
> . . . It is obvious that a man with a popgun can do nothing against a battery of heavy artillery and that if I wish to remain the head of my own creation of thirty-eight years' standing – namely the Promenade Concerts – I have no alternative but to fall in with your proposal contained in your astonishing letter of the 19th, which I therefore do, excepting that, as has already been explained to Mr Eckersley, I am not in a position to undertake to conduct during the January festival.

The last point referred to the offer of a concert in the British music festival which had replaced the winter promenade concerts in the BBC's plans. By then, Wood would be in Boston.

One phrase in the last-quoted letter from Gerald Beadle deserves emphasizing. If contractual agreement were not reached with Wood, then 'Boult would have to conduct the Promenade Concerts'. There was no suggestion that Wood 'owned' the Proms or had any legal or moral rights in their disposal. They were not, as they were later called, 'the Henry Wood Proms'. They represented a type of summer concert which had become traditional, but which had survived only because the BBC had taken over the enterprise. The BBC might run them in another way – or ditch the enterprise entirely, as World War Two would give it the pretext to do.

Chapter 17

Crisis

1933–5

'Oh, this dreadful Hitler. . .' exclaimed Jelka Delius in a letter of September 1933 to her husband's devotee and musical helper, Eric Fenby. The conductor Oskar Fried, one of Delius's staunchest German champions, had been forced out of Germany by the Nazis' anti-Jewish discrimination – the same fate that befell Schoenberg, Bruno Walter and so many other musicians. The coming years would give the highest public exposure to the Nazi politicisation of music in Germany (and, from 1938, in Austria). Toscanini's withdrawal – in protest against 'painful events' – from an engagement to conduct *Parsifal* at the Bayreuth Festival of 1933 was widely noted, and no less so the willingness of the complaisant, temporizing Richard Strauss to replace him.

Shielding himself as always from everything external to the work in hand, Wood made no comment on such events. Nor was he ever confronted, as both Beecham and Boult would be, by the necessity of reacting in a political context. Fascist Italy had not yet applied Nazi racial doctrine to the arts, so none but musical considerations were attached to his anticipation of conducting in Rome in January 1935. That engagement, however, was to precipitate a violent personal crisis.

In that crisis a poignant role was to be played by his elder daughter Tania. Henry J. Wood tried to project into her the spirit of artistic dedication which had been his own. Why, he asked in a letter written from a Cardiff hotel in April 1932, was she still 'listening to these terrible jazz records' and reading 'all these stupid cinema papers'? Such magazines were 'vulgar, really only fit for domestic servants'. As an art student, why was she not filling every hour with art?

The words tumbled ungrammatically from his pen and stayed uncorrected on paper:

You have heaps of material to hand – dozens of canvases, paints and brushes, yet you never go forth for one hour and paint in a sky, a foreground, a tree – the common – and a thousand objects and subjects that surround you at Chorley Wood.

Now why don't you make up your mind to cover a canvas every day with something, as Ruskin did for 3 years, you need not paint pictures – this will come later – but work – think pictorially – work at nature and colour, get atmosphere into your sketches. Personally I feel one never gets tired of painting, because you are putting down, not what you know already, but what you have just discovered. And this *daily*, gives you *Gusto*. A word that I as a boy heard every day of my life. *Remember*, every stroke of your brush, creating out of nothing, every stroke of your brush, a new field of knowledge and enquiry is opening out to you. Every day, every canvas, a new difficulty and a new problem is arising, and the *inner satisfaction* is a triumph. One part of your sketch always shames another, every object becomes lustrous from the light thrown back upon it, by the mirror of your art and talent. You know how I loathe this *Photographic vision*. Do see into the life of things in nature, no mechanical reproduction, no mechanical instruments, *you have* a craftsmans finger-sense – use it. I have always felt that the most sensible men were painters, I always liked them better than musicians because they are real observers of objects around them (I admit they often only see things from a painter's point of view, but never mind) they are staring at nature which is wonderful. I cannot tell you the inner joy and satisfaction, looking at the Eiger for four of[=or] five mornings, gave me – it is a living and lifelong experience.

Indolence in any form, is always a distressing state – I know you are always working at something – but divide your time, my treasure, between your art and your health – don't fritter your valuable young time away in drivelling tosh – rest and work – *life is so short*, and art is so long. We must be doing something *good*, to be really happy. And to put your daily art work on the floor after dinner and talk about it – criticise it, is so much more noble, useful and helpful, than playing Patience like an old lady of 70, who has accomplished and almost finished her life work. Games and Exercise as much as you like – get tired in the evening, after your day of beautiful art labour – not with looking at Film Photos and listening to bad Negro music!

. . .*Be as modern as you like*, but don't waste a moment of your precious life and time, on stupid, brainless pleasures.

Good night, my darling Tania. Mother does not know that I have written you this letter, but I do want it *to sink in* and *bear good fruit*, during the next few months my precious Tania.

Your devoted father
   Henry J. Wood

Tania adored her father, as she often said in later years. But he was pressing on her a destiny which she never felt was hers. The depth of his own feeling for the medium of paint was never so vividly expressed as in the above-quoted letter (which, in full, would be twice as long, all on the same note). When such an emotional link between father and daughter was eventually to be shattered – by *her* decision – the overtones would inevitably be bitter.

Meanwhile not only was Boston beckoning, but (for the third time) the Hollywood Bowl as well. Muriel, of course, did not miss the chance of accompanying him. Very likely it was her idea to preface the Boston engagement with a vacation in Bermuda during the first few days of 1934. Once arrived in Boston – where Koussevitzky's annual vacation regularly provided a place for guest conductors – Wood was made welcome by the city's music-lovers. In the biography printed with his programmes, there was naturally no mention of that fantasised visit to Boston during boyhood which was to make its appearance in *My Life of Music*.

The two concerts in Boston's Symphony Hall took place on Friday 19 January at 2.30 p.m. (for an evidently leisured audience) and on the following evening at 8.15. They were preceded by a concert on 16 January at Providence, the capital of Rhode Island, some forty-five miles south. Wood's programme was the same at all three occasions, and it was a programme that neither Koussevitzky nor anyone else would have given the New Englanders:

Suite	Purcell-Wood
Rondino for eight wind instruments	Beethoven
Andante from Cassation no.1, for strings	Mozart
Enigma Variations	Elgar

INTERVAL

Don Juan	Strauss
Norwegian Rhapsody	Lalo

The opening item was tagged as a first performance in Boston, the second and third only as 'first performance at these concerts': these favourite pieces of Wood's, respectively offering the limelight to the wind and string sections of the orchestra, might indeed have been previously given in chamber-music series. Press coverage was not merely local but national, the *Musical Courier* (27 January) noting that

Sir Henry's conducting technic is taken for granted. It remains but to emphasise the outstanding quality of his music-making – his authoritative and sensitive musicianship. This quality was especially noteworthy in the slight but delightful andante of Mozart and in the variations of Elgar. Every phrase, under Sir Henry's baton, had the greatest conviction, while in spacing and in tone quality there was exceptional balance. The conductor was obviously fortunate in having the assistance of an orchestra like the Boston Symphony, an orchestra of which Sir Henry sang voluble praises during the week.

Readers of *The Times* of London heard from its Boston correspondent that only once before had the orchestra played anything by Purcell, 'and then it was but the *Trumpet Voluntary*' (still generally attributed to Purcell). As to Elgar's *Variations*, 'both Koussevitzky and Toscanini have performed them here, but neither revealed in them the mingled strength and sweetness which the English conductor disclosed . . . The Variations had been heard before according to the musical letter; they were now enriched according to the spirit.' Not always did *The Times*'s London-based critics respond so warmly to Wood.

No other concerts were on his original American schedule. But Cadillac the car-makers, as the sponsor of a major radio series (in the broadcasting studio, but with audience), grabbed the distinguished visitor for a studio concert with the New York Philharmonic on 28 January – the Purcell, Mozart and Beethoven works performed in Boston, plus the *Academic Festival* overture of Brahms, with the pianist Josef Hofmann playing the first movement of Anton Rubinstein's concerto no.4. The *Musical Courier* reported that 'both artists addressed the radio listeners briefly' – probably a first time for Wood, who resisted until 1941 the temptation to address his British audiences, even those of the 'Last Night of the Proms'.

He was fascinated, the *New York Times* (on 4 February) reported, by the city's radio-equipped taxicabs, 'especially when he heard symphonic airs amid the traffic on Fifth Avenue. The Prince of Wales, of course, has a radio in his car; but few others are so provided with music in England,' he was quoted as saying. Three days later the same newspaper quoted his endorsement of a proposal by the soprano Lotte Lehmann and the conductor Fritz Reiner to have Wagner's operas performed in shortened versions: 'Sir Henry Wood thought [it] . . . would be a good way to make the Wagnerian drama available to the average man.'

It had been announced on 28 January that he would conduct the Rochester (NY) Symphony Orchestra 'next week' but he did not. He had decided to return to London earlier than planned, if the impression left by Muriel Wood is correct. 'My husband decided at the last minute that he must go by the [steamship] Manhattan yesterday,' she wrote on 1 February to Elizabeth

Sprague Coolidge, the distinguished patron of music. She herself, avid to see the sights of Charleston and Washington before leaving the United States, asked Mrs Coolidge (whose home was in Washington) 'whether you happen to have a leisured friend in either place, with a car, who might *very* kindly be able to show me as much as possible in my very short time in both places'.

Mrs Coolidge responded with the offer of a 'good guide and car' in Washington and an invitation to spend the night with her there. But first Muriel saw off her husband in the company of the baritone Keith Falkner, who had likewise booked passage on the *Manhattan*. 'Now you take good care of Henry,' Muriel told him. 'See that he has his topcoat and muffler whenever he goes on deck.' Falkner recalled that, as the ship left the dockside, Wood took his arm with boyish enthusiasm: 'Come on, my boy. Let's go and have a bottle of wine.' The British pair later gave a recital for their fellow-passengers, 'he looking just like Brahms in the famous portrait, seated at the piano'. Disembarking at Plymouth, they were met by the singer's wife, whom Wood asked to send a telegram notifying his daughter Avril of the time of the boat-train's arrival in London, with the additional instruction, 'Put bottle in bed.'

Muriel did not long delay her return. Her typed letter of 29 March 1934 shows the cordiality she maintained towards her husband's musical assistant:

> Dear Mr Sanders,
>   My husband is at the Langham Hotel until Monday as Avril has
> German measles (following hard upon ordinary measles) and is supposed
> to be infectious until Saturday. So I have sent your letter on to him.
>   . . . I hope that you and Mrs Sanders will come down and see us [at
> Appletree Farm] soon; perhaps one day before very long you may feel
> drawn daffodil-wards; they ought to be fully out soon, but they are late –
> the first one appeared on Sunday, but by next week there should be a
> large company.

Next day was Good Friday, always marked musically by the BBC: its offering from Queen's Hall was Bach's *St John Passion* under Wood's baton. (He was more often to conduct *The Dream of Gerontius* or a selection from *Parsifal* to mark that day.) Ahead lay an engagement to conduct massed Welsh choralists in a Handel oratorio, entailing a request dispatched to Sanders from Appletree Farm on 3 April:

> Would you very kindly time *Samson* for me, not too carefully as it is not for

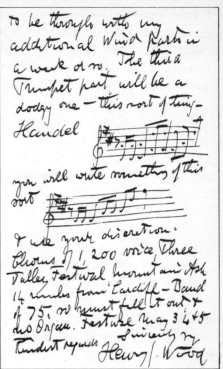

Arranging Handel: Wood instructs his musical assistant.

wireless purposes but for the Three Valley[s] Festival with a chorus of 1200 – what-ho! – and we want to know within twenty minutes as Lloyd George [the former Prime Minister] has got to speak at the interval and we must give him a time limit. Just roughly, the timing of Part I and Part II as I have marked it. Of course this is a business proposition, as they say in the business world.

The last sentence was Wood's typically tactful way of assuring Sanders that he would be paid for giving this preparatory help. Next, to balance the outsize choral force at that Welsh festival, Wood instructed Sanders to add double-bassoon and third trumpet to *Samson*, 'the third trumpet part will be a dodgy one' – Wood scrawling a music example of how an independent part could be contrived to add to Handel's two-part writing (see illustration, above).

257

Battling

For the trip to Hollywood in mid-year the Woods chose, as they had done before, the sea route from Liverpool to Montreal. Henry's handwritten letter from aboard the steamer *Duchess of Richmond* on 20 June tells Hubert Foss that 'we are enjoying our trip tremendously – fine boat, very few passengers and after our London rush most enjoyable'. Once again, reunions with former players awaited him: Alfred Brain had by now become manager of the Los Angeles Philharmonic, whose musicians were engaged for the Hollywood Bowl, and a violist from Queen's Hall days of long past, Emile Ferir, was to take the solo role in Strauss's *Don Quixote*.

This time Wood was the opening conductor of the Bowl season, drawing an enthusiastic 12,000 to the first concert on 10 July, with seven more concerts following. At the fifth concert Hindemith's *News of the Day* overture 'delighted everyone', said the critic of the *Los Angeles Times*: it is a fair deduction from the reception of this series that the Bowl audience had increased its musical sophistication since Wood's encounter with the lions and the Lions. The programmes showed Wood's boundless confidence in being able to deliver (even with an orchestra not 'his') music almost as unfamiliar to the players as to the audience.

As in Boston, here was the favoured Beethoven *Rondino* for eight wind instruments and Wood's own Purcell Suite. The strings faced that most exhilarating of tests, Elgar's *Introduction and Allegro*. Presumably for the first time in America, Wood gave the 'Klenovsky' version of the Bach Toccata and Fugue in D minor, of which he had not yet revealed himself as the arranger: the printed programme ascribed it not to the fictitious Paul Klenovsky but to the real Nikolay of that surname. There was an all-Wagner evening; there was Sibelius's Symphony no.1, Elgar's second *Wand of Youth* Suite, Bridge's *The Sea*, Smyth's overture to *The Boatswain's Mate*, and Bax's Third Symphony. Two movements from a *Moorish Suite* by a local composer, Juan Aguilar, formed an unexpected addition to Wood's list of first performances.

The same issue of the American *Musical Courier* which reported the success of Wood's Hollywood Bowl series also featured on its main news page the opening of the fortieth season of London's Proms on 11 August: CAPACITY AUDIENCE STANDS AND CHEERS INTREPID PIONEER. Elgar and Holst, both of whom had died earlier in the year, were respectively honoured by the inclusion in the opening programme of the prelude to *The Kingdom* and three of the *Planets*. (Wood seems never to have conducted *The Kingdom* as a complete oratorio.) Delius, more recently deceased, would be commemorated by a special programme on 23 August. Tchaikovsky's popularity was down, the American reporter commented, and Bach's was up.

258

There was still a danger that 'Intrepid Pioneer' would not be a label for Wood much longer. But the BBC allowed a few more premières this season – of which Kodály's *Dances of Galanta* won a lasting success. Constant Lambert appeared as conductor of his jazz-laden success of 1928, *The Rio Grande,* and Vaughan Williams as conductor of *A London Symphony*. Wood had always encouraged composers to take the baton for *first* performances (to show, once and for all, how the music should go) but privately did not share the BBC's liking for having them pop up casually. The 'Bach-Klenovsky' Toccata and Fugue was heard, with the hoax not yet divulged. In the final concert on 6 October Wood's old enthusiasm for Busoni's music resurfaced in a performance of his *Indian Fantasy* for piano and orchestra, with a young soloist destined for popularity: Eileen Joyce.

As journalism increasingly sought to bring its readers the private lives of celebrities, family photographs taken at Appletree Farm (with the Woods' dog, Robert) appeared not only in the BBC's *Radio Times* but also in the independent *Radio Magazine*. The interviewer for the latter publication, Gibson Young, had observed Wood over many years. 'In his purely Edwardian dinner-jacket his appearance is only slightly changed since the first time I saw him conduct one of the old Gentlemen's Concerts at the Midland Hotel, Manchester, before the [1914–18] war.' But the press never made public the violent disruption which was now to overtake Wood's life – entailing nothing less than the break-up of the Woods' marriage, the estrangement of Henry from his two daughters, and the dilemma imposed on friends when he set up a new relationship which was a marriage in all but name.

His friends and neighbours, Hubert and Dora Foss, had no inkling of what was to come. On the contrary: Dora was to remember 'as vividly as if it were yesterday' a scene at the Woods' dinner-table during that summer of 1934: 'Henry, who was on my right, had been discoursing on the amount of work he was committed to, and suddenly he looked at his wife, sitting at the end of the table opposite him; his eyes beaming, and in a voice conveying the deepest affection and emotion, [he] said "I don't know what I would do without Muriel." I was most moved by this and events of the subsequent years only served further to impress this scene on my mind and memory.'

Henry had indeed become as dependent on Muriel as Dora Foss's anecdote implied. But that dependence was on *her* terms, applied in an increasingly self-centred way; and since she herself could not cook, her failure to manage servants had become particularly destructive of domestic peace. Wood's complaint, in *My Confession,* of being forced to eat out in local teashops was perhaps (as his elder daughter Tania was to maintain) a large generalisation from an isolated example or two: but it evidently rankled. The price he paid for her management of irksome correspondence and day-to-day financial decisions was her insistence on working on correspondence during mealtimes.

She gave little impression of caring for his appearance: the thing everyone noticed when, eventually, he left her for his new companion was how much more spruce he looked. To escape the tension, Tania decided (apparently on the prompting of her mother's intimate friend, Helen Douglas Irvine) to leave home and stay with a London friend, Joan White; and it was (as she told the author of this book) her mother that she was runnning away from.

Muriel was worried. From the Langham Hotel in London (her husband's frequent base during Proms seasons) she wrote to Dora Foss on 29 August 1934:

> Henry and I would both be *so* grateful if you still felt you could write to Tania; she is fond of you both and we feel that a word of advice from a friend like you would be helpful to her and prevent her from saying things she will almost certainly regret when she no longer feels as she does now, poor child. . . .
>
> [P.S.] I know you understand how I feel. I can't say much to Henry now because *he* mustn't be worried during Proms.

From Appletree Farm House she alluded to her difficulty in finding servants when she wrote again on 5 September:

> Yes, I have been rather tired; no, nothing to do with domestic work, (I don't do any to speak of; neither does Avril, except that she 'gets' breakfast usually only for herself and Miss Douglas [Irvine], and sometimes tea, but she and I had quite a satisfactory business arrangement about this!) The weekends are very well taken care of professionally and the little house also every day! *Forgive* these details – only the circumstances justify this mention! If you hear of *guaranteed* domestic treasures capable and above all full of courage to face this 'lonely moor', 'wood' and 'great distance from a main road' do send them along!! One cannot really complain if after 19 years of domestic peace one strikes a bad patch.

'A bad patch', yes. In writing to her friend, Muriel was evidently anxious not to suggest any possible division between husband and wife, referring only to a period of '19 years' – the span of time since the younger daughter, Avril, was born. Childhood and adolescence could be seen as understandable problems, and the management of domestic servants likewise. Dora was not allowed to sense that there was more amiss than that.

While Tania was living with Joan White, Henry made a point of seeing her regularly, almost daily. The 1934 season of promenade concerts was now in full swing and she evidently enjoyed attending rehearsals and concerts. She had even been allowed in the artists' room while the orchestral players filed past their conductor to have their tuning checked. The deep mutual attachment of father and daughter is clear from the letter he wrote to her from the Langham Hotel on 29 August:

Dearest Tania,

I am feeling the strain of the Proms very much – especially now poor Woodhouse [Charles Woodhouse, for many seasons his orchestral leader] has cracked up. And though I have enjoyed our lunches and merry meetings in the intervals every day, especially as Mum has been so little by my side in Queen's Hall up to now, I feel I must keep on with so much. The BBC is worrying me all the time to make appointments about next seasons dates and I find with these trying piano rehearsals that I *must* lunch alone more often.

So you and I must have our little lunches on [only] two days a week, so please keep Mondays and Thursdays for Dad and come *alone* here at 1.30. So glad to have you with me at rehearsal every day and during every morning interval, but I want *you only to come* upstairs two nights a week in the interval and also two nights a week to the artists room before the concert, and not bring any friends to [seat number] 56 or the artists' room with you because I find it *very tiring*, and you know I don't like people with me when I am tuning and the Band hate it. I do need Mum during the interval and I know she will come when I tell her this, so I shall *not* be lonely when you are not there. Don't be cross with me, dear Tania – I couldn't bear it during this time of great strain and it will help me tremendously if [you] will keep to our days and come and see me Tuesday and Friday before the concert and during the interval and lunch, don't forget, on Monday and Thursday.

I shall keep these days free for you religiously. I am going to persuade Mum to sit in her old seats again so I am going to give *you two* special seats for yourself and a friend *every* night – here are some, I'll give next week's later, I've mislaid them for the moment.

Fondest love from

Daddy

What is clear also from this letter is Henry's continuing and willing dependence on 'Mum' – though her presence in the intervals of concerts seems to have been desired mainly to help the perspiring conductor with a change of clothing. Yet domestic friction must obviously have continued. Tania in 1990 was to recall her mother as increasingly unable, at that time, to fulfil the combined matrimonial and business role. 'She was utterly devoted to him and his work. Unfortunately she knew and cared nothing about music and finally got bored with the whole set-up, became selfish and impossibly difficult.'

Tania had further removed herself from the tension. She went to live in Paris at a boarding-house at 21 Rue Washington, ostensibly to further her art studies and to pursue a dietary regime designed to shed some of her excessive weight. Her father kept in touch in terms of a smothering affection ('Heaps of love, your adoring Daddy'). One letter was written after a BBC concert at Queen's Hall on 28 November 1934 at which Stravinsky conducted his *Persephone* and played the piano solo in his *Capriccio*:

> I am so glad you have lost 7lbs, bravo. I think Avril is looking *very well*
> . . . Did you hear [the broadcast of] the Stravinsky Concert? The Band
> played *Fireworks* and *L'Oiseau de Feu* splendidly but Stravinsky let us all
> down. After 4 hours' rehearsal his memory went wrong *4 times*, and he
> made a complete mess of the Capriccio, the Band were furious. If you
> heard any of the Concert do write and tell me your impressions.
> *Persephone* was a washout, it is the dullest 53 minutes I have ever gone
> through, a perfect performance. Ida Rubinstein [speaker] *fine*.
> Stravinsky kissed me in public – What ho!. . .

The friction was private and matrimonial: the attempt in Reginald Pound's biography to link it with a decline in Wood's musical powers (citing adverse notices from the Norwich Festival four years previously as if they were typical of the intervening period) cannot be sustained. It is clear that a sharp worsening of the marital relationship and a resolve to escape from it happened between the summer of 1934 and the following January.

In the later document headed *My Confession*, Wood attempted to paint the whole marriage retrospectively black. The accusations of being 'sent to Coventry' by Muriel, of being forced to consult his own diary in order to learn his schedule for the day, hardly suffice to justify an allegation of having endured for twenty years 'the most trying and difficult life that any married man could possibly endure'. Muriel's indifference to food ('a glass of milk and a bun were sufficient for her needs for hours on end') got on his nerves 'most terribly. . .'

Of such complaints, seemingly quite petty, Henry J. Wood made a justification for leaving Muriel in January 1935. The sequence and motivation of events cannnot be separated from a car accident which severely injured Muriel in September 1934. But the crucial event was the reappearance in Henry's life of Jessie Linton, who as Jessie Goldsack had been a favourite pupil of his and had so frequently sung in his concerts around 1900.

During her married years at Bowdon near Manchester, she had on just a few occasions greeted Wood at his Manchester concerts. Widowed at the age of fifty, she wrote to 'Dear Sir Henry' from a London address on 17 June 1933. She had perhaps read in the papers of his illness:

> I was very shocked to hear today how seriously ill you have been – and relieved indeed to know you are now on the high road to good health again.
>
> Where *would* the dear old Proms be without you – and good music in general? So *do* take care, and not try and do too much too soon!
>
> I lost my dear husband a month ago – the ultimate result of his war service – and for the time being am staying with my widow[ed] daughter, until I have sufficient courage to decide what is best to do – for my husband left me absolutely without means – owing to his failure in the awful depression of Manchester cotton!
>
> With kind regards to Lady Wood, and your dear self,
> Yours very sincerely
> Jessie Goldsack-Linton

She soon moved back to her youthful haunts (see p.68) at Ealing in outer London. After such a long absence from the concert platform, could she hope to earn an income through her singing once again? She resumed lessons with Wood at the Blüthner Studios where he regularly taught in central London. That they should enjoy each other's company was not surprising, nor that he should invite her to one of his Sunday parties at Appletree Farm. But it must also be suspected that Wood's request to Tania to restrict her lunches with him to two days a week was not made, as he told her (p.261), in order that on other days he could lunch *alone*.

Muriel's injuries in her car accident (Avril was the driver, but was not so badly hurt) caused her to spend some time in Hendon Cottage Hospital. According to Jessie Linton's own tape-recorded reminiscences of 1972, Henry asked her – as a family friend – to pay his wife a visit:

> Would I take her some green figs and some fruit? I remember that meeting so well, she was propped up in bed with her head bandaged, poor dear, and

there was Helen Gaskell, the lovely oboist. Oh dear, it was such a nice meeting, and also her aunt was there, Aunt Maud, and before I left that afternoon, Aunt Maud said the funniest thing, [asking me to] make him [Henry] some sandwiches and some fruit, make him a little parcel and take [it] to Queens Hall at night: 'I'm sure you go to some of the Proms – I know he doesn't get enough to eat because, you see, he's too late for lunch when his rehearsal is over and he's much too late for dinner when he comes home to the Langham Hotel at night! So he really, I suppose, just has a bit of cold ham or something and it's not good for him.' From that moment I seemed to sense that all was not quite clear in every way.

On 14 October Wood himself wrote to Hubert Foss that 'Muriel is going on *quite well* and will leave, I hope, Hendon Cottage Hospital in about a week'. His own musical life continued with BBC concerts in Belfast as well as London and was pleasantly seasoned by the press and public reactions to his admission of authorship of the 'Klenovsky' score. *The Times* gave it a heavy, would-be-humorous editorial; the *Daily Express* a cartoon by the popular Strube.

With a home life disarrayed by Muriel's absence in hospital, Jessie's sympathetic temperament – so different from Muriel's – must have made itself felt. Moreover, she could *talk music*, as his first wife Olga had done but Muriel could not. At first, according to Jessie, their relationship began innocently enough from her vocal lessons with him.

Time by time, I used to think how dirty he was and how unkempt he looked, how tired he was, and one day when I was having my lesson he said 'You know, Miss Goldsack, I would like to come over and have tea with you one day'.. . and he came over and had tea with me and we walked on the Common, and it was a very happy and easy going tea-party and those went on from time to time . . . and I never noticed in the slightest way any familiarity in thought or deed. But one postcard came which made me laugh . . . 'Dear Miss Goldsack, I would like if I may to call you Jessie instead of the more formal way. May I? If not, I shall just call you Madam!' . . . It did go on from time to time time, a little bit more familiar and more friendly . . . and of course in later years I learnt that he never called anyone by their Christian name, never mind how well he knew them. . .

And then one day he came and said 'The may is out, it would be so nice if we could go on the Common' . . . And then in the minute or two that we had been sitting on a seat in the main road, with the may behind us, he suddenly said 'Oh, I feel so ill . . .' I could see that he was in great stress . . . [She hailed a passing car to take him to her home, then telephoned her doctor] . . . He came very soon and said 'I think he's had a slight stroke . . .' And so he slept that night at my flat – I had two bedrooms there . . . He was all

right the next morning and went off in a hired car and went to his rehearsal
. . . And that was the beginning – although it was very, very difficult for me
to know exactly what to do now and how to take what had happened and
what might happen . . .

Pound's account of that incident safeguards the proprieties by having Wood
spend the night at 'a nursing-home' rather than at Jessie's flat. Moreover,
Pound crucially misdates it, placing it (omitting the reference to may-
blossom!) in February 1935, *after* Wood's break with Muriel instead of
before. The relationship with Jessie was plainly in place by mid-1934, even if
at that time it was seen by Wood as an occasional haven from his marriage
and not a replacement of it.

In January 1935 came his first engagement to conduct in Italy, preceded by
a two-week season of Winter Promenade Concerts at Queen's Hall for the
BBC from 31 December. He stayed at the Langham Hotel to be near
Queen's Hall while Muriel was convalescing at a hotel in Sidmouth in Devon
after her illness. 'I have written to Mother every day and sometimes twice a
day,' he told Tania in a letter from the Langham to her address in Paris. It is a
letter full of solicitude for his wife. Anxious to have her in Rome, he was
pleased that by breaking her journey to see their daughter in Paris she would
ease any strain.

> I am so glad she is going to Rome in easy stages and is only spending
> one night with me here – tomorrow (Monday) night, and unless the sea
> is very rough (Dover-Calais is nothing for such a world-wide traveller as
> Muriel) she will leave here on Tuesday morning. I am so glad her 'head
> throb' has stopped and I do hope the journey to Rome will not bring it
> on again – but I think it is only motoring that is bad for her. Please give
> her a happy time in Paris and love her very much.
> The 'Proms' are an enormous success, *sold out every night*.

For his two concerts at the Augusteo in Rome – with the city's principal
orchestra, that of the Accademia di Santa Cecilia – he made a typically
'ambassadorial' gesture. Vaughan Williams' *A London Symphony* was on the
first programme (Sunday afternoon, 20 January), and Bax's Symphony no.3
on that of the following Wednesday.

Not speaking Italian, he may well have been apprehensive of difficulties in
communicating with the orchestra. But the orchestra pleased him and he
judged the concerts 'a great success'. According to a British newspaper
report, 'Sir Henry's personality quite won the audience' at the first concert,
the Vaughan Williams symphony being rather coolly received but the

'Bach-Klenovsky' transcription (acknowledged as his own) bringing the audience to its feet. When he wrote to Tania from his Roman hotel on 25 January 1935, his only complaint was that the Augusteo was 'a death-trap', 'the coldest hall in the world', where twenty-five screens had to be put up at rehearsal to shield conductor and orchestra from the draughts.

That letter reproached Tania for supposed indolence and extravagance in Paris: 'I very much fear that you swank about as the daughter of Sir Henry Wood of Queen's Hall, and lead people to think I am a kind of cinema star.' She must, he insisted, gain her diploma and start earning her own living as an art teacher. There was no hint in that letter of any marital tension. Yet within a few days Henry and Muriel Wood quarrelled bitterly at their hotel in Rome, and parted – he returning on 5 February for engagements in London, she typically determined (whatever might have been Henry's need of her) to stay a further week in Rome and then to go on to Sicily for further sightseeing at her leisure. By telegram, she sent for nineteen-year-old Avril to be her companion for the trip. Avril had been living at the Elsworthy Road house under the supervision of a friend of Muriel's, a Mrs Mary Hillman.

Back at Appletree Farm, Henry J. Wood set his name on 12 February 1935 to two extraordinary letters. Tania had written reassuring him of the seriousness of her studies in Paris. Now he addressed her in what seems a desperately over-possessive manner ('I do know that we realize our devotion to each other and our everlasting love for each other – in fact *we* understand') and divulged that he had 'a very nice bedroom' in London at 19 Adam Street, Portman Square. 'I know you will keep my secret . . . no one knows this.' (He described it as a quieter alternative to the Langham Hotel.) He told her he had endured 'a terrible time in Rome' with her mother. But now the strain was over: 'M— has promised to stay in Italy a month, perhaps 2 or even 3 months, *until my nerves, as she says, have recovered.* So that's that. . . . I have *promised* not to write to Muriel and she has *promised* not to write to me for one month – a real Greatrex contract – we shall see.'

The second letter was to Muriel herself, not merely breaching that 'contract' but showing that – after a week in London – he had resolved on nothing less than a permanent break with her. He wanted to live with Jessie but still apparently hoped to do so without disturbing the formality of his marriage. His colleague Sir Landon Ronald could have set him an example: he maintained his mistress in a separate establishment for many years and married her only after his wife's death.

Darling Muriel,

The contents of this letter will possibly cause you a great shock and yet at the same time may not be entirely a surprise to you, after the very painful time we spent together in Rome.

You always ask for frankness and tell me of your great broadmindedness – and you will recall the many times you have offered and even suggested to me, to do what I liked and 'run off' on my own. Well darling – fate or the inevitable has happened – and a dear friend has fortunately crossed my path for all time.

You see we have *for a long time* been getting on each others' nerves, it seems unkind to say so, but during the last few years, you have (and it is no good denying it) been getting very much upon *my* nerves – although I have not mentioned it point blank before. It has not started with the Tania/Helen Douglas affair, but the beginning started in those long evenings at Chorley Wood, when even our drawing-room was half drawing-room and half office, and it was then that things began to get on my nerves, because to have you writing (I know you were doing my business) at the same time, I felt my home life was vanishing. Lately of course I have really suffered from the intense feeling (and this caused me to break down altogether at Sidmouth at Xmas) of possessing no real home, all this expense, all this trouble, all one's goods and chattels spread out – and yet not one little resting place in which one could rest in peace and tranquillity in front of a nice fire, enjoy a restful non-hurried dinner – and a quiet hour or so, without business, without worry. Of course you will say I had all this – yes – perhaps – in your way, but not in my way – and for the sake of peace, I accepted much and said nothing.

Well, darling – I am now 66 years of age and you will readily admit that I am not the only man that has kicked over the traces and chosen his own life. I do quite honestly feel that it is better for both our lives for us to be quite friendly but at the same time, *I must lead my own life in my own way*.

You have Appletree Farm and I have my Jessie and the happy evenings we spend together in her charming flat with lovely little dinners (for she is a lovely cook) and what I adore and have missed so terribly since the dear Olga days are the lovely heart-to-heart talks on music and musicians, and our music together – and fancy, after all these years, I have found one who understands my *Gentle Art of Singing* and perhaps I never told you that from 1901 to 1905 she was my favourite pupil, that *her* voice touched me *more deeply* than any of my other pupils, and her performance in the *Matthew Passion* at the Sheffield Festival of 1906 [correctly 1908] has always remained a living memory with me and always will. So you see my feelings for 'Jessie' are not a fleeting passing passion, but something I cannot help and must accept for the rest of my life.

Don't try to argue this matter out with me in any way, as it is so

267

much kinder and better for both of us to let the matter stand as it is – as I am quite determined in what I have told you, and this letter has not been written in haste, but calmly deliberated. Our secret can be kept from all our friends and relations, from our public life and the alteration in our 'régime' need never be known.

    Your dear old
      HEN

The twenty-two-year-old Tania was to find herself at the agonized pivot of the tension between her parents. Henry hoped that Tania would join the new household which he would set up with Jessie. Her presence would legitimize that household – a conductor sharing a home with his grown-up daughter and with a woman no longer young as his secretary. 'All would have been well in the eyes of the world,' as Tania put it in her taped reminiscences of that period. Had he not the right to *expect* such a gesture from a child so emotionally close to him? Had not Tania's own 'flight' from home given a clear realisation of how 'impossible' her mother had become? He met her in London on Saturday 16 February (she occasionally came home from Paris at weekends) and told her his resolve.

She was obviously sympathetic to her father. At his urgent invitation she consented to have lunch with him and Jessie at Pagani's Restaurant – still a favourite haunt of his. But at the last moment, after Mrs Hillman's expostulations on behalf of the absent Muriel, she telephoned her father and declined to come. She may have experienced a revulsion at the prospect of being asked to condone the desertion of her mother; equally strong, if her later recollections are to be relied on, was a determination not to be tied down in dependence on her loving but over-dominating father: 'I wasn't going to be a stooge; . . . if I once saddled myself with that, I would only be chauffeur, cook, everything else. . . .'

On the reasonable assumption that Muriel in Sicily had by now received Henry's letter and would be under severe emotional shock at its implications, Mrs Hillman telegraphed a message of comfort and support for her. Back came a telegram of bafflement. Muriel – roving to Palermo, Taormina, where else? – had not received the letter, which chased her from one address to another. Only when Mrs Hillman finally reached her by telephone at Palermo did she learn of the new situation now confronting her. According to Mrs Hillman, Muriel was at first remorseful, writing to her husband 'a beautiful letter begging him to reconsider his decision and to start afresh, [saying] that she would repair any mistake or mistakes she may have made, that he could continue his friendship, have a separate home if he liked, but continue the dignity of his life, coming to them all at Chorley Wood from time to time'.

But by then Henry's attitude had hardened – fortified by Jessie, it may be guessed. Desiring a divorce, he would receive no communication from his wife except through his solicitors. He gave orders for both the Elsworthy Road house and Appletree Farm to be sold – in the case of Appletree, minus the plot on which the barn stood, a plot which had been bought in Muriel's name alone. Tania then, whether or not prompted by Muriel, ordered the removal from the Elsworthy Road house of most of its contents, which she put into storage at Harrods. Who can now be sure of the motives for such an impetuous act – outrage, revenge, a genuine desire to safeguard what belonged to her mother's 'realm'? (Goods dating back to Olga's day were not removed.)

'My father never forgave me for that.' It was an act which in his eyes ranged her definitely on her mother's side against him. Sufficient excuse, perhaps, was provided by Henry's decision to sell Appletree Farm – dispossessing his wife of that lovingly cultivated garden which was her greatest treasure. Yet in that letter of 12 February which had failed to reach her in Sicily, he had seemed to offer her Appletree unconditionally as a place of residence, should she comply with his wishes.

When that letter eventually reached her on her return to England, Muriel refused to open it or to acknowledge its contents. (Her solicitor was allowed to open it.) She still hoped for a reconciliation with her husband. As late as 9 May she asked Sir John McEwen to mediate: he offered sympathy but declined to interfere. She, or some well-meaning friends, even approached the higher management of the BBC, in the hope of bringing Henry to a realisation of possible damage to his public esteem. As for divorce (on the available grounds of adultery), she would never consider it; the law gave Henry no grounds for divorcing *her*. But Henry's decision to sell the two homes put pressure on her. If she wanted to have her beloved Appletree, she would have to *buy* it back.

Here an ugly factor enters the case. As husband's and wife's solicitors sought to settle matters, it became clear that she had invested under her own name considerable sums drawn from her husband's earnings. That Henry had put his financial affairs entirely in her hands, and had been relieved to do so, is undoubted. Did she exceed that trust in placing investments under her own name? Henry was obliged, through his solicitors, to contend that she did; he now hoped to *recover* what he considered his own money. To the accusation that Muriel had cruelly mistreated him was added the accusation (articulated both by Henry and by Jessie) that she had robbed him.

More immediately, there was social embarrassment on all three sides. Muriel Wood made no *public* complaint of Henry's conduct, nor an admission of the breakdown of her marriage. Were Henry himself to make such a public admission, he would be seen to have deserted his wife of twenty-four years – and this in a society where at least the appearances of marital rectitude were strongly valued. As for Jessie Linton, formerly Goldsack, in what form and under what name could she be seen as the companion of Sir Henry J. Wood, knight and celebrity? Henry refused to keep Jessie hidden. The BBC was informed that his new address from the end of February 1935 was 19 Adam St (the formerly 'secret' address he had divulged to Tania); later in the year he wrote on business matters from Jessie's address, Cumberland Lodge, Ealing. Letters dealing with his contractual matters arrived at the BBC offices with the signature 'J. Linton, secretary'.

In dealing with this period, Jessie's tape-recorded reminiscences of 1972 are not without an element of self-defence, indeed exculpation. She was 'pitched into this cauldron'. She too would have preferred the apparently easy solution of a *ménage-à-trois* with Tania. But in the face of Henry's declaration that he wanted to live with her, what was Jessie to do when Tania, on the verge of saying 'Yes', instead said 'No'? 'I simply felt I could not say to him "This has stopped everything" . . . I felt it was quite impossible to say no to him. I was left carrying the baby . . . It was asking too much of me. How could I tell this poor man that I couldn't undertake it unless Tania was with us? . . . I couldn't say no to him.'

Henry J. Wood's new life was beginning – in the company not of the conventional 'wife-replacer', the much younger woman bringing glamour and perhaps the rejuvenating stimulus of a new fatherhood, but of a mature, motherly figure, a few weeks *older* than the wife with whom he had spent twenty-four years.

A heavy legacy of family bitterness was to be the result of the separation. But on his part there was not the faintest foot-shuffle of turning back. Appletree Farm House now being up for sale, he and Jessie apparently went and threw out all Muriel's possessions into the barn (which was on *her* land). With irony, an article written for *Woman's Journal* before the breakup appeared in January 1935, portraying the household which existed no longer. Its author was Joyce Wedgwood, who had contributed the previous summer's article to the *Radio Times*. An outdoor photograph showed the conductor enjoying the company of Robert the black labrador and of Lady Wood, who 'has made the garden her especial care, with the most delightful results'.

Chapter 18

'Love is a disease'

1935–6

Homeless, at least temporarily, Muriel threw herself on the hospitality of various friends including Mrs Edward Speyer, widowed the previous year. Soon an invitation arrived which offered a complete refuge from the scene. Muriel's younger brother Cecil Greatrex, British consul in Nagasaki, urged her to stay with him in Japan, bringing one or both of her daughters.

Among the small number of friends in whom she confided was Dame Ethel Smyth, whose response came in a shower of letters. Though she had considered herself a close friend of both Muriel and Henry, Ethel Smyth initially viewed the separation from only a single angle. Desertion of a devoted wife by her husband was despicable:

[8 May 1935]
Your letter touched me so terribly . . . but the gist of anything I could say – if I had hours before me to write in – is this. Love like yours is so big – such a wonderful thing to have felt and still to feel for another mortal – that I feel sure it will triumph in the end if you cling on to it and don't let anyone egg you on to bitterness even in the innermost folds of your own heart. It must be terribly difficult not to let bitterness in yet it seems to me that you, whatever your faults may be, are one of the rare beings who can achieve this. Love, especially at Henry's age *is* a disease. Nothing but this terrible madness can account for the way he has acted in this matter but no cruelty or cowardice on his part (for that has a great deal to do with it – I mean the dread of a scene) can prevent his being a deeply intelligent man who knows as well as I (or for the matter of that Shakespeare or God!) the transcendent worth of a love such as yours – surviving and silencing other reactions even while the wound is still bleeding. I feel *certain* the day will come when he will be ashamed of himself and go back to you and the children *and all depends on how you face the future*.

But Ethel Smyth's first reaction was soon tempered by Muriel's elusiveness. An undated letter, apparently from about 20–23 May 1935, asked

> Are we never to meet? . . . I feel that I know (really) so little about what your life with Henry and the girls has been of late years, and as I told you, since I no longer trusted H., there seemed no point in trying to take up the old relations. In fact I did feel that what I had once thought was a clear pellucid situation was not so: I felt that you were a little veiled from me . . . whether because you were shielding H. from my scrutiny, or had, on your side, things and elements in your mutual life that no longer corresponded to the picture I had of you as two hand-in-hand partners. I didn't know!
>
> Now too I feel I don't know where you stand – what you are aiming at – your wishing to go to Japan – your dread lest anyone should hear such is your intention (*if it is your intention*) – all this is bewildering.
>
> If a person is in a bag one must have an idea on which side of it they wish to emerge! and I feel that if you don't seem to want to see me, it may be that you don't know yourself. I feel this tragedy *is no surprise to you* – that you may have been ostrich-like about it and just drifted on till your accident brought things to a head.

Once more, in a letter of 24 May, Ethel Smyth wrote 'I do wish we could meet', and continued:

> I think I will risk saying this (1) that I found out some years ago that in some ways Henry is *not a strong character* (2) that I can imagine that nine times out of ten he would do a good deal to evade a row or a fight (3) that given his work I quite see that to act thus – to slip round a situation on 'anything for a quiet life' lines though it involves the person in a certain hypocrisy – is perhaps the only way if you have to deal with a very strong character (*on whose masterfulness in other ways you have leant!*). I feel quite certain that you may never have suspected how a weaker and terribly hard-worked person feels when a situation gets complicated by domestic confusions . . . in fact I know he told someone he had been meditating this present step ten years ago. I don't believe 'falling in love' has anything much to do with it *and that is one reason why I think Time will help*.

To her surprise, Ethel received a letter from Henry – not about the separation, however, but (as she told Muriel in a letter of 25 May) 'entirely about an odious speech Thomas Beecham made at the dinner for the British Women's Orchestra – a speech I made game of in yesterday's D. T.' [*Daily Telegraph*]. Having hesitated to approach Henry before, she now could not resist doing so.

I said I had been wanting to write to him for some days and felt I must . . . I wrote three sheets to him – all in the sense I told you. I simply told him that as an old friend of you both I could not be silent . . . I spoke of how I honour and admire the way you tackle the disaster – and I let him feel – or even said to him – that your anguish burnt all littleness and desire for revenge out of your heart – so it seemed to me. And I told him that though I knew that nothing could *now* make an impression on him – for probably as we all do when constrained to be cruel, he was justifying his action by looking away from anything but his grievances, still . . . a day would come – for certain . . . when, etc., etc.,. But I will not go on. I said all I felt, and all I thought might bear seed by and by. *I begged him not to answer* – to believe that though I cannot understand things that do not rhyme together with the Henry I know, I venture [?] to judge no one unless I know more than I can know (or wish to know) of your mutual story. Only I begged him just to *keep my letter* and later to read it again. I told him I was glad to know you were leaving England as soon as you can – that of course you could not bear life otherwise.

It was a letter that could not *anger* him against me and make him consider me an enemy (*I specially wanted to avoid that* – hoping for better times between you later on). And I think it *must* rend his heart. Anyhow (too) he knows now what is in mine.

I am having it typed in Woking today (names left out) as you say he cannot read my writing easily and shall send it off tomorrow Sunday.

[P.S.] Can you give me *no* permanent address?

By now Muriel had sent Ethel not only copies of correspondence from Henry's lawyers but, on Ethel's request, a copy (evidently via Muriel's own lawyers) of Henry's letter addressed to her in Sicily – which Muriel still refused to read for herself. Writing to Muriel (as she was now doing every three days or so), Ethel now allowed herself a more brutal tone (27 May):

My feeling is that Henry's brain is not in order. There is in him the inherent weakness (and in some points lack of truthfulness – of straightness) that, during the last few years, has very much affected my feeling for him. The surface seemed all right but one felt the root was not really sound. And as I knew your adoration for and loyalty towards him, I no longer besought you to let me come to Appletree Farm.

He now seems to be veering in all directions . . . To start with, the mad idea expressed in the letter (which, dear Muriel, I *do* think you ought to read) that your friends and relations 'need' know nothing. But I suppose this was at the time when he thought the 'Appletree' life would apparently go on as usual – that you and the girls would treat Mrs L. as his secretary and thus cover his tracks! And no doubt you are right in thinking that when Tania refused the luncheon trio he was persuaded by Mrs L. to make a deliberate break – and start the lawyers business. . .

If you did start a divorce it is obvious that none of your faults excuse the incredible caddishness and cowardice of his behaviour . . . his letter to you would be enough to damn him! I thought H looked rather dreadful at the Albert Hall – puffy, shifty, no *bone* in his face.

. . . I think I can believe that you *overdrove* him – for his own good. I was told by someone *he* didn't want to go to America; and I suppose you have thought for a long time he must not let himself be quite submerged by T.B. [Beecham]! If so H ought to have had the strength to resist you; but as all your friends agree 'what M. said *was law*; had to be done'; and in the same way he is now under the thumb of this woman. Hence all the self-contradiction.

By 31 May Ethel Smyth was advising Muriel to 'face the truth about him' – in a new sense, namely that all was over.

I feel I must take back the words I said that, I fear, gave you comfort – but that no longer correspond to my present feeling. That feeling I will only sum up by saying: I hope to Heaven you will find strength to . . . *face the truth* about him. And I trust that before long you will be as unable as I am for you, now! to desire future reunion with him. Only on this basis – *of facing the truth* – of *realising* and facing it – can a new life begin for you all three – you and the girls. I wish I had never written to him . . . I shall now write again and say . . . that for my own part I trust we shall not meet again – unless it is inevitable professionally (not very likely!).

In fact I shall make him feel no friendly relation is possible between us.

If we do meet I shall not greet him.

Far from holding to the idea that Henry had been thrown temporarily off-balance and would soon return to his marriage, she now (in a letter of 20 June) called on Muriel to recognize that:

at heart, Henry is a superficial, a *contemptible* human being. For you see I *don't* believe it is a sudden madness; I fully believe it is, as I told you, the case of dry rot eating away the heart of the beams of a house, so that it is bound to come down under a sudden strain (a ball on the first floor for instance!) or, if you prefer the picture, it is like elms that throw out roots *close under the surface*, instead of downwards; comes a storm . . . and over they go.

You have absolutely proved to me that your idea of getting away out of England as soon as possible is *not* running away from it all in the cowardly sense but a wise and sane decision.

Battling

In whom would Henry himself wish to confide? The answer was Francis G. Sanders, his musical assistant. His letter of 21 April 1935 was cool and firm:

> On 5 February I left Lady Wood for good, in Rome. We have kept up appearances wonderfully well but I could stick it no longer – I should have left her ten years ago, but my children were too young. She was certainly the worst-tempered woman in Great Britain and I toed the line of least resistance – anything for peace – and to fulfil my job; but how I conducted for the last five years, God only knows! Well, it is finished! and I never want to see a Greatrex or a Manuelle [his wife's mother's family] again, except by accident.
>
> I have found a marvellous business manager and secretary, in an old pupil of mine, Mrs Linton of Bowden [*sic*; rightly Bowdon], near Manchester. You may remember her as Jessie Goldsack in the old Newman days. Her husband died from the results of the War and she moved to London about two years ago and already my business has tremendously increased. I have just signed a five-year contract with Decca and been offered a fine series of concerts in America (sailing 19 June) but I have just cabled it 'off' – I want a peaceful summer holiday.
>
> Don't trouble to answer this, my dear friend, as I do not want to discuss my private affairs, and I am sure as man to man we understand each other, but when Tania left home *very suddenly last September*, and when one's daughter said four years ago, 'How does poor Daddy stick it?', it is serious. There are of course *two sides* to such a question and Lady Wood has gone round to many of my oldest friends giving her version, but Dr Cathcart and Rosa Newmarch are entirely on my side.

Rosa Newmarch was indeed quick to recognize, and accept, Wood's new liaison. Although she had known Henry for about forty years she had never been on greatly cordial terms with Muriel (as she had with Olga). As early as 11 April 1935 she wrote to 'Dear Mrs Linton', signing 'Yours sincerely and gratefully'. She had evidently been told of attempts to vilify Henry in the eyes of his friends and, perhaps, in those of the BBC:

> Thank you for your letter which pleased me very much. One has only to look at dear Henry to see that he is already a different man. He need not worry too much, for he is a good man and a big man and he can and will live down the attacks of a nonentity [Muriel], however cunningly planned. Nevertheless, as she has had nothing to do *really* for many years but spin complicated webs of veiled hostility around her too-kind husband and his friends, the situation does require deliberate and cautious handling.
>
> Please tell Henry from my daughter and myself that we shall be very pleased and proud to accept his invitation for dinner on 15 April. I do

think that as none of his true friends and old have felt very happy these last few years, even when they kept on going to Appletree for his sake, that it is a nice thought of his to rally them in this way. Of course *we* ought to be giving the dinner to him. But dear Henry, who is the most hospitable soul in the world, has, in spite of his two houses, been very cunningly kept from entertaining the right sort of people for a long time past.

At the same time I do feel very strongly that it would be best to make it a quiet, dignified rally. A conjuror certainly! But no speeches, no unsolicited testimonials from indiscreet semi-friends! We who are there will gladly show *by our presence* our affection and *respect* for Henry, and in our hearts we shall rejoice that he is his own man again, but the less demonstration the better! You won't mind my saying this, for I perceive you are wise as well as kind.

Has Henry invited anyone from the BBC? Herbert Heyner and his wife lunched here on Monday (she is a very nice little soul) and gave me a most amusing account of the rejoicings there over 'no more letters from Lady Wood'!

I should much like to meet you. We have of course met in the past . . .

She was not the only one of Henry's friends to have noticed something going badly wrong with the marriage, and to welcome Jessie as his rescuer. One of them, Muriel Saleeby (wife of Dr C. W. Saleeby), had noted that from about 1933 Henry seemed to be losing 'his serenity and good humour': '. . . We who knew him diagnosed the reason and were unhappy; also, the orchestras were unhappy! This changed immediately Jessie became his helpmate – as he said to us, "his perfect wife" . . . . He once remarked to us, "She can cook, type, sing, write and above all she gets on well with servants" (with a sigh). She has a great heart and a fine brain to control it.'

Would his other friends accept the new arrangement? The marital irregularities of conductors were nothing new in musical circles. Sir Thomas Beecham had been cited as co-respondent in a well-publicised divorce case and was himself to be divorced; Sir Hamilton Harty was known to be living in Manchester not with Lady Harty (the singer Agnes Nicholls) but with someone else. Divorce was no longer regarded as shocking. But the apparent desertion of a wife who did not want a divorce might well be thought less than honourable. It says much for Jessie, and for the general recognition of how much happier she made Henry, that nearly all those who knew Wood best came to accept her as the sharer and enricher of Henry's life.

By the summer Muriel had, at last, overcome her inward-turning disposition sufficiently to meet her friend Ethel Smyth after all those weeks of correspondence. Moreover her lawyers (Waterhouse & Co) had come to an understanding with those of her husband (Hastie's). The two firms drew up a set of 'Heads of Agreement' towards a settlement regarding property matters. The outcome must have given her no little satisfaction. On 9 July Hubert Foss wrote to his wife, who was away from home:

> Lady Wood didn't ring up till 10 to 12! She kept me over half an hour. She says that the whole HJW case has crumpled up like a pricked bubble and Henry has signed an agreement like a lamb. She is to have Appletree entire, with all the furniture, one-third of his income, all the alleged stolen money in trust for the girls, and Avril to have £3 a week as well. She says that her solicitors attribute the whole débâcle to a good counsel.
>
> Lady Wood says that someone who has seen HJ and JL together talks of her complete 'domination and proprietorship'! Rather distressing.

The provision of income for Avril was apparently a last-minute arrangement; it does not appear on the lawyers' typed 'Heads of Agreement'. As for 'the alleged stolen money', the terms of the agreement were a little more complex than Muriel gave Foss to understand. Trustees were to be appointed and Muriel would retain such investments standing in her name 'as shall be proved to the satisfaction of the trustees to be derived from her own moneys'. As to 'the remaining investments', they would be held in trust for Lady Wood for life (i.e. she would have access to the income, but not to the capital), then in trust similarly for Sir Henry if he survived her, 'with remainder to their daughters or their issue'.

This meant, crucially, that Henry did *not* recover for his own use the capital sum of which he alleged that Muriel had 'cheated and deceived' him. By signing the agreement and not going to court over this matter, he might be said to have conceded that she had acted in good (matrimonial) faith – or at least that he could not prove otherwise.

Appletree Farm was now Muriel's; by the terms of the agreement she paid £4100 for it from her own investments. If she were not residing there, she would be able to derive a substantial income from letting it, in addition to her investment income and the 'one-third' to be paid by Henry. (More precisely, it was to be 'one-third of the joint income from all sources', with some further stipulations on how that was calculated.) If not rich, she was now comfortably off – able to travel and to continue the kind of existence she was used to.

The passage to Japan in response to her brother's invitation was duly booked. One at least of the daughters was needed to give her company. For this Tania was chosen, not Avril – who, scholastically brighter, was thought more capable of developing her own career. Muriel and Tania sailed on 5 July on their long voyage, via the Mediterranean, calling at Hong Kong and Shanghai before arriving in Japan on 22 August. Prolonging her overseas stay in various locations, Muriel never saw her husband again; Tania was to meet her father only on one, bruising encounter. She remembered her mother's depressed state on that voyage: 'She used to stand by the rail and weep by the hour. . . . She could not face what had happened.' The disposition 'not to face' was characteristic: once under her brother's roof in Nagasaki she would, as Tania recalled, put aside the letters her own solicitors sent her: 'She didn't want to know.'

The terms of the property settlement were a private matter. It did not deal with personal separation – still less with divorce, the very possibility of which Muriel never admitted. She remained the wife of Sir Henry J. Wood, and the law would protect her against any imputation to the contrary. The property settlement had presumably helped to persuade Ethel Smyth that Muriel's decision to leave Britain was now 'wise and sane'.

In the eyes of others, however, it simply left the field to Jessie. Henry was the gainer, able to bask in the sun of Jessie's devotion. His career likewise benefited, for Jessie proved not merely an efficient manager but a positive – yet diplomatic – pusher. Far from easing him into retirement (as he alleged that Muriel planned to do), Jessie vigorously supported his determination to continue conducting wherever suitable engagements might be offered.

His income had been falling – 'dropping every year now by hundreds', according to that letter to Tania in which he had reproved her supposed extravagance in Parisian living. That was a reference to the fall in the number of his engagements since being stripped of an orchestra of his own in 1927.

In general he was in direct rivalry with younger conductors. His one specially privileged position was as conductor of the promenade concerts. Despite his feeling like 'a man with a popgun' against the BBC's heavy artillery, his contractual arrangements with it continued to look fair. For the financial year ending on 5 April 1934 the BBC had paid him £3650:

	£
2 monthly arrangements, April-May 1933	650
Summer promenade concerts, 1933	2300
2 Queen's Hall concerts, Dec. & Mar.	200
Good Friday concert, Queen's Hall	100
4 studio concerts	400
	3650

The sum would differ only slightly (£3700) in the following year. Though the fixing of the financial twelvemonth is not the same, it is instructive to range these BBC figures alongside his own 'draft financial account' (presumably for personal taxation purposes) for the calendar year 1935, which puts his earnings at £5651, his expenses at £1799.17s.6d., profit £3851.2s.6d. Of his total of fee-income, therefore, the proportion drawn from the BBC was thus about two-thirds, and well over half of that was derived from the Proms. Fortunately for him the Concerts Committee of the BBC had decided by January 1935 that in all likelihood Wood's health would allow him to undertake the Proms 'for another five years', and that instead of suggestions of retirement he should be asked 'whether he would like some assistance'.

No, he would not! And meanwhile, even in those months of his marital upheaval, he remained conspicuously busy. On 4 February he shared with Landon Ronald and Malcolm Sargent a concert at the Albert Hall in memory of King George V (who died on 20 January), in aid of the Musicians' Benevolent Fund. He performed Borodin's Second Symphony and the Schubert-Liszt *Wanderer* Fantasia (with Clifford Curzon) at the Bournemouth Festival, and Elgar's early choral work *The Banner of St George* at the Liverpool Philharmonic. He conducted a Holst-Delius-Elgar commemoration (including Holst's *Hymn of Jesus*) with local Watford forces in May. In June he repeated, this time from a BBC studio, Janáček's *Glagolitic Mass*. On the occasion of Wood's receiving his honorary doctorate at Cambridge on 13 June the University Orator did not actually mention Klenovsky but wondered *utrum inter Britannos vivos numerare expediat an defunctos Sclavonas* – whether the honoured musician 'should be counted among living Britons or deceased Slavs'.

He attempted also to brighten his image where it was fuzzy, in the relentlessly competitive world of gramophone recording. He wrote to Gerald Beadle of the BBC on 2 April 1935:

> I am about to sign a very important contract with a well-known Recording Co., for a number of years, and make a fine series of classical works starting with the six Brandenburg Concertos of Bach.
> I do not know if you are aware that I own all the shares in 'The Queen's Hall Orchestra Limited', and its registered title.
> I am very anxious to revive this title for the Recording – above mentioned – and the Recording Co. agree that the title, coupled with my name, would prove a valuable asset.
> I should be glad if you will let me know what your confreres think of

26 The earliest known photograph
of Henry J. Wood on the rostrum
of Queen's Hall – from *The Tatler*, 1903

27 Shaking hands with Rachmaninoff after the great pianist had performed at Wood's jubilee concert at the Royal Albert Hall in 1938

28 At one of Myra Hess's wartime concerts in the National Gallery, September 1939

Wood conducting

30

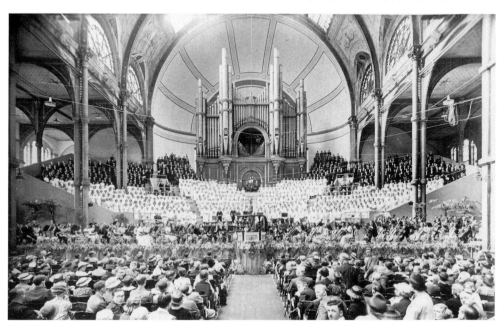

31 An open rehearsal at
Alexandra Palace, 1939

32 After the
destruction of the
Queen's Hall by
bombing in May
1941 the BBC
asked Wood to be
photographed
among the ruins.

33 The original
(above) shows him
with two BBC
officials; the more
heroic solo pose
was obtained by
doctoring the
photograph

34 Cartoon by *Spy*, 1907

35 Sir Bernard Partridge of *Punch* portrays Wood in 1926 – evidently conducting his student orchestra at the Royal Academy of Music

36 At Sheffield, where he first conducted the famous triennial festival in 1902, Wood is photographed with the typical floppy bow tie of his youth and with the jokey non-music emblem of his choice

37 A photograph of the 1930s much favoured by Wood himself

38 At a presentation in honour of his 75th birthday in 1944 Wood is seen with Ralph Vaughan Williams (seated) and Sir Adrian Boult

39 At the studio for the recording of Vaughan Williams's *Serenade to Music*, written to celebrate Wood's jubilee in 1938: (back row, left to right) Walter Widdop, Parry Jones, Frank Titterton, Heddle Nash, the composer, Roy Henderson, Harold Williams, Robert Easton, Norman Allin, and (front row, left to right) Isobel Baillie, Elsie Suddaby, Eva Turner, Stiles-Allen, the conductor, Margaret Balfour, Astra Desmond, Muriel Brunskill, Mary Jarred

40 Sir Henry J. Wood arrives with Lady Jessie Wood for a wartime Promenade concert at the Royal Albert Hall

41 In 1969, after a concert, Lady Jessie Wood is presented to Queen Elizabeth (now the Queen Mother) – 'legitimising' her position

42 The bust by Donald Gilbert which is kept at the Royal Academy of Music except when it is brought to the Royal Albert Hall and garlanded for the Proms

43 Meredith Frampton's portrait of Sir Henry J. Wood
hanging on the wall of his last home,
63 Harley House, Marylebone Road, London;
Wood holds his own juvenile painting, *Apples*

this, as of course I know you have taken over the Queen's Hall Promenade Concerts, but always advertise the orchestra as 'The BBC Symphony Orchestra'.

Your reply at the earliest possible moment, I shall deem a favour.

The 'well-known' company was Decca. The BBC would not bite, however; the Proms continued to be given by the BBC Symphony Orchestra. His pre-1914 welcome to women orchestral players was crowned in 1935 when, for the first time, the 1935 promenade concerts opened with a woman in the leader's chair – Marie Wilson. She had actually replaced the indisposed Charles Woodhouse at the end of the previous summer.

The *Morning Post* (14 August 1935) was one of a press chorus which greeted the opening of the 1935 season with unusual warmth:

> Nowhere else in Europe these forty years has it been possible to hear regular performances of fine works by so good an orchestra at so reasonable a price; and how much one indefatigable conductor has done for musical taste in his long span is beyond compute. . . . Today Sir Henry Wood has created an audience which adds discrimination to its fine fervour. No one, perhaps, realized how deeply the Promenades had played themselves into London's affections until they threatened to end eight years ago. If the BBC had done nothing besides, the Corporation would deserve our gratitude for giving these concerts a new and safer lease, and for making it possible for Sir Henry Wood's baton to beat in millions of listening rooms throughout the land.

The Proms had indeed been converted, through broadcasting, from a London to a national institution. A provincial paper like the *Sheffield Evening Telegraph* did not cover the London musical scene as such, but nevertheless its readers were sufficiently involved to be told on 5 October:

> It is generally agreed, even by those who are not 'fans', that the Promenade season which will end tonight in semi-riotous fashion with Sir Henry Wood's *Fantasia on Sea Songs*, has been the best, technically and musically, for many years.
>
> Sir Henry has never been more brilliant as a host, and the orchestra have backed him notably. Miss Marie Wilson, who has led the players throughout the strenuous eight weeks, has made an international reputation.
>
> But, strenuous as has been the famous conductor's role, he is not taking a rest, for tomorrow afternoon he is conducting a big programme [with the New Symphony Orchestra, and Solomon as soloist] at the Palladium. For a man of 66 this is a phenomenal record in the music world.

Battling

The BBC planners persisted in rescheduling at the Proms those newer works which had undergone baptism in the studio – confronting the promenaders with the label 'first concert performance' or 'first concert performance in England'. Shostakovich's Symphony no.1 was one such work heard in the 1935 Proms, one of several by which Wood freshened his speciality in Russian music. He was permitted a few Continental works genuinely new to Britain, including the orchestral version of Bartók's *Hungarian Peasant Songs* on 16 September and a concerto by Germaine Tailleferre for two pianos (Ethel Bartlett and Rae Robertson) with mixed chorus, saxophones and orchestra on 3 October.

The success of the Proms that summer emboldened the BBC to mount a fortnight's winter season of Proms beginning on 30 December. On 4 January 1936 Eileen Joyce was heard in the first British performance of Shostakovich's Concerto for Piano, Trumpet (Herbert Barr) and Orchestra. Three days later, in an all-Hungarian programme, Béla Bartók reappeared in person to perform his Second Piano Concerto – an occasion remembered by him when he wrote out four bars in full score as his contribution to an album of seventy-fifth-birthday tributes to Wood in 1944 (see p.385).

Leading soloists at the Proms (including Bartók on that occasion) were still encouraged to display their art without orchestra in the second half – pianists on their own, singers with piano accompaniment. Ballads had supposedly been banished as culturally inferior, but Peter Dawson was evidently able to persuade the BBC that those were what his public demanded. So, after fulfilling his first-half duty with Handel, he reappeared with 'A Smuggler's Song', to a favourite Kipling text ('Watch the wall, my darling, while the Gentlemen go by!'), set by C. G. Mortimer. This was to be the last time the BBC offered Wood a fortnight of winter promenade concerts.

Wood as choral conductor continued to be entrusted with the BBC's special Good Friday music-making. On 10 April 1936 it was *Parsifal* at Queen's Hall, with the generous provision of eleven solo singers – though sometimes Wood had filleted *Parsifal* for concert extracts with one or two singers or none at all.

Within a few months, however, came a change in broadcasting policy which seemed to indicate a lessened BBC commitment to the Proms. Previously it had broadcast, if not the whole of each concert, at least the 'defining' first half. Now it ceased to do so, claiming that by selecting just a portion of each concert ('maybe a complete symphony, maybe several works, covering from forty minutes to an hour and a half') it could offer more variety to its large listening audience. It must be remembered that the expedient widely used today, of recording a concert and then broadcasting it later, was not considered available. The move to selective broadcasting from the Proms aroused furious criticism in the musical press and elsewhere. It was suggested that the BBC had no mandate to spend its licence-money in setting up public, 'unbroadcast' concerts in competition with other promoters.

Wood cannot have been pleased with this lessened contact with radio listeners, nor with the dropping of the Winter Proms. He needed the oxygen of new exposure, not just such a generous retrospective tribute as the BBC's prospectus for the summer Proms of 1935 had given him: 'It is scarcely too much to claim that Greater London owes its orchestral education to Sir Henry and his "Proms".' The author was the veteran critic Edwin Evans, old enough to recall a pre-Wood, pre-Newman promenade concert of 1882. Evans accepted that Wood's role had changed. Formerly his Proms programmes virtually stood alone in educating the public to appreciate not only the classics, but also the best of the newest music; but now, with other promoters also engaged in pioneering, Wood was commendably nourishing his audiences in a taste for 'virtually the entire repertoire from Bach to the day before yesterday'. That was – though Evans did not put it so – the new role which the BBC saw for the Proms.

Evans calculated the number of promenade concerts in Wood's series as 2418 so far (of which, he might have added, Wood himself had missed hardly more than a dozen or two). Absent from Evans's summing-up, curiously, was any mention of admission price, a potent factor in retaining the younger and least affluent section of the musical public. Entrance to the promenade area of Queen's Hall, payable at the doors only, was still only two shillings; a promenade season ticket for all forty-nine concerts of 1936 was only 37s.6d. (a little under £2). The cheapest admission to the BBC's symphony concerts, in the same hall during the non-Proms season, was also 2s. – but, of course, to a far more restricted area of the hall, with the best seats priced at 10s.

The revived 'Queen's Hall Orchestra' which Wood took into Decca's recording studios had, of course, not been conjured out of nowhere. It was simply his own selection of available London players when free of other commitments. Its leader and manager was at first Charles Woodhouse, then from 1936 George Stratton, who was the regular leader of the London Symphony Orchestra: the critic of the *Monthly Musical Record* noticed a strong contingent of members of that orchestra.

Battling

Wood's previous recording contract with Columbia had lapsed; the company had failed to renew its three-year arrangement after the previous one expired at the end of 1933. (In a letter of *rapprochement* with Columbia in 1938, Wood blamed the original rupture on 'the unreasonable demands of the then Lady Wood, over whom I have [*sic*] no control whatever' – that is, having made his wife his business manager, he now blamed her for taking too firm a position on his behalf!). So he was in no position to resist Decca's offer of terms considerably *worse* than his former Columbia rate of £105 for a three-hour session. Decca's offer, in a letter from its director Edward Lewis (later Sir Edward) dated 9 April 1935, was for a basic twelve sessions at £50 per session:

Dear Sir Henry,
   I am writing to confirm the final arrangements we made yesterday, on the following terms:

(1) You will record exclusively for this company for a period of three years, in consideration of a fee of six hundred pounds (£600) per annum. This Fee will cover a maximum of Twelve (12) sessions per annum, any further sessions to be paid for at the rate of sixty pounds (£60) per session. The Fee to be payable as under:
   £150 at the beginning of the first series of six sessions,
   £150 at the end of the first series of six sessions
   £150 at the beginning of the second series of six sessions
   £150 at the end of the second series of six sessions
(2) The Records will be issued under the name of 'The Queen's Hall Orchestra', and we agree to pay a further Five guineas (£5.5s) per session for the exclusive use of this name.
(3) It is understood that you will supply us with Band parts free of charge.
(4) Although I understand it may be impossible, in certain cases, to record more than two or three sides at a session, it is understood that our scheme is based on at least four sides per session, and that you will make every endeavour to see that the average works out at a minimum of four sides.
(5) It is understood that at the end of three years we are to have the option to extend the contract for a further period of two years on the same terms.

I was delighted to have the opportunity of meeting you last night, and I am very much looking forward to a long period of happy association.
   Yours sincerely –

But what Wood gained was quantity. His Columbia recordings issued during 1933 had totalled a mere twenty sides, probably representing five or six sessions. Moreover, four of these sides were accompanying soloists

(Gieseking in Franck's *Symphonic Variations*, Irene Scharrer performing the Litolff *Scherzo* on two ten-inch sides). Decca's contract envisaged twelve sessions annually, with a yield of up to forty-eight sides. In the half-year of 1935 remaining, Decca indeed marketed twenty-six sides by the New Queen's Hall Orchestra, conducted by Sir Henry J. Wood – and these were all fully orchestral, none shared with a soloist.

As it turned out, there were to be no Decca recordings of the Brandenburg Concertos – whether because the company had other conductors lined up for Bach, or because Wood's concert performance of those works was already being judged as inappropriately heavy. Instead, Wood's Decca releases began with a disturbingly high proportion of 'remakes' of short, popular works which he had previously recorded for Columbia – Wagner's *Ride of the Valkyries,* Järnefelt's *Praeludium,* Wood's own arrangement of Rachmaninoff's Prelude in C sharp minor, and so on. Along with Eric Coates's popular *London Suite*, these were presumably intended as the company's money-spinners to offset the loss envisaged on recording one of the major works of modern English music, *A London Symphony* by Vaughan Williams, which required the investment of ten sides.

That recording was welcomed by the *Musical Times*, the *Monthly Musical Record* and particularly by the *Gramophone*. The editor of the *Gramophone* was the well-known novelist Compton Mackenzie, a layman in music who had earned the attention of the growing class of discriminating music-lovers concerned to build up their collections of records. In this case he took the step of seconding his reviewer's praise with his own (July 1936): 'I consider this recording the finest technical achievement of the Decca company to date. There is nothing to criticize in it and everything to praise, and if I were asked to name a set of discs to illustrate the effect of the various orchestral instruments I should find it hard to suggest a better set than this.'

A devastating review, however, came from *The Times* (21 August), which maintained its tradition of anonymous criticism (almost dead in the rest of the British press); one suspects in this case the pen of Frank Howes, who was staking out a claim to be an authority on Vaughan Williams. Wood's records

> hardly compare for clarity and brilliance with the best modern examples of orchestral recording: the tone in a *tutti* is too often at once thick and thin, i.e., it is opaque yet lacking in sonority.
>
> The orchestra is described as the Queen's Hall Orchestra, which presumably means the players formerly under the regular command of Sir Henry Wood and successors chosen by him for any necessary replacements. Their playing sounds undistinguished on these discs, but whether it

– new words adapted to the music of Mozart's *The Seraglio*,
inscribed by the celebrated soprano Elisabeth Schumann in the 1944 album of
tributes to Sir Henry J. Wood

is the fault of the recording machine, or of the players themselves, or of their conductor, it is not easy to say. Certainly Sir Henry Wood must take the responsibility for some extraordinary maladjustments of time and *tempo*. In the introduction, for instance, the opening phrase is in slow minims, but before the section is ended they have turned themselves into crotchets. On the other hand, in the course of the main body of the first movement the marks *animato* and *largamente* are ignored in a flat-footed, two-in-a-bar jog-trot. Again, in the finale there is a positive error where a triplet bar in two-two time is lengthened by 50 per cent, i.e., instead of being played as a triplet it is played as though it was an interpolated bar of three-two time. Our pleasure therefore in possessing the symphony is modified by the regret that a more sensitive performance was not more sensitively recorded.

Ill-advisedly (one would love to know whether, at this point, Jessie was urging him forward or vainly trying to restrain him), Wood wrote a remonstrating letter to the paper's editor. It was relegated to small print and a down-page position seven days later.

I am the last person in the world to question honest criticism: I go so far as to welcome it, and have done so for nearly 50 years of public work, knowing that our musical critics are in most cases absolutely beyond reproach.

I feel very much about this, because much intelligent thought, both before the recording and during the same, was given by myself and Messrs Decca, and the result, to my mind (not without many years of recordings and hearing recordings), is that this record in question, *The London Symphony*, excels both from the orchestral and engineer's point of view.

Dr Vaughan Williams tells me he has heard the record only on a very bad gramophone and thinks the discs excellent in every way!

For myself, I say that my *tempi* are not those of another conductor, just as his would not be mine: but I have played this symphony the world over, and always with great success. But I do feel, and feel very strongly, that when a British firm shows such remarkable enterprise as do Messrs Decca, by placing great music on the gramophone market at a price within the reach of the man in the street – at a cost to themselves equalling any other recording company (my fee and that of my orchestra) – it is so terribly wrong that we should be so unjustly and thoughtlessly criticized.

There is no error in my playing of this work, and I must ask you to deny this untrue statement.

I hope you will endeavour to hear the record in question and hope you will see my point of view. The orchestra comprises the finest orchestral musicians in London, whose names you are welcome to know if you wish, and I know from my years of vast experience that their playing in this symphony, rather than lacking, gives a more distinguished performance of orchestral playing than that of any record I have heard for years.

As an example of how not to deal with criticism this would be hard to beat.

Presumably with Decca's backing, Wood gained the possibility of a new audience by an appearance in a feature film with his new orchestra (under the title of Queen's Hall Light Orchestra). Here he was just in advance of Stokowski, who began with *The Big Broadcast of 1937* before going on to *A Hundred Men and a Girl* and *Fantasia*. Wood and the orchestra appeared 'as themselves' (along with such stage celebrities as Sir Cedric Hardwicke and George Robey) in *Calling the Tune,* released in July 1936. A brief trade description suffices: '*Musical:* Record manufacturer's daughter loves the son of the man he cheated.' Unlike the Stokowski films, it flopped. Wood never troubled to see it, which is no doubt why he got the 'story' wrong in *My Life of Music*. But he remembered with admiration the raked set constructed at Ealing for the effective display of the orchestra. The only work which he was seen to conduct, however, was Grainger's *Shepherd's Hey*.

On his schedule of coming engagements was a revival of Rachmaninoff's *The Bells* at the Sheffield Festival that autumn. The composer had made a substantial revision of his score which would entail the checking of new chorus parts. Rachmaninoff's double reputation as one of the greatest composers as well as one of the greatest pianists of the day had been maintained with the huge success of his *Rhapsody on a Theme of Paganini*, introduced to London in March 1935 with the composer as soloist and Beecham as conductor. With Rachmaninoff in both his capacities Wood was long and closely associated, yet showed towards him a deference which is surely touching. It is apparent in letters he typed himself, his punctuation and capitalization remaining as erratic as ever:

March 30th 1936

Dear Mr Rachmaninoff,

Your delightful signed Photograph has just arrived through our mutual friend, Mr Ibbs.

How very kind of you, and believe me I shall always treasure it, – and I have placed it on my Piano in my Music Room.

The Chorus part of your Bells is nearly ready, though it has taken me much longer than I anticipated, but I hope to let you have it during tomorrow.

I have a Concert to-morrow, that I always enjoy, my R.A.M. Orchestral Concert at Queen's Hall at 3 pm.

How I should like you to drop in for a few minutes, for the [*sic*] sometimes do very remarkable things.

They number 135 players, and I am very proud of them. I see you are playing my beloved No 3 Concerto tomorrow, and but for an engagement I should have given myself the pleasure of coming to hear you.

Kindest regards and best wishes in which, Lady Wood joins,

Very sincerely yours,

Henry J. Wood

During that summer, Rachmaninoff must have visited Wood at 4 Elsworthy Road and made the acquaintance of Jessie – and of her dog, which had originally belonged to her daughter Eileen.

13 September 1936

My dear Mr Rachmaninoff,

Just a few lines to tell you that our mutual friend, Nicolas Medtner, gave a most beautiful performance last Friday of Beethoven's 4th Concerto at Queen's Hall, he made the *deepest* impression upon all music lovers and we are looking forward to his own 2nd Concerto on Sept 24th.

Moiseiwitsch gave such a fine performance of your Rapsody [*sic*] on August 29th and he is playing it again at my regular Sunday afternoon Orchestral Concerts at Queen's Hall. . . My wife joins me in kindest regards and so does our dear dog Michael. We are looking forward to the Sheffield Festival October 21st.

No answer to this please!

Always sincerely yours

Jessie was already 'Lady Wood' and 'my wife' – and Michael was 'our dog'!

PART IV

Celebrating

'Nehmt meinen Dank mit tausend Freuden, Sir Henry, lebt
gesund und froh' – 'Accept my thanks with thousandfold
joy, Sir Henry, live in health and good cheer.'

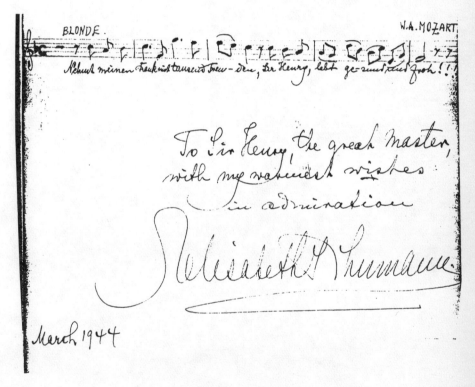

– new words adapted to the music of Mozart's *The Seraglio*,
inscribed by the celebrated soprano Elisabeth Schumann in the
1944 album of tributes to Sir Henry J. Wood

Chapter 19

Jousting with Sir Thomas

1936–7

Liberated from matrimonial ties (he considered he had no obligations remaining to Muriel), Henry J. Wood was a happy man. He gave Muriel her proper title in a letter to Francis G. Sanders, dated 17 January 1936. 'I learnt from my solicitors last week that Lady Wood and Tania are still in Japan but are shortly leaving for Chilee [*sic*] – the further away they are the better.'

For Muriel, a trans-Pacific hop would not have been in the least out of character. The attraction of Chile lay in the presence there of relatives of her friend Helen Douglas Irvine (and Helen herself, perhaps). That trip was not taken, however: Muriel went to Shanghai, and later to the interior of China.

Unknown to Henry, the 'haven' which had been offered to Muriel by her brother in Nagasaki had become a haven no longer. Once having made Muriel and Tania his house-guests, Cecil Greatrex soon enough formed the opinion that his sister was far from being a victim. The strain between uncle, niece and mother became considerable. He was himself on the point of returning to England, his term of consulship in Nagasaki being nearly over. While Tania was still under his roof he typed out and addressed a letter to her on 2 January 1936, with the prefatory caution that 'by showing it to your mother you will only make things more difficult for both of you':

> . . . From my impressions of your home in past years [he referred to his
> visits to England on leave] I assumed that I was writing to daughters
> who loved and respected their mother.
>   Well, soon after your arrival here you began to show me the other
> side of the picture: a mother who had long ago forfeited all claim to your
> affection or respect; a household where father and daughters were
> united in submitting, for the sake of peace needed for your father's
> work, to a reign of continual petty tyranny so that, in your own words,
> everyone who had an opportunity of judging has marvelled that your

father managed to stick it all these years; and finally the hundred and one
incidents which convinced you and others around her that your mother was
scarcely suffering except from injured pride and that self-exaltation, if
necessary or convenient at the expense of all others, continued to be her
principal aim in life. When I heard you describing your experiences to
George, I became convinced that at all events you were not *intentionally*
presenting me with a deceptive picture, and from my own observations
from day to day I was forced to the further conviction that the picture you
drew was an accurate one in its essential outlines.

Your mother then left us alone for six weeks, enabling me to judge
whether you were right in asserting that she is a bad influence for you. Just
before returning she wrote you that letter which I describe as gratuitous
calculated venom, and I told you I undertook to back you to the limit in
breaking away from her if you would promise to be guided by me, – which
you did, and we accordingly despatched that telegram warning her not to
come back unless prepared to change her tactics.

[In order to help Tania to free herself from her mother's domination, he
had offered to escort her back to England and pay any incidental expenses
of that journey.]

She [Muriel] then proceeded to work on your feelings until you fainted
and lay in bed babbling incoherently . . . And what happens next? I come in
one day to find you making merry with your mother and with nothing but a
discouraging scowl for me.

. . . I must have your final decision [on whether to return home with him]
during the next four or five days because boats are always full homeward-
bound in the spring . . . For the rest, I was quite serious in saying that
unless you accept my guidance I hope you will both leave my house at the
earliest possible date . . .

Tania did *not* return with her uncle. She went with her mother to Shanghai
and found independence by working there as a secretary. Then at Wei-Hai-
Wei, where Britain's China Fleet regularly spent the summer, she re-met a
childhood friend, the son of a Chorley Wood doctor. He was Lieutenant
George Jameson ('Jim') Cardew, a regular officer of the Royal Navy. They
became engaged, and Tania's destiny was now distanced from that of both
parents.

There is no doubt that the absence abroad of the real Lady Wood – that is,
Muriel – conveniently eased Henry's unofficial bestowal of the title on Jessie
Linton. The letters which he himself sent to her in and after 1936, during
brief absences while he was conducting BBC or other concerts outside
London, were addressed to 'Lady Wood' at 4 Elsworthy Road. These letters
were brim-full of love – and sometimes of nothing else:

My angel treasure!
    I adore you!
    I love you!
    I adore you!
    I love you!
    A million thanks to you for giving me your beautiful love,
which makes me the happiest man in the world – Dear darling
Jessie – that is all
    Henry

At other times the signature might be 'your loving and devoted little hubby Hen' or even a jocular 'Hen-ner-ry'. He would telephone Jessie long-distance (much rarer in social intercourse than today) and hear their dog Michael 'sing' down the instrument. For Henry that verb needed no quotation marks: 'I did love talking to you for five minutes last night and shall long for the same tonight . . . Michael sang awfully well. I thought so many times of you during the night and pictured you all alone in your little bed with Michael beside you – fondest love my precious treasure.'

'Thursday' (undated) was the inscription on each of the above letters, written from the Royal Station Hotel, Hull. The precaution of travelling to Hull on a Wednesday, to give himself a night's rest before the Thursday evening concert with his amateurs of the Hull Philharmonic, did not guarantee results:

> Thursday morning, 4.24 a.m.
>   My sweetest treasure
>   I simply cannot go to my room without a few words to you of love and adoration for all you are doing for me my treasure . . . Rotten journey, turned out [of train] at Selby, nice fire in Ladies Waiting Room, train came in at 3.30, got to Hull at 4.22, just had a W. and S. [whisky and soda] and now off to bed to dream of my beloved Jessie
>   Your loving Henry

Those with whom he had professional business were now introduced to Jessie as his secretary and manager, at first in her old name as 'Linton'. A letter to Gerald Beadle of the BBC on 12 February 1936 is signed by her 'With kindest regards/ Sincerely yours/ Henry J. Wood J.L.' Within Henry's private, loving letters to Jessie, there are some insertions concerning the business letters she was dealing with. Would he conduct another concert in Liverpool, for a charitable cause? Yes, he would: 'No fee, I expect, but they must pay my expenses.'

In that month a cable arrived for him (via the BBC) from New York:

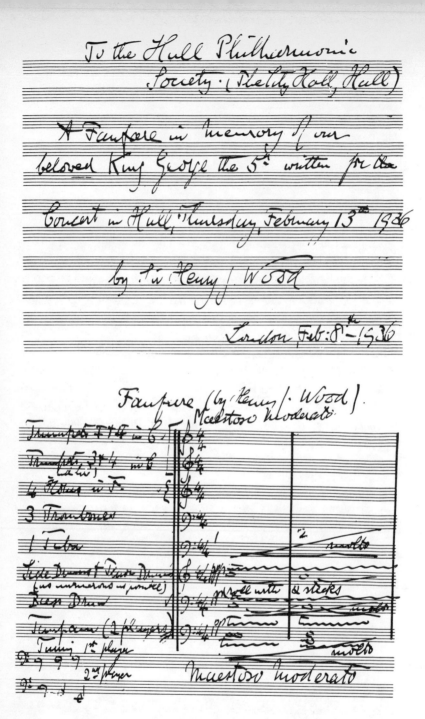

For his amateur orchestra in Hull, Henry J Wood jotted down
an immediate tribute on the death of King George V in 1936.

296

HAD GREAT PLEASURE CONDUCTING LAST NIGHT PHILHAR-
MONIC BACH-KLENOVSKY TOCCATA FUGUE ORCHESTRATED
BY YOU AM VERY HAPPY IT MET WITH ENORMOUS SUCCESS
REGARDS – TOSCANINI

There is an understandable sense of pride in Wood's reproducing this in his
autobiography, for at that time Toscanini was the icon of musical 'correctness'. As conductor of the New York Philharmonic-Symphony Orchestra (a
fusion of the two previously separate orchestras) since 1928, he was famed
for a supposedly absolute fidelity to the score. (In sober fact he did, on
occasion, impose his own changes.) In 1935 Toscanini's first visit to the
BBC Symphony Orchestra as guest conductor had evoked an extraordinary
prostration by the BBC establishment and many critics. But it was no part of
his approach (nor that of his eminent contemporaries) to reject transcription.

So Wood's Proms continued to feature such transcriptions – in 1936 not
only the 'Bach-Klenovsky' Toccata and Fugue in D minor, but also the
earlier Bach-Wood Toccata in F, the Bach-Elgar Fantasia and Fugue in C
minor, and a transcription by the Italian composer Casella of the *Chaconne*
for unaccompanied violin – as well as the Handel-Harty *Water Music*. Side by
side with these were heard Bach's Brandenburg Concertos, clavier
concertos and violin concertos in pretty much their original contours –
though always with piano rather than harpsichord and flute substituted for
recorder.

The shade of 'Klenovsky' himself was not reinvoked: Wood embarked on
no further examples of what might be called 'virtuoso' or 'showpiece'
orchestration. He had not changed his view, however, on the legitimacy –
indeed the necessity – of considerably touching up or reinforcing Bach and
Handel (usually anonymously) in order to conquer the modern audience. He
made his judgements completely *ad hoc*. The *St Matthew Passion* 'needed'
nothing but the multiplication of the original instrumentation. But Handel's
organ concertos – created as display pieces for the composer himself to play
on a pedal-less instrument – called for a complete re-edition. Far more was
required than a part for the modern instrument's pedal-board. Wood's work
had the enthusiastic collaboration of such master-organists as G. D.
Cunningham and Marcel Dupré:

> M. Dupré will improvise the cadenza. [Sir Henry] has not only added the
> necessary weight to the score by lending it woodwind, brass and drums but
> has, besides, substituted for the finale the one in the same key from the
> third concerto of the first set. The original last movement was a slight

> gavotte, by no means a big enough close, as modern ears expect it, for so
> imposing a work, and Sir Henry's wisdom on that point has been acclaimed
> by the whole organ world.

So the BBC's programme annotator had presented the performance of a Handel organ concerto (opus 7 no.1) at the previous winter's Proms. Different considerations occurred to Wood when looking ahead to the 1936 Sheffield Festival. The scheduled performance of Bach's Magnificat in D threatened to have many orchestral players 'sitting on the platform doing nothing'. So, he suggested on 19 March to the ever-available Sanders, 'How would it be if you wrote a third flute, cor anglais, 3rd clarinet, contra [-bassoon], 4 horn parts and 3 trombone parts and a new organ [part] – then I can use my existing printed parts [for the rest of the scoring]. You can take three months over it if you like.'

'Third clarinet' no doubt meant 'three clarinets', since Bach never used the instrument. Obviously Wood saw this work not in the devotional world of Bach's *St Matthew* and *St John Passions* but (with a cue from Bach's trumpets) as music charged with grand rhetoric and drama, like a Handel oratorio. Hence the different 'solution'.

Soon afterwards Wood changed his mind and instructed Sanders not merely to provide extra parts but to re-score the whole work – and 'damn the expense of the band parts'. His practice of *normally* brightening the upper string parts is evident: 'Do you think Bach's original string parts could be used, if so it would save expense'; but if Sanders considered Bach's parts 'too *low* and dull for your orchestration' he could freely rewrite them. The soprano aria 'Quia respexit', originally with an *obbligato* for *oboe d'amore* (lower in range than the normal oboe), was to be rewritten as 'an ordinary oboe solo for Léon Goossens'. But he did not want to lose the brilliancy of Bach's high trumpet writing, difficult though it was for players of the modern standard instrument: 'Perhaps B's original three trumpet parts might stand – I shall have a small D trumpet if wanted.'

On 28 June he wrote thanking Sanders for the work ('perfect'), adding that next day he was leaving for Paris *en route* for a holiday in Lucerne. On the return journey there would be six concerts at the Kursaal, Ostend, 'which will pay for the holiday'. The stay at the Palace Hotel, Lucerne, would provide time to begin dictating to Jessie the autobiography which was to be published as *My Life of Music*.

A week of nightly concerts at Ostend was a pretty humdrum task: at an equivalent British seaside resort such as Bournemouth, he would have conducted a single concert as a distinguished guest. It can only be supposed that he really did need the money. He made his usual ambassadorial display of British music with Elgar's second *Wand of Youth* Suite, Grainger's *Handel in the Strand*, Vaughan Williams's overture to *The Wasps* and, more surprisingly, Sullivan's *Overtura di ballo*, as well as his own arrangement of the 'Purcell' *Trumpet Voluntary* and his Suite from Purcell's dramatic works. Strauss's *Don Juan* was among his other items – all, presumably, on a single rehearsal each day with an unfamiliar orchestra! On the preceding Sunday (26 July) he also conducted a memorial concert at the neighbouring coastal town of Knokke, to mark the visit by King Edward VIII to the British war memorial at Vimy Ridge on that day.

On his return to London Wood's place was, of course, once more with the Proms and the BBC Symphony Orchestra, Marie Wilson again occupying the leader's chair. The BBC continued to show little concern for the dynamic element of the new. A work by Sibelius given its first British performance in 1936, *The Ferryman's Brides*, turned out to have been composed in 1897. It can hardly have helped that the (originally Finnish) text was sung by Muriel Brunskill neither in the original nor in English, but in German. A piano concertino by Elizabeth Maconchy, performed six years before in Prague, was now renamed a concerto and given with the popular Harriet Cohen as soloist. John Ireland's *A London Overture*, highly successful on 23 September and for decades afterwards, was at least new in its orchestral dress, though originating as *A Comedy Overture* for brass band.

Some elements of 'formula' in the planning of the Proms – Wagner on Mondays, Beethoven on Fridays – not only preserved tradition but also functioned as pillars between which the discriminating music-lover could thread his or her way. As ever, the 'first halves' continued to define the character of the concert, often given over to a single composer; the second halves were open to a diversity of composers. So David Cox's history of the Proms slightly misleads in saying that on 11 August 1936 'Walton, aged 34, was given a programme to himself for the first time'. Walton's music occupied only the first half (the composer conducting two works, and Wood another two); after the interval came the tuneful familiarity of Grieg's *Lyric* Suite and Borodin's *Prince Igor* Overture.

Toscanini had seized on Wood's 'Klenovsky' transcription through its published availability. An unpublished arrangement, however, Wood regarded more possessively. When Koussevitzky had wished to borrow the score and parts of his arrangement of Handel's *Solomon* for a projected performance of his own, Wood declined as gracefully as he could, on the plea that if he acceded then he would have to accommodate all such requests. He recommended an application to Sir Thomas Beecham, who, 'I believe, uses an edition by Mr [Armstrong] Gibbs . . . charmingly arranged and scored'. A brotherly gesture! But not much of that spirit emerged in the confrontation with Beecham which Wood was unwise enough to provoke at the 1936 Sheffield Festival.

Since the previous festival three years before, Wood had maintained his activity in Sheffield as conductor of the Sheffield Musical Union, the City's principal choral society. He did himself no good by openly criticizing the Musical Union for its choral standard, for the poor standard of its orchestra of local musicians, and for the business arrangements. A performance of the *St Matthew Passion* in March 1934 he apparently considered particularly inadequate, although he continued to conduct in the following season.

By 1936 he had resigned, but a letter written to the *Sheffield Star* and published on 23 April 1936 was petulant in tone and even implied that – given a reorganization – he was almost desperate to be reinvited.

> To begin with, a young, alert business manager and secretary must be found, [chorus-master] Miss Eva Rich must be given a free hand, and, in order to bring it into line with the modern orchestra, the chorus must rehearse twice a week (ladies one night, gentlemen another) and meet once a month for a full collective rehearsal . . . Regarding the orchestra: I *know* that if I were to take a rehearsal for two hours once a week – why not on a Sunday, when members are free? – I could train them to accompany choral works properly. . .
>
> You must have a conductor of European reputation, and boom him, but he must be an *expert* in the art of *singing*, as well as that of the *orchestra* . . . As for guest conductors, they are hopeless for a permanent choral society. The chorus have no time to become acquainted with their methods or their beat, and most of these guest conductors know very little about *singing*; and if you really inquire, how many orchestras have they *successfully trained and made*?

The hint was not taken up: Eva Rich was made conductor as well as chorus-master – that is, she was given the concerts as well as the rehearsals. After such intrusive behaviour on his part, the city's choralists may have felt none too well disposed towards Sir Henry J. Wood as the time for the 1936 Festival drew near.

Worse was to come. Bad feeling among orchestral players was raised by the quarrel which he picked over the participation of the London Philharmonic, which, as in 1933, was the orchestra chosen for the festival.

The orchestra's personnel had changed. Paul Beard had departed to become leader of the BBC Symphony Orchestra, and David McCallum had been appointed by Sir Thomas Beecham – who remained in both musical and financial control of the London Philharmonic – to Beard's place in the leader's chair.

It was doubtless necessary that Wood should have the completest *rapport* with the leader of the orchestra. Whether he genuinely doubted the abilities of the inexperienced McCallum or not, it is understandable that he should have preferred the man he knew. But he must have known that he was overstepping both contract and custom in telling the festival that he wished to call Paul Beard back and would not conduct unless that substitution was made. Beecham, of course, refused, and called Wood's request 'fantastic', verging on 'impertinence'.

'The position now is clear,' announced the *Sheffield Star* on 12 September. 'Sir Henry Wood must either accept Mr McCallum, the new leader of the Philharmonic Orchestra, or carry out his threat to resign.' A columnist burst into verse:

> Sir Thomas and Sir Henry were hardly hand in hand,
> They could not reach agreement on the leader of the band;
> 'Sir Thomas,' said Sir Henry, 'It is greatly to be feared
> That you do not grasp precisely that I cannot spare my Beard!'
> 'Sir Henry,' said Sir Thomas, 'you can hardly have your way;
> My leader is McCallum, and my leader he shall stay.'
> 'Sir Thomas,' said Sir Henry, 'when you're older you will know
> That *my* leader is essential'. Said Sir Thomas: 'Is that so?
> You are very rude, Sir Henry, and your comment issues hence
> From the region of fantastics into sheer impertinence!'
> And there we leave the champions, and we do not take the part
> Of the fiery knight Sir Henry, or Sir Thomas Beecham, Bart.
> But hope the Festival itself will in due course display
> Some more harmonious features than those we see today.

Wood climbed down, with an unconvincing reproach: 'I am sorry that Sir Thomas Beecham, whom I have often been glad to help, did not see fit to make a gesture to a brother artist about the leadership of the orchestra – the sort of gesture which great conductors have often made, and which I myself have made on other occasions . . .' When the *Musical Times* eventually reviewed the performance, Frank Howes dismissively referred to 'some preliminary skirmishings undertaken to establish a strange new doctrine that an orchestral leader is not so much a part of the orchestra as an appendage of the conductor, to be taken round with him in his suitcase like his dress clothes'.

According to the reminiscences forty years later of Philip Hodges, who sang in the 1936 chorus, the orchestral players showed their resentment at rehearsals and gave 'a terribly ragged performance of the *Haffner* symphony'. Another chorister of that festival, Charles F. Hatfield, writing in 1990, recalled Wood 'in a thoroughly bad mood' at an afternoon rehearsal for the evening's performance of the Verdi Requiem and Walton's *Belshazzar's Feast*. Eva Turner was scolded for arriving a little late. Individual instrumentalists were reproved and made to repeat passages: 'I want to hear a bass drum, not a tea-tray!'

Rachmaninoff arrived in the city not only to hear Wood conduct the revised score of *The Bells* but to perform in his popular Piano Concerto no.2. Other announced participants included the pianist Solomon, at the height of his fame, and the cellist Suggia. Owing to her illness, however, she was replaced by the pianist Irene Scharrer – a bad overweighting of pianists. Except for Vaughan Williams's *Sea Symphony*, which was entrusted to J. Frederic Staton, one of the chorus-masters, Wood conducted every item. *Belshazzar's Feast*, first given five years before under Malcolm Sargent's baton, had become the latest work to fix itself in the British choral canon. Rachmaninoff's *The Bells* would never achieve more than an occasional hearing, though the composer's revision had ironed out some of the difficulties of the choral parts.

The four festival concerts were not crammed, as in 1933, into two days, but even a three-day span must have stretched Wood's skills in planning and timing rehearsals. This was the last of Sheffield's festivals, and its programmes (the first two taking place on the same day) deserve quoting in full as a record of the repertory and the artists. The reader may well pause to contemplate the public appetite, sixty years ago, for Verdi's Requiem and *Belshazzar's Feast* in the same concert with two substantial orchestral works between, or (on the last night) for Beethoven's *Missa Solemnis* followed by Tchaikovsky, Delius and Handel. The soloists' names are added in brackets:

21 October, 2 p.m.
Te Deum [Parry Jones, tenor]   Berlioz
Violin Concerto [Adolf Busch]   Brahms
The Bells [Isobel Baillie, Parry Jones, Harold Williams]   Rachmaninoff

21 October, 7.30 p.m.
Magnificat [Jo Vincent, Jessie King, Mary Jarred, Parry Jones,
    Keith Falkner]   Bach
Piano Concerto no.2 [Rachmaninoff]   Rachmaninoff
Death and Transfiguration   R. Strauss
A Sea Symphony [Jo Vincent, Roy Henderson]   Vaughan Williams

22 October, 7.30 p.m.
Requiem [Eva Turner, Muriel Brunskill, Walter Widdop,
    Alexander Kipnis]   Verdi
'Haffner' Symphony   Mozart
Piano Concerto no.1 [Irene Scharrer]   Liszt
Belshazzar's Feast [Roy Henderson]   Walton

23 October, 7.30 p.m.
Missa Solemnis [Isobel Baillie, Muriel Brunskill, Parry Jones,
    Keith Falkner]   Beethoven
Piano Concerto no.1 [Solomon]   Tchaikovsky
Brigg Fair   Delius
The King shall rejoice   Handel

These were '£8-a-minute concerts', according to a calculation of festival expenditure by which the *Sheffield Star* tried to show its readers what a lavish feast was to be put before them. In the event, the takings were a disappointment, with a loss of £2000 reported. In the *Yorkshire Telegraph and Star*, Wood made a characteristically perky retort: 'As for the empty seats: I think every member of any music organization should go round and sell tickets. I always say: give me a car a month before any concert and I can guarantee a full house.' The *Morning Post* reported him as saying: 'I have been associated with the Sheffield Festival since 1905, but never have I heard such magnificent choral singing.'

Blaming Sheffield's new City Hall for dead acoustics and an awkward platform, the *Musical Times* did not manage to sum up Wood's performances by any adjectives beyond 'sound' and 'resourceful'. In *Belshazzar's Feast* 'he did not appear to be on his usual terms of comfortable familiarity' with the music. Though this was, in execution and reception, a damp farewell to Sheffield, nevertheless fifty years later his name would still be an emblem of past musical glories for the inhabitants of what once had been Steelopolis. The soloist in *Belshazzar's Feast* kept Wood's letter of 25 October 1936:

> My dear Mr Roy Henderson
>
> Just a few lines to thank you for your splendid singing at the 1936 Sheffield Festival. Your voice, your style and your interpretation gave me the greatest satisfaction and pleasure.
>
> My wife joins me in kindest regards and the best of good wishes –
>
> Sincerely yours –

That form of salutation (not 'Dear Mr Henderson' or 'Dear Roy') was Wood's compromise when a professional intimacy had been established, well short of the personal friendship of 'Dear Rosa'. The versatility of Rosa Newmarch was to be extended to the provision of English verse texts for Wood's second set (1937) of operatic choruses by Handel.

From his own Queen's Hall Orchestra in its revived form – using notepaper with the proud sub-heading 'Founded 1895' – Wood hoped for much. But past glories were not easily recoverable. Beginning on 4 October 1936, Chappell's engaged Wood and the orchestra for a series of Sunday afternoon concerts. Failing to bring in sufficient audiences, they were soon discontinued – a failure which Wood ascribed to the fact that they were not scheduled *every* Sunday, 'for it is only by pegging away that a Sunday afternoon audience in Queen's Hall can be regained'. But the fact was that there was now far more orchestral competition than in former days. Significantly enough, Beecham offered rival concerts with the London Philharmonic Orchestra at Covent Garden Theatre on the very Sunday afternoon of Wood's opening, with a further clash on 29 November.

Wood was not yet to celebrate a jubilee nor any such milestone. But in Bournemouth, Sir Dan Godfrey was honoured in March 1936 for forty years' service at the head of the town's orchestra, persistently championing new works. Wood was one of the conductors (the others were Beecham, Boult, Harty, Sargent and Lawrance Collingwood) who subscribed to the fund for the presentation of a portrait to Godfrey – a portrait which, when done, was embarrassingly unlike him. In Wood's telegram of congratulation there was surely something unnecessary, pointing attention the wrong way:

> SIR DAN GODFREY PAVILION BOURNEMOUTH – BRAVO YOU HAVE DONE IN BOURNEMOUTH WHAT I HAVE DONE IN LONDON FORTY AND MORE YEARS IN THE SERVICE OF MUSIC – HENRY J. WOOD.

Perhaps if he had not been worried about the danger of his own decline he might have achieved the simplicity of another well-wisher's telegram:

CONGRATULATIONS TODAY'S CEREMONY – BANTOCK.

Wood again conducted the Bournemouth Municipal Orchestra on 25 March when its strength was augmented to sixty-five for its annual festival. Jessie came with him, as he recalled when writing to 'Dear Sir Dan' on 16 August, presumably after receiving congratulations in return on beginning his forty-second season of promenade concerts:

> Thank you so very much for your kind letter – although I have always known you have supported me in my musical life, it is nice to hear you express it so unreservedly. . .
> We have the photograph of the three of us at Bournemouth – Linton is the name, but now of a necessity 'Wood' is Jessie's name.

In February he had received and accepted the BBC's proposal for his engagements covering a year from the coming summer: £2300 for the 1936 promenade concerts, £200 for two subsequent symphony concerts at Queen's Hall, £100 for his Good Friday (1937) *Parsifal* concert there, and £500 for 'a minimum of five other dates which may be either public or studio concerts at £100 each' – a total of £3100, which in the event was increased by three further concerts to £3400. As a total of fees it looks not unreasonable, but the squeezing-point was the restriction to two appearances in the chief shop-window of the BBC's orchestral year, the symphony concerts held at (and broadcast from) Queen's Hall.

Any suggestion that he needed assistance in his performances was furiously resisted. A glance at the preliminary announcements for the 1936 Good Friday *Parsifal* was enough to trigger a telegram to Owen Mase of the BBC's management (with a copy to Jessie), sent from Hull on 2 April:

> VERY DISTRESSED TO SEE AND CANNOT ALLOW ARNOLD PERRY'S NAME TO APPEAR AS MY ASSISTANT CONDUCTOR IN PRESS OR AS COACH IN PROGRAMMES OF PARSIFAL CONCERT IT IS NOT DONE IN THE CONCERT WORLD HAVE DIRECTED PARSIFAL CONCERTS AT QUEEN'S HALL FOR THIRTY YEARS AND NEVER EMPLOYED AN ASSISTANT OR COACH MANY OF THE SOLOISTS ARE MY OWN PRIVATE SINGING PUPILS I WILL PLAY FOR MY OWN PIANO REHEARSALS NEXT.

The last few words were, need it be said, ironic, as though he feared that even an accompanist would be given equal BBC billing with himself.

A new-ish work by Dohnányi seized Wood's fancy in 1936, curiously entitled *Symphonic Minutes* – about thirteen and a half of them, the critic W. R. Anderson helpfully pointed out, reviewing Wood's broadcast from January's Winter Proms. The work having been previously broadcast from the studio, this was announced as a 'first British concert performance' – a BBC description disliked by Wood, who rightly saw it as diluting the true distinction of a first (or first British) performance. Wood soon introduced Dohnányi's piece, variously under the French and German forms of its title, to both the Hallé Orchestra's audience and the Liverpool Philharmonic's, and also recorded it. On that Liverpool occasion (10 November 1936), his soloist in Strauss songs, and in an orchestrated version of Schubert's *Der Hirt auf dem Felsen*, was one of the most admired singers of her time, Elisabeth Schumann. The present author claims a link with that performance: the *obbligato* to the Schubert was played by his clarinet teacher, Pat Ryan.

The Liverpool Philharmonic relied largely on importing Hallé players from Manchester (such as Ryan) for its concerts, and still had no permanent conductor. Nor had the Hallé Orchestra itself moved to appoint a successor to Harty, who had acrimoniously resigned the conductorship in 1933. Guest conductors continued to plug the holes, Wood and Beecham being engaged in both cities. Writing to Jessie from Liverpool at 6 p.m. on 1 February 1937, between a rehearsal and concert, Wood told her that the Philharmonic Society committee 'were all over me' 'and marvelled at my directing the *Alpine Symphony* [of Richard Strauss] as if I had known it all my life – it is quite a decent work and sounds well and *after* the Vaughan Williams they all love it'.

Vaughan Williams's newest symphony, the unexpectedly discordant no.4, was on that programme. It must have indeed been a strange experience for Henry J. Wood to be conducting the *Alpine Symphony* apparently for the first time, some thirty-five years after he had first begun to nourish London's taste for Strauss's descriptive music.

In that same letter Henry commented to Jessie about an item of news which the papers announced that day: 'I told you Adrian would get it.' Boult's knighthood was included in the first honours list of George VI, following the short reign of Edward VIII. As chief conductor, Boult had added to the BBC Symphony Orchestra's prestige by successful concerts in Brussels (1935), Vienna (1936) and other Continental cities. Wood did not lack a proper appreciation of Boult's abilities, but the assertion that Boult had studied conducting with Nikisch drove Wood to stinging language in that letter to Jessie: 'I like the lie he drags in, "a pupil of Nikisch" – such rot, for he *does everything* that Nikisch loathed.'

One would give a lot to know just what Wood took exception to, on those grounds, in Boult's conducting. Certainly the 'Nikisch' label was persistently hung by journalists round Boult's neck, though it would have been Boult's own nature to say no more than the truth, namely that to observe Nikisch's conducting in Leipzig had been one of the most valuable experiences of his student years.

The Bournemouth Musical Festival again called on Wood in 1937 – at an earlier date than usual, 22 February. On his programme was not only Bridge's *The Sea* but Glazunov's Symphony no.6, a work Wood also revived elsewhere to mark the composer's death in the previous year. The amateurs of Hull also continued to have the benefit of his conductorship, bringing the participation of distinguished soloists – among them Medtner as performer of Beethoven's Fourth Piano Concerto and some solo pieces of his own on 18 February 1937. Printed programmes at Hull carried his testimonial for a brand of pianos ('Every Collard & Collard 5-ft. Grand is tested and approved by Sir Henry J. Wood and bears his signature'). It was the kind of sponsorship for which he could hardly be reproved, since so exalted a performer as Schnabel was doing a like service for Bechstein pianos in the same programmes.

Wood's Good Friday performances of *Parsifal* (or, rather, of a concert selection from that work) meant much to him. In the past Wood had sometimes managed with only one or two singers, compelling a heavy reliance on orchestral extracts. The BBC's provision of a complete cast and chorus as on 26 March 1937 significantly enlarged the experience. Such seasonal programming of Wagner's 'Christian' opera in English can be seen as prolonging – on the BBC's vastly extended horizon – Robert Newman's original policy of fitting concerts to the calendar.

With *Parsifal* as well as the Proms distinctively 'his', Wood's expectancy was that his annual contractual arrangements with the BBC would be, if not bettered, at least maintained. At the highest level of the BBC, however, his power to draw the public was sharply questioned. B. E. Nicolls, Controller of Administration, had minuted on 24 February:

> I have just had up the usual request for the renewal of Sir Henry Wood's contract. As you know, this gives him two Queen's Hall Symphony

Concerts in addition to the Good Friday *Parsifal* one, and I am wondering whether we need go on paying this blackmail. He has no drawing power in Symphony Concerts, and I think I am right in saying that he usually does not maintain the standard of playing. On December 9, he drew £108, and last week, with Arthur Rubinstein as a great draw, he only brought in £141, the capacity of the house being £400.

Couldn't we at least reduce him to one concert this coming year?

The reply made on 5 March by Sir Adrian Boult, as Director of Music, was tactful but evidently alluded also to another complaint – that Wood was inclined to a brusque treatment of his players:

I am afraid I cannot in any way contest what is said by Controller (A) on this matter, but I must confess that I find it very hard indeed to support the proposal. Sir Henry's work for us at the Proms is of enormous value and importance. He is treating the Orchestra very much better now and is altogether more amenable in regard to his negotiations with us. I remember how tremendously hurt he was when his six Symphony Concerts were reduced to two, and I feel that it would be extremely hard for us to suggest a further reduction. It is impossible to say how much longer he will be with us, but it is undeniable that the London musical public owes him a debt which it can never repay, and I cannot help feeling that our sacrificing (if this is the right word) two Symphony Concerts and Good Friday to him is only a small contribution to the debt which London music-lovers owe him and which we are the only people who can repay. Between us and the North of Ireland I think it is quite easy to use him for more than the five studio dates which I believe are in his contract.

The 'better' relationship with his orchestral players had indeed been noted. It was apparently an aspect of Wood's more settled and relaxed temperament since Jessie had begun to smooth and stabilize his domestic life, at the same time smartening his appearance. He himself, as will be seen, gratefully ascribed to her just such a renewal of his human qualities.

Did Wood know, when receiving a new contract which *did* maintain the old terms, that he had been 'saved' by Boult? He would certainly have measured with an expert and rueful eye the proportion of empty seats at his Queen's Hall symphony concerts to which Nicolls had alluded. At the Proms his pulling-power was undiminished. 'Almost four nights a week the doors had to be closed at 7.40 p.m.' (twenty minutes before starting-time), he claimed when writing about the 1937 Proms to his publisher, Hubert J. Foss of Oxford University Press. A redecorated, re-seated and reventilated Queen's Hall enhanced the season. Among the items conducted by the

Best Wishes for a Happy Christmas

49 HALLAM STREET
PORTLAND PLACE, W.I

In a greetings card, Henry designates Jessie as 'Lady Wood'.

Celebrating

BBC's chorus-master, Leslie Woodgate, was a second series of Handel opera choruses of which Wood was the nominal editor, though the re-orchestration was the (anonymous) work of Sanders.

Since Delius's death in June 1934 his music had not lost its attraction for Wood or his audiences, and the promenaders of that year heard the *Dance Rhapsody* no.1 and the familiar coupling of *On hearing the first cuckoo in spring* and *Summer Night on the River*. A few weeks before the series began, he wrote on 9 June 1937 to Eric Fenby, whose book on Delius captivated so many readers:

> Dear Mr Fenby,
> I have only just had time to read your *Delius as I Knew Him* although I purchased a copy when it came out.
> I cannot tell you how *deeply* it has touched me, and I am now reading it to my wife. You have accomplished your task *superbly* and all Delius lovers are your debtors.
> Many years ago I used to see him in Paris and stay with them later in Grez – I was playing him to my London pupils and public, long before Beecham came upon the scene – and I shall always remember the Sheffield Festival Committee were not *keen* upon *Sea Drift* at all, but I called a special meeting, took the train from London, played and sang them the great work, and it was accepted and made a tremendous impression and from this date notice was taken of this great talent.
> With kind regards,
> Sincerely yours

When asked by Wood to design a Christmas card for him as 1937 drew to its end, the *Daily Express* cartoonist Strube saw the sixty-eight-year-old conductor as a bundle of energy, depicting him as a strutting one-man band simultaneously playing the saxophone, accordion and assorted percussion. (See previous page.) Giving a new address, 49 Hallam Street, Portland Place (a return to the Queen's Hall area), the card circulated with the inscription in his own hand: 'From Sir Henry and Lady Wood'. Many recipients, and Jessie herself, must have wondered how long such a deceptive identification could continue – a form of words probably libellous, implying that Muriel was not his wife.

However, an ingenious way out would be found. As the Lord Chancellor in *Iolanthe* had put it when weighing up another matrimonial problem: 'The subtleties of the legal mind are equal to the emergency.'

Chapter 20

Jubilee

1937–8

The dating of Henry J. Wood's fiftieth anniversary as a conductor was rather arbitrarily decided (see Chapter 2, p. 17), but the achievement certainly merited its celebration on the grand scale – for which, in the London musical calendar, at least a year's notice was required. A handwritten letter dated 22 August 1937 went to one of his contemporaries that Henry J. Wood most admired. It is reproduced with the original punctuation:

My dear Mr. Rachmaninoff,

On the 1st of January 1938, I attain my jubilee, as a Conductor, and my many musical friends have determined to mark the event by organising a great Orchestral Concert at the Royal Albert Hall on the very appropriate day of St. Cecilia, on November 22nd 1938.

It has been my unique opportunity during these 50 years of presenting to the British public, all the great International Artists and Composers, and when I look back on this achievement, coupled with its very many happy associations, I find no name that gives me such great satisfaction as that of yourself and wonder, would you be willing to play for me, one of your concertos at this Concert. (no other artist.)

This is not to be a Benefit Concert, but will be arranged under the Patronage of Royalty, (we think the King and Queen) to provide a fund to give a Hospital Bed or Beds, entirely for [orchestral] musicians.

May I say that the *whole* proceeds derived from the sale of tickets for this Concert will go to the fund complete with no deductions, for fees etc:

In all my career I have never asked a musician to aid me in my personal scheme and I feel that I am asking a great deal of you, but at the same time, I feel I should have your sympathetic understanding. It will be purely an Orchestral Concert directed by myself.

With kindest regards
Very sincerely yours
Henry J. Wood

Celebrating

A November date gave the hope of the King (George VI) and Queen being present. In October they would not be available, but when Rachmaninoff could offer only an October date, that was of more importance. He would make the journey from his Swiss home specially, as Wood's next letter (29 August) gratefully acknowledged:

> My dear Mr. Rachmaninoff,
> How can I ever thank you for the great honour you do me, in consenting to play one of your Concertos at my Jubilee Concert, and not only to play, but to make the journey to England specially for this Concert.
> I know all my colleagues will feel the honour with me, and the undoubted success it is assured by your unstinted generosity.
> The Albert Hall will be pencilled in for October 4th, 6th and 7th (1938) and as soon as the necessary dates for Royalty etc: have been looked into, I will advise you which of these days is chosen.
> I would like to tell you that *my* contribution to the Fund will be that of meeting the fees of the three full orchestras.
> Once again my deepest and warmest thanks, for without your assistance nothing of such an ambitious character could have been undertaken and your kindly help has *encouraged* me beyond words,
> Believe me
> Very sincerely yours
> Henry J. Wood

In a further letter, Henry wrote that he and Jessie had 'dashed from Southport to London' on 18 November, arriving at Queen's Hall at 9.30 p.m. just in time to hear Rachmaninoff's recent Symphony no.3. The conductor, not mentioned in the letter, was Beecham! This performance under the auspices of the Royal Philharmonic Society constituted the first hearing of the symphony in Europe, Stokowski having given the première with the Philadelphia Orchestra a year before. Wood was looking forward to giving the work at Liverpool on the following 22 March and at a BBC studio concert on 3 April. 'If there is any advice you can offer me as regards your feelings or reading of the symphony, please do so, and I shall be most grateful.' A postscript mentioned that 300 players would form the orchestra for the jubilee concert – 'but they will not *all* play in your piano concerto, so don't be frightened'.

The date of the celebration at the Albert Hall was fixed for 5 October 1938. The BBC volunteered the services of its orchestra and chorus, and of its concerts manager W. W. Thompson as secretary to the organizing committee. Robert Mayer (the organizer of orchestral concerts for children,

ROYAL ALBERT HALL

THE
HENRY WOOD
JUBILEE
CONCERT

To celebrate Sir Henry Wood's 50th Anniversary as Conductor

The entire proceeds of the concert, together with Donations, will be devoted to the endowment of beds in London Hospitals for the benefit of Orchestral Musicians

Wednesday, October 5th, 1938, at 8.15

Combined

LONDON ORCHESTRAS and CHOIRS

Conductor

SIR HENRY WOOD

Soloist

RACHMANINOFF

BOXES: £26 5s., £21, and £10 10s.
TICKETS: £2 2s., £1 1s., 15/-, 12/-, 7/6, 6/-; PROMENADE 3/6
May be obtained at the Box Office, Royal Albert Hall (KENsington 3661);
Chappell's Box Office, Queen's Hall (LANgham 2823); usual Ticket Offices, and

IBBS & TILLETT, 124 WIGMORE STREET, W.1
Ticket Office, WELbeck 8418

BAINES & SCARSBROOK LTD., SWISS COTTAGE, N.W.6

313

knighted in 1939) was the committee's chairman, with Sir Hugh Allen, Sir Adrian Boult and Sir Landon Ronald as well as the music-loving physician Lord Horder among the members. Moreover the London Philharmonic and London Symphony orchestras also volunteered their services, as did members of Wood's own Queen's Hall Orchestra, relieving him of his undertaking to pay the instrumentalists. As the event drew nearer, a wholly exceptional gathering of goodwill was evident.

A new composition of a unique nature was to be included in the programme. It would not present any individual soloist to detract from Rachmaninoff's singularity, but none the less the concert would no longer be a 'purely orchestral' event. Ralph Vaughan Williams – firmly regarded, since the deaths of Elgar, Delius and Holst, as Britain's leading composer – gladly accepted Wood's invitation to write a short choral work. Wood's reply shows what may seem (as in his letter to Rachmaninoff) an excessive deference.

> Dear Dr Vaughan Williams,
>   I cannot tell you the gratitude I feel that you should write me so kindly regarding my request. I do not for a moment however propose that this work of yours should be written as an ode to myself, for I would like it to be a choral work that can be used at any time, and for any occasion. I would not think of asking you to write a work that might only be used the once, which would naturally be the case were it written round myself.
>   Perhaps for such a work you already have many poems by you.
>   With kindest regards,
>   Sincerely yours

By 2 June the composer had sent Wood 'a copy of my *Serenade* for you to look at and express your approval or otherwise. I am afraid I must ask you to send this copy back as this must be the one for the printer if it is printed.' By a stroke of inspiration, the *Serenade to Music* turned out to be a setting for sixteen solo voices, each one a named singer whose part was marked in the score – though, naturally, allowing the eventuality of performances by other soloists or by choral forces. Nothing could have been more appropriate than the Shakespearean text beginning 'How sweet the moonlight sleeps upon this bank', cunningly selected and joined together from the scene between Lorenzo and Jessica in *The Merchant of Venice*, ending in praise of music itself:

> Soft stillness and the night
> Become the touches of sweet harmony.

For the last sixteen months the BBC had been regularly transmitting programmes in the new medium of television. The cameras caught Henry J. Wood for an interview on his sixty-ninth birthday, 3 March 1938. World War Two would suspend the BBC's television service altogether; its resumption in 1946 and the first televising of the promenade concerts in 1947 belong to an era after his death.

There was a continuing contact with Rachmaninoff before the jubilee. Wood gave his two promised performances of the Symphony no.3 – at Liverpool on 22 March ('a rapturous reception', he told the composer in a letter next day), and in a BBC London studio on the evening of Sunday 3 April, the composer having been present at the rehearsal that morning. Keen to perform the work further, Wood expressed to the composer his regrets that the orchestral material was available only on rental:

> P.S. My wife wanted to come to our Sunday morning rehearsal but was afraid she might be in the way, but was so sorry when she learnt that Mrs Rachmaninoff and the Medtners dropped in round twelve o'clock. Please don't forget to do something about letting me have band parts of your 3rd symphony for my own use – I will look after performing fees all right. I should like the students of the Royal Academy of Music to give it at Queen's Hall (3 months rehearsal, twice a week).

In his typically dry way Rachmaninoff noted shortly afterwards that only three people really liked the work – Wood, 'the violinist [Adolf] Busch', and himself!

On Sunday 6 March, three days after his sixty-ninth birthday, Wood could still not stop himself from undertaking two concerts in a day. In the afternoon in the Albert Hall Menuhin played three concertos, the rarely heard Schumann (there was much fuss at the time about this supposedly 'lost' work) as well as Mendelssohn's and Brahms's. In the evening, at a BBC studio, came Mendelssohn's again, with an even younger violinist, aged thirteen – 'little Ida Haendel', as *My Life of Music* calls her. Next day, from Liverpool, he wrote to congratulate 'Dear Miss Haendel' on her 'tone, technique, phrasing and interpretation . . . Bravo! *it was splendid.* My wife joins me in kindest regards to yourself and your dear father.' Born in Poland in December 1924, Haendel was curiously stated at this time to be *older* than she really was (instead of younger, as commonly with child prodigy

MAHLER'S EIGHTH SYMPHONY

(The Symphony of the Thousand)

WEDNESDAY, 9 FEBRUARY AT 8.15 P.M.

IN THE QUEEN'S HALL, W.1

(Sole Lessees: Messrs. Chappell & Co. Ltd.)

Stiles-Allen	May Blyth
Laelia Finneberg	Muriel Brunskill
Margaret Balfour	Walter Widdop
Harold Williams	Robert Easton

Chorus of Boys

THE PHILHARMONIC CHOIR

THE BBC SYMPHONY ORCHESTRA
(Leader: Paul Beard)

CONDUCTOR:

Sir HENRY J. WOOD

TICKETS (*including Tax*)

AREA (Unreserved) 2/-   BALCONY (Reserved) 3/6

STALLS (Reserved) 4/-, 6/-, 7/6, 10/-   GRAND CIRCLE (Reserved) 6/-, 7/6, 10/-

May be obtained from THE BOX OFFICE, BROADCASTING HOUSE, W.1. (Telephone: WELbeck 4468)
Chappell's Box Office, Queen's Hall, Langham Place, W.1 (Telephone: LANgham 2823) and the usual Agents.

316

performers), in order to evade a London County Council restriction on very young performers.

The tide of critical opinion was turning slowly in Mahler's favour. Entrusting Wood with a revival of the Eighth Symphony (the 'Symphony of a Thousand') on 9 February 1938, the BBC engaged the advocacy of Ernest Newman, now something of a grand oracle of criticism. The reverse side of the handbill advertising the performance quoted him: 'It is high time that this country learned a little more about Mahler. Whether one "likes" his music or not is a matter of taste; but he is too big a figure to be ignored.' Wood's line-up of singers (Stiles-Allen, May Blyth, Laelia Finneberg, Muriel Brunskill, Margaret Balfour, Walter Widdop, Harold Williams, Robert Easton) partly drew on that of his pioneering performance of eight years before. Though Anton Bruckner's music was then even less commonly programmed than Mahler's, Wood boldly prefaced the Symphony with Bruckner's Overture in G minor, a work which he had pioneeringly recorded the previous year.

A Good Friday performance on 15 April of *The Dream of Gerontius* (replacing Wood's customary Good Friday *Parsifal* concert) likewise showed the BBC's continued confidence in Wood as a choral conductor. With the death of Elgar himself, and with Landon Ronald's a few months away, Wood was the only leading conductor who could offer a *Gerontius* based on the experience of this work from its earliest days (1900). *The Times* on 16 April 1938 reproved him for 'too literal' an obedience to the composer's detailed marking of expression (an interesting critical variant from the usual chastisement of conductors for an excessive freedom), resulting in a 'bumpy', 'aggressively prosaic' performance.

King George and Queen Elizabeth, though not to be available for Woods's jubilee concert itself, were present when he shared in the musical celebration of Empire Day, 24 May 1938, in a Command Performance at the Albert Hall. The choral and orchestral programme was not jingoistic (no 'Wider still and wider'), not even imperial, but simply representative of England, Scotland, Ireland and Wales. The items ranged from the thirteenth-century *Sumer is icumen in* to the present. Wood conducted Bax's new orchestration of his *Paean* (originally for piano), a Byrd transcription by Gordon Jacob, and short works by Delius, Herbert Howells and the twenty-seven-year-old Herbert Murrill. Other items were conducted by Malcolm Sargent, Hugh Allen, George Dyson and (for folk and national songs) local choral conductors. 'No encores whatever can be given,' the audience was warned: 'the applause may well be STRONG but not LONG.' The apparent impossibility of programming such a

317

Command Performance today in the presence of the Sovereign may be sadly noted.

Twice in this jubilee year Henry J. Wood's name appeared in authorship. He wrote a valuable introduction to a poor biography of his friend Percy Pitt (who had died six years previously) by J.D.Chamier; and his own *My Life of Music* was issued by the music-loving publisher Victor Gollancz. The contract for that autobiography had been signed as recently as 11 February, Wood making use of one of London's best-known literary agents, Curtis Brown. The payment – outright, not on a royalty basis – was the respectable sum of £2500. Gollancz was the publisher of such successful novelists as Dorothy L. Sayers and was the instigator (with Harold Laski and John Strachey) of a powerful voice of political opinion, the Left Book Club. He had lost money on the autobiography of Shalyapin, *Man and Mask*, and later noted that *My Life of Music* was one of only two of his many books on music that sold 'decently'. (The other was the compilation by A.L.Bacharach, *The Musical Companion*.)

It was a rush to get the autobiography ready in time to coincide with the jubilee concert itself. From Thursday to Sunday 5–8 May, each day in his diary bears the advance entry 'Memoirs absolutely nec[essary]' in his own strong, pencilled handwriting. On 13 May follows 'I must take scripts to Gollancz and Curtis Brown'. (Conveniently, the publisher and the literary agent both had their premises in Henrietta Street, Covent Garden.) That resolution evidently failed, because the inscription 'Script must be in today' is entered for 16 May, and was complied with. A social visit to 'Mr and Mrs Gollancz, 27 Charles Street, Berkeley Square' is noted for 5.30 to 8.30 p.m. on 1 June. Other diary entries such as 'Teach all day' (his vocal lessons remaining important to him) are likewise in his own hand. Others are in Jessie's, including monthly reminders of 'staff tips due' at their block of flats: 'Entrance [hall] £1, Restaurant £1, Maid 10 shillings'.

The planning of the Proms season in that jubilee year was, as usual, the occasion of tussles with BBC management. Asked to hold an audition for younger soloists who had been recommended by the BBC, but whose names had not been on the preliminary programmes he himself drew up ('my programmes'), Wood gave a reluctant consent:

> but may I say that I shall very greatly regret it if this audition is by way of placing unknown people on to the Promenade Concert programmes, who have not yet made what I call suitable London appearances. I shall greatly deplore the fact if such people as Michal Hambourg [Mark Hambourg's

pianist daughter], [the soprano] Nan Maryska, and other young artists whose names were embraced in my programmes, do not get an appearance at the Promenade Concerts this year. These artists have all given recitals, and have received good Press notices, and one should, I think, try to follow the precedent of Robert Newman in giving such young artists their trial at Queen's Hall, after which, having been given their chance, they find their own level.

Thus on 26 April. He had earlier submitted reports on various artists heard. Mary Bonin 'sings well, with go grip [*sic*] and dramatic intensity – let her sing the Bloch Psalm in G in Hebrew during the coming season – it will be a great novelty – *and it is a fine work*'. (It was not given, however.) The 21-year-old Moura Lympany, which he spelt 'Lympani', was 'a most excellent artist, good technique and power'. His recommendation for some reason was to engage her for the following year, 1939 – perhaps assuming that a sufficiency of pianists was already available for the current year – but in the event her Proms debut was advanced to 28 September 1938. Later, when the BBC had submitted further draft programmes and artists' names:

. . . Ruth Naylor is certainly hopeless as a concert [as distinct from operatic] artist – no good at all for a promenade concert.

I think we shall have to get in a Bax symphony – it would surely be very wrong to omit such when we do foreigners' works at these concerts.

I cannot take the responsibility for teaching my friend how to spell his name, and as a very recent photograph which he gave to me is signed RACHMANINOFF, we must not spell the name in our programme with a final V.

Roy Henderson has taken to TALKING to his audience before his song – I hope he can be told that beyond announcing the title and composer of an encore, this chatty business is not acceptable.

I am sorry to cut the Béla Bartók [*Music for strings, percussion and celesta*], but since our going over the score, I know it is an impossibility during a promenade concert season.

. . . I am in entire disagreement with a harpsichord solo. The hall is quite unfitted and the concerts are out of keeping entirely with such historical instruments. Wigmore Hall yes! Queen's Hall no. I hope you will reconsider this proposal.

To R. S. Thatcher, who had been appointed the BBC's deputy Music Director to Boult, he sent a complaint on 6 June over the BBC's 'extraordinary delay' in deciding on the programmes, so that his work in allocating and timing rehearsals would have to be done during his scheduled holiday period before the Proms were due to begin. The complexity of arrangements shows in an informal and evidently hasty communication to his concert manager, W. W. Thompson, on 19 June (here reproduced verbatim). References such as 'No.33' are to the BBC's chronological numbering of the concerts. A significant lengthening of orchestral rehearsal time, however welcome, brought its own problem:

> Could you possibly arrange a Sunday evening Chorus rehearsal for me with the BBC Choral Society on Sunday evening, September 11th for the Handel Chorus[es] from Judas, Acis, Israel & the Messiah. Now that the Band rehearsal on Thursdays has been changed from 10 to 1 to 1.30 to 6.30 I cannot manage a 6 pm rehearsal the day before this Handel Concert on Tuesday September 13th (no.33). The Chorus rehearsal for the Beethoven etc. Concert of Friday, September 30th (concert no.48) can be held at 6pm on Thursday September 29th. Please call the 5 solo singers also at 6 pm for this rehearsal for the Choral Fantasia and the 9th symphony (Beethoven).
>
> There is really only one, what I might call *very tight day*, and that is concert no.41 (Thursday Sept: 22nd) Piano Concerto, Delius, Heldenleben, Strauss, and Fountains of Rome Respighi – if only a well known piece, *that need not be rehearsed*, could be substituted for the Respighi piece, all would be well. No aria [received] for Joan Cross, concert no.49. Hope to see you this Thursday afternoon at 5 pm when I hope to hand you my completed rehearsal list.

The Respighi was duly replaced by the more familiar tone-poem of Franck's, *Le Chasseur maudit*.

Rigidly though the BBC timed the Proms broadcasts in advance, Wood insisted on marking the death of his friend Landon Ronald (14 August 1938) by the insertion of *Nimrod* from Elgar's *Enigma Variations* into next day's concert. He reassured the BBC, in capital letters, that it required only THREE MINUTES AND FORTY SECONDS and could be squeezed in without overrunning the radio schedule. A week previously, perhaps wishing for tactical reasons not to be considered an awkward negotiator, he had written to Thatcher of his pleasure in collaborating with the BBC's music department: 'I do not think that I remember such happiness and sweetness for years.'

A possible brush with Rachmaninoff was threatened: the composer evidently felt that the Prelude from his opera *The Avaricious Knight* (which Wood had scheduled as a first performance in Britain) would not 'work' on its own and wished to withdraw it. Wood was at his most tactful in a letter of 5 August: 'Unfortunately, the BBC have a very strong objection to changing any item after sending out thirty-five thousand promenade programmes to the public, so I took the liberty of using the last 24 bars of Act I (from figure 34 to the end) as a concert finish, and it certainly sounds quite delightful – and further, they did want a novelty of yours as nothing from any of your operas has ever been played at Queen's Hall.'

A further letter of assurance dated 6 September went from Wood to 'My dear friend,': 'You may trust me to give the very best of myself to your concert, and I am sure *The Avaricious Knight* will be received with enthusiasm.'

There was something else to be communicated to Rachmaninoff too:

> Dear Mr Rachmaninoff,
>   I have not had a moment this week in which to write you, with a Promenade Concert on every night for two months with a heavy classical programme, as I *wanted to do* immediately after Cyril Smith played your 3rd concerto at Queen's Hall last Saturday. He is playing it at nearly all his concerto engagements. I have rarely heard it played so wonderfully; certainly somewhat lacking in the fire and spirit that I associate with it, but technically perfect, and I think you would have been delighted, the reception of the concert was *terrific* and *marvellous*. I wonder if you were able to 'listen-in'?

Smith, twenty-seven years old, was at an early stage of a notable career; even younger at twenty-four was Benjamin Britten, who appeared on 18 August in the first performance of his own Piano Concerto. Wood took to the work immediately, and suggested to the BBC a repetition at the Proms in the following season. A new, second suite compiled by Walton from his *Façade*, of which Wood conducted the first British performance on 10 September, testified to the popularity which the first suite had won.

Young soloists continued to find Wood the most reassuring and helpful of conductors. 'Are you happy? Any wishes?' he asked Ida Haendel after they had rehearsed Brahms's Violin Concerto for her Proms performance on 31 August. His manner, 'looking down upon me with his benign smile', created a lasting impression on her as she sensed 'this important person's solicitude for a little girl'. Later, in one of the private notes to Jessie which he wrote while away on tour, he speculated on the possibility of 'Ida Haendel giving three concertos, some Saturday afternoon, with the Queen's Hall Orchestra – Bach, Beethoven and Brahms. . .this is what Kreisler, Szigeti etc. all did at their first season. A band of 60 would do – the Queen's Hall Orchestra and little timber.' [A rare self-reference to his own nickname – without a capital letter!]

Celebrating

No such concert eventuated. Nevertheless Ida Haendel, who settled in Britain and remained there through World War Two, often played for Wood, and regarded him with a daughter-like affection.

With his jubilee approaching, the audiences of that Proms season of 1938 gave the conductor an especially heart-warming reception. Vaughan Williams, in a broadcast of a few weeks afterwards, caught the mood that had been struck at the opening concert:

> On August 6 last, when the Prelude to *Die Meistersinger* started nearly five minutes late owing to the uncontrollable applause which greeted him when he appeared, one hopes that he felt that he had received his reward.

For the usual forty-nine programmes of that Proms season the BBC's fee was again £2300. In the following winter-to-spring season there were once again to be (only) two engagements in the Queen's Hall symphony concerts, with another Good Friday concert and at least five other 'public or studio concerts', a total of £3100. He was earning moderately but apparently saving nothing. He was naturally worried. What financial provision could he make for Jessie should he predecease her?

He could, and would, make a new Will. But he was evidently apprehensive that such a Will, cutting out his lawful wife and their daughters Tania and Avril, stood open to being challenged in court on their behalf. He went before a Commissioner for Oaths and signed 'for the purposes of the Inheritance (Family Provision) Act' a legal deposition or Statutory Declaration, setting out the grievances he claimed to have suffered at Muriel's hands and, to a lesser extent, those of his daughters.

The picture he paints of being insulted, maltreated, un-cared-for, ill-fed, kept short of money, punished like a naughty child and at least once physically belaboured by Muriel ('She called me all the vile things possible, and lay [*sic*] about me on the head and face with a book') makes astonishing reading. Sometimes, however, the reader's astonishment is that Henry on his own admission submitted with such docility and for so long. The following extracts are reproduced verbatim – not even Henry's own solicitor having tidied up the outpouring.

> . . . She refused to allow me to have a piano in my own Drawing room and I was gradually relegated to the state of a nonentity in our home and treated rudely before friends and business associates alike. Although I was always given the cheapest of everything my wife was always complaining about the cost of what I ate and drank. She could go all day on merely a cup of tea and

cake . . . My clothes were a disgrace. Soiled shirts were given me to wear again and again, as were my woollen underclothes which from the continual perspiration associated with my conducting, and which at times positively smelt, were so hard as to be disagreeable to wear from both causes . . .

. . . At social functions in various cities in England and on the Continent, where I have been invited in the course of my profession, perhaps having directed a Concert or Festival, I was naturally the person they wished to honour, but I have many a time had my tongue tied with fear of a scene, when my coat has been tugged from behind 'Henry, Henry introduce me to these people, and tell them they must talk of future engagements to me'. Or sitting at the other end of a Legation Luncheon table, I have felt far enough away from her to trust myself to speak, when in a loud voice she would chime in 'No, Henry, that is not correct, it was so and so, etc.' . . .

The telescoping within a few sheets of paper of all the disagreeable incidents of a twenty-four-year marriage no doubt produces an over-concentration; and some details of these incidents, as reproduced in Reginald Pound's book, are flatly denied by Tania. Nevertheless, this was a document which Wood intended if necessary to be produced in court where its veracity could be challenged – with his family pitting their testimony against that of such friends as Rosa Newmarch, who is invoked in his support (plainly identified, though not by name).

Stating further that 'my wife is now in possession of over half of my capital', he claimed that it would be 'inequitable' for him to have to make further provision. A separate paragraph ran:

To my friend Jessie Linton, I owe the greatest thing in my life – my regained self respect. My musician friends tell me that they know the real ME for the first time. My orchestral musicians are ever telling me what a difference there is in my music and as a matter of fact, the musical world generally, had been saying for years past, that I had died – musically, and how greatly they enjoy working with me now that only good humour accompanies my work, whereas hitherto I was quick tempered and unapproachable. I am dressed as becomes my position. I am given help in my work of music and my musical associates are treated with the respect their calling deserves. I would like everyone to know that were it possible, I would marry Mrs Linton tomorrow, and should she be left without me, I hope her people and my friends will look upon her union with myself as one of untiring loving and restoring comradeship in which no thought of herself or the discomfort of her position socially occurs.

A Will leaving everything to Jessie, as 'Jessie Linton', had probably been already signed. A new Will became necessary, however, and was signed on

Celebrating

27 September 1938, as a result of a change in Jessie's surname. Such a change (by deed poll) was (and is) not unusual where a man and woman are living together but not in marriage. 'Jessie Linton' might easily enough, and legally, become Jessie Wood. But Henry was introducing her as 'Lady Wood', which she was not. It was the apparently unique ingenuity of Henry's legal adviser, the solicitor Stanley Rubinstein (no relation to the musicians of that name), which led to Jessie's changing her forenames along with her surname, emerging in the form of Lady [as a forename] Jessie Wood.

'Lady' as a forename? The public was familiar with the American dance-band leader, Duke Ellington; there was also, as Jessie herself knew, a British circus proprietor whose posters named him as Lord George Sanger. In those cases, however, there was no deception or impersonation, any more than with the parliamentary candidate in the 1980s and 1990s, Screaming Lord Sutch. If 'Lady' were a genuine title, however, and not a name, then the wife of Sir Henry J. Wood would be *not* Lady Jessie Wood but Lady Wood. (The inclusion of a forename, as 'Lady Jessie Wood', would denote the daughter of a duke, marquess, or earl, as today's 'Lady Helen Windsor'.) The offence was, on Henry's part, to refer to Jessie as 'Lady Wood' – as he had already started to do. 'So I'm really Mrs Lady Jessie Wood – what a thing to start a new life with!' Jessie reminisced on tape around her ninetieth year. But it was inevitable that the 'Lady' in 'Lady Jessie Wood' would be taken as a title. The assumption was generally made that the pleasant, smartly dressed, matronly presence at Sir Henry's side was Sir Henry's wife; and in the narrow circle of those who knew the truth perfectly well, to accept the counterfeit appeared to be simply good manners.

Henry and Muriel's younger daughter Avril was still in London, unmarried. The letter from the Far East in which his elder daughter announced her engagement (she and her naval bridegroom were married in Hong Kong Cathedral on 30 April 1938) induced no softening of his hostility towards her for having 'betrayed' him:

My dear Tania,
   I did not reply to your first letter received some weeks ago, as its contents and views expressed therein considerably upset me. I am glad to hear that you are going to be married to Lieutenant George Jameson Cardew, I sincerely hope you will make him a good wife. I do remember his father, Dr Cardew, quite well.
   I am sure you don't or cannot expect a loving father's reply to your letters, for I can never bring myself to forgive your treatment of me, knowing so well as you do, that you could no longer live with your

324

mother and when I took the only possible step myself, you could range yourself so much on her side, as to take *my* home (4 Elsworthy Road) to pieces as you did, and later send to me the telegram which you despatched from Paris on a certain Bach night. I gave you girls an education and where-with-all up to the moment of the only obvious course for me to take – you both rallied yourselves against me, perhaps knowing that your mother has acquired so much of my capital, with the knowledge that it is to her, you must look for your future. On reflection, I can never understand how two young women could allow me to be so neglected as I was in those dreadful days at Chorley Wood, and how I kept my musical work together is a mystery, and my health another mystery. Naturally I wish you luck and happiness and I hope should you marry Cardew, you will make a great success of it, I wish I could write your *affectionate* father

    Henry J. Wood

His Will, however, had not quite excluded his daughters. Jessie was to have everything, should he predecease her; but if she predeceased him, then Tania and Avril would share his inheritance in three equal parts with Jessie's daughter Eileen (widowed some years before and now married a second time to Dr Gordon Calthrop). A clause in the Will noted that he had 'already made full provision for Lady Muriel Wood' – an inaccurate title for one who was still legally Lady Wood and would remain so until the day of her death.

Alas, there was a prior death to mourn – Michael's, the dog who 'sang' down the telephone and 'sent' his good wishes to Rachmaninoff. Wood heard the news after conducting the *St Matthew Passion* on 12 May at the Montgomeryshire Festival, to which he had been invited by its organizer, Sir Walford Davies. 'Wally-Wally' (as fellow-professionals irreverently called him) was an exceptionally successful radio talker on music and had been Master of the King's Music since the death of Elgar in 1934. Wood was due to proceed immediately to Mountain Ash to rehearse another performance of the *Passion* scheduled later that month at the Three Valleys Festival. From the Bear Hotel, Newtown, Henry wrote:

Friday [13 May] 12.30 am

My beloved one,

    Eileen [Jessie's daughter, who had telephoned] has just told me the sad news, how we shall miss him – he was a darling of the first water. I am sure you must be terribly distressed & I wanted to come home at once to console my darling – I am sure you must be absolutely *worn out* with your beautiful [dutiful?] vigil. I have felt he had been ill for some time because he slept *too* much.

    I should have come home only Eileen would not hear of it. All my plans are changed – they are fetching me at 2 p.m. for Aberdare where

Wood was sometimes criticized for such advertising, but (as Jessie Wood noted) he donated the £100 which he received to his fund for endowing hospital beds for musicians.

they give me tea & then I go on to Mountain Ash for my 6.30 rehearsal & shall not get to the Angel Hotel, Cardiff until 9.30 this evening. They are arranging a room for me to change after the rehearsal in Mountain Ash.

Wally-Wally is a great nuisance, he might just as well have conducted the Festival, because he will chime in and *talk* every now & then, & seems as fit as a fidler [*sic*] – I just long to hear your dear voice on the Phone between 6 & 7 this evening. Fondest love & many many kisses. This is a most excellent old town you can obtain everything here. Also the town is most up to date – even a Woolworth, 2 cinemas, splendid chemist. Don't worry about me I had a splendid rest until 12 this morning, woke from 4 am until 6 thinking about you & poor darling Michael.

Very warm here and raining a bit.

Your devoted Henry.

[P.S.] Eileen was so nice on the Phone – she is a good sort.

Henry was indeed 'devoted' to Jessie and she to him. To Eileen he became 'Daddy' or 'Daddles'. Henry J. Wood's new happiness, his new liveliness and spruce appearance under Jessie's gentle care made it hard for his friends not to accept his new life for what it was. Even Ethel Smyth, the former furious defender of Muriel, came completely round to his side. In a letter of 15 January 1938, which loses by being abbreviated in Pound's biography, she wrote:

Let me tell you that at the beginning of your domestic change I knew nothing of any complaint against M[uriel] except that you said you got on each other's nerves. And in cases like that – as I am sure you will see is only natural in a woman like me – my sympathy would always go to the one who still loves, and still hopes for reunion.

Well, as time went on, and [as] I began to realize what you accuse[d] her of having done about investments, at last I wrote to her (and there has been a good deal of beating about the bush in her replies) and said how report (*authorized, I believe, by you*) said she had behaved, and that in my opinion she ought to face the music!

Since that moment she, who used to write fairly often, has not said a word. Consequently I can but conclude the accusations that were flying about are merited! I myself have never written to her since.

As regards the fact of two people, to both of whom I used to be very much attached, seperating [*sic*] – there is nearly always one of them has got to care about someone else! and in such cases I am the last person to 'take sides', though, unless I know that the 'forsaken' has behaved badly in some way (humanly – or financially – or anything else), my sympathies would always go to the one who goes on loving the lost husband or lover. As it is, my sympathy has dried up!

She excused herself, on the grounds of her deafness, from not having made a personal contact with him. She intended to give him her copy of Sullivan's *The Golden Legend*, inscribed to her by its composer, and wanted him to have it immediately, not (as she had originally proposed) on her death. He replied, apparently suggesting she *ought* to retain the score until her death, but on 31 January she dismissed that idea and said that she was sending the score.

On 1 April, having met Jessie at the Bournemouth Festival, Smyth wrote to Henry of her delight in being acquainted with 'one who, as I felt at once, must infallibly make you happy and therefore further the great work of your life. *By the way, how ought I to address her?* "Lady Wood", I suppose?'

A signal of the new harmony between his personal and professional life was the holding of a grand post-Proms supper party at the Langham Hotel for members of his orchestra (that is, the BBC Symphony). There would be a conjurer and other forms of light entertainment – but, as he announced to the orchestra when issuing the invitation during a rehearsal, 'I promise you – there will be no music.' Jessie was the 'mother' of such occasions: Muriel could never have been.

Newspaper editors, interviewers, critics and photographers had marked the date of 5 October in advance as the jubilee occasion, and the publication of *My Life of Music* that same month elicited hundreds of further columns of press coverage. Most significant of all such attention was surely that given in the very first issue (1 October) of *Picture Post*, the weekly journal founded by the politically progressive Edward Hulton and edited by a refugee from the Nazis, Stefan Lorant. Its photo-journalism (a word not yet coined, however) made it a leader of progressive opinion in the War and immediate post-war years. Typical was the two-page article by Hulton himself in the first issue which exposed the scientific falsehood of Nazi race doctrine. Six pages of the magazine were given to Wood's achievement and to action photographs of himself, his promenading audiences and members of the BBC Symphony Orchestra.

An unlooked-for snag arose while that jubilee concert was being prepared. Rachmaninoff absolutely and on principle refused to broadcast, apparently because his experience in the United States had shown him that pirate recordings could be made from transmission, and marketed. He supposed that, as a substitute, the BBC when broadcasting the jubilee concert could put on air his gramophone recording of the same work, the Piano Concerto no.2. Henry Wood had to assure him the BBC would rule out any such substitution. He still hoped that Rachmaninoff would relax his custom:

Naturally it would be a very great day for England if you *would* broadcast my concert, and I know that, although they cannot pay the fee that should be yours for such a thing, they would be glad to pay a nominal fee, which I am sure could be readily discussed if you would agree to do so. At any rate, I have arranged now that, if you still are determined not to allow your performance to be broadcast, that only half my programme can be given over the air.

The composer-pianist was inflexible, and the BBC broadcast only the second half. It was a programme which reflected the devotion which Henry J. Wood had shown to vocal art no less than to orchestral, with a chorus formed from three of London's leading amateur groups, the BBC Choral Society, the Philharmonic Choir and the Royal Choral Society. In the presence of the Duke of Kent, a younger brother of the King, Part One began with the National Anthem and the unaccompanied 'O Gladsome Light' from *The Golden Legend* (Sullivan still signified much to him). Then came Beethoven's *Egmont* overture, the Rachmaninoff Concerto, and the Sanctus from Bach's Mass in B minor.

After the interval came the broadcast part:

London Pageant	Bax
Serenade to Music	Vaughan Williams
The Ride of the Valkyries	Wagner
The Hailstone Chorus (*Israel in Egypt*)	Handel
Pomp and Circumstance March no.1	Elgar

Vaughan Williams's *Serenade to Music* – a work of both serenity and exaltation which passed immediately into the repertory – was delivered to a rapt audience by the sixteen chosen singers. They were Isobel Baillie, Stiles-Allen, Elsie Suddaby, Eva Turner, Margaret Balfour, Muriel Brunskill, Astra Desmond, Mary Jarred, Parry Jones, Heddle Nash, Frank Titterton, Walter Widdop, Norman Allin, Robert Easton, Roy Henderson and Harold Williams.

To describe the ovations for Vaughan Williams, for Rachmaninoff, for Sir Henry himself is needless. (One of the most pleasant touches is that Rachmaninoff expressed deep admiration for the *Serenade*, and Vaughan Williams was much appreciative when told so.) Among all the hundreds of works of which Wood had given first performances few had carried a dedication to him personally, and no work so individually memorable as this one. His association with it must have pleased him no less than the feat of having raised, from ticket sales and donations, the sum of £9000 for his fund to endow hospital beds for orchestral musicians. Three of these were endowed at Charing Cross Hospital, two at St Bartholomew's, and one each at Westminster, University College, St Mary's and Wembley hospitals.

Among those who had telegraphed their congratulations was Sibelius. In a letter of 29 October Wood thanked him, but added:

> It is extraordinary for me today to scan the papers here and see that Sir Thomas Beecham – in large letters – is giving a so-called SIBELIUS FESTIVAL. The fact seems to be unaccountably overlooked that during the strenuous season of promenade concerts in 1937 I gave *what was indeed a Sibelius Festival*, and through the season did your seven symphonies. It seems to me that because this great undertaking was carried out in the stride of these [*sic*] series of concerts that it may have passed unnoticed and unrecognized. This has hurt your friend extremely. Never mind, I hope with all my heart that I shall be able to produce your EIGHTH SYMPHONY and many more symphonies to come.

He must have raised the topic again in the summer of 1939, to which Sibelius replied on 29 July, 'Nothing can be dearer to me than to know [*sic*] my Eighth Symphony performed by you, to whom I am much indebted.' The composer declined to say when the new work, 'which has already been so much discussed', would be ready. It never was.

Wood's letter of thanks to Vaughan Williams two days after the concert shows that even in that context his searching mind was thinking as usual about how to make performances *better*. '. . . We are *so* excited to hear this morning from Columbia that they are going to record it [the *Serenade to Music*], and sell it for the Hospital Fund, and I do hope you can run in and help me record it, as your advice and assistance will be most valuable. I should like a couple of Russian basses for the low D's – they don't tell, I fear.'

What the two British basses would have said to having their low notes reinforced by 'Russian' voices hardly bears thinking about. A similar wish for deep 'Russian' male voices, and Wood's fruitless hope of finding them in the Russian-Jewish community of East London, will be recalled from the account of the preparation of Mahler's Eighth (p.226). The point was not pursued.

The original solo singers and the BBC Symphony Orchestra reassembled ten days later at EMI's Abbey Road Number 1 studio to record the *Serenade* under Wood's baton, with the composer present. It marked Wood's return to the fold of Columbia records after his period with Decca. Columbia would have few years left, however, and those mainly of wartime restriction, for an exploitation of Wood's prestige and his distinctive repertory. There was a portent of the approaching conflict when in the middle of the promenade concert of 30 September, the Queen's Hall audience was allowed to hear the BBC's news broadcast in which the voice of Neville Chamberlain, the prime minister, announced that he had come home from Munich with 'peace with honour': 'I believe it is peace in our time.'

Political issues could not be shut off from artistic matters. Many musicians had already committed themselves in the general Leftist cause of opposition to fascism. A clear moral issue was seen in the Spanish Civil War (1936–9), in which Hitler's Germany and Mussolini's Italy helped to crush democracy in Spain. It was this which prompted Benjamin Britten to write his *Ballad of Heroes* to words by W. H. Auden. Even such an older composer as John Ireland produced the cantata *These Things Shall Be* (1937), which incorporated, for those able to identify it, a musical quotation from the Communist hymn, the *Internationale*.

The ever-unpolitical Wood accepted an invitation to conduct what anyone more astute would have identified as an obviously 'Leftist' concert. He reacted sharply, not converted to the cause but, on the contrary, disconcerted at the 'Red' menace he saw within it. He wrote a 'strictly private' letter to Boult on 14 December 1938:

I was approached some time ago to direct a concert at the Queen's Hall, viz: A Massed Concert of the Co-operative Societies Choral Units. I was very pleased to say yes! because I felt that it was good to get music among the masses, under such splendid conditions as put forward to me. It went so far, as booking the date and the rehearsals, but when the programme was put before me, I found that one item by Hans [Hanns] Eisler was impossible for me to direct in a British Concert Hall, or anywhere else, as an Englishman.

I am sending you copy of the translation of the words used in this Cantata, from which you will see what I mean.

[Extract from Eisler's *Lenin (Requiem):* 'Since that day fifteen years have passed. A sixth of the world has been freed from exploiters. At the call "Exploiters are coming", the people are ready, renewed for the struggle, prepared to fight them. Lenin is enshrined in the mighty heart of the people.']

They [the organizers] certainly agreed to remove this offending item from my programme, but the fact remained that those running this concert, and the Musical Director of this Choral Society, is a man *who would have allowed and expected his Choruses to declame [sic] these words, from a British platform, and worse still, at Queen's Hall in the heart of our Empire* . . . .

Celebrating

Though he sent the letter to Boult's private address rather than to his BBC office, Henry J. Wood obviously intended his warning to reach the BBC, where a watchful eye could be kept over such dangerous musicians as the one singled out though not named. It was probably Alan Bush, who had already conducted his own orchestral works three times at the Proms, but who would not dissociate his Communist affiliation from his work as composer. Evidence is lacking that the scheduled concert programme by Co-operative Choirs ever took place, at least in the form Wood referred to.

It is tempting to compare Wood's naïve alarm over communism with his silence on fascism – but the comparison is hardly fair. He was reacting impulsively to a work bearing a communist text; he was never asked, of course, to perform a fascist equivalent. Nevertheless his obstinate self-isolation from the issues of the impending conflict was hardly admirable. One looks in vain for any concern over the Nazis' cultural repression, even with reference to the forced emigration from Europe of composers with whom he had enjoyed personal contact, among them Schoenberg, Hindemith and Bartók. During the war years that followed, it was enough for him that he should just (to quote a banality which he himself used) 'keep on keeping on'.

Chapter 21

Into the Blackout

1938–41

By the end of 1938 the marital stresses, the legal complications, the social problems in initiating a new pseudo-marriage – all these, it might be supposed, were over. No one was harassing Henry J. Wood; though his daughter Avril was working in London she stayed out of his way. In the Statutory Declaration quoted earlier (p.322), he had already set down the grievances which he felt morally justified his decision. Just why he should scratch at the plastered wound, going over those grievances again – in a less controlled way – is hard to understand.

Yet that is what he did, in the extraordinary document headed *My Confession* which survives in the Wood papers deposited in the British Library and is reproduced as an appendix on p.415–17 of this book. The dating of it as 4 February 1939 both at the top and at the end is only one of the many signs of mental turmoil in writing it. It has far more than Wood's usual quota of mis-spelling, random punctuation, and clumsy phrasing: even his wife's middle initial (properly E. for Ellen) and her maiden name of Greatrex are wrongly given.

Three months *after* setting down this testimony, he asked his new solicitor Stanley Rubinstein to dig out the Statutory Declaration itself, as 'I wish to use the contents of the document to safeguard my interests while I am here [living] and Lady Jessie's should she survive me'. Once having reread what he had written in the Statutory Declaration, he may have planned to work up *My Confession* into some more coherent form in order that it could be produced as testimony.

He never did so, however. Nor was it shown to anybody else in his lifetime – not even to Jessie. She came across it some years after his death when going through his papers. She recognized it then as 'just your everlasting thought for me' – springing from his desire that, should he predecease her (as was probable), Jessie would have every claim on his estate and Muriel none.

Celebrating

His concern for Jessie's welfare in that eventuality must have been heightened when the outbreak of war in September 1939 made the civilian population (of London, especially) the likely target of enemy bombing. The special involvement of the BBC in that war was to alter Henry's professional schedule to an unimagined degree. Contingency plans for war had long since been made by the BBC, mainly in its role as a news and information channel. In September 1938, shortly after the pioneering Sir John Reith had left the post of director-general, to be succeeded by F.W.Ogilvie, the Munich crisis provided 'a useful rehearsal', as Asa Briggs was to put it, for what was to come. In anticipation of air raids, visitors to Broadcasting House during September and October 1938 would see anti-gas doors installed and sandbags positioned in the lobby.

During the year between the two Septembers the BBC's higher management set up emergency plans to remove various departments away from London – plans which, of course, had to be kept secret if the object of outwitting the enemy was to be achieved. Bristol was chosen as the location for the Symphony Orchestra. Boult as Director of Music must have been among those warned in advance (curiously enough, his biographer Michael Kennedy is silent on that point); Wood, merely a contracted artist, was not. Meanwhile on the practical level of music-making both inside and outside the BBC, it was 'business as usual'. The BBC maintained its friendly cultural relations with its counterpart in Nazi Germany. The Reichs Rundfunk station in Berlin thanked the BBC for 'the excellent broadcast of Sir Henry Wood's jubilee concert', transmitted there on 7 December 1938. Such deferred broadcasts were possible because the BBC had begun to make recordings of certain programmes for export, though instantaneous transmission remained the rule for domestic radio.

Wood's life continued in much the same busy fashion, and at the same rate of remuneration for his broadcast concerts – broadcast by radio, that is. The BBC's television service was still broadcasting only a few hours each day (one hour on Sundays), with at most 25,000 sets in use by mid-1939. Its fees to performers were correspondingly small. Accepting a contract 'to speak and conduct the Television Orchestra' on 11 February 1939 at a fee of ten guineas (as against £100, his normal fee for a radio concert) he wrote: 'May I say that it is many, many years since I signed a contract for such a fee, but I am very pleased to do this in the service of our young form of entertainment – television.'

The jubilee of 1938 he regarded as a milestone but in no sense a prelude to retirement. New music was as ever to be considered, plans made for well-shaped concert programmes. A great jotter-down of scraps of information and ideas he wanted to be reminded of, he would use odd pieces of paper or odd spaces in his desk diary for the purpose. Where his 1938 diary ended with the printed heading of 'Annual Cash Summary' he used the space to write instead: 'I would like to do Schumann *Paradise and the Peri* [a rarely performed cantata], Schumann Piano Concerto with Myra Hess, overture *Manfred*' – a complete Schumann programme of distinct originality, but one which he never brought to fruition. But as guest conductor of the Bournemouth Municipal Orchestra on 27 October 1938 he showed comparable originality in pairing his old enthusiasm for Busoni (the *Comedy Overture*) with his new enthusiasm for Benjamin Britten's Piano Concerto, finishing with Beethoven's Seventh Symphony, a most unusual three-Bs programme. As at the Proms, Britten himself was the soloist. Sir Dan Godfrey having retired from his Bournemouth post in 1934 (Richard Austin was his successor), Wood was regarded as an elder statesman and musical adviser there.

He continued his twice-weekly conducting of the student orchestra at the Royal Academy of Music. The Academy had for four years housed Wood's own music library, its 2800 orchestral scores and 1928 sets of complete orchestral parts constituting without doubt the largest private collection in Britain, if not in the world. In December 1938 he made the library over as a gift to the Academy, but asked that no announcement be made: 'If it were published now, Press etc. etc. might run away with the idea that I am retiring from public work.' He had continued to charge the BBC (see p.233) for the use of this material at the Proms, though not when he conducted other BBC concerts, and he levied similar hire fees on the Sheffield Festival and the Liverpool Philharmonic Society. At ten shillings per item this produced an income 'in the nature of £150' for each promenade season. All such fees he would now lose and suggested the Academy should allot them to a special fund for helping necessitous students.

Legally, since this was an absolute gift, he could impose neither this condition nor any other, as the Academy made him aware. But his deed of gift expressed the hope that an exemption from charges would continue to be granted to the Hull Philharmonic and to the Bournemouth and other 'seacoast' festivals for so long as he continued to conduct them; and, crucially, that he himself would be granted free use of the material, with the Academy paying for the despatch and collection of the parts. 'I need hardly say that those wishes will be respected,' wrote the Academy's Secretary, L.Gurney Parrott, in accepting the gift on 15 December. Wood had got a good bargain: he was free of the need to devote a large room to the many-shelved storing of such extensive material, and of paying a librarian. On its side, the Academy could not have foretold the strain which was to be caused by Wood's demands, under the difficult circumstances of war, for the delivery of 'his' material for performance in various locations.

The gift *was* formally announced, evidently with Wood's sanction, at the Academy's prizegiving on 18 July 1939. As well as continuing his twice-weekly conducting of the Academy's orchestra, he was still giving vocal lessons: 'Teach all day' continues to be found in his diary schedule. At last, however, he recognized that his service to the amateur Hull Philharmonic – with the added burden of long rail journeys and nights in a hotel – must be brought to a close. He gave the last of his thirty-nine concerts on 13 April, receiving while still on the conductor's rostrum the gift of an onyx cigarette-case. It is not any single one of Wood's programmes at Hull that is so remarkable, but rather the total record of his sixteen years – the symphonies alone including four by Beethoven, all those by Brahms, two by Glazunov and two by Sibelius, Rachmaninoff's no.2 and Vaughan Williams's *A London Symphony*. In *My Life of Music* he paid tribute to a former assistant conductor at Hull in terms that reflect his own workmanlike attitude: 'He is still the society's timpanist and does not mind being seen moving his drums to and from the hall on a handcart because there is no place in which to store them between rehearsals. He can do this and yet retain his dignity as one of the vice-presidents of the society.'

Wood's enthusiasm for choral Handel continued unabated. The BBC permitted him to devote one of his allotted Queen's Hall concerts in the 1938–9 season (30 November) to an un-cut *Judas Maccabaeus*, for which the programme note was written by a younger Handelian, Julian Herbage of the BBC Music Department. (His presentation of the BBC's *Music Magazine*, in co-operation with his wife Anna Instone, was to make Herbage one of the most familiar radio personalities to post-war music-lovers.) Herbage followed with a letter of congratulation which Wood, replying to it, took as a 'great personal compliment':

> As I believe Lady Wood told you over the telephone – Sir Adrian too
> was delighted with *Judas Maccabaeus* and suggested how splendid it
> would be to do it in the Studio in three sections, or failing *Judas* then to
> perform *Israel in Egypt*, under the same conditions.
>
> From every quarter, except Dr Colles, who is suffering from a very
> bad liver, I have had nothing but praise for the beautiful string quality of
> this performance. Certainly never have I heard finer playing myself.

P.S. And then there is *Joshua, Samson, Susanna, Athalia, L'Allegro* etc.
Semele, Theodora, Saul, Belshazzar, Solomon, Deborah, Jephtha etc: it
would be a splendid feather in the cap of the BBC if all these could be
presented in *sections* by the BBC – it would be a *monumental achievement*
and it could *only* be undertaken by you.

It was an ingenious attempt to catch Herbage's own enthusiasm on the
rebound, but the BBC mechanism was not so easily reactivated. Wood's
other engagements took him on 27 November to the London Palladium,
filling the place that his friend the late Landon Ronald would have occupied in
conducting the New Symphony Orchestra for the National Sunday League.
The programme offered was anything but routine: Mendelssohn's *Ruy Blas*
overture, both the first and second piano concertos of Tchaikovsky played
by Moiseiwitsch (in reverse order, one in each half), Haydn's Symphony
no.88, and the Sailors' Dance and Trio from Handel's opera *Rodrigo*. More
such Sunday concerts at the Palladium were to follow in the new year.

The campaign to standardize pitch at 'Continental' level – a cause that
might have been supposed to have been won long ago (see p.34) –
resurfaced. The Alexandra Palace, a popular centre of entertainment in
North London with a very large auditorium, had been effectively deprived of
massed choral performances because the organ had been originally built at
'high' pitch. Wood had been an early donor to funds for the adjustment to low
pitch – and when that alteration had been completed, what conductor of
greater choral authority could be asked to direct the concert celebrating the
re-opening of the organ? On 3 June 1939 forty local choirs combined as the
Alexandra Festival Choir to perform selections from Handel's *Judas
Maccabaeus, Israel in Egypt* and *Messiah*. Baillie, Balfour, Titterton and
Harold Williams were the soloists, with G. D. Cunningham at the restored
organ and an orchestra of students from both the Royal Academy and the
Royal College of Music.

It must have afforded Wood some satisfaction that the extracts from *Israel*
were broadcast, though the type of performance was larger-scaled and more
unwieldy than he had been proposing to the BBC via Herbage. A significant
encounter was with Charles Proctor, the chorus-master of that massive
vocal force: he would be Wood's regular choral associate in difficult wartime
days.

He continued to champion Rachmaninoff's Third Symphony, giving it at
Bournemouth on 16 March and writing on 3 July to tell the composer ('My
very dear Friend') of the BBC studio performance scheduled for 2 August.
In the same letter Wood thanked Rachmaninoff once more for the 'noble and

generous support' which had contributed so greatly to the fund-raising success of the jubilee concert. 'The memory of it will ever remain one of the most pleasurable and gratifying climaxes to a long life of service to the music I represent and love.' These performances of the symphony presumably incorporated the cuts which had been suggested to Wood (as he previously told the BBC) by the composer.

Rachmaninoff might be abridged but on the other hand Wood decided to give Schubert's Ninth at the Proms *without* cuts – a sudden decision which he must have known would upset the BBC schedules. 'I very much regret,' he wrote to W. W. Thompson on 15 August

> that in deciding to play Symphony No.9 in C (Schubert) without my usual 'cuts' I have disorganized your timing this evening.
>
> I cannot at this late hour, however, alter my decision to hear for myself, once again, whether my 'cuts' are not more helpful to the hearing public of [*sic*] this longish – but very lovely – symphony.

That was an awkward phrasing, but the note at least gave Thompson something to show his superiors. Doubtless Wood was conscious of the hostility his cuts had incurred in knowledgeable quarters. (The *Musical Times*, October 1935: 'There is no need to discuss the maltreatment of Schubert's C major symphony, for it cannot be done in the language of moderation.') Some further stimulus towards a rethinking about the 'Viennese' repertory may have also arisen from Wood's meeting and hearing Bruno Walter, who made further appearances with the BBC Symphony Orchestra earlier that year. Diary entries of 18 January 1938 (when Walter conducted Beethoven's Ninth at Queen's Hall) and other dates show Wood's plans to attend.

The Royal Philharmonic Society in previous seasons had elbowed Wood out of its programmes and may with some reason have thought Beecham and Weingartner more of a draw. But after the salutes of the jubilee they could hardly neglect one of their most distinguished living gold medallists. His programme on 26 January 1939, with Solomon playing the *Emperor* Concerto, began with Glazunov's *Carnival* Overture (of which he had given the first performance in Britain forty-one years before) and continued with Bax's *November Woods*, George Butterworth's *A Shropshire Lad* (of which he had given the first London performance in 1917) and Borodin's Symphony no.2.

A second Royal Philharmonic Society concert came his way that season – one of two (Beecham conducted the other) which the society contributed to a

'London Musical Festival'. By this time any orchestral programme Wood conducted could hardly fail to be commemorative of his own achievement: here (28 April) was *L'Après-midi d'un faune*, which Wood had introduced to London in 1904. On the programme also were Bach's Sixth Brandenburg Concerto, Rachmaninoff's second concerto (with Moiseiwitsch) and the *Enigma Variations*. This London Musical Festival, from 23 April to 28 May, was the largest ever: with Toscanini re-engaged to conduct the BBC Symphony Orchestra, it embraced various orchestral, choral, operatic, ballet and other events. Not even Robert Newman, who had first decided to import the term 'festival' into his London season four decades before, had contrived to have his operations sealed and sanctified by the patronage of the Sovereign and an opening service at Westminster Abbey.

'Workmanlike' as ever, Wood not only filled his prominent place in the Royal Philharmonic Society's contribution but took over the festival performance on 20 May at Queen's Hall by the London Junior Orchestra (of students), whose conductor, Ernest Read, was ill. His interest in early-instrument performance was shown when he suggested to the BBC that representatives should attend a concert to be given at the Grotrian Hall by the Arte Antica ensemble.

The BBC proposed in April 1939 to leave out the 'J' from announcements of Sir Henry J.Wood's performances, and he seems not to have objected. But he strongly resisted the BBC proposal to drop the 'Sir' in such cases as his own:

> Lady Wood has told me [he wrote to W.W.Thompson on 5 June] of your conversation today per telephone regarding the renunciation of Titles among musicians generally.
>
> I have no hesitation in saying at once, that I for one cannot agree to such an omission in bills posters or programmes in connection with music.
>
> I have been proud to hold the honour conferred upon me as long ago as 1911, which honour was conferred in the name of MUSIC IN ENGLAND, and I consider such renunciation as apparently is proposed, to be in the nature of a slight to the Crown, and to the music for which I stand – in differing degrees it must be admitted – in England and abroad.
>
> We as a Country are fast losing the fine traditions for which we have stood in the eyes of the World, and each fresh evidence of a wish to denounce traditions, is a nail in the coffin of our becoming a Nation so democratized as to fall into line with a Country whose very régime has brought us nigh unto war, and whose peoples are but serfs under an anti-tradition rule.

Celebrating

One can even less expect Sir Thomas Beecham, Bart., to have welcomed the proposal, and it sank from view.

He and Jessie had moved in May into a new flat (24 Fountain House, Park Street, almost adjoining Hyde Park). For the first time he removed his listing from the telephone directory, giving 'Grosvenor 3556' in his own hand-writing on letters to the BBC. Jessie's careful management of his own comforts is seen in her reminder for 6 August in the desk diary: 'Maids both out – out for supper'. During June and July she had shepherded him down to Mayfield in Sussex for four quiet weeks. Glyndebourne was not far away, and diary entries show several visits planned. Glyndebourne's owner-impresario, John Christie, invited them to be his guests on 11 July for *Le Nozze di Figaro*.

For *Così fan tutte* five days later the diary had the added reminder, 'take Gordon' – Dr Gordon Calthrop, of Upper Wimpole Street in London's fashionable medical district, to whom Jessie's daughter Eileen was married. The birth of 'Dear Eileen's baby' was noted in Jessie's hand on 7 September. The Calthrops named their child Henry Thomas, and Henry J. Wood became his doting, pram-pushing, surrogate grandfather.

The royal physician Lord Horder had become a friend of the couple as well as Henry's medical adviser. On 13 July Jessie's diary entry noted: 'Consulted Lord Horder. He is delighted with Henry, but says he *must* take things more quietly – give up teaching – and any speech-making – but take more "odd times" holiday and rest.'

Beecham's concert for the Royal Philharmonic Society had included the first European performance of Ernest Bloch's Violin Concerto (with Szigeti as soloist) – a première which, before the BBC downgraded the role of the Proms in giving first performances, might well have been secured for the Proms season. The BBC proposed that the concerto should nevertheless be given at the Proms, second-hand. Wood turned down the suggestion on the ground that he did not like the work – but, since he much admired Bloch's music in general, he was probably registering a protest against the BBC's obvious failure to secure the première. He asked instead that Arthur Catterall should play Busoni's Violin Concerto ('a fine work, rarely given, and he plays it well, and the public do not expect him to play this from memory'); he also wanted the BBC to engage Emil Telmányi to play the Violin Concerto by 'Nielson' (as he spelt him).

In his interest in Carl Nielsen, whose daughter Telmányi had married, Wood was – as so often – in advance of his time: Nielsen died in 1931 but his reputation in Britain as a composer of equal status with Sibelius was not made until the 1950s. Neither the Busoni nor the Nielsen concerto actually got through his later discussions with the BBC to the stage of incorporation in the Proms prospectus of 1939. Fewer still, in that war-torn season, achieved actual performance. But just before the promenade season Wood was able to programme a BBC studio performance of Dorothy Howell's *Lamia*, the work which had won such success with the promenade audience of twenty years before, writing on 7 August of his pleasure that she had been able to 'listen in'.

Wood had earlier deplored the scarcity of good new singers, especially for the Wagner items: 'Oh! – that we could find big voices, who can sing and declaim them in German.' He also suggested to the BBC that Beethoven's Ninth should be performed in German rather than in English as in all its appearances so far at the Proms. (A particular stumbling-block had always been the translation of the bass recitative.) But the summer of 1939 was not propitious for a call to universal brotherhood delivered in London in German: the Ninth was among war's casualties that season.

Only eighteen of the announced forty-nine promenade programmmes were given. They began on Saturday 12 August. Daily thereafter the threat of war tightened. 'Dear Mr Ogilvie', Wood wrote on 24 August to the BBC's director-general

> One cannot at the moment say what may happen during the next days, or for that matter, hours, but should war be determined I expect all public performances of cinema, theatre, or concerts will have to cease.
>
> Obviously music must play a part in helping to keep the older and younger folk as happy and interested in other subjects than war, and its horrors, and at the same time help the morale of those called upon to shoulder the burdens of actual participation in the services of our country.
>
> With this in mind, I would like to tell you that I have no intention of leaving London, and place myself unreservedly at the command of the British Broadcasting Corporation for studio work of any kind.
>
> Naturally, I should like to think that we could carry out our programmes from the studio or at least that part of each programme that has been earmarked for broadcasting from Queen's Hall during the Promenade concert season, as in this way we can still employ those artists engaged, who are not called for national duty.
>
> For obvious reasons, I cannot be of service in any other capacity, but should like to feel that although we cannot have our great public audiences we can go on giving pleasure and comfort to a large listening public during the trying days ahead.
>
> Believe me, the question of finance does not enter into this, and fees

could be adjusted to meet the requirements of the strain that all resources will naturally be subjected to in the event of war.

On Friday 1 September Hitler invaded Poland. That evening's concert (see p. 344–5) was to have included Frank Bridge's *A Dance Poem*, conducted by the composer. But after conducting Beethoven's *Pastoral* Symphony, the preceding item of the programme, Wood left the platform, returned and addressed his audience:

> Owing to the special arrangements for broadcasting which are now in force, the BBC very much regrets that the Symphony Orchestra will no longer be available for these concerts in London. I am therefore very sorry to say that from tonight the Promenade Concerts will close down until further notice. I must thank you again, my dear friends, for your loyal support, and I hope we shall soon meet again.

Ogilvie had appeared in person during that morning's orchestral rehearsal. He spoke appreciatively to the players of their and their conductor's work. But they were warned to stand ready to go to Bristol, the city which had been chosen as the orchestra's wartime base. The signal for them to do so would be the replacement of the usual announcement 'This is the BBC' by 'This is London' at the start of the BBC's 9 p.m. news bulletin. The fateful words were uttered by the BBC announcer next evening, 2 September. On Sunday 3 September Britain declared war on Germany.

Leaving Queen's Hall on the Friday of the curtailed concert, Wood was silent. As Jessie Wood was to recall in her book, *The Last Years of Henry J. Wood*:

> He ate no supper. There was just numb sorrow that night for him. We drove home in darkness – a blackout we were to endure for many years had already descended on London. Henry never again saw a street fully lit – he died before the end of the war.
>
> The BBC departed, we knew not where; there was no word – and no indication as to the rest of the season.

'We knew not where': Jessie's recollection, fifteen years later, must have been inaccurate. Wood had been present when Ogilvie addressed the orchestra and indeed wrote to him two days later 'to express my gratitude for the thoughtful kindness which brought you to Queen's Hall'. Praising not only the players but the members of the BBC's Music Department during weeks of suspense, he continued: 'We as a nation have just entered into war and I cannot but refer once again to the hope that the British Broadcasting Corporation will consider my kind of music as an essential part of the nation's uplift and comfort during the stress of the times through which we are all bound to pass, and that consideration will be given to the many older artists whose very living depends upon a little work here and there.'

That double concern – that the value of music should be recognized for its power of 'uplift', and that members of the orchestral profession should not suffer undue hardship – remained with him in the years that were left to him.

An incidental casualty of war was the cancellation of the degree ceremony at which the University of London was to have presented him with an honorary doctorate – following similar recognition from the universities of Cambridge, Oxford, Manchester and Birmingham. The degree had been formally announced in June, but war made it advisable for the university's central office to leave London and the parchment in its plush purple tube reached him by messenger.

His own resolution to remain in London despite the dangers had assumed that the BBC Symphony Orchestra would be there. Since that was no longer so, there was every reason for him and Jessie to follow the officially encouraged step of moving out of the capital, where heavy bombing was thought inevitable. They chose the area of Brighton, from which he could – and assiduously did – travel to London, Liverpool, Manchester and wherever the BBC or any other British promoter asked him. Sir Thomas Beecham disappeared in May 1940 to the United States, then to Australia, not returning to Britain until 1944; Wood never left.

At the outbreak of war, fearful of exposing concentrations of hundreds of people to the danger of air raids, the Government ordered the closure of all theatres, cinemas and concert-halls in London. The BBC, becoming the main channel of Governmment information, merged all its programmes into one network which it filled with news, records, variety shows and what Sir Adrian Boult's biographer, Michael Kennedy, calls 'seemingly endless cinema organ recitals'. As Boult was later to recall, in a frame of mind calmer than he showed at the time, 'My friend Sandy Macpherson, the organist, who did a grand job, had a sixteen-hour day. The Variety Department ran out of jokes, while the symphony orchestra went for long walks exploring the lovely country round Bristol.'

The Times published letters from Bernard Shaw and from the theatrical producer Basil Dean deploring the standstill, followed on 7 September by Wood himself. Music between the news bulletins would be to troubled minds

SIR HENRY J. WOOD

Baron

My dear Friends, I thank
You for your Loyal support -
and I hope we shall soon
meet again. *Spoken by
H.J. when Prom Closed 1939*

BEETHOVEN CONCERT
Friday 1 September 1939

CONDUCTOR: SIR HENRY J. WOOD

OVERTURE   Coriolan   *Beethoven*

SONG CYCLE   An die ferne Geliebte   *Beethoven*

CONCERTO No. 2, in B flat,
           for Pianoforte and Orchestra   *Beethoven*

SYMPHONY No. 6, in F (Pastoral)   *Beethoven*

INTERVAL OF FIFTEEN MINUTES

A DANCE POEM   *Frank Bridge*
            (Conducted by the Composer)

SONGS (with Pianoforte)
        (*a*) The Eve of Crecy   }   *Julius Harrison*
        (*b*) Marching Along   }

MINUTES SYMPHONIQUES   *Dohnányi*

JOHN FULLARD
Solo Pianoforte: HARRIET COHEN

Encores cannot be allowed in the First Part of the Programme

The last promenade concert given at Queen's Hall before the outbreak of World War II: (1) Wood's notes for his address to the audience at the interval; the second part of the printed programme was not performed.

> a new and consoling force, as opposed to the speaking voice. When I say 'music', I mean the fine orchestral and vocal and instrumental standard works, which should take their place in programmes so often given to the 'lighter flippant music', which, although so helpful to some minds, merely jars upon others.
>
> In the last Great War, I received thousands of letters from the trenches, all begging us to keep the 'Proms' going, and the Sunday Afternoon Concerts, as they were longing for 'leave' and wanted to come to hear and see the real things.
>
> Of course, we know that conditions of warfare have greatly changed, and that 'blackouts' have to be considered, but surely from 6 to 8 pm concerts and theatres could carry on without undue risks, now that we are so splendidly provided with adequate shelter [sandbagged or otherwise protected refuges from bombing].

Typically his letter ended with a plea not to impose 'dreadful poverty' on 'our British artists, vocal, instrumental and dramatic'.

Cautiously, restrictions on performance were lifted, the authorities not being unaware of the morale-building function of entertainment. At the National Gallery (whence pictures had been removed) the lunch-time concerts conceived and directed by Myra Hess became a symbol of defiant artistic survival. With the enthusiastic help of the director of the gallery, Sir Kenneth Clark, the concerts began at 1 p.m. on 10 October 1939 and continued daily from Monday to Friday. Myra Hess volunteered to give the first concert herself 'in case the whole thing is a flop'. By the time the doors had to be closed on the disappointed tail-end of the queue, roughly a thousand people had crowded in, in place of the 200 for which official permission had been granted by the Home Office.

The cost of admission was a shilling, and proceeds went to the Musicians' Benevolent Fund. Henry J. Wood appeared early in that famous, unbroken series (1698 concerts were to be given until 10 April 1946). He conducted the Boyd Neel String Orchestra on 23 November – 'against doctor's orders', according to the caption which the *Daily Mail* gave next day to multiple photographs of his gestures in conducting.

He had already given what the *Daily Telegraph* called 'the first symphony concert of the season' with the London Symphony Orchestra (and Moiseiwitsch as soloist) at Queen's Hall on 14 October. Three days later came his first studio broadcast with the BBC Symphony Orchestra in Bristol – at his old fee of £100, plus £1.11s.6d as first-class return rail fare from London. The LSO concert began with Elgar's *Polonia*, its political relevance in the First World War repeated in the Second. Boult had sent a telegram of

good wishes to Queen's Hall to which Wood replied with an enthusiastic
report: ∕

> . . .the LSO never played better though, owing to the call of the ARP
> [the civilian Air Raid Precautions service, in which some players had
> enrolled], we had a few deputies. . . . I was not allowed to start the
> concert until 2.42, as 200 or 300 people could not gain admission and at
> 2.30, Mr [George] Wood the Sec. went round the orchestra to try to
> gather a few tickets from members of the orchestra.

'What makes me so happy and contented', he added, was that 'every penny
in the house' went to the musicians who played. He was evidently taking *no*
fee in this case, and would often take a much reduced one in order to help
keep the London Symphony Orchestra afloat – and the London Philharmonic
Orchestra also, when it later became self-governing after its desertion by
Beecham, its founder. But he resolutely opposed any reduction of fees to
orchestral players or to soloists. The BBC having decided to mount regular
public concerts at Bristol (at the Colston Hall), he accepted an engagement
for 15 November: he had declined the BBC's original date of 29 November
'as I have an Academy rehearsal the previous day'. The RAM had reduced
its orchestral rehearsals to only one a week instead of two, with a
consequent cut in Wood's remuneration, but he felt an intense loyalty to the
effort to keep it going at all.

Henry and Jessie had spent some weeks in the Sussex countryside at
Mayfield but from October 1939 had established themselves in a flat at 4
Grand Avenue, Hove (adjoining Brighton). Some letters, however, perhaps
while the flat was being decorated, gave the address of the Old Ship Hotel at
Brighton itself. From there he wrote on 6 December to the composer
Elisabeth Lutyens, welcoming the proposal of the newly formed Association
of British Musicians to fund a series of winter promenade concerts under his
direction. He made a condition that the LSO be used, and laid it down firmly
that, 'much as I always wish to put in new works', the proposed two-week
season and the demands of the box-office would not allow it. The series
never took place, but the proposal was indicative of the interest of others in
sustaining the Proms tradition if the BBC would not.

And would it? After long years of difficult negotiation and what he regarded
as a discourteous severance in the previous summer, Henry J. Wood had
learnt to be wary of counting on BBC benevolence. (Here he made a
distinction, which was correct, between the professional goodwill of the
Music Department and the administrative mentality of its higher

management, which if necessary would call on Boult to be its public spokesperson.) He had, first of all, to face a demand that, since only eighteen of a proposed forty-nine promenade programmes had been given that summer, his previously agreed fee should be cut proportionately. Considerable wrangling took place before the BBC, having suggested a reduction from the original £3100 to £1050, accepted a compromise of £2127.10s.0d.

Wood desperately desired that the BBC would grasp the nettle, even in wartime, of staging a promenade season as usual in the summer of 1940. Throughout the early months of the year the BBC's higher management kept him in doubt whether it would do so – though, as David Cox's history of the Proms was to reveal, the professionals of the BBC Music Department expressed themselves strongly in favour. It was not until 5 April, after the BBC's failure to act, that Wood announced in the press that the Proms would continue – under the new auspices of the Royal Philharmonic Society and with the support of Chappell's as the lessors of Queen's Hall.

Stung, the BBC put up Boult as a stalking-horse for management. A letter over his signature in *The Times* on 9 April claimed that the BBC had wanted to be the promoters, 'subject to certain emergency safeguards', but had found the Queen's Hall already let. In a letter printed two days later which began: 'I feel sure Sir Adrian Boult had no intention to wound me', Wood had no difficulty in showing the extent of the BBC's temporizing, and a letter in the *Daily Telegraph* from Louis Dreyfus, chairman of Chappell's, confirmed the BBC's two-month delay. The BBC was compelled in May to issue in the *Radio Times* a disclaimer of any possible imputation that Wood had acted in bad faith.

So the wartime separation of the Proms from the BBC began. It was to last not one but two seasons and to end in acrimony. The 1940 season was announced to last eight weeks from 10 August, the orchestra being the London Symphony Orchestra. Despite the blackout, the old starting-time of 8 p.m. was given in the prospectus:

KEITH DOUGLAS AND OWEN MASE
under the auspices of
THE ROYAL PHILHARMONIC SOCIETY
announce
SIR HENRY WOOD'S
forty-sixth and
FAREWELL SEASON
of
PROMENADE CONCERTS

The involvement of the Royal Philharmonic Society not only lent some prestige but enabled Keith Douglas to place the royal arms on his prospectus. He was not only the honorary secretary of the Royal Philharmonic Society but, as a man of private wealth, was funding it. His partner, Owen Mase, had formerly worked for the BBC and had organized the successful London Musical Festival of the previous year. According to Jessie, Wood supposed Mase to be still linked in some way with the BBC: if he held such a belief he was naive, which in business matters indeed he was. How Wood can have consented to the announcement of a 'farewell season', even under the urging of such a clever persuader as Keith Douglas, is unfathomable.

The favourites of the traditional Proms repertory from Beethoven to Rachmaninoff were there, and on 13 August a distinctive clutch of Finnish works including Palmgren's Piano Concerto (Cyril Smith) – no doubt a token of British sympathy for Finland's vain resistance to the previous winter's Soviet invasion. A 'Bach Concert' (as ever, such labels indicating only that *most* of the music was drawn from that composer) featured Alec Rowley's Harpsichord Concerto played by Lucille Wallace (wife of Clifford Curzon), who had earlier contributed Bach's F minor Concerto. Wood was beginning to admit the harpsichord in Bach, in place of the modern piano.

To Wood a promenade season without first performances was hardly a promenade season at all, and the new management did not apparently demur. There was nothing new from abroad, but Lennox Berkeley's Two-Piano Concerto (6 September) was scheduled, with the composer and William Glock as soloists. Wood was determined that performances claimed as 'first' should genuinely be so – a principle which he felt had been eroded by the BBC. He had planned to perform Thomas F. Dunhill's *Divertissement* but had written asking the composer to confirm that it was, in capitals, 'a FIRST PERFORMANCE ANYWHERE IN ENGLAND' (in Britain, he presumably meant). On learning that it had been given before, probably in the theatre, he wrote again on 23 April 1940 declining with respect to perform the work 'since I am determined not to announce anything in such form as a *First Concert Performance*. This is all nonsense and, of course, has been created by the Broadcasting Corporation, as with their plugging in these Studio performances they have left themselves nothing for the public concert performance, and this year I am determined to put in only works that are first performances in England anywhere, anyhow. Otherwise I find the Press never come, which is not good either for the Management, the Publisher, or the Composer.'

Celebrating

A significant new participation was that of the Alexandra Choir, formed and directed by Charles Proctor at a time when older London choirs were disrupted. On 14 August its male members joined Roy Henderson in a revival of one of Stanford's suitably patriotic works, Proctor himself conducting. '*Songs of the Fleet* under Proctor good – choir dragged, but no rehearsal with the band', Wood noted privately. The impossibility of getting a choir and orchestra together to rehearse a weekday concert, especially in wartime, just had to be accepted: after separate rehearsals, such a master of the baton as Wood knew how to pull the forces together, but he made allowances for a less experienced hand.

At a time when firm musical support of his enterprise was of particular value to him, he rapidly came to appreciate Charles Proctor's artistic worth and business-like methods. Several letters of Wood's during the period of preparation from January to July 1940 (written from 4 Grand Avenue, Hove, or later from 7 Grand Avenue) show his lively encouragement of the younger musician. He had planned that Proctor should conduct not only *Songs of the Fleet* but the purely orchestral *Turkish March* of Musorgsky which was to follow, and apologized on discovering that the Douglas-Mase management had engaged Basil Cameron as a stand-by conductor for the whole series. Cameron's general availability in reserve came to be a useful insurance for the BBC and others, and later propelled that essentially dull musician to a questionable prominence.

Proctor and his choir were selected for further performances later in that Proms season, during which Henry and Jessie set themselves up temporarily in his old haunt opposite Queen's Hall, the Langham Hotel. 'From our room on the third floor we witnessed many terrible air raids,' she was to recall. With the lights turned out and the blackout screens removed, they saw St Paul's dome turn scarlet from the fires rising after the bombing of dockland in the East End of London. Opposite the hotel, Broadcasting House itself was hit, the hotel's regular lighting and the emergency plant both failed, and candles appeared on staircases and landings.

Mollie Panter-Downes, whose reports from wartime Britain in the *New Yorker* magazine became classics of journalism, referred to the concert of 26 August:

> At Queen's Hall, a Wagner concert ran to greater length than *Götterdäm-merung*, while the immortal Richard's compatriots droned somewhere in the vicinity; when Sir Henry Wood's official programme ended, members of the symphony orchestra obliged with solos and the indefatigable

audience filled in with community singing and amateur talent until the all-clear came, around three. 'Was it [the air-raid siren] Siegfried's horn or Fafner's growl or both together?' asked the *Times* music critic in a facetious mood that day.

Solo songs with piano being part of every programme in which singers appeared, an accompanist had been engaged for the season as in BBC days (and, indeed, as in Robert Newman's time). This season it was none other than Gerald Moore, whose command of 'any song that was asked for' enlivened those impromptu sessions, and who on one occasion joined in a performance of Schubert's *Trout* Quintet with string players from the orchestra. 'Basil Cameron would organize a music quiz for the 2000 or so who remained in the arena and the stalls,' recorded David Cox, and contributions by members of the orchestra included 'a take-off of Beecham to the T' – the impersonator being the violinist Ralph Nicholson.

The bombing got worse: *blitzkrieg* was the word as the German command, having failed to knock out the RAF bases in southeast England, turned its full force on London. For safety's sake the authorities brought the Proms to an end after four weeks, on 7 September. 'Happily enough, a new work had figured in the [last] programme,' wrote Jessie Wood, omitting to name it. The work was Elisabeth Lutyens' *Three Pieces*, on which Wood commented in his private annotation of the programmes: '[It] did not get a hand. Thank God, only five minutes of excessive boredom.' The conductor who had pioneered Schoenberg in Britain in 1912 had evidently little sympathy in 1940 for the only British composer to have followed Schoenberg's path.

Among 'first performances' originally scheduled but lost by curtailment of the season were Edmund Rubbra's Symphony no.3, a *Dialogue* by Elizabeth Maconchy for piano (Clifford Curzon) and orchestra, and *Three Divertissements* by Dorothy Howell (whose *Lamia* had been given earlier).

Memories of a sunnier period of music-making were evoked in a letter from John Barbirolli dated 29 October, accompanied by a photograph:

> Whilst conducting at the Hollywood Bowl this summer, I discovered that three old and very distinguished members of your own Queen's Hall Orchestra were still playing there. You will of course remember your old friends, Emile Ferir, Alfred Kastner, and Henri de Busscher. My wife was also with me in Hollywood, and you will perhaps remember her having played first oboe for you as Evelyn Rothwell, so that we found ourselves five old members of the Queen's Hall Orchestra suddenly thrown together in California.
>
> We had a grand talk about 'the good old days', and naturally we talked

much of you and all the work we had done with you. We had the enclosed picture taken to send you, and I hope that in these sad times you may find a little pleasure in the very warm place that you still hold in the hearts of your devoted ex-members of your Orchestra.

With warmest greetings to you and Lady Wood

The war had a particularly severe effect on orchestral music at Bournemouth, the only town in Britain where a symphony orchestra was under direct municipal management. On Wood's own recommendation its strength had been fixed in 1937 at sixty-one players, but under war conditions the numbers were slashed to twenty-four plus six part-timers – adequate for light entertainment only. From his acknowledged position as adviser Wood sent a 'private and confidential' letter to Bournemouth's mayor on 21 May 1940: 'When War came, you did not tell your gardeners to pull up your bulbs and your trees that require money spent on them – you did not give instructions for your picture galleries and your museums to be destroyed, which all cost money and which do not directly compensate the Municipal purse. Then why should music, with its great uplift at times such as these, be so treated?'

Much local protest was generated by the municipality's decision. When a substitute Wessex Symphony Orchestra was set up without municipal support, Wood conducted it without fee in four concerts during a single weekend in early September 1941.

In Manchester, there was no question of a dismemberment of the Hallé Orchestra (run under the management of local well-wishers) but it lost its historic home. The Free Trade Hall was at first taken over under wartime requisition as a store, and then bombed by enemy aircraft. The famous acoustics were irrecoverable, but Sunday concerts were given instead at the Paramount cinema, Britain's Sunday observance laws still not permitting cinemas to function as such on that day. Wood was welcomed to conduct not only at the Paramount but in other northern towns from October 1940 to the following January. For touring to smaller centres the Hallé, like other orchestras, had a lifeline of financial support from the American-based Pilgrim Trust.

Long drives in hired cars over blacked-out roads on the return journeys to Manchester were the penalty imposed on the seventy-one-year-old conductor. Occasional refuge was provided by friends in nearby rural Bowdon, where Jessie's years of marriage had been chiefly spent. It can have come as no surprise to Henry and Jessie to find that their friends were compulsory hosts to two of the hundreds of thousands of children officially removed from the endangered cities to safer areas. 'Evacuees', they were called, a word which Jessie, writing in 1954, was still able to use without quotation marks.

The war having seriously reduced civilian mail and train services, Henry J. Wood ran into foreseeable difficulty in getting 'his' scores from 'his' library at the Royal Academy of Music to the various places of performance. Not a few complaints were dispatched to the Academy's Secretary (administrator), L. Gurney Parrott. 'I could not of course keep faith with my audience on Saturday at Blackpool and had to apologize for *Polonia*', the music of which had not arrived (30 October 1940). 'Alas! another catastrophy [*sic*] today in Manchester at the Hallé Concert. Some new MS parts of the Love Duet from *Tristan & Isolde* were sent down which have *never been played from*' (instead of his own set of parts, corrected and marked); 'it took me 45 minutes to rehearse this [piece] of 20 minutes owing to no letters or section marks' (17 November). 'Candidly', he had written on 4 November, 'my gift to the RAM is the source of continual worry to me,' especially the inadequacy (as he saw it) of the orchestral librarian.

He was not unconscious of the Academy's own difficulties of staffing under the threat of call-up, and on at least one occasion had to apologize to Parrott for not having made his requirements clear. Understandably, however, his mind focused on his own difficulties of actual performance, with orchestral ranks weakened by the absence of players on active service. Minor personal problems he left gratefully to Jessie, who toured with him. Energetic as he always was at rehearsal and concert, his heavy perspiration demanded 'as many as twelve or fourteen sets of underclothes a week', according to her own account. After clothes rationing began on 1 June 1941 (food rationing had been in place since the beginning of the war), she wrote asking for an extra allowance – and got eight coupons, 'sufficient for a single set of woollen underwear'. When she reminded the Board of Trade that her request was on behalf of Sir Henry Wood, the response was that 'all dance band leaders are allowed the same number of coupons'. (Henry Hall, director of the BBC Dance Orchestra, had his own following.)

Wood's old and constant friend Rosa Newmarch died in April 1940, aged eighty-two and still pursuing her life's work of musical exposition: her books on Czechoslovak music and on Sibelius were published posthumously. That she, who had known him so well for fifty years, had taken with such warmth to Jessie was of particular solace to him. With Rosa's daughter Elsie Newmarch the Woods had already been in contact for many years – and Jessie was to remain so.

He continued to travel, responding to the spurt in public demand for orchestral concerts. His diary for April and May 1941 shows him in Bristol to rehearse and conduct his annual *Parsifal* concert for the BBC on 11 April, and a Sunday concert two days later with the London Philharmonic Orchestra at Queen's Hall. Four successive days with the London Symphony Orchestra took him to High Wycombe, then to Bath (two concerts on the same day), Cheltenham (two concerts) and Reading. This despite a 'slight seizure', as it was called, on 6 April at Bradford, where he had conducted the Hallé Orchestra the night before.

He was too ill for the train journey home. The expense of hiring a car to take him back from Bradford is noted in the diary as £15.15s. Not only expenses are noted in the diary, but almost daily (in Jessie's hand) a record of alcoholic and other drinks consumed – Wednesday 9 April: '2 large pink gins, $1\frac{1}{2}$ beer, 1 bottle Volnay, 1 large whisky and soda'; on the 11th, '$\frac{1}{2}$ champagne, $\frac{1}{2}$ red wine' and next day '2 pink gin, 1 bottle Volnay, 1 pint beer, 1 large whisky and soda'. These and later entries do not refer to purchases (they are never accompanied by a price, and include 'Water with lunch'): they perhaps fulfil a medical instruction to keep a record as a guide to health. But any medical warnings to 'go slow' or 'take it easy' he found it temperamentally hard to accept.

To his provincial concerts, often in inconvenient conditions and usually with only a single rehearsal, he brought the expertness and patience of his forty-five years of conducting in Queen's Hall. Now came a violent wrench with that past, not merely for Wood but for all his orchestral players, choralists and audiences. On 13 May 1941, in an air raid which caused London's highest casualty figures (1436 killed, 1792 injured) and which destroyed the chamber of the House of Commons and damaged Westminster Abbey, Queen's Hall was set alight. Lack of water hampered the firemen. By next morning, a Sunday, the hall was gutted, only a shell remaining. 'This now presents the appearance of a Roman arena,' wrote the music-loving theatre critic James Agate in his diary, 'and should be left as a memorial to Hitler.'

The concert of the previous afternoon – *The Dream of Gerontius*, with Malcolm Sargent conducting the Royal Choral Society and the London Philharmonic Orchestra – was the last to be given at Queen's Hall. Unusually, and only because they were due to give another concert there on the Sunday afternoon, many of the players had left their instruments in the hall. Few were recoverable. But a bust of Henry J. Wood, sculpted by Donald Gilbert and placed in the hall to mark the 1938 jubilee celebrations, remained intact. It now graces the platform at the Royal Albert Hall during each season of Proms.

A photograph which shows the bare-headed Wood inspecting the ruins (see plate 33) became famous and emblematic. He was himself the incarnation of musical survival. His pose in the photograph (he had been brought there specially so that the photograph might be taken) was forward-looking and earnestly defiant. But there was an element of fake: the figures of two other people in the original photograph were removed (see plate 32) to increase the impact of Wood standing alone, almost as a silent echo of the rallying oratory of Winston Churchill as Prime Minister: 'We shall never surrender' in June 1940; 'Give us the tools, and we will finish the job' in February 1941.

Two days after the bombing of Queen's Hall, on Thursday 15 May, a meeting in Broadcasting House with Julian Herbage, the BBC's music planner, went ahead as scheduled. 'Planned out Prom programmes' reads the Woods' diary. The BBC was not to undertake promotion of the coming season (Keith Douglas would again do that), nor to lend its orchestra, but it was to lend W. W. Thompson's services as concert manager and would broadcast twenty of the concerts. Fortunately another hall would be available as their home.

The survival of the Proms through the war reflected not merely the determination of those who planned them. For a complexity of reasons not yet fully investigated (there has been no proper history of Britain's wartime music-making), the war brought an astonishing surge in public receptivity to orchestral music. In the siege years, with military reverses abroad added to the terror of explosive and incendiary bombs at home, Wood's assertion of the 'uplifting' character of such music was seen to be more than pious hope. Concert-giving in cinemas, munition factories and Armed Services centres tapped new audiences. Not only the Pilgrim and Carnegie Trusts provided financial support, but also the newly created Council for the Encouragement of Music and the Arts (CEMA) – the first-ever instrument of State subsidy to music and the direct ancestor of the later Arts Council of Great Britain. R. J. Forbes of the Hallé management, in reporting the 1939–40 season, had described the CEMA subsidy as 'the most striking thing which has occurred in the history of music in England'.

Henry J. Wood in his seventies was a much-demanded conductor. In his private life one incident – or rather a non-incident – sets a puzzle. In an undated letter (presumably from 1941–2) to his publisher and friend, Hubert Foss, he wrote that he had been to see Walt Disney's film *Fantasia*, in which

Celebrating

Stokowski conducted the various items and also made a personal appearance: 'I was surprised to find that my Bach "Toccata and Fugue" is done as a purely orchestral piece and wonderfully directed by Leopold Stokowsky [*sic*]. It is a very great gesture on his part, as of course you know that he has orchestrated this same work himself – and to give my version seems to me an extraordinary decision.'

Stokowski did not use Wood's version, but his own – naturally enough. The difference between the two is enormous: a few seconds would have sufficed for an identification. Plainly, Wood never saw the film, and must have been relying on the (mistaken) word of someone else. Why not say so? He did not *have* to fabricate a story to Foss. In the days of his life with Muriel such a letter might be exceptionally 'explained' as having had Wood's signature on paper before the text was typed, but such a procedure is unknown on Jessie's part. Besides, Jessie watched over Henry's every step: she would certainly have known better than to say he had visited the cinema (quite out of his ordinary routine) if he had not. The biographer presents this episode to his readers as an unsolved enigma.

Chapter 22

'Somewhere in England'

1941–2

Other locations besides Queen's Hall had already been pressed into service to give orchestral music to Londoners in wartime. The orchestras themselves sought the suburbanites who might be reluctant to venture far afield in the blackout. Sunday afternoon concerts were offered at the Golders Green Hippodrome, where Henry J. Wood had conducted the London Symphony Orchestra in the early weeks of 1940 with such popular soloists as Myra Hess and Pouishnoff. But only one location was suitable to take a whole season of promenade concerts in the summer of 1941. The Royal Albert Hall it would have to be, with some 6000 seats (limited under wartime safety measures to 5000) as against Queen's Hall's 3000. It was a sign of the wartime musical boom that some of the concerts would indeed attract over 4000 patrons, who would take in their stride the type of notice appearing in the printed programmes:

> In the event of an Air Raid Warning the Audience is requested to leave the Auditorium immediately and carry out the instructions of the Stewards and Attendants. Shelter is provided in the various Corridors, but if any persons should wish to leave the building the nearest Public Shelters are:-
> Trenches in Kensington Gardens.
> Trenches in Hyde Park, Knightsbridge.

As well as this conspicuous relocation of the Proms, mid-1941 brought another removal – a secret transfer involving hundreds of people, and one which would shape the final years of Wood's music-making. Bristol had proved not to be a bomb-free home for the BBC Symphony Orchestra: on 24 November 1940 a particularly devastating raid occurred. After investigations of other possible havens it was decided that the orchestra's new home should be Bedford, a small town much nearer London but without the concentration of industry and docks which had made Bristol a target for the bombers. The move took place at the end of July 1941, by a special train which avoided London. The members of the orchestra, as also of the BBC Theatre Orchestra and the BBC Singers, were compulsorily billeted on householders in a town 'already packed with evacuees, homeless mothers and refugee foreign soldiers of every description'. The BBC Symphony Orchestra was to remain in Bedford for more than four years – its presence not to be announced in the Press until 1944, nor mentioned in broadcasts. Like so many other wartime activities of potential interest to the enemy, the location of its work was cloaked as 'somewhere in England'.

The Calthrops (Jessie's daughter Eileen, her husband and baby) meanwhile moved out of London for safety's sake to the village of Weston near Stevenage in Hertfordshire, though Dr Calthrop himself maintained his medical practice in Upper Wimpole Street, London. Preferring to be near them rather than on the vulnerable south coast at Hove, Henry and Jessie chose at this time to spend long periods at the Cromwell Hotel in Stevenage. From there, while the BBC Symphony Orchestra was winding down its schedule of performances during the last months at Bristol, Henry undertook the long, double train journey (Stevenage to Kings Cross, then Paddington to Bristol) to rehearse and conduct a Saturday afternoon concert at the Colston Hall on 22 February 1941, with Ida Haendel playing the Tchaikovsky concerto. Another, with Albert Sammons playing the Elgar violin concerto, was on Wednesday 11 June.

Wood was familiar enough with the experience of conducting in the Albert Hall on 'outsize' occasions with very large choruses and orchestras, but the adjustment to nightly Proms would need some consideration. On 31 May he went to hear the London Symphony Orchestra's concert there, conducted by Basil Cameron. Playing the third horn, he noticed, was a woman – Livia Gollancz, the daughter of his publisher. 'Dear Miss Gollancz,' he wrote next day from the Cromwell Hotel,

> A year or two ago your father told me you were studying the horn, and at yesterday['s] concert at the Royal Albert Hall, I had the pleasure of seeing you, particularly in the Brahms Second Piano Concerto with LSO.
>
> May I offer my warmest congratulations, your tone and phrasing in the solo passages allotted to the third horn rang splendidly in the body of the Hall – a real achievement for a woman artist – Bravo!
>
> I am proud of the fact that I was the first conductor to introduce women into our professional orchestras in all departments and my confidence and faith in them has never faltered.
>
> Believe me
> Sincerely yours
> Henry J. Wood

358

A woman brass-player was, however, a wartime innovation born of the depletion of male ranks. It was fortunate that such players had been accepted in the orchestras of the music colleges. Wood had indeed forgotten, if he ever knew, that Livia Gollancz had played under his baton in the massed student orchestra at the opening of the Alexandra Palace two years before.

Continuing to help various orchestras survive, Wood accepted two concerts with the Hallé in a single day in North Wales on Sunday 15 June (at Rhyl in the afternoon, Llandudno in the evening), funded by the Carnegie Trust – earning him the very modest fee of 35 guineas for each. At least there was the pleasure of a drive home next day over Llanberis Pass – 'Snowdon perfect', he jotted in the diary. With the Proms due shortly, a radio programme was devoted to him in the BBC's *Scrapbook* series presented by Leslie Baily, a kind of counterpart to television's later *This is Your Life*. Wood had always appeared to dislike public speaking of any sort, but the enjoyment he found under Baily's agreeable guidance perhaps gave him a greater readiness to add words to his music- making henceforth – on special occasions only. One such occasion was to take place at the end of the 1941 Proms.

The promoter, this time not in partnership with Owen Mase, was again Keith Douglas, whose complicated programme-headings managed to involve the Royal Philharmonic Society (again justifying his use of the royal arms) and even the bombed and silent auditorium. He announced 'Sir Henry Wood's / Forty-seventh Season / Of Queen's Hall / Promenade Concerts' at the Royal Albert Hall. The promenade season was scheduled to begin earlier than usual on 5 July to tempt patrons with the longer hours of daylight. Likewise with an eye to the continuing danger of air raids once darkness fell, and also to help audiences to get home before 'blackout time', the concerts would start at 6.30 p.m., changing on 11 August to 6 p.m.

Keith Douglas had taken the move to the Albert Hall seriously and conscientiously, installing a new overhead acoustic screen which reduced the notorious echo and improved the fidelity of sound. It was not surprising that, facing unknown box-office prospects at a larger hall away from the West End, he insisted on the exclusion of new works from the programmes, a decision which had to stand in Wood's name. Dorothy Howell, hoping for the inclusion of her *Divertissement*, one of the casualties of the curtailed 1940 season, received from Wood a letter dated 29 May: 'After grave and earnest consideration we have decided that it would be inadvisable during this purely experimental season to include any new works.'

'Experimental' – because the public's readiness to take to the Albert Hall was supposedly in doubt. The prospect had to be 'sold', as in an article headed PROMS AGAIN in the *Radio Times* of 4 July to introduce the BBC's coming selection of concerts to be broadcast:

> Of course the real advantage of the Albert Hall for the present series of Proms is the size of the auditorium. Latterly, at Queen's Hall, as we all know, there was never a promenade in the real sense of the word. Sometimes the hall was so packed that there was no room to move an arm, let alone stroll about! Here there will be plenty of room to breathe, and incidentally this will perhaps leave the St John Ambulance men freer for more vital work!
>
> Lastly, there is the interval. Instead of the busy thoroughfare of Langham Place, there are the cool gardens of Kensington. As Sir Henry remarked: 'It only remains for Prom-goers to acquire the habit of going to the Albert Hall. Then all will be much as before.'
>
> Certainly the programmes will be as before, though it may be noticed, possibly with regret in many quarters, that there is an absence of novelties. The explanation is the inevitable one: at the best of times the public is not interested in new music, particularly British, and now, at the worst of times, the box office must be considered.

That last sentiment must have irked Wood. Had forty-five years of pioneering implanted no taste for the new? But shrewd observers realized that wartime hunger for orchestral music was a hunger for the emotional assurance of 'the classics' – a series apparently terminated by Sibelius and Rachmaninoff. Though excluding absolutely new works, the 1941 prospectus at least had room for Bax as well as Bach. Among performers, Cyril Smith and Phyllis Sellick – husband and wife, hitherto pursuing entirely separate careers – were invited by Wood to make their first appearance as duo-pianists in Saint-Saëns' *Carnival of the Animals* on the opening night, the beginning of a famous concert partnership which continued even after Smith lost the use of his left arm in 1965.

As in 1940 the orchestra was the London Symphony Orchestra, led by George Stratton. But this time a major change was made in the appearance of Basil Cameron as a regular associate conductor, sometimes taking over the first or second 'half' of a programme from Wood, sometimes simply an item or two. The reason was obviously the anxiety over Wood's health, as he faced thirty-seven different programmes in a row, with daily rehearsals. One may grant sympathy towards Wood's attempts to mask the onset of the years. To C. B. Rees, a journalist who was to write much (and always with love and admiration) about him, he wrote on 16 July 1941 that he was 'certainly not feeling aged or ill':

My sole reason is that I want to accustom my public to have another conductor on the rostrum, otherwise what is to happen, when the natural course is run, and I am no more? I want to be assured that these concerts will proceed as they have done all these years, and remain, as they have been, the Cradle of Music in England – and I should not be honestly doing my duty by them, did I not endeavour to introduce a colleague.

The idea that a successor needed to be introduced piecemeal in such a manner can have deceived no one.

In advance of the season, Douglas upset Wood by pushing leading soloists to reduce their fees, as a recognition of his own financial difficulties of wartime enterprise. Most artists capitulated, but Solomon (through his agent, E. A. Michell) refused. With the utmost delicacy Wood wrote to Solomon as 'my dear friend' on 17 May: 'Do not think for a moment I *suggest* that any artist should reduce his fee . . . [but] it is obviously difficult to carry on when such heavy inroads are made on finances of those undertaking the management.' To Douglas, Wood maintained that Solomon *must* be engaged whatever his fee; but Douglas, having persuaded Hess, Moiseiwitsch and Pouishnoff to reduce their fee to 25 guineas, would make no exception for anyone else. Wood then asked Solomon whether he might accept 30 guineas if the other artists 'upped' their rate, and offered to pay the difference out of his own pocket. Solomon would have none of it; and, beneath Wood's keen regret at the absence of such a friend and public favourite from his prospectus, one senses his admiration for a properly professional stand.

Believing with some justice that he was always liable to be outsmarted by those whose business was business, Wood had always shunned an involvement in the financial management of his concerts. But as a condition of Keith Douglas and Owen Mase's 1940 enterprise he had been obliged to become a guarantor, and now accepted a like obligation for the 1941 season. Douglas seems to have held over Wood's head the threat to close down the series if the concerts failed to make enough at the box office – which, by contract, he was quite entitled to do. But the concerts did well and the six-week season suffered no closure, either through finance or through enemy action. For reasons not entirely clear, Wood developed an increasing animosity towards Douglas and his methods of management.

For the first time in his forty-seven seasons of promenade concerts, Wood decided to make a last-night speech to the audience on 16 August – and, in thanking all other collaborators, deliberately omitted Douglas's name. Resentment at that insult naturally hardened Douglas's attitude when, the season once over, a wrangle began about what was owed to the conductor. As usual avoiding face-to-face disputes, Wood resorted to calling on the services of his solicitor and friend, Stanley Rubinstein. To Rubinstein fell the duty of attempting to see justice done between his two 'Brother Savages' – Wood himself having become a member of the Savage Club, that haunt and circle of so many well-known men in the arts, the press and the law.

To Douglas's enterprise Wood had given a guarantee of £100 for each of the six weeks of the season, in the form of not immediately claiming the £100 due as his weekly fee for conducting. Douglas, though he had made a profit on the season, wished to balance that profit against a loss on the curtailed 1940 season, entitling him to diminish the £600 which Wood claimed as his due. Only after a prolonged postal siege by Rubinstein on Wood's behalf, with some savage rather than Savage-like personal exchanges between Rubinstein and Douglas, did Wood get (four months later, in December!) his £600. Rather unnecessarily, Wood had protested, in a letter to Rubinstein of 27 October, that the 1941 arrangements had been 'forced upon me against my own better judgement'. In truth Wood had been desperately anxious not to see 'his' Proms disappear beneath the waves of wartime, and only Keith Douglas had offered him a lifeline.

After the Douglas discomfiture, another followed. The centenary of Dvořák's birth, falling on 8 September 1941, was to be honoured by three concerts and by the participation of Jan Masaryk, the Foreign Minister of the London-based government-in-exile of Czechoslovakia. As a member of the organising committee, Wood had expected to be asked to conduct the final concert at the Albert Hall, following concerts under Sargent and Boult. But Basil Cameron ('not as innocent as he would like us to think', wrote Jessie to Stanley Rubinstein) allowed his name to go forward. Wood resigned from the committee.

If there were tensions here, they arose from Wood's understandable fear that offers of engagement would steadily diminish because organisers *perceived* him to be weaker (whether he was 'really' so or not) and would be increasingly worried about whether he would be able to appear on the platform as promised. How pleasant, then, to receive from Sir Hugh Allen an invitation of the utmost cordiality 'to play to your own people' – meaning Oxford University, of which he had become an honorary Doctor of Music fifteen years before. The fee, 'in view of the [small] size of the Sheldonian Theatre', would be 30 guineas. He fulfilled that engagement, for which the London Symphony Orchestra was engaged, on a Thursday afternoon, 23

October 1941. But he detected a drying-up of engagements originating from the LSO itself, and blamed that on a meddling Keith Douglas.

Without emulating Beecham's prolonged absence from Britain while the hardships of war lasted, Wood might well have taken an opportunity of 'ambassadorial' trips abroad. But he had declined an invitation to be guest conductor of the Vancouver Symphony Orchestra for the 1940–1 season, on the ground that 'my place is here'; he declined a similar invitation from the Australian Broadcasting Corporation to conduct its symphony orchestras at a time of his own choice between April and October 1942. A more bizarre offer, likewise declined but only after some deliberation, had invited him to raise 'at least one million dollars' for the British war effort by touring the United States with a young violinist, Grisha Goluboff, and by appearing in a Hollywood film in which he would act the part of a young violinist's (Goluboff's) conductor-father.

He would, nevertheless, find himself in an almost ambassadorial role without leaving home. Although the United States was not to enter the war until December 1941 after the Japanese attack on Pearl Harbor, the economic support initiated by President Roosevelt under the provisions of 'Lend-Lease' was publicly acknowledged. The American composer John Alden Carpenter's *Song of Faith* had been introduced to Britain on Independence Day (4 July) in a BBC broadcast, Leslie Woodgate conducting, and now reached London at an 'Anglo-American concert' during the Proms. Once again Wood had enlisted the Alexandra Choir and afterwards wrote to its conductor, Charles Proctor, that he had 'nothing but praise' for its performance. At that concert (5 August), ending with 'The Star-Spangled Banner' as well as 'God Save the King', Wood handed over to Cameron only the conducting of Samuel Barber's Symphony no.1.

The cause of even more conspicuous musical salutes, however, was the Soviet Union's entry into the war on 22 June 1941. It took some time – and not a little logistical difficulty – for a new wave of Soviet works to reach British programmes, but Russian music as a whole took on a new resonance. With the BBC Symphony Orchestra at Bedford (giving public concerts at the Corn Exchange and using the hall of Bedford School as an extra studio), Wood made his first appearance on 1 October with the overture to Rimsky-Korsakov's *Ivan the Terrible*, Stravinsky's *Firebird* Suite, the prelude to Musorgsky's *Khovanshchina* and Tchaikovsky's Fourth Symphony. Such an all-Russian (but curiously non-Soviet) programme must have awoken for him an echo of his early pioneering of the Russian repertory at bygone Queen's Hall.

Celebrating

For transmissions not involving its own orchestra the BBC still commanded studio space in London but, incredible as it seems, was still not using the facility of recording and replay in order to cater for overseas listeners. When the time-displacement from Greenwich so dictated, the orchestra had to work at all hours. At 11 p.m. on 9 October Wood and the London Symphony Orchestra were in the Paris Cinema, Regent Street, for a balance test prior to a transmission in the BBC's North American Service. The programme itself followed at 1.10 a.m.: Smyth's overture *The Boatswain's Mate*; Vaughan Williams's *Serenade to Music* in its orchestra-only arrangement, and Elgar's *Pomp and Circumstance* no.1. A room at the Hyde Park Hotel enabled Wood to sleep for what was left of the rest of that night, after which he and Jessie returned to Hove to take up residence in their flat. When conducting for the BBC at Bedford he frequently stayed in a hotel there or at the Cromwell Hotel at Stevenage.

The daily engagement diary, which continued to have entries in both Henry's and Jessie's hand (often supplemented by her *after* the event), indicates a significant new commitment on 30 October: 'Anglo-Soviet Public Relations Committee, emergency meeting, 2.30 sharp, 1 Grosvenor Place'. A later date (21 November) has 'Cannot attend Anglo-Soviet Committee': it was a Friday, when Wood's regular rehearsals with the orchestra of the Royal Academy of Music continued to carry absolute priority for him. But the result was to involve Anglo-Soviet relations at a high level, preluded by a BBC communication of 11 December, addressed to Wood at the Cromwell Hotel: 'This is to confirm that you are conducting the BBC Symphony in a Studio Concert in honour of Stalin's birthday in the Overseas Service on Sunday 21 December from 2.30–3.15 p.m. and at 10.38–11.25 p.m. in a repeat of the same programme on the Home Service – both broadcasts to come from Bedford.'

The overture to Glinka's *Ruslan and Lyudmila* was followed by Shostakovich's *Salute to Life* and Dunayevsky's *Song of Freedom* (two works in popular Soviet vein) then by Balakirev's *Russia* and a suite from Prokofiev's *Alexander Nevsky*. The presence at the afternoon concert of Agnes Maisky, wife of the Soviet Ambassador, and the sight of 'the stalwart Russian soldiers and sailors entering the Corn Exchange' was recalled by the music critic of the *Bedfordshire Times*, J. H. M. Sykes, in an article marking the orchestra's eventual farewell to Bedford in October 1945. An unattributed quotation in Nicholas Kenyon's book on the BBC Symphony Orchestra merely notes 'an invited audience of munition workers and members of the Russian Embassy'.

Kenyon astonishingly fails to name the conductor. Reginald Pound's biography of Wood goes one better in not even mentioning the event at all. But it was surely a historic occasion when the conductor who had warned the BBC against subversive Communist infiltration in 1938 hymned Stalin in December 1941. This was, of course, no more and no less remarkable a turn-round than had been executed by the British establishment as a whole – and by Churchill in pursuit of the aims of the war.

Wood complied with a request to send a message for the first issue of *Britansky Soyuznik* (*British Ally*), the magazine sponsored by the British Government for circulation from Moscow. He sent, via Ivan Maisky as the Soviet Ambassador, a cheque to the Soviet Red Cross and lent his name (though not his presence) to a celebration of Soviet National Day on 7 November 1942 at the Empress Hall, Earls Court. That was exceptional, and plainly prompted by his musical involvement. In general, Henry J. Wood remained as aloof from the actual struggles of war as he had during 1914–18. Jessie Wood comes as near as she ever did to exasperation in writing (in *The Last Years of Henry J. Wood*, 1954):

> He would not read newspapers unless some incident in music, art or science was brought to his notice. I doubt if he would ever have known much of the sad or brutal things – murders and so forth – happening in the world if someone had not discussed reports of them during conversation with him. So aloof was he from the daily Press that I urged him to read either *The Times* or *Daily Telegraph* leaders during the war. This he did because it was asked of him. But throughout the war I do not remember even a single comment, much less a discussion, on the progress of our arms, except about the weary length of the war for everybody.

Projects for future performances of works too big for wartime revival, including Mahler's Second and Eighth Symphonies, continued to occupy him, as did the pursuit of 'worthwhile new music' (Jessie's phrase). Simple patriotism, however, coupled with a consciousness of his own symbolic position, made its call. Along with such theatrical stars as Sybil Thorndike, Edith Evans, Leslie Howard and Eric Portman, he took part without fee in a daytime spectacle of national pride, 'Cathedral Steps', outside St Paul's on 24 September 1942, conducting the Alexandra Choir.

Wood's own battle of Bournemouth – to promote the restoration of a permanent symphony orchestra there – was able to register at least an interim victory. A new mayor, beset by a press campaign on this question, proved receptive. On 16 April 1942 Wood reappeared at the head of a partially replenished Bournemouth Municipal Orchestra – making it clear that this was to be regarded as a step towards the sixty-one players he considered essential for a symphonic sound. Again he sacrificed his fee, as he had done for the temporary Wessex Symphony Orchestra.

Meanwhile his continuing association with the BBC led to the fulfilment of a cherished wish – that the Proms should return to the BBC fold. Its bureaucracy might annoy, but there was a conscience to be appealed to. Wood found a sympathetic ear in the BBC's Controller of Programmes, B. E. Nicolls, who as 'Dear Benjie' was to remain a confidant of Jessie's long after Wood's death. By the end of 1941 the arrangements for the 1942 Proms under the BBC's management were in train, subject to the agreement of Reginald Askew, manager of the Albert Hall. Wood's fee would be, as in 1939, £2300 for the series.

There was to be one completely new feature. The undertaking of the whole series by a single orchestra was, for the first time, abandoned. The London Philharmonic was engaged for the first four weeks, the BBC Symphony for the remaining four. Basil Cameron would again be the associate conductor for the first four, but Boult would fill that role for the second. The associate conductors would always take a complete 'half' of the concert – sometimes the first half, sometimes the second, but not just an item or two at a time. Wood was given the proper glory of conducting the whole of the opening concert, and all three conductors would share the final night. In a letter of 23 February 1942 to Boult he declared himself determined to put behind him the unhappy experiences of the previous season under Keith Douglas's management, and welcome Boult's participation: 'I am happy and confident that the second month of the forthcoming season of Promenade Concerts at the Royal Albert Hall will be a real joy and pleasure.'

Yes! I am meeting Mr [Julian] Herbage and Mr [W. W.] Thompson tomorrow (Tuesday) morning to lay my plans and suggestions, and my list of British novelties, and I do hope, a short time after this, when my plans have been licked into shape, that you will be able to attend the meeting, and give your advice and suggestions.

We must all thank Lady Wood for bringing Promenade matters to a head for she conceived the idea of interviewing Mr Askew and securing the Hall for three years, *I* think a splendid gesture on her part, I should never have had the courage.

Your kind offer about rehearsals will be most helpful. . .

Jessie had, indeed, pulled off a managerial *coup*. The Albert Hall was the only place where promenade concerts could be held, and for the next three summers Wood had an option on it. His hope, but by no means an assured one, was that the BBC would continue to promote the enterprise. But, if they did not, he was free to seek an alternative management (certainly not Keith Douglas's!), and the BBC could not present the Proms *without him*, as he must always have suspected they might wish to. In his view the Proms as an institution were *his*. The BBC were too wary in legal and managerial practice to let such a point be taken for granted. The 1942 prospectus was issued under the heading:

The BBC presents
SIR HENRY WOOD'S
48th season of Queen's Hall
PROMENADE CONCERTS

That was a large step away from naming them the 'Henry Wood Promenade Concerts'. The inclusion of the words 'Queen's Hall' conformed to Wood's own desires – after all, Queen's Hall would surely be rebuilt and the Proms resume their proper residence!

Boult was in fact now able to take on a larger commitment as conductor. Arthur Bliss, who had been living in the United States (his wife was American), had cabled at the beginning of the war offering to return to Britain in the service of the BBC in London, and in April 1941 had been put in charge of its Overseas Music Department. He then made, without pretence of modesty, a proposal that he should be promoted to the post of Director of Music, taking over Adrian Boult's administrative load and leaving him free to concentrate on the baton. 'I have had an interview with Ogilvie, the chief Pooh-Bah,' wrote Bliss to his wife on 31 August, 'but I doubt whether I rise to such eminence immediately.' Boult had welcomed the proposal and Bliss was confirmed as Director of Music in April 1942. By then Pooh-Bah had split himself into two with a positively Gilbertian facility: Ogilvie had retired, and R. W. Foot and Cecil Graves were appointed joint Directors-General.

Though still based at Bedford, the BBC Symphony Orchestra came to London for the first time since the outbreak of war to present two Albert Hall concerts in a series 'under the patronage of the Allied Governments and the British Council'. That on 28 May included the British première of what was to become *the* representative American symphony of its time, Roy Harris's Third, conducted by Boult; at the concert on 4 June, Wood was to have introduced to Britain Shostakovich's Symphony no.7, the so-called *Leningrad* Symphony. The composer had begun it in Leningrad itself under Nazi siege in the previous autumn, completing it in the temporary Soviet capital, Kuibyshev on the Volga, where it was first performed on 1 March 1942.

But the score and parts failed to arrive in time for the Albert Hall date. So, in place of the BBC Symphony Orchestra, the London Symphony Orchestra was engaged to give the postponed performance of the Shostakovich symphony – as a broadcast before a small invited audience, not at Bedford but in the BBC's main London orchestral studio at Maida Vale. The date chosen was 22 June, the first anniversary of the entry of the Soviet Union into the war.

The score had arrived on 900 slides of microfilm and was discovered to be riddled with errors: in the Woods' diary for 17 June Jessie noted 'H. and copyist working on Shostakovich mistakes'. On the following two days the diary noted 'copyists' in the plural, sent by the publishing firm of Novello to the Woods' flat in Hove in a race to have the work ready for rehearsal. The Woods were about to move from their seaside home. They stayed at the Cadogan Hotel in London until the end of the promenade season, and thereafter took up residence in their new, and Henry's last, permanent home. It was a commodious flat at 63 Harley House, almost next to the Royal Academy of Music, with the green and flowered Regent's Park at the rear. London was no longer felt to be under the immediate threat of bombing, though the blackout remained.

Disaster threatened the *Leningrad* Symphony's première when the work was calculated as too long for the hour's broadcast allotted by the BBC. The performance was to be immediately followed by the 9 p.m. news – a totally unalterable, unpostponable programme in time of war (and long after). If the performance were not finished, it would simply be faded out. 'How Henry sweated over this,' wrote Jessie later, 'cutting short the intervals [pauses between movements?] and closing in on passages where he would have liked a little less rigidity.' He must also have made actual cuts to bring within an hour a work normally taking 75–80 minutes. At the final bar, 'he looked up at the huge studio clock and could hardly wait for the red light to fade before he said with great glee and a broad smile: "We've done it! And not a second either way."'

In the studio were Ambassador Maisky and his wife as well as Sir Stafford Cripps, lately British Ambassador to Moscow and now 'the dominant figure' (as A. J. P. Taylor calls him) in the Coalition Government, after Churchill himself. Not merely the first performance of the work in Britain but the first anywhere outside the Soviet Union, the occasion must be counted as a peak of all Wood's roll-call of new music. Indeed the achievement at the age of seventy-three with Shostakovich's symphony, amid the extraordinary pressures of wartime music-making, can be said to be no less remarkable than that of the forty-three-year-old conductor with Schoenberg's *Five Pieces for Orchestra* in its première of 1912.

Not without a grumble, Wood had to miss his customary holiday period because the BBC set the opening of the Proms even earlier than Douglas had done – Saturday 27 June – in order to make the most of the hours of daylight. For the same reason, as in 1941, the concerts started at 6.30, then for the last two weeks (from 10 August) at 6 p.m. Solomon was back – need it be said? – to join such other favourite pianists as Moiseiwitsch, Hess and Curzon, each of them appearing more than once. But soloists no longer played non-orchestral items in the second 'half'; the prospectus no longer named an 'accompanist' for the singers. The Albert Hall may well have been thought unsuitably large for such solo items.

Wood had always found stimulus and pride in presenting new and younger artists, but the larger-than-usual presence of veteran soloists in the 1942 roster showed all too well how the call of the Services almost strangled the flow of new talent, male and female. But when holding auditions for the Proms he had been 'completely bowled over', in Jessie's words, by the tone and technique of a young contralto, Janet Howe – and by her handsome appearance also, always a legitimate asset for a concert artist in Wood's eyes. It was rare in those days for a British artist to be heard in the two-octave coloratura dazzle of the final *rondò* from Rossini's *La Cenerentola* (*Cinderella*), as Howe was heard on 30 June, the first of her two appearances that season.

Wood was two years off his 'Proms Jubilee', the fiftieth season, but in programming Tatyana's 'Letter Song' from Tchaikovsky's *Yevgeny Onegin* he must have remembered that it was fifty years since he had introduced the opera itself to Britain. Nevertheless he made no sentimental occasion of it: sung by Oda Slobodskaya, a Russian soprano long settled in Britain, the item fell in Basil Cameron's half of the programme on 4 July. It was more important to Wood that he should conduct the 'first performance' of that night – a *Circus* Suite by Mary Anderson Lucas, who thus achieved her Proms 'début' at the age of sixty.

As the opening item of the whole season Wood delivered John Ireland's new *Epic March*. After the previous season's nil score in premières, it looked praiseworthy that the BBC should have scheduled eighteen first performances – if one counted Britten's *Sinfonia da Requiem*, already performed in the United States, and Alan Rawsthorne's new, fuller orchestration of his Piano Concerto no.1. By Wood's own standards, however, the deficiency was obvious: no new music by non-British composers, save for Aaron Copland's ballet suite, *Billy the Kid*. Characteristically adventurous, Wood himself took on that work, as well as the new violin concerto of E. J. Moeran, a composer much admired at the time, and Ruth Gipps's *Knight in Armour* (on the final night). The remaining premières of the season were conducted either by their composers or by Boult and Cameron, and are wrongly attributed to Wood's baton in Reginald Pound's and Jessie Wood's books.

The Promenaders also heard the *Leningrad* Symphony – in a repetition on 29 June, substituted by Wood for the announced Tchaikovsky's Fourth. The Maiskys again attended. 'Audience seemed most interested,' commented Wood himself in notes which he made on that season's performances (and the box-office takings). Characteristically, Wood's next step was to send a letter to Shostakovich inviting him to conduct his next symphony in the 1943 Proms: 'I should like to shake you by the hand, a young member of our fraternity of musicians.' Though the blatancy of its 'heroic' vein became a target of criticism - its march-theme being famously parodied in Bartók's *Concerto for Orchestra* – the symbolic impact of the *Leningrad* Symphony at the time, in the United States as well as in Britain, is a matter of record.

To immense relief all round, no concert had to be shortened or cancelled through enemy action. Having set a precedent for a last-night speech in the previous season, he could hardly refuse this time to thank his collaborators and his audience – including his radio audience. Jessie Wood kept a recording of the broadcast:

> My dear friends, this brings our glorious season to a close. It has been one of extremely happy co-operation with my colleagues, Mr Basil Cameron and Sir Adrian Boult, the London Philharmonic Orchestra and the BBC Symphony Orchestra. Before bidding you adieu, I must thank you and tell you what a wonderful audience you are. How you listen! Your attention is so encouraging and exhilarating. We look forward to meeting next year in this great old hall. . . I hope [at this point, Jessie noted, the audience interrupted with shrieks of delight, and Wood paused before adding] I hope, in days of peace.

Immediately afterwards, the *Daily Mail* left its readers in no doubt of the public enthusiasm:

> Millions of listeners to the BBC broadcast of the concert heard a quarter of an hour of the cheering that followed the final flick of Sir Henry's baton.
>
> And after the BBC switched off, the cheering, stamping, clapping of the audience went on for another 15 minutes.

The notes which Wood himself made as a reference for the future would have dismayed some of the soloists, had they read them. Pouishnoff: 'Never heard him play so badly'; 'Isobel Baillie has certainly gone off!' Even the admired Moiseiwitsch merited an ironical comment: 'Very fine [in Beethoven's Piano Concerto no.3], no slips, technique firm and sure (for a wonder).' Eileen Joyce: 'Such a poor performance [of Rachmaninoff's Piano Concerto no.2], her opening solo full of wrong notes. We never want her again. No good in concertos.' Nevertheless the popularity of that concerto and that performer had obviously helped to swell the box-office to an unusually large £612; Elgar's Cello Concerto, even with Beatrice Harrison to play it, was *not* then a popular work and the takings that night, with Noel Mewton-Wood playing Prokofiev's Piano Concerto no.3, were down to £272.

The Proms over, Wood not only fulfilled more guest engagements with the BBC Symphony Orchestra at Bedford, but also resumed the Sunday afternoon concerts begun earlier with the London Philharmonic Orchestra in the Albert Hall. They were promoted by Harold Holt, an impresario then personally managing the firm which long afterwards retained his name. There was some clever programme-planning here. On 25 October, between the *First* Symphony of Shostakovich and the crowd-pulling Tchaikovsky *Pathétique,* Wood presented his new discovery, Janet Howe, in the 'farewell' aria from Tchaikovsky's *The Maid of Orleans*, and the ever-admired Ida Haendel in Wieniawski's Violin Concerto no.1.

In his diary for 13 May 1942 had stood the reminder: 'Sullivan Centenary actual date'. (Sullivan, the leading British composer during Wood's first three decades, was born on 13 May 1842.) On Wood's own initiative, Holt's Sunday afternoon concert on 10 May became a 'Sullivan Centenary Festival' – the heading being printed in the programme in suitably Victorian Gothic type. Sullivan's Leeds Festival cantata *The Golden Legend* (1886) formed the first half, and was broadcast: Wood had reminded the BBC more than a year before that he was 'the only musician living who had daily contact with Sir Arthur Sullivan as an accompanist'.

Celebrating

In the second half of the concert were 'The Lost Chord', vocal selections from *Ivanhoe* and the Savoy Operas, and Sullivan's *In Memoriam* Overture. The soloists with the Alexandra Choir and the LPO were Joan Hammond, Astra Desmond, Muriel Brunskill, Henry Wendon, Dennis Noble (five front-rank names) and Leyland White.

Sullivan and Shostakovich! – it was a combination for 1942 which enshrined the musical range and character of Henry J. Wood.

Chapter 23

Ending

1943–4

OUR DEEPEST SYMPATHY GOES OUT TO YOU IN YOUR SORROW
STOP I MOURN YOUR DEAR HUSBAND NOT ONLY AS A FRIEND
BUT AS AN IRREPLACEABLE FIGURE IN THE WORLD OF MUSIC
STOP WE SHALL MISS HIM BUT HIS NAME WILL LIVE FOR ALL
TIME

Henry J. Wood's telegram was sent to 'Madame Sergi [*sic*] Rachmaninoff'
with no other address than 'Beverly Hills, California' on 29 March 1943. The
greatest composer-pianist of this century had died of 'a virulent, rapid
cancer' the previous day at the age of sixty-nine. No keener intimation of
mortality could have been provided for the British conductor who had just
passed his seventy-fourth birthday.

Throughout 1943 his role on the rostrum was conspicuous. At Liverpool,
not Russian but Chinese war relief claimed his services – China being, in a
loose sense, an ally of Britain by virtue of the separate Japanese hostilities
against both. Yehudi Menuhin, an American citizen, had volunteered to fly to
Britain exclusively to give concerts for war charities and was to have arrived
in time for an Aid to China concert on 14 March with the Liverpool
Philharmonic Orchestra. His plane was forced back. 'I am just as sorry as you
are that a very great artist is not playing this afternoon,' Wood told the
assembled audience on Sunday 14 March, promising that he and Menuhin
would appear instead on 23 March. And so they did (the violin concertos
were Mendelssohn's and Elgar's), neither taking a fee.

With Liverpool, however, Wood's wartime links were tenuous. It was the
Hallé Orchestra of Manchester, grateful for the touring which he had already
undertaken with them, that offered him the post of conductor-in-chief. R. J.
Forbes, a leading member of the Hallé committee and principal of the Royal
Manchester College of Music, wrote to Jessie on 30 March expressing the
hope that Henry would decide to live in the area during the season, 'as

Under the Patronage of

HER MAJESTY THE QUEEN

and

H. M. THE KING OF THE HELLENES

Concert

given for the benefit of

ROYAL   NAVAL   WAR   LIBRARIES

by

MYRA HESS

SIR HENRY WOOD

and the

LONDON   SYMPHONY   ORCHESTRA

Leader : GEORGE STRATTON

The Concert has the full support of

THE BOARD OF ADMIRALTY

Wednesday Evening, April 14th

ANALYTICAL
PROGRAMME

IBBS & TILLETT
124 Wigmore St. W.1

One of many wartime charity concerts (1943): Myra Hess played Beethoven's *Emperor* concerto and Franck's *Symphonic Variations*. Unusually, Wood concluded the programme with three movements from his celebrated *Fantasia on British Sea Songs*.

374

Richter used to do'. But Wood knew the physical demands of the post were beyond him and in a letter of 13 April recommended Basil Cameron and, among younger conductors meriting consideration, Richard Austin and Ian Whyte. He continued: 'Boult? Well, he might give up the BBC in favour of the Hallé, and I for one know that were such a swap offered me, I should plank [sic] for the Hallé, with the great musical tradition to live up to and live with, a joy and privilege given to few.'

All this time, as he cannot have realized, the Hallé management had been negotiating for the services of John Barbirolli, who since 1936 had been conductor of the New York Philharmonic as Toscanini's successor, and whose wish to return home to Britain was known. On 17 April 1943, as soon as Barbirolli's acceptance was announced, Wood congratulated the Hallé management on its choice of 'John Barbarolli' [sic], who had been, at sixteen, the youngest cellist in the Queen's Hall Orchestra. In the New York orchestra's annals the Barbirolli years are accounted pretty much of a disaster; with the Hallé and his new public he was a miracle-working saviour, to be hailed as 'Glorious John' in Vaughan Williams's inscription on the manuscript of his Eighth Symphony.

Wood likewise put forward Basil Cameron's name as his successor in what he foresaw as an early ending to his long, conscientious stewardship of the senior orchestra at the Royal Academy of Music. Sir Stanley Marchant, principal of the Academy since 1936, was not impressed by the suggestion – and indeed Wood's commendation of Cameron as 'a quiet, very nice man' hardly suggested the temperament required.

With the BBC Symphony Orchestra, still based at Bedford, he gave once again his 'traditional' Good Friday performance of *The Dream of Gerontius* – a public as well as broadcast performance on 23 April at the Corn Exchange. Janet Howe, Parry Jones and Dennis Noble were the soloists. In his audience was the twenty-seven-year-old Charles Groves, who had lately been appointed conductor of the BBC Revue Orchestra. Almost fifty years afterwards Groves recalled that performance of *Gerontius*: 'It was so beautiful . . . That was the last thing I ever heard him conduct and it remains in my memory. It's a performance I could model myself on: it was so true.' Like many others, Charles Groves had been initiated into orchestral music by a boyhood immersion in Wood's Proms and had noted the unusually long baton and the bold sweep of the conductor's gestures: 'The point of the stick came over his back and almost touched him on the shoulders, it was so long.'

On Sunday afternoons, a popular time for London concerts, the London

Celebrating

Symphony Orchestra embarked on a series of concerts at the Cambridge Theatre under the management of Jay Pomeroy. To make up its war-depleted ranks of string-players the orchestra was obliged to seek reinforcement from music students, one of whom was Hugo Cole, later to be a music critic for the *Guardian*. As an orchestral cellist between 1942 and 1944 he played not only under Wood's baton but under those of Malcolm Sargent, Basil Cameron, Albert Coates, Adrian Boult, George Weldon and John Barbirolli. He set down his recollections especially for this book:

> The wartime LSO was not a good orchestra, and many of the older players were tired, jaundiced and bitterly critical of conductors. Sargent and Cameron were actively disliked, Boult was thought to be – and was – boring (he wasn't at his best in one-rehearsal LSO concerts). But I never heard a word of criticism of Henry Wood, and the orchestra played consistently better for him than for any other of the above-mentioned conductors (Coates conducted one or two marvellous concerts, also some where everything seemed to go wrong).
>
> Wood could be testy but never bullied individual players, never wasted time and gave many helpful cues: his large and clear beat defied one to come in wrong. If an inexperienced player did, in spite of that, make a wrong entry, he was quick as a knife in getting things back on course – no doubt having learned the art in conducting many practically unrehearsed concerts. I was much surprised one day when he stopped in the aisle during the rehearsal interval and made some kindly remark to me, which none of the other supposedly great men would have deigned to do. Of the conductors mentioned, Boult, Cameron and Coates all threw quite dramatic fits of temperament at certain rehearsals in which I was involved; but Wood, never.
>
> He seemed to me magnificent in Tchaikovsky and in Beethoven, and in unfamiliar Russian music which we played at one wartime festival.

Two days after that Good Friday performance of *Gerontius* at Bedford, Wood was at the Albert Hall for another Sunday afternoon performance. This time it was under Harold Holt's management with the London Philharmonic Orchestra and with Katharine Goodson in that unsinkable favourite, Tchaikovsky's Piano Concerto no.1. The programme ended with Beethoven's Symphony no.7 – 'the most tiring work to direct, with not a let-up anywhere', as he told Jessie. Should he have been accepting two such engagements so closely spaced? The price was heavy. Hardly had Jessie taken him away for a few days' quiet at her daughter's home when he became delirious.

Suddenly, about one o'clock in the morning after our arrival, he insisted that a wind was blowing over his face – which was quite possible in the old oak-beamed house. I quickly obtained hot-water bottles and a screen with the help of that dear, kind family, but in half an hour a rigor intervened. Henry was soon delirious, sitting up in bed directing an orchestra, demanding attention in a stentorian voice such as no living orchestra had ever heard from him. We soon had our dear Dr Skeggs in from Stevenage, who in turn asked Lord Horder to come, which of course he did, and with the efficient help of the local nurse managed to cope with that foretold breakdown.

'Of course he did': Horder had become a warm friend of the Woods, and later that year sent 'Greetings, and my love, to two of the nicest people left in this mad world'. The Stevenage-based Dr Basil Skeggs was likewise both physician and friend. Two weeks' enforced rest was all Wood permitted himself: on 15 May he was back at the Albert Hall conducting the BBC Symphony Orchestra at a charity concert in aid of the Red Cross. It was a Saturday afternoon concert with two of the finest soloists, Eva Turner and Solomon – the Bax overture slipped in so as to give him a refresher before conducting it (with another orchestra) on the opening night of the 1943 Proms:

Overture, *A London Pageant*	Bax
'Ritorna vincitor' (*Aida*)	Verdi
Piano Concerto no.5 ('Emperor')	Beethoven
'In questa reggia' (*Turandot*)	Puccini
Symphony no.4	Tchaikovsky

In the form in which he jotted down the programme in advance in his diary, the composer of the *second* aria is also given as Verdi: a mental slip barely conceivable in Wood's earlier years. That his physical power was also dangerously liable to slip is evident in a letter which he was surely unwise to send to Adrian Boult after the performance (and the rehearsal on the same day) of the above programme:

Of your kindness on Saturday, I cannot but say thank you for the peace of mind you afforded me and the comfort you brought to Lady Wood, for she knew as well as I did, that my legs were very groggy, after a fortnight in bed. To give up your whole day was wonderfully kind, and to listen all day to such a stereotyped programme, made your generous contribution to my safety and comfort all the greater.

I am sure I need not tell you – since you were there – that I found the orchestra strangely unresponsive and inattentive – a fact which perhaps reflects tiredness either owing to an early morning, or to their recent travels. For instance, the Bax went reasonably well with what little rehearsal we had at our command, but what happened in the afternoon I fail to understand, unless someone had tampered with the desks after the rehearsal. I noticed with alarm that there was an exchange of parts in progress during the first part of the work!! – (first violins desks 1 & 2). Then Tchaikovsky, I could not get them to play the pizzicato movement as I directed it, in spite of my very definite markings – perhaps they thought 'this is old Wood's marking', but even so, they are there to do what is asked of them, never mind what, and my requests are never indefinite. As for getting the climax of tone on the seventh bar of this movement, well, they just want to play everything straight through. I may say here that all the markings throughout No 4, are notes made by myself on the spot, when Tchaikovsky directed the work in London at St James's Hall, in 1893.

No one could be more disposed than Boult to make allowances for Wood, but in an internal BBC memorandum he was candid:

The trouble was that he had badly over-rehearsed them in the morning, and they were thoroughly bored with the whole thing, particularly as his performance was listless. I did not hear any of the Tchaikovsky as I was behind the scenes and left at the beginning of the second movement, but Mr Beard himself commented to me on Sir Henry's apparent lack of interest in the Concert. I should very much like to tell him that no orchestra can play a Tchaikovsky symphony well twice in one day, but I suppose it is wiser to say some sweet nothings.

Even after that concert he would cancel only *some* and not all of his promised engagements in the interim period before the Proms were to begin. On 30 May he fulfilled an Albert Hall engagement – again with Solomon, this time in Brahms's Piano Concerto no.1 – under Harold Holt's management; on 7 June he was again at the hall to accompany Moiseiwitsch in three Rachmaninoff concertos at a concert in aid of Mrs Churchill's Aid to Russia Fund. Signing 'Ever yours, Benno M.', the soloist was deeply grateful: 'It was grand and typical of you to collaborate with me last Monday. It was a terrific physical and mental task for you, and I was delighted to see you as fresh at the end as you were at the beginning. It was a great joy to appear with you again.'

A week later he turned over to his deputy, Ernest Read, a concert of his student orchestra at the Royal Academy of Music, but nevertheless came to listen.

As in 1942, so in 1943 the London Philharmonic and BBC Symphony Orchestras were to divide the promenade season, with Basil Cameron and Adrian Boult as the respective associate conductors. Wood on his own, with the LPO, carried the first night, Saturday 19 June. Bax's *A London Pageant* was the first item; Heddle Nash sang, Moura Lympany played, and Wood conducted the first British performance of *A Negro Parade* by the American composer Lamar Stringfield. Sunday brought rest, but on the Monday morning he was back at the Albert Hall to rehearse the first half of the evening's programme, the remainder scheduled to be taken by Basil Cameron. At the concert Wood gave, as planned, Brahms's *Tragic* Overture, accompanied the soprano Noel Eadie in Mozart's *L'amerò, sarò costante* and Myra Hess in Mozart's piano concerto K450 in B flat, and returned to Brahms with the Symphony no.2.

Unusually, Jessie was not watching from the front but waiting at the point where Henry would leave the platform on the way to the conductor's room. She sensed a weakness in the beat, then saw him coming towards her, his body bent to the right: 'Damn silly, I've tried to keep upright, can't understand it . . . I had to direct beneath the desk – I couldn't get my arm up!' Horder prescribed at least a month in bed: the whole of Wood's remaining participation in the Proms was threatened. The prospectus of the whole season had clearly defined 'his' halves of each concert (after the first night), but the individual programmes for each night now simply announced 'Sir Henry Wood's Forty-Ninth Season' and the associate's name, so that the audience did not know whether they would see Wood on the rostrum at all.

Twenty-two consecutive concerts by the London Philharmonic Orchestra, therefore, fell in their entirety to Cameron. The stricken Wood missed the occasions of a tribute to Rachmaninoff and a Grieg centenary concert; he missed giving the first British performance of two Soviet works specially sent over, the *Overture on Russian Folk-Tunes* by Anatoly Alexandrov and the *Festival Overture* by Nikolay Budashkin. He missed a revival of his friend Landon Ronald's vocal scena, *Adonaïs*, with Stiles-Allen, and the first British performance (it had already been given in USA) of Benjamin Britten's *Scottish Ballad*, with the composer and Clifford Curzon as duo-pianists.

On 24 June, he sent a message of 'all possible good luck' to Vaughan Williams, who was to conduct his recent Symphony in D (no.5); 'I cannot tell you how touched I was by your letter,' responded the composer the next day. Wood could not long keep away from 'his' Proms, even when still lacking the strength to conduct them. Beaming, he was photographed in the audience at the Albert Hall, seated in the box which would normally have been at his disposal for guests. That was on 11 July – exceptionally a Sunday, to which the programme of 7 July had been transferred when the Government required the Albert Hall on the earlier date.

On 20 July, three days after the BBC Symphony Orchestra had replaced the LPO on the platform, fervent applause greeted the familiar figure as he remounted the Albert Hall rostrum at last. During the remaining five weeks, he maintained his presence but took charge of fewer items than had been scheduled. On Boult's shoulders fell a correspondingly greater load, including the whole of Wood's remaining quota of *new* works – by Aaron Copland, William Schuman, Aram Khachaturyan, Benjamin Dale and Edmund Rubbra. On 21 August the two orchestras and three conductors combined to end the series with an all-British programme – Wood's items, interspersed with the rest, being the opening *Crown Imperial* (Walton), Mackenzie's *Scottish* Concerto for Piano (Ivey Dickson) and Orchestra, and his own *Fantasia on British Sea Songs*. It was his last 'Last Night', with the *Sea Songs* entrenched in their original, purely orchestral dress and neither a *Pomp and Circumstance* nor a 'Jerusalem' to be heard.

Once again Wood was prevailed on to make a last-night speech to his concert and radio audience – but to save strain he had recorded it in advance. When he returned to the platform, the audience may well have supposed he had been speaking into the microphone from his dressing-room. Singing 'For he's a jolly good fellow', they mobbed his car as he left the Albert Hall.

The 1943 Proms, declared the violinist-turned-critic Ferruccio Bonavia in the *Monthly Musical Record*, had taken more money than any previous series and 'contemporary composers have been given a greater share of the programmes than ever before'. The latter claim was almost certainly untrue, unless Bonavia was calculating no further back than the BBC's first involvement. Around 1900, when 'contemporary composers' included Dvořák, Verdi, Rimsky-Korsakov, Grieg, Strauss and Saint-Saëns (to mention only foreigners), the quota was much higher. But at least the BBC had set the engine of new music awheel again; and whereas a taste for Russian music had never been lacking, a taste for American symphonic music was at last planted.

'The Proms will have their jubilee,' he had assured his last-night audience, in the Albert Hall and on radio. But would they be *his* Proms, not only in 1944 but beyond? He told Nicolls that he was considering the formation of a small private company to be called the Henry Wood Promenade Concerts Ltd, to which he would assign the goodwill subsisting in that name. He was quickly informed that the BBC would not work with or negotiate with such a company. In another unwise letter, he wrote to Nicolls (whom he should have recognized as his champion within the BBC) suggesting that if the BBC would not accept a longer term commitment he might have to go elsewhere. Nicolls was decent enough to reply 'unofficially':

> I was very much disturbed by the threat in your letter about 1945. (You say 'if the BBC . . . I shall feel obliged to offer my services to another management'.) I must say I could hardly believe my eyes when I read this, and I am sure you will realize that no genuine form of co-operation between yourself and the BBC is possible on these lines.

Wood withdrew apologetically, saying he had meant only to tell the BBC he had 'the annual option'.

After the 1943 Proms the baton was put away, the brushes taken out: with Jessie, Henry J. Wood spent his last painting holiday at Beaumaris on the island of Anglesey. It was a joy to contemplate the Snowdonian range across the strait, and a joy afterwards to be 'back in our dear home', as he wrote to his old friend, the baritone Herbert Heyner, on 19 September. 'After my not always happy experiences in a so-called home, the joy and happiness that dear Jessie has fixed up for me during the last few years is a thing I thank God for. I am eternally grateful.'

As an amateur painter he finally achieved recognition from his professional colleagues in an invitation to open the exhibition of the London Group at the Royal Academy of Arts. *Picture Post* in its issue of 13 November 1943 showed him and Jessie in the company of Elliott Seabrook, president of the Group, with such painters as David Bomberg and James Fitton also present at the opening – and Eva Turner, befurred and with lorgnette, examining one of the exhibits. Earlier in the year Wood himself posed in Oxonian academic robes for an official-type portrait by Frank Salisbury (a painter of more traditional outlook than that of the London Group). The original painting was to find its way to the National Portrait Gallery, Salisbury making another copy of his own work which is now in the Royal Academy of Music. An earlier, lounge-suited portrait of Wood by William Rothenstein, likewise in oils, remains in private hands.

To have passed the forty-ninth season of Proms was a relief: the fiftieth was a great event to be looked forward to in 1944. Invitations to send new works went to various composers. Benjamin Britten, just past his thirtieth

birthday, regretted in a letter of 13 December that he had no new orchestral
work to offer:

> I am just embarking on an enormous commitment – the writing of a full-
> length opera, scheduled for performance this next summer in the USA –
> so it doesn't look as if I can possibly get a new work written by the
> beginning of the season. Would you however like the first performance
> of an orchestral excerpt, or some kind of set-piece with voices out of it?
> . . . I am so glad that you are putting down the *Scottish Ballad*
> again . . .
> [P.S.] The title of the opera is *Peter Grimes*.

That may well have been the first mention of the title of the opera 'in public',
though among Britten's own circle of friends it was already spoken of. Wood
jotted on that letter, presumably for the BBC's eventual attention: 'All right
and also play piano concerto'. The opera, which in fact had its first production
not in the United States but at the post-war reopening of Sadler's Wells
Theatre in London, was indeed to yield a famous set of orchestral 'excerpts',
the *Four Sea Interludes*. They never made it, however, into the 1944 Proms
prospectus. Nor did the alcoholic Constant Lambert produce, as he
proposed to do, 'an overture of about the same length as *[Prince] Igor* or
Ivan the Terrible, as I feel the English repertoire is very short of such
pieces'.

Early in 1943 Wood had found among singers auditioning for him a young
contralto called Kathleen Ferrier. After hearing her sing 'Where'er you
walk' from Handel's *Semele* and 'Softly awakes my heart' from *Samson and
Delilah*, he wrote in his notes: 'Nice warm quality of voice, sings well and
deserves a show – should be a success.' Perhaps through BBC doubts of
whether her voice was big enough for the Albert Hall, her name was not on
the roster of singers at either the 1943 or 1944 Proms – though it was in the
first post-Wood season, that of 1945.

He continued to set days or half-days aside for teaching in a London studio,
his recent discovery Janet Howe now joining those who came to him for
advanced study. He found time to reply personally to letters arriving from
Servicemen on active duty. A former promenader, now serving in the Royal
Corps of Signals in the Middle East, told him of the pleasure of being able to
hear Proms by radio and mentioned hearing, while on leave in Cairo, the
concerts given by the visiting Palestine Orchestra (later to become the Israel
Philharmonic). Wood's reply, typed by himself on 26 September, gave news
of a planned scheme which had not yet been released to the newspapers:

Dear Mr Matthews

I am greatly touched that you should write me, and to learn that you are one of my large family of Promenaders.

It was indeed a sad blow when dear old Queen's Hall fell a victim, but we hope to build another or rebuild that same one by means of contributions from my public next year, and which a Committee with Lord Horder in the chair, hope to constitute a memorial to my work for music – for it will be the 50th season in 1944, and my 75th birthday in March of the same year.

I am interested and very glad to hear that you do get some first hand music and that there is such a fine orchestra as the Palestine Orchestra sometimes coming your way.

I hope my dear friend with you, that you may be home next year, and that we shall all again be able to resume some semblance of normal life again, although I know full well this thing will take a very long time to settle up even when peace is signed.

Thank you and your comrades for all you are doing for us here at home, and believe me, I shall do my best to be at my post for the 50th season, with you all, present, and over the air.

Sincerely yours,

The replacement or rebuilding of Queen's Hall, named in the letter to Matthews, was not mentioned in the original press announcement for the jubilee – though it soon became part of the fund-raising appeal. On 4 October *The Times* named the members of the 'Henry Wood Proms Jubilee Committee' under Horder's chairmanship, including Boult, Moiseiwitsch, Lord Keynes (J. M. Keynes, the distinguished economist) and Nicolls of the BBC, with Wood's ever-devoted W. W. Thompson as honorary secretary. The announcement continued: 'All the proceeds of the appeal and concerts will go into a general fund, and it will be left for Sir Henry to decide the appropriate musical cause to which the fund shall be devoted as a permanent commemoration of his life's work.'

During the whole of the war there had been many occasions which harnessed music to the national cause, but no occasion of personal homage such as was to mark Wood's double anniversary. His seventy-fifth birthday on 3 March 1944 would be followed by the fiftieth season of Wood's promenade concerts, the first concert of the unbroken series having taken place on 10 August 1895. The time seemed auspicious: the political and military prospects of the war had improved and the restrictions and anxieties of social life had somewhat abated. Church bells, silenced in 1939 so that their sounding could warn of an invasion, were permitted to be heard again on 15 November 1943 – as a signal of

Celebrating

rejoicing at Montgomery's Egyptian victory over the German army at El Alamein.

As with the celebration of his fifty years of conducting in 1938, his birthday celebration reached its apex with a concert of combined orchestras (the London Philharmonic, London Symphony and BBC Symphony) at the Albert Hall. There were to have been four conductors – Wood, Boult, Cameron and Malcolm Sargent. But air raid damage to the Albert Hall compelled the deferment of the concert from 4 to 25 March, and Sargent had to drop out owing to a previous engagement. Solomon was the pianist, all performers giving their services so that more than £3000 was raised for the Fund in aid of a new concert hall. 'As Wood entered, prompt at 2.30,' wrote the historian of the Albert Hall, Ronald W. Clark, 'the whole audience rose spontaneously and clapped for minutes. A few seconds later they were on their feet again as the Queen [later the Queen Mother] and the two Princesses entered the Royal Box.'

Wood opened the programme with the overture to *The Flying Dutchman*, followed by Bach's *Brandenburg* Concerto no.3; he closed it with *The Ride of the Valkyries*. Earlier,

> with one of the sly deceptions which have endeared him to audiences for 50 years and which have never really deceived anyone, Sir Henry came in . . . to conduct the Beethoven pianoforte concerto, hiding behind the broad back of Solomon. The audience were clapping both conductor and pianist, but Sir Henry pretended the cheers were only for Solomon and clapped his own hands as they walked in single file on to the platform. Everyone laughed, as they do when Sir Henry makes his famous hat, stick and coat exit at the Proms. This was the sort of fun we all wanted.

So wrote the reporter in the *Daily Telegraph,* the sponsor of this Saturday afternoon concert, describing it as 'the greatest musical event of the war'. The paper's music critic, Ferruccio Bonavia, was able to concentrate on the considerable problems set in co-ordinating such a large body of players. He was agreeably surprised.

> One could not have anticipated the fine effect Sir Henry Wood obtained in the overture and in the cavalcade of the Valkyries, not by the sheer weight of the attack but by its precision. Each strand stood out sharply outlined giving a picture finished to the last detail. [In the Brandenburg Concerto he] had taken pains to ensure that every woof and web should get its due, realizing every aspect of the composition, its dignity and elegance, intimacy and bewitching charm.

384

Among the many composers who sent musical salutes for inclusion in the 1944 birthday album was Béla Bartók.

Celebrating

The rest of the month had been marked by other celebrations. On 2 March a presentation was made at the Royal Academy of Music not by the Academy itself but by the Performing Right Society. Boult and Vaughan Williams were on the platform as Wood received not only a cheque for £1000 but an album of 267 pages in which hundreds of musicians (and a few others) had signed their names, many of them with appropriate musical quotations. Smyth, Bax, Quilter – it was obvious that these and many other British composers would be honoured to sign. Most ingeniously, Elisabeth Lutyens wrote out a tiny *Fanfare* with, over the first bar, the direction: 'For Wood' – the specified instruments being woodwind instead of the customary brass. Fritz Reiner of Chicago, Serge Koussevitzky, Pierre Monteux, Bruno Walter added their congratulations. Elisabeth Schumann expressed her thanks in the music given to Blonde in Mozart's *The Seraglio*, with words suitably modified (see p.291).

In the case of deceased musicians who would have wished to pay tribute, some widows or other relatives signed – among them Elgar's daughter, Carice Elgar Blake. Certain signatures were added to the book *after* its formal presentation, as is clear from a letter of Wood's to the widow of the composer Norman O'Neill. She had evidently sent Wood, much to his pleasure, a sketch of Nikisch, the conductor whom he never ceased to regard as a paragon. His reply gives a detail of the type of hall he had in mind: 'Of course you must sign the "album", but do you mind leaving it until the "Proms" start, when I shall be able to arrange for the Album to be available and in Town. I do hope you like my idea of a very comfortable new concert hall, to hold 4000, with 2000 seats at two shillings for the promenaders. I am delighted to have the delightful sketch of that great genius, Arthur Nikisch – only one Nikisch ever lived and we shall never see his like again.'

On 11 March his Brother Savages entertained Henry J. Wood to luncheon. On a grander scale, with a message from King George VI, was the luncheon on 24 March given for him at the Savoy Hotel by the Musicians' Benevolent Fund in acknowledgement of Wood's work for distressed musicians. A fanfare inaugurated the ceremony – not Lutyens's 'for Wood', but a more conventional one for brass instruments by Arthur Bliss. The BBC announcer Stuart Hibberd read out a specially written sonnet by John Masefield, showing that the versifier of *Sea Fever* was clearly wading out of his depth, even if he was the Poet Laureate:

> How many thousand times have you upheld
> A batonette between two multitudes,

Each hushed to ready and receptive moods,
Waiting your mind's impulsion, that will bring
Oneness to beat, to breath and stroken string,
And beauty's presence, holding the house spelled?

. . . and so forth. To equate the 'multitude' of an orchestra with that of an audience was crass, and if ever such a thing as a 'batonette' existed it was not Henry J. Wood's famously long stick. It would be charitable to call this a poemette. Wood read his acceptance of the tribute from a prepared text, alluding to 'this sad and foolish war' – an extraordinary insensitivity which was not allowed to mar the occasion.

During his birthday month he had been delighted to receive a booklet published by the London Philharmonic Orchestra called *Homage to Sir Henry Wood: A World Symposium*. 'You are truly a wonder to get out such a wonderful little Symposium for my 75th birthday,' he wrote to the orchestra's general manager, Thomas Russell, who had co-edited it with Felix Aprahamian (later well known as a music critic working for the *Sunday Times)* and Miron Grindea, editor of the international literary review, *Adam*. To have assembled and published such a range of international contributions at such a time of war was indeed a feat. Alongside tributes by such conductors as Klemperer and Stokowski, a cable from New York showed Beecham unable to rise to generosity:

HEARING THAT THE LPO HAS PREPARED A WORTHY TRIBUTE TO SIR HENRY WOOD ON HIS SEVENTY-FIFTH BIRTHDAY, IT GAVE ME GREAT PLEASURE TO LEARN THAT THE RELATIONS BETWEEN HIM AND THE LONDON PHILHARMONIC ORCHESTRA CONTINUE TO REMAIN ON THEIR OLD BASIS OF MUTUAL APPRECIATION.

Who would have guessed that George Cathcart (who supplied finance and faith to the very first season of Proms) was still alive to reminisce in that symposium? By this time in poor circumstances, Cathcart occasioned Wood some annoyance in soliciting aid from musical charities and proclaiming that he was being excluded from the anniversary celebrations. Wood assured him of free admission to his box at the Albert Hall – 'so please don't go round saying you cannot get a ticket for the opening night'.

A lifelong devotion to Russian music was recognized in birthday greetings that came to him from Moscow, mostly through the official All-Union Society for Cultural Relations with Foreign Countries. A cable sent on 2 March, the

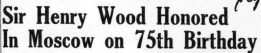

Russia pays tribute to a great promoter of Russian music – a report in the English-language *Moscow News*. *Inserted*: invitation to a reception.

day before his birthday, was signed by Prokofiev and Shostakovich, their fellow-composers Myaskovsky and Glière, the violinist David Oistrakh, the conductor Yevgeny Mravinsky and others. A letter from Shostakovich in his own handwriting, in Russian, thanked Wood for sending his photograph. The Skryabin Museum sent its congratulations to 'the first conductor of *Prometheus* in London'. A musicians' meeting in Moscow on 3 March in Wood's honour, with a Minister of the British Embassy present, was reported by the Soviet periodical *Literature and Life* in both its Russian and English editions.

Second only to the promenade concerts, Wood prized in his annual commitment to the BBC the Easter-tide performance of *The Dream of Gerontius*, which by now was preferred to *Parsifal* on such occasions. But on 22 March Jessie took it on herself to write to W. W. Thompson, still the liaison between Wood and the BBC, saying that the strain would be too much: 'I know he lives and *dies* with Gerontius.' Six days later Wood himself showed a defiant readiness to undertake the performance on 7 April: 'My doctor will give me the necessary Medical Certificate.' But his powers were too weak, and Boult conducted the performance. 'I shall listen to every note,' Wood telegraphed on the morning of the performance, 'and shall be with you all in spirit and affectionate regard.'

An oratorio could not be divided with another conductor in performance, but a band concert could – and so Wood finally made contact, at the very end of his life, with the vigorous amateur brass band movement which had long ago been favoured with original compositions from Elgar, Ireland, Vaughan Williams and others.

The massed bands of Foden's, Black Dyke, Fairey Aviation, Luton, Coventry and Enfield combined in a Saturday afternoon concert at the Albert Hall on 15 April, of which Wood conducted the broadcast second half: Meyerbeer's *Coronation* March, the Handel-Harty *Water Music*, Tchaikovsky's *1812* and the Prelude to Act 3 of Wagner's *Lohengrin*. For the last-named he insisted on having the band parts rewritten to his own specifications – a typical Wood touch, maintained to the end. Harry Mortimer, organizer of the concert for the BBC, was to remember the rehearsal – Wood seeming to grow in stature as he raised his baton, giving the single command 'Every eye!' (a favourite of his), and then beginning with such communicated power that, in an instant, 'every man knew, as never before, why he was a bandsman'.

At a time of such tributes, triumphs and memories, how often did thoughts of his sundered family cross his mind? His younger daughter Avril, still in the women's branch of the Army, was now an officer. His elder daughter Tania, with her two children, was living in Trinidad where her husband 'Jim' was on naval duty in a training role, having earlier survived the sinking of the aircraft-carrier *Courageous*. And Muriel? Suddenly, in a conversation towards the end of April 1944, Nicolls of the BBC had asked Jessie if she knew where 'Her Ladyship' was – he himself having learnt that Muriel had left China and was in New Zealand. But Nicolls reassured Jessie that the BBC recognized *her* position and told her: 'I am going to let you into a secret, but whether the BBC is strong enough to bring it about I don't know, but we certainly hope to see Henry [created] the first Lord in Music to celebrate his jubilee of Proms.'

The Proms, for which his BBC fee had been £2600, had for some years yielded the larger portion of his income. 'When I cease to be associated with them I shall be obliged to resort to a very small invested income,' he wrote to Rubinstein on 27 April. His wish that the BBC should perpetuate his name in the title of the Proms was not merely a bid for fame after his death, but a way of making sure that, as long as he could conduct them, he would be assured of his BBC income. The BBC officials, no doubt recognizing more clearly than he himself that his conductorship was not likely to last beyond the current year of 1944, were at last near to agreeing on a suitable formula with him.

After various preliminary drafts, on 30 May William Haley, as the BBC's new Director General, accepted 'the exclusive right to use the title "the Henry Wood Promenade Concerts" or some similar title involving the use of your name which you are so generously granting to the BBC . . . In the event of the BBC abandoning this intention, notice shall be given to you or your personal representatives within three months of the end of the season.' The BBC thus was not *quite* relinquishing its right to present promenade concerts under other arrangements, but the weight of intention was now clearly in Wood's favour. The BBC, after all, had every reason to rejoice in the name of the conductor under whose inspiration the Proms had reached their half-century.

The agreement was cordially celebrated by a lunch which the BBC gave him at Claridge's Hotel on 5 June. Two days after, Jessie thanked the BBC on receiving its handsome tribute in booklet form, with many contributors: *Sir Henry Wood: Fifty Years of the Proms*. On 25 June EMI Records were his hosts, handing him a cheque for one thousand guineas (£1050) towards the Fund. The directors of the company were also looking forward to a resumption of Wood's services as a recording artist on the Columbia label: a contract had been signed at the not-too-generous rate of £50 per three-hour session, and time allotted on 3 August. Failing health prevented his fulfilling an assignment which he must have dearly wished for. His recorded legacy was to be an inadequate representation of his work.

Over the signature of Winston Churchill a letter had announced that he was to be appointed a Companion of Honour. As a State recognition in the hour of national acclamation it was counted by many of his musical admirers as a disappointment. As Beatrice Harrison put it in a letter to Jessie on behalf of her sister Margaret and herself: 'We were thrilled when we heard about the Order but of course we thought he would be a Lord or have the OM.' The Order of Merit, limited to twenty-four persons at any one time, would have been a far greater distinction: it had already been given to Elgar in 1911 and to Vaughan Williams in 1935. To be made a Companion of Honour (an honour bestowed earlier in 1944 on Canon Edmund H. Fellowes, the Tudor music scholar) was in Wood's case 'a somewhat meagre reward', as the *Daily Mirror* put it: 'The OM would have been more appropriate. There is a peculiar honours standard in this country. The lesser orders are bestowed upon the giants of science and art. The big titles are mainly reserved for those who, having made a fortune in pickles, beer or tobacco, can be relied on to give a lump of it to party funds.'

The tabloid *Daily Mirror* had throughout the war been the voice of radicalism – purporting to represent 'us' against 'them'. It is a measure of Wood's place that its editor should have so fiercely ventilated the point. One can understand the Government and the Palace drawing the line short of a peerage: it would have raised once again the question of 'Lady Wood'. Against the Order of Merit it is difficult to find any valid objection.

Some measure of Wood's *popular* ranking was evident when the newspapers published photographs in June of the real Sir Henry facing a waxed Sir Henry. He had been modelled for exhibition at Madame Tussaud's – lending some of his own clothes, since clothes rationing by coupon would have prevented the famous museum from purchasing an outfit. He was the first conductor (and, so far, the last) to take his stand in that shrine.

Beginning on 10 June, the 1944 promenade concerts were to be undertaken in turn by the three orchestras which had united their strengths in the seventy-fifth birthday concert. The London Philharmonic was booked for two weeks and the London Symphony for the next two, Basil Cameron being Wood's associate conductor for this entire period; then the BBC Symphony Orchestra would take the platform for five weeks, with Boult as Wood's associate conductor. The series was still not called the Henry Wood

Promenade Concerts (that was to be a posthumous title); this was simply 'Sir Henry Wood's Jubilee Season'. There was a note of euphoria in London and throughout the Allied nations during that opening week: at long last, on 6 June, the 'second front' was opened with the invasion of the beaches of northern France.

The approach of a wave of new music in Henry J. Wood's honour was proclaimed by the BBC in its prospectus:

> More than usual interest attaches to this year's new works for a number of them have been specially written in response to invitation for Sir Henry Wood's Jubilee Season of Promenade Concerts. Among the British composers who are thus paying special tribute to this unique occcasion are Granville Bantock, Ian Whyte, Constant Lambert, Arnold Bax, and Alan Bush. Stravinsky offered to Sir Henry for his Jubilee Season the first performance in this country of his *Four Norwegian Moods*, so did Hindemith with his ballet overture *Cupid and Psyche*. From America comes a work by Roy Harris, *Chorale for orchestra*, specially written for this great season. From Russia Shostakovich, whose *Leningrad* was the sensation of the 1942 Promenade season, has sent Sir Henry the score of his Eighth Symphony for its first performance in this country.

Shostakovich had replied cordially to Wood's invitation to conduct, but without a promise, and in the event the work fell to Wood.

Almost immediately after the opening of the promenade season, however, the war brought a new menace. Direct air attacks on London began with the use of a new weapon, the V-1 – a small pilotless plane or 'flying bomb' which seemed to stutter as it approached; then the engine's sound would cut out altogether before the explosive cargo dropped to earth. As with the earlier type of air raids, few members of the promenade audience took the opportunity of leaving the hall when the red light indicated an imminent attack on London. On the day when the LSO began its share of the season, 24 June, Jessie Wood wrote in her and Henry's joint diary of 'a splendid evening' unspoilt even by 'Hitler's dreadful engines' (perhaps an allusion to Purcell's aria, 'Let the dreadful engines of eternal Will . . .'): 'The announcement was made advising the packed house to go to the corridors or trenches in Hyde Park: roars of laughter – including Henry on the rostrum – and the Delius Concerto with Clifford Curzon proceeded.'

A gratified Nicolls wrote to Wood on 26 June that the first two weeks had achieved 'a greater aggregate audience than last year in the first week and [an] equal audience in the second'. Wood was continuing to reply punctiliously to Servicemen who had written about his broadcasts. To D. J.

Borthwick at an RAF station in Orkney he wrote on 22 June: 'Please accept my thanks for your kind letter of appreciation of the Promenade Concerts, the broadcasts of which I am glad that some of you are able to enjoy. I hope it will not be long before conditions change, and you are able to visit London again and get to some of the concerts.'

Wood realized the dangers, however. On 19 June he wrote to Nicolls: 'Should the authorities insist on determining [terminating] the use of the Royal Albert Hall owing to the number of people attending at a given time under the vulnerable glass dome which is the roof of the Hall, I would like you to understand that my services remain at the disposal of the Corporation, and that I shall be willing to continue elsewhere.'

On 29 June, when Eda Kersey was playing Bax's Violin Concerto (Wood and Basil Cameron were sharing the conducting that evening), the approach of a V-1 was detectable in quieter passages. Then, Ronald W. Clark records, 'when the machine appeared to be directly above the Hall, the engine cut out. Eda Kersey continued, apparently oblivious to the fact that one ton of explosive was somewhere overhead. No one in the audience moved. It was a long wait. Then, at last, there came the muffled roar of the explosion.'

Next day, at 5.45 p.m. on Friday 30 June, W. W. Thompson came to see Wood and told him that, after the BBC had been in consultation with the Home Secretary, there would be no concert that night or until further notice. Wood declared himself 'completely dumbfounded, as I had not been consulted', but in view of his letter of the 19th he cannot have been really surprised. On 1 July Haley attempted to justify the decision as considerate to Wood and his fellow-artists: 'I know it has been a great strain for all of you to concentrate on performance with all these robots flying about . . . we were all very sorry indeed that it has been necessary in the interests of public safety to suspend your Jubilee season after such splendid persistence on the part of yourself and the artists and the public, and I sincerely hope we shall be able to resume the concerts later in the year.'

Wood certainly, and probably the majority of the orchestral players and solo artists, were in a mood to have 'soldiered on' and to enjoy the continuation of public enthusiasm for the jubilee season. But no more promenade concerts were given that season at the Albert Hall. The London Symphony Orchestra's portion of the concerts ceased immediately, in mid-stream, as it were – an episode strangely unmentioned in the quasi-official history of the orchestra by Hubert Foss and Noël Goodwin. From 3 July the BBC Symphony Orchestra from its Bedford base played only to radio listeners and only those items which had already been marked for broadcasting.

Celebrating

Wood of course betook himself (and Jessie) to Bedford. Her entry in their joint diary for Tuesday 4 July alludes to an incident which was often to be retold:

> Henry to orchestra: 'Gentlemen, I notice you are smoking under your desks, but I can see you. I thought it was only taxi drivers who smoked while doing their job' (all cigarettes vanished). Benno Moiseiwitch came then to rehearse – took off his coat and lit his customary cigarette – whereupon shouts from all over the orchestra – 'Taxi – taxi!'

The faithful Basil Cameron was on hand in Bedford to assist with those concerts (up to 7 July) which would have fallen to him and the LSO at the Albert Hall. On the following day, as planned, those concerts originally allotted to the BBC Symphony Orchestra began. The first 'opened with A.B.' (Boult), as Jessie's diary entry recorded, and then: 'Henry gave a marvellous performance of [Sibelius's] *En Saga* – Paul Beard came to see him in his dressing room and thanked him for his wonderful direction. "The orchestra is thrilled, and all talking about it – it is just the difference between the amateur and professional," he said. I have never seen Paul Beard so completely enthusiastic.'

This was a passage she diplomatically edited for her memoirs, *The Last Years of Henry J. Wood*, omitting the jibe at 'the amateur' – which, if Paul Beard really uttered it, would seem as unsuitable for Boult as for Cameron. On 13 July Wood gave the last in his unique tally of more than 700 first performances: Shostakovich's Eighth Symphony. After his death Jessie was to send to Moscow's official Society for Cultural Relations with Foreign Countries an album commemorating outstanding events in Wood's life, his performance of the Eighth Symphony being the last.

A letter Henry sent from Bedford on 16 July 1944 to L. Gurney Parrott of the Royal Academy of Music mentioned the Woods' worries over the condition of their London flat, which they had let to Elsie Newmarch.

> You will have heard that we were obliged to come to Bedford for daily rehearsals and broadcasts when they shut down the Promenade Concerts without warning, and [you] will know how sad it has all been. Lady Wood runs up and down to keep an eye on [things] – as last Monday, when she found many windows blown out in a back part of the flat. I understand the Academy caught it too . . .
> We are quiet overhead in this sleepy place, but the people are like herds of rather dirty sheep, which makes the slightest attempt at a walk

an exercise of patience, dodging up and down curbs [*sic*] and avoiding
prams and rowdy American soldiers.

On 19 July, according to the diary: 'Henry did Brahms Concerto in A [minor],
Violin, Cello and Orchestra and Symphony no.1 without any effort – as
rehearsal was good.' But a morning rehearsal on 26 July had Jessie watching
apprehensively. On a kindly suggestion from Vaughan Williams, Jelly
d'Arányi (who of late years had seen her engagements fall severely) had
been invited back to play Bach's Violin Concerto in A minor. The other
works were Bach's also: the Orchestral Suite no.4 and the Four-Keyboard
Concerto (with Joyce Riddle, Joyce Hedges, Ronald Smith and David Till).

> Orchestra disgraceful – no wish to rehearse – he had to ask them could they
> understand his beat. Yes! Then you didn't look at the beat. Now I shall
> have to go through that movement again – whereupon second violins put
> instruments down and chatted. . . . Paul Beard said 'They don't like
> Bach'!!! Poor Henry *made* them play at night. Dreadful, the strain of it.

Jessie put the blame on the players, but such a breakdown in the discipline for
which Wood was famous was surely a sign. On Friday 28 July he again
encountered a rebellious, or at least sullen, orchestra. With Joan Hammond
as soprano soloist and Maurice Cole as pianist, the rehearsal took place for a
programme which was to have consisted of the overture to Mozart's *Così
fan tutte*, Beethoven's vocal scena *Ah, perfido*, Mozart's Piano Concerto in
A, K488, and Beethoven's Symphony no.7. But, as is shown by the BBC's
duty-sheets for that day, the Mozart overture had been removed from the
bill. Boult, due to conduct the Symphony Orchestra in other items for
transmission later that day in the BBC's African Service, shared the
rehearsal-time:

> The orchestra [wrote Jessie] didn't want to rehearse because it was
> Beethoven [i.e., a familiar work]. Boult announced he didn't intend
> rehearsing for the following African Broadcast – Cheers – but made
> Henry's rehearsal the more difficult in consequence. Poor old Henry –
> coming over the bridge [on the way back to the hotel] he said he intended
> making them play Beethoven 7 as never before – he did – a wonderful
> performance – but at what cost!!! He was whacked.

It cannot always be told with certainty to what extent Jessie's diary entries
were, at this point, immediate and to what extent written-up afterwards as
an aid to memory. The preceding has an unvarnished intimacy about it, the

395

episode being more elaborately (and slightly differently) presented in *Last Years*. At the bottom of the diary page for 28 July the pencilled writing is fainter, with a bereaved woman's postscript: 'They killed my dear Hen.'

That performance of Beethoven's Seventh Symphony before an invited audience at Bedford was Henry J. Wood's last music-making. It was broadcast – but not recorded. The force of legend naturally would put a halo on such a final performance, but the timpanist Eric Pritchard recalled it almost fifty years later as 'a marvellous performance of Beethoven Seven – he was above himself, as it were'. Jessie Hinchliffe, one of the orchestral violinists, gave Jessie Wood a similar report. Boult, a man not given to exaggeration, said that the performance could have been taken by a radio listener to be that of 'some brilliant conductor in his early forties'.

We may well believe what Jessie Wood wrote in her book of memoirs – that Henry began by turning on the musicians 'a cold, steely-blue eye in place of that kindly "now we are about to enjoy ourselves" glance'; that he summoned his full reserves to deliver the music with its full energy and passion; and that in the car going back to his hotel he embraced her with the remark: 'I made 'em play, didn't I?'

Characteristically, while in Bedford he was looking and planning well ahead. Since the Proms would now end on 10 rather than 12 August, he had accepted an invitation from Steuart Wilson (at this time the BBC's Overseas Music Director) to conduct a concert in the BBC South African service on 12 August. He also undertook to 'pre-record' – the process at last being accepted! –

> another programme for your series called 'Carnival Concerts', as apparently other serious conductors are to adopt this somewhat 'light' style of programme to suit your special purpose. It is 'light' isn't it? Should the programme you suggest stand, will you bear in mind that I do the Weber-Weingartner *Invitation to the Waltz* [and not another arrangement]. Candidly, I do not think my *Sea Fantasia* a happy suggestion apart from the Prom audience of the last night – and it plays 17 minutes!. . . *Marche Militaire* (Schubert) in D would be a very [suitable] item (5 minutes) – my orchestration.

But on the night after his performance of the Beethoven Seventh, Henry became ill and delirious – 'rambling all night', noted Jessie. As the days passed, she must have realized from Horder that the end was not far off. 'Terribly ill – abscess' is her diary entry for Sunday 6 August.

On 10 August, the very day of the fiftieth anniversary of the first promenade concert which Wood gave for Robert Newman, not Wood but Boult conducted the BBC Symphony Orchestra, and not in London but in Bedford. On Broadcasting House notepaper, but with the word 'Bedford' written below, a letter was sent:

> My dear Sir Henry
>   Here we are, audience, orchestra, announcer, soloist and conductor all waiting to begin your Jubilee Celebration and very sad that you are not with us. We all send our love and wish you a quick recovery and many more Proms to come!
>   Yours always

The signatories were the leader of the orchestra Paul Beard and his deputy Marie Wilson, the orchestra's first trumpet Ernest Hall, the orchestral attendant William Fussell, the baritone George Pizzey, together with 'Adrian C.Boult' (as he signed himself) and, a serviceman representing the audience, 'James Crookes, Sgt'.

A message to his public, read by the BBC announcer Stuart Hibberd, was all that Wood could contribute to that event. In another room of the hotel, Jessie listened to the broadcast and (after the news bulletin which followed) to the appeal which the BBC allowed Horder to make on behalf of the Fund. The programme included Wagner's *Rienzi* overture, the opening item of the opening concert of the opening season in 1895, and also the first performance of Henry J. Wood's newest orchestration – Handel's Organ Concerto no.4 in F (opus 4/4) undertaken 'because Tovey said it was the best of them all'. The eighty-three-year-old organist of Salisbury Cathedral, Sir Walter Alcock, had accepted Wood's invitation to be the soloist, but with the removal of the Proms out of London a younger performer replaced him. As Jessie's diary noted on the day: 'Thalben Ball played it splendidly. I related the whole concert to my darling – and somehow – as soon as he knew the anniversary was over – 50 years – he seemed immediately to relapse into a sad despondent mood – in fact, I am afraid – so afraid.'

The public knew he had been ill but the press announcement had specified jaundice. Princess Mary wrote to him from Harewood House, Leeds, on 18 August:

> Dear Sir Henry,
>   I am so very sorry to hear you are laid up and I send you my sympathy. I realize what a very great disappointment it must be to you not to be able to conduct any more Promenade Concerts for the

present. It has been very remarkable the way these have been kept going in wartime in spite of innumerable obstacles and I know how much this is due to your indomitable spirit.

My eldest son [the future Earl of Harewood] and I had the pleasure of attending 2 Promenade Concerts at the Queen's Hall shortly before it was destroyed and enjoyed them enormously, this was his and my début at these concerts. . . .

This barley sugar comes with my best wishes.

Sweets, including barley sugar, were rationed: the gift was not trivial, but arrived too late. The dying man had been taken to Hitchin Hospital on Wednesday 16 August and was thereafter only intermittently conscious, with Jessie by his side. Having stayed on the Friday night at Dr Skeggs' house in Stevenage, she was called very early next day to his bedside. On Saturday 19 August 1944, at 1.22 p.m., Henry J. Wood's life was over. Dr Skeggs signed the death certificate: '(a) Coma, (b) Uraemia, (c) Arteriosclerosis'.

Among the papers left by the musician was a sheet torn from a lined exercise book, on which under the heading 'Singing' Wood had written in pencil:

'There is no gain in art apart from labour of mind and body.'

'Education is not a remedy for barbarism in the soul, but it is a ladder by which those who *will*, may rise out of it.'

Were these a pair of maxims recollected from Ruskin? To Wood's posterity they speak of the man himself, the labourer in music, the educator and thus the civiliser of his public. They would make no bad epitaphs for him.

Chapter 24

Fifty Years On

1944–94

'I'm off on holiday,' the vicar had told his curate. 'I am not coming back even if the war ends. You are in charge.' The young Rev. Roger Bagnall was unprepared when the undertaker called to say that Sir Henry Wood had died and it was desired to have the funeral at Hitchin Parish Church 'because of the size and convenience'. His churchwardens were consulted and gave their agreement. He had never even met or seen Wood, and must have wondered at the piously inventive report in the *Daily Telegraph* that 'for months he [Wood] had worshipped every Sunday in the church'.

The service on 24 August 1944, conducted jointly by Bagnall and by the Rev. Hugh Matthews from the Woods' 'home' parish of Marylebone, represented an act of national homage. The BBC Singers formed the choir, conducted by Leslie Woodgate; the local organist, W. M. Stretch, shared his instrument with a distinguished guest, George Thalben Ball. After the Blessing, the slow movement of Bach's Brandenburg Concerto no.6 was conducted by Sir Adrian Boult, and Wood's own arrangement of Chopin's funeral march by Basil Cameron. Did the phantom of a voice well known at Queen's Hall utter the complaint that the crowded church could not accommodate enough players to do that arrangement justice?

By train from London came hundreds of mourners, many attending on behalf of musical and other bodies. The provisional French government (de Gaulle's) and the Soviet embassy were represented. Wood's oldest associate, George Cathcart, was there, as was the violinist who had always looked up to him as to a guardian, Ida Haendel: 'I cried as if I had lost a member of my own family,' she told the present writer. At the head of its list of those attending the *Daily Telegraph* placed 'Lady Wood' – not true; it was Jessie. *The Times* skipped the difficulty by naming only the mourners 'in addition to members of the family'.

Avril Wood had received a telegram from 'Mrs Linton' (as she referred to

Jessie) with details of the funeral. 'I arrived far too early and sat in the churchyard,' she wrote by airmail to her sister in Trinidad.

> Hundreds of people came and tried to get seats but most of them had to remain outside. I saw dreadfully few people I knew and those I scarcely spoke to. I have never felt more alone in my whole life and I longed for you and Mummy to be there with me. . . .
> When the service was over, I followed the coffin out of the church. I knew that the cremation service was to be held privately in Cambridge. I turned to Mrs Linton's daughter at the door of the church and said 'I am coming with you to Cambridge'. She asked me 'Who are you?' My only answer was to get in the car where I sat between her and her mother and we followed the coffin to Cambridge. It was a terrible journey. Thank God no-one tried to speak. At Cambridge the service was very brief. I said goodbye to him, Tania, for the three of us.

Two days before the funeral the suggestion appeared in the Press that his ashes should find a place in Westminster Abbey. The Dean was on holiday, and the matter was then allowed to lapse in the usual English evasive hush. Presumably the Abbey would not accept the remains of a public offender against its canons of marriage. On Jessie, who was to work as assiduously in keeping Henry's memory green as she had in caring for him, fell the responsibility of finding some other place for a visible memorial.

She 'suddenly knew, as if Henry himself had spoken', where it should be – at St Sepulchre's, High Holborn, the London church in which his father had sung in the choir and Henry as a boy had learnt the organ. The burial of the ashes took place there on 14 June 1945, and a memorial window was designed by Gerald E. R. Smith in collaboration with Frank Salisbury. At the dedicatory service on 26 April 1946, Leslie Woodgate conducted the BBC Chorus in a setting by William Walton of newly written words by Masefield, 'Where does the uttered music go?' Vaughan Williams' *Serenade to Music* was performed with an ensemble of soloists which included several who had sung it at the original 'conductor's jubilee' performance in 1938.

The memorial window at St Sepulchre's portrayed St Cecilia. During his last years Henry J. Wood himself developed an enthusiasm for reinstating St Cecilia's Day (22 November) as an occasion for the national celebration of music. It had virtually lapsed since the eighteenth century, though the works written in her honour by Purcell and Handel were not quite forgotten – and the *Hymn to St Cecilia* by Benjamin Britten, whose birthday happened to fall on that day, had been first performed on 22 November 1942. Hoping to promote an annual celebration of the day, Jessie persuaded the *Daily Herald*, a Labour newspaper, to sponsor the first such celebration on 22 November 1946. A service was held at St Sepulchre's, marked by civic pomp and the participation of three cathedral choirs and that of Westminster Abbey. The luncheon that followed was attended by Clement Attlee as Prime Minister and an evening concert of British music at the Albert Hall was attended by the Queen.

That was the forerunner of what in later years was designated the Royal Concert (annually on or near 22 November), associated with the cause of the Musicians' Benevolent Fund. It still continues, though the bogus-historical association of music with an early Christian martyr was not likely to rally succeeding generations of secularized music-lovers. Not St Cecilia's Day but the blessed Henry's night – the annual Last Night of the Proms – was to give the world (via television) its image of British musical celebration.

Attlee's first Labour government (1945–50) looked favourably on the project to rebuild Queen's Hall – the purpose of Wood's seventy-fifth birthday appeal. A new name, the Henry Wood National Memorial Fund, identified the cause. Meanwhile no opportunity of keeping alive the sacred flame was missed by Jessie. The *Daily Telegraph*, which had sponsored the original concert marking Wood's birthday in 1944, was persuaded to support two more in March 1945 and 1946. In succeeding years, such birthday concerts were given at the Albert Hall by the Henry Wood Concert Society (Jessie was its founder and chairman, with Sir Arnold Bax as president) and from 1953 by the BBC. For some years from 1961 the celebration united the choirs and orchestras of the four leading London music colleges, usually under Malcolm Sargent (Sir Malcolm since 1947).

The Henry Wood Concert Society had also promoted an Elgar Festival in 1949 to which Bernard Shaw was asked to lend his commendation – which, in a letter to 'Dear Lady Wood', he refused in characteristic fashion: 'Neither Henry nor Elgar need any testimonials: such rubbish is an impertinence and would be a waste of your time. Cut all that stuff out: it would not sell a single extra seat and might even lose a few in my case, as there are many benighted wretches who loathe my name.'

Other promotions of the Society included a performance of Mahler's *Resurrection* Symphony under Bruno Walter (only its second hearing in Britain) in 1949. Stokowski, whom Jessie invited in 1946 to conduct, thanked her 'for offering me the privilege of paying tribute to your dear husband' and gave hope of an early date – but did not manage to find one. The chief commemoration of Wood, however, remained fixed on the hoped-for rebuilding. Negotiations with the Treasury and with the Crown

Commissioners and Chappell's (respectively owners and lessees of the old site) dragged on. On the South Bank of the Thames, the chief metropolitan site of the Festival of Britain, the Royal Festival Hall was opened in 1951 – but even then the proponents of the Queen's Hall scheme still saw their West End location as a winning card. Why should the public wish to trek to the Festival Hall with its inconveniently long approaches open to the weather?

The Queen's Hall plans came to a halt for quite a different, internal reason. By the later 1950s it became clear that the total of about £80,000 raised by public appeal would be quite inadequate to meet the costs now estimated for the rebuilding. Unwisely, no target figure had ever been attached to the appeal. There was parliamentary questioning and an appreciable public disappointment. The trustees of the fund found themselves legally compelled to return any contributions above a certain level, 'unless they are disclaimed or donors do not come forward'. The High Court directed that money not required to be returned could be devoted to an alternative fund for the advancement of music and the honouring of Wood.

As a result, London has no Queen's Hall nor any concert hall in Wood's name. The benefactions from what was left in the fund went on minor projects. Probably not one in a hundred of today's promenaders knows of the existence, south of the river, of Henry Wood Hall, a former church which serves as an orchestral rehearsal space, and of Henry Wood House, a hostel for music students. 'Henry Wood House' is also the designation which the BBC bestowed in 1964 on its new office block, standing on the very site of the old Queen's Hall. Round the back still stands the public house which Henry J. Wood nicknamed 'The Glue-Pot' because his orchestral players got stuck there when they should have been hastening back after a mid-rehearsal break.

The final act of the Henry Wood Memorial Trust (as it had become) was, in 1980, to endow at the Royal Academy of Music a scholarship for students of conducting. Wood's own fund-raising appeal to endow hospital beds for sick orchestral musicians had begun its good work in 1938 (see pp.329-30). The advent of a National Health Service in 1945 meant, however, that this and thousands of other such endowments lost their function. At its new (1970) site, the Charing Cross Hospital, to which three beds had been donated, displays a single plaque in the lobby: 'This bed is endowed to commemorate the Jubilee of Sir Henry Wood 1888-1938'. The earmarking to the musical profession is not mentioned. *Sic transit caritas!*

Approaching her sixty-second birthday when Henry J. Wood died, Jessie was reinforced in her determination to keep his memory vibrating by the stream of supportive letters she received from celebrities and non-celebrities, whether they had or had not previously made her acquaintance. 'My dear Jessie (if I may)', Myra Hess's first letter began; she later wrote to 'My dearest Jessie'. Solomon, acknowledging Jessie's gift to him of a clavichord Henry had owned, signed 'Yours affectionately, Solo'. Tosta de Bennich, the Swedish pianist who looked back on an association with Henry which had begun more than forty years before, wrote warmly to 'Henry's Jessie', recalling that Muriel used to write to her personally but had ceased to do so:

> I tried hard to see all her [Muriel's] good points and she had some such, but she was always peculiar and all out for adventures yet I do think she was genuinely fond of Henry in her way. How great a man he was she never realised . . . At the same time I wish things had been *done* differently. You see we [in Sweden] think nothing of divorce . . .

Muriel had done well out of her financial settlement: she was to leave £158,165. But Henry's death did not leave Jessie a rich woman. His Will, which made her his sole executrix, was proved at £6460. (The announcement of that in the *Daily Mail* also noted that the Yorkshire choral trainer Sir Henry Coward had left £12,367.) It seems quite likely that Henry and Jessie had been drawing on such capital as Henry retained in the separation from Muriel, but that Muriel despite all her expenses of travel kept her capital intact.

The day after Henry J. Wood's death, Jessie suggested to Stanley Rubinstein, who remained her legal adviser, that she should renounce her change of name. He advised against and she accepted that advice. So 'Lady Jessie Wood' she remained, a form of words inevitably shortened to Lady Wood. The wonder is not that occasional public unpleasantnesses occurred in consequence, but that they were so rare. At a so-called 'diamond jubilee' promenade concert in August 1954, Sir Malcolm Sargent directed some of the final applause towards Jessie in her box. The *Daily Mail* reported that 'Lady Wood' acknowledged the applause. Wood's daughter, Mrs Tania Cardew, protested to the editor, who was compelled to print a few days later a denial that any such person as Lady Wood was there – without saying who it really was!

Jessie's undoubted triumph came on 3 March 1969, the centenary of Henry J. Wood's birth, when she received the handshake of the Queen. The occasion was a reception following the performance of Verdi's Requiem at the Albert Hall, conducted in the Queen's presence by Sir John Barbirolli and presented jointly by the Memorial Trust and the Henry Wood Concert Society. The moment was duly photographed (see plate 41). It had been ascertained beforehand that in such a context the Queen had no objection to meeting one whom the public took to be, but was not, the widow of a man who had received a sovereign's honour. If anyone could have 'earned' such a widowhood, it was Jessie. On Tania's behalf a protest had been made to the Palace that neither she nor Avril was due to be presented; but the protocol already agreed was not changed to include them.

Having originally taken down from Henry's lips the narrative which became *My Life of Music*, Jessie was conscious of how much had been editorially excised (by way of shortening it) before it met the public eye. On its publication in 1938, Henry himself was made aware of some at least of the errors and tried to persuade his publisher, Victor Gollancz, to bring out a revised edition. In the stressed circumstances of wartime publishing it is not surprising that Gollancz declined. His firm did, however, bring out in 1954 *The Last Years of Henry J. Wood* by Jessie Wood (not designated 'Lady Jessie Wood'), which went beyond its title in filling in some earlier details of her hero's life also. Diplomacy still smudged the relationship of the author with her subject: the reviewer in the *Aberdeen Free Press and Journal* even supposed 'Jessie Wood' to be Henry J. Wood's daughter.

Purely by chance Jessie had lately met a schoolboy friend of Henry's, surnamed Bannister, son of the Woods' family doctor. Her book made good use of Bannister's boyhood memories (see p.6) and it is surprising that Reginald Pound in his centenary biography of Wood (1969) did not. Jessie made her memories and papers available to Pound, whose *Sir Henry Wood* exhibited the writer's craft which Pound had developed in several well-received biographies of non-musical figures. Though his sympathies were with Jessie (as were those of almost everyone he met), he made a point of consulting Avril Wood. She was a natural 'musical' contact for him, having become head of the music department of the British Council, the organization charged with official links between Britain and other countries.

For whatever reason, Avril did not direct him to her sister Tania, whose enormous store of printed, written and photographic material remained unknown to him. That material, as the reader will have gathered, was freely put at the disposal of the present writer, as was a comparably large store of material which had descended from Jessie to her daughter Eileen Calthrop. These two private archival sources, along with the Henry J. Wood papers at the British Library (deposited there by Jessie), form the main first-hand sources of this book.

Avril Wood died at Guildford on 10 May 1983, aged sixty-eight, unmarried. Tania and her husband George Jameson ('Jim') Cardew, living in Berkshire, celebrated their fifty-fifth wedding anniversary in 1993. Henry J. Wood never saw any of the four grandchildren born before his death: Carolyn, Sarah, and the twins Eve and Richard. A fifth, Rowena, was born in 1954.

Muriel had returned after the war to live in Britain. Her eccentricities – particularly in stealing up to a house and looking in, rather than presenting herself formally – continued to bemuse those who knew her. She renewed in Newcastle-on-Tyne and London her friendship with Professor John Findlay, the philosopher, and his wife Aileen, whom she had met in New Zealand: in 1993 Aileen Findlay remembered her as 'just like Mary Poppins, with long thin English feet' and breaking out into an 'eldritch laugh'. Her hunger to see new places never abated, her passport showing visits between 1954 and 1960 to Argentina, Mozambique, Uganda and Egypt, as well as to half-a-dozen European countries. Neither with Tania and Tania's husband Jim, nor with the Findlays, would she allow the breakdown in her marriage to be discussed. Lady Wood died at Roehampton, near London, on 21 May 1967, aged eighty-four.

Jessie spent her last years at Seaford, Sussex, living in a flat within the house occupied by her daughter, Eileen Calthrop, whose second husband, Dr Gordon Calthrop, had died in 1948. Having outlived Henry J. Wood by nearly thirty-five years, Jessie de Levante, then (for professional purposes) Goldsack, then (by marriage) Linton, then (by deed poll) Lady Jessie Wood, died in Seaford on 14 June 1979, aged ninety-six.

Had Wood died in 1930, the Proms would have been seen as only one part – admittedly a large part – of a grand and broad career. Thenceforward the Proms became central to his professional life. No longer having an orchestra of his own, and with choral festivals on the decline, he was dependent for his income more on the BBC than on any other source. His public increasingly saw him as the Man Who Made the Proms, and in *My Life of Music* he did not seek to suggest any different emphasis. It became rare for him to be honoured in a more general context. Quite exceptional in its breadth of reference was the centenary tribute in *The Times* (28 February 1969) headlining him as THE NATIONAL HERO OF ENGLISH MUSIC: significantly its author was not a regular music critic of the paper, but a social historian of music, Henry Raynor.

The Proms have thus become his monument. Wood's bust (by Donald Gilbert) is annually brought from the Royal Academy of Music to preside over the organ console at the Albert Hall: no smaller hall, even if it were available, could now hold the Proms. Like any living series, they have developed their own momentum. The reign of Sargent as chief conductor (1948–66) is well remembered – a period which did not lack Wood's popular touch, but in which the drive for new music was slowed down, and so-called 'novelties' (meaning works 'not previously performed at a Henry Wood Promenade Concert') were paraded by the BBC in place of genuine premières. The radical decisiveness of William Glock as the BBC's Controller of Music, 1959–73, rewound Wood's clock of modernity while asserting that its key should remain in the hands of the BBC's musical policy-makers, with no individual conductor's charisma predominating.

The later history of the Proms, examined in various other books (Barrie Hall's of 1981 being outstanding), is not of primary concern here. It may be noted, however, that with the label of 'Britain's biggest music festival' frequently affixed, the Proms became a principality on its own in 1992, when John Drummond was appointed the BBC's first Director, Promenade Concerts.

Since Wood's death, his name has been frequently invoked as a touchstone by those who complained of deteriorating behaviour on the part of promenade audiences – particularly on the final night of the season. Blame is sometimes put at the door of Sargent, with his careful milking of the applause and his annual closing addresses to 'my beloved promenaders'. More clearly, Barrie Hall saw the unruliness of the Last Night springing inevitably from the invasion of the Proms by television in 1947, the promenaders soon realizing that the cameras would not be pointed exclusively in the performers' direction. The way was open for dressing up, calling out, and what in Wood's Victorian boyhood would have been called 'larks' in general.

What must be mostly regretted is that the Last Night is presented and televised in such a way that the outside world can too easily take it to be the essence of the Proms, not as its end-of-term frolic. The content and sequence of the Last Night is now obviously chosen *for* the cameras and has been allowed to encourage, and to entrench, an unbridled jingoism which happily has no place in any other major artistic event among Wood's countrymen. The merest suggestion of a possible modification of that jingoism caused the instant dismissal of the conductor-elect, Mark Elder, in 1990: would Robert Newman have dismissed Henry J. Wood for opening his mouth in public?

The matter-of-fact answer is, of course, that Wood did not 'open his mouth in public'; a conductor's job was to conduct, a manager's was to manage (whether such decision-making was in the hands of Newman or Speyer or William Boosey of Chappell's or the executives of the BBC). The journalistic urge to turn a performer into a 'personality' was not exactly unknown, but throughout Wood's period was kept within fairly strict bounds. Partly for this reason, and despite the uncovering of letters and other private documents in the present book, the character of Henry J. Wood himself remains somewhat elusive.

The quota of fibbing and fantasy in *My Life of Music* is not so monstrous as Leopold Stokowski's construction of his phoney accent and faked national origin, yet seems at first curiously at odds with what is perceived as Wood's straightforwardness and lack of guile. 'He had the simplicity and directness of all great men,' said his admiring fellow-artist Clifford Curzon ten years after Wood's death. But underneath, as this book's exploration of his life suggests, there seems to have been an insecurity perpetually craving for extra assurance. As if the support of his parents in boyhood were not enough, he embellished it in the telling. As if his first achievements as conductor were not a sufficient testament of youthful prowess, he pretended (until mid-life) to be a year younger than he was. His first wife Olga had to be, not merely the daughter of a Russian princess, but a princess herself.

As if he feared that the flow of engagements might dry up, he undertook far too many concerts for far too many years, evolving for that excessive load a technique which stamped him a mighty worker first, a refining artist only second. Thus the wish to compensate, to insure, to be ceaselessly 'on the go' lest the wheel suddenly stop turning – this was what in the eyes of posterity (which is concerned not in the least with inward compulsions) has flawed his reputation.

Immersed in music, he never achieved an all-round adjustment to the buffeting of the world. An only child, he was cossetted by his parents. His marriage to Olga and his virtual marriage to Jessie succeeded because those partners were, in their different ways, his supporters in art and exclusively devoted to caring for him. He rushed into marriage with Muriel because she gave promise of businesslike management at least; the breakdown of that marriage was partly caused by the increasingly eccentric Muriel's unwilling-ness to submerge her *whole* personality in caring for him. (Jessie, said her daughter Eileen, 'waited on him hand and foot'.)

Once the break with Muriel was made, he had not the elasticity to cope with complexities of arrangements. ('He was a moral coward,' his daughter Tania once remarked.) From the moment he separated from his wife he cut himself off absolutely, unforgivingly, from his daughters – even though, with Muriel permanently absent from England (providentially for him) and his liaison with Jessie unchallenged, he could have sought a *rapprochement* with Tania and Avril without threat to himself. It was as if, possessed by his professional life as a relentless driving force, he could allow himself no negotiability outside it. His desertion of Muriel began with a letter (pp.267–8) in which he evidently saw himself as making quite a reasonable proposition for a bolt-hole from marriage. The likely effect the letter would have on its recipient was beyond his imagination.

Divorce would have been a consequence preferable to him, and no great shock to society's expectation of conductors' behaviour. Beecham's court appearance as a co-respondent in a divorce case had attracted maximum publicity but damaged his career not a jot; nor did Beecham's own subsequent divorce, long afterwards. Faced with Muriel's total refusal to entertain thoughts of divorce, Henry J. Wood allowed his strict pragmatism to take over: he had resolved to live with Jessie, so if she could not be his real wife, she would be his *de facto* wife. A change of surname by deed poll was an expedient commonly resorted to under such circumstances. The change not merely of surname but of forenames to give pseudo-legitimacy to 'Lady' (Stanley Rubinstein's brilliant suggestion) was thoroughly in line with such pragmatism. That any moral, religious, or legal issue might be involved seems not to have disturbed him in the slightest. At least (it might admiringly be said) hypocrisy and sanctimoniousness never came into it. He was concerned only with such convenience as would allow a social life to proceed without any consequence except to Nosy Parkers.

'Morality' in the superficial sense did not concern him. 'Morality' in the artistic sense was all: it is impossible to understand his self-driven urge towards musical accomplishment except in terms of a code, of a duty. The utmost conscientiousness went into it. That quality was picked out by Ernest Newman (who had observed virtually the whole of Wood's professional life) when obituarizing him in the *Sunday Times*:

> No one who has not seen him at close quarters can have the smallest conception of the care he took, the labour he imposed on himself, in the performance of his duties as he saw them. An episode such as that in Birmingham, when *Gerontius* came perilously near shipwreck on its first voyage [1900] through Richter's laziness, obtuseness and lack of conscientiousness, was never even remotely possible where Wood was concerned. The fact that a work did not really speak to his heart of hearts only made him work the harder at it, and see that everyone under him did.

It is not by his 'interpretation' of any particular composer that we shall remember him . . . To say this is not at all to disparage him, but simply to define him. No conductor – indeed, no performer of any species – has been or ever will be equally remarkable in music of every kind: each of them pays for his pre-eminence in one field by limitations in others. So I would not say that Wood 'missed' that sort of pre-eminence: I would prefer to put it that he escaped it – a lucky escape, on the whole, for if there is glory in being a 'star', there is also danger for the luminary as for the beholder. . . .

His great qualities were his thorough mastery of the whole language of music and the whole praxis of conducting, his amazing capacity for work, his conscientiousness, that made him, as a matter of course, do his best for whatever new work fell to him to introduce, and that insatiable interest in the musical activity of all countries, all periods, that for half a century kept his audiences abreast of all that was being done in every country.

Much the same praise – for Wood as a universalist – is to be found in what William Glock wrote (a month *before* Wood's death) in the *Observer*:

. . . Sir Henry is never over-in-love with the music, as Walter can be; nor does he preoccupy himself to Beecham's extent with problems of 'interpretation'. He is not one of those through whom music, if it happens to be the right music, pours as through its own private and appropriate channel. Rather its greatness is expressed in his general bearing, whilst his thoughts and energies are given to technical details; and those who have played under him would probably agree that one feels neither a conflict nor an identity of musical aim, but rather that one's path is made extraordinarily clear. This dualism of noble character and masterly technique falls short of genius, but rises above mannerism, and is an absolute condition both of Henry Wood's enormous repertoire and of the public's unfaltering belief in him.

The sharing of applause with the players of his orchestra – pioneered by him – was only the most visible sign of a deep sense of co-operation, a co-operation not incompatible with leadership. Earlier in these pages Barbellion's comparison of Wood with a sword-waving general was quoted. Wood's orchestral musicians, particularly those to whom World War One was vivid, would have better recognized the image of the subaltern officer going 'over the top' (of the trenches) with the troops he himself has trained. There is another 'model' for Wood's activity: the artist of John Ruskin's ideal, for whom art, work and morality are inseparable. The term 'workman', often applied with condescension to him, is in Ruskinian discourse a term of nobility.

His achievement perhaps reached its height in the kind of transfiguration that many music-lovers felt, and many went to seek. His future publisher, Victor Gollancz, experienced the Proms as a kind of communion, with Queen's Hall as a temple and Wood as its celebrant: 'His simple and unreflecting humanity, and his love of music and respect for his audience, combined to produce an atmosphere akin to that of an early Christian love-feast. We really did love everything and everybody on those prom nights: the music, the performers, our neighbour and Henry Wood.'

Whereas the Proms centenary season in 1995 maintained Wood's honoured presence, the 100th season in 1994 – the fiftieth anniversary of his death – had reasserted his musical achievements. Under the conductorship of Andrew Davis, the Last Night not only sustained tradition with Wood's *Fantasia on British Sea Songs*, but revived Vaughan Williams' *Serenade to Music* (one of Wood's most notable non-Proms premières), as well as Wood's own arrangements of Bach's *Toccata and Fugue in D minor* and of Percy Grainger's *Handel in the Strand*. During the Proms season of 1991 the American conductor Leonard Slatkin had re- explored Musorgsky's *Pictures at an Exhibition* by giving different movements in different orchestrators' versions, Wood's included.

Fifty years after his death, however, a question remains. How does Henry J. Wood 'rank' as a conductor? It is impossible to respond without first considering the criteria for any such ranking.

The conductor as a representative figure has changed almost unrecognizably since Wood began. In the 1880s the conductor had only lately emerged from quasi-anonymity; in the 1940s he had become, in the person of Arturo Toscanini, the most famous living musician in his (adopted) country, possibly in the world. 'He', indeed. It would have been as impossible in that time to imagine a female Toscanini as a female Mussolini.

The juxtaposition of those two names is not altogether ridiculous, as is shown by the title *Dictators of the Baton*, an admiring book by the American author David Ewen (1943). Toscanini's ferocity of glance, his intensity of manner, his conducting without a score, his demand for an 'impossible' number of rehearsals, his well-publicized tantrums – all helped to make him the supreme icon of such a type. Toscanini's image was that of the sacred interpreter, the priest or oracle through whom alone the gods of the classics revealed their message. Herbert von Karajan conducting with closed eyes, Leonard Bernstein leaping into the air in mid-Mahler were later phenomena similarly suggesting an awesome communication with something beyond: the one like a spiritualist medium, the other in the frenzy of Dionysiac possession.

At a sufficiently cooling distance it is possible to see in the adoration of the Toscanini-type and its successors just what caused Wood to be downgraded in the estimation of many. Toscanini established his position – but at a cost. A selection of classics was canonized as the 'essential' music to which the listener was directed. Toscanini's repertory was markedly small (in comparison not only with Wood, but with Koussevitzky, Stokowski and others in America). For contemporary music he did the minimum: even his famous 'première', Samuel Barber's *Adagio for Strings*, already existed in string quartet form.

Wood – with his huge repertory, his insatiable appetite for new music, his ability to manage where necessary on minimum rehearsal, his willingness to perform with students and amateurs – had evolved into a different kind of conductor. His feet were, in the metaphorical sense as well as in the precepts of his volume *About Conducting*, firmly on the ground. He was not included among Ewen's *Dictators of the Baton*. (Beecham was.) A builder, explorer and curator, he established for British listeners, by repetition as well as by first performances, the long-lasting basic orchestral repertory. Within the whole Bach-to-Britten range which he covered, only one composer (Vivaldi) has been added since his death to the canon of popular acceptance.

If we seek evidence for Wood simply as an outstanding interpreter, then it must be admitted that the greatest acclaim came mainly in his earlier decades. Not even Hans Richter's performances were always preferred to his then. When, with his own orchestra or with a festival chorus drilled through months of patient rehearsals, he rode the whirlwind of Tchaikovsky or re-sculptured a Handel oratorio, critics as well as audiences were in no doubt that they were experiencing the conductor's art at its height. When New York or Zurich invited Henry J. Wood, they looked to hear (and reports show they were not disappointed) deliveries of the classics no less individually arresting than a Mengelberg, a Weingartner, a Walter would provide. In presenting new-born works which bid to bridge the gap between the old romanticism and its newer forms – the music of Strauss, Sibelius, Elgar, Rachmaninoff – Wood had those composers' complete confidence that he knew the way from the printed page to the hearts of the audience. Soloists granted him an equal confidence: whether for voice, piano or other instruments, he was a superlative accompanist.

Celebrating

Wood's later period, where the BBC was a giant to be wheedled and cajoled, and where only the annual Proms placed him at dead-centre of British music-making, put the emphasis on the glory and variety of his repertory. Less and less did his reputation stand on finely shaped, wholly individualized performances. Frank Howes, chief music critic of *The Times* from 1943 to 1960 and the exerciser of an icy hand on the postwar British musical scene, pushed Wood into the past while he was still alive (1942):

> Every critic, professional and amateur, cuts his teeth on Sir Henry Wood, who has been the teacher of an uncountable host of grateful listeners – none the less grateful if perhaps they ultimately outgrow his interpretations. . . More sophisticated tastes miss in his work fine shades of expression and find his permanently broad outlines and bold effects apt to be oppressive.

In other words: slog away, dear Sir Henry, while we submit our souls to be ravished by the sophistications of Sir Thomas. Vaughan Williams had anticipated that with a defence of Wood which may seem to be a backhanded compliment but was assuredly not meant as such:

> The 'Proms' do not appeal, and are not meant to appeal, to the jaded hypercritical Aesthete – they are essentially 'popular'. The meticulous fidelity of a Toscanini is not only impossible, it is not even desirable in these circumstances. . .Is not the cult of super-perfection carried too far? If it is to be a question of quality versus quantity, I am for quantity every time. A listener with imagination and insight should want the music, not so-and-so's rendering of it. If the music is intelligibly played and above all with verve and vitality, why should we wish for more?

Vaughan Williams' words now seem antique. The expansion of music in recorded form, in ever greater immediacy of sound, leads us to praise no conductor for 'quantity every time'. We may now seek 'so-and-so's' renderings in almost unending extension. At the same time we can conjure many performances out of the past through modern reissues of older recordings. Some consideration of Wood's recordings in this light is made in Appendix 2. But his recorded output is too small, and too bitty, to raise any reasonable expectation that a new generation will rate him *simply as an interpreter* with Beecham or Stokowski, to name only two – two who were lucky enough, as he was not, to survive into the era of post-war recording technologies. Sharing with Stokowski a zeal for exploiting the orchestral palette, he did not share Stokowski's interest in the techniques of recording. *My Life of Music* is barren of any evocation of the recording studio.

412

As an interpreter he eludes us. Yet, seen in the widest historical perspective, Henry J. Wood is surely not to be denied the crown of greatness as a conductor. He wrought prodigiously on the musical life of his countrymen, at a time when personal exertion – of a performer in giving, and a listener in journeying to receive – was still the fundamental mode of musical experience, with the 'gramophone' and the radio a long way behind. Endlessly persistent in his work, and conveying a joy in that persistence, he left his country's music-making a sturdier and wider-spreading tree than he had found it.

Not that Britain had ever been a 'land without music'. The phrase itself is a phantom: much quoted in later indignant rebuttal, it was unknown in Victorian times. When first found in 1914 as 'Das Land ohne Musik', it was used in a German wartime polemic attacking Britain not for lack of music but for lack of 'soul'. If there was a charge to be laid against Victorian musical life, it was for an over-fascination with foreign musical names on the one hand, and a narrowly self-feeding musical culture (the oratorio and the ballad being examples) on the other. For this reason Wood's embrace of the widest concert repertory and his remoteness from any little-Englandism is deeply significant.

In person an essentially lower-middle-class Londoner-of-Londoners, never happier than when breathing English air, in music he was a cosmopolitan, as omnivorous of different countries' music as of different centuries' music. He presented that music to the widest audience in the land: he gave the people possession of it. Nobody grasped that better than the scholar, multiple linguist and Cambridge professor who became the first president of the International Society for Contemporary Music. 'All honour and gratitude', Edward J. Dent wrote in the 1944 album of tributes to Wood, 'to the man who has made England once again a musical country.'

Soon after Henry J. Wood's death, Jessie's doctor advised her to take a short holiday on the south coast. Leaving their flat, she took with her on the bus to the station a suitcase which still bore Henry's leather label.

> The case fell over rounding Marble Arch into Park Lane, and the conductor righting it popped his head round the corner. (I was sitting just inside.) 'Did you belong to *him*?' – 'Yes.' – 'Ah, we miss him at home. He taught us to love music. . . .'

Celebrating

When the bus arrived at the nearest stop to Victoria station, it was raining heavily.

> I went to pick up my case but the bus conductor quietly took me by the arm and, with my case, left his bus and passengers, and, taking me across to the station, gave me in charge of a porter. 'No,' he said (when I protested, 'You can't leave your bus!'), 'I'm going to carry this over for you. *He* did more for us.'

Appendix 1

'My Confession'

[This revelatory document, signed by Henry J. Wood and dated 4 February 1939 at both top and bottom, resides in the British Library's Henry Wood manuscript collection, file 56431. It takes up six folded double-page foolscap sheets, i.e. making twenty-four sides, of which only the odd numbers from 1 to 11 (i.e. not 12) are used.

The oddities of spelling and punctuation go markedly beyond Wood's usual carelessness in writing and possibly indicate the tense circumstances of its origin. All such oddities are retained here. They include a wrong middle initial for his wife and a wrongly spelt surname (properly Greatrex) for his father-in-law, as well as a mis-spelling of Helen Douglas Irvine, who was his own literary collaborator as well as his wife's close friend. Equally to be noted is the mis-spelling 'Goldsacks' as a surname: Jessie Goldsack, elsewhere referred to as Mrs Linton, was the person for whose benefit this 'confession' was evidently intended.]

I (Sir) Henry Wood of 49 Hallam Street, London W.1 wish to state and set forth the following statement about my private life. For nearly 20 years, I went through the most trying and difficult life, that any married man could possibly endure. My wife (Muriel M Wood) certainly possessed one of the worst and most difficult tempers, imaginable, inherited from her father (Major Gretrex [*no punctuation*!] for three days at a time and often longer she would send me into coventry and not speak a word to me for three whole days, and considering she looked after the business side of my musical life the difficulties were intensely difficult, and often when leaving Chorley Wood in the morning she would not tell me my day's work and it was only by looking in my diary, I found my day's work, further for months on end I used to catch the 6.30 pm train from Marylebone Station to Chorley Wood or Rickmansworth, arriving home in time for dinner, and the meal was rushed through in 30 minutes, after which correspondance [*sic*] was started (after a long day of musical work) and while I tried to rest a little bit from 9 to 11 pm and play games in the Drawing Room with my daughters, Tania and Avril, Mother would be tapping at the type writer all the evening – of course the whole day was taken up in her garden – this was the one thing she lived for and loved, and travelling. There was no part of the world she did not wish to visit. And my work in London was always made subservient to going away from December 15 to February 20 and from June 15 to August Bank Holiday, these

415

annual scamps abroad, either on the Continent or America, South Africa or Trinadad [*sic*], Bermuda etc were to her imperitive [*sic*] and essential.

We kept up appearances most wonderfully, but her temper became so violence [*sic*], that even her dearest friend – Miss Douglas Irving became broken-hearted, and many's the time she told me 'What has happened to Muriel, why does she treat everybody in this impossible manner?' Twelve years ago I remember my daughters telling me 'Dear Daddy, how ever do you stick it, we can't ['] and Tania took a flat in London at this time with Miss Joan White[.] I waited for several years to slipt [*sic*] away and leave her, but I was determined to try and stick it until my daughters were old enough to get their own living and lead their own lives. I lavished all the money I could lay hands out [*sic*] to give them a fine education, I kept three cars going for some years, one for Mother and one for Tania and Avril.

Tania went abroad a good deal, especially to Paris and stayed with my old friend Madame Aubertin (26 Avenue d'Eylau, Paris 16) who will confirm all I say.

Working as I do, and giving forth so much nervous energy in my Conducting and my Vocal teaching – it is essential that I have good and regular food – Muriel never cared for food and a glass of milk and a bun were sufficient for her needs for hours on end. This used to get on my nerves most terribly. I left all my money affairs entirely in her hands, and made few enquiries and only signed a dozen or so cheques per week. She dabbled in shares and speculated from time to time, entirely with my money, as she only had £35 per year of her own.

I was very delighted to be [away] four nights a week sometimes, in the Provinces, and then latterly I stayed a good deal at the Langham Hotel, as it was so convenient for my work.

Time after time she had a [*illegible word*] way of seeing me off on the boat at New York [or] Cape Town, and telling [me] when saying good bye on the tender, 'oh, you had better go to the Langham Hotel because Appletree Farm is let, 4 Elsworthy Road, N.W., is also let, and the daughters are staying with Miss Helen Douglas in Adam Street. After four or five weeks I shall turn up, [but first] I must go to Florida, or I must see the Victoria Falls ['] And she would walk in, to Chorley Wood or Elsworthy Road, without a word of warning to any of use [*sic*]'.

The crisis came in Rome, after I had conducted at the Augusteo, she became absolutely impossible, and I left her in the Hotel, she was going on to Sicily, and I had to come back for engagements in London, this was the last time I saw Muriel. Of course I had made up my mind, ten years before this, to leave her, if only the opportunity presented itself.

I came home to the Langham Hotel, fulfilled my Concert engagements, and went on with my Vocal teaching. Among my many pupils, a certain Mrs John Linton appeared, I knew her, as an old pupil in the early days of the Promenade Concerts under Robert Newman and she sang under [her] maiden name of Jessie Goldsacks. She had a most remarkable voice, and was a fine singer, but she married an Electrical Engineer and settled in Manchester for nearly 20 years, I never saw Mrs Linton, but when her husband died from War effects, and she had to take to her singing again, and went back to her native heath to live – Ealing. She obtained quite a good engagement in the BBC Singers, and went on with her weekly lessons with me. I fell very deeply in love with her, she was in full sympathy with my work, and of course gradually learned of my home difficulties and my unhappy existance [*sic*].

I want to very clearly state, that Mrs Linton never encouraged me and what ever happened is entirely my fault and my suggestion. I need not tell anyone how happy we have been together, in fact I feel 10 years younger, and the way my house is managed, my business is looked after and my musical friends all love and adore her, and we so often say, if we had only met 25 years ago how different my life and my musical success would have been. (for Muriel always hated and despised – musicians).

The terrible part of our life is that Muriel will not divorce me, so we have to live together as man and wife, but it is so terribly hard upon my darling Jessie. But I can do nothing. I must say my friends have rallied round me, and never given me an anxious moment, but my precious Jessie does feel the position, and if I pass away first it will be still more difficult for her – but she has been a guardian angel to me, and nothing I can say or write, can ever express my love, my adoration for my darling Jessie, who has given up and sacrificed everything to live with me and make my life a perfect joy – thank God for my good fortune and gratefulness to her for sharing my home and my life.

Henry Joseph Wood

[A note in Jessie Wood's hand is on the back page (side 1) of the manuscript, evidently added long after his death. It appears that at some point she gave it to her friend Leslie Regan for safe keeping but afterwards recovered it in order that it should survive in the British Library collection.

Dear Henry
This is just your everlasting thought for me, and which I saw only when going thro' our home library before giving it in its case to Leslie Regan in 1950 or later, maybe.

Leslie Regan FRAM, 10 Cavendish Avenue, NW8]

Appendix 2

The Recorded Legacy

When research for this book began, the modern CD collector found in the catalogues barely a surviving trace of Henry J. Wood's art as a conductor. Recent years have transformed that situation: some eight hours of Wood's conducting are now available on CD reissues, reprocessed from recordings originating in the days of 78 r.p.m. shellac discs. Taken collectively, these reissues sample almost the whole span of Wood's commercial recordings as conductor (1916–40), supplemented by a few originating in BBC performances. In the chronological survey which follows, an asterisk denotes those recordings now available on CD – more than thirty items in all, a few of them duplicated in reissues by different CD companies.

Death in 1944 debarred Wood from the technological advantages so notably reaped in recording by Thomas Beecham and every conductor since. But this is not the only reason why the harvest of Wood recordings is liable to disappoint. Purely as repertory, the sum of his recordings fails to represent the breadth or the specialities of his career. His early fame as a director of major choral masterpieces in performances by top-ranking festival choirs is not recoverable in a handful of *Messiah* choruses recorded from a 3500–strong Crystal Palace performance. Nor can the thrice-recorded *Ride of the Valkyries* (the *last recording, in 1935, sadly rough in ensemble) represent Wood's mastery of large-scale Wagner in concert, as in his Good Friday performances of *Parsifal* for the BBC in the 1930s.

Within Wood's own period, Albert Coates (1882–1953), a conductor now almost faded from public view, left a more solid orchestral legacy on record. So did Landon Ronald, beginning earlier than Wood (1911) and, thanks to his role as adviser and staff conductor at HMV, recording with such artists as Backhaus, Kreisler, Cortot, Casals, and Menuhin. Nevertheless Wood's recordings are of historical importance as evidence of performing style, and in some cases for their intrinsic worth as performances. A listing of his recorded works shows an overwhelming preponderance of composers of his own lifetime – *contemporary* music. Not a few were composers whom he had personally welcomed to his rostrum at Queen's Hall, or in whose presence he had conducted their music.

His orchestral work in the recording studio was preluded at the piano in accompanying the voice of his first wife Olga, née Mikhailov. As well as such giants as Patti, Caruso and Shalyapin, many singers of lesser historical importance recorded before 1914. 'Mrs Henry J. Wood, soprano', as Olga was identified in recording as

418

well as in concerts, was not a star; but the glimpse of her art in her last two years (1908–9) is touching. Only six single sides by her were ever issued, covering nine items, all sung in English. They remained only briefly in the catalogue of the oddly named 'Gramophone and Typewriter' company (G.&T.) of which the eventual successors were to be EMI Records.

Olga's artistic personality in combined verbal and musical interpretation (doubtless under her husband's guidance) is vivid in Arthur Somervell's 'Sleep, Baby, Sleep'. 'Farewell, forests' (Joan of Arc's aria in Act 1 of Tchaikovsky's opera *The Maid of Orleans*), necessarily much abbreviated in that era of recording, is feelingly delivered and has a presumed value in the closeness of the Woods to Tchaikovsky's era. It was the only one of Olga Wood's recorded songs to re-emerge in the LP era – on a disc (Rubini GV7), which fails to identify her husband as her accompanist.

As noted in Chapter 9, the unissued recordings ascribed to Olga's name in the company's ledgers include two songs, on a single side, actually sung by Henry J. Wood himself, to his own accompaniment: Schumann's *Die Lotosblume* (in English) and Hatton's *To Anthea* – both, especially the latter, performed in a deliberately mannered and parodied style. Wood has written the word 'Terrible' on the central label of the disc. It was obviously put on record as a private joke, not for issue, but now survives in the Royal Academy of Music collection.

After Olga Wood's death, it was another and more illustrious singer who effected Wood's first introduction to orchestral recording. For Clara Butt (1872–1936) Elgar had written his *Sea Pictures*: now the recordings in which Wood accompanied her in 1915–17 included four sides of linked extracts from Elgar's *The Dream of Gerontius*. Butt's delivery of the Angel's role, including *'Softly and gently', is highly persuasive, and a fine but now little-known tenor, Maurice D'Oisly, is heard as Gerontius. Remarkable, in view of the limited capacity afforded by recording techniques of the time, is the positive contribution by chorus and orchestra to the colouring and texture of the sound.

The other items represent not Butt's celebrated ballad repertory but a selection of favoured operatic and oratorio numbers, including *'Mon coeur s'ouvre à ta voix' ('Softly awakes my heart') from Saint-Saëns' *Samson et Dalila*. As expected, Wood's orchestral accompanying melts smoothly into the singer's phrasing and timing. Handel's *Largo ('Ombra mai fù' from *Serse*) is given not in one of its English adaptations but in Italian, with its introductory recitative. The laughter inserted by the singer into the Donizetti aria, 'Il segreto d'esser felice' ('The secret of being happy'), is charmingly individual. The original recordings were on nine single sides, soon to be reissued in double-sided couplings. (Some items were remade by Butt after 1924 with improved recording techniques and not with Wood conducting.)

Wood thus began work in the restrictive period of 'acoustic' recording, when the vibrations of musical sound were channelled through a large 'recording horn' to activate directly the movement of the needle on the wax disc. Orchestral sound could be reproduced much less well than that of the solo singer or instrumentalist. Smaller than full orchestras generally had to be used to achieve proximity to the horn, and instruments which did not register well were often omitted or replaced by others. Though the effect of enlarging public access to orchestral music can scarcely be exaggerated, the recordings themselves became rapidly outdated – first by technical advances within the 'acoustic' process and period, then by the introduction in the mid-1920s of electrical (microphoned) recording.

Though the orchestra was not formally named in the first half-dozen years of Wood's orchestral recordings, there is no doubt that it was recruited from his own Queen's Hall Symphony Orchestra (probably in reduced numbers). The appearance of that name on record labels from mid-1922 presumably denotes a formal agreement between the record company and the orchestra's owner, the music-publishing firm of Chappell's, which owned Queen's Hall. The use of his own players for recording allowed Wood to presume on familiarity with the music, with a consequent economy of rehearsal time; posterity may legitimately suppose that even the oldest records, with their now antiquated sound, represent the kind of music-making (at least in matters of tempo and expression) which Wood actually gave his Queen's Hall audiences.

The market had gradually to be probed. In his earlier years of orchestral recording, Wood (like other conductors) was restricted to short works or compelled to make drastic reductions of longer ones – Strauss's *Till Eulenspiegel* on two sides (about ten minutes), Beethoven's *Eroica* on six sides (his later, electrical recording required fourteen sides). The main interest in this period of his recorded output is in its strong representation of the special elements of his concert repertory, including Wagner's *Song of the Rhine-Daughters* (Wood's own transcription from the opening of *Götterdämmerung*, with the voice-parts taken by instruments), and a *Tambourin* by Rameau. Columbia even risked some fairly new works: Balfour Gardiner's *Shepherd Fennel's Dance*, various short pieces by Percy Grainger, and Holbrooke's *Three Blind Mice* variations.

Unfortunately the contemporary work of most interest, Delius's *Dance Rhapsody* no. 1, cannot be commended in Wood's recording (1923) – not only abridged but jerky in its gradations of movement. He recorded no further Delius, not even the second such *Rhapsody*, of which he gave the première in that year at Queen's Hall. Evidently neither Columbia nor Decca (his later company) was willing to challenge the competition of Beecham in the Delius field. Similarly with Sibelius: Wood was denied the recording of any Sibelius symphony, though he was the first conductor to present no. 1 to British audiences and would be the first also with no. 7, Sibelius's last symphony.

Nor, though acknowledged one of the greatest of Tchaikovsky conductors, was he to leave behind him any integral recording of a Tchaikovsky symphony. After an abridged, single-sided, single movement from no. 4 in 1915, he made a version of all four movements of no. 6 in 1923 which is poorly balanced in sound as well as markedly cut. The famous 'lamenting' melody in the first movement, scored by the composer as alternate notes for first and second violins, ludicrously emerges as a 'tune' on the first violins only, as melody-note, non-melody-note, melody-note, etc.

Those interested in the history of orchestral playing will expect to encounter in these early recordings a greater use of *portamento* in string-playing (the continuous sliding transition from one note to the next) than is customary today. But the difference has to be carefully listened for and does not fundamentally influence the approach to musical phrasing. As Robert Philip suggests in his book *Early Recordings and Musical Style* (a point brought out even more in his earlier, unpublished Ph. D.

dissertation), Wood in comparison with others of his time kept the use of *portamento* on a pretty tight leash and probably influenced such later conductors as Boult in this direction.

Philip quotes Wood himself (1927): 'String-players have been sliding about their fingerboards in a barbarous manner during the past few years, having acquired the habit, I fancy, in restaurant orchestras where the public seems to enjoy the wobble and the slide with certain dishes, possibly because tasteless and nauseating playing is suitable to similar kinds of food'. An exceptional, deliberately expressive use of *portamento* may be found in the rise to the top note of the first phrase of Mendelssohn's *Spring Song* – this on a performance of 1929 in the succeeding period of electrical recording.

Acoustic recording had itself improved by the time the new process of electrical recording arrived in the mid-1920s, but the benefits of the new process – with sound transmitted to the recording needle in the form of electrical impulses, via the microphone – were decisive. Works which Wood had originally recorded a dozen years before now came in newly minted versions, among them his *Götterdämmerung* transcription (*Song of the Rhine-Daughters*) and his own orchestration of Rachmaninoff's **Prelude in C sharp minor*. The improvement of sound also helped persuade the public to listen to recordings of longer works without the previous truncations, and the catalogue expanded accordingly. 'Columbia are celebrating Beethoven's centenary [the centenary of his death, 1927] with something like an orgy of his music . . . all the nine symphonies, an overture [*Coriolan*], twelve quartets and three sonatas', announced the *Gramophone* magazine.

Henry J. Wood's share of the 'orgy' was the symphony no. 3, the *Eroica*; but it ran up immediately against Albert Coates's version on the rival label, HMV. 'Sir Henry Wood is less thrilling than Coates in the *Eroica* and the general effect is less massive,' the *Gramophone* reviewer thought [March, 1927]. It is indeed a performance of somewhat neutral interpretation, though technically acceptable for its time. Wood's recording of Beethoven's *Leonora no. 3* overture, likewise issued in the centenary year, is strongly articulated and paced, and the clear pitch of the timpani is a feature not always evident even on some later recordings. In 1934 Wood brought the Haydn *Farewell* symphony (no. 45) into the British record catalogue for the first time – with solo instruments admirably registered and the vigour and grace of the music happily balanced.

The sum of these, together with Schubert's **Unfinished Symphony* in 1933, fell nevertheless short of winning for Wood the esteem granted to such conductors as Weingartner and Mengelberg in the classical (Viennese) symphonic style. Wood's individuality is perhaps most to be relished in highly characterised, lilting pieces like the Saint-Saëns *Danse Macabre* and the orchestrated version of a *Chant sans paroles* by Tchaikovsky. The relish may be extended to his pair of Bach's *Brandenburg Concertos* (nos. 3 and 6), if the listener of today suspends the search for 'authenticity'. With a full string force, **no. 3* preserves a vital clarity in texture as well as in structure.

This period of the Columbia releases between 1926 and 1934 found Wood also expounding short works by such composers as Mendelssohn, Sibelius (but only *Finlandia*), and Percy Grainger (**Molly on the Shore* and **Mock Morris*). In a class of its own was the full-length, 12-sided version of *Elgar's violin concerto with Albert Sammons as soloist – a work which had been stripped to a bare four sides for Wood's earlier recording with the same soloist. The full-length version has been accorded the status of a classic recording, acknowledged by reissues on both LP and CD. Reissues on CD also preserve the gratifying partnership between conductor and pianist in Franck's *Symphonic Variations* with Walter Gieseking and in 'the' Litolff *Scherzo with Irene Scharrer.

But by this time, when so many other British and foreign conductors were available, Columbia's use of Wood was far less enthusiastic than it had been in the pioneering period of ten years before. The opportunity of a move to Decca must have been welcome, bringing incidentally a first chance to record the highly popular 'Klenovsky' orchestration of Bach's *Toccata and Fugue in D minor*. But one wonders whether Wood knew of Decca's evident intention to issue much of his work (beginning with Beethoven's *Fifth Symphony in July 1935) on a 'cheap label', at a price of 2s.6d rather than five or six shillings per record. It was good marketing and good for musical culture, but inevitably reinforced Wood's 'Proms' image of the 1930s – that of a popular conductor rather than a great interpreter.

Using a reconstituted Queen's Hall Orchestra (see p.283), Decca can hardly be blamed for getting Wood to re-record, for the benefit of its catalogue, such items of his popular repertory as the *Ride of the Valkyries, Finlandia*, and the Järnefelt *Praeludium*. Eric Coates's *London Suite* (one of its numbers providing the signature tune to the popular radio show, 'In Town Tonight') and the separate *London Bridge March were also recorded. Among such items Grainger's *Handel in the Strand* deserves a special mention: brilliantly orchestrated by Wood himself (the composer has done no full-scale orchestration), it had not been recorded by Wood since pre-electric days, and now came over as one of the best-recorded and most exhilaratingly performed items of all his recorded output.

A bold expansion of the repertory came with Wood's recordings in 1937 of Bruckner's posthumous *Overture in G minor and Dohnányi's *Symphonic Minutes*, with the overture to Glinka's *Ruslan and Lyudmila* as a last (and rather perfunctory) evocation of his Russian speciality. To Handel, while he did not apply Klenovsky's brush, Wood was an 'improver' still, with modernised orchestrations of the *Samson overture and of the *Sailors' Dance and Rigaudon* (Wood's combination from two numbers from different Handel operas) which now seem a superfluous labour. But in the overture to *Berenice* the livelier movements fully support Wood's robust re-orchestration, and the celebrated Minuet is irresistible as a cello solo against muted orchestral strings.

Elgar having died in 1934, Wood's close relationship to him no doubt prompted Decca to include the *Enigma Variations* among the longer works Wood recorded. It is an attractive version, perhaps with a slight lack of weight in the final variation, but with a welcome freedom from mannerism (at the end of the *Dorabella* variation, for instance). There followed Brahms's *Variations on a Theme of Haydn*, more notable for expressive instrumental tone-colour than for depth of sympathy – whereas a rarer work, Dvořák's *Symphonic Variations*, found in Wood's treatment the happiest unity of pace, colour, and feeling. During rehearsals for the latter work, the Decca production team seized a moment to capture the sound of *Wood's voice exhorting his players – the resulting disc being presented to Wood for his private pleasure. Its survival in the Royal Academy of Music collection has permitted its universalisation via CD.

Decca's recording of Vaughan Williams's *A London Symphony*, having the approval of the composer (and despite the assault of *The Times*, as narrated in Chapter 18), retains historic importance. The urgency of flow and the specificity of orchestral colour in the composer's 'scene-painting' are notable. In Vaughan Williams's familiar *Fantasy on 'Greensleeves'*, recorded during the same week of 1936, Wood opted for a rather fast, dance-like lilt which may be preferred to the usual dreamy search for 'olde English' sentiment. These two, together with the *overture to *The Wasps*, were linked on CD in 1993 with Vaughan Williams's *Serenade to Music*: this Dutton Laboratories disc was the first to establish, with skilled technical remastering, how attractively Wood's orchestral sound could re-emerge.

The *Serenade to Music*, as the product of Wood's jubilee celebrations in 1938, belonged not to Wood's brief (1935–37) stay with Decca but to his return to the Columbia fold. The recording of the *Serenade*, made ten days after the première by the original conductor with the original sixteen soloists and orchestra (the BBC Symphony), represents a rare type of historical authenticity – similar to that which Britten was to impart to works he conducted on record *immediately* after their first performances. Columbia treated the occasion handsomely and the singers gave of their best: Isobel Baillie's soprano quietly soaring above the rest in the final 'touches of sweet harmony' is not easily forgotten.

What might have lain ahead for Wood in the Columbia studios, had war not supervened, is idle speculation. *Some* sessions, even in the darkest days, were carried through, using not a specially enlisted orchestra with a Queen's Hall tag but the two orchestras in whose wartime survival Wood played a generous part. He conducted the London Symphony Orchestra in a four-sided version of his own *Fantasia on British Sea Songs* (which he had not brought to the studio since his two-sided pre-electrical recording of 1916). Made in November 1939 to meet patriotic demand, it shows how different was Wood's score – longer, with fanfares, and without voices – from the modern BBC concoction. The last day he spent in the recording studio, 4 March 1940, yielded recordings with the London Philharmonic Orchestra of Elgar's *Pomp and Circumstance Marches* nos. *1 and *4, Gounod's *Funeral March of a Marionette* and a performance of Berlioz's *Carnaval romain* which has the old fire blazing anew from the baton. That was one day after his seventy-first birthday.

Begining in the 1930s, recordings also survive from a few of the BBC's studio performances or public concerts. Copies of these BBC recordings are available for public listening at the National Sound Archive (now part of the British Library), and a number of these recordings have also achieved CD reissue. Of these the most interesting is the sole recording which survives of a promenade concert at Queen's Hall, on 8 September 1936. It provides four items, or five if both the short pieces from Schubert's *Rosamunde* music are counted. Wood's treatment of the famous *Entr'acte in B flat – unusually slow, each phrase caressed – is to be cherished, and the *Ballet no. 1* gracefully follows. The violinist Jean Pougnet and the violist Bernard Shore are eloquent soloists in Mozart's *Sinfonia Concertante* (shortened); Elisabeth Schumann sings the aria *'L'amerò' from Mozart's opera *Il re pastore* as well as Mozart's familiar *Alleluia*. The BBC Symphony Orchestra is led by Marie Wilson, who also plays the violin *obbligato* for the operatic aria.

Wood's conducting of the Proms in their new home, the Royal Albert Hall, is represented in the BBC archives solely by the first performance of John Ireland's *Epic March* on 27 June 1942. Recording failed to perpetuate Wood's historic wartime performance of the Shostakovich *Leningrad* Symphony (22 June 1942): no more than a seven-minute extract of the broadcast is preserved in BBC archival stock. But the first performance in Britain of Prokofiev's Violin Concerto no. 2 (with Robert Soetens as soloist), recorded in the broadcasting studio on 20 December 1936, is preserved entire.

Likewise from the studio, the first performance of Bax's violin concerto (with Eda Kersey), a BBC commission, is preserved from 22 November 1943. Wood had broadcast all of Bax's first three symphonies and given the première of the third (dedicated to him), so the absence of any complete Bax symphony or even a complete symphonic movement is a particularly regrettable gap in his discography. Tantalizingly, two brief extracts from the first movement of *no. 3 are heard in the course of a recording taken by the BBC at a Proms rehearsal in the Royal Albert Hall on 24 June 1942, during which Wood is also heard rehearsing Bach's *Brandenburg Concerto no. 3.

Three items in an Albert Hall performance with brass bands (a medium he had never worked with until then) ironically survive from 1943 as Wood's last performance to be recorded – at any rate 'officially'. The qualification is necessary because private recordings 'off-air' (that is, transferred 'live' from radio broadcasts) had for some years been technically possible. The only two examples known in Wood's case, however, are of earlier date and both are fragmentary. They are (1) detached *extracts from Bax's Cello Concerto, from a BBC studio performance, 1 February 1938 (soloist, Beatrice Harrison); (2) sections of part 2 of Elgar's *The Dream of Gerontius*, with Muriel Brunskill, Parry Jones and Harold Williams, from the BBC's Good Friday performance in Queen's Hall, 15 April 1938.

A listing of Wood's recorded performances is thus a biographical necessity. The fullest possible discography has been deposited in the National Sound Archive of the British Library, which is also the repository of the recordings themselves. The Royal Academy of Music houses a unique archive of Henry J. Wood's and Olga Wood's joint recordings of 1908–9 and of the recordings Henry J. Wood made for Decca – not merely the published issues in these categories, but the rejected takes as well.

Such a discography would aim not only to list the published recordings by their catalogue numbers, but to identify each session in the recording studio by the matrix number and the number of the take, with dates. (The matrix is the single recorded disc in its first-processed form, whether eventually approved for issue or not.) The listing below confines itself to the issued discs only and their catalogue numbers, with dates of recording and first issue. Reissues are not included.

The listing in each section is chronological by date of recording. Actual dates in the studio are specified where known (direct from company ledgers, or from the research of Christopher Dyment). Where studio dates are not available, the chronological order has been fixed from the sequence of matrix numbers (not given here), against with Christopher Dyment's kind co-operation.

All records are 78 rpm (except for a few at 80 rpm). All are double-sided except as indicated for Olga Wood and Clara Butt. All are 12-inch except for the following label-prefixes on Columbia, which denote 10-inch:

D
5000 (and upwards)
DB

Other indications: *pt* (part), *s/ss* (side, sides), *w* (with).

The orchestra on all Columbia records up to L1478 (released August 1922) was anonymous; thereafter it was the NEW QUEEN'S HALL ORCHESTRA on Columbia and the QUEEN'S HALL ORCHESTRA on Wood's Decca recordings, with exceptions indicated in this listing as follows:

BBC SO   BBC Symphony Orchestra
BSO   British Symphony Orchestra (a made-up name)
LPO   London Philharmonic Orchestra
LSO   London Symphony Orchestra
SO   Symphony Orchestra (unnamed)

The soloists collaborating with Wood were (apart from Mrs Henry J. Wood, Dame Clara Butt, and Maurice D'Oisly, who appears as solo tenor with Butt):

violinist   Albert Sammons
pianists   Harriet Cohen, Clifford Curzon, Walter Gieseking, Irene Scharrer
singers   (in Vaughan Williams's *Serenade to Music* only) Isobel Baillie, Margaret
            Balfour, Stiles-Allen, Eva Turner, soprano
            Muriel Brunskill, Astra Desmond, Mary Jarred, Elsie Suddaby, contralto
            Parry Jones, Heddle Nash, Frank Titterton, Walter Widdop, tenor
            Norman Allin, Robert Easton, Roy Henderson, Harold Williams, bass

and, in BBC recordings mentioned at the end of this list, the violinists Eda Kersey, Robert Soetens and Jean Pougnet, the violist Bernard Shore, and the soprano Elisabeth Schumann.

I RECORDINGS AS PIANO ACCOMPANIST
  TO OLGA WOOD ('Mrs HENRY J. WOOD'), soprano

These records were issued by the Gramophone and Typewriter company. All were single-sided. The order of listing is by chronology of recording dates, followed by composer and short form of title, original catalogue number, date of issue.

RECORDING DATE	COMPOSER AND WORK		CAT.NO.	ISSUE DATE
17/07/08	TCHAIKOVSKY	'Farewell, forests' (*The Maid of Orleans*)	GC3778	1908
04/06/09	ALLITSEN	'Since we two parted'		
	ROGERS	'At Parting'	GC3833	1909
	SOMERVELL	'Sleep, baby, sleep'	GC3834	1909
	COATES	'Orpheus with his lute'		
	COATES	'Under the greenwood tree'	GC3835	1909
	PITT	'Love is a dream'		
	CAPEL	'Star and Rose'	03161	1909
	COATES	'Who is Sylvia?'		
	COATES	'It was a lover and his lass'	03162	1909

Henry J. Wood

II RECORDINGS AS CONDUCTOR OF ORCHESTRA
FOR CLARA BUTT, contralto:

These records were issued on the Columbia label. All were (in their first issued form, as given here) single-sided. Actual dates of recording are not known, but were probably only a few months before the respective dates of issue (and none before September 1915 – see Chapter 11).

Maurice D'Oisly, tenor, and an unnamed chorus participate in the extracts from Elgar's *The Dream of Gerontius*.

The order of listing is by chronology of recording sessions, though the exact dates are not known. The information for each record gives the composer and short form of title, original catalogue number, date of issue.

COMPOSER AND WORK		CAT.NO.	ISSUE DATE
GOUNOD	'When all was young' (*Faust*)	74003	12/15
SAINT-SAËNS	'Mon coeur s'ouvre' (*Samson et Dalila*)	74004	01/16
HANDEL	'Ombra mai fù' (*Serse*)	7121	02/16
ELGAR	(*The Dream of Gerontius*):		
	'My work is done'	75005	06/16
	'I see not those false spirits'	75006	06/16
	'We now have passed the gate'	75007	06/16
	'Softly and gently'	75008	06/16
MENDELSSOHN	'O rest in the Lord' (*Elijah*)	7127	09/16
GOUNOD	'O divine Redeemer'	7135	10/16
HANDEL	'Rend'il sereno' (*Sosarme*)	74009	10/16
DONIZETTI	'Il segreto' (*Lucrezia Borgia*)	74012	11/16
HANDEL	'He shall feed his flock'(*Messiah*)	7139	12/16
GLUCK	'Che farò' (*Orfeo*)	74038	09/17

III ORCHESTRAL RECORDINGS
COLUMBIA 1915–34

DATE OF RECORDING IF KNOWN	COMPOSER AND WORK		CAT.NO.	ISSUE DATE
	WAGNER	*Lohengrin*: Prelude Act 3		
	RACHMANINOFF	Prelude in C# minor	L1005	11/15
	– WOOD			
	GRAINGER	*Shepherd's Hey*		
	TCHAIKOVSKY	Symphony 4: Scherzo	L1006	11/15
	WAGNER	*Tristan*: Prelude and Isolde's Love Song	L1013	02/16
	BEETHOVEN	*Coriolan*: Overture		
	WAGNER	*Tannhäuser*: Grand March	L1021	02/16
	CHABRIER	*España*		
	GRAINGER	*Irish Tune from County Derry*	L1024	03/16
	WAGNER	*Götterdämmerung: Song of the Rhine-Daughters*		
	WAGNER	*Die Walküre: Ride of the Valkyries*	L1027	04/16
	WAGNER–WOOD	*Träume*		
	GARDINER	*Shepherd Fennel's Dance*	L1033	05/16

426

	WOOD	*Fantasia on British Sea Songs*	L1052	08/16
	BRAHMS	Hungarian Dances 5, 6	L1054	09/16
	GOUNOD	*Faust* Ballet Music 1, 2	L1063	09/16
	GOUNOD	*Faust* Ballet Music 3, 4, 5	L1064	10/16
	STRAUSS, R.	*Till Eulenspiegel*	L1067	10/16
	ELGAR	Violin Concerto *w* Sammons	L1071–2	10/16
	GOUNOD	*Faust* Ballet Music 6, 7		
	CORDER	*Prospero* Overture	L1066	11/16
	RAFF—WOOD	Cavatina		
	SAINT-SAËNS	*Danse Macabre*	L1118	11/20
	GRAINGER—WOOD	*Handel in the Strand*		
	WAGNER	*Die Meistersinger*: Dance of the Apprentices	L1125	02/17
	HOLBROOKE	*Three Blind Mice*	L1134	03/17
	RIMSKY-KORSAKOV	*Capriccio Espagnol*	L1148	04/17
	DUKAS	*The Sorcerer's Apprentice*		
	WAGNER	*The Flying Dutchman*: Overture	L1172	06/17
	WAGNER	*Rienzi*: Overture	L1182	09/17
	WAGNER	*Tannhäuser*: Overture	L1196	09/17
	BIZET	*Carmen*: Overture, entr'actes, Ballet Music	L1208–9	12/20
	GRANADOS	Five Spanish Dances, 1–4	L1214–5	02/18
	GRANADOS	Five Spanish Dances, 5		
	ALBENIZ	*Catalonia*	L1216	03/18
	TCHAIKOVSKY	*Capriccio Italien*	L1230	11/18
06/18	MUSORGSKY—WOOD	*Pictures at an Exhibition*, pts 1&2	L1341	02/20
06/18	MUSORGSKY—WOOD	*Pictures at an Exhibition*, pts 3&4	L1342	03/20
08/18	HEROLD	*Zampa*: Overture	L1247	06/19
08/18	BEETHOVEN	*Leonora*: Overture 3		
	BEETHOVEN	Minuet from Septet op.20 (1s)	L1319–20	10/19
08/18	MASSENET	*Le Cid*: Ballet Music	L1327–9	12/19
08/18	MASCAGNI	*Cavalleria Rusticana* excerpts	L1354	05/20
07/19	SCHUBERT	Symphony 8	L1360–1	06/20
07/19	LALO	*Symphonie Espagnole w* Sammons	L1365	08/20
07/19	CARR	*Lt Warneford VC*	L1367	08/20
	TCHAIKOVSKY	*The Battle of Poltava*		
07/19	WAGNER	*Tannhäuser: Venusberg* Music	L1378	09/20
07/19	GOUNOD	*Funeral March of a Marionette*		
	ARCADELT—WOOD	*Ave Maria*	L1379	10/20
07/19	DVOŘÁK	Slavonic Dances 1, 2	L1387	10/20
07/19	ROSSINI	*Semiramide*: Overture	L1395	01/21
07/19	LISZT—WOOD	Hungarian Rhapsody 1	L1412	10/20
08/19	LISZT—WOOD	Hungarian Rhapsody 2	L1415	05/26
11/20	MUSORGSKY	*Night on the Bare Mountain*	L1417	02/22
12/20	AUBER	*Fra Diavolo*: Overture	L1402	03/21
12/20	MEYERBEER	*Le Prophète: Coronation March*		
	HANDEL—WOOD	*Largo*	L1403	04/20
15/06/21	GOUNOD	*Mors et Vita*: 'Judex'		
14/11/21	WAGNER	*Das Rheingold: Entry of the Gods into Valhalla*	L1427	06/22
12/12/21	FRANCK	*Le Chasseur Maudit*	L1423	03/22
20/06/22	ROSSINI	*William Tell* Overture		
	MASCAGNI	*Cavalleria Rusticana*: Intermezzo (1s)	L1435–6	09/22
30/06/22	BEETHOVEN	Symphony 3	L1447–9	11/22

4,11/12/22	MENDELSSOHN	*A Midsummer Night's Dream* Overture	L1462	02/23
11/12/22	BANTOCK	*The Pierrot of the Minute*	L1463	03/23
13/12/22	TURINA	*Danzas Fantasticas*	L1467–8	04/23
17,18/4/23	TCHAIKOVSKY	Symphony 6	L1489–92	10/23
24/04/23	MENDELSSOHN	*Fingal's Cave*	L1478	08/23
16/05/23	RAMEAU	*Tambourin*	L1506	12/23
16/05/23	BACH	Gavotte in E		
	BEETHOVEN	Rondino for wind	L1515	01/24
16/05/24	LALO	Aubade in D		
		Aubade in G minor	L1531	03/24
30/05/23	DELIUS	Dance Rhapsody 1 (3ss)	L1505–6	12/23
2,9/07/24	FRANCK	Symphony in D minor	L1569–72	10/24
9,10/7/24 & 16/7/24	ELGAR	*Enigma* Variations	L1629–32	05/25
24/09/24	BACH	Clavier Concerto in D minor *w* Cohen	L1624–6	04/25
05/02/25	BACH–WOOD	Suite 6	L1684–5	01/26
5/02/25 & 25,26/3/25	HAYDN	Symphony 94 (5ss)		
	JÄRNEFELT	*Praeludium*	L1668–70	10/25
26/03/25	WEBER	*Oberon* Overture	L1677	11/25

Electrical recordings begin here

07/12/25	NICOLAI	*The Merry Wives of Windsor* Overture	L1723	05/26
07/12/25	GOUNOD	*Faust* Ballet Music	L1794–5	01/27
14/04/26	LISZT–WOOD	Hungarian Rhapsody 2	L1796–7	01/27
15/04/26	WAGNER	*Götterdämmerung: Song of the Rhine-Daughters*	L1993–4	05/28
15/04/26	WAGNER	*Lohengrin*: Prelude, Act 3		
	RACHMANINOFF–WOOD	Prelude in C# minor	L1005R	08/29
20/04/26	TCHAIKOVSKY	*1812* Overture	L1764–6	09/26
22/04/26	TCHAIKOVSKY	*Chant sans Paroles* op.2/3	L1746	09/26
23/04/26	SCHUBERT	Symphony 8	L1791–3	01/27
12/06/26	HANDEL	*Messiah*: 'And the glory', 'Behold the Lamb of God', 'He trusted in God', 'Let us break their bonds' *w* Handel Festival Choir	L1768–9	09/26
28/11/26 & 2,5/12/26	BEETHOVEN	Symphony 3	L1868–74	03/27
9/12/26 & 13/04/27	SAINT-SAËNS	*Danse Macabre*	L1987	09/27
28/02/27	BEETHOVEN	*Leonora* Overture 3	L1978–9	07/27
13/04/27	WAGNER	*Die Walküre: Ride of the Valkyries*	L1994	05/28
13/7/28	ROSSINI	*William Tell*: Overture	5058–9	11/28
13/7/28	MENDELSSOHN	*A Midsummer Night's Dream*: Overture (side 4 not Wood)	9559–60	12/28
04/03/29	JÄRNEFELT	*Praeludium w* SO	DX194	02/31
04/03/29	SIBELIUS	*Finlandia*	9655	06/29
04/03/29	DVOŘÁK	Slavonic Dance op.46/8 (s.2 not Wood)	L2313	08/29
04/03/29	MENDELSSOHN	*Fingal's Cave* Overture	9843–4	10/29
04/03/29	MENDELSSOHN	Songs Without Words Op.62/6 (Spring Song), Op.67/4 (*Bees' Wedding*)	9844	10/29
18/3/29 & 10/04/29	ELGAR	Violin Concerto *w* Sammons	L2346–51	12/29
19/06/29	LISZT–WOOD	Hungarian Rhapsody 2	DX9–10	03/30
19/06/29	BACH–WOOD	Partita in E: Prelude	DX10	03/30

12/06/30	BACH	*Brandenburg* Concerto 6 *w* SO	LX41–2	09/30
12/06/30	RACHMANINOFF	Prelude in C# minor *w* SO		
	—WOOD			
	TRAD—WOOD	*Volga Boat Song w* SO	DX87	10/30
12/06/30	MASCAGNI	*Cavalleria Rusticana*: Intermezzo *w* SO	DX194	02/31
16/06/32	BACH	*Brandenburg* Concerto 3 *w* BSO	LX173	10/32
10/10/32	QUILTER	*A Children's Overture w* LPO	DB951–2	11/32
16/10/32	GRAINGER	*Molly on the Shore w* BSO		
		Mock Morris w BSO	LX200	02/33
16/10/32	BACH—	*Air on a G String w* BSO		
	WILHELMJ			
	BACH—WOOD	Gavotte in E *w* BSO	DX475	08/33
31/10/32	LISZT	Piano Concerto 1		
		w Gieseking & LPO	LX181–2	01/33
31/10/32	FRANCK	Symphonic Variations *w* Gieseking &		
		LPO	LX192–3	03/33
30/10/33	SCHUBERT	Symphony 8 *w* LSO	DX551–3	12/33
30/10/33	LITOLFF	Concerto Symphonique 4: Scherzo *w*		
		Scharrer & LSO	DB1267	12/33
19/04/34	MOZART	*Don Giovanni* Overture *w* LSO	DX587	08/34
19/04/34	HAYDN	Symphony 45 (*Farewell*) *w* LSO	LX323–5	10/34

IV ORCHESTRAL RECORDINGS
DECCA 1935–37

DATE OF RECORDING	COMPOSER AND WORK		CAT.NO.	ISSUE DATE
26,29/4/35 & 3/5/35	BEETHOVEN	Symphony 5	K757–60	07/35
30/4/35	GRAINGER	*Handel in the Strand*		
		Mock Morris	K767	08/35
29,30/4/35	BRAHMS	Variations on a Theme by Haydn	K763–4	09/35
01/05/35	WAGNER	*Die Walküre: Ride of the Valkyries*	K761	07/35
01/05/35	WAGNER	*Götterdämmerung: Song of the Rhine-*		
		Daughters	K765–6	08/35
02/05/35	RACHMANINOFF	Prelude in C# minor	K762	07/35
	—WOOD			
02/05/35	BACH—	Toccata and Fugue in D minor	K768	08/35
	KLENOVSKY			
08/05/35	DVOŘÁK	Humoreske	K762	07/35
08/05/35	JÄRNEFELT	*Praeludium*	K766	08/35
08/05/35	SIBELIUS	*Valse Triste*	F5582	12/35
06/11/35	ELGAR	*Enigma* Variations	K837–40	10/36
07/11/35	COATES	*London Suite: London Bridge* March	K800–1	12/35
07/11/35	HANDEL	*Samson* Overture	K812	02/36
07/11/35	HANDEL	*Berenice* Overture	K819	05/36
07/11/35	HANDEL	*Solomon* Overture	K840	10/36
21/04/36	VAUGHAN WILLIAMS	*A London Symphony*	X114–8	06/36
22/04/36	VAUGHAN WILLIAMS	*The Wasps* Overture (3*ss*) *Fantasia on Greensleeves*	K821–2	08/36
31/03/37	GRANADOS	Spanish Dances 1, 4, 5	X180–1	08/37
31/03/37	DOHNÁNYI	*Symphonische Minuten*	X190–1	11/37
01/04/37	DVOŘÁK	Symphonic Variations	X182–4	09/37

Henry J. Wood

01/04/37	SCHUBERT–LISZT	*Wanderer Fantasy w* Curzon	X185–7	10/37
02/04/37	HANDEL	*Sailors' Dance (Rodrigo)* & *Rigaudon (Almira)*	X184	09/37
02/04/37	BRUCKNER	Overture in G minor		
	GLINKA	*Ruslan and Lyudmila* Overture	X192–3	12/37
02/04/37	PURCELL–WOOD	Suite	K975–6	10/41

V ORCHESTRAL RECORDINGS
COLUMBIA 1938–40

DATE OF RECORDING	COMPOSER AND WORK		CAT.NO.	ISSUE DATE
15/10/38	VAUGHAN WILLIAMS	*Serenade to Music w* Desmond, Brunskill, Jarred, Baillie, Stiles-Allen, Suddaby, Turner, Balfour, Nash, Widdop, Jones, Titterton, Henderson, Easton, Williams, Allin, BBC Chorus, BBC SO	LX757–8	11/38
3,21/11/39	WOOD	*Fantasia on British Sea Songs w* LSO	DX954–5	12/39
04/03/40	ELGAR	*Pomp and Circumstance* Marches 1 & 4 *w* LPO	DX965	04/40
04/03/40	GOUNOD	*Funeral March of a Marionette w* LPO	DX969	05/40
04/03/40	BERLIOZ	*Carnaval romain* Overture *w* LPO	DX982	11/40

VI BBC RECORDINGS

Though the BBC does not grant public access to its own recorded archives, the recordings are available for public listening at the National Sound Archive (British Library), on the same basis as commercially recorded material.

In these BBC archives are several recordings (on disc or tape) alluding to Wood: they include other conductors' performances of Wood's arrangements, Wood's own spoken words, other people's spoken words about him, and a few extracts from his own *Fantasia on British Sea Songs* in performances from the Last Night of the Proms (various seasons).

Complete performances by Wood of musical works, however, are confined to the following. Date and place of recording, performance details, and National Sound Archive (NSA) reference numbers are given. (One NSA tape or disc may take in more than one item or performance.)

8/09/36	Queen's Hall, items from promenade concert: Schubert, Entr'acte & Ballet Music 1, *Rosamunde*; Mozart, Sinfonia Concertante for violin (Jean Pougnet) and viola (Bernard Shore); Mozart, 'L'amerò' (*Il re pastore)* and 'Alleluia' (Elisabeth Schumann), with BBC SO	NSA Tape T28007
20/12/36	BBC studio: Prokofiev, Violin Concerto no.2, Robert Soetens with BBC SO	NSA Tape T28007
27/06/42	Royal Albert Hall: Ireland, *Epic March* with LPO	NSA Tape T11048W
22/11/43	BBC studio: Bax, Violin Concerto, Eda Kersey with BBC SO	NSA Tape T11048W
3/05/44	Royal Albert Hall: Wagner, Prelude to Act 3, *Lohengrin;* Meyerbeer, Coronation March (*Le Prophète);* Handel–Harty, *Water Music* Suite, with Massed Brass Bands	NSA BBC Archive LP 10394, 12789, 12790–1–2

Two incomplete items are of special interest: the extract from Shostakovich's *Leningrad* Symphony (22 June 1942) with the London Symphony Orchestra on NSA Tape 11048R and the Proms rehearsal recording (24 June 1942), with the London Philharmonic Orchestra, NSA Tape 101W.

Appendix 3

Musical Works by Henry J. Wood

[For literary works see Bibliography, p.493]

I: Original Compositions;
II: Arrangements and Editions;
III: Collections.

I: ORIGINAL COMPOSITIONS

A booklet of eight pages, by 'F.T.S.', entitled *Henry J. Wood, Composer, Conductor*, described by H. G. Farmer in the *Musical Times*. September 1961, pp.560–1, lists thirty-four works and gives opus numbers for each (but omitting opus numbers 1, 7, 10, 13, 20, 26–29, 31–33). No copy of this booklet, dated by Farmer 'about the close of 1889', has been traced. Those works which are identified only in this source and were apparently unpublished and unperformed – including two symphonies! – are marked * here.

According to the programme of the Sheffield Musical Festival of 1902, which he conducted, 'In 1893 Mr Wood destroyed the whole of his compositions and devoted himself entirely to conducting.' It will be noted, however, that one song had a 'first performance' in 1894, and that a hymn is dated 1914. Works more in the nature of adaptations, such as the celebrated *Fantasia on British Sea Songs* (1905), are also evidently exempt from this self-imposed abstention.

(a) CHURCH AND CHORAL

* *New Year's Song*, cantata, op.3
* *Come, Jesus, Come*, anthem, op.11
And Suddenly There Came, anthem for bass solo and chorus, op.14 (Novello, 1889, 1902)
* *Oswald's Rock*, cantata, op.22
St Dorothea, op.25, dramatic oratorio, text by Meta Scott. Grosvenor Hall, 15 February 1889 [MS–RAM]
Nacoochee, dramatic cantata, words by F. Grove Palmer, 1890?, composed for Redruth Choral Society but apparently never performed
Mass in E flat for solos, choir and orchestra, op.55.Full score, MS–RAM, marked 'Composed for the centenary of St Mary's, Lowe House, St Helen's', 1893; vocal and organ score, naming St Joseph's Retreat, Highgate, June 1896 (Tuckwood, 1896)
'O God Our Strength', hymn, words by W. Boyd Carpenter (Skeffington, 1914)

(b) SOLO INSTRUMENTS

Romance in C, op.2, for violin and piano (Weekes, 1887), performed by H. C. Tonking (violin) and the composer, 19 November 1886, Grosvenor Hall, London SW, and later elsewhere

* Abendlied, for violin and piano, op.5
* Two Sketches for piano, op.6
* Theme with Variations in F sharp minor, op.9
* Adagio patetico for violin and piano, op.12
* Abendlied for cello and piano, op.23
Fantasie [sic] on a Welsh Air, for violin and piano, op.20 (J. Williams, c.1890)

(c) SOLO VOCAL

(With piano accompaniment unless otherwise stated)

Six Songs with pianoforte accompaniment, op.15 (Weekes, 1888): no.1 'A flower thou resemblest', no.2 'The sea hath its pearls', no.3 'Every morning rise I crying', no.4 'The Dying Child', no.5 'Tell me, ye shepherds', no.6 'When on my couch I'm lying' (nos. 2 and 6 performed at Royal Academy of Music chamber concert, 16 Mar 1888)
'The Silent Land', op.16 no.1. Song, words by Salis, translated by Longfellow (Weekes, 1888)
'Love thee as only a mother can love', op.16 no.2. Lullaby, words by Hermann Smith, performed at Royal Academy of Music students' concert, 23 Jun 1888 (Weekes, 1888)
'Life and Death', op.17 no.2. Song, words by Meta Scott (Jefferys, c.1889)
'The Poacher', op.18 no.1. Song, words by Hermann Smith (Weekes, 1888)
'The King and the Miller', op.18 no.2. Song, words by C. Mackay (Weekes, 1889)
'Darling Maiden', op.19. Song, words translated from Heine (Weekes, 1886)
'My Perfect Love', op.28 no.2. Song, words by Hermann Smith (Ditson, Boston MA, 1891), sung by Alice Esty, various locations, October/November 1890
'To One I Love', op.17 no.1. Song, words by Meta Scott (Weekes, 1888)
* 'My Darling, For You', op.24. Song, words by ?, c.1890
'I care not for love'. Song, words by ?, sung by Marie Garcia in London, 16 May 1893
'Jacob's Lament'. Song, text from Bible, for bass voice and full orchestra, Kendal Amateur Orchestral Society [in Wood's scrapbook, 'first time'], 18 May 1894
'A Twilight Dream'. Vocal waltz, words by Edward Oxenford (B. Mocatta, 1893), sung by Marie Roze on her 1893–4 concert tour
'Will her heart to me incline'. Song, words by Hermann Smith (Chappell, 1893)
'Darling, how I love thee'. Song, words by Hermann Smith (Boosey, 1894)
'A waif and a stray', op.21. Song, words by Edward Oxenford [comp. before 1890] (Forsyth, 1897; also orchestrated) [MS – RAM]
Album of Six Songs [MS-RAM] 'My lassie is a bonny girl', words by Hermann Smith, 'I gave him my heart for ever', words by Hermann Smith, 'Ave Maria', Latin traditional words, 1894, 'Anything for thee', words by Charles T.C.James, 'I once believed', words by Hermann Smith, 1892, 'The fairest bloom in the garden', words by Charles T. C. James, 1890

(d) STAGE WORKS

(Operas or operettas, except for last-named; locations London unless otherwise stated)

Daisy, comedy-opera, two acts, op.36, libretto by F. Grove Palmer, Kilburn Town Hall, 1 May 1890 [MS – RAM; lyrics privately printed]
Returning the Compliment, op.35, operetta, one act, libretto by F. Grove Palmer [in later references, Otto Waldau and F. Grove Palmer], Royal Park Hall, 5 November 1890
A Hundred Years Ago, 'pastoral operetta', one act, libretto by 'Alec Nelson' (Edward Aveling), Royalty Theatre, 16 July 1892 [lyrics privately printed] [some numbers MS–RAM]
Zuleika, the Turkish Slave, op.30, three acts, written 1889–90; not produced, but an entr'acte performed orchestrally (?Harrogate) and as organ solo, Bow, 9 November 1889; entr'actes published as piano arrangement (Williams, c. 1895)
Francine, or a Butterfly Queen, libretto by Robert Ireton and F. Grove Palmer, lyrics by Hermann Smith, announced *Daily Chronicle* 29 January 1893, not produced
Jean-Marie, libretto by H. A. Ransom and Ernest Delsart, announced *Sunday Times* 10 September 1893, not produced

433

Henry J. Wood

The Frog, incidental music to play by 'Alec Nelson' (Edward Aveling), Royalty Theatre, 30 October 1893

(e) ORCHESTRAL

* Symphony no.1 in C, op.4 [before 1890]
* Marche Elégie, op.8
* Symphony no.2 in D minor, op.34 [before 1890]
Fantasia on British Sea Songs, first performed 21 October 1905, Queen's Hall, published ('arranged by George L. Zalva from the original score of H.J. Wood') 1944 [MS-RAM]
Fantasia on Welsh Melodies, first performed 19 August 1909, Queen's Hall [MS-RAM]
Fantasia on Scottish Melodies, first performed 28 August 1909, Queen's Hall [MS-RAM]
Fanfares for the Norwich Musical Festival, 26–29 October 1927[MS-RAM]
Fanfare for the Hull Philharmonic Society (see p.296)

II: ARRANGEMENTS AND EDITIONS

(All for orchestra with or without voices, unless noted)

(a) PUBLISHED

Anon, 'God Save the King/Queen' (Curwen, 1924)
Arne, 'Rule Britannia'. . . from the *Fantasia on British Sea Songs* (Chappell, 1943)
Bach, Motet no.4, 'Be not afraid' BWV 228 (Breitkopf & Haertel, c. 1905)
Bach, Motet no.6, 'Praise the Lord, o ye heathen' BWV 230 (Breitkopf & Haertel, 19??)
Bach, *Brandenburg* Concerto no.3 in G (Boosey & Hawkes, 1944) [the preface suggests this was intended as the first of an edition of all six *Brandenburg* Concertos]
Bach, [so-called] 'Suite no.6' (Murdoch, 1923) [in six movements arranged from various works of Bach, BWV 848/1, 992/3, 827/6, 811/5 & 6, 827/1, 1006/1]
Bach–Klenovsky, 'Organ Toccata and Fugue in D minor' BWV 565 (OUP, 1934)
Chopin, *Funeral March* from Piano Sonata in B flat minor (Breitkopf & Haertel, 19??) [in B minor; full orchestra with organ; MS-RAM, dated 1905]
Grainger, *Clog Dance* (Handel in the Strand) (Schott, 1933)
Handel, *Five Operatic Choruses* [chorus and orchestra] (OUP, 1927)
Handel, *Five Operatic Choruses* [another set, chorus and orchestra] (OUP, 1937)
Handel, *Largo*, E [Larghetto from Grand Concerto op.16 no.12] (OUP, 1928)
Handel, *Largo*, D [as preceding, for violin and piano, transposed] (OUP, 1929)
Purcell (attributed to, really by Jeremiah Clarke), *Trumpet Voluntary* (arr. for brass, organ and drums, Murdoch, 1933; arr. for full orchestra, Chappell, 1945; also for piano solo, 1923)
Purcell, 'Suite in Five Movements' [Prelude to Act 3 of *Dioclesian*; Minuet from *Distressed Innocence*; Largo from Sonata Z794/3; Song of the Birds from *Timon of Athens*; Vivace from Sonata Z790/2] (Murdoch, 1936)
Purcell, 'Suite of Five Pieces' [piano arrangement of preceding] (Murdoch, 1936)
Rachmaninoff, 'Prelude in C sharp minor', op.3 no.2 (Novello, 1914)

(b) UNPUBLISHED

(Apart from a few privately printed, nearly all remain in MS, with score and parts held at Royal Academy of Music)

Transcriptions for orchestra of works by other composers

The indication (S) denotes an orchestration by F. G. Sanders from instructions given him by Henry J. Wood. The sign + indicates a solo instrument in addition to orchestra.

(S) Albéniz, *Córdoba*
Arcadelt, [attrib.], *Ave Maria*
Bach, [so-called] 'Suite no.5' [in three movements arranged from BWV 592/1, 528/2, 530/1]
(S) Bach, *Passacaglia*, C minor

434

Bach, Toccata in F
Bach, Concerto for Two Violins in C minor, from Concerto for 2 Keyboards, BWV 1060
Bach, Overture in G minor, BWV 1070
Bach–Gounod, *Meditation*
Bach–Kreisler, *Gavotte*, E
Beethoven, 'Adelaïde' (orchestra only)
Boccherini, *Minuet*, A, + viola da gamba
Debussy, *La cathédrale engloutie*
Dvořák, *Humoresque*, op.101/7
Elvey, *Gavotte*
Gluck, Ballet music, Act 2, from *Alceste*
Granados, *Five Spanish Dances*
Grieg, *Funeral March*, A minor
Handel, Grand Concertos op.6 nos. 4, 7, 12
Handel, Organ Concertos 1, 2, 4, 7, 9, 10, 11
Handel, Overture and Ballet Music, *Alcina*
Handel, Sailors' Dance and Trio, *Rodrigo*
Handel, Dead March, *Samson*
Handel, Dead March, *Saul*
Handel, Overtures to *Berenice, Ottone, Samson, Semele*
Handel, *Largo* [= 'Ombra mai fù']
Haydn, *Largo*, F sharp minor, from String Quartet op 76/5
Liszt, Hungarian Rhapsody 1
Liszt, Hungarian Rhapsody 2
Liszt, *Liebesträume* no.3
Mendelssohn, *Fairy Revel* (*Songs Without Words*, op.19/4)
(S) Mozart, *Fantasia*, F minor, K608
Musorgsky, *Pictures at an Exhibition*
Musorgsky, 'The Song of the Flea'
Paderewski, *Minuet*, G
Paganini, Violin Concerto 1
Prowinsky, *A Passing Serenade*
Quantz and Woodall, *Adagio and Serenade*, + alto flute
Rachmaninoff, *Vocalise*, op.34/14 + viola
Raff, *Cavatina*, op.85/3
Saint-Saëns, *Romance*, D, + viola da gamba
Scharwenka, *Three Polish National Dances*
Schubert, *Marche militaire*, D
Sharp and Vaughan Williams, *Three Somerset Folksongs* ('Come all ye worthy Christian men';
    'Bingo'; 'Admiral Benbow')
Vitali, T.A., [attrib.], *Ciaconna*, + violin
(S) Vivaldi, Concerto, B minor, + 4 violins
Wagner, 'Träume', + violin
Wagner, various selections (some with concert endings, some with reduced orchestrations) from
    Der fliegende Holländer, Lohengrin, Parsifal, The Ring
(S) Widor, *Allegretto & Toccata*, + organ (from Organ Symphony no.5)

Hymns and national songs, arranged for orchestra with or without chorus

(i) Hymns
    'O God our help in ages past' (Croft)
    'Mine eyes have seen' (H. Walford Davies)
    'Eternal father' (Dykes)
    'Nearer, my God, to thee' (Dykes)
    'When I survey the wondrous cross' (Miller)
    'All hail the power' (Shrubsole)

Henry J. Wood

(ii) British national songs
'Auld Lang Syne', 'Scored for the opening night of the Christmas Promenade Concerts, 31 Dec 1932' (standard orchestra)
'Auld Lang Syne', 1932 (large orchestra including organ)
'Gathering Peascods', English folksong
'God save the King', 'for large chorus (in unison) and orchestra', Sheffield Festival, 1936 [begins percussion and organ]
'God save the King', orchestra only, 'New version, Promenade Concerts, 1928' [begins full orchestra including harp glissando]
'God save the King', orchestra only [begins with full orchestra including organ and harp, 2/4], undated, = Curwen Edition
'God save the King', unison voices and orchestra [begins with drum-roll], undated; so-called 'Version B'

(iii) Other national anthems and songs from World War I
Australia: 'Song of Australia' (Linger)
Belgium: 'La Brabançonne' (Campenhout)
Belgium: 'Le chant du départ' (Méhul)
Canada: 'The Maple Leaf for Ever' (Muir)
Canada: 'La belle Canadienne'
Czechoslovakia: 'Kde domov muj' (Skroup)
Czechoslovakia: National Hymn (preceding) & Song (rescored 1941)
France: 'La Marseillaise' (R.de Lisle)
France: ditto, 'official version'
Italy: 'Fanfare & Marcia reale d'ordinanza' (Gabetti)
Italy: 'The War Hymn of Garibaldi' (Olivieri)
Japan: 'Kimiga yowa' (Hayashi)
Portugal: 'A Portuguêsa' (Keil)
Romania: 'Traiasca regele în pace' (Hübsch)
Russia: 'Bozhe, tsarya khrani' (Lvov)
Serbia: 'Boze pravde, ti, sto spase' (Yenko)
USA: 'The Star-spangled Banner' (J. S. Smith)

(iv) Other traditional
'The Haulers [sic] on the Volga: Russian Boatmen [sic] Song', 1917

Song and choral accompaniments orchestrated or re-orchestrated

MS scores (mostly also with separate parts) are held at the Royal Academy of Music. The titles are given in their original languages or in English translation, as Wood left them and as catalogued by the RAM. Most are orchestral versions of an original keyboard accompaniment, but those for oratorios, cantatas, operatic excerpts, etc., are re-orchestrations.

The indication (S) denotes an orchestration by F. G. Sanders from instructions given him by Henry J. Wood.

Aikin, 'Sigh no more'
Aikin, 'Shakespeare Sonnet no.18'
Anon., 'Gathering peascods'
Anon., 'The last rose of summer'
Arensky, 'Song of the water-nymph'
Arne, 'The soldier tir'd of war's alarms' (*Artaxerxes*)
Arne, 'Decrepit winter'
Arne, 'Where the bee sucks'
Arne, 'In Infancy'
Austin, E., 'Life I know not'
Bach, J.S., Mass in B minor
Bach, J.S., Sanctus in D, BWV 238
Bach, J.S., St Matthew Passion

Bach, J.S., St John Passion
Bach, J.S., Magnificat in D
Bach, J.S., Cantatas (complete) BWV 203, also (ascribed to, really by Telemann) 160
Bach, J.S., Cantatas (extracts) BWV 3, 7, 8, 12, 13, 18, 20, 21, 28, 39, 41, 51, 53 [spurious], 57, 68, 70, 81, 82, 93, 94, 99, 129, 135, 144, 145, 149, 151, 152, 159, 202, 206, 209, 210, 212
Bach, J.S., 'Schemelli Song-book': 'Come sweetest death', 'Beloved soul', 'In faith and quiet wait'
Bach, J.S., [spurious?] 'Bist Du bei mir' ('Abide with me'), BWV 508
Bach–Gounod, 'Ave Maria'
Balakirev, 'Sleep, my darling'
Beethoven, 'Ah! perfido'
Beethoven, 'Busslied'
Beethoven, 'Es war einmal ein König'
Beethoven, 'In questa tomba oscura'
Beethoven, 'Creation's Hymn'
Beethoven, 'An die ferne Geliebte'
Beethoven, 'The Quail'
Beethoven, 'The Erl-King'
Beethoven, 'Knowest thou the land'
Beethoven, 'Tears of love'
Bemberg, 'Chant Hindou'
Bishop, 'Home, sweet home'
Bishop, 'Should he upbraid'
Bizet, 'Pastorale'
Bizet, 'Agnus Dei' (adapted from L'Arlésienne)
Boïeldieu, 'Pauvre Dame Marguerite' (La Dame blanche)
Borodin, 'Konchakovna's aria' (Prince Igor)
Boyce, 'Hearts [sic] of Oak'
Braham, 'The Death of Nelson'
Brahms, 'To the Nightingale'
Brahms, 'Vergebliches Ständchen'
Brahms, 'Feldeinsamkeit'
Brahms, Trios for female voices, op.17
Caccini, 'Amarilli'
Caldara, 'Come raggio di sol'
Carey, 'A Spring Morning'
Carey, 'Flocks are sporting'
Carissimi, 'Vittoria, vittoria'
Davy, 'The Bay of Biscay'
David, 'Charmant oiseau' (La Perle du Brésil)
Debussy, 'Mandoline'
Debussy, 'Fantoches'
Debussy, 'Green'
Debussy, 'De fleurs'
Dell'Acqua, 'Villanelle'
Duparc, 'Le Testament'
Durante, 'O vergin tutto amor'
(S) Durante, 'Danza, danza'
Eccles, 'This way, mortal' (The Judgement of Paris)
Flégier, 'Le Cor'
(S) Franck, 'Panis angelicus'
Giordani, 'Caro mio ben'
Gluck, 'O malheureuse Iphigénie' (Iphigénie en Tauride)
Gluck, 'Adieu d'Iphigénie à Achille' (Iphigénie en Tauride)
(S) Gluck, 'Armez-vous d'un noble courage' (Iphigénie en Tauride)
Gluck, 'Einen Bach' (The Pilgrimage to Mecca)
Gluck, 'Beaux lieux' (Echo et Narcisse)
Gluck, 'De la femme médecine' (L'île de Merlin)
Gluck, 'Che farò' (Orfeo)
Gluck, 'J'ai perdu mon Eurydice' (Orphée)

Henry J. Wood

Gordigiani, 'Ogni sabato'
Gounod, 'Le Vallon'
Grechaninov, 'Le captif'
Gretry, 'Air de la fauvette' (*Zémire et Azor*)
Gretry, 'Ariette de Colombine'
Grieg, 'A Dream'
Hahn, 'Si mes vers avaient des ailes'
Handel, choruses from *Israel in Egypt, Judas Maccabaeus, Samson, Dettingen Te Deum*
Handel, Coronation Anthems 'The King Shall Rejoice', 'Zadok the Priest'
Handel, Chandos Anthem 6
Handel, *Messiah, Solomon* (complete oratorios)
Handel, 'Cangio d'aspetto' (*Admeto*)
Handel, 'Verdi prati' (*Alcina*)
Handel, 'Ne trionfi. . . Lusinghe più care' (*Alessandro*)
Handel, 'Revenge, Timotheus cries' (*Alexander's Feast*)
Handel, 'S'estinto è l'idol mio' (*Amadigi*)
Handel, 'Care selve' (*Atalanta*)
Handel, 'Riportai gloriosa palma' (*Atalanta*)
Handel, 'Tell fair Irene' (*Atalanta*)
Handel, 'Tears such as tender fathers shed' (*Deborah*)
Handel, 'Dignare Domine' (*Dettingen Te Deum*)
Handel, 'Droop not, young lover' (*Ezio*)
Handel, 'Nasce al bosco' (*Ezio*)
Handel, 'Piangerò la mia sorte' (*Giulio Cesare*)
Handel, 'V'adoro, pupille' (*Giulio Cesare*)
Handel, 'Caro più amabile beltà' (*Giulio Cesare*)
Handel, 'The Lord is a man of war' (*Israel in Egypt*)
Handel, 'Deeper and deeper still. . . Waft her, angels' (*Jephtha*)
Handel, 'The peasant tastes' (*Joseph*)
Handel, 'Oh, had I Jubal's lyre' (*Joshua*)
Handel, 'From mighty kings' (*Judas Maccabaeus*)
Handel, 'Sound an alarm' (*Judas Maccabaeus*)
Handel, 'Arm, arm, ye brave' (*Judas Maccabaeus*)
Handel, 'O let eternal honours' (*Judas Maccabaeus*)
Handel, 'Sweet bird' (*L'Allegro*)
Handel, 'The trumpet shall sound' (*Messiah*)
Handel, 'Prophetic visions' (*The Occasional Oratorio*)
Handel, 'When warlike ensigns' (*The Occasional Oratorio*)
Handel, 'Sorge infausta' (*Orlando*)
Handel, 'Vinto è l'amor' (*Ottone*)
Handel, 'Qual farfalletta' (*Partenope*)
Handel, 'Furibondo spira il vento' (*Partenope*)
Handel, 'Yes, I tremble'; 'Demons of darkness' (*La Resurrezione*)
Handel, 'Thou shalt die' (*Rodelinda*)
Handel, 'Mio caro bene' (*Rodelinda*)
Handel, 'Giacché morir non posso' (*Radamisto*)
Handel, 'Lascia ch'io pianga' (*Rinaldo*)
Handel, 'Let the bright seraphim' (*Samson*)
Handel, 'Return, O God of hosts' (*Samson*)
Handel, 'Honour and arms' (*Samson*)
Handel, 'Hear me, ye winds and waves' (*Scipio*)
Handel, 'Where'er you walk' (*Semele*)
Handel, 'Ombra mai fù' (*Serse*)
Handel, 'Dearest daughter' (*Tamerlano*)
Handel, 'Angels ever bright and fair' (*Theodora*)
Handel, 'Rend'il sereno al ciglio' (*Sosarme*)
Hatton, 'The Enchantress'
Hatton, 'Revenge'
Hawley, 'Riding through the broom'

Hawley, 'Abou ben Adhem'
Haydn, 'Hark what I tell to thee'
Haydn, 'My mother bids me bind my hair'
Haydn, 'The mermaid's song'
Hedgcock, 'On the road to Mandalay'
Hook, 'Mary of Allendale'
Horn, 'I've been roaming'
Knight, 'Rocked in the cradle of the deep'
Koto-Uta, 'Sakura'
Koto-Uta, 'Hotaru'
Lassen, 'All souls' day'
Lawes, 'Go young man'
Leroux, 'Le Nil'
Loewe, 'Sir Oluf'
Loewe, 'Archibald Douglas'
Lully, 'Triomphe de l'amour' (*Jupiter*)
Mack, 'Song of the Shulamite'
(S) Marcello, 'Quella fiamma'
Méhul, 'Air d'une folle'
Mendelssohn, 'On wings of song'
Monro, 'My lovely Celia'
Monteverdi, 'Con che soavità'
Monteverdi, 'Tu sei morta' (*Orfeo*)
Mozart, 'Batti, batti' (*Don Giovanni*)
Mozart, 'L'addio', K621a
Musorgsky, 'The Musician's Peepshow'
Musorgsky, 'In the corner'
Musorgsky, 'Prayer at bed-time'
Musorgsky, 'The Hobby-horse man'
Musorgsky, 'The song of the flea'
Musorgsky, 'Gopak'
Pasquini, 'Verdi tronchi' (*Erminia*)
Pergolesi, 'A Serpina penserete' (*La serva padrona*)
Purcell, 'An evening hymn'
Purcell, 'Ye twice ten hundred deities' (*The Indian Queen*)
Purcell, 'I attempt from love's sickness to fly' (*The Indian Queen*)
Purcell, 'Arise, ye subterranean winds' (*The Tempest*)
Purcell, 'Come if you dare' (*King Arthur*)
Purcell, 'From rosy bowers' (*Don Quixote*)
Purcell, 'Kind fortune smiles'
Purcell, 'Ah, how sweet'
Purcell, 'Ah, Belinda, I am prest with torments' (*Dido and Aeneas*)
Purcell, 'When I am laid in earth' (*Dido and Aeneas*)
Purcell, 'Anacreon's defeat'
Rameau, 'Tristes apprêts, pâles flambeaux' (*Castor et Pollux*)
Ricci, 'Sulla poppa' (*La Prigione di Edimburgo*)
Rimsky-Korsakov, 'The rose enslaves the nightingale'
Rossini, 'Salce' (*Otello*)
Rossini, 'Fac ut portem' (*Stabat Mater*)
Sacchini, 'Tout mon bonheur' (*Oedipe à Colone*)
Sacrati, 'E dove t'aggiri' (*Proserpina*)
Saint-Saëns, 'La cloche'
Schindler, 'Eternel roman'
Schubert, 'Ellen's three songs', D.837–9
Schubert, 'The Erl-King'
Schumann, 'The Two Grenadiers'
Sharpe & Vaughan Williams, 'Three Somerset Folksongs'
Spross, 'Will o' the wisp'
Stange, 'Damon'

Henry J. Wood

Stradella, 'Pietà, signore'
Strauss, 'Heimliche Aufforderung'
Sullivan, 'The Lost Chord'
Tchaikovsky, 'Don Juan's Serenade'
Tchaikovsky, 'A heavy tear'
Tchaikovsky, 'Nay, though my heart' [= 'None but the lonely heart']
Tchaikovsky, 'To the forest'
Tchaikovsky, 'Only for thee'
Tchaikovsky, 'Hear me, friends' (*The Queen of Spades*)
(S) Tchaikovsky, cantata 'Nature and Love'
Verdi, 'Invocazione' (*Un ballo in maschera*)
Verdi, 'La luce langue' (*Macbeth*)
Wagner, 'Träume'
Weingartner, 'Du bist ein Kind'
Weingartner, 'Nelken'
White, 'How do I love thee'
Wolf, 'Auf ein altes Bild'
Wolf, 'Auch kleine Dinge'
Wolf, 'Wer sich der Einsamkeit'
Wolf, 'Tretet ein, hoher Krieger'
Wolf, 'Die Zigeunerin'

III: COLLECTIONS

Music of all Nations. 'A serial collection of the world's best music, in 30 parts, edited by Sir Henry
  Wood' (Amalgamated Press, 1927–8)

First Performances conducted by Henry J. Wood

Between 1889 and 1944 Henry J. Wood conducted the first performance (**) or the first British performance (*) of at least 716 works by 356 composers, as shown in the following list. The order is alphabetical by composers, and chronological within that. In the indication of dates, the endings 89 to 99 refer to the years 1889–99, the remainder being understood as prefixed 19–.

The location of performances is London, Queen's Hall, except as otherwise indicated: AH (Royal Albert Hall, London), BBC (BBC studio), H (Hollywood Bowl), OT (Olympic Theatre, London), SJ (St James's Hall, London), LL (Liverpool), M (Manchester), N (Norwich), PP (People's Palace, London), RAM (Royal Academy of Music, London), S (Sheffield), SS (South Shields).

The names of composers and the titles of works are amended from the original programmes, where necessary, to conform with general modern usage. Titles of works are, for reasons of space, given in the briefest identifiable form, opus numbers generally omitted, and an indication such as 'No.1' is replaced by a simple numeral. Titles of songs and arias (only) are in quotation marks.

Abbreviations used: bar(itone), bsn = bassoon, fl(ute), h(or)n, h(ar)p, ob(oe), orch(estra), org(an), pf = pianoforte, sax(ophone), str(ings), vc = violoncello, v(io)la, vln = violin.

NOTES

(1) So-called 'first concert performances' or 'first public performances' (e.g. when a piece had been previously given in a theatre or on radio) are not included. Wood himself objected (see p.349) to the classification of these as 'first' performances. Among Wood's performances so excluded are those of the *Three Fragments from 'Wozzeck'* (8 March 1933) by Alban Berg and of the same composer's Violin Concerto (9 December 1936) – both given at Queen's Hall, but previously broadcast from BBC studios under other conductors. Performances prepared under Wood's supervision but conducted by their composers are also excluded.

(2) Orchestral arrangements of works originally for other musical media (the arranger usually but

not always being Wood himself) are included – e.g., after the listing of works by Grieg, under the heading 'Grieg–Wood' will be found the *Funeral March for Richard Nordraak*, originally composed for military band. Of Wood's own original works only the orchestral fantasias are included, the most famous being the *Fantasia on British Sea Songs;* for other works, mostly early, see pp.432–40.

(3) The principal sources are:

Cox, David, *The Henry Wood Proms*, 1980

Kenyon, Nicholas, *The BBC Symphony Orchestra*, 1981

Newmarch, Rosa, *Henry J. Wood*, 1904

Newmarch, Rosa, *A Quarter of a Century of Promenade Concerts*, 1920 [two copies: one belonging to Lewis Foreman with inked corrections of main list, one belonging to Arthur Jacobs with typescript additional list]

Thompson, Kenneth, *A Dictionary of Twentieth Century Composers*, 1973

Wood, Henry J., *My Life of Music*, 1938

Individual concert programmes and press reports

The contribution of Lewis Foreman and Stephen Lloyd is gratefully acknowledged.

Aguilar, Juan
 2 movts, *Moorish Suite*   **H   20 Jul 34
Akimenko, Fyodor
 Ange   *   17 Aug 26
Albéniz, Isaac
 Catalonia   *   4 Mar 00
 Nivian's Dance (*Merlin*)   **   12 Sep 17
 Cordoba   **   22 Oct 19
Albert, Eugène d'
 'The Sleigh of Life'   *   6 Sep 04
 'Slumber Song'   *   6 Sep 04
 Aschenputtel   *   26 Sep 25
Alfvén, Hugo
 Symphony 2   *   17 Sep 01
 Midsommervaka   *   31 Aug 11
Alwyn, William
 Five Preludes   **   22 Sep 27
Ames, John Carlowitz
 Petite Suite   **   28 Nov 96
 Last of the Incas   **   5 Oct 01
Arcadelt–Wood
 Ave Maria   **   29 Aug 18
Arends, Henri (Genrikh)
 Viola Concertino   *   8 Oct 07
Arensky, Anton
 Silhouettes   *   30 Jan 96
 Symphony 1   *   1 May 97
 Piano concerto   *   14 Oct 03
 Variations on Tchaikovsky Theme   *   16 Oct 06
Ashton, Algernon
 Three English Dances   **   24 Oct 12
 Three Scottish Dances   **   24 Oct 14
Aubert, Louis
 Fantasia, pf & orch   *   27 Sep 11
 Suite Brève   *   11 Sep 17
 Habanera   *   15 Aug 22
Austin, Ernest
 Variations, *Vicar of Bray*   **   6 Oct 10
 Stella-Mary Dances   **   26 Sep 18
Austin, Frederic
 Spring   **   16 Oct 07

Averkamp, Anton
   Elaine and Lancelot   *   28 Aug 02
Bach, J.S.
   Solo cantata, *Amore Traditore*, BWV 203   *   18 Sep 07
   Brandenburg Concerto 1   *   28 Nov 08
   Clavier Concerto 2, BWV 1053   *   13 Sep 12
   'Hört doch, der sanften Flöten Chor' from
      BWV 206   *   26 Sep 13
   Violin concerto in G minor [after BWV 1056]   *   11 Sep 18
Bach–Casella
   Chaconne   *   3 Oct 36
Bach–Gounod–Wood
   Meditation   **   16 Sep 16
Bach–Klenovsky [= Wood]
   Toccata & Fugue in D minor   **   5 Oct 29
Bach–Mahler
   Suite for Orchestra   *   20 Oct 11
Bach–Raff
   Chaconne   *   20 Feb 97
Bach–Respighi
   Prelude & Fugue in D   *   29 Sep 34
Bach–Sanders
   Passacaglia in C   **   18 Sep 18
Bach–Wood [see also Bach–Klenovsky]
   Suite 5   **   9 Oct 09
   Toccata in F   **   10 Sep 13
   Concerto, 2 violins, C minor   **   1 Oct 15
   Suite 6   **   15 Sep 16
   Suite in G, ob, org, orch   **   14 Oct 21
Bagrinovsky, Mikhail
   Fantastic Miniatures   *   19 Aug 15
Bainton, Edgar L.
   Pompilia   **   8 Oct 03
   Elegy & Intermezzo (from 3 Pieces)   **   20 Sep 19
Balakirev, Mily
   Overture on 3 Russian Themes   *   26 Sep 99
   Symphony in C   *   26 Sep 01
Bantock, Granville
   Prelude, *Sappho*   **   25 Sep 06
   Lalla Rookh   **   19 Sep 07
Barber, Samuel
   Essay for Orchestra 1   *   24 Aug 39
Barker, F. C.
   Violin concerto   **   3 Sep 07
Barns, Ethel
   Concertstück, vln & orch   **   17 Oct 07
Bartók, Béla
   Suite 1   *   1 Sep 14
   Dance Suite   *   20 Aug 25
   Rhapsody, pf & orch   *   15 Oct 21
   Hungarian Peasant Songs (orch)   *   26 Sep 35
Bath, Hubert
   2 Sea Pictures   **   28 Sep 09
   African Suite   **   31 Aug 15
Bax, Arnold
   In the Faery Hills   **   30 Aug 10
   Four Sketches, nos 1 & 4   **   23 Sep 13
   Scherzo   **   3 Sep 19

Symphonic Variations, pf & orch   **   23 Nov 20
Overture, Elegy and Rondo   **   3 Oct 29
Symphony 3   **   14 Mar 30
Violin concerto   **BBC 22 Nov 43

Becker, Reinhold
   Huldigungsmarsch, *Frauenlob*   *   22 Sep 97
Bell, William Henry
   Prelude, *Agamemnon*   **   13 Oct 08
Benjamin, Arthur
   Piano Concertino   **   1 Sep 28
   Prelude to Holiday   *AH   6 Aug 42
Bendl, Karel
   South Slavonic Rhapsody   *   11 Feb 99
Berkeley, Lennox
   Introduction & Allegro, 2pfs & orch   **   6 Sep 40
Berners, Lord
   Fantaisie Espagnole   **   24 Sep 19
Blake, Ernest
   Alastor   **   21 Jan 02
   Introduction, *The Bretwalda*   **   15 Sep 03
Bleichmann, Jules
   Suite de Ballet   *   19 Oct 99
Bliss, Arthur
   2-Piano Concerto   **   5 Sep 29
   Conquest of the Air   **   3 Sep 38
   Piano Concerto   *   17 Aug 39
Bloch, Ernest
   Schelomo, vc & orch   *   11 Oct 22
   Three Jewish Poems   *   13 Jan 23
   Concerto grosso [1]   *   19 Feb 25
   Israel Symphony   *   20 Apr 28
Bloch, Josef
   Suite Poétique   *   10 Oct 01
Blockx, Jan
   5 Flemish Dances   *   6 Sep 99
   Symphonic Triptych   *   18 Sep 06
Boehe, Ernest
   Episode from *Odysseus*   *   11 Sep 06
Borodin, Alexander
   Polovtsian Dances, *Prince Igor*   *   3 Apr 97
Borsdorf, Oscar, jun.
   Concert Overture in D   **   30 Sep 09
   Glaucus and Ione   **   26 Sep 14
Bossi, Enrico
   Organ Concerto   *   6 Aug 04
Boughton, Rutland
   Into the Everlasting   **   22 Sep 03
   Love and Night   **   20 Oct 14
Bourgault-Ducoudray, Louis
   Prelude to Act 2, *Thamara*   *   3 Apr 97
   Le Carnaval d'Athènes   *   17 Feb 01
Bowen, York
   Lament of Tasso   **   1 Sep 03
   Piano Concerto 3   **   8 Sep 08
   Violin Concerto   **   28 Sep 20
Bradford, Hugh
   Variations on a Popular Theme   *   10 Sep 31

Bretón, Tomás
  Violin Concerto   **   21 Aug 23
Brewer, Herbert
  Two Pieces: Age and Youth   **   15 Oct 08
Brian, Havergal
  For Valour   **   8 Oct 07
Bridge, Frank
  Isabella   **   3 Oct 07
  The Sea   **   24 Sep 12
  Lament   **   15 Sep 15
  Sally in our Alley, orch version   **   26 Sep 16
  Cherry Ripe, orch version   **   26 Sep 16
  Sir Roger de Coverley   **   21 Oct 22
  Rebus Overture   **   23 Feb 41
Bright, Dora
  Liebeslied   **   6 Mar 97
  Theme and Variations   **   8 Apr 17
  Suite Bretonne, fl & orch   **   22 Sep 17
Britten, Benjamin
  Piano concerto   **   18 Aug 38
Bruch, Max
  Suite on Russian Folk-Tunes   *   22 Aug 05
Bruckshaw, Kathleen
  Piano Concerto   **   10 Sep 14
Bruneau, Alfred
  Four Preludes from *L'Ouragan*   *   4 Sep 02
  Entr'acte, *Messidor*   *   13 Sep 06
  Suite, *L'Attaque du Moulin*   *   6 Sep 10
Bryson, Ernest
  Voices   **   15 Sep 10
Buck, Percy
  Croon   **   22 Sep 17
Bunning, Herbert
  Shepherds' Call   **   28 Aug 95
Burgmein, J. [= Giulio Ricordi]
  Fantaisie Hongroise   *   13 Mar 97
Busoni, Ferrucio
  Suite, *Turandot*   *   21 Aug 06
  Comedy Overture   *   20 Oct 06
  Violin concerto   *   24 Sep 13
  Rondo Arlecchinesco   *   14 Mar 21
Caetani, Roffredo
  Prélude Symphonique   **   5 Oct 09
Carpenter, John Alden
  Adventures in a Perambulator   *   15 Aug 18
  Concertino, pf & orch   *   12 Oct 21
Carr, Howard
  The Three Heroes   **   5 Sep 15
  The Jovial Huntsmen   **   18 Oct 19
  The Shrine in the Wood   **   17 Sep 25
  The Sun God   **   17 Sep 25
Carse, Adam von Ahn
  In a Balcony   **   26 Aug 05
Casella, Alfredo
  Le Couvent sur l'eau   *   28 Aug 19
  Pagine di Guerra   *   19 Aug 20
  Italia   *   20 Nov 20
  Partita for pf & orch   *   13 Sep 28

Violin Concerto	*	26 Oct 28
Cassadó, Joaquín		
Hispania, pf & orch	*	11 Sep 23
Catoire, Georgy		
Piano concerto	*	25 Aug 20
Celega, Nicolo		
The Heart of Fingal	*	1 Oct 01
Chabrier, Emmanuel		
Joyeuse Marche	*	12 Sep 96
Slavonic Dance, *Le Roi malgré lui*	*	19 Sep 96
Chadwick, George		
Symphonic Sketches	*	23 Sep 09
Chaminade, Cécile		
Suite, *Callirhoë*	*	3 Sep 96
Chausson, Ernest		
Poème, vln & orch	*	17 Jun 99
Viviane	*	31 May 00
Chanson Perpetuelle	*	24 Feb 17
Chopin–Wood		
Funeral March	**	17 Aug 07
Christesen, Ernest		
Belphegor (opera)	**SS	2 Nov 89
Clutsam, George Howard		
Carnival Scenes	**	11 Sep 95
Coates, Eric		
Suite, *Miniatures*	**	17 Oct 11
Idyll	**	14 Oct 13
Cobb, Gerard		
Romance	**	31 Oct 01
Coleridge-Taylor, Samuel		
Toussaint L'Ouverture	**	26 Oct 01
Violin concerto	*	8 Oct 12
Converse, Frederick		
The Festival of Pan	*	18 Aug 04
Flivver Ten Million	*	31 Aug 29
Copland, Aaron		
Billy the Kid	*AH	1 Aug 42
Corder, Paul		
Preludes to I, II, *Rapunzel*	**	14 Sep 15
Coverley, Robert		
Four Sketches	*	27 Sep 99
Cowen, Frederic		
The Butterfly's Ball	**	2 Mar 01
The Language of Flowers, Suite 2	**	19 Sep 14
Cox, Garnet Wolseley		
Ewelme	**	10 Sep 03
The Mysterious Rose-Garden	**	10 Sep 07
Crowther, G. W. F.		
Concertstück, pf & orch	*	3 Apr 97
Cui, César		
Suite miniature	*	1 Sep 97
Scherzo	*	29 Sep 99
Davies, H. Walford		
Songs of Nature	**	12 Oct 09
Conversations, pf & orch	**	14 Oct 14
Davis, John David		
Miniatures Suite	**	9 Sep 05
Two Pieces, vc & orch	**	8 Oct 14

Debussy, Claude
    L'après-midi d'un faune   *   20 Aug 04
    La Damoiselle élue   *   29 Feb 08
    Song, *Le Jet d'eau*   *   29 Sep 08
    L'Enfant prodigue   *S   8 Oct 08
    Rondes de printemps   *   23 May 11
    Children's Corner (orch Caplet)   *   12 Sep 11
    Ibéria   *   18 Sep 13
    Symphonic extracts, *Le Martyre de S. Sébastien*   *   24 Aug 15
Delibes, Léo
    Polonaise & Ballet from *Kassya*   *   9 Jan 97
Delius, Frederick
    Sea Drift   *S   7 Oct 08
    Piano Concerto   *   22 Oct 07
    Eventyr   **   11 Jan 19
    Double Concerto   **   21 Feb 20
    A Song before Sunrise   **   19 Sep 23
    Dance Rhapsody 2   **   20 Oct 23
    A Song of Summer   **   17 Sep 31
    Idyll   **   3 Oct 33
Depret, Edmond
    Requiem Mass   *   10 Dec 98
Dieren, Bernard van
    Introit (*Les propous des Beuveurs*)   **   6 Sep 21
Dittersdorf, Carl D. von
    Actaeon   *   20 Oct 99
Dohnányi, Ernö
    Suite   *   9 Oct 13
    Ruralia Hungarica   *   5 Oct 26
Dorlay, Georges
    Das Lied von der Glocke   **   22 Sep 09
    Concerto Passionné, vc & orch   **   30 Sep 13
    La Lutte et l'Espoir, pf & orch   **   18 Oct 16
    Mirage   **   28 Sep 20
Draeseke, Felix
    Miniature Suite   *   8 Oct 01
    Tragic Symphony 3   *   27 Feb 97
Drysdale, Learmont
    A Border Romance   **   8 Oct 04
Dubois, Theodore
    Three Pieces from *Xavière*   *   5 Sep 96
    Fantaisie Triomphale, org & orch   *   24 Aug 12
Dunhill, Thomas F.
    The King's Threshold   **   9 Sep 13
Duparc, Henri
    Phidylé, voice & orch   *   20 Aug 08
    Aux Etoiles   *   11 Sep 18
Dupré, Marcel
    Cortège et litanie, org & orch   *   6 Sep 27
    Symphony   *   9 Sep 30
Dvořák, Antonín
    The Water Sprite   *   14 Nov 96
    The Noonday Witch   *   21 Nov 96
Elgar, Edward
    The Snow; *Fly, singing bird* (versions with orch)   **   12 May 04
    Pomp and Circumstance 4   **   24 Aug 07
    Wand of Youth Suite 1   **   14 Dec 07
    Sospiri   **   15 Aug 14

447

Pomp and Circumstance 5	**	20 Sep 30
Elvey, George		
Gavotte à la mode ancienne	**	5 Dec 96
Enescu, George		
Romanian Rhapsody 1	*	29 Aug 11
Suite	*	5 Oct 11
Romanian Rhapsody 2	*	22 Aug 12
Enna, August		
Overture, *Cleopatra*	*	13 Sep 02
Erlanger, Frédéric d'		
Suite Symphonique 2	**	18 Sep 95
Andante Symphonique, vc & orch	*	29 Oct 04
Sursum Corda	**	26 Aug 19
Fairchild, Blair		
Tamineh	**	16 Sep 13
Fauré, Gabriel		
Ballade, pf & orch	*	20 Oct 13
Fantaisie, pf & orch	*	2 Sep 20
Fibich, Zdenko		
A Night at Karlstein	*	27 Sep 06
Floersheim, Otto		
Miniature Suite: *A Love Tale*	*	8 Oct 01
Fogg, Eric		
Suite from *The Golden Butterfly*	**	21 Sep 20
Foote, Arthur		
Suite for strings	*	25 Aug 10
Ford, Ernest		
Scènes des Bacchanales	**	16 Jan 97
Forsyth, Cecil		
Viola concerto	**	12 Sep 03
Four Studies from Victor Hugo	**	23 Sep 05
Foulds, John		
Epithalamium	**	9 Oct 06
Music Pictures, Group 3	**	5 Sep 12
Fox, George		
The Boy and the Butterfly	**	6 Nov 00
Franchetti, Alberto		
Symphony	*	8 Oct 98
In the Black Forest	*	29 Aug 05
Franck, César		
Le Chasseur Maudit	*	20 Mar 97
Les Eolides	*	29 Aug 14
Frewin, T. H.		
The Battle of the Flowers	**	31 Aug 95
Mazeppa	**	26 Sep 96
The Seven Ages of Man	**	10 Sep 97
Bellona	**	13 Oct 98
Frischen, J.		
Herbstnacht and Rhenish Scherzo	*	11 Oct 02
Gardiner, H. Balfour		
English Dance	**	21 Oct 04
Symphony [2]	**	27 Aug 08
Shepherd Fennel's Dance	**	6 Sep 11
In Maytime	**	3 Oct 14
Gatty, Nicholas		
Concert Allegro, pf & orch	**	6 Oct 03
Geehl, Henry E.		
Fairyland	**	10 Oct 14

Gilbert, Henry F.
  The Dance in Place Congo   *   2 Oct 23
  Comedy Overture on Negro Themes   *   3 Oct 18
Gipps, Ruth
  Knight in Armour   **AH   22 Aug 42
Glazunov, Alexander
  Scènes de Ballet   *   24 Sep 96
  Symphony 5   *   30 Jan 97
  Carnaval   *   8 May 97
  Symphony 6   *   1 Jan 99
  Suite from *Raymonda*   *   25 Nov 99
  Les Ruses d'Amour   *   1 Nov 00
  Chant du Ménéstrel, vc & orch   *   24 Sep 01
  The Seasons Part I   *   17 Oct 01
  The Seasons Part II   *   19 Oct 01
  Ouverture Solennelle   *   29 Oct 01
  Introduction and Dance of Salome   *   10 Sep 12
  Piano concerto   *   28 Aug 13
  Paraphrase on Allies' National Anthems   *   9 Sep 16
Glazunov, Lyadov, Sokolov
  Polka from *Fridays*   *   21 Oct 99
Glière, Reinhold
  Symphony 1   *   26 Aug 06
  Les Sirènes   *   30 Nov 12
Gluck–Mottl
  Ballet suite from the operas   *   16 Jan 97
Gnessin, Lev
  Symphonic Fragment   *   19 Sep 17
Goedicke, Alexander
  Trumpet Concerto   *RAM   27 Feb 36
Goens, Daniel van
  Cello Concerto 1   *   13 Aug 04
Goldmark, Carl
  Intro, Act 2, *Die Kriegsgefangene*   *   19 Sep 99
  In Italien   *   21 Oct 04
Golestan, Stan
  Romanian Rhapsody   *   13 Sep 19
Goossens, Eugene
  The Eternal Rhythm   **   19 Sep 20
  Oboe concerto   **   2 Oct 30
Gouvy, Théodore
  Serenade, fl & str   *   8 Sep 04
Graener, Paul
  From Valleys and Heights   **   15 Sep 09
  Variations on a Russian Folk Song   *   8 Sep 25
Grainger, Percy
  Over the hills and far away   *   22 Oct 19
Grainger–Wood
  Handel in the Strand   **   26 Aug 16
Granados, Enrique
  Dante and Beatrice   *   28 Oct 16
Granados–Wood
  Five Spanish Dances   *   8 Sep 17
Greenbaum, Hyam
  Parfum de Nuit, ob & orch   **   12 Oct 22
  A Sea Poem   **   14 Aug 23
Grieg, Edvard
  Two Norwegian Melodies   *   6 Oct 96
  Symphonic Dances   *   28 Jan 99

Grieg–Wood
   Funeral March for Richard Nordraak   **   16 Oct 07
Hadley, Henry
   Salome   *   24 Aug 09
   The Culprit Fay   *   25 Sep 19
Hahn, Reynaldo
   Le Bal de Béatrice d'Este   *   11 Sep 13
Hale, Alfred Matthew
   Elegy   *   12 Sep 12
Hales, Hubert
   Twelfth Night   *   8 Oct 25
Hall, Marshall
   Symphony   **   20 Aug 07
Halvorsen, Johan
   Boyard's March   *   2 Oct 95
   Vasantasena   *   15 Jun 98
   Norwegian Folk-Song   *   8 Sep 98
Handel, George Frideric
   [ascribed] Aria, 'Dank sei Dir'   *   19 Oct 04
Hanson, Howard
   Pan and the Priest   **   28 Sep 26
Harrison, Julius
   Cleopatra   **N   30 Oct 08
   Variations on 'Down Among the Dead Men'   **   22 Oct 12
Hartmann, Emil
   Overture, *Ragnhild*   *   14 Sep 97
Harty, Hamilton
   Symphony (*Irish*)   *   14 Oct 05
   Comedy Overture   **   24 Oct 07
   Three Pieces, ob & orch   **   7 Sep 11
Hathaway, Joseph William George
   Sunshine   **   4 Oct 10
Haussegger, Sigismund von
   Barbarossa   *   10 Oct 05
Haydn, Joseph
   Violin concerto 2   *   1 Sep 09
   Violin concerto 1   *   20 Oct 09
Haydn, Michael
   Symphony, op.1/3   *   14 Sep 99
Heath, John Rippiner
   Rhapsody   **   8 Oct 19
Henriquez, Fini
   Suite in F, ob & str   *   23 Aug 06
Herbert, Victor
   Cello Concerto 2   *   11 Sep 09
Hindemith, Paul
   Nusch-Nuschi Dances   *   13 Oct 23
   Concerto, orch, op.38   *   14 Sep 26
   Kammermusik 2, op.36/1   *   3 Sep 27
   Kammermusik 5, op.36/4   *   22 Nov 29
   Konzertmusik, op.50   *   17 Feb 32
   Philharmonic Concerto   *   2 Jan 33
   Konzertmusik, op.48   *BBC 19 Mar 33
   Das Unaufhörliche   *   22 Mar 33
Hinton, Arthur
   Three Orchestral Scenes from *Endymion*   **   5 Sep 07
Holbrooke, Josef
   Variations on *Three Blind Mice*   **   9 Nov 00
   Ulalume   **   26 Nov 04

Symphony 1: *Les Hommages*	**	25 Oct 06
Imperial March	**	16 Sep 14
Holland, Theodore		
Ellingham Marshes	**	15 Aug 40
Hollander, Benno		
Fantaisie Pastorale, vln & orch	*	24 Feb 00
Honegger, Arthur		
Prelude, *The Tempest*	*	8 Jan 27
Rugby	*	7 Sep 29
Cello concerto	*	9 Sep 30
Symphonic Movement 3	*	16 Sep 33
Horrocks, Amy E.		
The Romaunt of the Page	**	6 Oct 99
Undine	**	6 Feb 97
Howell, Dorothy		
Lamia	**	10 Sep 19
Piano concerto	**	23 Aug 23
Koong Shee	**	20 Oct 21
The Rock	**	6 Oct 28
Howells, Herbert		
Procession	**	29 Aug 22
Merry-Eye	**	30 Sep 20
Huber, Hans		
Symphony 2	*	31 Jan 02
Hughes, Herbert		
Four Parodies, voice & orch	**	29 Aug 20
Humperdinck, Engelbert		
Introduction, Act 2, *Königskinder*	*	27 Feb 97
Ibert, Jacques		
Concertino da camera, sax & orch	*	12 Sep 36
Indy, Vincent d'		
Chansons et Danses	*	23 Sep 99
Wallenstein, pts 2 & 3	*	2 Sep 02
L'Etranger	*	23 Oct 03
Symphonie Montagnarde, pf & orch	*	23 Oct 07
Ippolitov-Ivanov, Mikhail		
Caucasian Sketches	*	7 Sep 99
Ireland, John		
The Forgotten Rite	**	13 Sep 17
Piano concerto	**	2 Oct 30
A London Overture	**	23 Sep 36
Epic March	**AH	27 Jun 42
Itasse, Léon		
Rhapsodie Espagnole	*	8 Oct 96
Janáček, Leoš		
The Fiddler's Child	*	3 May 24
Sinfonietta	*	10 Feb 28
Taras Bulba	*	16 Oct 28
Lachian Dances	*	19 Aug 30
Glagolitic Mass	*N	23 Oct 30
Järnefelt, Armas		
Korsholm	*	18 Sep 02
Jervis Read, Harold		
Two Night Pieces	**	8 Sep 10
Jongen, Joseph		
Fantasia on Two Popular Walloon Carols	*	18 Aug 15
Lalla Rookh	*	20 Sep 20

Juon, Paul
Symphony   *   6 Sep 04
Keyser, Harry Assur
Preludes Acts 4 & 5, *Otello*   **   16 Oct 13
Kistler, Cyrill
Festklänge   *   23 Sep 95
Festmarsch   *   19 Sep 96
Klughardt, August
Festival Overture   *   17 Oct 01
Kodály, Zoltán
Summer Evening   *   16 Sep 30
Dances from Galanta   *   22 Sep 34
Dances of Marosszek   *BBC   29 Mar 31
Ballet Music   *   24 Aug 37
Koessler, Hans
Symphonic Variations   *   28 Jan 02
Korbay, Francis A.
Hungarian Overture   **   11 Sep 12
Korngold, Erich Wolfgang
Theatre Overture   *   17 Oct 12
Music for *Much Ado About Nothing*   *   15 Aug 23
Kufferath, Hubert Ferdinand
Mirages   *   14 Oct 25
Labey, Marcel
Overture 'pour un drame'   *   20 Apr 28
Lalo, Edouard
Suite 1, *Namouna*   *   24 Oct 96
Suite 2, *Namouna*   *   9 Oct 00
Laurence, Frederick
Legend   **   2 Oct 18
The Dance of the Witch Girl   **   12 Oct 20
Lekeu, Guillaume
Fantasia on Two Popular Angevin Airs   *   21 Aug 13
Lenormand, René
Piano concerto   *   1 Oct 03
Leo, Leonardo
Sinfonia from *S. Elena al Calvario*   *   13 Sep 99
Leroux, Xavier
Le Nil   *   27 Aug 08
Liszt–Burmeister
Concerto Pathétique, pf & orch   *   15 Oct 07
Liszt–Wood
Idyl   *   27 Aug 08
Litolff, Henri
Scherzo from Concerto Symphonique 4   *   19 June 97
Loeffler, Charles Martin
The Death of Tintagiles   *   17 Aug 15
A Pagan Poem   *   11 Oct 17
La Villanelle du Diable   *   23 Aug 19
Luard-Selby, Bertram
A Village Suite   **   9 Sep 08
Lucas, Clarence
Overture, *Othello*   **   20 Sep 98
Overture, *As You Like It*   **   20 Sep 99
Overture, *Macbeth*   **   28 Sep 01
Lucas, Mary Anderson
Circus Suite   **AH   4 Jul 42
Lyadov, Anatol
Valse-Badinage   *   26 Aug 99

Eight Russian Folk-Songs	*	25 Aug 06
Baba-Yaga	*	30 Aug 06
A Fragment from the Apocalypse	*	25 Aug 14
Kikimora	*	18 Sep 17
Lyadov, see also Glazunov		
Lyapunov, Sergey		
Solemn Overture	*	21 Sep 01
Rhapsody, pf & orch	*	7 Sep 09
MacDowell, Edward		
Indian Suite	*	23 Oct 01
Poème érotique	*	3 Oct 16
Scotch Poem	*	3 Oct 16
MacEwan, Desirée		
Uam-Var	**	5 Oct 21
McEwen, John		
A Winter Poem	**	12 Sep 22
Mack, Albert A.		
Song of the Shulamite	**	25 Aug 10
Mackenzie, Alexander		
St John's Eve	**	27 Sep 23
Maconchy, Elizabeth		
The Land	**	30 Aug 30
Macpherson, Charles		
Hallowe'en	**	27 Aug 04
Mahler, Gustav		
Symphony 1	*	21 Oct 03
Symphony 4	*	25 Oct 05
Adagietto from Symphony 5	*	31 Aug 09
Symphony 7	*	18 Jan 13
Das Lied von der Erde	*	31 Jan 14
Symphony 8	*	15 Apr 30
Malipiero, G. F.		
Il Molino della Morte	*	24 Aug 26
Manén, Joan		
Concerto Espagnol, vln & orch	*	9 Sep 26
Marsick, Armannd		
Tableaux Grecs	*	29 Sep 36
Martin, Easthope		
Two Eastern Dances	**	18 Aug 10
Marx, Joseph		
Romantic Piano Concerto	*	30 Sep 26
Mascagni, Pietro		
The Sun from *Iris*	*	21 Aug 15
Mascheroni, [Angelo?]		
Grande valse espagnole	**	9 Sep 99
Massenet, Jules		
Overture, *Le Cid*	*	1 Oct 96
Rhapsody and March from *Le Cid*	*	3 Oct 96
Le Sommeil de Cendrillon and Menuet	*	11 Sep 99
Matras, Maud		
Ballade for vln & orch	**	13 Mar 97
Migot, Georges		
Le Paravent de Laque aux Cinq Images	*	5 Sep 22
Miguez, Leopoldo		
Ave Libertas	*	12 Sep 99
Milhaud, Darius		
Suite Symphonique 2	*	31 Aug 22

453

Moeran, E. J.
    Violin concerto   **AH   8 Jul 42

Moniuszko, Stanislaw
    Mazur from *Halka*   *   8 Oct 98

Moór, Emmanuel
    Violin concerto   *   30 Nov 07

Mossolov, Alexander
    Three Songs with Orchestra   *   19 Sep 35

Moszkowski, Moritz
    Excerpts from *Laurin*   *   17 Sep 96
    Polish Dances   *   7 Oct 99

Mozart, Wolfgang Amadeus
    Allegro in D (finale of a symphony)   *   17 May 00
    Concerto in F, K242, 3 pfs & orch   *   12 Sep 07

Mozart–Pitt
    Andante, wind   **   8 Oct 13

Mozart–Sanders
    Fantasia in F minor   **   22 Aug 19

Musorgsky, Modest
    Night on the Bare Mountain   *   19 Feb 98
    March in A flat   *   5 Mar 98
    Gopak   *   6 Oct 06
    Intermezzo   *   4 Sep 16
    Persian Dance (*Khovanshchina*)   *   18 Sep 16

Musorgsky–Tushmalov
    Pictures from an Exhibition   *   7 Sep 16

Musorgsky–Wood
    Song of the Flea   **   25 Aug 09
    The Peep-Show   **   31 Aug 09
    King Saul   **   15 Sep 09
    The Nursery, voice & orch   **   19 Aug 19
    Pictures at an Exhibition   **   17 Apr 15

Myaskovsky, Nikolay
    Alastor   *   4 Oct 23
    Silentium   *   30 Sep 29

Napravnik, Edward
    Romance and Fandango   *   3 Sep 97

Nesvera, Josef
    Overture, *Lesní vzduch*   *   3 Oct 03

Noren, Heinrich
    Kaleidoscopic Variations and Double Fugue   *   19 Aug 09

Offenbach, Jacques (compiled from)
    Serenade (*The Goldsmith of Toledo*)   *   15 Oct 21

Olsen, Ole
    Asgardsreien   *   16 Sep 99

O'Neill, Norman
    In Autumn   **   26 Oct 01
    Death on the hills, voice & orch   **   8 Sep 04
    Variations on an Irish Air   **   14 Sep 11

Paderewski–Ford
    Minuet in A   **   10 Oct 96

Paur, Emil
    In der Natur   *   13 Oct 10

Petri, Egon
    Concertstück, pf & orch   **   6 Oct 06

Pezel, Johann
    Two Suites   *   18 Sep 07

Pfitzner, Hans
   Three Preludes, *Palestrina*   *   3 Sep 25
Phillips, Montague
   Fidelity   **   10 Sep 08
   Phantasy, vln & orch   **   16 Oct 17
Pick-Mangiagalli, Riccardo
   Sortilegi, pf & orch   *   4 Oct 23
Pierné, Gabriel
   Izéyl   *   23 Jan 97
   Paysages Franciscains   *   7 Sep 22
Pitt, Percy
   Suite in Four Movements   **   28 Aug 95
   Coronation March   **   23 Sep 96
   Fêtes Galantes   **   12 Dec 96
   Concertino, cl & orch   **   9 Oct 97
   Overture, *The Taming of the Shrew*   **   12 Mar 98
   Air de Ballet   **   9 Sep 99
   Cinderella   **   14 Oct 99
   Ballade, vln & orch   **   24 Feb 00
   Le Sang des Crépuscules   **   30 Apr 00
   Dance Rhythms   **   7 Nov 01
   Aria, strings   **   21 Oct 13
   Suite from *Sakura*   **   17 Sep 14
Poldowski [= Lady Dean Paul]
   Nocturne   **   8 Oct 12
   Pat Malone's Wake, pf & orch   **   2 Oct 19
Pratella, Francesco Balilla
   La guerra   *   9 Sep 19
Prokofiev, Sergey
   Humorous Scherzo, 4 bsns   *   2 Sep 16
   Piano Concerto 1   *   24 Aug 20
   Violin Concerto 2   *BBC   20 Dec 36
Prowinsky–Wood
   A Passing Serenade   **   9 Sep 16
Purcell-Colles
   Hornpipe   **   2 Sep 15
Purcell–Wood
   Suite in 5 Movements   **   21 Sep 09
   From Rosy Bowers   **   24 Sep 13
   (ascribed) Trumpet Voluntary   **   5 Sep 23[1]
Quilter, Roger
   Serenade   *   27 Aug 07
   Suite from *Where the Rainbow Ends*   **   26 Sep 12
   A Children's Overture   **   18 Sep 19
Rabaud, Henri
   Poème Virgilien   *   21 Sep 99
Rachmaninoff, Sergey
   Piano Concerto 1   **   4 Oct 00
   The Isle of the Dead   *   25 Aug 15
   The Bells   *LL   15 Mar 21
   Chansons Russes   *LL   17 Mar 30
Rachmaninoff–Wood
   Prelude in C sharp minor   **   20 Sep 13
Raff–Wood
   Cavatina   **   30 Aug 11
Rameau–Mottl
   Suite de Ballet   *   5 Oct 99

---

[1] date of first performance at the Promenade Concerts: date of actual first performance not known

Ravel, Maurice
    Introduction and Allegro   *   4 Sep 07
    Rapsodie Espagnole   *   21 Oct 09
    Pavane pour une Infante défunte   **M   27 Feb 11
    Ma mère l'oye   *   4 May 12
    Valses Nobles et Sentimentales   *   25 Sep 13
    La Valse   *   3 May 21
    Piano Concerto, left hand   *   16 Aug 32
Rebikov, Vladimir
    The Christmas Tree   *   28 Sep 16
Reed, William Henry
    Valse Brillante   **   22 Sep 98
    Touchstone   **   17 Oct 99
    Valse Elégante   **   30 Oct 00
    Among the Mountains of Cambria   **   1 Feb 02
Reger, Max
    Serenade in G [divided]   *   21, 28 Aug 07
    Variations and Fugue   *   26 Aug 09
    Symphonic Prologue to a Tragedy   *   14 Sep 09
    Psalm 100   *   22 May 11
    Comedy Overture   *   16 Nov 12
    Piano Concerto   *   9 Oct 23
Reinecke, Carl
    Flute Concerto   *   9 Sep 09
Respighi, Ottorino
    Vetrate di Chiesa   *   9 Mar 28
Ricci, Vittorio
    Two Forest Scenes, bar & orch   *   25 Sep 06
Rimsky-Korsakov, Nikolay
    Capriccio Espagnol   *   24 Sep 96
    Scheherazade   *   5 Dec 96
    Suite from *Mlada*   **   12 Nov 98
    Fantasia on Serbian Themes   *   15 Jan 99
    Fantaisie Russe   *   31 May 00
    Symphony 2   *   19 Sep 00
    Piano concerto   **SJ   22 Jun 03
    Suite from *Christmas Eve*   *S   8 Oct 08
    Night on Mount Triglav (*Mlada*)   *   10 Oct 10
    Pan Voyevoda   *   10 Oct 16
Rimsky-Korsakov–Wood
    Cradle Song (*The Maid of Pskov*)   **   16 Sep 16
Rogister, J.
    Fantaisie Concertante,vla & orch   *   27 Aug 10
Ronald, Landon
    Suite de Ballet   **   3 Nov 00
Rootham, Cyril
    A Passer-by   **   3 Oct 11
    Overture to *The Two Sisters*   **   19 Sep 18
Roussel, Albert
    Evocation   *   24 Mar 17
    Le Festin de l'araignée   *   23 Oct 20
    Pour une Fête de Printemps   *   3 Oct 22
    Piano concerto   *   14 Dec 37[1]

---

[1] Listed both by Kenyon and Thompson (see above) with a query as a first British performance; no independent confirmation is available.

Rowley, Alec
    Harpsichord Concerto   **   4 Sep 40
Roze, Raymond
    Antony and Cleopatra   **   21 Sep 11
Rubinstein–d'Indy
    Melody in F   *   24 Sep 98
Saint-Saëns, Camille
    Prélude et Cortège (*Déjanire*)   *   5 Sep 99
    Les Barbares   *   7 Dec 01
    Le Carnaval des Animaux   *   11 Aug 23
Sainton, Prosper
    Harlequin and Columbine   **   1 Oct 25
    Two Orchestral Pictures   **   4 Sep 23
Santoliquido, Francesco
    Il Profumo delle Oasi Saharine   *   6 Oct 21
Scarborough, Ethel
    Promise   **   19 Oct 22
Scharwenka, Xavier
    Prelude to *Mataswinka*   *   2 Oct 95
Scharwenka–Wood
    3 Polish National Dances   **   23 Sep 19
Scheinpflug, Paul
    Comedy Overture   *   16 Sep 09
Schillings, Max
    King Oedipus   *   27 Sep 02
Schmitt, Florent
    Suite, *Reflets d'Allemagne*   *   5 Sep 14
    Rêves   **   16 Oct 19
    Rapsodie Viennoise   *   25 Oct 19
Schoenberg, Arnold
    Five Orchestral Pieces   **   3 Sep 12
Schreker, Franz
    Suite, *Der Geburtstag der Infantin*   *   27 Aug 25
Schumann, Georg
    Dance (*Amor and Psyche*)   *   24 Oct 01
    Variations, 'Wer nur den lieben Gott'   *   23 Jan 02
    Liebesfrühling   *   25 Jan 02
    Ruth   *S   27 Apr 11
Schumann, Robert
    Concertstück, 4 hns & orch   *   8 Oct 09
Schumann–Pfitzner
    Eight Choruses, female voices & orch   *   19 Oct 11
Schumann–Sanders
    Canon   **   19 Oct 11
Schytte, Ludwig
    Piano Concerto   *   21 Jan 02
Scott, Cyril
    Symphony 2   **   25 Aug 03
    Rhapsody 1   **   10 Sep 04
    Overture, *Princess Maleine*   **   22 Aug 07
    Twilight of the Year & *Paradise Birds*   **   26 Aug 13
    Britain's War March   **   23 Oct 14
Serov, Alexander
    Cossack Dance   *   15 Sep 97
Shostakovich, Dmitri
    Piano Concerto 1   *   4 Jan 36
    Symphony 7   *BBC   22 Jun 42
    Symphony 8   *BBC   13 Jul 44

Sibelius, Jean
   King Christian II   *   26 Oct 01
   Symphony 1   *   13 Oct 03
   Suite, *Karelia*   *   23 Oct 06
   Dance Intermezzo 2   *   31 Aug 07
   Violin Concerto   *   1 Oct 07
   Overture, *Karelia*   *   25 Oct 07
   Suite, *Swan-White*   *   29 Sep 09
   Romance in C   *   12 Feb 10
   Symphony 6   *   20 Nov 26
   Canzonetta & Valse Romantique   *   2 Dec 11
   Symphony 7   *   8 Dec 27
   Tapiola   *   1 Sep 28
   The Ferryman's Brides   *   10 Sep 36
Simonetti, Achille
   Madrigali   *   30 Sep 99
Sinding, Christian
   Episodes Chevaleresques   *   11 Nov 99
Singigaglia, Leone
   Danze Piemontesi 1 & 2   *   6, 19 Oct 09
   Piemonte   *   22 Aug 12
Sjögren, Emil
   Wüstenwanderung der heiligen drei Könige   *   25 Feb 99
Skilton, Charles Stanford
   Two Indian Dances   *   17 Oct 18
Skryabin, Alexander
   Prometheus: The Poem of Fire   *   1 Feb 13
   Scherzo   *   19 Sep 16
Smith, D. Stanley
   Prince Hal   **   20 Aug 19
Smyth, Ethel
   Four Choral Preludes   **   29 Aug 23
   Double Concerto   **   5 Mar 27
   Suite from *Entente cordiale*   **   3 Jan 35
Sokolov, Nikolay, see Glazunov
Sowerby, Leo
   Comes Autumn Time   *   23 Aug 28
Spain-Dunk, Susan
   Idyll   **   13 Oct 25
   Romantic Piece, fl & str   **   13 Oct 25
Speight, Joseph
   Queen Mab Sleeps & Puck   **   30 Aug 17
Spelman, Timothy Mather
   Barbaresques   **   20 Sep 23
Squire, William Henry
   Summer Dreams   **   4 Sep 97
   Sweet Briar   **   24 Sep 98
   Slumber Song   **   16 Sep 99
Stanford, Charles Villiers
   Suite of Dances   **   28 Aug 95
Steggall, Reginald
   Oreithyia   **   24 Oct 01
Stenhammar, Wilhelm
   Piano Concerto 2   *   9 Oct 20
Strauss, Richard
   Prelude Act I, *Guntram*   *   2 Oct 95
   Festmarsch   *   6 Oct 98
   'Wanderers Sturmlied'   *S   2 Oct 02
   Aus Italien, pts 1 & 2   *   27 Aug 03

Symphonia Domestica	*	25 Feb 05
Parergon to the Symphonia Domestica, pf & orch	*	25 Aug 28
Stravinsky, Igor		
Suite, *The Firebird*	*	4 Sep 13
Scherzo Fantastique	*	26 Aug 14
Fireworks	*	29 Aug 14
Stringfield, Lamar		
A Negro Parade	*AH	19 Jun 43
Strong, George Templeton		
The Night	*	17 Aug 20
Suk, Josef		
A Fairy-Tale	*	6 Oct 03
Svendsen, Johan S.		
Andante Funèbre	*	2 Oct 95
Swert, Jules de		
Cello Concerto 2	*	18 Sep 02
Tailleferre, Germaine		
Ballade, pf & orch	*	22 Sep 26
Tansman, Alexandre		
Piano Concerto	*	16 Aug 28
Tapp, Frank		
Metropolis	**	30 Aug 34
Taylor, Deems		
Through the Looking Glass	*	11 Aug 25
Tchaikovsky, Pyotr Ilyich		
Yevgeny Onegin (opera)	*OT	17 Oct 92
Marche Solennelle	*	2 Oct 95
Suite, *The Nutcracker*	*	17 Oct 96
Overture to *The Storm*	*	20 Feb 97
Overture to opera *The Voyevoda*	*	15 May 97
Suite 3	*	15 May 97
Suite 4, *Mozartiana*	*	24 Sep 97
Overture on Danish National Anthem	*	15 Jun 98
Manfred	*	28 Sep 98
The Tempest	*	5 Oct 98
Overture to *Cherevichki*	*	22 Sep 99
Cossack Dance (*Mazeppa*)	*	28 Sep 99
Fatum	*	28 Oct 99
Suite from *Swan Lake*	*	14 Sep 01
Pastoral Play (*The Queen of Spades*)	*	6 Nov 01
The Battle of Poltava	*	16 Aug 04
Air (*Yolanta*)	*	15 Oct 04
Intro & Dance (*The Oprichnik*)	*	21 Sep 05
The Voyevoda op.78	*	28 Sep 05
Tchaikovsky–Erdmannsdörfer		
Chant sans paroles (op.2/no.3)	*	3 Oct 99
Tcherepnin, Nikolay		
The Romance of a Mummy	*	16 Sep 25
Thieriot, Ferdinand		
Sinfonietta	*	7 Nov 96
Thuille, Ludwig		
Romantic Overture	*	11 Sep 02
Ticciati, Francesco		
Poema Gregoriano, pf & orch	**	25 Aug 21
Tinel, Edgar		
Godoleva	*	27 Sep 00
Toch, Ernst		
Symphony, pf & orch	**	20 Aug 34

Tommasini, Vincenzo
   Prelude, Fanfare and Fugue   *   7 Sep 29
Valentin, Karl
   Festmarsch   *   22 Sep 98
Vasilenko, Sergei Nikiforovich
   Epic Poem   *   13 Aug 04
   To the Sun   *   23 Oct 13
Vaughan Williams, Ralph
   A Norfolk Rhapsody 1   **   23 Aug 06
   Fantasia on English Folk Songs   **   1 Sep 10
   Flos Campi   **   10 Oct 25
   Serenade to Music   **AH   5 Oct 38
   Serenade to Music (orch version)   **   10 Feb 40
Verhey, Theo. H. H.
   Flute Concerto   **   5 Oct 07
Vicars, Harold
   Rosalind   **   2 Oct 95
Villa-Lobos, Heitor
   Choros 8   *   12 Aug 30
Vivaldi–Ziloti
   Concerto in D minor   *   22 Aug 14
Volbach, Fritz
   Es waren zwei Königskinder   *   12 Oct 01
   Ostern   *   2 Nov 01
   Alt Heidelberg   *   23 Aug 04
Volkov, Nikolay
   Cossack Dance   *LL   9 Sep 99
Vreuls, Victor
   Poème 1, vc & orch   *   25 Oct 07
Vycpálek, Ladislav
   Cantata of the Last Things of Man   *LL   20 Mar 28
Wagner, Siegfried
   Intro Act 3, *Der Bärenhüter*   *   15 Sep 99
   Valse at the Fair (*Herzog Wildfang*)   *   31 Oct 01
Wallace, William
   Sir William Wallace   **   19 Sep 05
Walthew, Richard H.
   Caprice Impromptu, vln & orch   **   24 Sep 04
   Friend Fritz   **   19 Aug 14
Walton, William
   Façade Suite 2   *   10 Sep 38
Waud, J. Haydn
   Comedy Overture   **   9 Oct 99
Weber, Carl Maria von
   Theme & Vars, basset-hn & orch   **   21 Sep 04
Weber–Weingartner
   Invitation to the Dance   *   8 Sep 99
Webern, Anton
   Passacaglia   *   22 Aug 31
Weingartner, Felix
   Symphony 2   *   24 Sep 01
West, John E.
   King Robert of Sicily   **   8 Oct 96
White, Felix H.
   Shylock   **   26 Sep 07
Widor, Charles-Marie
   Sinfonia Sacra, org & orch   *   17 Sep 19

First Performances conducted by Henry J. Wood

Widor–Sanders
    Symphony in F minor, org & orch   **   23 Oct 19
Wolf, Hugo
    Penthesilea   *   12 Nov 04
    Christmas Night   *N   30 Oct 08
Wolf-Ferrari, Ermanno
    Chamber Symphony   *   4 Sep 03
Wood, Henry J.
    Fantasia on British Sea Songs   **   2 Oct 05
    Fantasia on Welsh Melodies   **   19 Aug 09
    Fantasia on Scottish Melodies   **   20 Aug 09
Woods, F. Cunningham
    Suite in F   **   19 Sep 01
Wyk, Arnold van
    Symphony 1   **BBC   31 May 43
Ysaÿe, Théophile
    Piano concerto   *   29 Sep 21
Zilcher, Hermann
    Concerto, 2 vlns   *   22 Sep 04
Zöllner, Heinrich
    'O, buzzing golden bee' (*Die versunkene Glocke*)   *   8 Oct 13

Appendix 5

Paintings by Henry J. Wood

Those oil-paintings by Henry J. Wood which remained with him up to his death were afterwards arranged by Jessie Wood in the apparent sequence of date, and photographed. An album of the photographs served as a documentation of Jessie Wood's disposal of the paintings themselves in 1956. All were made over, by deed of gift, to the Royal Academy of Music, save for those either to be retained by her or given to named individuals or to Trinity College of Music. Signatures beside the respective photographs in the album serve as receipts. A note in Jessie Wood's hand shows that Malcolm Sargent signed in error for the *wrong* picture: the correct one is indicated in the list below. The indication 'J.W.' in the album identified those pictures Jessie Wood had reserved for herself.

It appears, however, that she also took possession of numbers 16, 30, 35, and 39. Numbers 16 and 39 were given by her family (after her death) to the Musicians' Benevolent Fund for a charity auction in 1987. Numbers 30 and 35, together with numbers 56, 57, and 58, are now (1995) in the custody of her grandson and literary executor, Henry T. Calthrop. He also has the original album of photographs, together with their negatives.

The titles and dates in the album, reproduced below, are not in the painter's hand. In the documentation held by the Royal Academy of Music itself the titles sometimes differ slightly, and no. 17 is said to be of 'Chantilly'. Those paintings from this list which are still (1995) located at the Academy are denoted by an asterisk. The Academy also holds four other paintings, one entitled 'Llangollen', one 'The Little Bay, St Emogat [?], Brittany' and two landscapes of uncertain title.

* 1 Apples, 1880
  2 Self Study, age 14, 1884
  3 By the Leg of Mutton Pond, Hampstead, 1884 [JW]
* 4 Study for a Larger Canvas: Near Crick-heath hall, Oswestry (Mother's Relations), 1890 [JW]
  5 Near Crick-heath hall, Salop (Mother's Relations), 1890
* 6 Thunder in the Air, Ranmoor near Sheffield, 1900
* 7 Near Sheffield, 1900
  8 For my Breakfast, 1900
  9 Near Bettws-y-Coed, North Wales, 1900
*10 6 a.m. off the Isle of Wight on board *Majestic*, 1904
 11 After the mid-day Meal, 1905
 12 Squally weather at sea: on my way to New York, 1905 [JW]

13 The Bridge at Bruges, 1905 [JW]
14 Silent Woods: The haunt of the heron, 1905
15 The River runs into the Sea, Wareham, 1905
16 Evening Seascape, 1905
17 The Avenue, Coire, near Paris, 1906
18 A Ploughfield in rainy weather (one-hour sketch), 1907 [JW]
*19 A windy morning, Chorley Wood Common, 1907
20 Sandy Shallows at Parkstone, near Bournemouth, 1907
21 Study in nude, 1908
22 High Street, Coire, near Paris, 1908
23 Old Farm House, Arvica, Sweden, 1908
24 A Calm Sea, 1908 [Norman Allin]
25 Looking towards Brownsea Island, Sunset, 1908
*26 Brownsea near Poole, 1908
27 Wareham St Martin, Dorset, 1908
28 Sunlit Cornfield, Norwich, 1908 [Sir Malcolm Sargent]
*29 Bettws-y-Coed, Valley and Hills, 1908
30 The Land of Mountain and Flood, 1909
31 Coniston Water from the foot of Ruskin's Garden, Brantwood, 1909 [JW]
32 Corfe Castle, 1909
33 Christchurch, near Bournemouth, 1909 [Phyllis Sellick]
34 Evening in Richmond Park, near Kingston Gate, 1910
35 An October morning, Richmond Park, 1910
*36 The Estuary, Bournemouth, 1910
*37 Shipping at Poole, 1910
38 Cottage, Arvica, Sweden, 1913
39 Early morning Sea at Brighton, 1913 [JW]
40 September Sunset: a Cornfield near Chorley Wood, 1920 [Elsie Newmarch]
*41 Arvica, Sweden, 1921
42 Meadows near Burnside, Westmorland, 1921
43 A Garden near Woking, 1922 ['Dr Skeggs' Daughter']
44 Chorley Wood Common, 1927 [Sir Reginald Thatcher]
45 The Alps, Montreux, 1928 [Tufton Beamish, MP]
46 Old Barn, Apple Tree Farm, Chorley Wood, 1930 [W. Greenhouse Allt]
*47 The Eiger, Mürren, Switzerland, 1931 [JW]
48 The Jungfrau, Interlaken, Switzerland, 1931
49 Lake Brienz, Interlaken, Switzerland: evening view after a storm, 1931 [Solomon]
50 Stormy weather, Lake Brienz, Interlaken, Switzerland, 1931 [Solomon]
*51 Trees, 1933
52 Burgenstock from the Balcony of Palace Hotel, Lucerne (with view of Triebschen), 1936
53 The Sisters, Lucerne, 1936 [Trinity College of Music]
54 The Cairngorms, from the Ladies Turn, Speyside, 1937 [Trinity College of Music]
55 Oban Bay from the Great Western Hotel, 1938 [Stanley Rubinstein]
56 Early morning over the Estuary from Beaumaris, 1943 [JW]
57 Stormy weather; the Welsh Hills from Beaumaris, 1943 [JW]
58 Welsh Hills at low tide on the Estuary from Beaumaris: his last finished sketch, 1943 [JW]

A listing of his paintings made on 5 January 1938 by Wood himself includes the following titles (without dates) which cannot be readily identified with any of the above:

1 Lilies
2 A Pool near Western Turville
3 Evening near Amersham
4 Christmas, Château d'Oex
5 Scotland ('with apologies to D. Y. Cameron')
6 The Lake near Château d'Oex
7 Erdig Hall (Sir Phillip [sic] Yorke) near Wrexham

Henry J. Wood

 8 On the Coast of Cornwall ('copy')
10 Lake Louise ('copy')

The first of these, with the date 1906, is in the possession of Henry T. Calthrop.

The following paintings are owned by the painter's daughter, Tatiana Cardew:

1 Stanmore Park, September 1907
2 The Aylesbury Valley, Winter, November 1913
3 Evening, looking across from Montreux, July 1926
4 Champéry above Martigny, Switzerland, ?1928–9
5 ?Chorley Wood, undated
6 [unidentified, damaged]

The following paintings (plus one in water-colour) are owned by the painter's grandson, Richard Cardew:

1 Autumn Trees and a Pond [undated]
2 The Black Horse [public-house], Chorley Wood, seen from Appletree Farm [undated]
3 [Landscape, unidentified, undated]

A number of other paintings may be presumed to have been given away by him during his lifetime.

Appendix 6

Honours and Dedications

Henry J. Wood was created Knight Bachelor in 1911 and Companion of Honour in 1944, and also held two foreign decorations: member of the Order of the Crown of Belgium, 1920, and officer of the Légion d'honneur (France), 1926.

He became a Gold Medallist of the Royal Philharmonic Society in 1921 and an honorary freeman of the Worshipful Company of Musicians in 1938. He received honorary doctorates of music from the Universities of Manchester, 1923; Oxford, 1926; Birmingham, 1927; Cambridge, 1935; and London, 1939. He became a Fellow of the Royal Academy of Music in 1920 and of the Royal College of Music in 1923.

The following works were dedicated to him or, in the case of those by Alwyn and Walton, to his memory. The dates are those of the first performance:

Pitt, Percy	*Fêtes galantes*	1896
Pitt, Percy	*The Taming of the Shrew*	1898
Bantock, Granville	*Dante and Beatrice*	1901
Cowen, Frederic Hymen	*The Butterfly's Ball*	1901
Elgar, Edward	*Grania and Diarmid* (incidental music)	1901
O'Neill, Norman	*In Autumn*	1901
Hervey, Arthur	*In the East*	1904
Holbrooke, Josef	Symphony 1: *Les Hommages*	1908
Coates, Eric	Miniature Suite	1910
Reed, W. H.	*Suite Vénitienne*	1910
Gardiner, H. Balfour	*Shepherd Fennel's Dance*	1911
Goossens, Eugene	Miniature Fantasy	1911
Delius, Frederick	*Eventyr*	1917
Howell, Dorothy	*Lamia*	1919
Greenbaum, Hyam	*A Sea Poem*	1922
Smyth, Ethel	Double Concerto (violin & horn)	1927
Bax, Arnold	Symphony 3	1930
Dupré, Marcel	Symphony in G minor	1930
Vaughan Williams, Ralph	*Serenade to Music*	1938
Rubbra, Edmund	Symphony 4	1942
Dale, Benjamin J.	*The Flowing Tide*	1943
Bliss, Arthur	*Birthday Fanfare for Sir Henry Wood*	1944
Walton, William	*Memorial Fanfare*	1944
Walton, William	'Where does the uttered music go?'	1946
Alwyn, William	Concerto grosso 3	1964
Bax, Arnold	*Spring Fire* (composed 1913)	1970

Source-Notes

References

BBCWA = BBC Written Archives

BL   = British Library Additional Manuscripts: Sir Henry Wood and (Loan 42) Royal Philharmonic Society

Diary   = Henry J. Wood's annual diaries (MSS), 1935–44, with some entries by Jessie Wood

DT   = *Daily Telegraph*

LC   = manuscript material in the US Library of Congress

LY   = Jessie Wood, *The Last Years of Henry J. Wood*, 1954

MLM = Henry J. Wood, *My Life of Music*, 1938

MMR = *Monthly Musical Record*

MT   = *Musical Times*

NG   = *The New Grove Dictionary of Music and Musicians*, 1980

QH   = Robert Elkin, *Queen's Hall*, 1945

RAM = Royal Academy of Music

RP   = Reginald Pound, *Sir Henry Wood*, 1969

SAN   = collection of letters from Henry J. Wood to Francis G. Sanders, in the possession of the author

Tape   = audiotape interviews by Arthur Jacobs 1991–3

Books are referred to as listed in the Bibliography; a date is given only if there is more than one by the same author, and an indication of title only if there is more than one work of the same year. Periodical, newspaper and manuscript references are given in full.

Foreword

p.xxii mis-spellings: in a list of conductors from whom he profited, [Max] Fiedler becomes simply 'Fielded' (p.44)

p.xxii 'It is – as you say. . .': Abse, 312

PART I

p.1 'Orchestral virtuosity. . .': R. Vaughan Williams, 267

Chapter 1

p.3 'as if every nerve': Shaw, II, 347
p.4 he himself maintained: MLM, 11
p.5 which owned 7 Pond Street: Census returns 1871, 1881
p.5 became no.185: Kelly's Post Office Directory, London (1882)
p.5 The description: MLM, 23ff
p.6 'Mr Wood practised. . .': BL 56429, 23–41
p.6 'much older': MLM, 13
p.6 'one of the best mixed choirs': MLM, 16ff for this and the following paragraph
p.7 'nearly nine. . . Mr and Mrs Vie': MLM, 13, 20
p.8 'wore the kilt for best': MLM, 45
p.8 'My father never missed. . .': MLM, 26
p.9 'a period of stagnation. . .': LY, 11
p.9 'my greatest of colleagues. . .': letter 18 January 1910, in the possession of Christopher Fifield
p.10 'a little man with jet-black hair': MLM, 26
p.11 'Mr Henry J. Wood gave his first. . .': Scholes, 388
p.12 the *Era*: 24 March 1888
p.12 'a further Academy concert': MLM, 31, reverses the order of these two concerts
p.12 'much above the average': MT, July 1888, 430
p.12 'cannoned me to the floor': MLM, 30
p.13 his own account: MLM, 35
p.14 various trips abroad: MLM, 38–9
p.14 *The Yeomen of the Guard*: MLM, 39. The 'puff' planted by Wood himself in mid-1895 (see Chapter 3, p. 35) also fails to mention this supposed early association with Sullivan, which would have been immediately deniable while Sullivan was still alive. Likewise in *The Sketch*, 7 September 1898, p. 312, Wood's association with Sullivan is dated only from 1890.
p.14 Mary Frances Ronalds: MLM, 41
p.15 'What a filthy trick!': MLM, 32

Chapter 2

p.17 he later maintained: MLM, 37
p.18 'travelling every Sunday. . .': M. Goossens, 2
p.19 'In one small town': E. Goossens, 28
p.19 'on the wrong side of the cow-horse': interview with Wood in the first issue (3 November 1927) of *Music of All Nations*, of which he was the nominal editor. The incident is also mentioned in the news report of an after-dinner speech by Wood ('New Role for H.Wood': *Daily Telegraph*, undated, mid-1920s). See also MLM, 55-6
p.19 'a tremendous tea': MLM, 54
p.20 'some difficult letters': MLM, 56

p.21 *Mignon, The Mock Doctor: My Life of Music* wrongly places both these performances *before* the Rousbey tour.

p.21 'often refusing to go away': MLM, 58

p.21 'a splendid orchestra of ten': MLM, 57

p.22 *A Hundred Years Ago:* information on this and other theatrical dates from George Hauger (unpublished)

p.22 'the best-paid operatic engagement': MLM, 58

p.24 *Daily Graphic*: 19 October 1892; also *The Times*, 18 October; *The People*, 21 October; *The World*, 26 October (reprinted in Shaw II, 717)

p.26 'couldn't conduct for nuts': Sims, 224

p.26 *The Lady Slavey:* according to Kurt Gänzl, the historian of the light musical theatre (private communication), Wood was also one of the song-composers for the show.

p.26 'the most extraordinary prima donna': MLM, 67; see also the interview with Wood in *Music of All Nations*, part 1 (3 November 1927), 7

Chapter 3

p.28 'uncomfortable, long, narrow. . .': H. Henschel, 81

p.29 'armchair accommodation': QH, 16

p.29 work was in progress: QH, 18

p.29 'attenuated Cupids. . .': ibid.

p.29 'orgie of suburbia': Gilbert Burgess in Sims 1990, I, 59

p.30 *Illustrated London News*: Carse, 1951, 112

p.31 'Mr Levy the cornet': *The Orchestra*, September 1874, quoted in Jacobs, 107

p.31 Cowen as conductor: MT September 1893, 538, where G. R. Betjemann is named as leader and deputy conductor
as assistant: letter from Newman's daughter Eileen to Jessie Wood BL56430, 30

p.32 2 December 1893: the organist was W. G. Wood, see press reports

p.32 You Be Quiet Club: MLM 63 gives 'U.B.Quiet', but the club's surviving documentation shows this to be erroneous. (Information from the custodian of the material, Norman McCann.)

p.33 'The Wagner Choir': MT, June 1895, 381

p.33 attended the Bayreuth Festival: in *My Life of Music* Wood claimed improbably to have made a first visit to the festival in 'the year Liszt died' (1886), when Wood had not even entered the RAM.

p.33 'as a boy prodigy': Hambourg, 18–9

p.34 'two or three thousand pounds': MLM, 69

p.36 'Herr Nikisch is. . .': NG vol.13, 245

p.36 'To me he was. . .': Flesch, 148

p.36 'We are so spoilt. . .': Jacobs, 368

p.38 'got the movement into its stride': Shaw, II, 347

p.38 Agnes Nicholls: Hall, 34

p.38 'who do not care for ambulation': *The Year's Music*, 1896, 195

p.38 'handsome palms and shrubs. . .': ibid.

p.39 'The members of the orchestra . . .': ibid., I, 58

p.40 Kelly's Post Office Directory: confirmed by a scrawled note in Lady Jessie Wood's handwriting on the dust-jacket of *My Life of Music*

p.40 in an article in 1992: *CD Review* (Michael Collins), October 1992, 92

p.40 'Wood conducted excellently. . .': Grainger *Selected Letters*, 79
p.41 'Some may be in doubt': Brian, 217
p.41 'installing my dear mother': MLM, 65

Chapter 4

p.44 'The tone had changed completely': Cox, 34
p.45 'he did not claim': typescript *Sir Henry J. Wood* signed Adrian C. Boult, dated 24 January, 1962, in the possession of the author
p.46 The excellence of Wood's performances: MT November 1895, 744–5
p.46 'The type of audience. . .': QH, 27
p.47 *Monthly Musical Record*: April 1896, 79
p.47 Gustav Holst: MLM, 88; Holst, 18–19
p.47 'an appalling work': MLM, 92
p.50 'Mr Wood, will you permit me to suggest. . .': MLM, 109
p.52 'will be made more efficient': MMR, September 1897, 208
p.52 'no less than thirty new players': MT, September 1897, 622
p.53 absence of her name: see E. T. Cook, *The Life of John Ruskin* (1911), etc. But she was called on to sing at Ruskin's funeral.

Chapter 5

p.57 'I have a fairly long experience. . .': Jacobs, 391
p.58 compliment Wood on his performances: 2 February 1897
p.58 'on the doorstep of his flat. . .': RP, 63
p.59 allusions to her in the British Press: MT, 1898, 525
p.59 her mother died there on 24 February 1897, aged 62: Ikonnikov KI, 232; L2, 354
p.59 A letter from Ermilovka: RP, 61, where 'Ermilovka' is given erroneously as 'Emilovka'
p.60 'She had become. . .a very welcome visitor. . .': MLM, 117
p.60 'I think I should have gone under. . .': MLM, 119–20
p.61 about 50 strong: *Nottingham Daily Express* 28 December 1897
p.61 orchestra's début on 8 December 1898: MT January 1899, 44
p.61 'The orchestra has received. . .': *Nottingham Daily Express*, 9 December 1898
p.62 'hit on the admirable idea. . .': MLM, 122
p.63 'With regard to your concert. . .': Carley, 148
p.64 'When engaged upon French music. . .': MT June 1899, 391
p.64 première of Elgar's *Enigma Variations*: Moore, 268
p.65 'he outdated all the schools. . .': Casals, 128

Chapter 6

p.67 recital by Svyatlovskaya: St James's Hall, 8 June 1896
p.68 Harry's wife (who was also his cousin): see also Jessie Wood's notes on family in BL 56430, 140
p.70 in November 1900: *The Times*, 25 November 1900 (the work was Beethoven's Piano Concerto no.4)
p.72 'the most important ever given. . .': MT, December 1900, 817
p.74 'I shall never forget the scene. . .': MLM, 154

Chapter 9

p.118 'Never in England. . .': Smyth/ Crichton, 285
p.119 'After having played with Beecham. . .': Coates, 137–8
p.121 also the first performance anywhere: the 'first performance' listed in Orenstein, 595, is later (25 December 1911).
p.122 'discovered to my relief. . .': Bax, BBC broadcast 4 March 1944, quoted in Foreman, 1983, 74
p.123 German conducting a bad name: NG, article 'Stransky'
p.125 'the thematic and counterpoint lines. . .': MT, June 1911, 386–7
p.125 'a more closed cavity. . .': Scholes I/46, quoting the Sheffield conductor and critic J. A. Rodgers (1912)
p.126 'with whom Casals has risked. . .': MLM, 246
p.126 Kennedy's biography of the composer: Kennedy 1968, 234
p.128 'There were twenty-nine Sunday afternoon concerts. . .': MLM, 246
p.128 occasional concert pianist: as in the first British performance (conducted by Eugene Goossens) of Falla's *El Amor Brujo*, 23 November 1921
p.129 Wood's working life revealed: SAN passim
p.129 'has lately taken her place. . .': MT, December 1921, 847
p.130 Tania was to observe: tape 1992

Chapter 10

p.131 'for having introduced the fashion. . .': MMR, July 1918, 151–2
p.131 concerts before 1900: *Nottingham Daily Express* 28 January 1899
p.132 'Sir Henry Wood managed to play. . .': MMR April 1914, 96
p.133 to conduct it himself: Carley, II, 89
p.133 company of Rosa Newmarch: Tawaststjerna, II, 219
p.134 'Herr [Willem] Mengelberg. . .': *Times*, 25 May 1912
p.135 'I was rather badly cut. . .': MLM, 277
p.136 'This baffling novelty. . .': E. Goossens, 'Sir Henry Wood at Rehearsals', *New York Times*, 3 September 1944
p.137 'It is not often that an English audience. . .': quoted by David Lambourne in MT, 1987, 423
p.137 'as almost inconceivable': Stuckenschmidt, 177
p.139 'I shall *never* forget the performance. . .': Rapoport, 199
p.139 a 'splendid success': Carley, II, 89
p.139 'disgracefully badly': Tomlinson, 1977, 8
p.142 'mixed bathing in the sea of music': Crichton, 340
p.142 opened their ranks to women: Maitland, 42
p.142 'If they are pretty. . .': St John, 192
p.142 'I shall never conduct. . .': ibid.
p.142 'Generous-minded Sir Henry Wood': ibid.
p.143 'I remember her conducting. . .': MLM, 282
p.143 'in spite of protests. . .': Crichton, 284–5
p.143 'so much more favourable. . .': MMR March & April 1914

Chapter 11

p.146 'Harmless old men. . .': A. J. P. Taylor, 19
p.147 'I had been a member. . .': Speyer, 216

p.174 'The tumultuous applause refused to die down. . .': *Neue Zürcher Zeitung*, 9 July 1921. (The critic rewrote his notice for the following month's *Schweizerische Musikzeitung.*)

p.174 'When we parted on the quay. . .': MLM, 440

p.174 critic of the *Manchester Guardian*: 9 January 1921

p.175 return by railway sleeping-car: BL 56419, 4

p.176 until the following December: S. de B. Taylor, 20–1

p.177 It was reported: Eaglefield-Hull, 356

p.179 France made him. . .: he was careless enough to describe himself in *My Life of Music* as an Officier *du* Légion d'honneur

p.180 'It is my little baby. . .': all documentation relating to Dorothy Howell from family collection

p.181 'interesting mainly on antiquarian grounds': MMR, 1922 September 220

p.181 'the timing was impeccable': MT, 1922, 873

p.182 'All we Londoners. . .': MMR, November 1923, 329

p.182 'No one enjoys a joke. . .': RP, 147–8

PART III

Chapter 13

p.187 'rarely if ever darkened its doors': Kitching

p.189 'He had turned one of the small barns. . .': BBC programme KP371H, broadcast 14 September 1975

p.190 Tania was to maintain in 1991: tape

p.190 revealed it to her in 1993: tape

p.192 'He expected everybody to run round. . .': tape, Tania Cardew's comment on RP, 183

p.193 'With much to be rehearsed. . .': Shore, 194–5

p.193 '.. .When really pressed for time. . .': Shore, 196

p.194 'Few conductors, if any, help their players. . .': Shore, 198

p.194 Marie Goossens, recalled: M. Goossens, 50, 58

p.195 'The orchestral works of the older masters': Wood, in Eaglefield-Hull, 362

p.195 'whose *Sea-Drift*, a work for soli, chorus and orchestra. . .': ibid., 363

p.195 'The composer of the future. . .': ibid., 364

p.197 'As the work has been gramophoned. . .': Brian, 109, from *Musical Opinion*

p.200 'perfect felicity and mutual understanding': MT, 1924, 937

Chapter 14

p.206 'well-chosen remarks in the British accents. . .': *Los Angeles Times* 23 July 1926

p.206 'Sir Henry apparently had not been told. . .': Koopal, 107

p.206 'near tears when her husband rushed to her aid. . .': Koopal, 107–8; cf. Pound, 154, where the acccount is rather different but no source is given.

p.207 'half-a-dozen times in the opening chorus. . .': MLM, 319

p.207 'I have spent the day on your score. . .': 6 March 1922

p.207 'Will nobody revive for us. . .': MT, October 1927, 397

p.207 'The levelling-up of all sorts and conditions. . .': *Daily Express*, 19 November 1926 p.207 In March of that year: MT, April 1926, 345

p.208 Next day the *Daily Telegraph*: 10 April 1926

p.208 'in ten years' time. . .': Scholes MM, 798

p.208 broadcasting cable to the hall: Chamier, 208–10

p.209 'Every concert-giver. . .': Chamier, 208–10; similarly next extract

p.209 Ronald had broadcast as early as 1924: MT, October 1924, 927

p.209 estimated as £60,000: Cox, 84

p.210 'Saving the Promenades': Cox, 86

p.212 noticed for the first time: *Westminster Gazette*, 15 August 1927

p.212 'I do not think I ever conducted. . .': MLM, 321

p.212 'The trash in the Prom programmes. . .': Cox, 87, 89

p.212 Watson Lyle in the *Musical Standard*: 27 August 1927

p.213 'a very minor role. . .': Herbage, unidentified magazine article 1963

p.213 as *The Times* did on 20 August 1927: Cox, 90

p.213 'to hear Wagner at the Proms. . .': Briggs II, 173

p.213 two and a quarter million: BBC Handbook 1928

p.214 of which the *Monthly Musical Record*: October 1927, 305

p.214 drawn from the Royal Academy of Music: MT, November 1927, 1030

p.215 'has been brought to a high pitch. . .': MT, May 1927, 459

p.215 'I have really at last entirely broken down. . .': Briggs II, 173

p.216 'Beecham has not replied. . .': Kenyon, 41

p.216 'Beecham remained an angry judge. . .': Briggs II, 174

p.216 'the joy of a *daily rehearsal*. . .': MLM, 321

Chapter 15

p.218 'When I got to my chair. . .': Jackson, 85

p.218 obituary of Wood in the *Daily Express*: 21 August 1944

p.218 Norman Carrell, however: Tape

p.221 'Walk through the passages. . .': Wood, *The Gentle Art of Singing* I, 12–17

p.221 Wood's suggested 'DAILY TIMETABLE. . .': ibid., I, 17

p.223 reviewing one of his performances: MT April 1926, 344

p.223 'Audiences have learnt. . .': MT, April 1934

p.224 'the worst orchestral performances ever heard . . .:' MT, January 1928, 70

p.224 trip with Muriel to Norway: Letter 30 July 1928

p.225 'gallantly accepted': S. Walton, 68

p.225 *two* rehearsals daily: the detail of Wood's demands is seen in his letter of 27 April 1929 (Patrick Prenter collection) to the violinist F. Waldo Channon, who had applied for an engagement.

p.225 'meaningless vandalism': Britten's diary (MS, Britten-Pears Library), 2 January 1933

p.225 'sending for his director': Kenyon, 39–40

p.229 the one simply 'merged': MLM, 321

p.229 'The tone in every section. . .': Kenyon, 46

p.229 has the fictitious 'reminiscence': Rubinstein, 250

p.230 'euphemistically called the Queen's Hall Orchestra': MMR, December 1930, 364

p.230 'sung to selected phrases. . .': MMR, December 1930, 365; in MLM both Bliss's première and the performance of the Janáček Mass are wrongly allotted to the 1927 Norwich Festival.

p.231 'Sir Henry's orchestral arrangements. . .': MT, September 1929, 843

p.231 Havergal Brian in *Musical Opinion*, September 1927, 1172–3
p.231 Capell: MMR, September 1931, 271. Capell mis-identified the work as Bach's 'Dorian' Toccata and Fugue (BWV 538) instead of BWV 565.
p.233 'I have often said. . .': *Star*, 10 August 1925
p.233 'I believe that wherever he goes. . .': BBC internal memorandum 16 January 1930 to Assistant Director of Programmes
p.233 'With the whole-hearted support. . .': Briggs, II, 184
p.233 'the biggest percentage increase. . .': Briggs II, 253

Chapter 16

p.235 relieving his feelings: letter to John Ireland (May 1931) in BL 56421
p.236 In the judgement of the *Musical Times*: August, 718
p.236 'No Newcomers Need Apply': *The Times*, 1 October
p.238 'The eighteen symphony concerts. . .': MT, October, 887
p.238 'strangely out of sympathy. . .': MMR, February 1932, 38
p.239 'well built': MMR, May 1933, 85
p.240 from Trinidad to Bermuda: ibid.
p.240 anticipatory letter to Sanders: SAN, 19 January 1933
p.240 'I had one or two batons with me. . .': MLM, 339
p.241 in Holland the following month: MT, August 1932, 750
p.241 the *Neue Zürcher Zeitung*: 29 April 1932
p.241 in Hamburg in November 1933: ML, 340
p.242 'The strongest impression I have. . .': BBC 'Music Magazine' broadcast 2 March 1969
p.244 'I really must write and tell you. . .': SAN, 24 March 1932
p.246 'I take pleasure in paying him tribute. . .': MMR, December 1933, 230
p.247 'Sir Henry gave us a magnificent performance. . .': Wright, 1988, 8
p.247 'no longer the staple entertainment. . .': Kennedy, 1960, 269
p.247 'nine months' tour abroad. . .': BBC internal memorandum from Gerald Beadle 3 January 1933

Chapter 17

p.252 musical helper, Eric Fenby: Carley, II, 423
p.252 Richard Strauss to replace him: Kennedy, 1976, 96
p.254 The *Musical Courier*: 3 February 1934
p.255 It had been announced: *New York Times*, 28 January 1934
p.257 Wood instructed Sanders: SAN, 13 April 1934
p.258 'delighted everyone': *Los Angeles Times*, 18 July 1934
p.258 on its main news page: *Musical Courier*, 15 September 1934
p.259 in the BBC's *Radio Times*: 10 August 1934
p.260 Tania was to maintain: Tape
p.263 according to Jessie: her taped reminiscences of about 1972
p.265 'Sir Henry's personality quite won the audience': apparently DT, 20 January 1935
p.266 The second letter: typescript copy supplied by Tania Cardew

Chapter 18

p.272 'Your letter touched me so terribly. . .': 8 May 1935
p.278 'Lady Wood didn't ring up. . .': Sparkes MS
p.281 'Nowhere else in Europe. . .': *Morning Post*, 14 August 1935

p.283 by George Stratton: BL 56429, 138–40; Stratton in 1944 misremembered it as the 'New' Queen's Hall Orchestra

p.285 'I consider this recording. . .': *Gramophone*, July 1935, 49

p.285 came from *The Times*: 21 August 1935

p.288 trade description suffices: Gifford, section '1936'

PART IV

Chapter 19

p.293 and Helen Douglas (Irvine) herself, perhaps: letter from Helen Douglas Irvine to Muriel Wood, 5 September 1944 (in possession of Tania Cardew) refers to Chile

p.294 brim-full of love: letters all in Eileen Calthrop's collection

p.297 HAD GREAT PLEASURE IN CONDUCTING. . .: MLM, 335; actual cable in BL56428 has telegraphic errors

p.298 Soon afterwards: 14 April

p.300 'charmingly arranged and scored': letter 15 November 1934, LC

p.302 Charles F. Hatfield: personally communicated by Stephen McClarence

p.304 a failure which Wood ascribed: MLM, 337

p.306 January's Winter Proms: MT, March 1936, 320

Chapter 20

p.312 'but they will not *all* play. . .': letter from Wood to Rachmaninoff in LC

p.314 'I cannot tell you the gratitude. . .': 25 January 1938

p.315 'PS My wife wanted to come. . .': all letters LC

p.317 restriction on very young performers: private information

p.318 compilation by A. L. Bacharach: Gollancz, 171

p.318 'but may I say that I shall very greatly regret it . . .': letter 26 April 1938

p.320 'I do not think that I remember such happiness. . .': letter, 8 August 1938

p.321 'I have not had a moment this week. . .': 17 September 1938

p.321 'this important person's solicitude. . .': Haendel 93

p.322 regarded him with daughter-like affection: author's personal interview with Ida Haendel, 1992

p.322 'On August 6 last. . .': RVW, 270

p.328 'I promise you – there will be no music': Carrell, Tape

p.329 'Naturally it would be a very great day for England. . .': 22 July 1938

p.332 'keep on keeping on': letter to Charles Proctor (in Proctor's posession), 23 June 1940

Chapter 21

p.333 his new solicitor Stanley Rubinstein: on 16 May 1939

p.333 'I wish to use the contents. . .': BL Wood 56423, 122

p.334 'a useful rehearsal', as Asa Briggs was to put it: Briggs II, 645

p.334 25,000 sets in use by mid-1939: ibid., 620

p.336 'As I believe Lady Wood told you. . .': letter, 2 December 1938 BBCWA

p.338 'There is no need to discuss the maltreatment. . .': MT, October 1935, 939 p.339 whose conductor, Ernest Read, was ill: QH, 82

p.341 'Oh! – that we could find big voices. . .': letter to W.W.Thompson, 19 December 1938

p.342 'Owing to the special arrangements. . .': Cox, 110

p.342 'He ate no supper. . .': LY, 76

p.343 reached him by messenger: LY, 76

p.343 'My friend Sandy Macpherson. . .': Kennedy, 1987, 187

p.346 The cost of admission was a shilling: Ferguson, 91

p.348 expressed themselves strongly in favour: Cox, 115

p.348 a letter in the *Daily Telegraph*: 11 April 1940

p.349 According to Jessie: LY, 80–1

p.350 'From our room on the third floor. . .': LY, 85

p.350 'At Queen's Hall, a Wagner concert. . .': Panter-Downes, 93

p.351 'a take-off of Beecham. . .': Cox, 116

p.351 'Happily enough, a new work had figured. . .': LY, 87

p.351 '[It] did not get a hand. . .': RP, 265

p.353 had not arrived: this and following letters from Royal Academy of Music Archives

p.354 'This now presents the appearance of a Roman arena. . .': QH, 129

p.355 'the most striking thing which has occurred. . .': Kennedy, 1960, 282

p.355 sets a puzzle: typed copy of letter kindly supplied by Diana Sparkes. (It is reproduced in RP, 185, with corrected spelling of Stokowski's name.)

Chapter 22

p.357 limited under wartime safety measures to 5000: Clark, 218

p.358 'already packed with evacuees. . .': David Heald, 'The Bedford Plan', *Music and Musicians International*, September 1989, 15–16

p.361 'My sole reason is that I want to accustom my public. . .': letter in the possession of June Rees

p.361 a properly professional stand: BL 56428, 127

p.363 'my place is here': *Daily Province*, Vancouver, 15 June 1940

p.363 between April and October 1942: BL 56428, 142

p.363 (Goluboff's) conductor-father: BL 56428, 18

p.364 'This is to confirm that you are conducting the BBC. . .': BBCWA 901/WOO, 10

p.364 farewell to Bedford in October 1945: *Bedfordshire Times*, 27 October 1945

p.365 at the Empress Hall, Earls Court: BL 56426, 15, 26

p.365 'He would not read newspapers. . .': LY, 108

p.365 'worthwhile new music': LY, 108

p.367 'I have had an interview with Ogilvie. . .': Kenyon, 172

p.368 sent by the publishing firm of Novello: LY, 115

p.368 'he looked up at the huge studio clock. . .': LY, 115–6

p.368 'the dominant figure': A. J. P. Taylor, 544

p.370 the box-office takings: BL 56431 [pages unnumbered]

p.370 'I should like to shake you by the hand. . .': 27 October 1942, BL 56426, 43

p.370 'My dear friends, this brings us. . .': LY, 118–9

p.371 'Millions of listeners to the BBC broadcast. . .': *Daily Mail*, 24 August 1942

p.371 '.. . No good in concertos': BL 56431 [pages unnumbered] p.371 'the only musician living who had daily contact': letter to Douglas Clarke, Director of programme planning, 9 January 1942, refers to earlier letter of September 1941

Chapter 23

p.373 'a virulent, rapid cancer': Norris, 78
p.375 'as Richter used to do': BL 56428, 164
p.375 'Boult? Well, he might give up. . .': BL 56428, 17
p.375 'a quiet, very nice man': RAM 8 August 1943
p.375 'it was so beautiful. . .': tape
p.376 'the most tiring work to direct. . .': LY, 128
p.377 'Greetings, and my love. . .': 8 September 1943, BL 56420, 19
p.377 'Of your kindness on Saturday. . .': letter, 17 May 1943
p.378 'he had badly over-rehearsed. . .': memo at BBCWA, 25 May 1943
p.378 'It was grand and typical of you. . .': RP, 295
p.379 'Damn silly, I've tried to keep upright. . .': Diary 21 June 1943; slightly different in LY, 130
p.379 'I cannot tell you how touched I was. . .': letter in possession of Ursula Vaughan Williams
p.380 On 20 July: date from MT, 254; see also Fisher BL 56428, 182
p.380 as he left the Albert Hall: DT, 23 August 1943
p.380 Ferrucio Bonavia in the *Monthly Musical Record*: September 1943, 158
p.381 negotiate with such a company: RP, 312
p.381 'After my not always happy experiences. . .': RP, 300
p.381 in private hands: it was placed on auction by Sotheby's of London on 28 September 1994 but did not reach the seller's reserve price
p.382 'I am just embarking on an enormous commitment. . .': BL 56428, 194, letter, 13 December 1943
p.382 'All right and also play piano concerto': BL 56428, 194
p.382 'an overture of about the same length. . .': letter, 11 November 1943 in BL 56428, 192
p.384 German army at El Alamein: A. J. P. Taylor, 560
p.384 'the whole audience rose. . .': Clark, 222
p.384 'with one of the sly deceptions. . .': DT, 27 March 1944. On 11 March: RP, 308
p.387 'You are truly a wonder. . .': *London Philharmonic Post* II, 7, September 1944, 5
p.387 'Hearing that the LPO has prepared. . .': LPO *Homage*, September 1944, 6
p.387 Society for Cultural Relations with Foreign Countries: BL 56426, 37, 43
p.389 'every man knew. . .': Mortimer, 135–6
p.390 was now an officer: letter from Helen Douglas Irvine to Muriel Wood, 29 April 1943, in possession of Tania Cardew
p.390 knew where 'Her Ladyship' was: letter from Wood to Rubinstein, 27 April 1944 in BL 56425, 87
p.390 'I am going to let you into a secret. . .': this and following quotations from BL 56425
p.391 time allotted on 3 August: HJW note in BL 56431 (pages unnumbered)
p.391 'The OM would have been more appropriate. . .': *Daily Mirror*, 13 June 1944
p.392 'The announcement was made. . .': Diary, 24 June 1944
p.393 'when the machine appeared to be directly above. . .': Clark, 222

p.393 From 3 July: memo from Dorothy Wood (of BBC staff; unrelated to Henry J. Wood) in BBCWA

p.394 'You will have heard. . .': letter at RAM

p.395 'didn't want to rehearse. . .': Diary, 28 July 1944

p.396 Pritchard recalled it almost fifty years later: tape

p.396 gave Jessie Wood a similar report: Diary 3, August 1944

p.397 'Thalben Ball played it splendidly. . .': Diary, 10 August 1944

p.397 'I am so very sorry. . .': RP, 322

p.398 'There is no gain in art. . .': found in miscellaneous material sent by Jessie Wood to the late Leslie Regan and now in the possession of his son, Christopher Regan

Chapter 24

p.399 'for months he [Wood] had worshipped. . .': DT 25 August; letter, Roger Bagnall to the author, 14 May 1990

p.399 'I cried as if I had lost. . .': Tape 1992

p.400 'Hundreds of people came. . .': 26 August 1944

p.400 The Dean was on holiday: DT 22 August 1944

p.400 She 'suddenly knew. . .': LY, 165

p.400 an ensemble of soloists: those of 1946 were Stiles-Allen, Elena Danieli, Mary Hamlin, Eva Turner, Muriel Brunskill, Janet Howe, Emelie Hooke, Mary Jarred, Jan van der Gucht, Heddle Nash, Walter Widdop, Henry Wendon, Trevor Anthony, Owen Brannigan, Henry Cummings and Roy Henderson (see LY, 172)

p.401 'for offering me the privilege. . .': BL 56429, 189

p.402 By the later 1950s it became clear: *Evening Standard*, 7 September 1957

p.402 'unless they are disclaimed': *The Times*, 31 August 1966, under the heading 'Returning Money Is Not So Simple'.

p.402 The final act of the Henry Wood Trust. . .: MT, September 1980, 517

p.403 'I tried hard to see all her [Muriel's] good points. . .': BL 54619, 120

p.403 she was to leave £158,165: RP, 325

p.403 announcement of that in the *Daily Mail*: 4 October 1944

p.403 she accepted that advice: letter Stanley Rubinstein to Baroness de Bush, 6 October 1944

p.404 It had been ascertained beforehand: ibid.

p.404 to bring out a revised edition: letter from files at Victor Gollancz Ltd

p.406 Barrie Hall saw: Hall, 1932, 129

p.407 ten years after Wood's death: BL 56430, 17, letter to Jessie Wood 1954 on publication of *The Last Years of Henry J. Wood*

p.407 Tania once remarked: Tape

p.408 obituarizing him in the *Sunday Times*: 20 August 1944

p.409 Glock. . . wrote in the *Observer*: 30 July 1944

p.410 Toscaini. . . Mussolini: see Horowitz, passim

p.412 'Every critic, professional and amateur' : Howes, 1942, 158

p.412 'The "Proms" do not appeal. . .': Vaughan Williams, 267–8

p.414 'The case fell over': BL 56440, 5

Bibliography

I   Books (not by Henry J. Wood)
II   Articles in Magazines, etc. (not by Henry J. Wood)
III   Manuscripts
IV   Writings by Henry J. Wood

I Books

The list is in alphabetical order of author and, within one author's works, by date. Titles are in short form, with the addition of a name if the (auto)biographical content is not obvious. All works were published in London unless otherwise noted.

The list could have been much extended, since references to Wood are to be found in most books about British musical life of his period. But where a book serves merely to confirm a dating of performance which is independently ascertainable, it is not listed here. The standard dictionaries of music and musical performers, and also works of the *Who's Who* type, are likewise excluded.

Abraham, Gerald, *A Hundred Years of Music*, 3/1964
Agate, James, *Ego 3*, 1938
Aldrich, Richard, *Concert Life in New York, 1902–23*, New York 1941
Allen, J. Mason, *Henry J Wood, Composer and Conductor* [William Reeves], 1891
   [reviewed in contemporary press, but no copy traced]
Allfrey, Anthony, *Edward VII and his Jewish Court*, 1991
Alvarez, Marguerite d', *Forsaken Altars*, 1954
Alwyn, William, *Winged Chariot*, 1933
Alwyn, William, *Ariel to Miranda*, 1967
Anderton, H. O., *Granville Bantock*, 1915
Anon., *The Year's Music*, 1896, 1897
Arditi, Luigi, *My Reminiscences*, 1896
Ayre, Leslie, *The Proms*, 1968
BBC Handbook, 1929
BBC Yearbook, 1931
BBC, *Sir Henry Wood: Fifty Years of the Proms*, 1944
BBC, *The Proms: A Living Tradition*, 1994
Bailey, Cyril, *Hugh Percy Allen*, 1948

Henry J. Wood

Baillie, Isobel, *Never sing Louder than Lovely*, 1982
Bamberger, Carl, *The Conductor's Art*, New York, 1945
Bantock, Myrrha, *Granville Bantock*, 1972
Barbellion, W. P. N., *The Diary of a Disappointed Man*, 1919
Bates, Frank, *Reminiscences of a Musician in Retirement*, 1930
Batley, Thomas, *Sir Charles Hallé's Concerts in Manchester*, 1895
Batten, Joe, *Joe Batten's Book: The story of sound recording*, 1956
Baughan, E. A., *Sixty Years of Music*, 1897
Baughan, E. A., *Ignaz Jan Paderewski*, 1908
Beaumont, Antony, *Busoni the Composer*, 1985
Bedarida, François, *A Social History of England 1851–1990*, 1979
Beecham, Thomas, *A Mingled Chime*, 1944
Bennett, Arnold, *Letters to his Nephew*, 1936
Bennett, Joseph, *Forty Years of Music*, 1908
Benson, E. F., *As We Were*, 1930
Berger, Francesco, *Ninety-Seven*, 1931
Blaukopf, Kurt, *Great Conductors*, 1959
Bliss, Arthur (ed. G. Roscow), *Bliss on Music*, 1991
Boden, Anthony, *Three Choirs*, 1992
Boosey, William, *Fifty Years of Music*, 1935
Booth, J. B., *Palmy Days*, 1957
Boult, Adrian, *A Handbook on the Technique of Conducting*, 1920
Boult, Adrian, *Thoughts on Conducting*, 1963
Boult, Adrian, *My Own Trumpet*, 1973
Bournemouth Municipal Orchestra, *Twenty-one Years of Municipal Music*, 1914
Bowers, Faubion, *Scriabin*, vol II, 1969
Bowles, Michael, *The Conductor*, 1961
Brand, Juliane, and others, *Berg–Schoenberg Correspondence*, 1987
Brian, Havergal (ed. Malcolm Macdonald), *On Music*, vol. 1, 1986
Briggs, Asa, *Victorian Cities*, 1963
Briggs, Asa, *The History of Broadcasting in the United Kingdom*, vols. II & III, 1965, 1970
British Music Society Annual, 1920
Brock, Michael and Eleanor, (eds.) *H. H. Asquith: Letters to Venetia Stanley*, 1982
Brook, Donald, *Conductors' Gallery*, 1945
Brooks, Collin, *Devil's Decade*, 1948
Brown, Howard and Stanley Sadie (eds.), *Performance Practice*, 1989
Bruneau, Alfred, *Musique de Russie & Musiciens de France*, 1903
Burgess, Harry, *My Musical Pilgrimage: An Unconventional Survey of Music & Musicians*, 1911
Busoni, Ferruccio, *Letters to His Wife*, 1938
Camden, Archie, *Blow by Blow*, 1982
Campbell, Margaret, *Dolmetsch*, 1975
Campbell, Margaret, *The Great Cellists*, 1988
Cardus, Neville, *Full Score*, 1970
Carley, Lionel, *Delius: A Life in Letters 1909–34*, 1988
Carpenter, Humphrey, *Benjamin Britten*, 1992
Carr-Saunders, A. W., *The Professions*, 1933
Carse, Adam, *Orchestral Conducting*, 1929
Carse, Adam, *The Orchestra*, 1949
Carse, Adam, *The Life of Jullien*, 1951

Casals, Pablo, *Joys and Sorrows*, 1970

Castle, H. G., *Fire Over England*, 1982

Chamier, J. Daniel, *Percy Pitt of Covent Garden and the BBC*, 1938

Clapham, John, *Dvořák*, 1979

Clark, Ronald W., *The Royal Albert Hall*, 1958

Coates, Eric, *Suite in Four Movements*, 1953

Cohen, Harriet, *A Bundle of Time*, 1969

Cole, G. D. H., and Raymond Postgate, *The Common People*, 1938

Cole, Hugo, *Malcolm Arnold*, 1989

Coleridge-Taylor, Avril, *The Heritage of Samuel Coleridge-Taylor*, 1927

Colles, H. C., *Walford Davies*, 1942

Columbus (Ohio) Gallery of Fine Arts, *British Art 1890–1928*, n.d.

Cook, E. T., *Life of John Ruskin*, 1911

Corder, H. F., *Royal Academy of Music: Souvenir Centenary Programme*, 1922

Corder, H. F., *History of the Royal Academy of Music*, 1922

Coward, Henry, *Reminiscences of. . .*, 1919

Cox, David, *The Henry Wood Proms*, 1980

Craggs, Stewart R., *John Ireland – a Catalogue, discography and biography*, 1993

Crump, Jeremy, 'The identity of English music: the reception of Elgar', in R. Colls
    and P. Dodd, *Englishness*, 1986

Cumberland, Gerald, *Set Down in Malice*, 1919

Dahlström, Fabian, *The Works of Jean Sibelius*, Helsinki 1987

Dawson, Peter, *Fifty Years of Song*, 1951

De Lara, Isidore, *Many Tales of Many Cities*, 1928

Delius, Clare, *Frederick Delius*, 1935

Dent, Edward J., *Busoni*, 1933

Dent, Edward J., *Selected Essays*, 1979

Dibble, J., *C. Hubert H. Parry*, 1991

Draper, Muriel, *Music at Midnight*, 1929

Duckenfield, Bridget, *O Lovely Knight* [Landon Ronald], 1991

Durant, Alan, *Conditions of Music*, 1985

Eaglefield-Hull, A., *A Dictionary of Modern Music and Musicians*, 1924

Ehrlich, Cyril, *The Piano, a History*, 1976

Ehrlich, Cyril, *The Music Profession in Britain Since the 18th Century*, 1985

Ehrlich, Cyril, *Harmonious Alliance: A History of the Performing Right Society*, 1989

Ellison, J. Audrey, *Norman Tucker, Musician*, 1978

Elkin, Robert, *Queen's Hall: 1893–1941*, 1944

Elkin, Robert, *Royal Philharmonic*, 1947

Elkin, Robert, *The Old Concert Rooms of London*, 1955

Elwes, Winefride and Richard, *Gervase Elwes*, 1935

Ensor, R. C. K., *England 1870–1914*, 1936

Evans, Edwin, *The Promenade Concerts* in BBC promenade concert prospectus, 1936

Evans, Edwin and Harold C.Hind, *The orchestra and its instruments*, 1936

Evans, Eric N., *Mark Hambourg*, n.d.

Ewen, David, *The Man with the Baton*, 1936

Ewen, David, *Dictators of the Baton*, 1943

Fenby, Eric, *Delius As I Knew Him*, 1937

Ferguson, Howard (ed.), *Myra Hess by Her Friends*, 1966

Festing, Sally, *Gertrude Jekyll*, 1991

F. T. S., *Henry Wood, Composer and Conductor*, *c.*1890, untraced: see note on p.432

Fifield, Christopher, *True Artist and True Friend. . . Hans Richter*, 1993

Finn, William J., *The Conductor Raises his Baton*, 1944

Floud, Roderick and Donald McCloskey, *The Economic History of Britain: vol.2*, 1981

Ford, Ernest, *A Short History of Music in England*, 1912

Foreman, Lewis, *A Percy Grainger Companion*, 1981

Foreman, Lewis, *Bax: A Composer and his Times*, 1983

Foreman, Lewis, *From Parry to Britten: British Music in Letters 1900–1945*, 1987

Foreman, Lewis (editor), *Music in England 1885–1920*, 1994

Forsyth, Cecil, *Orchestration*, 2/1935

Foss, Hubert J., *Music in my Time*, 1935

Foss, Hubert, *Ralph Vaughan Williams*, 1950

Foss, Hubert and Noël Goodwin, *London Symphony*, 1954

Foster, Myles Birket, *History of the Royal Philharmonic Society*, 1912

Foulds, John, *Music Today*, 1934

Ffrangcon-Davies, Marjorie, *David Ffrangcon-Davies*, 1938

Fuchs, Carl, *Musical and other recollections*, 1937

Furtwängler, Wilhelm, *Notebooks 1924–54*, 1989

Fussell, Paul, *Wartime*, 1991

Gaisberg, F. W., *Music on Record*, 1946

Galkin, Elliott W., *A History of Orchestral Conducting in theory and practice*, New York 1988

Ganz, W., *Memories of a Musician*, 1913

Geissmar, Berta, *The Baton and the Jackboot*, 1946

German, Sir Edward, *Radio & The Composer; The Economics of Modern Music*, 1933

Gifford, D., *British Film Catalogue 1895–1985*, 1986

Gillies, Malcolm, *Bartók in Britain*, 1989

Gilmour, J. D., *Sir Thomas Beecham – Fifty Years in the New York Times*, 1988

Glock, William, *An Autobiography in Music*, 1991

Godfrey, Sir Dan, *Memories and Music*, 1921

Goldbeck, Fred., *The Perfect Conductor*, 1960

Gollancz, Victor, *Journey Towards Music*, 1964

Goossens, Eugene, *Overture and Beginners*, 1951

Goossens, Marie, *Life on a Harp String*, 1987

Grainger, Percy, *The Farthest North of Humanness*, 1985

Grainger, Percy (ed. Kay Dreyfus), *Selected Letters 1911–14*, 1985

Graves, C. L., *Hubert Parry*, 1926

Gray, Cecil, *A Survey of Contemporary Music*, 1924

Gray, Cecil, *Peter Warlock*, 1934

Gray, Cecil, *Musical Chairs, or Between Two Stools: Being the Life and Memoirs of. . .*, 1948

Gregg, Pauline, *A Social and Economic History of Britain 1760-1965*, 1965

Gretton, R. H., *A Modern History of the English People*, 1930

Grierson, Mary, *Donald Francis Tovey: A Biography based on Letters*, 1952

Grisewood, F., *My Story of the BBC*, 1959

Grun, Bernard, *Private Lives of the Great Composers, Conductors and Musical Artists of the World*, 1954

Hadden, J. C., *Modern Musicians*, 1928

Hadow, Sir Henry, *The Revival of Music*, in The Times, *Fifty Years: Memories and Contrasts*, 1932

Haendel, Ida, *Woman with Violin*, 1970

Hall, Barrie, *The Proms and the Men Who Made Them*, 1981

Hambourg, Mark, *From Piano to Forte*, 1931

Hanslick, Eduard (ed. Henry Pleasants), *Vienna's Golden Years of Music*, 1951

Harries, Meirion and Susie, *A Pilgrim Soul: The Life and Work of Elisabeth Lutyens*, 1989

Harrison, Beatrice, *The Cello and the Nightingales*, 1985

Haskell, Harry, *The Early Music Revival*, 1988

Hast, Harry Gregson, *The Singer's Art*, 1925

Haste, Cate, *Keep the Home Fires Burning*, 1977

Hawkins, Frank V., *A Hundred Years of Chamber Music*, 1987

Henschel, Sir George, *Musings and Memories of a Musician*, 1918

Henschel, Helen, *Music When Soft Voices Die*, 1944

Hetherington, John, *Melba*, 1967

Hind, Harold C., *The Orchestra and its Instruments*, 1936

Holmes, John L., *Conductors on Record*, 1988

Holst, Imogen, *Gustav Holst*, 1938, 2/1969

Hoggart, Richard, *The Uses of Literacy*, 1957

Horowitz, Joseph, *Understanding Toscanini*, 1988

Horsbrugh, Ian, *Leoš Janáček*, 1981

Howe, M. A. de Wolfe, *The Boston Symphony Orchestra*, 2/1931

Howes, Frank, *Full Orchestra*, 1942

Howes, Frank, *The English Musical Renaissance*, 1966

Hudson, Derek, *Norman O'Neill*, 1945

Hulme, Derrick C., *Dmitri Shostakovich*, 1991

Huneker, James G., *The Philharmonic Society of New York and its 75th Anniversary*, 1917

Hurd, Michael, *Immortal Hour* [Rutland Boughton], 1962

Hurd, Michael, *Rutland Boughton and the Glastonbury Festivals*, 1993

Ikonnikov, Nicolas, *La noblesse de Russie*, Series K.1, L.2, Paris, 1960

Inghelbrecht, D. E., *The Conductor's World*, 1953

Jackson, Gerald, *First Flute*, 1968

Jacob, Archibald, *Musical Handwriting*, 1934, 1947

Jacobs, Arthur, *Arthur Sullivan: A Victorian Musician*, 2/1992

Jacobson, Bernard, *Conductors on Conducting*, 1979

James, Robert Rhodes, *The British Revolution*, vol.2, 1977

Jarman, Richard, *History of the London Coliseum 1904–1981*, 1981

Joachim, Joseph, *Letters to and from. . .*, 1914

Johnson, Arthur, *The Nottingham Sacred Harmonic Society: a Retrospect* [Nottingham, privately printed], 1905

Johnson, H. Earl, *First Performances in America to 1900*, Detroit, 1979

Kabalevsky, D. (ed.), *Prokofiev/ Myaskovsky Correspondence* [in Russian], Moscow, 1977

Kallaway, William, *London Philharmonic*, 1972

Kapp, Edmond X. and Yvonne Cloud, *Pastiche* [drawings of musicians], 1926

Kennedy, Michael, *The Hallé Tradition*, 1960

Kennedy, Michael, *Richard Strauss*, 1976

Kennedy, Michael, *Portrait of Elgar*, 1968, 1987

Kennedy, Michael, *Adrian Boult*, 1987

Kenyon, Nicholas, *The BBC Symphony Orchestra 1930–80*, 1981

Kirk, H. L., *Pablo Casals*, 1974

Klein, Hermann, *Thirty Years of Musical Life in London*, 1903

Henry J. Wood

Klein, Hermann, *Musicians and Mummers*, 1925
Klemperer, Otto (ed. Martin Anderson), *Klemperer on Music*, 1986
Koopal, Grace, *Miracle of Music: The History of the Hollywood Bowl*, 1972
Koven, Mrs Reginald de, *A Musician and his Wife*, New York, 1927
Kramer, Lawrence, *Music as a Cultural Practice, 1800–1900*,1990
Kuhe, Wilhelm, *My Musical Recollections*, 1896
Lahee, Henry C., *Annals of Music in America*, 1922
Lambert, Constant, *Music Ho!*, 1934
Lang, Paul Henry, *Music in Western Civilization*, 1941
Langford, Samuel, *Musical Criticisms*, 1929
Lassimonne, Denise (ed.), *Myra Hess by Her Friends*, 1966
Layton, Robert, *Sibelius*, 1965/1992
Lebrecht, Norman, *The Maestro Myth*, 1991
Leinsdorf, Erich, *The Composer's Advocate*, 1981
Lesure, François and Roger Nichols, *Debussy Letters*, 1987
Levine, Lawrence, *Highbrow/Lowbrow*, 1988
Ley, Wilfrid, *Promenade*, 1932
Lloyd, Stephen, *H. Balfour Gardiner*, 1984
Lochner, Louis P., *Fritz Kreisler*, 1951
Lockspeiser, Edward, *Debussy: his life and mind*, 1965–6
Lowe, George, *Josef Holbrooke and his work*, 1928
Lowe-Dugmore, Rachel, 'Documenting Delius' in *Studies in Music* (University of
    Western Australia) 12–14 (1978–80)
Lucas, John, *Reginald Goodall*, 1993
Lutyens, Elisabeth, *A Goldfish Bowl*, 1972
McCabe, Joseph, *Biographical Dictionary of Modern Rationalists*, 1920
MacDonagh, Michael, *In London during the Great War*, 1938
MacDonald, Cheryl, *Emma Albani, Victorian Diva*, 1984
McIntyre, Ian, *The Expense of Glory* [Sir John Reith], 1993
McKenna, Marian C., *Myra Hess*, 1976
Mackenzie, Sir A. C., *A Musician's Narrative*, 1927
Mackenzie, Compton, *A Musical Chair*, 1939
Mackenzie, Compton, *My Record of Music*, 1955
Mackenzie-Grieve, A., *Clara Novello*, 1955
Mackerness, E. D., *A social history of English music*, 1964
Mackerness, E. D., *Somewhere further north*, 1974
MacKinlay, M. Sterling, *Antoinette Sterling and Other Celebrities*, 1906
MacKinlay, M. Sterling, *Garcia the Centenarian*, 1908
Macleod, Joseph, *The Sisters d'Aranyi*, 1969
Macqueen-Pope, W., *Goodbye Piccadilly*, 1960
Magidoff, Robert, *Yehudi Menuhin*, 1955, 1973
Maine, Basil, *Reflected Music and Other Essays*, 1930
Maine, Basil, *The BBC and its Audience*, 1939
Mair, Carlene, *The Chappell Story*, 1961
Maitland, J. A. Fuller, *A Door-Keeper of Music*, 1929
Malko, Nicolai, *The Conductor and his Baton*, 1950
Martyn, Barrie, *Rachmaninoff: composer, pianist, conductor*, 1990
Marwick, Arthur, *Britain in Our Century*, 1984
Matthay, J. H., *The Life and Works of Tobias Matthay*, 1945
Matthews, Denis, *In Pursuit of Music*, 1966

Mayer, Sir Robert, *My First Hundred Years*, 1979
Meadmore, W. S., *The Story of a Thousand Concerts*, 1927
Mellers, Wilfrid, *Percy Grainger*, 1992
Midgley, Samuel, *My 70 Years' Musical Memories (1860–1930)*, 1934
Miller, Geoffrey, *The Bournemouth Symphony Orchestra*, 1970
Millington, Barry, and Stewart Spencer, *Wagner in Performance*, 1992
Minns, R. J., *Model Railway Engines*, 1969
Moiseiwitsch, Maurice, *Moiseiwitsch*, 1965
Monrad-Johansen, David, *Edvard Grieg*, 1945
Monteux, Doris, *It's All in the Music* [Pierre Monteux], 1969
Moore, George, *Hail and Farewell*, 1911
Moore, Gerald, *Am I Too Loud?*, 1962
Moore, Jerrold Northrop, *Edward Elgar: A Creative Life*, 1984
Moore, Jerrold Northrop, *Edward Elgar, Letters of a Lifetime*, 1990
Mortimer, Harry, *Harry Mortimer on Brass*, 1981
Mueller, John H., *The American Symphony Orchestra*, Bloomington, IN, 1951
Mussulman, Joseph A., *Music in the Cultured Generation*, Evanston, IL, 1971
Nettel, Reginald, *Music in the Five Towns*, 1944
Nettel, Reginald, *The Orchestra in England*, 1946
Newman, Ernest, *Richard Strauss*, 1908
Newman, Ernest, *From the World of Music*, 1956
Newmarch, Rosa, *Queen's Hall: Analytical programmes and books of words of concerts 1897–1914*, 1897–1914
Newmarch, Rosa, *Henry J. Wood*, 1904
Newmarch, Rosa, *Mary Wakefield: A Memoir*, 1912
Newmarch, Rosa, *A Quarter of a Century of Promenade Concerts at Queen's Hall*, 1920
Newmarch, Rosa, *The Concert-goer's Library of Descriptive Notes*, 1928–48
Newmarch, Rosa, *The Music of Czechoslovakia*, 1942
Newmarch, Rosa, *Jean Sibelius*, 1944
Newton, Ivor, *At the Piano*, 1966
Nichols, Roger, *Debussy Remembered*, 1992
Norris, Gerald, *A Musical Gazetteer of Great Britain & Ireland*, 1981
Norris, Gerald, *Stanford, The Cambridge Jubilee and Tchaikovsky*, 1980
Opperby, Preben, *Leopold Stokowski*, 1982
Orenstein, Arbie, *A Ravel Reader*, 1990
Orga, Ates, *The Proms*, 1974
Paderewski, I. J. and Mary Lawton, *The Paderewski Memoirs*, 1939
Palmer, Christopher, *Dyson's Delight*, 1989
Panter-Downes, Mollie, *London War Notes 1939–1945*, 1971
Parker, Maurice, *Sir Thomas Beecham: A Calendar of his Concert and Theatrical Performances* [privately printed], 1985
Parrott, Ian, *The Spiritual Pilgrims*, 1969
Peacock, Alan, and Ronald Weir, *The Composer in the Market Place*, 1975
Pearsall, Ronald, *Victorian Popular Music*, 1973
Pearsall, Ronald, *Edwardian Popular Music*, 1975
Performing Right Society, *Radio and the Composer*, 1936
Pettitt, Stephen, *Dennis Brain*, 1976
Philip, Robert, *Some Changes in Style of Orchestral Playing, 1920–50, as shown by gramophone recordings*. Cambridge University Ph.D. dissertation, 1974

Philip, Robert, *Early Recordings and Musical Style*, 1992
Pincherle, Marc, *Albert Roussel*, Geneva, 1957
Pincherle, Marc, *The World of the Virtuoso*, 1964
Ponder, Winifred, *Clara Butt*, 1928
Pound, Reginald, *Sir Henry Wood*, 1969
Priestley, Harold, *The What It Cost the Day Before Yesterday Book*, 1979
Priestley, J. B., *Trumpets over the Sea*, 1968
Procter-Gregg, H., *Beecham Remembered*, 1976
Prokofiev, Sergey, *A Soviet Diary and Other Writings*, 1991
Queen's Hall Orchestra Ltd., *List of Compositions performed for the first time at the concerts founded by Mr Robert Newman in 1893 and taken over by the Queen's Hall Orchestra Ltd in the autumn of 1902* [untraced; referred to in *Musical Times*, January 1908]
Rainbow, Bernarr, *The Land Without Music*, 1967
Rapoport, Paul (ed.), *Sorabji*, 1992
Raynor, Henry, *Music and Society since 1815*, 1976
Raynor, Henry, *The Orchestra*, 1978
Raynor, Henry, *Music in England*, 1980
Read, Donald, *England 1868–1914*, 1979
Reader, J. W., *Professional Men*, 1966
Redwood, Christopher, *An Elgar Companion*, 1982
Rees, Brian, *A Musical Peacemaker* [Edward German], 1986
Reich, Willi, *The Life and Work of Alban Berg*, 1963
Reid, Charles, *Thomas Beecham*, 1962
Reid, Charles, *Malcolm Sargent*, 1968
Reid, Charles, *John Barbirolli*, 1971
Reith, J. C. W., *Into the Wind*, 1949
Rigby, Charles, *Sir Charles Hallé*, 1952
Rivière, Jules, *My Music Life & Recollections*, 1893
Robinson, Harlow, *Sergei Prokofiev*, 1987
Ronald, Sir Landon, *Variations on a Personal Theme*, 1922
Ronald, Sir Landon, *Myself and Others*, 1931
Rosen, Carole, *The Goossens*, 1993
Rosenthal, Harold (ed.), *The Mapleson Memoirs*, 1966
Routh, Francis, *Contemporary British Music*, 1972
Rothenstein, William, *Men and Memories*, 1931
Rubinstein, Arthur, *My Many Years*, 1973
Ruskin, John (ed. K. Clark), *Selected Writings*, 1964
Russ, Michael, *Musorgsky: Pictures at an Exhibition*, 1992
Russell, Charles Edward, *The American Orchestra and Theodore Thomas*, Garden City, NY, 1927
Russell, Thomas (ed.), *Homage to Sir Henry Wood: A World Symposium*, 1944
Russell, Thomas, *Philharmonic Decade*, 1945
Russell, Thomas, *The Proms*, 1949
Sayers, W. C. Berwick, *Samuel Coleridge-Taylor, Musician*, 1915
Sassoon, Siegfried (ed. R. Hart–Davis), *Diaries 1918–25*, 1981
Scannell, Paddy and David Cardiff, *A Social History of British Broadcasting*, 1991
Schoenberg, Arnold, *Letters*, 1964
Scherchen, Hermann, *Handbook of Conducting*, 1933
Schnabel, Artur, *My Life and Music*, 1961

Scholes, Percy A., *The Second Book of the Gramophone Record*, 1925
Scholes, Percy A., *The Mirror of Music, 1844–1944*, 1947
Schonberg, Harold C., *The Great Conductors*, 1968
Schwarzkopf, Elisabeth, *On and Off the Record*, 1982
Scott, Cyril, *Bone of Contention*, 1969
Scott, William Herbert, *Sir Edward German*, 1932
Searle, Muriel V., *John Ireland*, 1979
Self, Geoffrey, *In Town Tonight* [Eric Coates], 1986
Seroff, Victor, *Rachmaninoff*, 1951
Shanet, Howard, *Philharmonic: A History of New York's Orchestra*, New York, 1975
Shaw, George Bernard, *Shaw's Music*, 1981
Shead, Richard, *Constant Lambert*, 1973
Shirakawa, S. H., *The Devil's Music Master* [Wilhelm Furtwängler], 1992
Shore, Bernard, *The Orchestra Speaks*, 1938
Sidgwick, A. H., *The Promenade Ticket*, 1914
Simpson, Harold, *A Century of Ballads, 1810–1910*, n.d.
Sims, George R. (ed.), *Edwardian London*, 1990 [reprinted from *Living London*, 1902]
Sims, George R., *My Life*, 1917
Skelton, Geoffrey, *Paul Hindemith*, 1975
Slattery, Thomas C., *Percy Grainger*, Evanston, IL, 1972
Smith, Barry, *Peter Warlock*, 1994
Smith, Martin Seymour, *Rudyard Kipling*, 1989
Smith, William Ander, *The Mystery of Stokowski*, 1990
Smyth, Ethel, *A Final Burning of Boats, Etc.*, 1928
Smyth, Ethel, *Female Pipings in Eden*, 1933
Smyth, Ethel, *As Time Went On*, 1936
Smyth, Ethel (ed. Ronald Crichton), *Memoirs*, 1987
Sorabji, K. S., *Mi contra fa*, 1947
Sotheby's, Catalogue for sale 4 December 1992, item 682 [re Francis G. Sanders]
Sousa, J. P., *Marching Along*, 1928
Speyer, Edward, *My Life and Friends*, 1937
Squire, J. H., . . . *And Master of None*, 1937
St John, Christopher, *Ethel Smyth*, 1959
Stanford, Charles V., *Pages from an Unwritten Diary*, 1914
Stanford, Charles V., *Interludes*, 1922
Stevenson, Ronald, *Alan Bush*, 1981
Stewart, Margaret, *English Singer: The Life of Steuart Wilson*, 1970
Storr, Anthony, *The Dynamics of Creation*, 2/1976
Storr, Anthony, *Solitude*, 1989
Stuckenschmidt, H. H. (trans. Humphrey Searle), *Arnold Schoenberg*, 1977
Stradling, Robert and Meirion Hughes, *The English Musical Renaissance 1860–1940*, 1993
Strutt, the Hon. William Maitland, *The Reminiscences of a Musical Amateur*, 1915
Suchoff, Benjamin (ed.), *Béla Bartók Essays*, 1976
Szigeti, Joseph, *With Strings Attached*, 1949
Tawaststjerna, Erik, *Sibelius*, vol.1, 1976, vol.2, 1986
Taylor, A.J.P., *English History 1914–1945*, 1965
Taylor, Stainton de B., *Two Centuries of Music in Liverpool*, n.d. [1976]
Tchaikovsky, P. I., *Letters to his Family*, New York, 1982
Temperley, Nicholas (ed.), *The Romantic Age 1800–1914*, 1981

Tertis, Lionel, *My Viola and I*, 1974
Tetrazzini, Luisa, *My Life of Song*, 1921
Thomas, Theodore A. (ed. George Upton), *A Musical Autobiography*, Chicago, 1964
Threlfall, Robert, *Sergei Rachmaninoff*, 1973
Threlfall, Robert and Geoffrey Norris, *Catalogue of the Compositions of Sergei Rachmaninoff*, 1982
Tomlinson, Ernest, *Delius and Warlock*, 1976
Tomlinson, Fred, *A Peter Warlock Handbook*, 1974, 1977
Toye, Francis, *For What We Have Received*, 1950
Toye, Francis, *Truly Thankful?*, 1957
Trend, Michael, *The Music Makers*, 1985
Turner, W. J., *Music and Life*, 1921
Turner, W. J., *Variations on the Theme of Music*, 1924
Turner, W. J., *Facing the Music*, 1933
Turner, W. J., *English Music*, 1941
Van der Merwe, P. *Origins of the Popular Style*, 1991
Vaughan Williams, Ralph, *National Music and other Essays*, 1963
Vaughan Williams, Ursula, *RVW*, 1964
Verne, Mathilde, *Chords of Remembrance*, 1936
Victoria and Albert Museum, *The Garden*, 1979
Vogel, Jaroslav, *Leoš Janáček*, 1962, 1981
Wagner, Richard, *On Conducting*, 1887, 1940
Wakefield, Mary (ed.), *Ruskin on Music*, 1891
Walbrook, H. M., *Gilbert and Sullivan Opera*, 1922
Walter, Bruno, *Theme and Variations*, 1948
Walter, Bruno, *Of Music and Music-Making*, 1961
Walton, John K. and James Walvin (eds.), *Leisure in Britain 1780–1939*, 1983
Walton, Susana, *William Walton: Behind the Façade*, 1988
Weingartner, Felix, *On Conducting*, 1925
Westrup, J. A., 'Conducting' in *NG*, 1980
Whelbourn, Hubert, *Celebrated Musicians, Past and Present*, 1930
White, Eric Walter, *The Rise of English Opera*, 1951
White, Eric Walter, *A History of English Opera*, 1983
White, Eric Walter, *A Register of the First Performances of English Opera*, 1983
Whyte, A. Gowans, *The Story of the R.P.A.*, 1939
Whittaker, W. Gillies, 'The Business of a Musical Editor', in *Collected Essays*, 1940
Wild, S., *E. J. Moeran*, 1973
Wilsher, Peter, *The Pound in Your Pocket*, 1970
Wilson, Elizabeth, *Shostakovich*, 1994
Wilson, H. L., *Music and the Gramophone and Some Masterpiece Recordings*, 1926
Wister, Frances Anne, *Twenty-five Years of the Philadelphia Orchestra*, 1925
Wood, Jessie, *The Last Years of Henry J. Wood*, 1954
Wooldridge, David, *Conductor's World*, 1970
Wright, D. (ed.), *Cardus on Music*, 1988
Wyndham, H. Saxe, *August Manns and the Saturday Concerts*, 1909
Young, Filson, *More Master-singers*, 1911
Young, Kenneth, *Music's Great Days in the Spas and Watering- places*, 1968
Young, Patricia, and others, *The Story of the Proms*, n.d. [1955]
Young, Percy M., *Kodály*, 1964

II Articles in Magazines, etc (not by HJW)

Apart from innumerable reviews, announcements of concerts, etc., the following articles deal more generally with Wood's achievement and personality. They are in order of *date*. Country of origin is UK unless otherwise indicated.

Anon., 'Gossip about the Theatres', *The Sketch*, 7 September 1898, p. 312

Anon., 'Mr Henry J. Wood, Conductor', *British Musician*, April 1896, p.85

Anon., 'The Queen's Hall Orchestra', *Tatler*, 27 November 1901, p.425

Our Special Correspondent, 'Henry Wood, Conductor of the Queen's Hall Orchestra', *Musical World* (Boston, New York, Leipzig), April 1903, pp.62–3

Anon., 'Is choral singing played out? – a Chat with Mr Henry J. Wood about his Choir', *Tatler*, 17 June 1903, p. 450

Bauer, Emilie Frances, 'Some Visiting Conductors', *The Musician* (Boston), March 1904, pp.108–9

Blackburn, Vernon, 'Henry J. Wood', *New Music Review* (New York), July 1906, pp.1014–17

Erckmann, Fritz, 'Henry J. Wood', *Musikalisches Wochenblatt* (Leipzig), 30 January 1908, pp.101–2

Anon., 'Mr Henry Wood' in *Musical Observer*, 1910, pp.25–7

Anon., 'Sir Henry J. Wood' in *Musical Times*, 1911, pp.153–6

Parker, D. C., 'Sir Henry J. Wood as Educator' in *Musical Standard*, 1918, vol.12 pp.158–9

Anderton, H. Orsmond, 'The Wizard of Queen's Hall', in *Musical Opinion*, 1919, pp.119–21

'Our Music Critic', 'Promenade Concert' in *Morning Post*, [day unidentified] July 1922

Anon., 'Sir H. Wood in New Role', in *Daily Telegraph*, [date unidentified, *c*. 1922]

Wortham, H. E., 'Great Conductors – Sir Henry Wood' in *Morning Post*, 21 November 1923

Snowden, W. Crawford, 'To a New Promenader', in *Evening News*, 15 October 1924

Goodbody, Terence E., 'Gramophone Celebrities, vii, Sir Henry Wood' in *The Gramophone*, February 1925

Boult, Adrian C., 'The conductor of the Proms' in The *Star*, 10 August 1925

Snowden, W. Crawford, 'Sir Henry, the Evergreen' in *Evening News*, 10 August 1925

Anon., 'Notable Musicians – Dame Ethel Smyth' in *Music of All Nations*, part 13, 19 April 1926

Anon., interview with Wood in *Music of All Nations* part 1, 3 November 1927, p.7

Newmarch, Rosa, 'Four Phases of the Promenade Concerts' in Prom programme 10 September 1928

Smyth, Ethel, 'Who Hath Honour? – Some Reflections' in *Daily Telegraph*, 12 March 1929

Newmarch, Rosa, 'Henry J. Wood' in *The Chesterian*, September, 1930, pp.16–18

Wood, Ralph W., 'The Prom Audience' in *Music and Letters* vol.II, 1930, pp.177–81

Russell, Thomas, 'Sir Henry Wood' in *Musical Opinion*, 1934, pp.864–5

Young, Gibson, 'Broadcasting – Here and in U.S.A.', *Radio Magazine*, April 1934, pp.17–18

Wedgwood, Joyce, 'A Glimpse of Sir Henry Wood at Home' in *Radio Times*, 10 August 1935

Terry, Sir Richard, 'A glimpse of the old Proms', in *Radio Times*, 7 December 1935, p.13

Henry J. Wood

Anon., 'We Visit Sir Henry Wood' in *Weekly Illustrated*, 15 August 1936

Evans, Edwin, 'The Proms Then and Now', in *The Listener*, 28 July 1937, p.212

Rees, C. B., 'The Man with a Load of Music' in *Daily Dispatch*, 5 October 1938

Foss, Hubert, in *London Calling*, Jan/Feb 1944

Anon., 'London Lives – No. 4: Timber!' in *Daily Mail*, 3 March 1944

Blom, Eric, 'The Story of Queen's Hall' in *The Listener*, 29 June 1944

Newman, Ernest, obituary notice in *Sunday Times*, 20 August 1944

Mackenzie, Compton, Editorial tribute in *The Gramophone*, August 1944

[Anderson, W. R.], 'Henry Joseph Wood' in *Musical Times*, September 1944, pp. 265–8

Anon., 'Sir Henry Wood and the Gramophone' ['written by one who enjoyed the closest contact with him in his recording work'], *The Voice* (EMI internal publication) XXXVII/3, autumn 1944

Brian, Havergal, 'The Passing of Henry Wood' in *Musical Opinion*, September 1944, p.377

Anon, 'Sir Henry Wood' (obituary) in *Musical America*, September 1944

Goossens, Eugene, 'Sir Henry Wood at Rehearsals' in *New York Times*, 3 September 1944

Sampson, George, 'H. J. W.: Or, 'Tis Fifty Years Since' in *Music and Letters*, 1944, vol.25 pp127– 31

Sharp, Geoffrey, 'Henry Wood' in *Music Review*, 1944, vol.5 p.261

Lambert, Constant, 'My Promenading Life' in *Radio Times*, 13 July 1945 (and correction, 3 August 1945)

Rees, C. B., 'The Story of the Proms' in *London Calling*, 5 June 1952

'Baron' [photographer], 'This was my life', *Sunday Express*, 26 December 1956

Farmer, Henry G., 'The Youthful Henry J. Wood' in *Musical Times*, September 1961

Herbage, Julian, 'Prom Progress', source unidentified, September 1963

Thompson, Kenneth, 'Sir Henry Wood, Composer' in *Musical Opinion*, November 1964

Thompson, K. L., 'Holbrooke: Some Catalogue Data' in *Music and Letters* vol. 46 (October 1965), pp.297–305

Mason, Colin, 'World of Music: Sir Henry was more than the Proms' in *Daily Telegraph*, 8 March 1969

Wood, Avril, 'Life in Elsworthy Road in the 1920s' in *Primrose Hill Magazine*, November 1980, pp.13–16

Lambourn, David, 'Henry Wood and Schoenberg' in *Musical Times*, August 1987, pp. 422–5

Irving, John, 'Schönberg in the News: the London Performances of 1912–1914', in *Music Review*, 1988, pp.52–70

Jacobs, Arthur, 'Henry Wood's operatic baptism' in *Opera*, August 1991, pp.894–8

Fuller, Mollie, 'Wood Felled by Dame Ethel's Charm' in *RAM Magazine*, Winter 1991

Keal, Minna, 'Back to the Future' in *RAM Magazine*, Winter 1991

Lebrecht, Norman, 'Into the Woods' in *Independent*, 5 December 1992 [see also letter in *Independent* from Arthur Jacobs, 9 December 1992]

Mráček, Jaroslav, 'The Reception of Leoš Janáček in the West from 1928 to 1988' in *Proceedings of the International Conference on Janáček and Czech Music*, ed. Michael Beckerman and Glen Bauer, 1993

Jacobs, Arthur, 'A Heart of Oak' in *RAM Magazine*, spring 1994

Lebrecht, Norman, 'Worrying Noises at the Proms' in *Daily Telegraph*, 15 July 1994

Cox, David, 'Warlock at the Proms' in *Peter Warlock Society Newsletter*, summer 1994

Jacobs, Arthur, 'Dear John Drummond' in *Independent*, 9 September 1994
Bisby, Iris, *Recollections of Sir Henry J. Wood* in Hull Philharmonic Orchestra concert programme, 26 November 1994

III Manuscripts

Boult, Adrian C., *Sir Henry J. Wood*, script of broadcast talk?, 1962
Falkner, Keith, *Sir Henry Wood 1869–1944*, undated, received 1990
Hauger, George, *Seventy Years of Musical Theatre* [typescript, 1977]
Prenter, Patrick, collection of letters from Henry J. Wood and others to the violinist F. Waldo Channon
Regan, Leslie, collection of materials originating from Henry J. Wood
Sparkes, Diana, collection of letters from her father and mother (Hubert and Dora Foss) in connection with Henry J. Wood, 1927–38
Wood, Avril, *Sir Henry Wood: A Personal Portrait by his Daughter Avril Wood* (BBC radio script), 1975

IV Writings by Henry J. Wood

i. Books by:

The Influence of the Gramophone on Musical Culture, 1924 ['a paper read before the Federation of British Music Societies Convention, 21 May 1924', original typescript with many MS corrections at Royal Academy of Music]
The Gentle Art of Singing, [4 vols.] 1927; [abbr. 1 vol.] 1930
My Life of Music, 1938
About Conducting, 1945; Russian translation, Moscow, 1958

ii. Contributions to others' books

Introductions to: Walbrook, 1922; Chester, 1924; Maine, 1930; Jacob, 1934; Chamier, 1938 [see main list, pp. 481–90]
'Setting out of an orchestra and directions for tuning' in H. Hind, 1936
Article 'Orchestration' in A. Eaglefield-Hull, *A Dictionary of Modern Music and Musicians*, 1924

iii. Articles and Letters in Newspapers and Periodicals

'Why I became a conductor' in *The Musical Leader and Concert Goer* (Chicago and New York), 26 May 1904
'Henry Wood looks back' in *Radio Times*, 30 September 1938
'Concerts in War Time' in *The Times*, 7 September 1939
'Help for the Orchestras' in *Daily Telegraph*, 19 January 1940
'The Promenade Concerts' in *The Times*, 9 April 1941
'Britain Needs Music' in *Star*, 12 July 1941
'The Future of Music in Britain' in unidentified newspaper, May [1943, 1944?]
'Handel's Messiah' in *The Times*, 8 April 1943
'Fifty Years of Music-Making' in *Radio Times*, 2 June 1944

iv. Programme-notes

'Till's Merry Pranks (A Rogue's Rondo)': descriptive notes 'specially written by
  Henry J. Wood', issued with his Columbia recording L1067, 1916
Also programme notes for festivals at Sheffield from 1902 and Norwich from 1908 –
  some of which, not always clearly attributable, were written by Wood.

v. Unpublished material, held at Royal Academy of Music – the first-named
  privately printed, the rest in typescript:

To my pupils: brief notes to be kept in memory, 1896
The cultivation of the singing voice: a lecture delivered at Nottingham University College
  [6 February 1900]
Singing as an art: a lecture delivered at Nottingham University College [7 February
  1900]
John [sic] Sebastian Bach. The times he lived in and his life's work. 1685 to 1750
  [Nottingham University College, 17 July 1901], with printed programme of synopsis
  and musical illustrations directed by Arnold Dolmetsch
The brass-wind instruments of the orchestra: *a lecture delivered on Friday 7 April at the
  Albert Hall, Sheffield*, 1904
The wood-wind of the orchestra: *a lecture delivered on 21 March, 1904 at the Albert
  Hall, Sheffield*; for Literary and Philosophical Society of Sheffield, illustrated by
  members of the Queen's Hall Orchestra (flute, clarinet, oboe, bassoon, horn);
  ends, 'And finally, if time will allow, we shall hear a quintet in E flat for the
  woodwind instruments and pianoforte'.
Ditto, 'second edition', for St Anne's-on-Sea, 16 December 1904
The voice and musical pitch: a lecture delivered at the Nottingham University College, 28
  March 1904
A lecture on choral singing, 1904
Analytical notes for the choristers on Bach's Mass in B minor, 1910 [Separate notes for
  Soprano I, II, contralto, tenor, bass]
*A list of arias and songs with orchestra, classified under voice, dramatic and lyrical,
  and which I have taught for 50 years*, 1938 [Notes giving duration have been added
  to many items]

Index

This index of names covers the main narrative text (Chapters 1 – 24) and Appendixes 1,2,5 and 6. Attention is also drawn to the alphabetical lists in Appendixes 3 and 4.